A HISTORY OF
ENGLISH DRAMA
1660-1900

A HISTORY OF
ENGLISH DRAMA
1660-1900

BY

ALLARDYCE NICOLL

*Professor of English Language and Literature
in the University of Birmingham*

VOLUME VI

A SHORT-TITLE
ALPHABETICAL CATALOGUE OF PLAYS
PRODUCED OR PRINTED IN ENGLAND
FROM 1660 TO 1900

CAMBRIDGE UNIVERSITY PRESS

CAMBRIDGE

LONDON . NEW YORK . MELBOURNE

Published by the Syndics of the Cambridge University Press
The Pitt Building, Trumpington Street, Cambridge CB2 1RP
Bentley House, 200 Euston Road, London NW1 2DB
32 East 57th Street, New York, NY 10022, USA
296 Beaconsfield Parade, Middle Park, Melbourne 3206, Australia

© Cambridge University Press 1959

ISBN 0 521 0583 2 5

First published 1959
Reprinted 1965, 1973, 1979

First printed in Great Britain at the
University Press, Cambridge
Reprinted in Great Britain by Redwood Burn Limited,
Trowbridge & Esher

PREFATORY NOTE

IN the earlier volumes of this series grateful acknowledgement has been made to several students of English theatrical history, and in particular to Sir St Vincent Trowbridge, who have kindly drawn my attention to obscure plays, as well as to sources of information concerning authorship and production dates for plays already recorded. In preparing the present catalogue, further help has come from Professor Beecher Hogan (who provided me with a list of hitherto un-noted Dublin performances) and from Mr Anthony M. Parish (who has given me items of information based on his examination of nineteenth-century printed texts). I wish also to take this opportunity of thanking Mr P. F. Hinton for furnishing me with a catalogue of the R. Crompton Rhodes Collection now in the Birmingham Reference Library.

A. N.

THE SHAKESPEARE INSTITUTE
(UNIVERSITY OF BIRMINGHAM)
STRATFORD-UPON-AVON

February 1958

INTRODUCTION

THIS volume is much more than an index.

Normally, and properly, an index is dependent upon the book to which it acts as a guide, and consequently it does not pretend to possess other than a subsidiary value. It is true that the pages of this volume do have as their first aim the object of thus serving as a guide, but they are designed to go considerably beyond such an immediate purpose and thus to have a positive, and to a certain extent independent, value of their own. In one sense, while the catalogue presented here may be regarded as an index to what is more fully given elsewhere, it seeks to be a substantive list, as complete as possible, of dramatic works produced in England from the Restoration to the end of the nineteenth century.

If this had been merely an index, nothing more would have been required, or expected, than short-title entries of plays, followed by volume and page references. The present list provides further information in three specific ways:

First, it indicates, in addition to the play-titles, the names of their authors (where known), together with the years of original production, publication or submission to the licensing authority. For immediate reference, therefore, the catalogue stands independent of the Handlists in the other volumes of this series, even although, of course, these contain more detailed information than could here be presented.

Secondly, it should be observed that this catalogue presents some material not in the Hand-lists themselves. During its compilation a number of fresh titles from the earlier periods came to light, as well as new information on the authorship of some dramas previously classed as anonymous. Such additional material has been incorporated here, with symbols to indicate the items or the supplementary information provided for the first time.

Thirdly, there has been introduced into the catalogue an element of a unique kind. From Archer's primitive play-catalogue of 1656, on through Langbaine's *An Account of the English Dramatick Poets* (1691) and Baker's *Biographia Dramatica* (1812), to the *Stage Cyclopaedia* of 1909, various efforts have been made to provide alphabetically-arranged records of English dramatic activity; but in none of these is any attempt made to list more than the main titles (quite apart from the fact that, as the Hand-lists have demonstrated, hundreds and indeed thousands of plays remained unrecorded). Often, however, short main titles fail to offer the help that a student needs: everyone working in this field must realise that frequently a play originally presented under one title was later acted under another name and that even more frequently dramas with sub-titles became popularly, and even professionally, known not by their main but by their alternative titles. A student unacquainted with Dryden's works, for example, might search in vain for *The Maiden Queen*, the name under which his *Secret Love* was usually performed, and he would fail to find *The City Wives' Confederacy*, the name under which Vanbrugh's *The Confederacy* was commonly acted. These are but two examples out of many. Now, it is obvious that a student engaged in elucidating theatrical references in contemporary diaries, correspondence or playhouse documents may be saved a great deal of trouble, or even may be provided with information which otherwise might elude him, if he has available a catalogue not only of main titles but of sub-titles and alternative titles as well. Accordingly, although it has entailed a great deal of additional labour, the present catalogue has been expanded so as to include at least the majority of such alternative names for plays of the period 1660–1900.

Expansion of the catalogue, however, had to be halted somewhere. The original plan called for the listing of all sub-titles and for the attaching to these of author and date references similar to those used for the main titles. The carrying out of a plan of this kind would obviously have swollen this volume, already lengthy, to inordinate proportions, and some modifications had perforce to be adopted. To save space, most of the Italian operas which appear in the Hand-lists have been omitted here—the only exceptions being those early operas of Addison's time which mingle English with their Italian and those of later date which have English translations prepared by known dramatic authors. Since the Italian operas are given alphabetically in the Hand-lists, their omission should not cause any difficulty if reference has to be made to them. Similarly, the repertoire of the French and Italian comedians presented in London early in the eighteenth century has not been included in the catalogue.

While the leaving out of this material resulted in a certain saving, clearly more was demanded; and hence arose the two chief modifications in the plan originally proposed. First, no author or date references are given for the sub-titles. This means that anyone consulting the catalogue may on occasion be referred back from a sub-title to a main title which belongs to two or more separate plays and that consequently a further short search may be necessary before the particular drama concerned is located. Clearly, it would have been best to make all the references specific: equally clearly, this could not have been done within reasonable limits—and between a choice of adopting the present procedure or leaving out the sub-titles altogether no doubt can be felt which is the preferable. In any case, for the majority of references no problem arises.

A second modification concerns those many pantomimes which so actively attracted audiences during the eighteenth and nineteenth centuries. Not only were these very numerous, they often indulged in sprawling titles, such as *King Hal the Bluff, Anne Boleyn the Fair; or, Harlequin Herne the Hunter and the Good Little Fairies of the Silver Ferns* and *Harlequin Blue Beard; or, The Red Rover, the Fairy of the Golden Locks and the Genie of the Magic Key*. Because of the number and length of these titles it was decided that only the main titles should be recorded except for the pantomimes of the early eighteenth century, which, as a scrutiny of Weaver's list shows, are often unlocatable unless we know the alternative names under which they were performed. Perhaps the loss here is not so serious: after all, the student is less likely to require the aid of sub-titles in this pantomimic sphere than when he is dealing with the more formal categories of plays.

The method followed in the catalogue may be briefly outlined. With the exceptions noted above, all the entries in the Hand-lists to the volumes of this series are recorded alphabetically and, save for pantomimes after 1750, all sub-titles and alternative titles are given with indications of the main titles to which they belong.

(1) The normal entry presents the short main title with (in brackets) the author's surname and initials followed by the year, and the appropriate volume and page references, as in:

> Way of the World (Congreve, W., 1700),
> I. 74, 190, 193, 236, 242–3, 341, 398;
> II. 125, 147

The year date usually is the earliest recorded, whether of production, publication or submission to the Lord Chamberlain's Office. For a few plays two dates appear: this indicates that a drama published at a certain time was not acted until several years later. To save space the various dates of similarly named pantomimes are given together, not separately. For plays written by two authors only references to the main entries in the Hand-lists are given.

(2) All initial definite and indefinite articles are omitted, except (*a*) when they form part of a proverb or quotation, as in *The Greatest of These*—; and (*b*) when the deliberately archaic 'Ye' is employed, as in *Ye Battell of Bosworth Field*.

(3) The original spelling forms are retained, as in *Old Batchelour*, but minor variations, such as *Busie-Body* and *Busie Body* are ignored. When confusion might arise, cross-references are supplied from the old-spelling to the modern-spelling forms.

(4) Occasionally plays appear in the Hand-lists twice, once under the name by which they were performed and once under that by which they were licensed. In such instances the form used is as in:

Fisherman's Hut (Tobin, J., 1819)=
Fisherman, IV. 413, 461, 614, 625

Those consulting the catalogue should observe that for some of these double entries part of the relevant information appears in one Hand-list entry, part in another. Thus in the example given above, IV. 413 gives the title under which this melodrama was performed and the date, IV. 461 records the title it had when submitted to the Lord Chamberlain and gives reference to the manuscript, while IV. 614 gives information concerning a printed version of the songs included in the production. Entries under both titles should be consulted.

(5) A + sign before an entry indicates that the play in question does not appear in the Hand-lists but has been added to this catalogue. Similarly a + sign before an author's name or a date draws attention to additional information incorporated here. Other notes are given in square brackets.

(6) Sub-titles and alternative titles are presented with the symbol =, followed by the main title to which they belong, as in:

Manoeuvring=Two make a Pair

It should be observed that the = sign may indicate (*a*) a sub-title (e.g. 'Mayor in a Hamper=Peeping Tom' refers to a play entitled *Peeping Tom; or, The Mayor in a Hamper*); (*b*) an original title abandoned before production (e.g. 'Bertrand and Suzetta=Marriage of Reason' refers to a play acted as *The Marriage of Reason* but submitted to the Lord Chamberlain as *Bertrand and Suzette*); or (*c*) a title substituted at a revival of the play or in a printed text (e.g. 'Brothers = Wolf and the Lamb' refers to a piece acted as *The Wolf and the Lamb* but later published as *The Brothers*). In addition, the same symbol is used to call attention to divergent spellings (e.g. *Boadicia* for *Boadicea*).

(7) In all instances, adaptations and translations are given under the names of the authors concerned in adapting or translating: thus, for example, Kemble's *Hamlet* is listed under Kemble's name, not under Shakespeare's, and *Rosmersholm* under Archer's, not under Ibsen's. Fundamentally, this is a catalogue of dramatic activity in England and any procedure other than that adopted here would have raised serious problems. *Rosmersholm* is, of course, only a translation, but it would have been impossible to draw an exact line between such a drama and *Breaking a Butterfly*, which is an adapted version of *A Doll's House*: Kemble's *Hamlet* is, in the main, merely a cut version of Shakespeare's tragedy, but from this we move on to adaptations of all kinds, going so far even as an independent melodrama called *Hamlet Prince of Denmark*, with songs for Hamlet and Ophelia. Apart from the fact that some of the 'Shakespeare' titles refer to lost plays concerning the text of which we have no other information, clearly it would have been inadvisable to list all of these under 'Shakespeare', and precisely the same conclusion must be reached in dealing with dramas derived from foreign originals, stretching all the way from literal versions to what are virtually separate works.

(8) Where a single title applies to several plays, the order of entry is (*a*) by authors, alphabetically; (*b*) by dates for anonymous pieces; and (*c*) by sub-titles. For example:

> Adrift on the World (Bousfield, F.,
>   1868), v. 270
> — (Twist, J. C., 1894), v. 605
> — (1874), v. 638
> — = Outcast Joe

This indicates (*a*) that there are two plays of known authorship, in 1868 and 1894; (*b*) that there is one, in 1874, which is anonymous; and (*c*) that the same title is attached as a variant to a drama the main title of which is *Outcast Joe*.

(9) The arrangement of entries is strictly alphabetical, so that, for example, *Only a Farmer's Daughter* comes before *On Parade* and *Son's Revenge* before *Son Tricked*. Where a title has *Dr Faustus*, this is not altered to *Doctor Faustus*: where it has *No. 17*, this is not altered to *Number 17*.

(10) Numbers are inserted alphabetically as they are commonly pronounced. Thus £110 *Pounds* appears as though it were 'A Hundred and Ten Pounds', and 1873 as though it were 'Eighteen Seventy Three'. Names of monarchs followed by numbers (as in *Henry VIII*) are placed in numerical order first in their appropriate categories, and variants, such as *Henry the Fifth* for *Henry V*, are regularised. Thus the Henry monarchs come before, say, *Henry Adams* and *Henry VIII* comes after, not before, *Henry V*.

Undoubtedly, there must be a number of duplicates in this catalogue, even although a considerable amount of effort has been made to identify entries of the same piece listed under two varying titles. It has, however, been thought wiser to leave possible duplicates standing without comment rather than risk guesses which might wrongly bring two distinct dramas under one name. No doubt the detailed study of individual dramatists, with the exact examination of manuscripts and printed texts, will result in the identification of many among the 'Lord Chamberlain' plays with plays listed under other names; but until such detailed examination is made the titles must perforce remain separately recorded. It is tempting, for example, to hazard the suggestion that *Under Suspicion*, licensed on 5 June 1894 for a minor London hall, is a revised version of another *Under Suspicion* licensed for Margate on 22 April 1893, and acted there on 29 May of that year as *The New Boy*; but we cannot be sure. It might be thought that *Little Ben Bolt*, licensed for the Bijou, Nashville Gardens, in 1876, is the same as Edwin Keene's *Little Ben Bolt*, acted at the Subscription Ground, Gravesend, in 1879; but again any basis for making a sure judgment is denied us. In the present state of knowledge concerning dramatic activity of these years the student is far more likely to be aided by having as full a list of titles as possible, even if he comes to discover that some of them are variant duplicates, than by having these variant titles attached together on no certain foundation of proof. Similarly, he is less likely to be confused if the attempt is made to keep as strictly as possible to the contemporary ascriptions of authorship for the plays recorded here.

A SHORT-TITLE
ALPHABETICAL CATALOGUE OF PLAYS
PRODUCED OR PRINTED IN ENGLAND
FROM 1660 TO 1900

A Apple Pie (1866), v. 638

Abaellino, the Great Bandit (Dunlap, W., 1802), IV. 582

+Abandondero, the Bloodless (Byron, H. H.: *Dicks* (in *Sensation Dramas*))

Abandoned Irishman=Pat and his Potatoes

Abarbance the Hebrew (1849), IV. 423

Abbaye de Castro (Boucicault, D., 1851), v. 779

Abbé Buonaparte (1891), v. 638

Abbé de l'Epée=Deaf and Dumb

Abbé Laffarge (1876), v. 638

Abbess of Santa Maria=Modern Vittoria Bracciano

Abbé Vaudreuil and the Court of Louis XV (Addison, H. R., 1860), v. 235

Abbey Lands (1824), IV. 423

Abbey of Glenthorn=Murderer's Dream

Abbey of San Marco=Proof Presumptive

Abbey of St Aubert=Ellinda

Abbot (Beverley, H. R., 1820), IV. 94, 267, 572

Abbot of San Martino (Dibdin, T. J., 1819), IV. 302

A.B.C. (Dibdin, T. J., 1833), IV. 423, 619

— (Newton, H. C., 1898), v, 503

Abdalla (Delap, J., 1803), IV, 165, 289

— (Wallace, J., 1845), IV, 416

Abdallah (Barham, F. F., 1820), IV. 569

— (1891), v. 638

Abdelazer (Behn, A., 1676), I. 101, 120, 390

Abd el Kador, the Napoleon of Algeria (1848), IV. 423

Abdellac the Terrible (1824), IV. 619

Abdicated Prince (1690), I. 11, 439

Abdication of Ferdinand (Mayo, R. W., 1809), IV. 423, 619

Abduction of Bianca (Sapte, W., Jr. and Yorke, C. M., 1888), v. 556

Abduction of the Jew's Daughter= Fortune-teller

Abelard and Heloise (Buckstone, J. B., 1837), IV. 275

Abel Drake (Taylor, T. and Saunders, J., 1874), v. 594

Abel Drake's Wife (1872), v. 638

Abel Flint (Hazlewood, C. H., 1868), v. 797

Abelino (1805), IV. 423

Abigail (1849), IV. 423

Abimelech (Jago, R., 1784), III. 348, 388

Abon (Tabrar, J., 1885), v. 589

Abon Hassan (1793), III. 318

— (O'Neil, A., 1869), v. 507

Abou Hassan (Dimond, W., 1825), IV. 145, 307, 581

— (Gilbeigh, and Grimes, G., 1850), v. 638, 793, 795, 826

— (Talfourd, F., 1854), v. 590

— (Upton, W., 1810), IV. 423, 619

Abou Hassan, the Sleeper of Bagdad and the Fairy Elves of the Enchanted Mosque (Marchant, F., 1862), v. 638, 805, 826

Aboukir Bay (Sicklemore, R., 1799), III. 307

About Town (À Beckett, A. W., 1873), v. 233

Above and Below (Stirling, E. 1846), IV. 37, 408

— (1847), IV. 423

Above Suspicion (Capel, G., 1882), v. 302

Abradates and Panthea (Edwards, J., 1808), IV. 309

1

Abradates and Panthea (Roberts, W., 1770), III. 302

Abraham Parker (Addison, H. R., 1846), IV. 251

Abraham's Faith (Lesley, G., 1684), I. 420

Abra-Mule (Trapp, J., 1704), II. 20, 79–80, 360

Abroad and at Home (Holman, J. G., 1796), III. 271

Absence of Mind (Poel, W., 1884), v. 529, 811

Absent Apothecary (Smith, J. and Smith, H., 1813), IV. 403

Absentee (Bernard, W. B., 1844), IV. 266

Absent Man (Bickerstaffe, I., 1768), III. 186, 237, 377

— (Hull, T., 1764), III. 274

— (Roberts, G., 1870), v. 544

— (Smollett, T. G.), II. 444

Absent-minded Beggar (Shirley, A., 1899), v. 565

Absent-minded Man (1884), v. 638

Absent One (Wigan, H.), v. 622

Absent Son (Buckstone, J. B., 1828), IV. 273

Absent without Leave (1824), IV. 423

— (1837), IV. 423

Absolution (Murray, H., 1892), v. 500

Absurdities of a Day (À Beckett, G. A., 1844), IV. 250

Abudah (Planché, J. R., 1819), IV. 376

— (1817), IV. 423

Abu Hassan (1870), v. 638

Abyssinia (Dibdin, T. J., 1825), IV. 304

Abyssinian War and the Death of King Theodore (Travers, W., 1868), v. 603

Abyss of Thorns (Faucquez, A., 1861), v. 791

+ Academic Sportsmen; or, Seven Wise Men of Gotham (12°? 1775; Dublin)

Academie (Barnes, J., 1675), I. 389

Academy (1897), v. 638

— (1898), v. 638

Acanor = Arab

Accepted by Proxy (Kingsley, E., 1893), v. 444

Accidental Son (1859), v. 638

Accomplish'd Fools = Tender Husband

Accomplish'd Maid (Toms, E., 1766), III. 312

Account Rendered (Harrison, W. B., 1894), v. 407

Accusation (Payne, J. H., 1816), IV. 368, 603

— (1840), IV. 423

Accused of Murder = Crocodile

Accuser (Lee, R., 1890), v. 453

Accusing Son = Maid of the Forest

Accusing Spirit (Suter, W. E., 1860), v. 588

— = (1) Castle of Wolfenstein; (2) Force of Conscience

Ace of Clubs (Shirley, A., 1889), v. 564

Ace Soir (Mayer, H., 1897), v. 482

Achille et Deidamia (Degville, 1804), IV. 579

Achilles (Boyer, A., 1699), I. 393; II. 72, 75, 85, 299, 432; III. 86

— (Gay, J., 1733), II. 122, 237, 241, 332; III. 116

Achilles and Iphigenia in Aulis = Achilles

Achilles in Petticoats (Colman, G., 1773), III. 116, 246

— = Achilles

Achilles in Scyros (Bridges, R. S., 1890), v. 275

— (Hoole, J., 1800), III. 387

Acis and Galatea (Burnand, F. C., 1863), v. 288, 781

— (Gay, J., 1731), II. 236, 332, 437

— (Motteux, P. A., 1701), II. 44, 259, 260, 345, 441, 447

— (Oxberry, W. H., 1842), IV. 367

— (Plowman, T. F., 1869), v. 528

— (1838), IV. 423

Acis et Galathe (1818), IV. 423

Acrobat (Barrett, W., 1891), v. 250

Across her Path (Irish, A., 1890), v. 432

Across the Atlantic (1871), v. 638

Across the Continent (McCloskey, J., 1871), v. 468

Act at Oxford (Baker, T., 1704), II. 21–2, 175, 297

Actaeon and Diana (Cox, R., 1656), I. 251, 417

Acteon and Diana (Byrus, J., 1800), IV. 423, 619

Acting in Earnest = Garrick

Acting Mad (1820), IV. 423

— = In Place or out of Place

Acting Run Mad (1835), IV. 423

3

Adventures of a Night = Alasnum and his Cottage Queen

Adventures of an Umbrella = Memoirs of an Umbrella

Adventures of a Sealed Packet = Nabob's Fortune

Adventures of a Servant Girl = Mary Price

Adventures of a Shilling (1845), IV. 424

Adventures of a Ventriloquist (Moncrieff, W. T., 1822), IV. 359

— (1826), IV. 424

Adventures of a Young Man (Lee, N. Jr., 1860), V. 802

Adventures of Becky Sharp (1899), V. 638

Adventures of Charley-wag (1846), IV. 424

Adventures of Cheek and Plant = Cheek and Plant

Adventures of Don Quixote = Don Quixote

Adventures of Five Hours (Tuke, Sir S., 1663), I. 2, 9, 26, 33, 38, 66, 69, 101, 127, 171, 192, 197, 219, 264, 346, 347, 348, 435; III. 114

Adventures of Florio the Foundling Prince = Dark King of the Black Mountains

Adventures of Four Years = Abdicated Prince

Adventures of Half an Hour (Bullock, C., 1716), II. 211, 301

Adventures of Harlequin in Spain (1741), II. 365

Adventures of Robin Hood, Earl of Huntingdon (1730), II. 365 [Probably = Robin Hood, II. 448]

Adventures of Jerry Abbershaw (1826), IV. 424

Adventures of John Sheppard = Prison Breaker

Adventures of Paddy O'Rafferty = Irishman's Fortune

Adventures of Prince Headstrong and Princess Bloomingbell = Enchanted Tower

Adventures of Roderick Random (Dibdin, T. J., 1818), IV. 96, 301

Adventures of Roderick Random, and his Friend Strap = (1) Pretenders; (2) Volunteers

Adventures of the Count de Monte Cristo (Smith, H. J., 1899), V. 572

Adventures of the Halibut Family = Life in Paris

Adventures of the Prince of Seville (1790), III. 318

Adventures of the Weasel Family = Pop goes the Weasel

Adventures of Tom and Jerry = Ashantees

Adventures of Tom Trip (Siddons, H., 1796), III. 307

Adventures of Twelve Hours = Love in the East.

Adventures of Ulysses (Mendham, 1811), IV. 355

Adventures of Venice = Perjur'd Husband

Adventuress (Amory, T. S., 1882), V. 240

— (Hilton, B. H., 1871), V. 422

Adversity (1861), V. 638

Advertisement (Burges, Sir J. B., 1817), IV. 276

— (Fennell, J., 1791), III, 259

— (Gardner, Mrs Sarah, 1777), III. 262

Advertisement for a Husband (Lawler, D., 1814), IV. 342

Advertisements (1868), V. 638

Advertisement—Wanted, Wives and Husbands (1854), V. 638

Advice Gratis (Dance, C., 1837), IV. 288

Advice to Husbands (Lancaster, C. S., 1846), IV. 341

— = Hints to Wives

Advocate (Lander, C., 1886), V. 447

— (1859), V. 638

— = Last Cause

Advocate and his Daughter (Ebsworth, J., 1852) = Advocate's Daughter, v. 353, 789, 826

Advocate of Durango (Wynne, J., 1853), V. 634

Advocate's Daughter (Ebsworth, J., 1856) = Advocate and his Daughter, v. 638, 789, 826

Advocate's Wife = Fatal Duel of the Glacis

Adzuma (Arnold, Sir E., 1893), V. 243

Æneas (Granville, H. S., 1868), V. 388

Alasnum and his Cottage Queen (1816), IV. 424

Alban and Aphanasia (O'Keeffe, J.), III, 294

Albanio = Fatal Accusation

Alberic, the Consul of Rome (Dwarris, Sir F. W. L., 1832), IV. 582

Alberta (Carter, J., 1787), III. 242

Albert and Adelaide (Birch, S., 1798), III, 45, 101-2, 238, 378

Albert and Elmira (1820), IV. 425

Albert and Emma = Treacherous Baron

Albert and Louise = Soldier Girl

Albert and Rosalie (Wharton, F. F., 1808), IV. 419

— = Fire King

Albert Arnall = Adolph Arnal

Albert de Rosen (Lane, Mrs S., 1875), v. 448

Alberto and Lauretta (Lynch, T. J., 1806), IV. 425, 619

Alberto and Rosabella = Brazen Mask

Albert's Mystery (1899), v. 640

Albina, Countess Raimond (Cowley, Mrs H., 1779), III. 83, 248

Albion (Cooke, T., 1724), II. 260, 316

Albion and Albanius (Dryden, J., 1685), I. 40, 43, 44-8, 65, 135, 141, 158-9, 406

Albion Queens (Banks, J., 1704), I. 52-3, 167, 389

Albion Restored (Stevens, G. A., 1758), III. 318, 396, 398

Alboin (Gurney, A. T., 1846), IV. 322

Album (James, H., 1895), v. 433

Albumazar (?Garrick, D., 1747), II. 437

— (Garrick, D., 1773), III. 113, 263, 385

Album of Beauties (1884), v. 641

Album of Beauty (1879), v. 641

Alcaid (Kenney, J., 1824), IV. 144, 337, 592

Alcamanes and Menalippa (Phillips, W.), I. 423

Alcantara (Woolf, B. E., 1879), v. 632, 824

Alcestis (Spicer, H., 1855), v. 576

— (Todhunter, J., 1879), v. 600

Alcestis burlesqued (Styrke, I., 1816), IV. 409

Alcestis, the Original Strong-minded Woman (Talfourd, F., 1850), v. 590

Alchemist (Shillingford, O., 1897), v. 563

— (1782), III. 318. See also Alchymist

Alchemist of Modena (Charlton, F., 1868), v. 308

Alchymist (Fitzball, E. and Bayly, T. H., 1832), IV. 314, 584

— (Garrick, D., 1774), III. 264

— (Moser, J. additional scene, 1809), IV. 364

Alchymy (Dibdin, C. I. M., 1817), IV. 294

Alchymyst's Daughter (Oxenford, J., 1844), IV. 367

Alcibiades (Otway, T., 1675), I. 39, 40, 120, 165, 348, 422

Alcide (1821), IV. 425

Alderman (Mortimer, J., 1887), v. 494

Alderman No Conjurer = Cuckolds-Haven

Alderman's Bargain = Luckey Chance

Alderman's Gown (Abrahams, H., 1851), v. 235

Alderman's Last Wish = Bow Bells

Aldgate Pump (Faucit, J. S., 1841), IV. 311, 583

Alerame, the Knight of the Lion (Denvil, 1833), IV. 290

Alexander and Statira (Wallis, G.), III. 314

Alexander Balus (Morell, T., 1748), II. 388

Alexander Selkirk (1845), IV. 425

Alexander's Successors = Humorous Lieutenant

Alexander the Great (Egville, J. d', 1795), III, 258, 398

— (Kemble, J. P., 1795), III. 279

— (Ozell, J., 1714), II. 347, 442

— (1715), II. 388

— (1770), III. 59, 318

— = Chiselling

Alexander the Great and Thalestris the Amazon (Dibdin, C. I. M., 1822), IV. 295

Alexander the Great! in Little (Dibdin, T. J., 1837), IV. 305

Alexander the Little (1764), III. 318

—— (1791), III. 318

Alexandra (1893), v. 641

Alexina (Knowles, J. S., 1866), v. 445

Alexis (Vallings, H., 1885), v. 606

Alexis (1831), IV. 425

Alexis and Dorinda (1725), II. 365

Alexis's Paradise (Newton, J., ?1722), II, 346

Alfonso and Claudina, the Faithful Spouse (1862), V. 641

Alfonso, King of Castile (Lewis, M. G., 1801), IV. 163, 195, 345

Alfred (Garrick, D., 1773), III. 263

— (Gower, Lord F. L., 1840), IV. 320

— (Home, J., 1778), III. 94, 272

— (Lindsay, Sir C., 1848), IV. 595

— (Mallet, D. and Thomson, J., 1740), II. 343, 440, 445

— (Mallet, D. and Thomson, J., 1751), III. 286

— (O'Keeffe, J., 1796), III. 295

— (Rhodes, E., 1789), III. 61, 318, 394, 398

— (1861), V. 641

Alfred and Elvida = Patriot King

Alfred and Emma (1806), IV. 87, 425

Alfred and Matilda (1825), IV. 425

Alfred le Grand, roi d'Angleterre (Aumer, 1823), IV. 425, 619

Alfred the Great (Almar, G.), IV. 253

— (Brough, R. B., 1859), V. 278

— (Faucit, Mrs J. S., 1811), IV. 311

— (Hamilton, S., 1829), IV. 425, 619

— (Knowles, J. S., 1831), IV. 79, 112, 172, 339

— (Lawler, D., 1811), IV. 425

— (Lonsdale, M., 1798), III. 318, 391, 398

— (Magnus, T., 1838), IV. 597

— (Milner, H. M., 1824), IV. 357

— (Pocock, I., 1827), IV. 46, 112, 387

— (1823), IV. 425

— = Alfred

Alfred the Great at Athelney (Redcliffe, Lord Stratford de, 1876), V. 536

Alfred the Great, Deliverer of his Country (1753), III. 318

Alfred the Ingrate (Bayley, W. V., 1871), V. 253

Al Fresco (1899), V. 641

Algerian (McDonough, G., 1893), V. 469

Algerine Corsair = Alzira

Algerine Slaves (Cobb, J., 1792), III. 244

Algernon the Blind Guide (Pitt, G. D., 1847), IV. 374

Algonah (Cobb, J., 1802), IV. 280

Alhambra (Smith, A. R., 1851), V. 572

Alhamor the Moor (Fitzball, E., 1849), IV. 317 [The entry under *Almahar* on IV. 425 should be deleted]

Ali Baba (Byron, H. J., 1863), V. 296

— (Colman, G. the Younger, 1806) = Forty Thieves, IV. 425

— (Locke, F., 1898), V. 462

— (Moreton, F. L. and Mountford, H., 1897), V. 493

— (O'Neil, J. R., 1852), V. 808

— (Pratt, F. W., 1892), V. 641, 811, 826

— (Taddei, E., 1871), V. 590

— (1811), IV. 425

— (1850), V. 826

— (1865), V. 641

— (1868), V. 826

— (1873, 1879, 1883, 1895), V. 641

Ali Baba à la mode (Reece, R., 1872), V. 537

Ali Baba and the Forty Thieves (À Beckett, G. A., 1866), V. 233

— (À Beckett, G. A., 1871), V. 233

— (Byron, H. J., Gilbert, W. S., Burnand, F. C. and Reece, R., 1878), V. 299

— (Chatterton, F. B. and Grattan, H. P. 1881), V. 308

— (Douglass, J. T., 1878), V. 348

— (Green, F. W., 1872), V. 794

— (1878, 1879, 1880, 1884, 1896), V. 641

Ali Baba, M.P. (Scarlett, W., 1893), V. 557

Alice Aukland (Parry, T., 1843), IV. 368

Alice Gray (1833), IV. 425

Alice Grey (Haines, J. T., 1839), IV. 323, 587

Alice Home (1843), IV. 425

Alice in Wonderland (Clarke, H. S., 1886), V. 313, 826

— (1886), V. 641, 826

Alice Lowrie, the Forger's Victim (1861), V. 641

Alice May (Fitzball, E., 1852), V. 368

Alice Wingold (Lacy, M. R., 1862), V. 446

Alienated Manor (Baillie, J., 1836), IV. 258

Aliens (Rowe, B., 1889), V. 552

Alina (1844), IV. 425

Alina (1851), v. 641

Aline (Stirling, E., 1843), IV. 407

Aline, reine de Golconde (Aumer, 1823), IV. 425, 619

Ali Pacha (Payne, J. H. and Planché, J. R., 1822), IV. 377

Ali Pasha (1836), IV. 425

Alive and Merry (Brown, 1796), III. 240

— (Dance, C., 1839), IV. 289

Alive or Dead (Hall, R. W., 1876), v. 400

— (Webb, C., 1843), IV. 425, 619

All about a Bonnet (Harraden, H., 1891), v. 404

All about a Lost Will = Capers

All about Love and Jealousy (Bolton, G., 1846), IV. 425, 619

All about the Battle of Dorking (Burnand, F. C. and Sketchley, A., 1871), v. 290

All Abroad (Burnside, W., 1892), v. 293

— (Hall, O. and Tanner, J. T., 1895), v. 400

— (Law, A., 1890), v. 450

Alladine and Palmonides (Archer, W., 1899), v. 242

All a Fetch (Dibdin, T. J., 1826), IV. 304

All Alive and Merry (Johnson, S., 1737), II. 340

— (1740), II. 451

— = (1) Happy Hero; (2) Wanton Trick'd

All Alive at Liverpool (1809), IV. 619

All Alive at the Races = Epsom Downs

All Alive in Auld Reekie = Royal Visit

All Alive, Oh! (1897), v. 641

All a Mistake (Phillips, Mrs N., 1890), v. 523

— (1825), IV. 425

+ Allario and Adelina; or, The Village Inn and the Count Out (Byron, H. J.: *Dicks* (in *Sensation Dramas*))

All Asleep at Noon = Modern Breakfast

All at C (Millet, and Wilcox, 1873), v. 489

All at Coventry (Moncrieff, W. T., 1816), IV. 358

All at Home (1804), IV. 425

All at Cross Purposes = Contrarieties

All at Sea (Grundy, S., 1873), v. 205, 396

All at Sea (Law, A., 1881), v. 449

All at Sixes and Sevens (Dibdin, C. I. M., 1829), IV. 296

All Bedevil'd (Browne, M., 1723), II. 215, 300

All but lost (Warrington, F., 1869), v. 615

All but One (Travers, W., 1868), v. 602

All by Chance (Belverstone, J., 1879), v. 257

All Change Here (Keith, R., 1898), v. 442

All comes to he who waits = Waiter

All Correct = Marriage of Gamacho

Allegro, il Penseroso ed il Moderato (Jennens, S., 1740), II. 388, 439

Allendale (Phillpotts, E. and Burgin, G. B., 1893), v. 524

All Fair in Fair Time = Cousin Campbell's Courtship

All for Error = What a Blunder!

All for Fame! (Cherry, A., 1805), IV. 279, 576

All for Gold (Griffiths, J. C., 1878), v. 394

— (Hopkins, F., 1878), v. 426

— = Found Dead in the Streets

All for her (Simpson, J. P., 1875), v. 568

All for himself (Wills, C., 1874), v. 626

All for Love (Dryden, J., 1677), I. 115, 136, 172–3, 177, 179–80, 350, 406; II. 70

— (Coyne, J. S., 1838), IV. 284

All for Money (Thierre, G. le, 1869), v. 595

All for Nothing (Aidé, H., 1880), v. 236

All for Number One = Gay Musketeers

All for our Country = Inundation

All for St Paul's = Britain's Brave Tars!!

All for the Best (1846), IV. 425

— (1880), v. 641

All for the Better (Manning, F., 1702), II. 50, 140, 160, 170, 343, 440

All for Them (Lyste, H. P., 1876), v. 465

All Hallows' Eve (Forbes, Mrs and Whitbread, J. W., 1891), v. 370

— (Leclercq, M., 1859), v. 641, 802, 826

— (Towers, E., 1865), v. 821

— (1838), IV. 425

— (1882), IV. 641

All Hallows' Even (1831), IV. 425

All her own Way (Dibdin, T. J., 1826), IV. 304

Allies Victorious = Buonaparte Burnt Out

All in a Bustle (Lathom, F., 1795), III. 280

All in a Family Way (Brown, H., 1832), IV. 574

All in a Fog (Williams, T. J., 1869), V. 626

All in a Good Humour (1872), V. 641

All in Confusion (1806), IV. 87, 425

— = Reasonable Fool

All in Good Humour (Oulton, W. C., 1792), III. 296

All in Honour = Sweet Revenge

All in Hot Water (Bruton, J., 1858), V. 284

All in One (1826), IV. 425

All in One Night (Dibdin, T. J., 1825), IV. 304

— (1829), IV. 425

All in the City = Cheapside

All in the Clouds = Air Balloon

All in the Dark (Horne, F. L., 1839), IV. 328

— (Impey, E. B., 1822), IV. 590

— (Planché, J. R., 1822), IV. 377

— (Planché, J. R., 1861), V. 527

All in the Downs (Jerrold, T., 1881), V. 436

— = (1) Black Eyed Susan; (2) William and Susan

All in the Dumps = Blackeyed Sukey

All in the Right (Hull, T., 1766), III. 274, 388

— (1761), III. 318

All in the Wrong (Dibdin, C. I. M., 1822), IV. 295

— (Murphy, A., 1761), III. 14, 117, 163, 290

— = (1) Mixed; (2) Rebellion

All is Vanity = Cynics' Defeat

All is well that ends well = Humours of Portsmouth

All Jackson's Fault (O'Connell, A., 1889), V. 506

All Jealous = Perplex'd Couple

All Lost (Craven, T., 1881), V. 329

All made up again = Forget and Forgive

All Mistaken (Howard, J., 1667), I. 52, 201, 232, 414

All my Eye and Betty Martin = Hit or Miss

All My Eye-Vanhoe (Hayman, P., 1894), V. 411

All of a Mind = Three Paddies

All on a Summer's Day (Inchbald, Mrs E., 1787), III. 275

All on the Wing = Three Deep

Allow me to apologise (Wooler, J. P., 1850), V. 632

Allow me to explain (Gilbert, W. S., 1867), V. 379

All Pleas'd at Last (1783), III. 318

All-Plot (Stroud, 1662–1671), I. 433

All Puzzled (?1702), II. 365

— = Is He Alive?

All Right at Last = Petticoat Colonel

All's a Delusion (1847), IV. 619

All's a Mistake = All a Mistake

All's Fair in Fair Time = Day's Fun

All's Fair in Love (Tobin, J., 1803), IV. 413

All's Fair in Love and War (Brougham, J., 1859), V. 280, 811

— (Price, M., 1862), V. 811

All's not Gold that Glitters (1790), III. 318

All's Not Well That Seems So (Lott, W., 1843), IV. 596

All's Right (Planché, J. R., 1827), IV. 378

— (1832), IV. 425

All's Well that Ends Well (Kemble, J. P., 1793), III. 279

— (Pilon, F., 1785), III. 298

— (1832), IV. 425

All that glitters is not gold (Morton, J. M. and Morton, T., 1851), V. 495

All the Comforts of Home (Gillette, W. and Duckworth, H. C., 1890), V. 381

All the Difference (McDonald, R., 1896), V. 468

All the World at Colchester = Law, Latin and Love

All the World's a Fair (McLaren, A., 1822), IV. 352

All the World's a Stage (Jackman, I., 1777), III. 186, 276

— (1819), IV. 425

— = Footlights

All the Year Round (1862), V. 641

All through a Wire (Herbert, F. H., 1894), v. 418

All Topsy Turvy = Our Three Hats

All to St Paul's (O'Keeffe, J.) = Britain's Brave Tars = Our Wooden Walls, III. 295, 393

All up at Stockwell (1772), III. 318

All Vows Kept (Downes, 1733), II. 319

All without Money (Motteux, P. A., 1697), I. 421; II. 437

Ally Croaker (Dibdin, C. I. M., 1804), IV. 291

Alma (Fitzball, E.), IV. 316

Almahide and Hamet (Malkin, B. H., 1804), IV. 353.

Alma Mater (Boucicault, D., 1842), IV. 269

— (1892), v. 641

Almanzar the Traitor = Petraki Germano

Almanzor and Almahide = Conquest of Granada by the Spaniards

Almazaide (1824), IV. 425

Almena (Rolt, R., 1764), III. 197, 303

Almeyda (Howard, G. E., 1769), III. 273

— (1801), IV. 425

Almeyda, Queen of Granada (Lee, S., 1796), III. 83, 281

Almida (Celisia, D. and Garrick, D., 1771), III. 40, 60, 82–3, 242, 378

Almighty Dollar (Wood, W., 1888), v. 631

Almira (1786), III. 318

Almirina (Jackman, I., 1788), III. 276

Almoran and Hamet (Amherst, J. H., 1822), IV. 253

— (1799), III. 318

Almost a Life (Henderson, E., 1882), v. 416

Almshouse (Lockhart, W. and Fernie, L., 1892), v. 462

Almyna (Manley, M., 1706), II. 79, 343

Alom Pram (Groves, E., 1832), IV. 321

Alone (Simpson, J. P. and Merivale, H. C., 1873), v. 103–4, 568

Alone in London (Buchanan, R. and Jay, H., 1885), v. 285

Alone in the Pirate's Lair (Hazlewood, C. H., 1867), v. 413

Alone in the World (Fuller, F., 1871), v. 374

— (Galer, E. J. N., 1871), v. 375

Alone in the World (Ingram, P., 1892), v. 431

— (1863), v. 641

Alonzo (Home, J., 1773), III. 40, 94, 272

Alonzo and Imogen (1895), v. 641

Alonzo and Imogene (Bird, W. W., 1869), v. 262

— (Fitzball, E., 1821), IV. 312

Alonzo and Imogine (Dibdin, T. J., 1797), III. 318, 382, 398

— (Dibdin, T. J., 1801), IV. 297

— (1808), IV. 425

Alonzo of Castile (1833), IV. 426

Alonzo the Artless (1892), v. 641

Alonzo the Brave (Burnand, F. C., 1855), v. 287

— (Lee, N. Jr., 1861), v. 803

— (Milner, H. M., 1826), IV. 357

— (1832), IV. 426

— (1864), v. 641

Alonzo the Brave and the Fair Imogene (Craven, H. T., 1855), v. 641, 786

— (Dibdin, T. J., 1821), IV. 303

— (Dibdin, T. J., 1826), IV. 304

— (Didelot, 1801), IV. 581

— (Fitzball, E., 1850), v. 367

Alonzo the Patriot (Somerset, C. A., 1830), IV. 426, 619

Alonzo ye Brave and ye fayre Imogene (Harrison, S. M., 1876), v. 407

Aloyse (1828), IV. 426

Alphonso, King of Castile (Warrington, W., 1813), IV. 616

Alphonso, King of Naples (Powell, G., 1690), I. 52, 157, 425

Alphonsus (Hyde, G., 1825), IV. 329

Alphonzo Algarres (Stuart-Wortley, Lady Emmeline, 1841), IV. 613

Alpine Hold (Haines, J. T., 1839), IV. 323

Alpine Maniac = Isaure

Alpine Romance = Paul of the Alps

Alpine Tourists (Phillips, Mrs N., 1888), v. 523

Alps (1886), v. 641

Alp, the Renegade (Almar, G., 1824), IV. 426, 619

Alp, the Tartar Khan (Raymond, R. J., 1831), IV. 426, 619

Alsatian Dialogue = Happy Result

Alta (1884), v. 641

Altamira (Victor, B., 1776), III. 313

Altamira = Generall

+Altamont and Lavinia (Smock Alley, Dublin, 8/3/1776)

Altar of Revenge = Nick of the Woods

Altemira (Boyle, R., 1701), I. 100, 106–7, 394; II. 299, 432

Alternative (1796), III. 318 [The date of acting should be 6/1/1796]

Alternative, Tyranny or Liberty = King Henry VII

Altogether (Dowsett, E., 1894), v. 350

Altogether Moral Trilby (Kay, C. B., 1896), v. 442

Alva (1840), IV. 619

+Alvarez (Talfourd, F., 1850), v. 819

— (1835), IV. 426

Always Intended (Wigan, H., 1865), v. 622

Always Ready (Callender, E. R., 1873), v. 300

Always sit up for your Husband (Sorrell, W. J., 1873), v. 574

Always Wrong and Try Again (1829), IV. 426

Alwyn and Bertholdy (Almar, G., 1831), IV. 426, 619

Alzira (Hill, A., 1736), II. 65, 72, 109, 336, 438

— (1809), IV. 426

Alzora and Nerine (+Leclerq, P., 1818), IV. 426

Alzuma (Murphy, A., 1773), III. 43, 53, 76–7, 290

Amadan (Boucicault, D., 1883), v. 269

Amadis (Rich, J., 1718), II. 133, 253, 365

— (1724), II. 446

Amakosa (Fitzball, E., 1853), v. 368

Amalasont, Queen of Goths (Hughes, J., 1696), I. 415

Amalderac the Black Pirate (1840), IV. 426, 593

Amalderac, the Black Rover (Lancaster, E. R.), IV. 426, 593

Amana (Griffith, Mrs E., 1764), III. 266

Amanthis (1820), IV. 426

Amasis King of Egypt (Marsh, C., 1738), II. 39, 58, 71, 111, 343

Amateur Detective (Lloyd, A., 1898), v. 461

Amateur Wife (Lancaster-Wallis, E., 1897), v. 447

Amateurs and Actors (Peake, R. B., 1818), IV. 145, 369

Amazonian Warriors (1861), v. 826

Amazon Queen (Weston, J., 1667), I. 101, 437

Amazon Queen of Denmark and Norway = Landgartha

Amazons (Pinero, Sir A. W., 1893), v. 525

Amazon's Oath (1858), v. 641

Amazon Sisters = (1) Ida and Carelia; (2) Sisters

Ambassador (Hobbes, J. O., 1898), v. 422

+ — (8°, 1832)

Ambassador from Below = Mephistopheles

Ambassador's Lady (Wilkes, T. E., 1843), IV. 421

Ambassadress (À Beckett, G. A., 1838), IV. 84, 250

— (Mellers, H., 1848), IV. 84, 355

— (Reece, R., 1868), v. 537, 812

Amber Box (1800), IV. 426

Amber Girl (Gordon-Clifford, E. and H., 1894), v. 385

Amber Heart (Calmour, A. C., 1887), v. 300

Amber Witch (Chorley, H. F., 1861), v. 784

— (?Faucit, J. S., 1851), v. 363, 791

Ambiguous Lover (Sheridan, Miss, 1781), III. 184, 305

Ambition (Fomm, L., 1899), v. 370

— (Mayhew, T., 1830), IV. 355, 598

— (Phillips, F. L., 1857), v. 641, 810, 826

— (Walford, H. L., 1870), v. 611

— (1836), IV. 426

— (1854), v. 641

Ambition's Slave (Fox, J., 1883), v. 371

Ambitious Father = Injur'd Lovers

Ambitious Mrs Moresby (White, E., 1898), v. 620

Ambitious Queen = Siege of Memphis

Ambitious Slave (Settle, E., 1694), I. 101, 149–50, 429

Ambitious Statesman (Crowne, J., 1679), I. 56, 150, 399

Ambitious Step-Mother (Rowe, N., 1700), II. 50, 98, 351, 443

Ambitious Vengeance (Merry, R., 1790), III. 287

Ambitious Widow (Woty, W., 1770), III. 317

Amboyna (Dryden, J., 1673), I. 78, 405

Ambrose Gwinett (Jerrold, D. W., 1828), IV. 331

+ Ambrosius (Berry, Alice, 8°, 1879)

Ambuscade at Inkerman (1860), v. 641

Amelia (Carey, H., 1732), II. 31, 32, 235–6, 302

— (Cumberland, R., 1768), III. 251, 381

Amergau (McSwiney, P., 1881), v. 472

America (Barber, J. H., 1805), IV. 258

— (Dibdin, T. J., 1812), IV. 299

American (Derrick, J., 1882), v. 343

— (James, H., 1891), v. 433

— (Wood, G. M., 1883), v. 630

American Adventurers = Coup de Main

American Assurance (Sidney, F. W., 1894), v. 565

American Belle (Seton, H., 1897), v. 561

American Bride (Young, Sir W. L. and Noel, M., 1892), v. 637

American Citizen (Ryley, M. L., 1899), v. 554

American Girl = (1) Sunny Florida; (2) Spin for Life

American Heiress (Branscombe, A. and Day, G. D., 1899), v. 274

American Heroine (1790), III. 318

— (1792), III. 319

— (1796), III. 319

— (1797), III. 319

American Indian (Bacon, J., 1795), III. 235

American in England (1855), v. 641

American Lady (Byron, H. J., 1874), v. 298

Americans (Arnold, S. J., 1811), IV. 255

Americans Abroad = Jonathan in England

American Savage = Tombo-Chiqui

American Singer Downstairs (Locke, T. and Downes, J. F., 1899), v. 462

American Sketches = Belle of the Hotel

American Slavery (1862), v. 641

American Slaves (McLaren, A., 1792), III. 284

American War of 1780 = Spy of the Neutral Ground

Amethyst Ring (1838), IV. 426

Amiable Mistake = Ranger in Wedlock

Am I a Princess? = Rosine

Amilie (Haines, J. T., 1837), IV. 322

Am I Myself or Another? = Irishman's Dream

Aminta (Dancer, J., 1660), I. 400

— (Du Bois, P., 1726), II. 224, 320, 435

— (Oxenford, J., 1852), v. 509

Amintas (Ayre, W., 1737), II. 224, 296, 432

— (Oldmixon, J., 1698), I. 422; II. 347, 442

— (Rolt, R. and Tenducci, F., 1769), III. 303

Amintas et Sylvie (1802), IV. 426

Amínte et Sylvie (1814), IV. 426

Among the Amalekites (Bennett, E., 1889), v. 258

Among the Breakers (Brougham, J., 1868), v. 281

Among the Mormons (Ward, A., 1866), v. 613

Among the Relics (Palmer, T. A., 1869), v. 511

Amorel of Lyonnesse (Brown, W. H. and Lawrence, S. B., 1890), v. 282

Amores da Gileso Scroggini e Molli Brownini (Lemon, M., 1843), IV. 344

Amorous Adventure (1730), II. 365

Amorous Adventures = Marriage A-la-Mode

Amorous Alderman (1773), III. 319

Amorous Bigotte (Shadwell, T., 1690), I. 187, 431

Amorous Fantasme (Lower, Sir W., 1660), I. 420

Amorous Fryars = Rome's Follies

Amorous Gallant = Amorous Orontus

Amorous Goddess (1744), II. 365

Amorous Jilt = Younger Brother

Amorous Knight, and the Belle Widow = Valentine's Day

Amorous Miser (1705), II. x, 209–10, 233, 365, 441, 446

Amorous Old-woman (1674), I. 17, 439

Amorous Orontus (Bulteel, J., 1664), I. 101, 394

Amorous Prince (Behn, A., 1671), I. 83, 140, 266–7, 390

Amorous Quaker = Fox and Geese

Amorous Quarrel (Foote, S., 1762), III. 384

Amorous Sportsman (1732), II. 365

Amorous Widow (Betterton, T., 1670), I. 17, 188, 259, 281, 347, 392; III. 114

Anne Boleyn (Dodson, R., 1873), v. 346
— (Grover, H. M., 1827), IV. 321
— (Lee, N., 1856), v. 642, 802, 826
— (Milman, H. H., 1826), IV. 167, 356
— (Taylor, T., 1876), v. 594
— (1825), IV. 426
Anne Bracegirdle (1847), IV. 426
Annette (1837), IV. 619
Annette Carline (Pitt, G. D., 1848), IV. 375
Annette and Lubin (Dibdin, C., 1778), III. 118, 255, 381
Anne Mie (Scott, C. W., 1880), v. 558
Ann Grandet (1835), IV. 427
Annie Laurie = Bonnie Annie Laurie
Annie Monksworth (Seaman, W., 1859), v. 642, 815, 826
Annie of Edenside (Vynne, C., 1868), v. 609
Annie of Tharau (Zoblinsky, Mme, 1880), v. 637, 825
Annie Tyrell (Serle, T. J., 1852), v. 561
Annira (Waterhouse, B., 1822), IV. 616
Anniversary (1758), III. 319
— = (1) Guilt; (2) Waterloo Bridge
Anniversary of St Patrick = Shamrock
Ann Jane Thornton (1835), IV. 427
Anno Domini 1838 = Murphy's Weather Almanac
Anno Domini 670 = Shadow of the Cross
Anonymous (1838), IV. 427
Anonymous Letter (Ambient, M. and Latimer, F., 1891), v. 240
— (Talfourd, F., 1854), v. 642, 819, 826
Anonymous Letters (Jacques, F., 1888), v. 432
Another (Hodson, E., 1885), v. 423
Another Cup (1881), v. 642
Another Daughter of the Danube (1847), IV. 619
Another Drink (Clarke, H. S. and Clifton, L., 1879), v. 312
Another Elopement (De Lara, F., 1888), v. 341
Another Fish out of Water = Recommendations
Another Glass = Drunkard's Glass
Another Maid and Another Magpie (+Dibdin, C. I. M., 1815), IV. 148, 427

Another Man's Crime = Forgery
Another Man's Money (Payne, W. B., 1884), v. 518
Another Man's Wife (Vaughan, W. J. and Mackay, R. F., 1893), v. 607
Another Matinée = Stage Coach
Another Mistake (1883), v. 642
Another Mummy (1833), IV. 427
Another Pair of Shoes (Hay, F., 1875), v. 411
Another Piece of Presumption (Peake, R. B., 1823), IV. 427, 619
Another Retreat from Moscow = Great Russian Bear
Anster Fair (Pocock, I., 1834), IV. 385
Answer Paid (Burnand, F. C. and Austin, W. J., 1878), v. 291
Antarctic (Farnie, H. B., 1875), v. 362
Anthony and Cleopatra (1891), v. 642
Anthony, Cleopatra and Harlequin (Dibdin, C. I. M., 1804), IV. 91, 291
Anthony Jolt (Bedwell, H., 1896), v. 255
Anthony's Legacy (Charleson, A. J., 1891), v. 308
Anthropos (1898), v. 642
Antichristian Opera (Paul, G., 1755), III. 296
Antigallican = Heiress
Anti-garotte (Collins, C. J., 1857), v. 642, 785, 826 [and see under My Knuckleduster, v. 628]
Antigone (Bartholomew, B., 1845), IV. 262
— (Blanchard, E. L., 1845), IV. 268
— (Fitzball, E., 1821), IV. 312, 427, 584
— (Whitelaw, R., 1890), v. 621
Anti-matrimonial Society (Beauchamp, E., 1876), v. 254
Antiochus (Mottley, J., 1721), II. 110, 346
— (Shuckburgh, C., 1740), II. 355
Antiochus the Great (Wiseman, Mrs J., 1702), II. 104, 160, 364, 446
Antipodes (Allen-Jefferys, J., 1896), v. 239
— (Taylor, T., 1867), v. 593
Antiquarian (Stead, G., 1889), v. 580
Antiquary (Murray, W. H., 1820), IV. 93, 365
— (Pocock, I., 1818), IV. 93, 384
— (Pocock, I. and Terry, D., 1820), IV. 28, 66, 77, 93, 384

Appius (Moncrieff, J., 1755), III. 287

Appius and Virginia (Betterton, T., 1669), I. 392

— (Dennis, J., 1709), II. 20, 31, 56, 86, 214, 318

Apple Blossoms (Albery, J., 1871), v. 237

Apples (Sturgis, J., 1887), v. 586

Appointed Spot (1845), IV. 427

Apprentice (Murphy, A., 1756), III. 21, 179–80, 188, 289

— = Acting Mad

Apprentice's Opera (Dibdin, C. I. M., 1826), IV. 296

April Day (O'Hara, K., 1777), III. 208, 291

— (1782), III, 319

April Folly (Hurst, J. P., 1885), v. 431

April Fool (Fitzball, E., 1841), IV. 316

— (Halliday, A. and Brough, W., 1864), v. 400

— (Macnally, L., 1786), III. 113, 285

— (1788), III. 319

— (1822), IV. 427

— (1895), v. 642

— = Davenport Done

April Fools (Dibdin, C. I. M., 1817), IV. 294

— (1883), v. 642

April Jest (1893), v. 642

April Rain (Outram, L. S., 1886), v. 509

April Showers (Romer, F. and Bellamy, G. S., 1889), v. 549

Apt Pupil (1896), v. 642

Aquatic Harlequin (1809), IV. 427

— = Fashion's Fools

Aquatic Prize (Dibdin, C. I. M., 1805), IV. 291

Aqua Triumphalis (Tatham, J., 1662), I. 434

A qui le victoire? = Cannon-mouth and Pistol-shot

Arab (Cumberland, R., 1785), III. 79, 252

— (1809), IV. 427

— (1812), IV. 427

Arab and his Steed (Rede, W. L., 1846), IV. 391

Arab Boy (1846), IV. 427

Arabella (Moser, J., 1808), IV. 364

Arabella Stuart (Neil, R., 1879), v. 502

Arabian Courtezan = Harlequin Hermit

Arabian Eve (1894), v. 642

Arabian Martyr = Abdallah

Arabian Nights (Grundy, S., 1887), v. 396

Arabian Night's Entertainments (1847), IV. 427

Arabian Vow = Almyna

Arab of the Desert (1831), IV. 427

— = Caliph Haroun Alraschid

Arab of the Desert and his Faithful Steed (Cooke, W., 1856), v. 324

Arab of the Niger = Mungo Park

Arab of the Red Desert = Battle of Navarino

Arab's Faith (Farrell, J., 1822), IV. 427, 619

— = Elphi Bey

Arab's Leap = Hassan Pacha

Arabs of the Desert (1837), IV. 427

— = Bedouins

Arab Spy = Lily of the Desert

Arab's Sacrifice = Leah and Nathan

Arajoon (Coyne, J. S., 1838), IV. 284

Aramanthus (Smith, H., 1821), IV. 402

Arbitration (Reynolds, F., 1806), IV. 391

Arcades of Flora = Florist

Arcadia (Blanchard, E. L., 1841), IV. 268, 573

— (Lloyd, R., 1761), III. 282

— (1849), IV. 427

— (1860), v. 642

Arcadian Brothers (O'Neil, J. R., 1852), v. 507

Arcadian Nuptials (1764), III. 319

Arcadian Pastoral (Craven, E., 1782), III. 249

Arcadie (Burton, J., 1888), v. 294

Archer rides to win = Demon Jockey

Archers of Islington and the Hog of Highbury = Red Cow

Archers of Ludgate = Citizen's Daughter

Archibald Danvers (Southam, G. and Armitage, E., 1893), v. 575

Archibald of the Wreck = Press-Gang

Archie Lovell (Burnand, F. C., 1874), v. 290

Architect (Gypsum, N., 1807), IV. 322

Architopia, Unlimited (Earle, A. E. and Sim, E. H., 1894), v. 353

Archives of the Poor = Halfpenny Club

Archon's Daughter = Lazaria the Greek

Archy Moore (Young, H., 1859), v. 642, 826

Arctic Expedition = North Pole

Arctic Story (1842), IV. 427

Arden of Faversham = Abbey Lands

Arden of Feversham (Lillo, G. and Hoadly, J., 1755, 1759), II. 71, 342; III. 58, 89–90, 281, 390

— (1736), II. 71, 365

— (1799), III. 319

Area Belle (Brough, W. and Halliday, A., 1864), v. 279

Area Bell rung too many times = Cooketish Cook

Area Sylph (1840), IV. 427

Aretoeus (Fuller, C. F., 1881), v. 374

Are You Coming to Bed? (1847), IV. 427

Argalus and Parthenia (1745), II. 365

Argentile and Curan (Mason, W., 1796), III. 286

Argus and his Hundred Eyes (1821), IV. 427

Ariadne (Amcotts, V.), v. 240

— (D'Urfey, T., 1721), II. 32, 236, 320

— (Oxenford, J., 1849), v. 642, 809, 826

— (Perrin, P., 1674), I. 31, 39, 43, 50, 80, 95, 133, 323, 423

— (1859), v. 642

Ariadne in Crete (Colman, F., 1733), II. 389, 434

Ariane (Praed, Mrs C. and Lee, R., 1888), v. 160, 530

— = Ariadne

Arianween (Parry, J., 1890), v. 514

Ariel (Burnand, F. C., 1883), v. 291

Arion (Burnand, F. C., 1871), v. 290

Aristocratic Alliance (Greville, Lady V., 1894), v. 394

Aristocratic Assassin (Siddons, H., 1875), v. 565

Aristocratic Burglar (Dering, C. E., 1897), v. 343

Aristodemus (Burney, F., 1818), IV. 277

— (Favalli, J. A., 1809), IV. 311

— (1802), IV. 427

— (1838), IV. 619

Aristomenes (Finch, Anne, 1713), II, 329

Ark on the Sands (Rennell, C. R., 1870), v. 541

— = Em'ly

Arkwright's Wife (Taylor, T. and Saunders, J., 1873), v. 594

Arline (Brough, W. and Brough, R. B., 1851), v. 278

Arline the Lost Child (Bellingham, H. and Best, W., 1864), v. 257

Arling Lodge (Turner, L. C., 1872), v. 605

Armada (Hamilton, H. and Harris, Sir A., 1888), v. 402

Armadale (Collins, W. W., 1866), v. 318

Armand (Mowatt, A. C., 1849), IV. 427, 601

Armed Briton (Burke, W., 1806), IV. 277

Armenian Queen (?1676), I. 439–40

Armful of Bliss (Moncrieff, W. T., 1843), IV. 427, 619

Armgart (Eliot, G., 1874), v. 356

Armidei (1845), IV. 619

Arminius (Knight, C., 1814), IV. 592

— (Murphy, A., 1798), III. 77, 290

— (Paterson, W., 1740), II. 23, 112, 348, 442

Armistice (Payne, J. H., 1822), IV. 368

— = Peter Smink

Armourer (Cumberland, R., 1793), III. 252

— (Dodson, R., 1876), v. 346

— (Hope, N., 1894), v. 426

Armourer of Nantes (Bridgeman, J. V., 1863), v. 275

Armourer of Paris (1837), IV. 428

Armourer's Daughter (Arnold, H. T., 1866), v. 243

Armourer's Forge (1834), IV. 428

Arms and the Man (Shaw, G. B., 1894), v. 90, 189, 195, 197, 201, 203, 204, 562

Armstrong the Shipwright (Haines, J. T., 1839), IV. 323

Army and the Navy = Watchman

Army of the North (Planché, J. R., 1831), IV. 379

Army, the Navy and the Volunteers (1870), v. 642

Arnold of Winkelried (Lemon, M., 1836), IV. 343

Army without Reserve = British Amazons

Arrah-ma-Beg (1866), v. 642

Arrah-na-Pogue (Boucicault, D., 1864), v. 89–91, 268

Arrah Niel (1872), v. 642

Arrah-No-Brogue (Shelley, 1865), v. 642, 816, 826

Arrangement (De Trueba, J. T., 1831), IV. 428, 619

Arrant Knave (Mackaye, J. S., 1889), v. 471

Arrested on Suspicion (1877), v. 642

Arrival of Redgauntlet = Practical Jokes

Arrivals (Lennox, W., 1821) = Incog., IV. 428, 619

Ar-rivals (Banero, J. M. and Pincroft, A. D., 1884), v. 248

Arrivals and Marriages = Love and Gout

Arrivals from College = Honour

Arrived at Crow-Street (1796), III. 319

Arrived at Last (1823), IV. 428

Arrived at Portsmouth! (Pearce, W., 1794), III. 204, 297

Arrogance brought down (McLaren, A., 1824), IV. 352

Arrogant Boy (1802), IV. 428

Arrow, the Apple and the Agony = William Tell

Arrow which killed the King = Knight of the Sepulchre

Arsaces (Hodson, W., 1775), III. 70, 83, 270

Arsinoe (Henderson, A., 1752), III. 268

Arsinoe, Queen of Cyprus (Motteux, P. A., 1705), II. 36, 226, 231, 234, 266, 389

Art (Brigdman, C., 1874), v. 275

— (Reade, C., 1855), v. 536, 812

— (1881), v. 642

Art and Love (Dubourg, A. W., 1877), v. 351

Art and Nature (Miller, J., 1738), II. 13, 146, 182, 203-4, 344, 441

Artaxerxes (Arne, T. A., 1762), III. 28, 69, 197, 233

— (Hoole, J., 1767), III, 387

— (1811), IV. 428

Artful Automaton (Law, A. and Hall, K., 1878), v. 449

Artful Cards (Burnand, F. C., 1877), v. 290

Artful Dodge (Blanchard, E. L., 1842), IV. 268

Artful Girl (Ridge, W. P., and Pearce, J. E., 1892), v. 543

Artful Husband (Taverner, W., 1717), II. 157, 171, 358; III. 116, 170

Artful Little Spouser (Robertson, L. and Comerford, M., 1882), v. 545

Artful Patriot = Patriot

Artful Plans (1895), v. 642

Artful Trick and Love in the Dark = Fireman and the Volunteer

Artful Wife (Taverner, W., 1717), II. 197, 358

Arthur and Emmeline (1784), III. 58, 319

Arthur, Monarch of the Britons (Hilton, W., 1776), III. 269

Arthur Orton (Stephens, W., 1874), v. 581

Arthur's Bakery Co. (Silvester, F., 1898), v. 566

Arthur's Round Table Restored = Institution of the Garter

Article 47 = Louisiana Creole

Artifice (Centlivre, Mrs S., 1722), II. 156, 306; III. 115

— (Miles, W. A., 1780), III. 287

Artificial Flower Maker (Hazlewood, C. H., 1871), v. 414

Artipadiades, King of Queeramania (1822), IV. 428

Artisan's Daughter (1842), IV. 428

— (1861), v. 642

Artisan's Triumph (Wood, A., 1861), v. 630, 642, 826

Artist (Wibrow, G. V., 1894), v. 621

Artist and his Family (Phillips, F. L., 1859), v. 642, 810, 826

Artiste de Terracina (1853), v. 643

Artistic Dilemma (Fenton, C., 1893), v. 365

Artist of Cas (1846), IV. 428

Artist of Rome = Graven Image

Artist's Ghost = Love and Art

Artist's Model (Hall, O. and Greenbank, H., 1895), v. 400

— (Lynn, N., 1892), v. 465

— (1894), v. 643

Artist's Muddle = Eugénie

Artist's Wife (À Beckett, G. A., 1838), IV. 250

— (1854), v. 643

Artizan and his Daughters (Archer, T., 1845), IV. 255

Artless Cinderella (Field, H. K. H., 1895), v. 365

Art of Love = Calypso

Art of Management (Charke, Mrs C., 1735), II. 23, 261, 306

Art of Modern Poetry = Harlequin-Horace

Art of Pleasing = Chameleon

Art of Seeing = Eyes and No Eyes

Arts and Crafts (James, A. and James, D., 1897), V. 432

Arts in an Attic = Lofty Projects

Arviragus (Tasker, C., 1795), III. 310

As a Man sows (Ramsay, A. and De Cordova, R., 1898), V. 534

Asancesado (1837), IV. 428

Ascot (Fendall, P., 1879), V. 364

Asgard, the Demon Hunter (Scott, J. M., 1812), IV. 397

As Gold through Fire (1873), V. 643

— (1879), V. 643

As Good as Gold (Coghlan, C. F., 1869), V. 316

Ashamed to Own It = All in the Dark

Ashantee Prince (1842), IV. 428

Ashantees (Almar, G., 1825), IV. 568

Ashantee War (Lowe, W., 1874), V. 464

— (Sandford, J., 1874), V. 555

— = King Coffee

Ashbrooke Blacksmith = Ding Dong Will

Ashby Manor (Allingham, W., 1883), V. 59, 239

Ashes (Collins, E. and Saunders, R., 1894), V. 318

Ashlynn (1870), V. 643

Ashore and Afloat (Hazlewood, C. H., 1864), V. 412

Asiatic (Yeo, 1790), III. 318, 398

As in a Glass (Rodway, J. and Lauri, C., 1887), V. 548

As in a Looking Glass (Grove, F. C., 1887), V. 160, 395

As it Should Be (Oulton, W. C., 1789), III. 185, 296

Ask No Questions (Selby, C., 1838), IV. 398

— = Father Matthias

As Large as Life (Shirley, A., 1890), V. 564

Aslan the Lion (Barrymore, W., 1824), IV. 262

Aslar and Ozines (Haines, J. T., 1842), IV. 323

Asleep or Awake (1823), IV. 428

As Like as Two Peas (Lille, H., 1854), V. 459

Asmodeus (1885), V. 643

Asmodeus, the Devil on Two Sticks (1859), V. 643

Asmodeus, the Little Demon (Archer, T., 1843), IV. 84, 254

Aspacia (Hughes, Mrs A., 1790), III. 274

Asprand (1805), IV. 428

As Pretty as Seven (1887), V. 643

A.S.S. (Maddox, J. M., 1853), V. 472

Assassin (Bell, R., 1816) = Watchword, IV. 428, 619

— (Hill-Mitchelson, E., 1890), V. 422

— = Man in the Cloak

Ass-ass-ination (Hook, T. E., 1810), IV. 328

Assassin Labourer (1827), IV. 428

Assassin of Dijon (1831), IV. 428

Assassin of Nantes = Julie de Moin

Assassin of Silesia = Fatal Precept

Assassin of Stebonheath = Man of Mile End

Assassin of the Rocks = False Friend

Assassins of Aveyron = Wild Girl

Assassins of Istria = Bertha

Assassins of Paris = Courier

Assassins of the Forest = Frederick the Great and the Deserter

Assassins of the Roadside (Douglass, J. T., 1865), V. 643, 788, 826

Assassins of the Roadside Inn = Assassins of the Roadside

Assault and Battery = Welcome Visit

+Assembly (Worsdale, J., Smock Alley, Dublin, 18/4/1740)

— (1722), II. 365

— (1752), III. 319

Assignation (À Beckett, G. A., 1837), IV. 249, 567

— (Dryden, J., 1672), I. 191, 230, 405

— (Fisher, 1812), IV. 318, 583

— (Lee, S., 1807), III. 281; IV. 343

— (1826), IV. 428

Assignation, Dissipation and Starvation (1830), IV. 428

Association = Downfall

Assommoir (Foote, J., 1879), V. 370

— (Sidney, W., 1879), V. 566

— (1879), V. 643

— (1882), V. 643

Assumptions (1823) = Guardians Outwitted, IV. 428, 619

Assurance Company (Fitzball, E., 1836), IV. 315

Assyrian Spy (1852), V. 643

As the Night Cometh (Grogan, W. E., 1899), V. 395

As the World Goes (Horde, T.), III. 273

Aston Hall (1854), V. 643

Astonishment (1818), IV. 428

Astounding Phenomena (Mathews, C. J., 1847), IV. 354

Astray from the Flock (1881), V. 643

Astrea Appeased (Olivari, F., 1797), III. 295

Astrologer (Dibdin, C. I. M., 1810), IV. 292

— (Ralph, J., 1744), II. 350

Astrologer's Star = Bertha the Broom Girl

Astronomer (Amphlett, 1802), IV. 254

+ — (Dibdin, C. I. M.: R.A., 1798)

Astronomy a Farce = Philosophic Whim

As You Find It (Boyle, C., 1703), II. 154, 232, 299, 432

As You Like It (Kemble, J. P., 1815), IV. 335

— (Macready, W. C., 1842), IV. 353

— (Moser, J., additional scene, 1809), IV. 364

— (1746), II. 365

— (1824), IV. 428

+ As you make your bed so you must lie in it (French)

At a Health Resort (Paull, H. M., 1893), V. 516

Atala and Chactas (Dibdin, C. I. M., 1825), IV. 295

Atalanta (Hawtrey, G. P., 1888), V. 410

— (Talfourd, F., 1857), V. 590

Atalanta in Calydon (Swinburne, A. C., 1865), V. 589

At All in the Ring (Dibdin, T. J., 1817), IV. 301

At Anchor in the Bay of Naples (1794) = Naples Bay, III. 319, 398

At any cost = Desperate Man

At Bay (Lander, C. and Cassilis, I. L., 1888), V. 447

At Break of Day (Tracey, F. T., 1894), V. 602

Atchi— (Morton, J. M., 1868), V. 496

At Dead of Night (Whyte, H., 1897), V. 621

At Duty's Call (Gerant, J., 1898), V. 377

Athalia (Humphreys, S., 1733), II. 390, 439

Athaliah (Duncombe, W., 1724), II. 320, 435

Athanase (Roberts, E. F., 1847), IV. 608

Atheist (Otway, T., 1683), I. 188, 423

Athelstan (Brown, J., 1756), III. 82, 240

Athelstane (1854), V. 643

Athelwold (Hill, A., 1731), II. 108–9, 116, 336, 438

— (Smith, W., 1843), IV. 303 [The author's full name is William Henry Smith]

Athenian Captive (Talfourd, T. N., 1838), IV. 48, 142, 177, 410

At Home (1813), IV. 428

At Home and Abroad = Face to Face

Atlantic Jack (Travers, W., 1860), V. 822

Atlantis (Dalton, M. and Genet, E., 1886), V. 333

Atlantis Destroyed = Apostate

At Last (Clarance, L., 1883), V. 311

— (Gough, H. and Edwards, M., 1896), V. 386

At Mammon's Shrine (Landeck, B., 1887), V. 447

Atonement (Fisher, C. A., 1894), V. 367

— (Poole, J., 1836), IV. 387

— (Muskerry, W., 1872), V. 500

Atreus and Thyestes (Sinnett, E., 1821), IV. 401

Atrocious Criminal (Simpson, J. P., 1867), V. 567

At Santa Lucia (Grist, W., 1894), V. 395, 795

At Sea (1882), V. 643

At Stake (Killick, J. M., 1870), V. 444

Attack of the Caravan = Horse Banditti and their Forty Steeds

Attack of the Diligence (Amherst, J. H., 1829), IV. 254

Attack of the Dragoons = Brigands of Ancona

Attack on Monterreau = Grand Army

Attack on the Convoy (1828), IV. 428

Attack upon the Mail = Courier of Lyons

Attar Gull (Almar, G., 1832), IV. 252

Attempt to please = Touch at the Times

At the Cross Roads (Dilley, J. J., 1894), v. 345

At the Ferry (Fawcett, Mrs, 1897), v. 364

At the Foot of the Altar (Jarman, F., 1897), v. 434

At the Foot of the Ladder (Travers, W., 1869), v. 603

At the Harbour Side (Pinkerton, P. and Grist, W., 1900), v. 525, 810

At the Kirk Arms (Malyon, E. J. and James, C., 1897), v. 473

At the Madonna's Shrine (1847), IV. 428

At the Mercy of the World = Wrecked in London

At the Pantomime (Grain, R. C., 1890), v. 388

At the Sword Point (Lashbrooke, H. and Perry, R. D., 1884), v. 449

Attic Drama (James, F., 1898), v. 433

Attic Science and Mimic Art = Scheming and Seeming

Attic Story (Morton, J. M., 1842), v. 352

+ Attila (8°, 1840)

Attila, my Attila (Field, M., 1896), v. 366

At Zero (Teale, L. and Hughes, T., 1898), v. 594

Auberge des Adrets (Selby, C., 1834), IV. 428, 619

— = Two Murderers

Auchindrane (Scott, Sir W., 1830), IV. 397

Auction (Cibber, T., 1757), II. 314, 437; III. 116, 243

Auctioneer (Dibdin, T. J. ?1796), III. 382

— (Morton, J. M. and Reece, R., 1898), 497

Auction of Pictures (Foote, S., 1748), II. 329

Augusta (Poole, J., 1823), IV. 386

Augusta's Triumph = Brutus of Alba

August First (1831), IV. 428

Augustus (Biddle, E., 1717), II. 298

Augustus and Gulielmus (Holland, W. A., 1806), IV. 328

Augustus Buggins (Selby, C., 1834), IV. 428, 619

Au Japon (1896), v. 643

Auld Acquaintance (Dilley, J. J., 1878), v. 345

Auld Lang Syne (Gordon, G. L., 1877), v. 385

— (Hood, B., 1892), v. 425

— (Lee, N., 1846), IV. 342

— (Leigh, N., 1891), v. 454

— (Stirling, E., 1843), IV. 407

— = Rob Roy Macgregor

Auld Robin Gray (Arnold, S. J., 1794), III. 19, 206, 234

— (Byrne, J., 1814), IV. 277

— (Fitzball, E., 1858), v. 368 [probably = the play listed without date, IV. 317]

— (Hazlewood, C. H., 1856), v. 643, 796, 826

— (Macfarren, G., 1828), IV. 350

— (Roy, G., 1883), v. 552

Aunt Agatha's Doctor (Harraden, H., 1891), v. 404

Aunt Charlotte's Maid (Morton, J. M., 1858), v. 486

Aunt Chimpanzee (Williams, R. A. P., 1897), v. 625

Aunt Dorothy (1855), v. 643

Aunt Hannah (1899), v. 643

Auntie (Byron, H. J., 1882), v. 299

Auntie's Motor (John, G. and War, C., 1899), v. 437

Auntie's Young Man = What! More Trouble!

Aunt Jack (Lumley, R. R., 1889), v. 464

Aunt Jemima (1894), v. 643

Aunt Madge (1898), v. 643

Aunt Margaret (Pease, S., 1897), v. 518

Aunt or Uncle (Wilson, A. J., 1885), v. 628

Aunt Rebecca (Atwood, A. and Vaun, R., 1895), v. 245

Aunt's Advice (Sothern, E. A., 1861), v. 575

Aunt Tabitha (Morland, F. H., 1894), v. 493

Aurelia = Roman Empress

Aurelian (1897), v. 643

Aurelio = Aurelio and Miranda

Aurelio and Miranda (Boaden, J., 1798), III. 72, 238, 378

Aureng-Zebe (Dryden, J., 1675), I. 24, 68, 101, 115, 345, 346, 405; III. 58

Au Revoir (1896), v. 643

Auromania (Pritchard, J., 1871), v. 531

Aurora (Noble, 1817), IV. 428, 620

— (1865), v. 643

— (1893), v. 643

Aurora Floyd (Ashley, J. B. and Melton, C., 1885), v. 244

— (Cheltnam, C. S., 1863), v. 309

— (Hazlewood, C. H., 1863), v. 412

— (Johnstone, J. B., 1863), v. 800

— (Webster, B. the Younger, 1863), v. 618

— (1863), v. 643

Aurora's Nuptials (1734), II. 365

Austerlitz (Haines, J. T., 1831), IV. 322

Australia (Stanley, A. G. and Archer, W., 1881), v. 579, 778

Australia Felix (1862), v. 643

Austrian Peasant (1791), III. 319

Author (Foote, S., 1757), III. 172, 259

— (Greville, E. E., 1891), v. 394

Author on the Wheel (1785), III. 319

Authors (Jones, L., 1755), III. 277

Author's Box (1896), v. 643

Author's Farce (Fielding, H., 1730), II. 21, 41, 232, 255, 263, 323, 381

Author's Triumph (1737), II. 366

Automaton (Beckwith, 1832), IV. 428, 620

Autumnal Dream = Camille

Autumn Manoeuvres (Stow, W. R., 1871), v. 585

Autumn Sheaves (1872), v. 643

Avalanche (Harris, A. G., 1854), v. 404

— (Taylor, T. P.), IV. 614

Avare (Ozell, J., 1732), II, 347, 442

Avare corrigé (1790), III. 319

+Avarice (Emson, F. E., 8°, ?1877)

— (? Johnstone, J. B., 1857), v. 643, 800, 826

Avenger (Lee, H., 1824), IV. 428, 620

— (Lovell, G. W., 1835), IV. 347

— (Moule, F., 1899), v. 498

— (1838), IV. 428

— (1846), IV. 428

Avenger's Vow (Linders, G., 1863), v. 804

Avenging Gift = Storm Visitor

Avenging Hand (Bartlett, H., 1899), v. 252

Avenging Hand of Fate and the Shilling Legacy = Life of Guilt

Average Man (Courte, S. X., 1895), v. 325

Avventura di Scaramuccia (1836), IV. 428

Awakening (Benham, A., 1892), v. 257

Awaking (Clarke, C., 1872), v. 151, 311

Away down East = Yankee Courtship

Away with Melancholy (Morton, J. M., 1854), v. 495

Awful Experience (Dening, Mrs C., 1893), v. 342

Awful Rise in Spirits (Taylor, T., 1863), v. 593

Awkward (1885), v. 643

Awkward Affair (Hay, F., 1878), v. 411

Awkward Dilemma (Scarlett, W., 1893), v. 557

Awkward Mistake (1881), v. 643

Awkward Recruit (1805), IV. 428

Axe and the Sword = Headsman

Axel and Valborg (Chapman, J. F., 1851), v. 783

Ayesha (1836), IV. 428

Aylma's Dream (1886), v. 643

Aylmere (Conrad, R., 1846), IV. 282

Ayrshire Tragedy = Auchindrane

Azael (Fitzball, E., 1851), v. 367, 792

— (Rodwell, G. H., 1851), v. 548

— = Prodigal Son

Azael the Prodigal of Memphis (Fitzball, E., 1851), v. 367, 792

Azamoglan (Dixon, W. H., 1845), IV. 581

Azel the Arab (James, C. S., 1851), v. 433

Azim (Dibdin, T. J., 1818), IV. 301

Azim and Alzira = Silver Valley

Azor and Zemira (Ball, W., 1831), IV. 428, 620

Azurine (1860), v. 643

Bab (1882), v. 643

Babbage's Puppets (1884), v. 643

Bab-Ballad Monger (Lindo, F., 1892), v. 460

Babbler (1762), III. 319, 398

Babble Shop (Rose, E., 1893), v. 550

Babes (Paulton, H., 1884), v. 516

Babes and Beetles = Babes in the Wood

Babes in the Wood (À Beckett, G. A., 1867), v. 233

— (Bailey, W. E., 1898), v. 247

Babes in the Wood (Bowyer, F., 1898), v. 272
— (Byam, M. and Wyke, E. B., 1891), v. 294
— (Byam, M., Graham, F. and Vincent, W. T., 1897), v. 295
— (Capel, G., 1884), v. 302
— (Chute, J. H., 1858), v. 784
— (Daly, B. and East, J. M., 1896), v. 334
— (Gordon, G. L. and Anson, G. W., 1877), v. 384
— (Grahame, J. C. and Artlett, B., 1895), v. 387
— (Hall, F., 1880), v. 399
— (Jones, J. W., 1894), v. 441
— (Jones, J. W., 1898), v. 441, 800
— (Jourdain, J., 1888), v. 442
— (Lander, G., 1873), v. 448
— (Locke, F., 1886), v. 804
— (McArdle, J. F., 1881), v. 644, 804, 827
— (McCabe, C. W. and Belmore, G., 1893), v. 467
— (Mead, T., 1873), v. 483
— (Merion, C., 1875), v. 485
— (Ramsdale, T., 1891), v. 534
— (Rice, C., 1874), v. 542
— (Robson, W., 1843), IV. 395
— (Roe, J. E., 1870), v. 814
— (Rogers, T. S., 1884), v. 644, 814, 827
— (Sturgess, A. and Collins, A., 1897), v. 586
— (Summers, W. J., 1899), v. 645, 818, 827
— (Taylor, T., 1860), v. 593
— (Thorne, G., 1888), v. 598, 820
— (Thorne, G., 1890), v. 598
— (Thorne, G., 1894), v. 821
— (Woolfe, J. H., 1896), v. 644, 824, 827
— (1824), IV. 428
— (1855), v. 643, 827
— (1856), v. 645
— (1857, 1858), v. 826
— (1859, 1860), v. 827
— (1869), v. 643
— (1872), v. 827
— (1875, 1876, 1877, 1878, 1879, 1880, 1881, 1884, 1885, 1886), v. 643-4
— (1887), v. 827

Babes in the Wood (1887, 1889), v. 644
— (1889), v. 827
— (1890, 1892, 1893, 1894, 1896, 1897, 1898, 1899), v. 644-5
— (1899), v. 827
Babes in the Wood and Bold Robin Hood (Lennard, H., 1892), v. 455, 803
— (1894), v. 645
Babes in the Wood and the Good Little Fairy Birds (Byron, H. J., 1859), v. 295
Babes in the Wood, Robin Hood and his Merry Men, and Harlequin who killed Cock Robin (Harris, Sir A. G. H., Blanchard, E. L. and Nichols, H., 1888), v. 405
Babes of the Castle (Dibdin, C. I. M., 1809), IV. 292
Babes out of the Wood = Little Offsprings
Babette (Murray, A. and Mosenthal, J. G., 1888), v. 500
Babil and Bijou (Boucicault, D. and Planché, J. R., 1872), v. 269
Babington (Doubleday, T., 1826), IV. 428, 582, 620
Babiole (Reece, R., 1879), v. 538
Baboon of Paraguay (1830), IV. 428
Baboo or Prince? (Daly, C., 1897), v. 334
Baby (Cowell, A. E., 1892), v. 327
— (Greville, Lady V., 1890), v. 394
— (Hook, W., 1888), v. 425
— (Soutar, R. and Herbert, F. H., 1890), v. 575
— (Waldron, W. R. and Ellis, L., 1896), v. 611
— (1883), v. 645
Baby and the Bachelor = Runaways
Baby and the Regimentals (Graham, J. H., 1850), v. 387
Baby Bunting (1897), v. 645
Baby's Birthday (Bucklaw, A., 1893), v. 286
Baby's Engagement (Rogers, R., 1892), v. 549
Baby's Hat (1891), v. 645
Baccarat (Suter, W. E., 1865), v. 588
Bacchanalian Festival = Charioteers
Bacchus (1855), v. 645

Bacchus and˙Ariadne (Leclercq, 1841), IV. 594
— (Mereweather, C., 1891), v. 806
— (1734), II. 366
— (1861), v. 645
Bacchus and Cupid (1715), II. 366
Bacchus Festival (Jordan, T., 1660), I. 415
Bachelor of Arts (Hardwicke, P., 1853), v. 403
Bachelor of Duddington (Ebsworth, J.), IV. 309
Bachelor Quarters = Bungalow
Bachelors (Aldred, A. A., 1884), v. 238
— (Buchanan, R. and Vezin, H., 1884), v. 284
— (Wharton, C. H. M., 1885), v. 619
Bachelors and Married Men = Balance of Comfort
Bachelor's Box (1882), v. 645
Bachelor's Buttons (Stirling, E., 1837), IV. 406
Bachelors' Fare = Helpless Animals
Bachelors' Hall (Gordon, G. L., 1877), v. 384
— = Bachelors
Bachelors' Miseries (1818), IV. 429
Bachelor's Romance (Morton, M., 1896), v. 497
Bachelor's Vow (Phillips, E., 1849) = Prejudice, IV. 429, 604, 620
Bachelor's Widow (O'Hare, J. F., 1897), v. 506
Bachelor's Wife (Watson, F., 1858), v. 615
Bachelors' Wives (Beazley, S. Jr., 1817), IV. 263
— (Bousfield, F., 1886), v. 270
— = P.Q.
Bachelor, the Maid, the Wife and the Widow = Domestic Arrangements
Back-Biter (1836), IV. 429
Back from India (Stevens, P. and Dick, C., 1879), v. 583
Back from the Grave = Church and Stage
Back from the Land of Yesterday = Not Guilty
Back in Five Minutes (Johnson, H. T., 1891), v. 437
Backing the Favourite (Gordon, G. L., 1875), v. 384

Back in Town (Grain, R. C., 1894), v. 388
Backsheesh (Grain, R. C., 1884), v. 387
Backslider (Shillingford, O., 1895), v. 563
Backwoodsman's Daughter = David Hunt
Back to Life = Mad
Bad Bargain (Grundy, S., 1879), v. 396
Bad Boys (Scott, C. W., 1885), v. 558
Bad Business (1832), IV. 429
Bad Customers (1810) = Who Pays the Piper, IV. 429, 620
Baden Baden (Bateman, R., 1872), v. 253
Bad D(j)inn and the Good Spirit = Camaralzaman and the Fair Badoura
Badinage de Provence (1735), II. 366
Bad Lot (Paulton, H. and Tedde, M., 1887), v. 517
Bad Luck's Good Luck with Good looking after = Leprechaun
Bad Neighbours (Arnold, S. J., 1810) = Plots, IV. 429, 620
Bad Penny (Lestocq, W., 1882), v. 457
Bad Quarter of an Hour (Costello, Miss, 1896), v. 325
Baffled (1878, 1881, 1884), v. 645
Baffled Crime (McCabe, C. W., 1896), v. 467
Bagging a Barrister (Stockton, E., 1896), v. 585
Baghran-Ho (1812), IV. 429
Bag of Gold (Hillyard, J., 1852), v. 422
Bag of Tricks (Potter, M., 1896), v. 529
Bagpipes (1895), v. 645
Bagshot Heath Camp (1792), III. 319
Bailie Bewitched = Bogle of the Clyde
Bailiff (Broughton, F. W., 1890), v. 282
Bailiff and the M.P. = Contrivances
Bailiff's Bet = Walk for a Wager
Bail Up (Hughes, J., 1893), v. 430
Bairn (Duncan, G., 1878), v. 352
Bakarak, the Miser (1824), IV. 429
Baker's Bride = Kitchen
Baker's Daughter = Fire of London
Baker worried by Buckstone = Keeley worried by Buckstone
Balaam (Davy, C., 1787), III. 351, 381
Balaclava (Johnstone, J. B., 1878), v. 438
Balaclava Day (1856), v. 645

Balaclava Heroes = Duty

Balaclava Joe (Emery, C. P., 1892), v. 358

Balance of Comfort (Bernard, W. B., 1854), v. 259

— (Raymond, R. J., 1836), IV. 389

Balcony Beau = My Wife's Dentist

Bald Head (1840), IV. 429

Baldur (Anderton, H. O., 1893), v. 241

Balet de la Paix (1660), I. 440

Ballad Girl (1866), v. 645

Ballad Monger (Besant, W. and Pollock, W. H., 1887), v. 260

Ballad Singer (Craven, T., 1891), v. 329

— (Moncrieff, W. T., 1839), IV. 361

Ballanasloe Boy (Hazlewood, C. H., 1867), v. 413

Ballet des Sauteurs et Voltigeurs (1788), III. 319

Ballet et Musique pour le divertissement (1674), I. 440

Ballet Girl (Tanner, J. T., 1897), v. 591

Ballet-girl and the Jew = Honour and Shame

Balloon (Darnley, J. H. and Fenn, G. M., 1888), v. 337

— (1812), IV. 429

Balloonacy (Burnand, F. C. and Stephens, H. P., 1879), v. 291

Balloon Agent = Mad or Not Mad

Balloon in Turkey (1837), IV. 429

Ball upon Deck = On Board the Mars

Ballybaggerty Bequest (Cleaver, M., 1852), v. 314

Ballyhooley (Bogue, J. R., 1898), v. 266

Ballynavogue = Row of Ballynavogue

Ballyvogan (Lloyd, A., 1887), v. 461

Bal Masqué (Ward, A. H., 1898), v. 613

— (1848), IV. 429

— = Any Port in a Storm

Baltic Fleet (1854), v. 645

Bamboozell = Lock and Key

Bamboozle (1860), v. 645

Bamboozling (Wilks, T. E., 1840), IV. 421

Bambuzleum (1872), v. 645

Bamfyde Moore Carew (Jerrold, D. W. + Surrey, 21/5/1824), IV. 331

Bampfyde Moore Carew (+ Moncrieff, W. T., 1816), IV. 331, 620

Bandalero the Bandit (Barrie, Sir J. M., 1877), v. 778

Bandit (Burges, Sir J. B., 1817), IV. 276–7

— (1814), IV. 429, 635

Bandit Farmer = When the Clock Strikes

Bandit Host (Rogers, W., 1839), IV. 609

Bandit Innkeepers (1832), IV. 429

Bandit King (1895), v. 645

Bandit Merchant (1847), IV. 620

— = Maid of Genoa

Bandit of Bohemia = Geraldi Duval

Bandit of Corsica (1840), IV. 620

Bandit of Otranto = Justinio

Bandit of Sicily (Courtney, J., 1860), v. 786

Bandit of the Blind Mine (Milner, H. M., 1821), IV. 356

Bandit of the Charmed Wrist = Spoglioni

Bandit of the Rock = Female Courage

Bandit Queen (1861), v. 645

Bandits = Malak the Jew

Bandit's Bride = Hag of the Glen

Bandit's Daughter = Salvatori

Bandit's Revenge = Castle of de Courcy

Banditti (D'Urfey, T., 1686), I. 221, 274, 409

— (O'Keeffe, J., 1781), III. 292

Banditti of the Cavern = When the Bell Tolls

Band of Death (1821), IV. 429

Band of Patriots = Constantine Paleologus

Bang Up! (Dibdin, C. I. M., 1810), IV. 292

Banished Brother (1818), IV. 429

Banished Cavalier = Rover

Banish'd Duke (1690), I. 440

Banished from Home (Griffiths, J. C., 1875), v. 394

Banished General (1731), III. 366

+ Banished Lord (8°, 1842)

Banished Star (Buckstone, J. B., 1840), IV. 275

Banishment of Cicero (Cumberland, R., 1761), III. 77, 125, 251

Banish't Cavaliers = Rover

Banker's Clothes Philosophy = Fact and Fancy

Banker's Daughter (Foster, W. C., 1876), v. 371

Banker's Son (1883), v. 645

Banker's Son and the Felon's Daughter
= Leap for Life

Banker, the Thief and the Will = Two
London Locksmiths

Bank Holiday (Cooper, H. B., 1886), v.
324

Bank Note (Macready, W., 1795), III.
116, 170–1, 285

Bank Robbery (Dawson, F., 1896), v.
339

Bankrupt (Campbell, A. V., 1835), IV.
278

— (Foote, S., 1773), III. 174, 260

Bankrupt Cobbler (1806), IV. 429

Banks and Breaks (O'Byrne, 1869), v.
506

Banks of Allan Water (Barnett, C. Z.,
1831), IV. 259

Banks of the Boyne Water (1884), v. 645

Banks of the Delaware = Recluse

Banks of the Elbe = All in the Dark

Banks of the Hudson (Dibdin, T. J.,
1829), IV. 305

Banks of the Lee = Bells of Shandon
+ Banner (Pemberton, C. R.; 8°, 1843,
(in *The Life and Literary Remains*))

Bannian Day (Brewer, G., 1796), III.
239

Bannister's Budget with the Shipwreck
(1814), IV. 429, 620

Bannockburn (Milner, H. M., 1827), IV.
429, 620

Banquet (Freeth, F., 1888), v. 373

Banquet Gallery = (1) Feudal Times;
(2) Silver Knight

Banquet of Wiles = Bilker Bilk'd

Banshee (Levey, J. C., 1876), v. 458

Banshee's Spell (Watson, J. S. W.,
1882), v. 616

Bantry Bay (Bond, S., 1897), v. 267

— (Reynolds, G. N., 1797), III. 301

Bar and the Stage = T.T.S.

Barark Johnson (Reeve, W., 1844), IV.
391

Barataria (Pilon, F., 1785), III. 114, 298

Barbara (Jerome, J. K., 1886), v. 436

— (Kenney, J., 1838), IV. 338

Barbara Allen (Dibdin, C. I. M., 1803),
IV. 291

Barbarossa (Brown, J., 1754), III. 82,
208, 240

Barbarous Idea (1857), v. 827

Barbazon (Matthison, A., 1887), v. 481

Barbe Bleue (Kenney, C. L., 1869), v.
801

Barber (Fitzball, E., 1822), IV. 312, 584

— (1892), v. 645

Barber and his Brothers (1826), IV.
429

Barber and the Bravo (Vernier, I.,
1846), IV. 415

Barber and the Hairdresser (1828), IV.
429

Barber and the Olive Merchant = Mill of
Bagdad

Barber, Barber, Shave the Cat (Seaman,
W., 1859), v. 645, 815, 827

Barber Baron (Thackeray, T. J., 1828),
IV. 412

Barber Barrister (1838), IV. 429

Barber Blue (1869), v. 645

Barber Bravo (Reynoldson, T. H.,
1846), IV. 393

— (1846) = Barber and the Bravo, IV.
429 (*and see* 415)

Barber Duellist = Modern Honour

Barber of Bagdad (Browne, E. M.,
1891), v. 283, 780

— (1826), IV. 429

Barber of Bath (Farnie, H. B., 1879), v.
362

Barber of Bishopsgate = Blood-spiller

Barber of Cadiz (1869), v. 645

Barber of Fleet Street = Sweeney Todd

Barber of Paris (O'Neil, J. R., 1853), v.
507

— (1842), IV. 429

Barber of Pera (Moser, J., 1808), IV.
364

Barber of Seville (Fawcett, J. and
Terry, D., 1818), IV. 311, 583

— (Griffith, Mrs E., 1776), III. 119,
266, 386

— (1824), IV. 429

— (1831), IV. 429

Barbers at Court (Mayhew, H. and
Smith, G., 1835), IV. 429, 620

Barbers of Bassora (Morton, J. M.,
1837), IV. 362

Barber's Petition (1796), III. 319

Barber's Secret (Archer, T., 1846), IV.
255

Barber's Trip to Paris (1876), v. 645

Barbier de Cadiz (1855), v. 827

Barcarolle (1847), IV. 429, 620

Bard and his Birthday = Shakespearian Reverie

Bard Bewitched = Christabelle

Bardes = Ossian

Bard, the Baron, the Beauty = Princess Charming

Bardwell versus Pickwick (Hollingshead, J., 1871), V. 424

— (Gem, T. H., 1881), V. 377

Barefaced Imposters (Taylor, T., 1854), V. 592

Barely Possible (1869), V. 646

Bargain Broken = Canterbury Guests

Bargeman of the Thames (1866), V. 646

Bargeman's Secret = Roving Meg

Bargemaster's Daughter (1863), V. 646

Barley Mow (Frith, W., 1892), V. 374

Barmaid (Dance, G., 1891), V. 335

Barmaid's Career = Jenny Vernon

Barmecide (Milner, H. M., 1818), IV. 356

Barnaby Brittle (1781), III. 114, 319

— (1811), IV. 429

Barnaby Rudge (Barnett, C. Z., 1841), IV. 97, 570

— (Phillips, W. and Vining, 1866), V. 523

— (Selby, C. and Melville, C., 1841), IV. 97, 398

— (Stirling, E., 1841), IV. 97, 407, 429, 620

— (1876), V. 646

Barn at Beccles (Hughes, G. and Bickley, A. C., 1891), V. 430

Barn Ball = Wagustur

Barn Burners (Rede, W. L., 1833), IV. 429, 607, 620

Barnes of New York (Collier-Edwards, H., 1888), V. 317

Barnet Fair = Black Legend

Barney Brallaghan (1830), IV. 429

Barney Brallaghan's Courtship (1827), IV. 429

Barney Buntline Ashore (Rogers, W., 1845), IV. 396

Barney Burke (1845), IV. 430

Barney's Mistake (1881), V. 646

— = Dhrame

Barney the Baron (Lover, S., 1857), V. 463, 804

Barn in a Bustle = Swiss Revels

Barnwell, the London Apprentice (1822), IV. 430

Baron (Holcroft, F., 1805), IV. 326

Baron and his Brothers = Three Crumpies

Baron de Trenck (1820), IV. 256, 430, 620

Baroness (Dick, C., 1892), V. 344

Baroness of Bruchsal = Disbanded Officer

Baronet (Sinclair, H., 1893), V. 570

— (Vincent, E. H., 1885), V. 609

— (1840), IV. 430

Baronet Abroad and the Rustic Prima Donna (Horne, F. L., 1864), V. 426

Baronet and the Bandit = Pimple the Pirate

Baronet Bit (1741), II. 366

Baronets (1870), V. 646

Baronet's Wager (Keeble, Mrs, 1869), V. 442

Baron Fitzarden (1845), IV. 620

Baron Golosh (1895), V. 646

Baron Kinkvervankotsdorsprakingatchdern (Andrews, M. P., 1781), III. 8, 204, 233

Baron Munchausen (Fenton, F. and Osman, W. R., 1864), V. 646, 792, 808, 827

— (Lonsdale, M., 1795), III. 319, 391, 398

— (1839), IV. 430

— (1840), IV. 430

Baron of Corvelle (Green, F. and Hanson, E., 1892), V. 392

Baron Rudolph (Howard, B., 1881), V. 428

Baron's Bride = Sylvia

Baron's Daughter (Bowles, E. W. and Phillips, G. R., 1893), V. 271

Barons of Ellenbergh (Weston, F. F., 1808), IV. 418

Barons of Ubaldo = Red Banner

Baron's Wager (Young, Sir C. L., 1881), V. 636

Baron, the Bride and the Battery = Last of the Legends

Baron Trenck (Arnold, S. J., 1830), IV. 256

— (Osbaldistone, W., 1831), IV. 256, 602

— (1899), V. 646

Barrack Room (Bayly, T. H., 1836), IV. 263, 571

Barren Island (1734), II. 366

Barren Land (Byatt, H. and Magnay, W., 1888), V. 295

Barricade (Holt, C., 1869), V. 424

Barringtons (Fitzgerald, S. J. A. and Merrifield, J. H., 1884), V. 369

Barrington Geo = Barrington, the Gentleman Pickpocket

Barrington's Busby (Fraser, J. A., 1883), V. 372

Barrington, the Gentleman Pickpocket (Marchant, F., 1862), V. 646, 805, 827

Barrington, the Pick-Pocket (1833), IV. 430

Barrister (Fenn, G. M. and Darnley, J. H.), V. 365

— (Reynoldson, T. H., 1852) = Home Truths, V. 542, 693, 813

Barry the Dauntless (Gatward, Hal. and Thompson, W. T., 1890), V. 377

Bar Sinister = David

Barsissa (Dibdin, C. I. M., 1816), IV. 294

Bars of Gold (Rae, J. and Sidney, T., 1892), V. 533

Bartholomew Fair (?1668), I. 446

Bartonmere Towers (Barrington, R., 1893), V. 251

Bartons of Barton Wold (Montgomery, B. S., 1865), V. 491, 646, 827

Barwise's Book (Craven, H. T., 1870), V. 329

Bas Bleu (Logan, W. H., 1835), IV. 430, 595, 620

Base Coin = Downward Path

Base Impostor (Wigan, H., 1859), V. 622

Basement to Let = Faith and Hope

Base Metal and Sterling Coin = Crooked Ways

Bashaw (1801), IV. 430

— (1809), IV. 430

Bashaw and the Bear = Bruno

Bashful Irishman (Lemon, M., 1843), IV. 344

— (1843), IV. 430

Bashful Lovers (1861), V. 646

Bashful Man (Moncrieff, W. T., 1824), IV. 359

Bashful Virgin (1760), III. 399

Basil and Barbara, Children of the Bottle (Pitt, G. D., 1848), IV. 430

Basiliska (1870), V. 646

Basil's Faith (1874), V. 646

Basket Girls of Liverpool (Hazlewood C. H., 1875), V. 415

Basket-Maker (O'Keeffe, J., 1790), III. 294

— (1831), IV. 430

— = Claudine

Basoche (Harris, Sir A. H. G. and Oudin, E., 1891), V. 406, 795

Basque Roads (1809), IV. 430

Bassett-Table (Centlivre, Mrs S., 1705), II. 196, 304

Bastard Brother = Charter

Bastard Child (1768), III. 319

Bastille (Atkyns, S., 1845), IV. 257

— (Dent, J., 1789), III. 19, 34, 54, 254

— (1842), IV. 430

Bastille of Calvados = No. 20

Bat and Ball (Russell, F., 1881), V. 553

Batchelors (1799), III. 63, 319, 399

Bateman (1703), II. 366

Bath (D'Urfey, T., 1701), I. 14; II. 194, 320, 435

Bath Bridge in 1830 = Maiden Lane Murder

Bathing (Bruton, J., 1842), IV. 272

Bathing Machine (1796), III. 319

Bath Intrigues, II. 366

Bath Road (Poole, J., 1830), IV. 430, 620

Bath Roll (Knight, C. J., 1894), V. 445

Bath Struggle = Dromio the Drinker

Bath Unmask'd (Odingsells, G., 1725), II. 178, 347

Bath Waters = Hot and Cold

Battered Batavians (Cawdell, J., 1798) = Down with the Dutch, III. 242, 400

Battle (Villiers, G., 1704), I. 436

Battledore and Shuttlecock (Lee, N., 1847), IV. 342

Battle Field = (1) Flag; (2) Victories of Edward the Black Prince

Battle of Agincourt (Milner, H. M., 1825), IV. 430, 620

— (1834), IV. 430

— = Harry of England

Battle of Aughrim (Ashton, R., 1728), I. 100; II. 262, 295

Battle of Austerlitz (1859), V. 646

Battle of Bannockburn = Robert the Bruce

Battle of Barnet (1845), IV. 430

Battle of Blenheim (Haines, J. T., 1841), IV. 430, 620

Battle of Bosworth Field (1824), IV. 430

— (1827), IV. 90, 430

— = (1) King Richard III; (2) Life and Death of King Richard III; (3) White Rose and the Red Rose

Battle of Bothwell Brig (Calcraft, J. W., 1823), IV. 93, 278

— (Middleton, 1827), IV. 598

— (Townsend, W. T., 1858), v. 646, 821, 827

Battle of Bothwell Brigg (Farley, C. 1820), IV. 93, 310

Battle of Bovines (Mildenhall, T., 1840), IV. 598

Battle of Brunanburgh = Ethelstan

Battle of Chevy Chase (1875), v. 646

Battle of Ching Ho = Chinese War

Battle of Clontarffe = Brian Boroihme, the Victorious

Battle of Cressy = Edward the Black Prince

Battle of Cronstad (1828), IV. 430

Battle of Drumclog = Covenanters

Battle of Eddington (Penn, J., 1792, 1797), III. 297

— = Alfred the Great

Battle of Flodden Field = Marmion

Battle of Garra-muir = Perkin Warbeck

Battle of Hastings (Cumberland, R., 1778), III. 13, 78, 251

— = (1) Invasion of England, by William the Conqueror; (2) King Harold

Battle of Hexham (Colman, G., the Younger, 1789), III. 247, 379; IV. 140

— (1812) IV. 140, 430

Battle of Inkerman (1854), v. 646

Battle of Jersey (1881), v. 646

Battle of Life (Atkyns, S., 1847), IV. 98, 257

— (Dickens, C., Jr., 1873), v. 344

— (Lyon, T. E., 1847), IV. 98, 348

— (Parry, A. W. and Dobb, T., 1894), v. 514

— (Pitt, G. D., 1847), IV. 98, 374

— (Robertson, T. W., 1847), v. 546

Battle of Life (Smith, A. R., 1846), IV. 98, 402

— (Somerset, C. A., 1847), IV. 98, 405

— (Stirling, E., 1847), IV. 98, 408, 613

— (Stocqueler, J. H., 1893), v. 646

— (1847), IV. 98, 430

— = 1870

Battle of Lincoln = King Stephen

Battle of Luncarty (Galloway, G., 1804), IV. 318

Battle of Navarino (1828), IV. 430

Battle of Otterburn = Chevy Chase

Battle of Philippi = Death of Caesar

Battle of Poictiers = Edward the Black Prince

Battle of Pultawa (Raymond, R. J., 1829), IV. 430, 620

— = (1) Charles XII and Peter the Great; (2) Peter the Great

Battle of Salamanca (Dibdin, C. I. M., 1812), IV. 292

Battle of Sedgemoor (Almar, G., 1837), IV. 253

— (1707), II. 366

Battle of Stirling Bridge = Wallace

Battle of Televera (1809), IV. 430

Battle of the Alma (Stocqueler, J. H., 1854), v. 646, 818

— (1856), v. 646

Battle of the Amazons (Wilks, T. E., 1848), IV. 421

Battle of the Bridges = Blood will have Blood

Battle of the Dandies = Half-way House

Battle of the Fairies (1836), IV. 430

Battle of the Greybeards = Humorous Quarrel

Battle of the Heart (Wilkins, J. H., 1865), v. 646, 823, 827

Battle of the Inch = St Valentine's Eve

Battle of the Nile (1799), III. 19, 71, 320

— (1815), IV. 14, 430

Battle of the Poets (Cooke, T., 1730), II. 316

Battle of the Season (Towers, E., 1867), v. 821

Battle of the Sexes (Saunders, J. D., 1898), v. 556

Battle of the World = Slaves of London

Battle of Trafalgar (1806), IV. 430

— (1824), IV. 14, 430

Battle of Vittoria (1813), IV. 431

Battle of Waterloo (Amherst, J. H., 1824), IV. 254, 568
— (1815), IV. 431
— (1825), IV. 431
— (1854), V. 646
Battle of Woman (1851), V. 646
Battle of Worcester (1825), IV. 431
— = King Charles II
Battle of Worcester and the Royal Oak = England's Monarch
Battle Royal (Matthison, A., 1878), V. 481
— (1785), III. 320
Battles of Parnassus and Fall of Bob = Fall of Bob
Battles of the West = Siege of Isca
Battle through Life (Mitchell, W. H., 1890), V. 490
Battle with the World (Courtney, J., 1861), V. 786
Bauble and Co. = Stella
Bauble Shop (Jones, H. A., 1893), V. 440
Baucis and Philemon (1740), II. 366
Bavarian Girl (Suter, W. E., 1869), V. 588
Bawd turn'd Puritan = Bragadocio
Bawdy-House School (1744), II. 366
Bayadère (Deshayes, 1831), IV. 431, 620
— (Horncastle, J. H., 1844), IV. 328, 589
— (1845), IV. 431
Bayaderes = Race for a Rarity
Bayes at Parnassus = Macheath in the Shades
Bayes no Poetaster = Two Queens of Brentford
Bayes's Art of Acting = Meeting of the Company
Bayes's Opera (Odingsells, G., 1730), II. 347
Bayes the Younger = New Rehearsal
Bay of Biscay (+ Rogers, W., 1841), IV. 620
— (Somerset, C. A., 1841), IV. 404
Bayonet (Hart, J. P., 1836), IV. 431, 620
Bays in Chromatics = Music Alamode
Bays in Petticoats = Rehearsal
Bazilette (Fitzsimon, J. F., 1881), V. 369
Bazzard d'Algier (Didelot, 1814), IV. 581
B.B. (Burnand, F. C. and Williams, M., 1860), V. 288, 781
Beacon (Baillie, J., 1812), IV. 258
Beacon Light (Clarance, L., 1891), V. 311

Beacon of Liberty (Bailey, P., 1823), IV. 431, 620
Beacon Tower = Mountain Maid
Beam of Fate = Watch-word
+ Bear (Norton, Mrs Caroline, ?1880)
+ Bear and Forbear (Bell, G., French)
Beard and Moustache Movement (1854), V. 646
Bearding the Lion (Fawcett, C. S., 1884), V. 364
Beard's Night (1760), III. 320
Bear-Hunters (Buckstone, J. W., 1825), IV. 272
Béarnaise (Murray, A., 1886), V. 500, 808
Bears, not Beasts (Capel, G., 1880), V. 302
— (Faucit, J. S.), IV. 583
— (Milner, H. M., 1821), IV. 356
— (1823), IV. 431
Bear, the Eagle and the Dolphin = Magic Horn
Bear the worse, and hope for the better = Unfortunate Youth
Beast and the Beauty (Burnand, F. C., 1869), V. 289, 781
Beasts' Burletta = Lions for a Lark
Beata (Fryers, A., 1892), V. 374
Beaten at Last = Man in a Thousand
Beaten by a Shadow (1882), V. 646
Beatrice (Blake, T. G., 1844), IV. 268
Beatrice Maxwell (1896), V. 646
Beatrice of Ferrara (Plunkett, A. H., 1837), IV. 606
Beau Austin (Henley, W. E. and Stevenson, R. L., 1884), V. 61, 187, 417
Beau bedevill'd = Cure for a Coxcomb
Beau Blandish the Rake (Calmour, A. C., 1887), V. 300
Beau Brummel (Jerrold, M. W. B., 1859), V. 436, 800
Beau Defeated (Pix, Mrs M., 1700), II. 171–2, 349, 419, 442
Beau Demolished (1715), II. 366
Beau Ideal (Lover, S., 1835), IV. 347
Beau in the Sudds = Female Parson
Beaujolais the Necromancer = Is She his Daughter?
Beau Lavender (Glennie, G., 1896), V. 382
Beau Metamorphos'd = Happy Lovers

Beau Nash, the King of Bath (Jerrold, D. W., 1834), IV. 332

Beau of the Belles = Dick

Beau outwitted (1788), III. 320

— = Sop in the Pan

Beau's Adventures (Bennet, P., 1733), II. 215, 297

Beau's Duel (Centlivre, Mrs S., 1702) II. 61, 166, 303

Beau! the Belle! and the Blacksmith!!! = Acis and Galatea

Beauties of Canterbury = Oaks

Beauties of the Harem (1854), v. 646

— (1871), v. 827

Beauties of the Poets = Blazing Comet

Beauties Triumph (Duffett, T., ?1675), I. 408

Beautiful Armenia (Ball, E., 1778), III. 235

Beautiful as a Butterfly = Cupid and Psyche

Beautiful Bride and the Bouncing Bachelor (1866), v. 646

Beautiful Duchess (1886), v. 646

Beautiful for Ever (Hay, F., 1868), v. 411

— (Hodgson, G. S., 1868), v. 423 [The two plays may be identical although they were credited to separate authors]

Beautiful Galatea (1882), v. 646

Beautiful Haidee (Byron, H. J., 1863), v. 296

Beautiful Helen of Troy = Helen of Troy up-to-date

Beautiful Insane (McLaren, A., 1824), IV. 352

Beauty and the Bard = Merry Mignon

Beauty and the Beast (Blanchard, E. L., 1869), v. 264

— (Blanchard, E. L. and Greenwood, T. L., 1874), v. 264

— (Brennan, J. C., 1871), v. 274

— (Chambers, T., 1861), v. 783

— (Davey, P., 1897), v. 338

— (Denny, J. T., 1884), v. 342

— (Denny, J. T., 1888), v. 342

— (Green, F. W., 1877), v. 391

— (Hazlewood, C. H., 1874), v. 797

— (James, C. S., 1851), v. 433

— (McArdle, J. F. and Stimson, F. J., 1883), v. 647, 804, 827

Beauty and the Beast (McLelland, H. F., 1892), v. 468

— (Oxenford, J., 1863), v. 510, 809

— (Planché, J. R., 1841), IV. 381

— (Roe, J. E., 1866), v. 814

— (Shaw, W. B., 1860), v. 816

— (Stimson, F. J. and Seymour, F., 1885), v. 818

— (Stratford, W., 1894), v. 585

— (Walden, R., 1879), v. 610

— (Yardley, W. and Harris, Sir A., 1890), v. 634, 825

— (1812, 1819, 1821), VI. 431

— (1854), v. 646

— (1857, 1860), v. 827

— (1875, 1876, 1877, 1879, 1881), v. 646

— (1882, 1884, 1887, 1889), v. 647

— (1891), v. 827

— (1891, 1893, 1894, 1895, 1899), v. 647

— = Azor and Zemira

Beauty and the Bey (Dibdin, T. J., 1820), IV. 431, 620

Beauty and the Brigand (1858), v. 827

Beauty and the Brigands = Fra Diavolo Travestie

Beauty and Virtue (1762), III. 320

Beauty in a Box (Dibdin, T. J., 1825), v. 294

Beauty in Distress (Motteux, P. A., 1698), I. 19, 63, 170, 421

Beauty of Bruges (1842), IV. 431

Beauty of Buttermere = Edward and Susan

Beauty of Ghent (Albert, 1844), IV. 251

Beauty of Lyons = Perourou, the Bellows Mender

Beauty or the Beast (Oxenford, J., 1863), v. 510

Beauty's Awakening (1899), v. 827

Beauty Show (Manley, H., 1899), v. 474

Beauty Stone (Pinero, Sir A. W. and Carr, J. W. C., 1898), v. 525

Beauty's Trials (Fawcett, C. S., 1893), v. 364

Beauty's Triumph = Beauties Triumph

Beauty the Best Advocate = Measure for Measure

Beauty the Conqueror (Sedley, Sir C., 1702), I. 428

Beaux Merchant (?Blanch, J., 1714), II. 261, 299

Beaux Stratagem (Farquhar, G., 1707), II. x, 131, 132, 134, 135, 136, 137, 138, 149, 183, 184, 322, 420, 436; III. 115, 127; IV. 140
— (Lawler, D., 1810), IV. 431, 620
Because of Billy Rudd (Hamilton, C., 1898), v. 401
Becket (Cattermole, R., 1832), IV. 576
— (Tennyson, Alfred Lord, 1879), v. 208, 595
Becky Sharp (Barrie, J. M., 1893), v. 211, 251
Bedding Makes the Bargain = Twice Married and a Maid Still
Bedlam Broke Loose = John Brown
Bed of Roses (Jones, H. A., 1882), v. 439
Bedouin and the Fire-Worshipper = Silver Veil
Bedouins (Irwin, E., 1801), IV. 329
Bedroom Window (Stirling, E., 1848), IV. 409
Beds for Two (Stirling, E., 1843), IV. 407
Bee and the Orange Tree (Planché, J. R., 1845), IV. 382
Beechborough Mystery (Galer, E. J. N. and Mew, J., 1889), v. 375
Beef Tea (Greenbank, H., 1892), v. 392
Bee Hive (Millingen, J. G., 1811), IV. 356, 599
— (1827), IV. 431
Beelzebub on Horseback = Tam o' Shanter
Beelzebub's Belles = Devil's Daughter
Been had (Pleon, H., 1889), v. 528
Beeswing in Port (1855), v. 647
Beethoven (Hein, G., 1879), v. 416
Beethoven's Romance (Raphael, S. A., 1894), v. 535
Before and After Luncheon = Double Courtship
Before and Behind the Curtain = Masks and Faces
Before Breakfast (Peake, R. B., 1826), IV. 370
Before, During and After the French Revolution = Three Generations
Before the Dawn (Byatt, H., 1895), v. 295
Before the Mast (Broughton, F. W., 1884), v. 281
Before the Play = Our Opera

Before the Sun goes Down (Hamilton, C., 1899), v. 401
Beggar (Broughton, F. W., 1889), v. 281
Beggar and the Soldier (1841), IV. 431
— = (1) Assassin of Dijon; (2) Smugglers of Dieppe
Beggar Girl of Lambeth Marsh = Green Mantle
Beggar Marquis (Howe, J. B., 1863), v. 798
Beggar my Neighbour (Morton, T., 1802), IV. 363
— (1870), v. 647
Beggar of Bethnal Green (Knowles, J. S., 1834), IV. 339
Beggar of Brussels (1860), v. 647
Beggar of Cripplegate (Moncrieff, W. T., 1830), IV. 360, 600
Beggar of Crosby Hall = Fool of Finsbury
Beggar on Horseback (O'Keeffe, J., 1785), III. 293
— (Sullivan, R., 1846), IV. 409
Beggar's Banquet (1862), v. 647
Beggar's Bush (1815), IV. 431
— = (1) Merchant of Bruges; (2) Royal Merchant
Beggar's Daughter of Bethnal Green (Knowles, J. S., 1828), IV. 339
Beggar's Grave = Sexton of Stepney
Beggar's Haunt (Blink, G., 1837), IV. 573 [By error, the date is wrongly given in the text as 1847]
Beggars of Flanders = White Hoods
Beggars of London = Seven Dials
Beggars of the Sea = Veva
Beggars of Tivoli = Four Hunchbacks
Beggars of Toulouse (1832), IV. 431
Beggar's Opera (Gay, J., 1728), II. 2, 3, 10, 134, 135, 136, 137, 138, 211, 237, 239–40, 241, 243, 245, 249, 250, 251, 269, 300, 331, 396, 412, 424; III. 116, 191, 192; IV. 1
— (Thompson, E., 1777), III. 116, 311
— (1781), III. 320, 399
— (1781), III. 320
— (1811), IV. 431
Beggar's Opera Burlesqued (1840), IV. 431
Beggar's Opera (parody on) (Hogg, C., 1809, IV. 326
Beggar's Opera Reversed (1781), III. 399

36

Belle of the Barley Mow (Arnold, H. T.,
1867), v. 243
Belle of the Bath (Eliot, A., 1897), v. 356
Belle of the Hotel (1842), IV. 431
Belle of the Season (?Heron, M., 1866),
v. 647, 827
— = New Year's Eve
Belle of the West = Wild Violet
Belle Russe (Belasco, D., 1881), v. 255
Belles and Bailiffs = Married and Single
Belles and the Ring (1847), IV. 432
Belles' Association (1780), III. 320
Belle Sauvage = (1) Ko and Zoa; (2)
Pocahontas; (3) Wild Girl; (4) Zora
Belles Have at Ye All (1831), IV. 431
Belles of the Kitchen (1869), v. 647
Belles of the Shannon = Garry Owen
Belles of the Village (Foster, H., 1889),
v. 371
Belle's Stratagem (Cowley, Mrs H.,
1780), III. 165–6, 167, 181, 248, 380;
IV. 190
— (Waldron, F. G., 1782) = Imitation,
III. 320, 397, 399
— (1781), III. 320
Belles without Beaux (1819) = Young
Prude, IV. 432, 620
Belle, the Baron and the Bear Hunter =
Daughter of the Danube
Belle Vue (Price, J., 1883), v. 531
— (Quittenden, R., 1877), v. 532
Bell in Campo (Cavendish, M., 1662),
I. 396
Belling the Cat (Becher, M., 1886), v.
254
Bell of Belle-Hawke (1873), v. 647
Bell-ringer (Barnett, C. Z., 1834), IV.
259, 570
— (Shirley, A. and Vane, S., 1897), v.
564
Bell-Ringer of Notre Dame (Abel,
W. H., 1871), v. 234
Bell-Ringer of St Paul's and his Daugh-
ter (Townsend, W. T., 1839), IV. 414
Bells (Lewis, L. D., 1871), v. 149, 459
Bells all gone wrong = Faust Reversed
Bells Bellesqued and the Polish Jew
Polished Off (1883), v. 647
Bells in the Storm (Hazlewood, C. H.,
1874), v. 415
Bells of Fate (Darbey, E., 1891), v.
356

Bells of Haslemere (Pettitt, H. and
Grundy, S., 1887), v. 521
Bells of Notre Dame = Midnight
Bells of Shandon (1863), v. 647
— (1868), v. 647
Bells of the Sledge (Allen, H., 1891), v.
239
Bells of Varnavale (1895), v. 647
Bells that Rung an Old Year Out and a
New Year In (1862), v. 647
Belly Wager = Selfe Interest
Belmont and Constance (1841), IV. 432
Belmonti (1830), IV. 432
Below London Bridge (Dowling, R.,
1896), v. 349
Belphagor (Wilson, J., ?1675), I. 262,
301, 438
Belphegor (Andrews, M. P., 1778), III.
204, 233
— (Buckingham, L. S., 1856), v. 286
— (Jones, J. W., 1889), v. 441
— (1851), v. 647
Belphegor the Buffoon (Higgie, T. H.
and Lacy, T. H., 1851), v. 421, 798
Belphegor the Itinerant (Courtney, J.,
1851), v. 326
Belphegor the Mountebank (Webb, C.,
1856), v. 647, 823, 827
— (Webster, B. N., 1851), v. 618
Belphegor, the Mountebank to any
Amount of Property (Hazlewood,
C. H., 1866), v. 647, 796, 827
Belshazzar (Harrison, T., 1727), II. 334
— (Milman, H. H., 1822), IV. 167, 356
— (More, Mrs H., 1782), III. 288
— (1745), II. 390
Belshazzar's Feast (Ball, W., 1834), IV.
569
Belveder (Almar, G., 1831), IV. 82, 252
Ben and Bob, the British Bulldogs =
Triumph of the Standard
Ben Block (1835), IV. 432
Ben Bolt (Johnstone, J. B., 1854), v. 438
— (1854), v. 647
Ben Brace (Faucit, J. S., 1836), IV. 432,
583, 620
Ben Bradshaw (Fitzball, E., 1844), IV.
316
Ben Child (Young, Mrs H., 1863) =
Swallows' Nest, v. 648, 755, 827, 847
Beneath the Lamps of London =
Beggar's Banquet

Beneath the Stars (Ellis, B., 1899), v.
357
Beneath the Surface (Murdoch, J. M.,
1873), v. 499
— = Dutch the Diver
Beneath the Three Spires (1876), v. 648
Beneath the Waters (1899), v. 648
Benedetto Mangone (Holl, H., 1836),
IV. 432, 620
Benefice (Wild, R., 1689), I. 437
Benefit Night (1844), IV. 432
Benefit of Hanging = Miser Smoked
Benefit of the Doubt (Pinero, Sir A. W.,
1895), v. 525, 810
Benevolent Cut-throat (1800), III. 320;
IV. 432
Benevolent Israelite = Conrad, the Rob-
ber Chief
Benevolent Jew (1821), IV. 432
Benevolent Jew of St Mary Axe =
Goodman's Fields in the Olden Time
Benevolent Man (Walker, M. C., 1773),
III. 314 [This was first acted Smock
Alley, Dublin, 18/2/1773]
Benevolent Planters (Bellamy, T.,
1789), III. 236
Benevolent Tar (1823), IV. 432
— = Purse
Benevolent Tars of Old England = Poor
Jack
Bengal Tiger (Dance, C., 1837), IV. 288
Ben Hur (?Young, W., 1899), v. 648,
827
Benicia Boy = B.B.
Benighted Monarch = Harry le Roi
Benliel (Travers, W., 1857), v. 648, 821,
827
Benliel, the Son of the Night (1884), v.
648
Ben Lighterware (Rayner, A., 1859) =
Foundling of the Sea, v. 648, 812
Ben-my-Chree (Caine, H. and Barrett,
W., 1888), v. 299
Ben Nazir, the Saracen (Grattan, T. C.,
1827), IV. 320
— (1842), IV. 432
Ben the Boatswain (Wilks, T. E., 1839),
IV. 421
Bentivoglio (Masterton, C., 1824), IV.
353
Benvenuto Cellini (Walby, 1853), v.
610

Benyowsky (Kenney, J., 1826), IV. 87,
337
Bequeathed Heart = Gabrielli
Bereaved Wife and Mother (1857), v.
648
Berta (Smart, H., 1855), v. 571
Bertha (Fitzball, E., 1819), IV. 312, 584
— (1851), v. 827
Bertha and Durimel (1821), IV. 432
Bertha Gray (1859), v. 648
Bertha Gray, the Pauper's Child (1851),
v. 648
Bertha's Bridal = Kiss
Bertha the Broom Girl (Pitt, G. D.,
1845), IV. 373
Bertram (Maturin, C. R., 1816) = Castle
of St Aldobrand, IV. 167, 354, 598
Bertrand (Harper, S. B., 1837), IV. 587
Bertrand and Burkenstaff (1834), IV. 432
Bertrand and Matilda = Rival Cavaliers
Bertrand and Suzetta = Marriage of
Reason
Bertrand de Courcy (1863), v. 648
Bertulfe, the Provost of Bruges = Pro-
vost of Bruges
Beside a Cradle (Latham, G., 1888), v.
449
Beside the Bonny Briar Bush (McArthur,
J., 1898), v. 467
Bess (Beringer, Mrs O., 1891), v. 259
Bessie (Brooke, E. H., 1878), v. 276
Bessie Bell and Mary Gray (McLaren,
A., 1808), IV. 351
Bess of the Bell (Blake, T. G., 1854), v.
262
Bessy Moore (Hazlewood, C. H., 1860),
v. 796
Best Bidder (Andrews, M. P., 1782), III.
233
Best Heart in the World (Moser, J.,
1807), IV. 364
Best Intentions (Marshall, P. F. and
Purdon, R., 1890), v. 478
Best Man (Lumley, R. R., 1894), v. 465
— (Playfair, G. M. H., 1898), v. 528
Best Man Wins (Melford, M., 1890), v.
484
Best of Husbands (Buckstone, J. B.,
1832), IV. 432, 620
Best of Mothers = Medea
Best People (Fairfax, Mrs, 1890), v.
360

Best Room in the House = Grim Griffin Hotel

Best Way (Wigan, H., 1866), v. 622

Be Sure You've Got on Your Own (1880), v. 648

Betha the Betrayer (1881), v. 648

Bethnal Green in the Olden Time = Wilkins the Weaver

Betly (1838), IV. 432

— (1841), IV. 432

Betrayed (Mansell, R., 1886), v. 474

— (1873), v. 648

— = Mary Lister

Betrayed by a Kiss (Saintsbury, H. A., 1891), v. 554

Betrayed Innocence = Lyddy Beale

Betrayer of his Country = Earl of Westmoreland

Betrothal (Boker, G. H., 1853), v. 266, 779

Betrothed (Fitzball, E., 1826), IV. 95, 313

— (1836), IV. 95, 432

— = (1) Betrothal; (2) Minerali

Betrothed Lovers (1881), v. 648

Betsey Baker (Morton, J. M., 1850), v. 495

Betsy (Burnand, F. C., 1879), v. 291

Betsy Baker (Hanray, L., 1895), v. 403

Betsy's Bailiff (Shute, E. A., 1893), v. 565

Betsy's Found (1856), v. 648

Better Angel (Reeve, W., 1868), v. 540

Better Days = Next of Kin

Better Half (Williams, T. J., 1865), v. 625

— (1896), v. 648

Better late than Never (Andrews, M. P. and Reynolds, F., 1790), III. 176, 233

— (Burnand, F. C., 1874), v. 290

— (Davies, W., 1786), III. 253

— (Palmer, E., 1870), v. 511

— = (1) Early Bird; (2) Invitation; (3) Legion of Honour; (4) Look on the Bright Side; (5) Nanette

Better Luck Next Time (Moore, R., 1870), v. 492

Better Man = Darkest Hour

Better Self (1882), v. 648

Better than Gold (East, J. M. and Dodson, E., 1894), v. 353

— = Divorce

Betting Boy (Webb, C., 1852), v. 617

Betting Boy's Career (James, C. S. and Johnstone, J. B., 1852), v. 433

— (1852), v. 648

Betting Boy's Career, from his Home to the Hulks (1852), v. 648

Betting Boy's Career, from the Counting House to the Hulks (1852), v. 648

Betting Boys, from the Counting House to the Hulks (1852), v. 648

Betty (Carey, H., 1732), II. 302, 432

Betty Martin (Robertson, T. W., 1855) = Clockmaker's Hat, v. 546

Between the Acts (Norman, G. T., 1898), v. 505

Between the Lights (Lampard, E. J., 1894), v. 446

Between the Posts = Indécis

Between Two Stools (Gray, L., 1886), v. 390

Betwixt the Cup and the Lip (Lonergan, Mrs E. A., 1896), v. 462

Beulah Spa (Dance, C., 1833), IV. 190, 288

Beverley Bogey (Hingeston-Randolph, M. and Giffard, A., 1897), v. 422

Beware of Jealousy (1891), v. 648

Beware of Man Traps (Younge, A., 1851), v. 637

Beware of the Centenier (1877), v. 648

Bey of Bagdad (Carlton, Charles, 1897), v. 303

Beyond (1894), v. 648

Beyond the Breakers (Vane, S., 1893), v. 606

Bianca (Robson, W. J., 1856), v. 547

— (Shepherd, R., 1772), III. 305

— (1846), IV. 432

Bianca Capello (Thompson, B., 1796), III. 311

Bianca Contarini (Greenwood, T., 1840), IV. 321

Bianca de Molino (Webb, C., 1845), IV. 417

Bianca, the Bravo's Bride (Simpson, J. P., 1860), v. 567

Bianca Visconti (Willis, N. P., 1843), IV. 422

Biarritz (Jerome, J. K. and Ross, A., 1896), v. 436

Bibb and Tucker (Clayton, J., 1873), v. 648, 784, 828

Bibbins and Figgins (Suter, W. E., 1860), v. 648, 818, 828

Bibboo (Somerset, C. A., 1842), IV. 405
— (1839), IV. 432

Bickerstaff's Burying (Centlivre, Mrs S., 1710), II. 168, 210, 305

Bickerstaff's Unburied Dead (1743), II. 215, 366

Bicycle (Bell, Mrs H., 1896), v. 256

Bicycle Belle = Lady Cyclist

Bicycle Girl (Osborne, C., Stuart, E. M. and Seton, H., 1896), v. 508

Biddy O'Neal (Pitt, W. H., 1869), v. 527

Bier Kroeg (Barnett, C. Z., 1830), IV. 259

Bigamy = His Wives

Bigamy, Trigamy and Quadrigamy = Everybody's Husband

Big Bandit (Watson, T. M., 1894), v. 616

Big Blue Bowl (Castles, F., 1888), v. 306

Big-bodied Bill, Big Belzebub's Boy (1850), v. 648

Big Fortune (Bourne, W., 1891), v. 270

Big O and Sir Glory (Cobbett, W., 1825), IV. 281

Bigot (Grove, F. C., 1890), v. 395

Bijou Residence to Let (Van de Velde, Mme, 1889), v. 606

Bilbery of Tilbury (Dauncey, S. and Day, G. D., 1898), v. 337

Bilious Attack = Chamber of Horrors

Bilker Bilk'd (1742), II. 364, 384

Bill Adams the Sailor = Mutineer's Widow

Bill and Me (1883), v. 648

"Bill due Sept. 29th" = Wanted a Partner

Billee Taylor (Stephens, H. P., 1880), v. 580

Billet Doux (1860), v. 648

Billet-master (Ward, W., 1767), III. 317 [By error this appears in III. 317 under W. Wood. The author's name was William Ward]

Billing and Cooing (Oxenford, J., 1865), v. 510
— = Old Turtles

Bill Jones (Amherst, J. H.), IV. 254

Bill of Exchange (Fisher, D., 1879), v. 367

Bill of Fare (Dibdin, C. I. M., 1822), IV. 295
— (Dibdin, T. J., 1822), IV. 303

Bill-Sticker (Jerrold, D. W., 1836), IV. 333, 590

Bill Stickers Beware (1875), v. 648

Bill! the Belle!! and the Bullet!!! = Freischutz

Bill! the Whole Bill!! and Nothing but the Bill!!! = More Reform!

Billy (Cooper, G. and Ross, A., 1898), v. 324

Billy and Mrs Button's Journey = Election

Billy Button's Disaster (1807), IV. 432

Billy Button's Journey to Brentford (Lee, N., 1853), v. 452

Billy Button's Ride to Brentford (1854), v. 648

Billy Doo (Rae, C. M., 1874), v. 532

Billy Duck (Dibdin, C. I. M., 1822), IV. 295
— (Dibdin, C. I. M., 1826), IV. 296

Billy Snivel and Sally Sly (1834), IV. 432

Billy Taylor (Buckstone, J. B., 1829), IV. 273
— (George, G. H., 1871), v. 377
— (Mowbray, T., 1861), v. 807

Billy Taylor, the Gay Young Fellow (1831), IV. 432

Binbian Mine (Praed, Mrs C. and McCarthy, J., 1888), v. 530

Binke's Blues (1884), v. 648

Binks' Photographic Gallery = Dream

Binks the Bagman (Coyne, J. S., 1843), IV. 284, 578
— (1842), IV. 432

Binks the Downy Photographer = Dream

Biorn (Marshall, F. 1877), v. 478

Birdcage Walk (Bennett, H. L. and Tapping, A. B., 1892), v. 258

Bird Catchers (1750), III. 320

Birdcatchers of Whitechapel (1859), v. 648

Bird Fancier = Isn't it a Duck?

Birdie's Nest (1884), v. 648

Bird in a Cage (1786), III. 320

Bird in the Bush = Rossignol

Bird in the Hand worth Two in the Bush (Phillips, F. L., 1857), v. 522, 810

Bird of Paradise (Thompson, A., 1869), v. 597

Bird of Paradise (1800), IV. 432

Bird of Passage (Webster, B. N., 1849), IV. 418

Birds, Beasts and Fishes (Lee, N., 1854), V. 648, 802, 828

Birdseller of Paris = Otto the Outcast

Birds in their little nest agree (Rae, C. M., 1876), V. 532

Bird's Nest (Lindo, F., 1898), V. 460

Birds of a Feather (Hatton, J.), V. 796
— (1796), III. 320

"Birds" of Aristophanes (Planché, J. R., 1846), IV. 382

Birds of Bloomsbury Bower = Bloomers

Birds of Paradise (Jerrold, D., 1835), IV. 432, 620
— = Love Birds

Birds of Prey (Hawkins, Mrs P. L., 1884), V. 410
— (Robertson, T. W.), V. 123, 547
— = Mouth of the Pit

Birds without Feathers (1824), IV. 432

Birmingham Bagsmen = Forty Winks

Birmingham Girl (1844), IV. 432

Birmingham in 1643 = Aston Hall

Birth (Robertson, T. W., 1870), V. 546

Birth and Adventures of Harlequin (1735), II. 366

Birth and Breeding (Jerome, J. K., 1890), V. 436

Birthday (Bancroft, G. P., 1894), V. 248
— (Dibdin, T. J., 1799), III. 122, 256, 383
— (O'Keeffe, J., 1783), III. 293, 393
— (Penny, Mrs A., 1771), III. 297
— (1788), III. 320
— (1799), III. 320
— = (1) Portraits; (2) Parson's Nose; (3) Reconciliation

Birth Day Dinner = Parson's Nose

Birthday Festivities = Merrymaking

Birth-Day Loyalty = Fourth of June

Birthdays (Roberts, G., 1883), V. 544

Birthday Tribute (Sicklemore, R., 1805), IV. 401

Birth-Night (1796), III. 320

Birth of Beauty (Akhurst, W. M., 1872), V. 237

Birth of Hercules (Shirley, W., 1763), III. 306

Birth of Jupiter (Olivari, F., 1797), III. 295

Birth of Merlin, the British Enchanter (1724), II. 378

Birth of the New Year (1860), V. 828

Birth of the Prince of Wales = Caernarvon Castle

Birth of the Steam Engine (Blanchard, E. L., 1846), IV. 265

Birthplace of Podgers (Hollingshead, J., 1858), V. 424

Birthright (Douglass, J. T., 1894), V. 349
— = Sea-Captain

Birthright of Britons = Magna Charta

Bishop (Field, W. F., 1894), V. 366

Bishop of the Fleet (Clarke, C. A. and Mouillot, F., 1889), V. 312

Biter (Rowe, N., 1704), II. 209, 352

Biter Bit (1731), II. 366, 385
— (1827), IV. 432
— = (1) Big Bandit; (2) Gripe in the Wrong Box; (3) Harlequin Disaffected; (4) Impostor

Biters Bit = (1) Fox and the Wolf; (2) Lynn Wives; (3) South-Sea

Bit of Brummagem = Bowled Out

Bit of Drapery (Hope, P., 1897), V. 426

Bit of Fun (Saxby, A., 1898), V. 557

Bit of Human Nature (Corbett, Mrs G., 1899), V. 324

Bit of Old Chelsea (Beringer, Mrs O., 1897), V. 259

Bit of Scandal = Little Nun

Bit of the Breast (1861), V. 648

Bitter Bargain = Mabel's Life

Bitter Cold (Coates, A., 1863), V. 315, 784
— (1865), V. 648
— (1868), V. 648

Bitter End = Knights of Knavery

Bitter Fruit (Dubourg, A. W., 1873), V. 351

Bitter Lesson (Harris-Burland, J. R. and Weatherley, A., 1896), V. 407

Bitter Love = For Wife and State

Bittern Swamp (1880), V. 648

Bittern's Swamp = Rover's Bride

Bitter Reckoning (Hazlewood, C. H., 1871), V. 414

Bitter Repentance (Samuels, W. R., 1889), V. 555

Bitter Sweet (Kitts, C. S., 1895), V. 445

Bitter Sweets (Parry, A., 1880), V. 514

Bitter Wrong (Lander, G. and Douglass, J. T., 1884), v. 448
— (1896), v. 648
— = In Black and White
Bivouac of Life = White Cuirassier
Bivouac of the Hills (1849), IV. 432
Black Adder (Pitt, G. D., 1850), v. 526
Blackamoor's Head (Thomson, J., 1818), IV. 432, 620
Blackamoor wash'd White (Bate, H., 1776), III. 236
— = Knights of the Post
Black and Blue (1898), v. 649
Black and Red Galleys (1854), v. 649
Black and White (Collins, W. W., 1869), v. 318
— (Melford, M., 1897), v. 484
— (1823), IV. 432
— (1843), IV. 432
— (1851), v. 649
— (1881), v. 649
Black and White Milliners (1788), III. 320
Black Armour (Sicklemore, R., 1813), IV. 611
Black Ball (Darcy, F., 1895), v. 336
Black Band (Young, Mrs W. S., 1861), v. 649, 825, 828
— (1835), IV. 432
— (1862), v. 649
Black Banner (1825), IV. 433
— = Montaldi
Black Banner of Heppenheff = Burgraves
Black Bayaderes (Pitt, G. D., 1847), IV. 375
Black Beard (Cross, J. C., 1798) = Genoese Pirate, III. 250, 380
Blackberries (Melford, M., 1886), v. 484
Blackbirding (Hazlewood, C. H., 1873), v. 414
Black Bishop (Williams, B., 1898), v. 624
Black Boarder (Johnstone, H., 1897), v. 438
Black Book (Simpson, J. P., 1857), v. 567
Black Bottle = Sicilian Hussars
Black Brand of Rome = Royal Crusader
Black Buccaneer (Taylor, T. P., 1841), IV 411, 614

Black Business (Matthison, A., 1878), v. 481
Black but comely (Forrester, S., 1882), v. 371
Black Caesar (Dibdin, C. I. M., 1825), v. 285
Black Captain (Faucit, H. S. and Fisher, W. D., 1867), v. 792
Black Castle (Amherst, J. H., 1801), IV. 253
Black Cat (Rodney, C. M., 1893), v. 548
— (Todhunter, J., 1893), v. 600
Black Cat of Coventry = Ronald Dhu
Black Charger = Brewer of Preston
Black Country (Leslie, H. T., 1867), v. 457
Black Crook (Paulton, J. and Paulton, H., 1872), v. 517
Black Diamonds (Mackay, R. F. and Denbigh, L. S., 1890), v. 470
Black Doctor (Archer, T., 1846), IV. 255
— (Bridgeman, J. V., 1846), IV. 270, 593
Black Domino (À Beckett, G. A., 1838), IV. 83, 250 [See also Queen's Ball]
— (Chorley, H. F., 1861), v. 310, 783
— (Coyne, J. S., 1838), IV. 83, 433
— (Sims, G. R. and Buchanan, R., 1893), v. 569
— (Mathews, C. J., 1838), IV. 83, 354
— (Morton, J. M. and Kenney, J., 1838), IV. 83, 433, 591, 601, 620
— (Webster, B. N., 1846), IV. 418, 616
— (Wilks, T. E., 1838), IV. 83, 420
Black Dove (Gordon-Clifford, E. and H., 1894), v. 385
Black Dwarf (1817), IV. 95, 433
Black Eagle (Almar, G., 1831), IV. 252
— (1841), IV. 433
Blackenberg (Dibdin, C. I. M., 1800), IV. 290
Black Enchanter = Island of Darkness
Black Ey'd Susan (Redgrave, R., 1898), v. 537
Blackeyed Sukey (Cooper, F. F., 1829), IV. 148, 283
Black Eyed Susan (Jerrold, D. W., 1829), IV. 148, 332
— (1829), IV. 433
— (1884), v. 649

Black Eyed Susan = (1) All in the Downs; (2) Davy Jones's Locker

Blackeyed Susan at Dunstable (1830), IV. 433

Black Festival (1800), IV. 433

Black Fisherman (Pitt, G. D., 1845), IV. 373

Black Flag (Pettitt, H., 1879), v. 521

Black Flag and the Vow of Vengeance = Elmira, the Female Pirate

Black Flag of Toraldi (1847), IV. 433

Black Forest (Birch, S., 1798) = Albert and Adelaide, III. 320, 378, 399

— = Lost and Found

Black Forester (1831), IV. 433

Black Forest of Istria = Mine

Black Friday (1838), IV. 433

Black Gang Chine = Storm Deed

Black Gentleman (1842), IV. 433

Black God of Love (Graves, J., 1836), IV. 320

Black Gondola (Hazlewood, C. H., 1856), v. 649, 796, 828

— = Tower of Nesle

Black Hand (Fitzball, E., 1834), IV. 433, 621

— (Towers, E., 1864), v. 821

Black Hawks (1893), v. 649

Black Heart = Crime

Black Hearts (Towers, E., 1868), v. 601

Black Helmet = Bavarian Girl

Black Hugh (Rogers, W., 1832), IV. 396

Black Hugh the Outlaw (1836), IV. 433

Black Huntsman of Bohemia = Freischutz

Black Hussar = Statue Steed

Black Inn of the Heath = Coupe Gorge

Black Justice (1897), v. 649

Black King (1830), IV. 433

— (1839), IV. 433

Black Kitten (1894), v. 649

Black Knight (Byrne, J., 1803), IV. 575

Black Knight of Ashton (Stanhope, B., 1874), v. 578

Black Knight of Chelmsford = Tilbury Fort

Black Law of Martinique (1842), IV. 433

Blackleg (Stanhope, B., 1886), v. 578

Black Legend (1837), IV. 433

Black Legend of Rotherhithe (1838), IV. 433

Black Lion of Finsbury (Taylor, T. P., 1839), IV. 411, 614

Blackmail (Dabbs, G. H. R., 1887), v. 332

— (Phillips, W., 1880), v. 523

— (Stanley, H. J., 1896), v. 579

— (1873), v. 649

— = Thumbscrew

Blackmailed Warrior = Athelstane

Blackmailers (Gray, J. and Raffalovitch, A., 1894), v. 390

— = Harvest of Wild Oats

Black Man (Kirkman, F., 1673), I. 418

Blackman and the Blackbird = Negro Slaves

Black Mask (Watson, F. M., 1899), v. 616

Black Monk and the Emperor's Secret = Gunmaker of Moscow

Black Musket (1835), IV. 433

Black Opera (Gay, B., 1847), IV. 318

Black Phantom (1828), IV. 433

Black Pig (Dibdin, C. I. M., 1800), IV. 290

Black Pirate = Roderick of Ravenscliff

Black Prince (Boyle, R., 1667), I. 55, 106–8, 344, 393

— (Farnie, H. B., 1874), v. 362

— (Lindsay, Sir C., 1846), IV. 595

Black Prince in Spain = Peter the Cruel

Black Rainbow (1855), v. 649

Black Reefer = Contraband Captain

Black Robber of the Mountains = Old Swiss Church

Black Rollo (Pitt, C.), v. 810

Black Rover (Searelle, L., 1890), v. 559

Black Seal = With the Colours

Black Sentinel (1840), IV. 621

Black Sheep (Coyne, J. S., 1861), v. 328

— (Raffalovich, A., 1894), v. 533

— (Simpson, J. P. and Yates, E., 1868), v. 567

Blacksmith (Collier, W., 1834), IV. 281

— (Maeder, F., 1892), v. 472

Blacksmith and the Baron = Sons of the Forge

Blacksmith of Antwerp (O'Keeffe, J., 1785), III. 293

— (1816), IV. 433

Blacksmith of Barnet = Irish Girl

Blacksmith of Ghent (Courtney, J., 1848), IV. 284

Blacksmith of Warsaw = Hans of the Iron Hand

Blacksmith's Daughter (Goldsworthy, A., 1888), v. 384, 794

Blacksmith's Daughter and the Mock Marriage = Geoffrey Kurdistan

Blacksmith's Daughter and the Red Hand (Haden, T., 1893), v. 398

Black Somnambulist (1848), IV. 433

Black Spectre = Anna

Black Spider (1831), IV. 433

Black Spirits and White (Dibdin, T. J., 1826), IV. 304

— = Scraps

Black Squire (Stephens, H. P., 1896), v. 580

Black Statue (Hazlewood, C. H., 1874), v. 649, 796, 828

Black Swan at Liverpool (1853), v. 649

Black's White = What's in a Name?

Black Tom of Tyburn (1850), v. 649

Black Tower (1832), IV. 433

— = Montalbert

Black Tower and the Spanish Patriots (1823), IV. 433

Black Tower of Linden (Pitt, C., 1869), v. 526

Black Tribunal = Rinaldo Rinaldini

Black Tulip (Grundy, S., 1899), v. 397

Black Valley (1822), IV. 433

Blackville Derby (1897), v. 649

Black Vulture (Fitzball, E., 1830), IV. 313

Black Walloon = White Wolf

Black Woodsman (Milner, H. M., 1827), IV. 433, 621

Blade Bone (1788), III. 320

Bladud (1777), III. 399

Blaize in Amaze = Conjuror

Blanca Rubea, the Heroine of Padua (1824), IV. 433

Blanche (Sketchley, A., 1870), v. 571

— (1897), v. 649

Blanche and Brunette (1862), v. 649

Blanche de Maletroit (Mason, A. E. W., 1894), v. 480

Blanche de Valmy (Bernard, W. B., 1844), IV. 266

Blanche Dhu, the Spectre Dog (1854), v. 649

Blanche Farneau (Calvert, W., 1890), v. 300

Blanche Heriot (Smith, A. R., 1842), IV. 402

Blanche of Chillon (Paul, H. M.), v. 515

Blanche of Jersey (Peake, R. B., 1837), IV. 370

Blanche of Navarre (James, G. P. R., 1839), IV. 590

Blanche of Nevers (Hyde, W. S., 1863), v. 799

Blanchette (Grein, J. T. and Churchill, M. L., 1898), v. 394

Blanche Westgarth (Lucas, J. T., 1871), v. 464

+ Blank; or, The Tar and the Ticket (Dibdin, C. I. M., R.A., 1797–8)

Blank Cartridge = How to Die for Love

Blarney (Creamer, A., 1875), v. 329

— (Logue, J. D., 1875), v. 462

Blarney Stone (1895), v. 649

— (1898), v. 649

Blasé (1844), IV. 434

Blasé Roué = Ruy Blas

Blaza the Beautiful (Righton, E., 1864), v. 813

+ Blazing Burgee (Bowles, T. G., French)

Blazing Comet (Johnson, S., 1732), II. 268, 340

Bleak House (Burnett, J. P., 1875), v. 80, 292

— (Elphinstone, J. and Neale, F., 1853), v. 80, 358

— (Lander, G., 1876), v. 80, 448

— (Thorne, E., 1876), v. 80, 598

— (1853), v. 649

— (1854), v. 649

— (1892), v. 649

— = No

Bleeding Nun of Lindenburg = Robber's Wife

Bleeding Rose of Normandy = Charlotte Corday

Blessing of Education = Only My Cousin

Blessings of Pxxx and a Scotch Excuse (1763), III. 320 [The last word in the title is 'Excuse', not 'Excise', as in the text]

Blessings of Peace = (1) Farmer Emigrant; (2) Farmer of Labian

Blessings of Two Wives at Once = Thelyphthora

Bletchington House (Craven, H. T., 1846), IV. 285
— (Gaspey, 1836), IV. 434, 621
Blight and Bloom (1855), v. 649
Blighted Bachelors (Lee, N. Jr., 1875), v. 453
— (Williams, H. L., 1881), v. 624
Blighted Being (Taylor, T., 1854), v. 592
Blighted Flower (1851), v. 649
— = (1) Linda di Chamouni; (2) Warrior and his Child
Blighted Home (Howe, J. B., 1864), v. 649
Blighted Hopes (1871), v. 649
Blighted Joys (1852), v. 649
Blighted Love (Masterton, C., 1832), IV. 353
— = Clara Charette
Blighted Moor = Fire-Raiser
Blighted One = Traviata
Blighted Willow (1839), IV. 434
Blight of Ambition (Almar, G., 1832), IV. 568
Blind (1877), v. 649
Blind among Enemies (1885), v. 649
Blind Bargain (Reynolds, F., 1804) = Hear It Out, IV. 391, 607
— = Rejected Addresses
Blind Beggar of Bethnal Green (Dodsley, R., 1741), II. 205, 249, 319, 435
— (Milner, H. M., 1834), IV. 357, 599
— = Injured General
Blind Beggar of Moorfields (1832), IV. 434
Blind Beggars of Burlington Bridge (Clements, A. and Malone, J., 1874), v. 314, 784
Blind Boy (Kenney, J., 1807), IV. 336
— (1899), v. 649
Blind Boy's Murder = Smuggler's Dog
Blind Child of Africa (1851), v. 649
Blind Father (Moncrieff, W. T., 1837), IV. 434, 621
Blind Fiddler (1872), v. 649
Blindfold (Soutar, R., 1882), v. 575
Blind Foundling (Phelps, C. H., 1899), v. 522
Blind Girl (Morton, T., 1801), IV. 363, 601
— = Augusta

Blind Girl of Tessaly = Last Days of Pompeii
Blind Girl's Fortune (1874), v. 649
Blind Girl's Inheritance = Dead Man's Cliff
Blind Girl's Protegée = Lamplighter
Blind Hearts (Collins, C., 1877), v. 317
Blind Justice (Bertrand, E. C., 1886), v. 260
Blind Lady (Howard, Sir R., 1660), I. 214, 414
Blind Love = Hester Gray
Blind Man (Dibdin, C., 1782) = None so Blind as those who won't see, III. 320, 382, 399
Blind Man of the Pyrenees = Cloud of Life
Blindman's Buff (Dibdin, T. J., ?1796, 1802), III. 382; IV. 297, 580
— (1815), IV. 434
Blind Marriage (Francis, F., 1896), v. 372
Blindness (1821), IV. 434
Blindness among Enemies (1878), v. 649
Blind Orphan (1833), IV. 15, 434
Blind Prince = Blindness
Blind Singer (Dabbs, G. H. R., 1898), v. 332
Blind Sister (Lacy, M. R., 1849), IV. 434, 621; v. 649, 801, 828
— (Meritt, P. and Conquest, G., 1874), v. 486
— = Mountain Robber
Blind Wife (Powell, T., 1843), IV. 387
— (1850), v. 649
Blind Wife and the Detective = Stolen Fortune
Blind Witness (Blythe, J. S., 1899), v. 266
— = Bararck Johnson
Blind Witness of Aberdare (1872), v. 649
Blister (1814), IV. 621
Blobb's Holiday (Crozier, C., 1892), v. 331
Blodwin (Parry, J., 1878), v. 514
Blonde or Brunette (Wooler, J. P., 1862), v. 632, 824
Blondin (1861), v. 650
Blondinette Melodists (1873), v. 650
Blondin on the Tight Rope (1873), v. 650

Blood demands its Victim (Amherst, · J. H., 1828), IV. 254, 568

Blood for Blood = Shade

Bloodhound (1845), IV. 434

Bloodhound of Cuba (Pitt, G. D. 1847), IV. 375

Blood of the Faithful (1898), v. 650

Blood-red Knight (Amherst, J. H., 1810), IV. 253

— (Barrymore, W.), IV. 262

— (Male, G., 1810), IV. 597

Blood Royal (Archer, T., 1843), IV. 254

— (1843), IV. 434

+ Blood-spiller; or, The Barber of Bishopsgate and the Fair Maid of Finsbury (C.L. ?1832)

Blood-stained Bandit = Crimson Crimes

Bloodstained Banner (Amherst, J. H.), IV. 254

Blood Stain on the Grass = Bravoes of London

Blood will have Blood (Dibdin, T. J., 1811), IV. 299

— (1813), IV. 434

Blood will tell (1895), v. 650

Bloody Contest between Charles the Twelfth, King of Sweden, and Peter the Great, Czar of Muscovy = Northern Heroes

Bloody Duke (1690), I. 11, 440

Bloody Plot Discovered (1780), III. 320

Bloomer Costume (James, C. S., 1851), v. 433

— (Stirling, E., 1851), v. 584

— (1851), v. 650

Bloomerism (Nightingale, J. H. and Millward, C., 1851), v. 504

Bloomers (Somerset, C. A., 1851), v. 574

Bloomer's Bride (Higgie, T. H., 1851), v. 421

Bloomer Wives = Bloomers

Blossom of Churnington Green (Hoskins, F. R.), v. 427

Blot in the 'Scutcheon (Browning, R., 1843), IV. 178, 273

Blotted Out (James, D. S., 1884), v. 433

Blot upon Humanity = Quadroona

Blower Jones (1881), v. 650

Blow for Blow (Byron, H. J., 1868), v. 114, 297

Blow in the Dark (Townsend, W. T., 1855), v. 602

Blown Up (1895), v. 650

Blue above and the Blue below = Lily Laburnem

Blue Anchor (Pocock, I., 1830), IV. 385

— (1832), IV. 434

— (1844), IV. 434

Blue and Buff (Ward, E. V., 1880), v. 613

Blue Baron (Dibdin, T. J., 1821), IV. 303

Bluebeard (Blanchard, E. L. and Greenwood, T. L., 1879), v. 265

— (Bridgeman, J. V., 1860), v. 275

— (Burnand, F. C., 1883), v. 291, 782

— (Butler, F., 1890), v. 294

— (Byron, H. J., 1871), v. 298, 782

— (Colman, G., the Younger, 1798), III. 27, 32, 51, 61, 98, 104–6, 248, 380

— (Dance, C., 1842), IV. 289

— (Danville, A., 1898), v. 336

— (Gower, Lord F. L., 1841), IV. 320

— (Hazlewood, C. H., 1865) = Harlequin Bluebeard and his Seven Headless Wives, v. 650, 828, 834

— (Lennard, H., 1883), v. 455, 803

— (Lennard, H., 1894), v. 456

— (North, W. S., 1894), v. 505

— (Planché, J. R. and Dance, C., 1839), IV. 381

— (Risque, W. H., 1892), v. 650, 813, 828

— (Woolfe, J. H., 1897), v. 824

— (1791), III. 320, 381, 399

— (1847), IV. 621

— (1858), v. 828

— (1859), v. 828

— (1863, 1864), v. 650

— (1865), v. 651

— (1869), v. 828

— (1870), v. 828

— (1874, 1875, 1876, 1877, 1878, 1879, 1880, 1881, 1882, 1883, 1884, 1885, 1886, 1887, 1888, 1889, 1890, 1892, 1894, 1895, 1896), v. 650

— (1898, 1899), v. 651

— = Barbe Bleue

+ Blue Beard; or, Dangerous Curiosity and Justifiable Homicide (Egerton, Lord Francis: printed in *Juvenile Plays for Home Performance* (*French*))

Blue Beard, according to Act of Parliament = Hints to the Curious

Blue Beard and Fat Emma (Green, F. W., 1877), v. 390

Bluebeard and Son (1883), v. 651

Bluebeard, Cinderella and Prince Pretty-step (1872), v. 651

Blue Beard done Brown (Spry, H., 1881), v. 577

Blue Beard from a New Point of Hue (Byron, H. J., 1860), v. 296

Blue Beard, his Blue Chamber (Suter, W. E., 1860), v. 819

Bluebeard in a Black Skin (Williams, M., 1875), v. 625

Bluebeard Re-paired (Bellingham, H., 1866), v. 257, 778

Bluebeard Re-trimmed (1877), v. 651

Blue Beard Re-wived (Douglass, J. T., 1879), v. 348

Bluebeard the Grand Bashaw (Muskerry, W., 1887), v. 501

Bluebeard the Great (1878), v. 651

Bluebeard the Great Bashaw (Arnold, H. T., 1869), v. 243

Bluebeard Trimmed (1895), v. 651

Blue-bells of Scotland (Buchanan, R., 1887), v. 285

Blue Bird of Paradise (Conquest, G. and Spry, H., 1860), v. 651, 785, 817, 828

— = King Charming

Blue Boar (Parker, L. N. and Carson, S. M., 1894), v. 513

Blue Dahlia (Sutcliffe, H. and Bartlett, H., 1898), v. 587

Blue Devils (Colman, G., the Younger, 1798), III. 248, 380

— (1842), IV. 434

— (1862), v. 651

Blue Dwarf (Marchant, F., 1862), v. 651, 805, 828

Blue-eyed Blue Beard, the Masher Pasha (Thorne, G., 1885), v. 598

Blue-eyed Mary (Nantz, F. C., 1835), IV. 434, 621

— (Pitt, G. D., 1835), IV. 373

Blue-eyed Susan (Sims, G. R. and Pettitt, H., 1892), v. 569

Blue-eyed Witch (Hazlewood, C. H., 1869), v. 413

Bluejackets (Stirling, E., 1838), IV. 406

— (1896), v. 651

Blue Jeans (Arthur, J., 1891), v. 244

Blue-legged Lady (Hill, W. J., 1874), v. 421

Blue Man (1834), IV. 434

Blue Monkey (1891), v. 651

Blue Mountain Spirits (1800), v. 424

Blue or Green? (Bell, Mrs H., 1896), v. 256

Blue Ribbon of the Turf (Williams, F., 1867), v. 823

— = Jack o' Lantern

Blue Ribbons (Browne, G. W. and Soden, J. E., 1887), v. 283

Blue Skin (Marchant, F., 1863), v. 651, 828

— (Mildenhall, T., 1846), IV. 598

Blue Stocking = M.P.

Bluff (1888), v. 651

Bluff King Hal (Lee, N. Jr., 1868), v. 453

— (Maddy, J. M., 1848), IV. 434, 621

— (Marchant, F., 1868), v. 475

— (O'Neil, C., 1877), v. 507

— (Spry, H., 1882), v. 577

— (1872), v. 651

— (1876), v. 651

— (1878), v. 651

— (1883), v. 651

Bluff King Hal and the Forest Maid = Herne the Hunter and his Demon Band

Blunderer (Foote, S., 1762), III. 384

Blunders (1898), v. 651

Blunders at Brighton = Irish Mimic

Blunder upon Blunder, yet all's Right at Last = Ephesian Duke

Blunt Tar (1791), III. 320

Blush Rose (D'Arcy, G., 1876), v. 336

— = Banshee's Spell

Blutzherranbhothrum (Marchant, F., 1868), v. 475

Boabdil el Chico (Burnand, F. C., 1866), v. 288

Boa-Constrictor and the Buffalo = Anaconda

Boadacia (Glover, R., 1753), III. 80–1, 265

Boadicea (Bealing, R.), II. 432

— (Dibdin, C. I. M., 1800), IV. 290

— (Hopkinson, A. F., 1888), v. 426

— (Lindsay, Sir C., 1857), v. 804

— = Boadicia

Boadicea Queen of Britain (Hopkins, C., 1697), I. 32, 40, 152, 413

Boadicea Unearthed (Rix, W. F. and Gillett, F. J., 1895), v. 544

Board and Residence (Edwardes, C. T. M., 1870), v. 354

Boarded and Done For = Jenkinses

Boarder (Ryan, R., 1832), IV. 434, 621

Boarding House (Beazley, S., Jr., 1811), IV. 263

Boarding House for 1862 (1862), v. 651

Boarding School (Bernard, W. B., 1841), IV. 266

— (Coffey, C., 1733), I. 275; II. 142, 237, 244, 315

— = Love for Money

Boarding School Ball (1853), v. 651

Boarding School Dissected = Governess

Boarding School Miss (Dibdin, C. I. M., 1816), IV. 294

— (Jodrell, R. P., 1787), III. 277

Boarding School of Montesque = Assurance Company

Boarding School Romps = Boarding-School

Board of Conviviality (1806), IV. 434

Boaster (?1698), I. 446

Boat-builder's Hovel = Negro of Wapping

Boat Builders of Brugen = Crossing the Line

Boatman of Deal = Deal Boatman

Boatmen of the Shannon (Towers, E., 1877), v. 601

Boatswain's Whistle (1859), v. 651

Bob (Marsden, F., 1888), v. 477

Bobbo (Tanner, J. T. and Ross, A., 1895), v. 590

Bob Bradshaw's Dream (Thomas, B. W., 1899), v. 595

Bob Bragshawe (Brown, W., 1876), v. 282

Bob Bretton, the Dead Shot of the Woods (1877), v. 651

Bobby No. 1 (Hodgson, G. S., 1872), v. 423

Bobby's Bride = Constable Jack

Bob Cherry, Rough and Ready (1860), v. 651

Bobinet the Bandit (1815), IV. 434

Bob Lumley's Secret (Pitt, C., 1869), v. 526

Bob Ridley (Lee, N., Jr., 1861), v. 803

Bob Short (Lemon, M., 1840), IV. 344

Bob the Outcast (Lyon, W. F., 1881), v. 465

Boccaccio (Farnie, H. B. and Reece, R., 1882), v. 363, 791

Boccagh (Gomersall, W., 1884), v. 384

Bodack Glas = Waverley

Bodagh of the Boyne = Gramachree Molly

Body in the Boskeen = Ghost Hunter

Bogey (Esmond, H. V., 1895), v. 359

Bogie (1876), v. 651

Bo Girl up-to-date = Romany Lore

Bogle of the Clyde (1836), IV. 434

Bogus Agent (Batho, R., 1895), v. 253

Bogus Bandit (Montague, L. A. D., 1896), v. 491

Bohemia and Belgravia (O'Neil, A., 1872), v. 507

Bohemian (Danvers, G. J. B., 1833), IV. 579

— (Parker, L. N., 1892), v. 513

— (Soane, G., 1817), IV. 403

Bohemian Bandit (Florance, Mrs B. E., 1843), IV. 317

Bohemian Banditti = Trenck the Pandour

Bohemian Gipsy and the Duel at the Willows (Webb, C., 1862), v. 617

Bohemian Girl (Bunn, A., 1843), IV. 276

— (1861), v. 651

Bohemian G'ywl and the Unapproachable Pole (Byron, H. J., 1877), v. 298

Bohemian Miller = Miller and his Men

Bohemian Mother (Ebsworth, J., 1831), IV. 434, 621

— = (1) Infanticide; (2) Rosalie

Bohemians (Farnie, H. B., 1873), v. 361

— (Grist, W. and Pinkerton, P. E., 1897), v. 651, 795, 828

— (Stirling, E., 1843), IV. 407

— (1843), IV. 434

Bohemians of Paris (Barnett, C. Z., 1843), IV. 260

Bohemian's Prophecy = Gold Guitar

Boiling Water (Cross, J., 1885), v. 330

Bold Advertisement (Parker, L. N., 1895), v. 513

Bold Bad Baron (Addison, J., 1889), v. 236

Bold Bucaniers (1826), IV. 434
— = Robinson Crusoe
Bold Buccaneer = Captain Kidd
Bold Dick Turpin (Simpson, J. P., 1878), v. 568
Bold Dragoons (Barnett, M., 1830), IV. 261
Bold Recruit (Stephenson, B. C., 1870), v. 582, 818
Bold Robin Hood (Lee, N., 1848), IV. 434
— (1882), v. 651
Bold Stroke for a Husband (Cowley, Mrs H., 1783), III. 167, 181, 248
— (1862), v. 651
— = Advertisement
Bold Stroke for a Wife (Centlivre, Mrs S., 1718), II. 135, 137, 144, 156, 241, 305, 385, 433; IV. 140
— (1810), IV. 434
— = Guardians Outwitted
Bold Stroke for Dinner = Travelling Incog.
Bold Stroke for Success = Stage Letter
Bolivar (Wills, W. G., 1879), v. 627
Bomb (1894), v. 651
Bombardment and Capture of Canton (Stocqueler, J. H., 1858), v. 651, 818, 828
Bombardment and Capture of St Jean d'Acre = War in Syria
Bombardment of Algiers = Slaves in Barbary
Bombastes Furioso (Rhodes, W. B., 1810), IV. 149, 394
Bombastio Furioso (1889), v. 651
Bombay Brothers = Joker
Bombay to Henley (Parke, W. and Maxwell, C., 1895), v. 512
Bombo the Dwarf (Grover, J. H., 1880), v. 396
Bonafaiso (1804), IV. 434
Bona Fide Travellers (Brough, W., 1854), v. 279
Bonaparte in Egypt (Somerset, C. A., 1852), v. 574
Bond (Gore, Mrs C. G. F., 1824), IV. 319
Bondage (1883), v. 651
Bond and Free = One Shade Deeper
Bondman (Bunn, A., 1846), IV. 277
— (Cumberland, R., 1779), III. 78, 251

Bondman (1719), II. 366
Bondman of Kent = Aylmere
Bondocani (Dibdin, T. J., 1880), IV. 297, 580
Bond of Life (Faucit, H. S., 1870), v. 363
Bond of Love (1854), v. 651
Bondsman (Caine, H., 1892), v. 299
Bond Street, 4 p.m. (Grain, R. C., 1894), v. 388
Bonds Without Judgment (Topham, E., 1787), III, 312
Bonduca (Colman, G., 1778), III. 246
— (Dibdin, C. I. M., 1823), IV. 295
— (Powell, G., 1695), I. 266, 338, 425
Bone for the Lawyers = Will and No Will
Bone of Contention (Harding, C., 1870), v. 403
Boneshaker (1894), v. 651
Bone Squash (1839), IV. 435
Bone Squash Diabolo (Rice, T. D., 1836), IV. 394
Boney Defeated = Peep at the Danube
Bonifacio and Bridgetina (Dibdin, T. J., 1808), IV. 148, 298
Bonnet Builder's Tea Party (Hazlewood, C. H., 1854), v. 412
Bonnie Annie Laurie (Daly, C., 1898), v. 334
Bonnie Babies in the Wood (Craven, T., 1894), v. 329
Bonnie Bo-Peep and Little Boy Blue (Anderton, J., 1893), v. 778
Bonnie Boy Blue (Stephens, V., 1892), v. 581
Bonnie Dundee (Boyd, M., 1881), v. 272
— (Falconer, E., 1863), v. 360
Bonnie Fish Wife (Selby, C., 1858), v. 560
Bonnie Prince Charlie (Exley, C., 1878), v. 359
— (Johnstone, J. B., 1868), v. 438
— (Lowe, W., 1875), v. 464
— (Terriss, T. H., 1889), v. 595
— = Our Bonnie Prince
Bonny Bohemia = Zamet
Bonny Lass of Leith (1793), III. 320
Bon Ton (Garrick, D., 1775), III. 134, 169, 263-4
Boodles (Lee-Bennett, H., 1894), v. 453

Bookmaker (Piggot, J. W., 1889), v. 524

Book of Fate = Captive Princess

Book the Third, Chapter the First = Novel Expedient

Book with the Iron Clasps = Vendetta

Bookworm (Aveling, E. B., 1888), v. 246

Boor's Hut (1820), IV. 435

Bootblack (Jefferson, A., 1897), v. 435

Bootle's Baby (Moss, H., 1888), v. 498, 807

Boot on the Right Leg (1863), v. 651

Boots at the Holly Tree Inn (Webster, B. N., 1856), v. 618

Boots at the Swan (Selby, C., 1842), IV. 398

Bo-Peep (Terry, E., 1863), v. 595

— (1874, 1876, 1894, 1897, 1898, 1899), v. 651

See Little Bo-Peep

Bo-Peep and Boy Blue (1876), v. 652

Borachio the Bandit (Pitt, G. D., 1850), v. 526

Boraldi the Outlaw (Gomersal, E. W., 1862), v. 794

Border Chief = Johnnie Armstrong

Border Chieftains = White Plume

Borderers (Wordsworth, W., 1796), IV. 192-3, 422

Borderer's Son (Coates, A., 1874), v. 652, 784

Border Feuds (1811), IV. 435

Border Heroine (Burnette, C., 1896), v. 293

Border Marriage (Sorrell, W. J., 1856), v. 104, 574

Borders of the Ukraine = True Satisfaction

Borgia (Brown, T., 1874), v. 282

Borgia Ring (Slous, A. R., 1859), v. 571

Born of Hilda (France, E. S., 1878), v. 372

Born to Good Luck (Power, T., 1832), IV. 387

Born to save (Clarke, G. H. and Douglas, L., 1883), v. 312

Born with a Caul (Almar, G., 1850), v. 652, 777, 828

Boro' Bench (1887), v. 652

Borough Elections = M.P. for Puddlepool

Borough Politics (Marston, J. W., 1846), IV. 353

Borrachio, the Outlaw (1824), IV. 435

Borrowed (Warren, E., 1885), v. 614

Borrowed Feathers (Millingen, J. G., 1836), IV. 356 [Attributed also to M. Barnett]

Borrowed Plumes (Maltby, A., 1866), v. 473

— = Hope of the Family

Borrowing a Husband (Moncrieff, W. T., 1843), IV. 361

Borrowing Boots (Little, A., 1899), v. 461

Boscabel (Springate, H. S., 1880), v. 576

Bos'en and the Middy (1854), v. 652

Bosjesman (1851), v. 652

Bosjesnans (1847), IV. 621

Bosom Friend (1844), IV. 435

Bosom Friends (Wigan, H., 1871), v. 622

Bossu (1863), v. 652

— (1866), v. 652

Bo'sun's Mate (Browne, G. W., 1888), v. 283

Botany Bay (1791), III. 399

Botheration (Oulton, W. C., 1798), III. 185, 296

Both of Them (1889), v. 652

Both Sides of the Question (Salaman, M. C., 1891), v. 555

Both Sides of the Water = Raft

Both Sides of the World (Bailey, 1882), v. 247

Bothwell (Swinburne, A. C., 1874), v. 589

— (Ware, J. R.), v. 614

Bottle (Taylor, T. P., 1847), IV. 411

— (1847), IV. 435

Bottle and the Glass (Barnett, C. Z., 1847), IV. 261

Bottle at Sea = Patriot

Bottle Bane (Pitt, G. D., 1847), IV. 375

Bottle Conjuror Out-done = Amours of Harlequin

Bottle Imp (Conquest, G. and Spry, H., 1865), v. 652, 828

— (Hale, W. P. and Talfourd, F., 1852), v. 398

— (Peake, R. B., 1828), IV. 370

Bottle of Champagne (Fitzball, E., 1832), IV. 314

Boys Together (Chambers, C. H. and Carr, J. W. C., 1896), v. 307
— (Howell-Poole, W., 1887), v. 429
Boz-i-a-na = Peregrinations of Pickwick "Boz's" Oliver Twist (Greenwood, T., 1838), IV. 97, 321
Brace of Gaol Birds (Melford, M., 1889), v. 484
Brace of Partridges (Ganthony, R., 1897), v. 376
Brace of Uncles (1876), v. 652
Bracewell's Adventures with a Russian Princess (1878), v. 652
Brachman (Dibdin, C. I. M., 1813), IV. 293
Bracken Hollow (Bright, Mrs A., 1878), v. 275
Brag (Wills, W. G., 1879), v. 627
Bragadocio (1691), I. 218, 440
Braganza (Jephson, R., 1775), III. 56, 94-5, 156, 276, 389
Braggadochio (1742), II. 384
Brahman's Curse (1829), IV. 435
Brain Reviver (Barrow, P. J., 1898), v. 252
Brand (Hereford, C. H., 1893), v. 419
Branded (Lee, R., 1881), v. 453
Branded Race (Wooler, J. P., 1858), v. 632
Brand of Cain (Gordon, G. L., 1875), v. 384
Brand of Crime = Walter Lorimer
Brand of Shame = Icebound
Brand of Time and the Mystery of 20 Years = Marianne Duval the Vivandière
Branksome Castle (1811), IV. 435
Brantinghame Hall (Gilbert, W. S., 1888), v. 380
Bras de Fer (Manuel, E., 1875), v. 475
Brass (Rowe, G. F., 1877), v. 552
Bravado (Smale, Mrs T. E., 1889), v. 571
Bravado the Swindler (Travers, W., 1864), v. 822
Brave and the Fair (Bourden, 1816), IV. 435, 621
Brave as a Lion (Douglass, J. T., 1872), v. 348
Brave Cossack (Astley, J., 1807), IV. 435, 569, 621

Brave Coward (Blythe, J. S., 1886), v. 266
Brave Gordons (1898), v. 652
Brave Harry Thorn (Stanley, H. J., 1874), v. 579
Brave Hearts (Comer, G. and Benton, F., 1898), v. 319
— (Matthison, A., 1881), v. 481
Brave Irishman (Sheridan, T., 1737), II. x, 144, 215-16, 355, 444; III. 396
— (1755), III. 396
Bravery and Ingratitude = Jew of Wilna
Brave Scottish Hearts (Hall, K. E., 1873), v. 399
Braving the Storm (Sheen, W. P., 1890), v. 562
— (Woodruffe, A., 1871), v. 631
Bravin's Brow (Fox, J. S., 1863), v. 652, 828
Bravo (Barnett, C. Z., 1833), IV. 97, 259
— (Buckstone, J. B., 1833), IV. 97, 274
— = Red Mask
Bravo and the Venetian Conspirators (1819), IV. 435
Bravoes of Calabria = Black Band
Bravoes of Chiozza = Maid and the Monk
Bravoes of London (Young, Mrs H., 1863), v. 652, 828
Bravo Ix (1854), v. 652
Bravo of Castille = Charles Ganganelli
Bravo of Venice = Rugantino
Bravo Rouse!!! (Pitt, G. D., 1851), v. 526
Bravo's Son (1819), IV. 435
Bravo turn'd Bully (1740), II. 366
Brazen Bust = Hungarian Cottage
Brazen Mask (Dibdin, T. J., 1802), IV. 297, 580
Brazen Nose College (1831), IV. 435
Brazen Water-Tower (1824), IV. 435
Brazilian (Pemberton, M. and Lestocq, W., 1890), v. 518
Brazilian Jack (1834), IV. 435
Brazilian Monkey = Jocko
Breach of Promise (Freund-Lloyd, M., 1891), v. 373
— (Robertson, T. W., 1869), v. 546
— (1841), IV. 435
— (1884), v. 652
— (1892), v. 652

Breach of Promise of Marriage (Rodwell, G. H., 1842), IV. 84, 395, 603, 608

Bread Winner (Calmour, A. C., 1892), v. 300

Break but not bend (Hazlewood, C. H., 1867), v. 413

Breakers Ahead (Haines, J. T., 1837), IV. 322

— = He would be a Sailor

Breakfast Appointment (1862), v. 652

Breakfast for Two (1851), v. 652

Breakfast of Love (1822), IV. 435

Breaking a Butterfly (Jones, H. A. and Herman, H., 1884), v. 439

Breaking it off (Doone, N., 1898), v. 347

— (1899), v. 652

Breaking the Bank = Lady Guide

Breaking the Ice (Thomas, C., 1878), v. 596

— = Holly Branch

Breaking the News (Heathcote, A. M., 1893), v. 415

Breaking the Spell (Farnie, H. B., 1870), v. 361

Break of Morn (1862), v. 652

Bred in the Bone (Lingham, F. T., 1890), v. 460

— (1896), v. 652

Breeze from New York (Raphael, F., 1893), v. 535

Breeze in the Baltic (1801), IV. 435

Breezy Morning (Phillpotts, E., 1891), v. 524

Brenda's Choice (1896), v. 652

Brennus (Maclean, W., 1871), v. 471

— (1832), IV. 435

Bressac (1886), v. 652

Brewer of Preston (Reynoldson, T. H., 1839), IV. 393

— (1876), v. 652

Brewer of Tadcaster (Rodgers, A., 1897), v. 547

Brewing a Bruin (Gee, L., 1873), v. 377

Brian Born (B., J. T., 1879), v. 653

Brian Boroihme (Knowles, J. S., 1811), IV. 170, 338

— (Mara, S. D., 1810), IV. 597

Brian Boroihme, the Victorious (1820), IV. 435

Brian, the Probationer (Hill, I., 1842), IV. 325

Briarly Farm (Conquest, G., 1858), v. 653, 785, 828

Briars and Blossoms (Hazlewood, C. H., 1873), v. 414

Bribery on Both Sides (1784), III. 320

Bric-a-Brac (Coghill, Sir J. J., 1888), v. 316

Bric-a-Brac Will (Fitzgerald, S. J. A. and Moss, H., 1895), v. 369

Brickdustman (1773), III. 399

Bricklayers' Arms (1830), IV. 435

Bridal (Knowles, J. S., 1837), IV. 339

— (Macready, W. C.), IV. 353

— = House of Colberg

Bridal Eve (1847), IV. 435

— = (1) Doom Light; (2) Wedding Eve

Bridal Gift = Bivouac of the Hills

Bridal Night = Conscience

Bridal of Armagnac (Streatfield, T., 1823), IV. 409

Bridal of Beatrix (1859), v. 653

Bridal of Beauty (Blanchard, E. L., 1863), v. 653, 779, 828

Bridal of Death = Red Mantle

Bridal of Flora (Byrne, J., 1816), IV. 435, 621

Bridal of Netherby = Lochinvar

Bridal Phantom (Conquest, G., 1863), v. 653, 828

Bridal Promise (Oxenford, J., 1833), IV. 435, 621

Bridal Ring (Reynolds, F., 1810), IV. 392, 607

— = (1) Bull-Fighter; (2) Mulatto Murderer; (3) Robert the Devil

Bridals (Cavendish, M., 1668), I. 396

Bridals of Messina = John of Procida

Bridal Spectre = (1) Alonzo and Imogine; (2) Alonzo the Brave and the Fair Imogene

Bridal Supper = Witch of Ravensworth

Bridal Three Centuries Back = Ladye of Lambeth

Bridal Tour (Boucicault, D., 1877), v. 269

— (1877), v. 653

Bridal Trip (Mortimer, J., 1876), v. 494

Bridal Wreath (Hazlewood, C. H., 1861), v. 412

Bride (Baillie, J., 1828), IV. 258

— (Bell, A., 1847), IV. 572

— (Korner, 1808), IV. 340

— (Rice, C.), v. 813

Bride and Bridegroom (1828), IV. 435

Bride and No Bride = National Guard

Bride and the Proscribed (1840), IV. 435

Bride at Fifty = Spring and Autumn

Bridegroom from the Sea = Wreck Ashore

Bridegroom of the Wave = Essex Rover

Bride of Abydos (Byron, H. J., 1858), V. 295

— (Dimond, W., 1818), IV. 47, 110, 306

— (1847), IV. 435

Bride of a Day = Barbara

Bride of Albi (Harding, C., 1853), V. 403

Bride of Aldgate (1859), V. 653

Bride of Corsica = Paali

Bride of Everton (1852), V. 828

Bride of Garryowen (1861), V. 653

Bride of Genoa = Valasco

Bride of Golconda (Jones, R. St C., 1852), V. 441

Bride of Lammermoor (Dibdin, T. J., 1819), IV. 94, 302, 436, 581

— (Calcraft, J. W., 1822), IV. 94, 278

— (Moncrieff, W. T., 1819), IV. 94, 436, 621

— (1831), IV. 94, 436

— (1848), IV. 94, 436

— (1863), V. 653

Bride of Love (Buchanan, R., 1890), V. 285

Bride of Ludgate (Jerrold, D. W., 1831), IV. 332

Bride of Messina (Irvine, G., 1837), IV. 329

— (Lockwood, P., 1839), IV. 346

— (Lodge, A., 1841), IV. 346

— (Müller, H., 1887), V. 499

— = John of Procida

Bride of Mexico = Indian Father

Bride of Milton and the Merchant of Gravesend (1859), V. 828

Bride of Munster = Kathleen

Bride of Parma = Carbonari

Bride of Poland (1856), V. 653

Bride of Portugal = Inez

+ Bride of Sicily (Downing, Helen, 4°, 1830)

Bride of Song (Farnie, H. B., 1864), V. 361

Bride of the Battlefield = Strongbow

Bride of the Bleeding Heart (1832), IV. 436

— = Emilie de la Roche

Bride of the Grave = Raven's Nest

Bride of the Isles = Vampyre

Bride of the Nile (1845), IV. 436

Bride of the Prairie (1847), IV. 436

Bride of the Thames = Carpenters of Lambeth

Bride of the Wave (Travers, W., 1867), V. 602

Bride of Two Isles = Bright Days

Bride of Venice = Queen of Cyprus

Bride's Death Sleep (Hazlewood, C. H., 1868), V. 413

Bride's Journey (Courtney, J., 1846), IV. 283

Brides of Florence (Fitzeustace, R., 1824), IV. 584

Brides of Garryowen = Colleen Bawn

Brides of Venice (Bunn, A., 1844), IV. 436

Brides' Tragedy (Beddoes, T. L., 1822), IV. 201–2, 264

Bride, the Bullet and the Bobby = Freischutz

Bridge of Baltaz = Secret Twelve

Bridge of Kehl (Blake, T. G., 1841), IV. 268

Bridge of Notre Dame (Hudson, E. N., 1847), IV. 329

— = Orphans

Bridge of Sighs (Leigh, H. S., 1872), V. 454, 803

— = Bravo

Bridge of Tresino = Forest Oracle

Bridge that carries us safe over (Peake, R. B., 1817), IV. 369

Bridget O'Brien (Lyster, F. and Sheridan, J. F., 1887), V. 466

Bridget's Blunders (Smith, L., 1892), V. 573

Brier Cliff (Morris, G., 1842), IV. 361

Brigadier (Reynoldson, T. H., 1845), IV. 393

Brigand (Douglass, J. T., 1865) = Brigand in a New Suit for Easter, V. 653, 788, 828

— (Osbaldistone, D. W., 1830), IV. 602

Brigand and his Banker (Taylor, T., 1860), V. 593

Brigand and his Son = (1) Bandit of Corsica; (2) Matteo Falcone

Brigand Chief (Planché, J. R., 1829), IV. 378

Brigand Chief = Fra Diavolo

Brigand Chief and the Dog of the Chateau = Diavolo Abruzzi

Brigand Deserter = First Claim

Brigand in a New Suit for Easter (Douglass, J. T., 1865) = Brigand, v. 653, 788, 828

Brigand Marquis = High Road of Life

Brigand Monk and the Dog of Mount St Bernard (1845), IV. 436

Brigand of Albans = Italian Sister

Brigand of Barcelona (1852), v. 653

Brigand of London (Travers, W., 1864), v. 653, 828

Brigand of Savoy = Corse de Leon

Brigands (Gilbert, W. S., 1889), v. 380

— (Leigh, H. S., 1884), v. 454

— = Falscappa

Brigand's Daughter (1845), IV. 436

— = Marinette

Brigand's Doom = Abduction of Bianca

Brigands in the Bud (Mildenhall, T., 1849), IV. 356

Brigands of Ancona (1844; 1845), IV. 436

Brigands of Bluegoria = Joan

Brigands of Calabria (Suter, W. E., 1866), v. 588

— (1831), IV. 621

Brigands of Sicily = Mysterious Hermit

Brigand's Ransom = Birthright

Brigand's Secret (1858), v. 653

Brigand, the Marchese and the Deserter = Perizzi

Briganzio the Brigand (Marshall, F.), v. 805 [A play of this name by F. Hall was printed by French]

Briggate (Bell, C., 1884), v. 255

Bright Beam at Last (Macdermott, G. H., 1872), v. 468

Bright Days (Wheatley, H. and Aldin C. A., 1889), v. 619

Brighter Days in Store (Towers, E., 1867), v. 601

— = Our Lot in Life

Brighter Future (1897), v. 653

Bright Future (Parry, S., 1883), v. 515

Brighthelmstone (Collier, J., 1853), v. 785

Bright Idea (Law, A., 1881), v. 449

Brighton (Howard, B. and Marshall, F., 1870), v. 428

Brighton Cliff (Bew, C., 1831) = White Hawk Lady, IV. 436, 621

Bright Road of Honesty and the Dark Path of Crime = Tom Sheppard

Bright Star of the Morn = Noureddin and the Fair Persian

Brig o' Doon = Tam o' Shanter

Brilliants (1799), III. 320

Brine Oge (Patmore, W. J., 1896), v. 515

Bringing Home the Bride! (Moncrieff, W. T., 1831), IV. 135, 360

Brisket Family (Jerrold, D. J., 1822) = Dolly and the Rat, IV. 436, 621

Bristol Diamonds (Oxenford, J., 1862), v. 510, 809

Bristol Sailor (Bernard, J., 1786), III. 320, 377, 399

Bristol Tar (1792), III. 321

Britain in her Glory = What We Have Been, and What We May Be

Britain's Allies (1813), IV. 436

Britain's Best Bulwarks = Mast and the Ploughshare

Britains Brave Tars!! (O'Keeffe, J., 1797) = All to St Paul's = Our Wooden Walls, III. 321, 393, 399

Britain's Defenders (1797), III. 321

Britain's Genius (Kennedy, R., 1840), IV. 336

Britain's Glory (Benson, 1794), III. 207, 236

— = Naval Volunteers

Britain's Happiness (Motteux, P. A., 1704), II. 346, 441

Britain's Jubilee (Arnold, S. J., 1809), IV. 255

— (Barrett, C. F., 1809), IV. 436, 621

Britains Rejoice = St George's Day

Britannia (Lediard, T., 1732), II. 35, 236, 341

— (Mallet, D., 1755), II. 343; III. 286

— (1734), II. 366

— = Love and Glory

Britannia and Batavia (Lillo, G., 1740), II. 342

Britannia and the Gods in Council (Averay, R., 1756), III. 234

Britannia in full Glory at Spithead = Love and Honour

Britannia, Mistress of the Seas (1895), v. 653

Britannia Rediviva (1746), II. 367

Britannia Rules the Waves = Nelson

Britannia's Relief (1789), III. 321

Britannia's Triumph = Fairy

Britannia Triumphans (1703), II. 447

Britannia Triumphant = (1) Fall of Martinico; (2) Naval Pillar

Britannicus (Boothby, Sir B., 1803), IV. 269

— (Ozell, J., 1714), II. 347

— = Brittanicus

British Admiral and the Seaman's Son (1812), IV. 436

British Amazon = Boadicea

British Amazons (Dibdin, C. I. M., 1803), IV. 291

British and Norman Feuds = Henry I

British at Brussels = Bachelors' Wives

British Beauty (Addison, H. R., 1848), IV. 251

British Born (Meritt, P. and Pettitt, H., 1872), v. 485

British Bravery Triumphant = Point at Herqui

British Brothers (Buchanan, J., 1868), v. 284

British Bull Dogs (Johnstone, J. B., 1868), v. 800

British Captain and the Indian Chief (Simpson, 1822), IV. 401

British Captives = Johnnie Armstrong

British Captives in France = Coronation!!

British Carpenter (McLaren, A., 1808), IV. 351

British Champion = St George and the Dragon

British Courage (1805), IV. 436

British Enchanters (Granville, G., 1706), I. 141; II. 234–5, 333, 437

British Esquimaux = Voyage to the North Pole

British Exile = Earl of Warwick

British Flag of the South American Pirate = Silver Store Island

British Fortitude, and Hibernian Friendship (Cross, J. C., 1794), III. 250

British Freeholder = Eldred

British Glory in Egypt (Astley, P. Jr., 1801), IV. 256

British Gratitude and Hibernian Friendship = British Fortitude and Hibernian Friendship

British Hero (Landeck, B., 1894), v. 447

British Heroes (1808), IV. 436

British Heroine (Jackson, J., 1777), III. 86, 276

— = Bonduca

British Heroism = Death of Captain Faulknor

British Inchanter, and King Arthur, the British Worthy = Merlin

British Intrepidity Triumphant = Northern Fleet

British Kings (Mylne, J., 1790), III. 290

British Legion (Bayly, T. H., 1838), IV. 263

British Liberty = Battle of Eddington

British Lion (1830, 1848), IV. 436

— = Plum Pudding Pantomime

British Loyalty (Moser, J., 1809), IV. 364

— (1789), III. 321

British Officer = Lindor and Clara

British Orphan (Starke, M., 1790), III. 308

British Peasant (1799), III. 321

British Pluck and Yankee Valour = Old World and the New

British Queen (1840), IV. 436

— = (1) Boadicea; (2) Bonduca

British Recruit = To Arms!

British Sailor (1786), III. 321, 377

British Sailor Abroad and at Home (1830), IV. 436

British Sailors in America = French Flogged

British Sailors in 1797 = (1) Mutiny at the Nore; (2) Mutiny of Spithead and the Nore

British Seaman's Fidelity = Faithless Friend

British Seaman's Story = Juan Fernandez

British Seamen at Anchor = Naples Bay

British Slave (Howe, J. B.), v. 428

British Soldier (1805), IV. 436

British Stage (1724), II. 256–7, 367

British Tar in Storm and Sunshine = Afloat and Ashore

British Tars (1859), v. 653

British Tars and Austrian Troops = Double Defeat

British Tars at Spithead = England's Glory

British Tars in 1782 = Youthful Days of William IV

British Tars regaling after Battle = Vanguard

British Troops Triumphant = Glorious Queen of Hungary

British Valour Triumphant = Cape St Vincent

British Vengeance = Slaves in Barbary

British Workman (1894), v. 653

British Worthy = King Arthur

Britomarte (Schofield, W. M., 1866), v. 653, 815, 828

Britomart, the Man-hater (1866), v. 653

Briton (Philips, A., 1722), II. 54, 106, 107, 116, 348

Briton and Boer (1899), v. 653

Briton Chief = Caswallon

Britons Abroad (Davis, H., 1861), v. 787

Britons at Navarino (Milner, H. M., 1827), IV. 436, 621

Britons in China = Ching-Li-Wang

Britons in the East = Siege of Acre

Britons in the East Indies = Massacre of Rajahpoor

Britons' Jubilee in Honour of their King (Cherry, A., 1809), IV. 576

Britons, strike home (Dibdin, C., 1804), IV. 290

— (Phillips, E., 1739), II. 349, 442

— = Volunteers

Britons to Arms (McLaren, A., 1803), IV. 350

Brittanicus (D'Oyley, E., 1695), I. 403

Brittany Folk (Frith, W., 1889), v. 373

Brixton Burglary (Sidney, F. W., 1898), v. 565

Broad Arrow (Holcroft, G., 1885), v. 424

Broadbrim and Co. (1828), IV. 436

Broad but not Long (1814), IV. 436

Broad Grins (1815, 1829), IV. 436

— = Whackham and Windham

Broad Path and the Narrow Way (1899), v. 653

Broad Road (Marshall, R., 1898), v. 478

Broadsea Cliffs (1835), IV. 436

Brocken Vows = Faust and Loose

Broken Bail (Gordon, G. L., 1878), v. 385

Broken Bonds (Calmour, A. C., 1883), v. 300

Broken Branch (Du Terreaux, L. H., 1874), v. 352, 789

— (1888), v. 653

Broken Chain (Haines, J. T., 1839), IV. 587

— (Suter, W. E., 1859), v. 653, 818, 828

— (1838), IV. 436

Broken Coupling (Moonie, J. A., 1890), v. 491

Broken Faith (1855), v. 653

— = Clouds

Broken Fetters (Thursby, C., 1897), v. 600

— = Convict's Daughter

Broken Gold (Dibdin, C., 1806), IV. 290

Broken Heart (Jerrold, D. W., 1832), IV. 332

— = (1) Agnes de Vere; (2) Beatrice; (3) Chimes; (4) Destiny; (5) Farmer's Daughter; (6) Farmer's Daughter of the Severnside

Broken-Hearted Club (Coyne, J. S., 1868), v. 328

Broken Hearts (Gilbert, W. S., 1875), v. 138–9, 140, 145, 380

Broken Home (Wilkins, J. H., 1859), v. 653, 823, 828

Broken Hot Cross Bun = Spectre of Shooter's Hill

Broken Idol (1874), v. 653

Broken Life = Chris

Broken Lily (Towers, E., 1878), v. 601

— (Willis, A., 1846), IV. 617

Broken Link = Dick's Repentance

Broken Links (Holmes, H., 1882), v. 424

Broken Marriage = Passion's Peril

Broken Melody (Keen, H. and Leader, J., 1892), v. 442

Broken Off (Phillips, Mrs N., 1892), v. 523

— (1891), v. 653

Broken Pearls (Archer, W. J., 1867), v. 242

Broken Promises (Arnold, S. J., 1825), IV. 256

Broken Reed = Stepmothers

Broken Sixpence (Thompson, Mrs G. and Sinclair, K., 1889), v. 597

Brother's Sacrifice (Lemon, M., 1841),
IV. 344
— = Express
Brothers Salacarro = Corsicans
Brother Tom (Buckstone, J. B., 1839),
IV. 275
Brought to Bay (1885), V. 654
— = Buried Alive
Brought to Book (Hay, F., 1875), V.
411
— (Macdermott, G. H. and Pettitt, H.,
1876), V. 468
Brought Together (Mouillot, F., 1894),
V. 498
Brought to Justice (Pettitt, H. and
Meritt, P., 1880), V. 521
Brought to Light (Darbey, E., 1889), V.
336
— (Palmer, T. A., 1868), V. 511
— (Percival, J., 1872), V. 520
— (1876), V. 654
Brought to the Test (1884), V. 654
Brown and the Brahmins (Reece, R.,
1869), V. 537
Brown Devil (Nantz, F. C., 1830), IV.
437, 621
Browne the Martyr (Lucas, J. T.,
1872), V. 464
Browne with an E. (Montague, L. A. D.,
1893), V. 491
Brown Fanny (1834), IV. 437
Brownie of the Brig = All Hallows' Even
Brownies (1894), V. 654
Brown, Jones and Robinson (1838), IV.
437
— (1850), V. 654
— (1866), V. 654
Brown, Jones and Robinson at Brighton
= Where's Brown?
Brown Man (1819; 1820), IV. 437
Brown Man of the Moor = Wizard
Brown's Boarders (1888), V. 654
Brown's Horse (À Beckett, G. A., 1836),
IV. 567
Brown Studies = My Absent Son
Bruce (Davidson, J., 1886), V. 338
Bruin and the Bashaw = Bears not
Beasts
Bruin the Brave (1854), V. 654
Brum (Desprez, F., 1880), V. 343
Brumley's Wife (1863), V. 654
Bruno (1821), IV. 437

Bruno the Black and the Knight
Champion (Dibdin, C. I. M., 1826),
IV. 296
Bruscino = Accidental Son
Brutus (Payne, J. H., 1818), IV. 368
— (1829), IV. 437
— (1854), V. 654
Brutus and Caesar (1866), V. 654
Brutus of Alba (Powell, G., 1696), I.
252, 425
— (Tate, N., 1678), I. 39, 40, 42, 54,
160, 434
Brutus Ultor (Field, M., 1886), V. 366
Bubble (Kirkman, F., 1662), I. 417
Bubble and Squeak (Hay, F., 1871), V.
411
Bubble Reputation (Willing, J. and
Douglass, J., 1885), V. 626
Bubbles (Fawcett, C. S., 1881), V. 364
— (Moser, J., 1808), IV. 364
Bubbles in the Sudds (1887), V. 654
Bubbles of the Day (Jerrold, D. W.,
1842), IV. 185, 333
Bucanier's Bridal = Wreck
Bucaniers of 1660 = Lolonois
Buccanier (1824), IV. 437
Buccaneers (Pendred, L. St L., 1894), V.
519
— = (1) Captain Kidd; (2) Montbar
Buccaneers of the Arctic Regions =
England Ho!
Buccaneer's Revenge = Rokeby
Buccaneer's Wife (Conquest, G., 1859),
V. 654, 785, 828
Buckaneer and the Little Dear = Zampa
Buckingham (Edwards, J., 1877), V.
355
— (Wills, W. G., 1875), V. 627
— = Favourite of the King
Buckle of Brilliants = Crown Prince
Buckram in Armour = Disappointed
Gallant
Buck's Interlude (1761), III. 321
Buck's Lodge (1790), III. 321
Buckstone's Adventure with a Polish
Princess (Lewes, G. H., 1855), V. 459
Bud and Blossom (Campbell, Lady C.,
1893), V. 301
Budget of Blunders (Greffulhe, 1810),
IV. 321, 437, 586
— (1819), 437
Buffalo Bill (Roberts, G., 1887), V. 545

Buffalo Bill (Stanley, H. J. and Hermann, C., 1887), v. 579

Buffalo Girls (Stirling, E., 1847), IV. 408

Buffalo Hunter of the Death Prairies = White Chief

Buffooning (1887), v. 654

Bugle Call (Parker, L. N. and Bright, A. A., 1899), v. 514, 654

— (1899), v. 654

Bugle Horn = Cumnor

Bugler of the Twentieth (1856), v. 654

Building of the Ship = King of Steel

Built on Sand (Harvey, F., 1886), v. 408

Bull and the Magpie = My Uncle's House

Bull by the Horns (Byron, H. J., 1876), v. 298

Bulldogs, Ahoy! (Daly, B. and Syms, A., 1899), v. 334

Bull-fighter (Almar, G., 1838), IV. 253

— (1855), v. 828

Bull in a China Shop (Mathews, C. J., 1864), v. 480

Bulls and Bears (1715), II. 367

Bull's Head (Beazley, S., Jr., 1818), Saracen's Head removed from Snow Hill, IV. 263, 571

Bully-Huff catch's in a Trap = Boaster

Bulse (Jodrell, R. P., 1787), III. 277

Bumble (Clement, F. A., 1891), v. 314

Bumble's Courtship (Emson, F. E., ?1874), v. 358

Bumbrusher (1786), III. 321

Bumpkin's Dream = St Stephen's Well

Bump of Benevolence (Faucit, J. S., 1841), IV. 311

Bunch of Berries (Blanchard, E. L., 1875), v. 264

Bunch of Keys (Hoyt, C. H. and Gordon, G. L., 1882), v. 429

Bunch of Roses (1897), v. 654

Bunch of Shamrocks (Bateman, F. and Douglass, J. T., 1896), v. 253

Bunch of Violets (Grundy, S., 1894), v. 397

Bundle of Prologues (1777), III. 321

Bungalow (Horner, F. and Wyatt, F., 1889), v. 427

Bungles (De Svertchkoff, A. and Morphew, H., 1892), v. 343

Bunkum Muller (Craven, H. T., 1864), v. 328

Bunthorne's Bride = Patience

Buonaparte (Ripon, J. S., 1803), IV. 394

Buonaparte at the Military School of Brienne = Little Corporal

Buonaparte Burnt Out (1813), IV. 437

Buonaparte in the Dumps = Admiral Nelson's Triumph

Buonaparte's Destiny (1831), IV. 437

Buonaparte's Fatalities (1828), IV. 437

Buonaparte's Invasion of Russia (Amherst, J. H., 1825), IV. 254

Buondelmonte (Woodrooffe, S., 1826), IV. 422

Burch and his Detractors (1875), v. 654

Burden of Guilt = Life for a Life

Burglar Alarm and the Detective Camera (Gannon, J., 1893), v. 375

Burglar and the Bishop (Coghill, Sir J. J., 1893), v. 316

Burglar and the Judge (Philips, F. C. and Brookfield, C. H. E., 1892), v. 522

Burglars (Melford, M., 1885), v. 484

Burglar's Baby (Douglass, J. T. and Williams, C., 1897), v. 349

Burglar's Fate = Struggle for Life

Burgomaster of Sardaam (Reynolds, F., 1818), IV. 392

Burgomaster's Daughter (1863), v. 654

— = Sexton of Cologne

Burgomaster Trick'd = (1) Apollo and Daphne; (2) Daphne and Apollo

Burgraves (Oxberry, W. H.), IV. 602

Burgundy the Bold (1832), IV. 437

Buried Alive (Macpherson, H., 1899), v. 471

— (1874), v. 654

— = (1) Caffres; (2) Cruel Brother; (3) Savage Chieftain; (4) Tom Cobb

Buried Secret = My Lady Hilda

Buried Talent (Parker, L. N., 1886), v. 513

Buried Titan (Leifchild, F., 1859), v. 453

Burlesque Steeplechase (1835), IV. 437

Burletta of Errors (Planché, J. R., 1820), IV. 376, 604

Burley and Morton = Old Mortality

Burlington Arcade (Dance, C., 1838), IV. 289

Burmese = Burmese War

Burmese War (Amherst, J. H., 1826),
IV. 254, 568

Burning Bridge (Fitzball, E., 1824), IV.
312

Burning Forest = Thunderbolt

Burning Gulf = Hawaia

Burning his Fingers (1880), v. 654

Burning Mountain (1804), IV. 437

— = Iron Casket

Burning of Moscow = Russian Sacrifice

Burning of the Kent East Indiaman
(1825), IV. 437

Burning Ship (1850), v. 654

Burning Sword = Thalaba the Destroyer

Burnt at Sea (Cooper, F. F., 1844), IV.
577

Burnt Offering (Fryers, A. and Fisher,
J. M., 1894), v. 374

Bury-Fair (Shadwell, T., 1689), I. 69,
188, 193, 198, 209, 215, 272, 431

Bush King (Lincoln, W. J., 1893), v.
459

Bushrangers = Australia

Bushrangers and the Last of the
African Settlers = Bosjesman

Busie Body (Centlivre, Mrs S., 1709),
II. 130, 131, 132, 133, 135, 136, 137,
138, 142, 167, 304, 433

Busie Body, Second Part of the = Mar-
Plot

Business is Business (Wigan, H., 1874),
v. 622

Busiris, King of Egypt (Young, E.,
1719), II. 26, 57, 113, 264, 364, 446

Bussy D'Ambois (D'Urfey, T., 1691),
I. 409

Bustle's Bride (Capes, B., 1884), v. 302

Bust Peter (Danvers, G. J. B., 1826), IV.
579

Busy Body = Busie Body

Butcher, Butcher, Kill an Ox (Neale, F.,
1845), IV. 437, 621

Butcher Butcher Killed the Ox, Ran
away with the Money Box (1859), v.
654

Butcher versus Baker (Talfourd, F.,
1852), v. 590

"But however—" (Mayhew, H. and
Baylis, H., 1838), IV. 355

Buthred (1779), III. 321

Butler (Merivale, H. C. and Mrs H.
Merivale, 1885), v. 487

Butler in the Suds = Nursery Maid
Mistress

Buttercup and Daisy (Dance, G., 1895),
v. 335

Butterflies' Ball (1860), v. 654

Butterflies' Ball and the Grasshoppers'
Feast (1855), v. 654

Butterfly (Carr, Mrs J. C., 1879), v. 304

— (Rhoades, W. C., 1887), v. 542

Butterfly Fever (Mortimer, J., 1881), v.
494

Butterfly of Fashion = Beau Lavender

Butterfly's Ball (Addison, H. R., 1833),
IV. 567 (= Butterfly Ball, IV. 437;
correct date, 19/11/1833)

Butterfly's Ball and the Grasshopper's
Feast (1853), v. 828 [See Butterflies'
Ball and the Grasshoppers' Feast]

Buttermilk Volunteers (Selby, C., 1850)
= White Serjeants, v. 560, 654

Buxom Joan (Willet, T., 1778), III. 316

"Buy a Broom?" (Milner, H. M.,
1827), IV. 437, 621

Buy-em-dears, alias Bay-a-deres
(Rouse, E., 1838), IV. 396

Buz and Mum = Birds of a Feather

Buz buz (1891), v. 654

By Accident or Design = Over the Cliff

By Advertisement (1896), v. 654

— = One, Two, Three, Four, Five, by
Advertisement

By and By (1896), v. 654

By Command of the Czar (Glover, R.
and Hermann, C., 1877), v. 382

By Command of the King (Towers, E.,
1871), v. 601

Byeways (Payne, G. S., 1897), v. 518

Bygone Days (Harrison, C., 1899), v.
407

— = Tramp

Bygones (Pinero, Sir A. W., 1880), v.
524

By Hat and Trap (1898), v. 654

By Land and Sea! (Campbell, J. M. and
Shine, J. L., 1886), v. 301

By Road and Rail (Grain, R. C., 1893),
v. 388

By Royal Command (Stirling, E., 1845),
IV. 408

By Special Appointment (1849), IV. 437

By Special Licence (Marryat, F., 1887),
v. 477

By Special Licence (1895), v. 654

By Special Request (Watson, T. M., 1887), v. 616

By the Deeps Nine (1850), v. 654

By the Hand of Woman = Life's Mistakes

By the King's Command = By Command of the King

By the Midland Sea (McCarthy, J. H., 1892), v. 467

By the Sea (Aveling, E. B., 1887), v. 246

— (1872), v. 654

By this Token (Angus, J. K., 1884), v. 241

Byways of London = Outcast Poor

Byzantium (Poole, R., 1823), IV. 387

Cabal (1763), III. 321

Cabal and Love (Timäus, J. J. K., 1795), III. 63, 321, 397, 399

Cabdriver (Buckstone, J. B., 1830), IV. 575

Cabin Boy (Archer, T., 1846), IV. 255

— (Stirling, E., 1846), IV. 408

— (1836), IV. 437

Cabinet (Dibdin, T. J., 1802), IV. 33, 142, 297

— (1806), IV. 437

Cabinet and Two Wives (Parry, J., 1824) = Two Wives, IV. 368, 603

Cabinet Minister (Pinero, Sir A. W., 1890), v. 525

Cabinet of Bronze = Fairy Lady

Cabinet of Fancy (Stevens, G. A., 1780), III. 309

Cabinet Question (Planché, J. R., 1845), IV. 382

Cabinet Secret (Du Terreaux, L. H., 1872), v. 352

— (1832), IV. 437, 621

— (1856), v. 654

Cabman No. 93 (Williams, T. J., 1867), v. 625

Cabman's Career (1859), v. 654

Cadi (Matthison, A., 1880), v. 481

— (1851), v. 654

Cadi gulled = Tit for Tat

Cadijeh (Jameson, Mrs A., 1825), IV. 590

Cadi's Daughter (Fizball, E., 1851), v. 367

Cadi's Flat = Ocular Misfortunes

Cadmus et Hermione (Quinault, P., 1686), I. 425

Cad of the Buss = Tiger at Large

Cady (1815) = Honesty the Best Policy, v. 437, 621

— = Cady of Bagdad

Cady of Bagdad (Portal, A., 1778), III. 299

Caedmon (Bantock, G., 1892), v. 248

Cælia (Johnson, C., 1732), II. 89, 105, 122, 124, 340

Cælina (Wallace, J., 1802), IV. 416

Caernarvon Castle (Rose, J., 1793), III. 303

Caesar and Clara = Koromantyns

Caesar and Cleopatra (Shaw, G. B., 1899), v. 189, 195, 200, 201, 562

Caesar, Bob and Lucy Neal (1847), IV. 437

Caesar Borgia (Barnett, C. Z., 1831), IV. 259

— (Lee, N., 1679), I. 79, 130, 146, 419

Cæsar in Ægypt (Cibber, C., 1724), II. 15, 70, 71, 103, 312

Caesar's Triumph over the Gauls (1815), IV. 437

Caesar's Wife (1880), v. 654

Caesar the Half-breed = Bloodhound of Cuba

Caesar, the Watch Dog of the Castle (Moncrieff, W. T., 1844), IV. 361

Caffres (Eyre, E. J., 1802), IV. 310

Caffres and Settlers = Cape of Good Hope

Caffre's Vengeance = Olga the Dreaded Witch

Cagliostro (1860), v. 654

Cagliostro the Magician (Clarke, C. A., 1875), v. 311

— = Cagliostro

Cagot (Falconer, E., 1856), v. 360

Cahill Euve Dha Rhug = Red Hand

Caid (1849), IV. 437

Cain (Byron, Lord G. G., 1821), IV. 169, 278

— (1878), v. 655

Cain and Abel (1890), v. 655

Caitiff of Corsica (1807), IV. 437

Caius Gracchus (Joshua, J., 1810), IV. 334

— (Knowles, J. S., 1815), IV. 171, 339

Caius Gracchus (Russell, Lord J.), IV. 396

Caius Marius (Doubleday, T., 1837), IV. 437, 582, 621

— (Otway, T., 1679), I. 68, 162–3, 338, 357, 422

Caius Silius, the Warrior Captive (1859), V. 655

Caius Toranius (Bell, A., 1841), IV. 264

Calabrian Asassin (Ebsworth, J.), IV. 309

Calaf (1826), IV. 437

Calas (1820), IV. 437

Calaynos (Boker, G. H., 1848), IV. 573

Calcutta (Cobb, J., 1788) = Love in the East, III. 321, 379, 399

Calderon, the King's Favourite (1862), V. 655

Caldron (1788), III. 321

Caleb (Johnson, S. A., 1893), V. 437

Caleb Quotem and his Wife! (Lee, H., 1809), IV. 342, 594

Caledonia (Thomson, W., 1818), IV. 614

— (1700), I. 440

— (1812), IV. 438

Caledonian Assassin (1824), IV. 438

Caledonian Feuds = Edgar

Caledonian Laurels (Byrne, J., 1815), IV. 277

Caledon's Tears (Nesbit, G., 1733), II. 346

Calenderer's Horse = Johnny Gilpin

Calife de Bagdad (Dibdin, T. J., 1809), IV. 438, 580

Calife voleur (1814), IV. 438

California Joe (Rainbow, J. G., 1878), V. 533

Caligula (Crowne, J., 1698), I. 124, 151, 400

Caliph and the Cadi (Planché, J. R., 1819), IV. 376

Caliph and the Cobler = Justice

Caliph and the Slave (1830), IV. 438

Caliph Haroun Alraschid (1824), IV. 438

Caliph of Bagdad (Brough, W., 1867), V. 280

— (1858), V. 655

Caliph Robber = Bondocani

Caliph Vathek (Milner, H. M., 1823), IV. 428, 621

Calisto (Crowne, J., 1675), I. 43, 60, 305, 357–60, 399

Call again to-morrow (Trueba, J. T., 1832), IV. 414

Called back (Chute, J., 1884), V. 310

— (Conway, H. and Carr, J. C., 1884), V. 323

— (1884), V. 655

— (1885), V. 655

Called back again (Chevalier, A., 1885), V. 309

Called there and back (Merivale, H. C., 1884), V. 487

Called to the Bar (Poel, W., 1892), V. 655, 811, 829

Called to the Front (Towner, Sergeant and Beaumont, F., 1885), V. 20, 602

Callendrack Callebrando, the Giant Zugic (1852), V. 655

Callirrhoe (Field, M., 1884), V. 366

Callista (1731), II. 262, 367

Call me at Three = Melo-dramatist

Call of Fate = Right and Might

Calthorpe Case (Goodrich, A., 1887), V. 384

Calumny (Watson, T. M., 1889), V. 616

Calydonian Chace = Meleager and Atalanta

Calypso (Cumberland, R., 1778), III. 251

— (Houlton, R., 1785), III. 273

— (Thompson, A., 1874), V. 597, 820

Calypso and Telemachus (Hughes, J., 1712), II. 235, 337, 439

— (1865), V. 655

Calypso, Queen of Ogygia = Telemachus and Calypso

Camaralzaman (Burnand, F. C., 1884), V. 291

— (James, G. P. R., 1849), IV. 590

Camaralzaman and Badoura (Brough, W. and Brough, R. B., 1848), IV. 152–3, 271

Camaralzaman and the Fair Badoura (Byron, H. J., 1871), V. 298

Camberwell Brothers (Selby, C., 1852), V. 560

Cambrian Hero (Sotheby, W., 1800), IV. 405

+ Cambridge Dionysia (Trevelyan, G. O.; 8°, 1869 (in *Ladies in Parliament and other Pieces*: apparently acted privately at Cambridge))

Cambridge Dunns = Academie

Cambro-Britons (Boaden, J., 1798), III. 238

— (1797), III. 321

Cambyses King of Persia (Settle, E., 1671), I. 40, 55, 66, 83, 116–7, 130, 428

Cameleon (1817), IV. 438

Cameleopard = Giraffe

Camelford (1822), IV. 438

Camelia (1861), V. 655

Camera Obscura (Browne, G. W., 1879), V. 282

Cameronians (Suter, W., 1863), V. 655, 829

Camilla (MacSwiny, O., 1706), II. 32, 58, 79, 227–8, 231, 234, 266, 274–5, 391

Camilla of Camden Town (Stuckey, H. D., 1893), V. 586

Camilla's Husband (Phillips, W., 1862), V. 523

Camilla the Amazon (1817), IV. 438

Camilla, the Wild Flower of the Wilderness (Hillier, A., 1874), V. 421

Camille (Wills, W. G., 1877), V. 627

— (1853), V. 655

— (1883), V. 655

— (1888), V. 655

Camillus and Columna (Powell, T., 1806), IV. 606

Camoens (Tucker, H. St G., 1832), IV. 615

Camp (Sheridan, R. B., 1778), III. 305, 395

— (1825), IV. 438

Campaign (Jephson, R., 1784), III. 277, 389 [This was acted Smock Alley, Dublin, 31/1/1784]

Campaigners (D'Urfey, T., 1698), I. 23, 273, 277–8, 409–10

Campaigning (1879), V. 655

Camp and the Convent (1820), IV. 438

Campanello (1837), IV. 438

Campano (Day, G. D., 1898), V. 340

Camp at Chobham (Lemon, M., 1853), V. 455

Camp at the Olympic (Planché, J. R., 1853), V. 82–3, 110, 117, 527

Camping Out (Howard, B., 1886), V. 428

Camp of Pleasure = Wags

Camp of Silesia (1847), IV. 438

Camp of the Wilderness = Siege of Jerusalem

Camp, the Cottage and the Court = King's Wager

Camp Visitants (Miller, J., 1740), II. 441

Canadian Basket Maker = Iroquois

Canadian War (Hart, J. P.), IV. 587

Canal Boat (1871), V. 655

Canary (Fleming, G., 1899), V. 369

Candida (Shaw, G. B., 1895), V. 189, 195, 204, 562

Candidate (Dent, J., 1782), III. 254

— (McCarthy, J. H., 1884), V. 467

Candidates for Rottenburgh = Election

Can he forgive her? (Calvert, Mrs C., 1891), V. 300

Can Love Kill? (1836), IV. 438

Cannibal (1838), IV. 438

Cannie Soogah (1873), V. 655

Cannon-mouth and Pistol-shot (1828), IV. 438

Canonburg (1834), IV. 438

Canonburg Tower (1831), IV. 438

Canonbury Tower (1857), V. 655

Canon's Daughter = Dione

Cantab (Robertson, T. W., 1861), V. 546

Cantabs (1787), III. 321

Canterbury Guests (Ravenscroft, E., 1694), I. 188, 256, 426

Canterbury Pilgrims (À Beckett, G. A., 1884), V. 234

Can't I do what I like with my own? (1831), IV. 438

Can't Sing Girl (1891), V. 655

Can't ye come out tonight? = Buffalo Girls

Canute's Birthday in Ireland (Buchanan, R., 1868), V. 284

Canute the Great (Field, M., 1887), V. 366

Canvass (1765), III. 321

Cape Mail (Scott, C. W., 1881), V. 558

Cape of Good Hope (Barrymore, W., 1819), IV. 438, 621

Capers (Marriott, F. and Matthews, A. K., 1899), V. 477

— (Stahl, R., 1885), V. 578

Capers and Coronets (Barnett, M., 1854), V. 250

— (Lunn, J., 1835), IV. 348

Capers and Crushers (1847), IV. 621

Capers at Canterbury (Planché, J. R., 1821), IV. 377

Capers of Cupid (1899), V. 655

Cape St Vincent (Sheridan, R. B., 1797), III. 306

Capillary Attraction = Man's Coming

Capital and Labour (Patmore, W. J. and Moss, A. B., 1890), V. 161, 515

— (1895), V. 655

Capital Idea (Arlon, F. and Rushton, A., 1871), V. 243

Capital Joke (De Lara, F., 1889), V. 341

Capital Match (Morton, J. M., 1852), V. 495

— (Parker, W., 1897), V. 514

Capital Pair = Charming Pair

Capitan (Klein, C. H., 1899), V. 445, 801

Capitola (Hazlewood, C. H., 1859), V. 412

Capochio and Dorinna, II. 445

— = Happy Captive

Capochio e Dorinna (1768), III. 321

Caprice (Broughton, F. W., 1889), V. 281

— (McCarthy, J. H., 1892), V. 467

Capriciosa (1880), V. 655

Capricious Beauty (D'Arcy, Major, 1886), V. 336

Capricious Lady (Cooke, W., 1783), III. 248, 380

— (Pye, Mrs J. H., 1771), III. 300

Capricious Lovers (Lloyd, R., 1764), III. 116, 118, 282, 390

— (Odingsells, G., 1725), II. 347; III. 116

Captain (Carlos, Don, 1883), V. 303

— (Field, W. F., 1886), V. 366

— (1677), I. 346, 440

— (1781), III. 321

Captain Bertram (1836), IV. 438

Captain Bertram and Jack Junk (1837), IV. 438

Captain Billy (Greenbank, H., 1891), V. 392

Captain Birchell's Luck (Parker, L. N., 1899), V. 514

— = Chris

Captain Blarney (1898), V. 655

Captain Brassbound's Conversion (Shaw, G. B., 1899), V. 195, 562

Captain Cartouche (1864), V. 655

Captain Charlotte (Stirling, E., 1843), IV. 407

Captain Cook (Faucit, J. S.), IV. 583

Captain Cuttle (Brougham, J., 1880), V. 281, 780

Captain Dreyfuss (Rackow, N., 1898), V. 532

Captain Firebrand (Pitt. C., 1872), V. 655, 810, 829

Captain Fritz (Hamilton, H., 1897), V. 402

Captain Gerald (Archer, W. J., 1867), V. 242

— (Howe, J. B., 1867), V. 428

Captain Hawk in the Coffin Cell = Shadow of Death

Captain is not A-Miss (Wilks, T. E., 1836), IV. 420

Captain Jack (1870), V. 655

Captain Jack, the Little Sheppard, and the Black Sheep, Jonathan Wild (1894), V. 655

Captain J. D. Pitman (1899), V. 655

Captain John Hall, the First Highwayman (1872), V. 655

Captain John Luck (1850), V. 655

Captain John Rock = Tale of the O'Hara Family

Captain Kidd (Abbott, C. H., 1883), V. 233

— (Kummer, C., 1898), V. 446

Captain Leigh, V.C. = Sister Mary

Captain Macheath (Travers, W., 1865), V. 655, 821, 829

Captain MacShane (1802), IV. 438

Captain O'Blunder = Brave Irishman

Captain of the Guard (Wood, F., 1882), V. 630

Captain of the Night Hawk (Jecks, A. E., 1897), V. 435

Captain of the Vulture (Lewis, J. and Falconer, H., 1888), V. 459

— (Vandenhoff, H., 1864), V. 655, 822, 829

— (1863), V. 655

Captain of the Watch (Planché, J. R., 1841), IV. 381

Captain Pop and the Princess Pretty Eyes! = Brown and the Brahmins

Captain pro tem (Lemon, M., 1840) = Captain (Query?), IV. 344, 438, 621

66

Carl Carlsruhe (1840), IV. 439

Carl et Lisbeth (1814), IV. 439

Carline (1831), IV. 439

Carline, the Female Brigand (Stirling, E., 1837), IV. 406

Carlists of La Vendée = Memoirs of the Duchess de Berri

Carlmilham (Fitzball, E., 1835), IV. 314

Carlo (Millingen, J. G., 1837), IV. 439, 621

Carlo Broschi = Ma Part

Carlo Brunari (1856) = Horse of the Cavern, V. 655, 694, 836

Carlo Foscari, the Italian Boy (1861), V. 655

Carlo Leoni (Hazlewood, C. H., 1859), V. 655, 796, 829

Carlos Gangenelli (Pitt, G. D., 1847), IV. 374

Carlowitz and Orloff (1831), IV. 439

Carl's Folly (Greene, C. M., 1891), V. 392

Carl the Clockmaker (Starr, H., 1894), V. 579

Carlyle's Wife (1883), V. 656

Carlyon Sahib (Murray, Sir G., 1899), V. 500

Carl Zeitter and his Bride (1835), IV. 439

Carmelite (Cumberland, R., 1784), III. 49, 78–9, 251

Carmelites (Fitzball, E., 1835), IV. 315

Carmen (Hamilton, H., 1896), V. 402

— (Hersee, H., 1879), V. 419, 797

— (Reece, R., 1879), V. 538

Carmen up-to-date (Sims, G. R. and Pettitt, H., 1890), V. 569

Carnac Sahib (Jones, H. A., 1899), V. 440

Carnation of Carnation Cottage (1862), V. 656

Carnaval de Venise (1821), IV. 439

Carnival (Charke, Mrs C., 1735), II. 306

— (Porter, T. ?1663), I. 219–20, 264, 425

Carnival at Naples (Dimond, W., 1830), IV. 439, 621

Carnival Frolic = One Hour

Carnival of Venice (Tickell, R., 1781), III. 312

— (1824), IV. 439

— (1859), V. 656

Carnival Time (Watson, T. M., 1890), V. 616

Carolan (Victor, H., 1892), V. 608

+ Caroline and Henrietta (*French*)

Caroline's Pupils (Vaun, R. and Atwood, A., 1896), V. 607

Caroona (Ray, E., 1899), V. 535

Carp (Desprez, F., 1886), V. 343

Carpenter (Moreau, 1813), IV. 600

Carpenter of Rouen (Jones, J. S., 1844, 1853), IV. 334; V. 440, 800

Carpenter's Family = Robert Ryland

Carpenters of Lambeth (1847), IV. 439

Carpenters of Paris (Archer, T., 1846), IV. 255

Carpet Bag (Blanchard, E. L., 1869), V. 264

Carpio (Finnamore, J., 1886), V. 367

Carrier and his Dog (1854), V. 656

— = Old Toll House

Carrier of London (Halford, J., 1854), V. 656, 795, 829

Carron Side (Planché, J. R., 1828), IV. 378

Carrot and Pa-snip (Green, F. W., 1872), V. 390

Carry's Breach of Promise (De Frece, M., 1872), V. 341

Carry's Triumph = Carry's Breach of Promise

Carte de Visite (Williams, M. and Burnand, F. C., 1862), V. 624, 824

Cartel at Philadelphia = Seventeen Hundred and Eighty One

Carte over Arm = Roland

Carter of Liverpool (1879), V. 656

Carthusiana (Stephenson, B. C., 1899), V. 582

Carthusian Friar (1793), III. 321

Cartouche (Strauss, F., 1860), V. 656, 818, 829

— (Travers, W., 1859), V. 656, 821, 829

— (1722), III. 367

Cartouche and Co. Ltd. (Newton, H. C., 1892), V. 503

Cartouche, the French Robber (1860), V. 656

Cartouche, the Renowned Robber of France (Travers, W., 1840), IV. 414

Carynthia (Towers, E., 1867), V. 600, 821

Caryswold (Herman, H. and Mackay, J., 1877), V. 419

Casanova (1837), IV. 439

Castle of Limburg (1822; 1840), IV. 439
Castle of Lindenbergh = Raymond and Agnes
Castle of Lochleven = Mary Stuart
Castle of Minski = Mines of Poland
Castle of Monte Falcon = Hag of the Lake
Castle of Montval (Whalley, T. S., 1799), III. 315
Castle of Morosino (Loveday, W., 1812), IV. 347
Castle of Olival = Wandering Boys
Castle of Otranto (À Beckett, G. A., 1848), IV. 251
— (Bradwell, W., 1840), IV. 573
— (Siddons, H., 1793) = Sicilian Romance, III. 321, 399
— (1859), V. 656
— = (1) Manfred; (2) Sicilian Romance
Castle of Paluzzi (Raymond, R. J., 1818), IV. 388
Castle of St Aldobrand (Maturin, C. R., 1816) = Bertram, IV. 439, 598, 622
— (1832), IV. 439
Castle of Sorrento (Heartwell, H. and Colman, G., 1799), III. 121, 268
Castle of Steinberg (1831), IV. 439
Castle of Sunderwald = Fire Fiend
Castle of Tarento (1819), IV. 439
Castle of the Forest = Fatal Sisters
Castle of Udolpho (Weston, F. F., 1808), IV. 418
Castle of Valenza (Courtney, J., 1851), V. 326
Castle of Wolfenstein (Thackeray, T. J., 1828), IV. 439, 622
Castle of Wonders (Andrews, M. P., 1786) = Enchanted Castle, III. 321, 377, 399
— (Johnson, 1819), IV. 333, 582, 590
Castles in Spain (Montague, L. A. D.), V. 491
Castles in the Air (Dibdin, C. I. M., 1809), IV. 292
— (Ryley, S. W., 1818) = Castle of Glyndower, IV. 396, 439, 622
— (Rae, C. M., 1879), V. 532
— (Robertson, T. W., 1854), V. 546
— (1832), IV. 439
— = In the Clouds
Castle Sombras (Smith, R. G. and Mansfield, F., 1896), V. 573

Castle Spectre (Lewis, M. G., 1797), III. 50, 52, 62, 72, 98, 99-100, 152, 281; IV. 113
Castle Walstenfurth (1801), IV. 439
Cast of the Lead (1899), V. 656
Cast on the Mercy of the World (Hazlewood, C. H., 1862), V. 412
Cast on the World = Alone in the World
Castruccio (Newbound, E., 1878), V. 502
Casual Acquaintance (Cooke, J. F., 1893), V. 324
Casual Ward (Cave, J. A., 1866), V. 306
Caswallon (Walker, C. E., 1829), IV. 416
Caswallon, the King of Britain (Gandy, E., 1826), IV. 318, 439, 622
Cataclysm = Noah's Flood
Catacombs of St Agnes = Nun
Catalina (Woodville, H., 1892), V. 631
Catalonian Marriage (1763), III. 321
Cat and Dog (Brown, J. R., 1871), V. 282
Cat and the Cherub (Fernald, C. B., 1897), V. 365
Cataract of Amazonia = White Witch
Cataract of Sostenza (1825), IV. 440
Cataract of the Ganges! (Moncrieff, W. T., 1823), IV. 359
Cataract of the Giant's Rock = Pirate Queen
Cataract of the Mountain = Hate
Catarina (Campbell, C., 1844), IV. 83, 440, 622
— (1844), IV. 83, 440
— (1861), V. 656
— (1862), V. 656
— = Crown Jewels
Catch a Weazel (Morton, J. M., 1862), V. 496, 807
Catch Club (1788), III. 321
Catch 'em alive = Bravo Rouse!
Catch 'em alive, oh! (Wild, G., 1851), V. 622
Catch him who can! (Hook, T. E., 1806), IV. 327
Catching a Gander (1854), V. 656
Catching a Governor = Pas de Fascination
Catching a Husband (1862), V. 656
Catching a Mermaid (Coyne, J. S., 1855), V. 327, 786
Catching an Heiress (Selby, C., 1835) IV. 397

Cause of the Greeks = Son of Evin
Cause of the present high Price of
    Provisions = Inquiry
Causes and Effects = Glass of Water
Caution to Young Ladies = Elopement
Cautious Coxcomb = Sir Salomon
Cavalearyer Costercana (Landeck, B.
    and Turner, E., 1893), v. 447
Cavalier (McCarthy, J. H., 1894), v. 467
— (Whitehead, D. C., 1836), iv. 419
— = Woodstock
Cavalier in Edinburgh = Woodstock
Cavalier of Wildinghurst = Charles at
    Tunbridge Wells
Cavaliers (1832), iv. 440
Cavaliers and Roundheads (Pocock, I.,
    1835), iv. 93, 385
— = Days of Oliver Cromwell
Cavalier, the Count and the Italian =
    Fair Circassian
Cave of Daroca = Moorish Banditti
Cave of Glenmore = Outlaws
Cave of Hecate (1797), iii. 399
Cave of Idra = Heroine of the Cave
Cave of Neptune (Holford, G., 1799),
    iii. 271
Cave of Plunder = Moorish Banditti
Cave of St Cataldo = Mysterious
    Stranger
Cave of St Robert = Eugene Aram
Cave of Trophonius (Hoare, P., 1791),
    iii. 269, 387
Cavern (Isdell, Sarah, Lady Morgan,
    1825), iv. 330, 601
Cavern in the Rock (1804), iv. 440
Cavern of Calabria = Murdered Monk
Cavern of Glotzden = Tower of Zauffen
Caverns of Hoenhelbe = Imperial
    Victims
C.D.I.T.D. Now Find it Out (1823), iv.
    440
Cead Mille Failthe (Murdoch, J. M.,
    1877), v. 499
Cedar Chest (Almar, G., 1834), iv. 253,
    568
Ceinture (1790), iii. 322
Celadon and Florimel (Kemble, J. P.,
    1796), iii. 115, 279, 389
Celebrated Case (Arthur, A., 1888), v.
    244
— (1890), v. 656
— = Proof

Celeste (1839), iv. 440
Celeste, the French Spy (1831), iv. 440
Celestia (Dalrymple, 1835), iv. 288
Celestial Institute (Sim, E. H., 1896), v.
    566
— = Institute Abroad
Celestials (Abbott, C. H. and Houghton,
    J. W., 1898), v. 233
Celestina (Savage, J., 1708), ii. 353
Celia the Gipsy Girl (Galer, E. J. N.,
    1879), v. 375
Cellar Spectre (1833), iv. 440
— = The Earls of Hammersmith
Cell of Mystery = Iron Tower
Cenci (Shelley, P. B., 1819), iv. 196–7
    221, 401
Cenia (1752), iii. 61, 322
Census (Brough, W. and Halliday, A.,
    1861), v. 279
Cent. per Cent. (Pocock, I., 1823), iv.
    124, 384 [The entry, iv. 277, under
    Butler, R. is in error]
Century Gone = St Ann's Well!
Cent Vierges (Grantham, J., 1874), v.
    388
Central Figure (Lloyd, H. H., 1897), v.
    461
Cephalus and Procris (1730), ii. 136,
    367, 451
Cephisa (Moser, J., 1804), iv. 364
Cerise & Co. (Musgrave, Mrs H., 1890),
    v. 500
Certain Age (1851), v. 656
Cervantes Knight = Spanish Gala
C'est l'amour (1820), iv. 440
C'est l'amour, l'amour, l'amour (1828),
    iv. 440
C'est la vie (Vaun, R., 1898), v. 607
Cestus (Dibdin, C., 1783), iii. 256
Cetewayo at Last (1882), v. 656
Cetewayo in South Shields (1882), v. 656
Chachechichochu (Pitt, G. D., 1845),
    iv. 374
Chaff (1877), v. 656
Chained to Sin and Brought up to Beg
    (1881), v. 656
Chain Gang (Harcourt, F. C., 1881), v.
    403
Chained to the Oar (Byron, H. J., 1873),
    v. 298
Chain of Events (Lewes, G. H. and
    Mathews, C. J., 1852), v. 458

Change of System (Paul, H. M., 1860), v. 516

Change Partners (1825) = Turn Hands and Change Partners, IV. 440, 545

Changes (Aylmer, J., 1890), v. 246

— (Proctor, H., 1876), v. 531

— (1843), IV. 440

Changes and Chances (1891), v. 657

Change upon Change (1805), IV. 440

Changing Servants (1836), IV. 440

Changing Years (1896), v. 657

Chaos (Dibdin, C. I. M., 1800), IV. 290

Chaos is come again (Morton, J. M., 1838), IV. 362

Chapel in the Wood = Invisible Witness

Chapel of Miracles = Idiot Queen

Chaperon (Brummel, H., 1899), v. 284

Chaperoned (Harrison, E., 1887), v. 407

Chaplain of the Fleet (1890), v. 657

Chaplain of the Regiment (1849), IV. 440

Chaplet (Mendez, M., 1749), II. 237, 260, 344, 440; III. 287

Chaplet of Innocence = Rose Wreath

Chapter from Don Quixote (Wills, W. G., 1895), v. 628

Chapter of Accidents (Douglass, J. T., 1870), v. 348

— (Lee, S., 1780), III, 120, 281

Character of Solomon Swop (1832), IV. 440

Charade (1852), v. 657

Charcoal Burner (Almar, G., 1832), IV. 252

Charcoal Burner of Charing = Fair Maid of Tottenham Court

Charcoal Burners of the Hartz = Steel Pavilion

Charibel (Green, F. W., 1885), v. 391

Charioteers (1810), IV. 440

Charitable Association (Brooke, H., 1778), III. 240

Charitable Man (Barry, H., 1887), v. 252

Charitable Quixote = Where is She?

+ Charity (Gardner, Mrs S, see Theatre Notebook, VII. 1953, 76–9)

— (Gilbert, W. S., 1874), v. 379

— (Hazlewood, C. H., 1862), v. 412

Charity begins at home (Stephenson, B. C. and Scott, C. W., 1872), v. 582

Charity Boy (Cross, J. C., 1796), III. 250, 380

Charity's Cloak (Dauncey, Sylvanus, 1891), v. 337

Charity's Love (Wilkins, J. H., 1854), v. 623

Charlatan (Aylmer, Mrs J., 1889), v. 246

— (Buchanan, R., 1894), v. 285

Charlemagne (Ducrow, A., 1841), IV. 308

— (1838), IV. 74, 440

Charles I (Brewer, E. C., 1828), IV. 270

— (Butler, A. G., 1874), v. 294

— (Flocton, C., 1879), v. 369

— (Mitford, M. R., 1834), IV. 358

— (Wills, W. G., 1872), v. 38, 627

Charles I and Charles II (1899), v. 657

Charles II (À Beckett, G. A., 1872), v. 234

— (Griffith, G., 1867), v. 394

— (Payne, J. H., 1824), IV. 369

— (1842), IV. 440

Charles II and Pretty Nell Gwynne (Soutar, R., 1867), v. 575

Charles VIII of France (Crowne, J., 1671), I. 64, 124, 347, 398–9

Charles XII (Planché, J. R., 1828), IV. 378

Charles XII and Peter the Great (Dibdin, T. J., 1828), IV. 440, 622

Charles at Tunbridge Wells (Forster, J., 1828), IV. 584

Charles Edward Stuart the Pretender in Scotland (Macdonald, 1823), IV. 441, 622

Charles Edward, the Last of the Stuarts (1828), IV. 441

Charles Ganganelli (1847), IV. 441

Charles O'Malley (Somerset, C. A., 1841), IV. 404

— = Galway Go Bragh

Charles O'Malley, the Irish Dragoon (Macarthy, 1843), IV. 349

Charles the Bold (Arnold, S. J., 1815), IV. 82, 256

Charles the Great = Charles the Eighth of France

Charles the Terrible (Faucit, J. S., 1830), IV. 82, 441, 583, 622

— (Raymond, R. J., 1821), IV. 82, 441, 622

Charley over the Water (1831), IV. 441

Charley's Aunt (Thomas, B., 1892), v. 183, 596

Charley Stuart (Belverstone, J., 1875), v. 257

Charley Wag (1861), v. 657

Charley Wag, the Outcast of the Thames (1861), v, 657

Charlie (Harraden, H., 1891), v. 404

Charlie's Uncle (1894), v. 657

Charlotte (Cullum, Mrs, 1775), III. 251

Charlotte and Werther (1810), IV. 441

Charlotte Corday (Bellew, H. K., 1894), v. 256

— (Bernard, W. B., 1855), v. 259

— (Mortimer, J., 1876), v. 494

— (1832, 1840), IV. 441

Charlotte Hanwell (Fitzball, E., 1842), IV. 316

Charlotte Hayden (Pitt, G. D., 1844), IV. 373

Charlotte Maria (Macrae, F. and Phillips, Mrs N., 1892), v. 472

Charm (Besant, W. and Pollock, W. H., 1884), v. 260

— (Ross, C. H., 1870), v. 551

Charmed Charger (1834), IV. 441

Charmed Harp (Courtney, J., 1852), v. 326

Charmed Horn = Oberon

Charmed Horse of the Black Valley = Golden-footed Steed

Charmed Lesson = Eulalie and Vermilion

Charmed Life (Whittaker, J. H. G., 1875), v. 621

Charmed Man and the Charming Woman = Ebon Wand

Charmed Pirate = Brown Devil

Charmed Rifle = Ora and the Red Woodman

Charmian and Badoura (Horsman, C., 1873), v. 427

Charming Cottage (Halliday, A., 1863), v. 657, 829

Charming Dreams = Did I dream it?

Charming Mrs Gaythorne (Cheltnam, C. S., 1894), v. 309

Charming Pair (Williams, T. J., 1863), v. 625

Charming Plaything (D'Arcy, G., 1873), v. 787

Charming Polly (Haines, J. T., 1838), IV. 322

Charming Widow (Oxenford, J., 1854), v. 509

Charming Woman (Wigan, H., 1861), v. 622

Charm of Iamblichus (Levy, J., 1896), v. 458

Charms (Young, Sir C. L., 1871), v. 635

Charter (Campbell, A. V., 1830), IV. 441, 622

— (1831), IV. 441

Charter of the Forest = All in One Night

Chartley the Fatalist (Pitt, G. D.), IV. 376

Chartreuse (Ganthony, R., 1899), v. 376

Chase (Suter, W. E., 1853), v. 587

— (1772), III. 322

— = Belford and Minton

Chasse (Noble, 1818), IV. 441

— = Cupid's Mistake

Chasseur Royal (1735), II. 367

Chasseurs (1831), IV. 441

Chastelard (Swinburne, A. C., 1865), v. 589

Chaste Nimph = Calisto

Chaste Salute (1831), IV. 441

— = Pay to my Order

Chaste Susanna (1711), II. 367

Chateau de Beauvais = Veiled Portrait

Chateau of Sevigny = Pauline

Chateau of Valenza (1851), v. 657

Chatelaine (1896), v. 657

Chatterbox (Jerrold, M. W. B., 1859), v. 436

Chatterton (Forster, J., 1888), v. 371

— (Herman, H. and Jones, H. A., 1884), v. 419

Chaubert (Villiers, J. C., 1789), III. 313

Chaunting Ben of Spitalfields (Lee, N., Jr., 1860), v. 802

Cheap Bargain (Dibdin, C. I. M., 1825), IV. 296

Cheap Excursion (Stirling, E., 1851), v. 584

— = London Barber

Cheap Jack (Towers, E., 1874), v. 601

Cheap Living (Reynolds, F., 1797), III. 46, 133, 301

Cheapside (1783), III. 322

Cheapside Beau = Squire Basinghall

Cheater Cheated (Kirkman, F., 1673), I. 418

Cheats (Wilson, J., 1663), I. 78, 212, 288, 318, 437

— (1717), II. 135, 367, 447

Cheats of Chick Lane = Murder House

Cheats of Harlequin (1729), II. 134, 367

— (1735), II. 367

Cheats of Scapin (Otway, T., 1676), I. 188, 258, 308, 422

— (Ozell, J., ?1715), II. 347, 442

— (1736), II. 137, 367

— = Cure for Covetousness

Check and Checkmate (1868), V. 657

Checkmate (Halliday, A., 1869), V. 401

Checkmated (1869), V. 657

Checkmate to Mr King (1886), V. 657

Check to the King (1846), IV. 441

Cheek and Plant (Fenton, F., 1864), V. 657, 829

Cheer, Boys, Cheer! (Harris, Sir A. H. G., Raleigh, C. and Hamilton, H., 1895), V. 406

Cheerful and Musical (Cassilis, I. L., 1891), V. 306

Cheerful Opinions = Alarmist

Chelsea (Stafford, J. J., 1832), IV. 441, 622

Chelsea Pensioner (Dibdin, C., 1779), III. 255

— (Soame, G., 1835), IV. 404

Cheque on my Banker (Moncrieff, W. T., 1821), IV. 441, 622

Cheque on my Banker's = Wanted a Wife

Chequer Board (1899), V. 657

Cherokee (Cobb, J., 1794), III. 367, 244

Cherokee Chief (1833), IV. 441

Cherries (1875), V. 657

Cherry (Hewson, J. J., 1895), V. 420

Cherry and Blue (1860), V. 657

Cherry and Fair Star (Blanchard, E. L., 1861), V. 263

— (Cheatham, F. G., 1862), V. 657

— (Green, F. W., 1874), V. 390

— (Hazlewood, C. H., 1867), V. 413

— (Stoman, C., 1845), IV. 409

— (1822), IV. 441, 622

— (1832), IV. 441

Cherry Blossom (1889), V. 657

Cherry Bounce (Raymond, R. J., 1821), IV. 388

Cherry Chance (1848), IV. 441

Cherry Garden Stairs (1895), V. 657

Cherry Hall (Dawson, F., 1894), V. 339

Cherry Tree Farm (Law, A., 1881), V. 449

Cherry-tree Inn = Elfie

Chertsey Curfew = Blanche Heriot

Cheshire Comics (Johnson, S., 1730), II. 340

Cheshire Huntress (1740), II. 367

Cheshire Knight outwitted = Love conquers all

Chess Board (1899), V. 657

Chester Fair (Hall, Mrs A. M., 1844), IV. 323

Chesterfield Thinskin (Maddox, J. M., 1853), V. 472

Chevalier de Maison Rouge and Marie Antoinette (Pritchard, 1859), V. 811

Chevalier d'Epsonne (Horncastle, J. H., 1848), IV. 441, 622

— (1848), IV. 441

Chevalier de St George (Robertson, T. W. 1845), IV. 608; V. 546 [Although this play is ascribed also to T. H. Reynoldson, T. W. Robertson seems to have been the author; if so, the entry at IV. 393 is in error]

— (Somerset, C. A., 1853), V. 574

— (1853), V. 657

Chevalier de St Georges (1853), V. 657

Chevalier of the Moulin Rouge (Hazlewood, C. H., V. 412, 796

Chevy Chase (Dibdin, T. J., ?1796), III. 382

— (Dibdin, T. J., 1816), IV. 300

— (Milner, H. M., 1832), IV. 357

— (Planché, J. R., 1836), IV. 380

Chez l'avocat (1877), V. 657

Chiara in Rosenberg (1837), IV. 441

Chicago, the City of Flames (Beverley, H. R., 1872), V. 261

Chicotte = Dangerous Game

Chi Chow Chi Chan (Marchant, F., 1869), V. 476

Chi Chu Ali (1851), V. 657

Chi Chu Ali, the Charmed Pirate (1831), IV. 441

Chickabiddies (1889), V. 657

Chickabiddy (1882), V. 657

Chicks (Field, W. F., 1886), V. 366

Chickweed and Groundsel (1884), v. 657

Chicot the Jester (Saintsbury, H. A., 1898), v. 554

Chief of the Arbutzi = Marco Schiarro

Chiefs of Erin = Cormac and Swaran

Chieftain (Burnand, F. C., 1894), v. 292

Chieftain's Banquet (Goff, H., 1824), IV. 585

Chieftain's Daughter = Retribution

Chieftain's Oath (Jerrold, D. W., 1821), IV. 331

Chieftains of Scotia (1809), IV. 441

Chieftains of the Glen = Outlaw's Oath

Chieftains of the Orkney Isles = Cattarans •

Chieftain's Vengeance = Kafrali Kara-bush

Chien du zouave (1856), v. 829

Child has found his Father = Birth of Merlin, the British Enchanter

Childhood's Dreams (Young, Sir C. L., 1881), v. 636

Child Lost (Douglass, J. T.), v. 789

Child of Air (1844), IV. 441
— = Fountain of Zea

Child of a Soldier = Home of the Brave

Child of a Tar = Wapping Old Stairs!

Child of Babylon = Hebrew Son

Child of Chance (Kemble, C., 1812) = Love's Errors, IV. 334, 496, 591, 631
— (Poole, W. H., 1886), v. 529
— (Travers, W., 1860), v. 822

Child of Concealment (Bromley, G. P., 1816), IV. 441, 622

Child of Crime = St Hilda's Cave

Child of Fortune = (1) Emmeline; (2) Ida May, the Kidnapped Child

Child of Love = Lover's Vows

Child of Mistery = Elfrida of Olmutz

Child of Mystery (1821), IV. 441
— = (1) Borrachio, the Outlaw; (2) Monk's Cowl; (3) Pride of the Blood; (4) Zilia

Child of Nature (Inchbald, Mrs E., 1788), III. 121, 144, 275, 388
— (1896), v. 657
— = Amanthis

Child of Science (1881), v. 657

Child of Sorrow = Julia Ackland

Child of the Army = Soldier's Sister

Child of the Desert = (1) Æthiop; (2) Æthiop's Oath; (3) Wild Horse, Mazeppa

Child of the Fire = Flamma

Child of the Foundling Hospital (1856), v. 657
— = Madeleine Dumas

Child of the Hempen Widow = (1) Horsemonger-Lane Joe; (2) Poor Joe of Horsemonger Lane

Child of the Island = Mad Woman through Love

Child of the Storm = Catherine of Russia

Child of the Sun (Brougham, J., 1865), v. 281

Child of the Waves = Life's Trials by Sea and Land

Child of the Wold (Faber, M. A., 1867), v. 790

Child of the Wreck (Planché, J. R., 1837), IV. 381
— = Ida Lee

Children (Hoare, P., 1800), III. 270; IV. 325, 588

Children in the Wood (Blanchard, E. L., 1872), v. 264
— (Blanchard, E. L. and Greenwood, T. L., 1874), v. 264
— (Clay, T. L., 1879), v. 313
— (Douglass, J. T., 1875), v. 348
— (Morton, T., 1793), III. 289
— (Osman, W. R., 1871), v. 508
— (Powell, T., 1805), IV. 387
— (Stirling, E., 1842), IV. 441, 622
— (Suter, W. E., 1860), v. 657, 818, 829
— (1850, 1875, 1876, 1877, 1878), v. 657

Children of Cyprus = Cherry and Fair Star

Children of Kings = Children of the King

Children of Mexico = Black Forester

Children of Mystery = Edwin and Angelina

Children of the Abbey = Fair Words and Foul Deeds

Children of the Alps = Brothers of Turin

Children of the Castle (Fitzball, E., 1857), v. 368

Children of the Earth = Spirit Bride

Children of the Ghetto (Zangwill, I.,
1899), v. 637
Children of the King (Armbruster, C.
and Davidson, J., 1897), v. 243, 778
Children of the Mist (1868), v. 657
— (1819), IV. 94, 442
— = Montrose
Children of the Sun = Incas of Peru
Children of the Wood (Blanchard,
E. L., 1859), v. 263
Children of the Zincali = Gitanilla
Children's Theatricals (Angus, J. K.,
1879), v. 241
Child Stealer (Suter, W. E., 1866), v.
588
Child, the Chouse and the Cheese =
Taffy was a Welshman
Chili Widow (Bourchier, A. and Sutro,
A., 1895), v. 270
Chilperic (Reece, R. + in association
with Marshall, F. A. and Mansell, R.,
1870), v. 537, 812
— (1875), v. 657
— (1884), v. 657
Chiltern Hundreds (Pemberton, T. E.,
1882), v. 519
Chimæra (Odell, T., 1721), III. 347
Chimes (À Beckett, G. A. and Lemon,
G., 1844), IV. 98, 250
— (Atkyns, S., 1844), IV. 98, 257
— (Edwards, E., 1844), IV. 98, 309
— (Travers, W., 1863), v. 657, 829
— (1845), IV. 98, 442
— (1863), v. 658
Chimes, A Goblin Tale (Stirling, E.,
1845), IV. 98, 307, 613
Chimes of Big Ben (1899), v. 658
Chimney Corner (Craven, H. T., 1861),
v. 328
— (Porter, W., 1797), III. 299
Chimney Piece (Rodwell, G. H., 1833),
IV. 395, 608
Chimney Sweeper (1736), II. 367
Chimney-Sweeper Prince (1788), III.
322
Chimney Sweeper's Opera (1728), II.
367
Chimpanzee in France = Return of
Perouse
Chinaman (Tresahar, J., 1894), v. 603
China Tale from a Delph Point of View
(McLelland, H. F., 1878), v. 468

China Wedding (Digges, W., 1877), v.
345
Chinese Divertisement (1824), IV. 442
Chinese Exhibition (1844), IV. 442
Chinese Festival (Noverre, J. G., 1755),
III. 291 [The author's christian name
was Jean Georges]
Chinese Giant (Soutar, R.), v. 817
Chinese Honeymoon (Dance, G. and
Talbot, H., 1899), v. 335
Chinese Insurrection (Almar, G., 1853),
v. 240
Chinese Invasion of 1960 (1863), v.
658
Chinese Junk (1848), IV. 442
Chinese Orphan (Hatchett, W., 1741),
II. 112, 334
Chinese Romance (Horne, F. L., 1862),
v. 426
Chinese Sorcerer (Dibdin, T. J., 1823),
IV. 304
Chinese Triumph (1747), II. 367
Chinese War (1844), IV. 442
Chinese Wedding (Hullin, 1824), IV.
589
Chinese Wonders (1833), IV. 442
Ching-a-Maree (1884), v. 658
Ching-Chow-Hi (Brough, W. and
Reed, G., 1865), v. 658, 780, 813, 829
Ching-Li-Wang (1879), v. 658
Ching's Bull Pup (1883), v. 658
Chink of Gold (1894), v. 658
Chip of the Old Block (Knight, E. P.,
1815), IV. 338
— (McLaren, A., 1823), IV. 352
— (1844), IV. 442
— = Veteran Tar
Chiromancy (Poel, W., 1888), v. 658,
811
Chirruper's Fortune (Law, A., 1885), v,
450
Chiselling (Albery, J. and Dilley, J.,
1870)
Chispa (Greene, C. M., 1889), v. 392
Chit-Chat (Killigrew, T., 1719), II. 18,
132, 187–8, 340
— (Walwyn, B., 1781), III. 314
Chivalry (Lee, R., 1873), v. 453
Chiverton Hall (1828), IV. 442
Chizzle's Choice (Francks, F. H. and
Wood, M., 1888), v. 372
Chloris (Newbound, E., 1876), v. 502

Chocolate-Makers (Stayley, G., 1759), III. 309

Choice (Cord, D. M., 1887), v. 325

— (McEwan, N., 1893), v. 469

— (Murphy, A., 1765), III. 290

— (1772), III. 322

Choice of Apollo (Potter, J., 1765), III. 299

Choice of Harlequin (1782), III. 322

Choice of Hercules (1753) = Hercules's Choice of Pleasure and Virtue, III. 322

Choknosoff (1871), v. 658

Cholera Morbus (1831), IV. 442

Choleric Count = Otto of Wittelsbach

Choleric Father's (Holcroft, T., 1785), III. 123, 203, 271, 387

Choleric Man (Cumberland, R., 1774) III. 126, 251
+ Choosing a Bride (*French*)

Choose your own path (1857), v. 829

Chopper's Wedding Morn (Turner, E., 1889), v. 604

Chops of the Channel (Hay, F., 1869), v. 411

Chopsticks and Spikins (Meritt, P., 1873), v. 485

Chorus Girl (1897), v. 658

— = Theatrical Duchess

Chosen for Life (Selby, H. C., 1882), v. 560

Chris (Parker, L. N., 1892), v. 513

Christabelle (À Beckett, G. A., 1872), v. 233

Christening (Buckstone, J. B., 1834), IV. 274

— (1860), v. 658

Christian (Caine, H., 1897), v. 300

Christian and his Comrades = Island

Christian Captives (Bridges, R. S., 1890), v. 275

Christian Hero (Lillo, G., 1735), II. 26, 50, 75, 84, 342

Christians and Moors (1824), IV. 442

Christian's Crime (Mortimer, L. and Wilson, P., 1899), v. 494

Christian's Cross (Oakley, F. and Claypole, C., 1897), v. 808

Christian's Cross and Martyr's Crown = Christian's Cross

Christian Slave (1856), v. 658

Christie Johnstone (Reade, C.), v. 812

Christina (Lynwood, P. and Ambient, M., 1887), v. 465

Christine (Broughton, F. W. and Jones, J. W., 1879), v. 281

— (1842), IV. 442

— (1862), v. 658, 829

— = Youthful Queen, Christine of Sweden

Christine of Sweden = Young Queen

Christmas at Brighton (Mathews, C. J., 1820), IV. 354, 597

Christmas Boxes (Mayhew, A. and Edwards, H. S., 1860), v. 483, 806

— (1825), IV. 442

— = New Year's Gift

Christmas Box System = Christmas Boxes

Christmas Capers (1835), IV. 442

Christmas Carol (Barnett, C. Z., 1844), IV. 97, 260

— (Cooper, F. F., 1854), v. 786

— (Stirling, E., 1844), IV. 97, 407, 613

— (Webb, C., 1844), IV. 97, 442, 622

— (1859), v. 658

Christmas Chimes (Williams, A., 1873), v. 624

Christmas Dinner (Taylor, T., 1860), v. 593

Christmas Eve (Cheltnam, C. S., 1870), v. 309

— (Deffell, C. and Browne, M., 1865), v. 341, 788, 842 [Probably = Oracle, below]

— (Fitzball, E., 1860), v. 368, 792

— (1840), IV. 442

— = (1) Oracle; (2) Yule Log

Christmas Gambol = (1) Country 'Squire; (2) Spendthrift; (3) Whim

Christmas Gossips (1812), IV. 442

Christmas Log (1846), IV. 442

Christmas Ordinary (R., W., 1682), I. 440

Christmas Pantomime (Vicars, W. A., 1871), v. 608

Christmas Party (1879), v. 658

Christmas Stocking (À Beckett, G. A. and Hall, K., 1879), v. 234

Christmas Story (Irving, L. S. B., 1893), v. 658, 799, 829

— (1852), v. 658

— = (1) Dot; (2) Holly Tree Inn

Christmas Tale (Garrick, D., 1773), III.
27, 118, 263, 385
— (1817), IV. 442
— = Zapolyta
Christopher Junior = Jedbury Junior
Christopher's Honeymoon (Watson,
T. M., 1889), v. 616
Christopher Tadpole (Brown, W.,
1877), v. 282
Christ's Passion (Sandys, G., 1687), I.
427
Chronicle of the Life and Death of Jane
Shore = Goldsmith's Wife
Chrononhotonthologos (Carey, H.,
1734), II. 241, 267–8, 302; IV. 1
Chrystabelle (Falconer, E., 1860), v.
360
Chrystal Cross and Glittering Fountains
= Knights of St Albans
Chrystaline (Layton, G. M., 1871), v.
451
Chuck (1736), II. 367
Chuck and Ruck a Roo (1866), v. 658
Chums (Warren, T. G., 1885), v. 615
— (1899), v. 658
— = Ned's Chum
Chuneelah (Campbell, A. V., 1826), IV.
278
Church and Stage (Reynolds, W., 1888),
v. 541
Churchwarden (Cassel, H. and Ogden,
C., 1886), v. 305
Chymical Counterfeits (1734), II. 367
— = Fate of Narcissus
Ciceley's Secret (Hawkins, Mrs P. L.,
1895), v. 410
Cicilia and Clorinda (Killigrew, T.
1664), I. 416
Cicisbea alla Moda (1759), III. 322
Cicisbeo (1837), IV. 622
Cid (Addison, J. and Howell, J. H.,
1878), v. 236
— (Neil, R., 1874), v. 501
— (Ozell, J., 1714), II. 347, 442
— (1691), I. 440
— (1802), IV. 442
Cigale (Burnand, F. C., 1890), v. 292,
782
— = Stroller
Cigarette (D'Arcy, G., 1876), v. 336
— (St Leger, E. W., 1892), v. 554,
815

Cinderella (Akhurst, W. M., 1874), v.
237
— (Allan-Fisher, C., 1895), v. 238
— (Allen, O., 1886), v. 239
— (Almar, H., 1831), IV. 252
— (Barwick, E., 1897), v. 252
— (Barwick, E., 1898), v. 252
— (Blanchard, E. L., 1844), IV. 268
— (Blanchard, E. L. and Greenwood,
T. L., 1864), v. 263, 779
— (Blanchard, E. L., 1874), v. 264
— (Blanchard, E. L., 1878), v. 265
— (Blanchard, E. L., 1883), v. 265
— (Burnand, F. C., 1885), v. 291
— (Byron, H. J., 1860), v. 296
— (Clair, H. B., 1891), v. 310
— (Daly, B. and East, J. M., 1897), v.
334
— (Douglass, J. T., 1884), v. 349
— (England, A. and Noble, C. R.,
1896), v. 358
— (French, H. P., 1889), v. 373
— (French, H. P., 1895), v. 373
— (Green, F. W. and Allen, O., 1883),
v. 391
— (Green, F. W. and Clay, T. L.,
1879), v. 391
— (Harris, Sir A. H. G., Raleigh, C.
and Sturgess, A., 1895), v. 406
— (Hazlewood, C. H., 1872), v. 797
— (Hewson, J. J., 1899), v. 660, 798,
829
— (Jones, F., 1898), v. 439
— (Jones, J. W., 1878), v. 440
— (Lacy, M. R., 1830), IV. 340
— (Leigh, H. S., 1883), v. 454
— (Lemon, H., 1870), v. 454
— (Lennard, H., 1888), v. 455, 803
— (Lennard, H., 1893), v. 456
— (Locke, F., 1892), v. 462
— (Logan, W. H., 1863), v. 804
— (McArdle, J. F., 1875), v. 804
— (McCabe, C. W., 1893), v. 467
— (McLelland, H. F., 1896), v. 468
— (Muskerry, W., 1886), v. 501
— (Rice, C., 1875), v. 542
— (Robertson, T. W., 1892), v. 547
— (Rogers, T. S., 1897), v. 549
— (Rogers, T. S., 1898), v. 549
— (Sturgess, A., Raleigh, C. and
Matthews, E. C., 1898), v. 586
— (Summers, W., 1898), v. 587

4

Citizen Outwitted = Miraculous Cure

Citizen Pierre (Coghlan, C. F.), v. 316

Citizen Robespierre (Perth, and Condie, 1899), v. 520

Citizen's Daughter (1775), III. 322

— (1847), IV. 622

— = Mark Fresland

Citizen's Wife = Delicate Ground

Citizen turn'd Gentleman (Ravenscroft, E., 1672), I. 76, 83, 188, 254, 347, 348, 425–6

Cits and Sights = Lord Mayor's Day

City Apprentice (1840), IV. 442

City Association (1780), III. 322

City Besieged = Patriots

City Bride (Harris, J., 1696), I. 39, 54, 412

City Customs (1703), II. 368

City Farce (Weddell, Mrs, 1737), II. 363

City Festival = Lord Mayor's Day

City Friends (Collins, C. J., 1855), v. 660, 785, 829

City Games (Rede, W. L., 1833), IV. 607

City Guard (1883), v. 660

City-Heiress (Behn, A., 1682), I. 79, 224, 391

City Intrigue = Why did I marry?

City Lady (Dilke, T., 1697), I. 54, 56, 218, 403

City Madam (Love, J., 1771), III. 283

— (1844), IV. 442

City Match = Schemers

City Merchant (Clinton, J. W., 1841), IV. 577

City Nymph = Tender Husband

City of Pleasure (Sims, G. R., 1895), v. 569

City of Small Trades = Golden Hearts

City of Stars = Valley of Diamonds

City of the Plague (Wilson, J., 1816), IV. 422

City of the Plague and the Great Fire of London (1825), IV. 442

City Outcast (Ellis, B., 1892), v. 357

City Politiques (Crowne, J., 1683), I. 10, 23, 24, 56, 58, 271, 350, 399

City Prison (1861), v. 829

City Ramble (Knipe, C., 1715), II. 341, 375

— (Settle, E., 1711), II. 31, 266, 354

City Rivals (Kenney, J., 1814) = Debtor and Creditor, IV. 443, 622

City Wives = Lesson for Gentlemen

City Wives Confederacy = Confederacy

Ciudad Rodrigo (1812), IV. 443

Civilian (Ryley, S. W., 1789), III. 304, 395

Civilization (Wilkins, J. H., 1852), v. 623, 846

Civil War (Merivale, H. C., 1887), v. 487

Civil War of Poetry (Bolton, G., 1846), IV. 98, 443, 622

Civil Wars between York and Lancaster = Civil Wars in the Reign of King Henry VI

Civil Wars In the Reign of King Henry VI (Cibber, T., 1723), II. 313

Clachan of Aberfoil = Roy's Wife

Claimant (Grattan, H. P., 1871), v. 389

Claimants (Vezin, H., 1891), v. 608

Claire (Bernhardt-Fisher, Mrs, 1887), v. 259

— = Cash for Coronets

Clairval (1877), v. 660

Clairvoyance (1845), IV. 443

Clandestine Marriage (Colman, G. and Garrick, D., 1766), III. 51, 167–9, 182, 246

Clans of Yore = Caledonia

Claperton Chisel (1850), v. 660

Clara (1809), IV. 443

— = Prisoner

Clara Charette (Collier, J. W., 1849), IV. 281

Clara Vere de Vere (Rae-Brown, C., 1888), v. 533

Clare Cottage (James, S., 1888), v. 434

Clarence Clevedon, his Struggles for Life or Death (Stirling, E., 1849), IV. 409

Clari (Payne, J. H. and Planché, J. R., 1823), IV. 377, 605

Claribel's Mystery (Towers, E., 1865), v. 660, 821, 829

Clarice (Browne, G. W. and Roberts, F., 1886), v. 283

Clarice de Clermont (Naden, A. T., 1892), v. 501

Claricilla (Killigrew, T., 1641), I. 416

Clarissa (Buchanan, R., 1890), v. 285

— (Porrett, R., 1788), III. 72, 299

Clarissa Harlowe (?Lacy, T. H. and
  Courtney, J. or ?Reynoldson, T. H.,
  1846), IV. 340–1, 393
— (Wills, W. G., 1889), V. 628
— (1831), IV. 443
— (1847), IV. 443
Clarisse (Robertson, T. W., 1855), V.
  660, 814, 829
— (Stirling, E., 1845), IV. 408
Clash of Steel (1894), V. 660
Classical Trip = Nicandra
Claude Duval (Bowyer, F. and Payne
  Nunn, 1894), V. 272
— (Burnand, F. C., 1869), V. 289, 781
— (Haines, J. T., 1841), IV. 323
— (Stephens, H. P., 1881), V. 580
— (Taylor, T. P., 1842), IV. 411
Claude Gower (Lancaster, E. R.), IV.
  593
Claudian (Herman, H. and Wills,
  W. G., 1883), V. 419
Claudia's Choice (Neil, Ross, 1883), V.
  502
Claudine (Dibdin, C. I. M., 1803), IV.
  291
Claudine of Switzerland = Outcast of
  Lausanne
Claudio (Thurgood, A. V., 1888), V. 600
Clavidgo (Leftley, F., 1798), III. 63,
  322, 390, 399
Clavigo (1847), IV. 443
— (1895), V. 660
Claychester Scandal = Intruders
Clean Sweep = Fluff
Cleanthes (Woodrooffe, S., 1826), IV.
  422
Clean Your Boots (Bruton, J., 1858), V.
  660, 781, 829
Clear ahead! (Clarke, C. A., 1885), V.
  311
Clear Case (À Beckett, G. A., 1835), IV.
  249
Clear Conscience (Walter, T. N., 1889),
  V. 612
Clearing the Toll = Lady Godiva and
  Peeping Tom of Coventry
Clear the Way (Harcourt, F. C., 1892),
  V. 403
Cleft Stick (Oxenford, J., 1865), V. 510
Clemence (Ebsworth, J.), IV. 309
Clementina (Kelly, H., 1771), III. 13, 15,
  18, 47, 79–80, 278, 389

Clementina (Moncrieffe, E., 1892), V.
  491
Clementine (1843), IV. 443
Clemenza (Ainslie, W., 1822), IV. 251
Clench and Wrench (1879), V. 660
Cleomenes (Dryden, J., 1692), I. 79,
  145, 407
Cleon (Maltby, A., 1874), V. 473
— (Thom, R. W., 1855), V. 595
Cleone (Dodsley, R., 1758), II. 319; III.
  9, 40, 43, 45, 49, 74, 257
Cleonice, Princess of Bithynia (Hoole,
  J., 1775), III. 59, 83, 197, 272
Cleopatra (Shirley, A., 1889), V. 564
Cléopatre, Reine d'Egypte (Aumer,
  1825), IV. 569
Cleora (1736), II. 368
Clergy (1876) = Unequally Sentenced,
  V. 660, 762, 829, 848
Clergyman's Daughter (Tanner, J. T.,
  1896), V. 591
Clergyman's Widow and her Orphans =
  Faith, Hope and Charity
Clerical Error (Jones, H. A., 1879), V.
  162, 439
Clerkenwell Election = Law versus
  Physic
Clerke's Well (1841), IV. 622
Clerk of Clerkenwell (Almar, G., 1834),
  IV. 253
Clerk of the Weather (Osborne, K. and
  Hodgson, A. H., 1892), V. 508
Clerkship and Cookery = Fish out of
  Water
Clever Alice (Thomas, B., 1893), V.
  596
Clever Capture (Melford, M., 1890), V.
  484
Cleverest Man in China = Shadows on
  the Water
Cleverest Man in Town = Amorel of
  Lyonesse
Cleverly Managed (Longmuir, A.,
  1887), V. 463
Clever People (Rose, E., 1889), V. 550
Clever Sir Jacob (Graves, A. P. and
  Toft, P., 1873), V. 389
Click Clack (Dibdin, C. I. M., 1804), IV.
  291
Clifford Castle (1809), IV. 443
Cliff, Steine, and Level = Humours of
  Brighton

Climbing Boy (Peake, R. B., 1832), IV.
370

Clinton (Phillips, F. L., 1858), V. 660,
810, 829

Clio (Campbell, B., 1878), V. 301

Clip (1899), V. 660

Cliquot (1892), V. 660

Clito (Grundy, S. and Barrett, W.,
1886), V. 396

Cloacina (Man, H., 1775), III. 286

Cloak and the Bonnet (1841), IV. 443

Cloches de Corneville (Farnie, H. B.
and Reece, R., 1878), V. 362, 791

Clock-Case (1777), III. 322

Clock has Struck=(1) Demon of the
Woods; (2) Wood Daemon

Clock House (Lee, N., 1840), IV. 594

Clock Maker (1892), V. 660

Clockmaker of Bishopgate (1860), V. 660

Clockmaker of Clerkenwell (1860), V.
660

Clockmaker of Mardyk=Old Father
Time

Clockmaker's Daughter (1874), V. 660

Clockmaker's Hat (Robertson, T. W.,
1855)=Betty Martin, V. 546

— =Sally Smart

Clock on the Stairs (Hazlewood, C. H.,
1862), V. 412

Clock Struck Four=Murdered Maid

Clockwork (Reece, R., 1877), V. 538

Clodhopper's Fortune (1872), V. 660

Clodpole's Mistake (1818), IV. 443

Clod, the Bellows Mender=Lady of
Lions

Clorinde's Revenge=Leontine

Cloris (Wycombe, M. and Shael, V.,
1885), V. 633, 824

Close of the Poll=Humours of an
Election

Close Shave (Speight, T. W., 1884), V.
575

— (Thalberg, T. B., 1895), V. 595

— =You mustn't laugh

Close Siege (Dance, G., 1839), IV. 289,
579

Closet Cordial=Married Man

Clotilda (1709), II. 229, 391

Cloud and Sunshine (Anderson, J. R.,
1858), V. 240

Cloud and the Silver Lining=Phyllis
Thorpe

Cloud King (Cross, J. C., 1806), IV. 286

Cloud of Life (Mead, T., 1859), V. 660,
806, 829

Cloud of Smoke (Squier, C., 1881), V.
577

Clouds (Bowkett, S., 1894), V. 271

— (Percival, A., 1872), V. 519

— (Theobald, L., 1715), II. 359, 444

— (White, J., 1759), III. 315

— (1885), V. 660

Clouds and Sunshine in a Life (Faucquez, A., 1862), V. 363

Clouds of Aristophanes (Cumberland,
R., 1797), III. 252

Clouds of Sorrow and Rays of Sunshine
=There are Secrets in all Families

Cloven Foot (Mouillot, F. and Steer, J.,
1890), V. 498

Clown and the Captain (Dibdin, T. J.,
1827)=Turn and Turn, IV. 305, 545
[Originally produced S.W. 26/7/1827]

Clown of China=Whang Fong

Clown's Chronology=April Fools

Clown's Fireside (1809), IV. 443

Clown's Stratagem (1730), II. 368

Clown's Trip to the Moon (1829), IV. 443

Clown turned Beau (1788), III. 322

Club (1891), V. 660 .

Club Baby (Sterner, L. and Knoblauch,
E., 1895), V. 583

Club-men (Kirkman, F., 1662), I. 417

Club Night=Rum Ones

Club of Fortune Hunters (1748), II. 368

Clump and Cudden (Dibdin, C., 1785),
III. 256

Cluricanne's Tower (Grover, J. H.,
1871), V. 395

Clutch of the Law=Notice to Quit

Clutterbucks (Pocock, I., 1832), IV. 385

Clytemnestra (Galt, J., 1812), IV. 585

Clytie (Hatton, J., 1875), V. 409

Coach Drivers (1766), III. 322

Coal and Coke (Harding, C. and Swanborough, W. H., 1868), V. 403

Coalition (Graves, R., 1793), III. 265,
386

— (Macnally, L., 1783), III. 285

— (1779), III. 322

Coal-ition (Hardman, T. H. and
North, H., 1881), V. 403

Coal Mine (Johnstone, J. B., 1867), V.
438, 800

College Chums (Kenney, C. H., 1895), v. 443

College Friends (1856), v. 660

+Collegian (Smock Alley, Dublin, 17/4/1776)

Collier Boy (1895), v. 660

Collier's Daughter (Bosworth, H., 1873), v. 267

Collier's Wife (Beverley, H. R., 1869), v. 261

Collision in the Mersey = Cry in the Darkness

Colomba (Hueffer, F., 1883), v. 429

Colomba, the Corsican Sister (1846), IV. 443

Colombe's Birthday (Browning, R., 1844), IV. 272; v. 20, 283

Colombina (1735), II. 368

Colombine Cameron = (1) Harlequin Incendiary; (2) Harlequin Invader

Colombine-Courtezan = Cupid and Psyche

Colombine in her Teens = Harlequin Captain Flash

Colombine Made Happy at Last = Escapes of Harlequin by Sea and Land

Colombine turn'd Elephant = Harlequin in the City

Colonel (Burnand, F. C., 1881), v. 291
— (1830), IV. 443
— (1894), v. 660

Colonel and the Soldier = Martial Law

Colonel Blood (1846), IV. 443

Colonel Bombomb (1893), v. 660

Colonel Gardiner (Barham, F. F., 1823), IV. 569

Colonel Jack (Coates, A., 1863), v. 784
— (Towers, E., 1860), v. 660, 821, 830

Colonel of Hussars = Libertine of Poland

Colonel's Belle (White, R. M., 1846), IV. 419

Colonel's Choice = Three and One

Colonel's Come (Dibdin, C. I. M., 1825), IV. 295

Colonel's Contrivance = Soldier's Stratagem

Colonel Sellers (Twain, Mark, 1874), v. 605

Colonel Split-Tail (1730), II. 368

Colonel's Tactics (1889), v. 660

Colonel's Wife (Reid, B. and Smith, L., 1888), v. 541

Colonel, the Captain and the Corporal = Broken Promises

Colonists (Ravani, E. C., 1895), v. 535
— = America

Colorado Beetle (Minto, W., 1877), v. 490

Coloured Commotion (1852), v. 660

Colour Sergeant (Thomas, B., 1885), v. 184, 595

Columbine (1717), II. 447 [This is evidently the same as Harlequin turn'd Judge, II. 374]

Columbus (Morton, T., 1792), III. 34, 50, 99, 101, 120, 288
— (Thompson, A., 1869), v. 597, 820

Comala (Burrell, Lady S. R., 1793), III. 72, 241
— (1792), III. 322

Comb-seller of Victoria Park = Mysteries of Shoreditch

Come and See (Langsdorff, 1814), IV. 341

Comedy and Tragedy (Gilbert, W. S., 1884), v. 380
— = Tragedy Queen

Comedy and Tragedy of War = Tit for Tat

Comedy Farce (1864), v. 660

Comedy in Embryo = Sir Harry Gaylove

Comedy of 1854 = John Bull

Comedy of Errors (Hull, T., 1779), III. 274
— (Kemble, J. P., 1811), IV. 335
— (Reynolds, F., 1819), IV. 392
— (1762), III. 322
— = Twins

Comedy of Sighs (Todhunter, J., 1894), v. 600

Comedy of Terrors (1855), v. 830
— = Nap

Comedy of Trifles (Beach, W., 1899), v. 253

Come Here (Daly, A., 1876), v. 333

Come if you can (Dibdin, T. J., 1824), IV. 304

Come of Age (1837), IV. 443

+Comet (Dibdin, C. I. M., 1797)
— (Moser, J., 1807), IV. 364
— (1789), III. 322
— (1832), IV. 443
— (1835), IV. 443

Comète (Pinero, Sir A. W., 1878), v. 524

Come to Town (Rede, W. L., 1836), IV. 390

Comfortable Conclusion = Merry Midnight Mistake

Comfortable Lodgings (Peake, R. B., 1827), IV. 370

— (1831), IV. 443

Comfortable Service (Bayly, T. H., 1835), IV. 263, 571

Comic = Modern Faust

Comical Complications = Jacko

Comical Countess (Brough, W., 1854), v. 279

Comical Disappointment (1736), II. 368

Comical Distresses of Pierrot (1729), II. 368

Comical Duel (O'Keeffe, J.), III. 292

Comical Gallant (Dennis, J., 1702), II. 8, 140, 318, 435

Comical Hash (Cavendish, M., 1662), I. 396

Comical Humours of Sir John Falstaff (1733), II. 384

Comical Lovers (Cibber, C., 1707), II. 142, 310, 434; III. 115, 389

Comical Resentment (1759), III. 322, 399

Comical Revenge (Etherege, Sir G., 1664), I. 38, 66, 67, 68, 101, 186, 235, 321, 346, 347, 410

— (1732), II. 368

Comical Rival = School-Boy

Comical Transformation = Devil of a Wife

Comic Extravaganza (1760), III. 322

Comic Muse Triumphant = Melpomene's Overthrow

Comic Robbers (1830), IV. 443

Comic Tragedians (1879), v. 660

Coming Clown (Melford, M., 1886), v. 484

Coming Events (Reece, R., 1876), v. 538

Coming Home (Walker, G. R., 1873) = Sithors to Grind, v. 611, 822

Coming Member (Silvester, F., 1893), v. 566

Coming of Age (Carpenter, J. E., 1869), v. 303

— (1855), v. 660

Coming of Peace (Achurch, J. and Wheeler, C. E., 1900), v. 777

Coming Out = Tom Jones

Coming Up, Sir! (1827), IV. 443

Coming Woman (1887), v. 660

Comin' thro' the Rye (Rosier, J. A. and Mainprice, W. T., 1886), v. 550

Commandant (Trevor, H. and Trevor, L., 1894), v. 603

Commencement of a Bad Farce but which however it is hoped will prove to be Wright-at-last (1853), v. 660

Commerce (Ebsworth, J.), IV. 309

Commercial Room (1887), v. 661

Commissary (Foote, S., 1765), III. 117, 174, 260

Commission (Grossmith, W., 1891), v. 395

Committed for Trial (Gilbert, W. S., 1874), v. 380

— (Towers, E., 1878), v. 601

Committee (Howard, Sir R., 1662), I. 27, 69, 214, 288, 308, 338, 343, 344, 345, 350, 351, 414; III. 114

— (1822), IV. 443, 622

Commodity Excis'd (1733), II. 368

Commodore (Farnie, H. B. and Reece, R., 1886), v. 363, 813

— = Creole

Commodore and the Colonel = Veterans

Commodore Bouilli (Ford, T. M., 1888), v. 370

Common Sense (Towers, E., 1878), v. 601

Common-Wealth of Women (D'Urfey, T., 1685), I. 37, 39, 408–9

Compact (Planché, J. R., 1832), IV. 379

— (1859), v. 661

Compact of Life and Death = Three Brothers of Normandy

Compact with the Ghost = Haunted Man

Companions of Midnight = Black Band

Companions of the Chair = Nellie

Company in One = Blackeyed Susan at Dunstable

Competition (Miller, E. T. W., 1889), v. 488

Competitors (Cubitt, S., 1893), v. 331

Complete Bulwer-tement of the Classical Drama = Very Last Days of Pompeii

Complete Change (McDonald, B. P., 1896), v. 468

Conquerors (Potter, P. M., 1898), V. 530

Conqueror's Steel (1831), IV. 622

Conquest of Amoy by British Arms = Chinese War

Conquest of Canada (Cockings, G., 1766), III. 245

Conquest of China by the Tartars (Settle, E., 1675), I. 39, 118, 128, 130, 348, 428

— (Wilmot, J., ?1678), I. 437

Conquest of Corsica, by the French (1771), III. 323

Conquest of Cupid (Rede, W. L., 1842), IV. 390

Conquest of France = (1) Henry V; (2) King Henry V

Conquest of France, by the English = King Henry V

Conquest of Granada (Almar, G., 1843), IV. 568

— (1811), IV. 444

— = Gonsalvo de Cordova

Conquest of Granada by the Spaniards (Dryden, J., 1670–1), I. 42, 96, 99, 102, 110, 114–15, 144, 234, 346, 404

Conquest of Ireland = Royal Flight

Conquest of Magdala (Stacqueler, M., 1868), V. 578

Conquest of Mexico (1832), IV. 444

— = (1) Cortez; (2) Hernando Cortez; (3) Indian Emperour

Conquest of Mysore = Arajoon

Conquest of Peru = Indian Empress

Conquest of Queen Judith = Prince's Ball

Conquest of St Eustacia (1781), III. 323

Conquest of Scinde (1845), IV. 444

Conquest of Spain (Pix, Mrs M., 1705), II. 70, 97, 181, 350

Conquest of Taranto (Dimond, W., 1817), IV. 306

Conquest of the Eagle (Sloman, C., 1853), V. 571

Conquest of the Golden Pagodas (1827), IV. 444

Conquest of the Sikhs = Mooltan and Googerat

Conquests of Ivanhoe = Lists of Ashby

Conrad and Christine (1828), IV. 444

Conrad and Lizette (1880), V. 661

Conrad and Medora (Brough, W., 1856), V. 279

Conrad Converted (Allan, A. W., 1873), V. 238

Conrad the Corsair (1858), V. 661, 830

Conrad, the Ghost Lover (Travers, W., 1865), V. 822

Conrad the Invincible (1865), V. 661

Conrad, the Robber Chief (1828), IV. 444

Conrad the Usurper (Barnett, C. Z., 1848), IV. 444, 622

— (Bunn, A., 1818), IV. 179, 444, 622

Conscience (Ashton, J., 1815), IV. 569

— (Haynes, J., 1821) = Lorenzo, IV. 324, 588

— (Litton, E., 1888), V. 461

— (Thompson, B., 1800), IV. 412

— (Vandenhoff, H., 1877), V. 606

— (1863), V. 661

— (1897), V. 661

Conscience Money (Byron, H. J., 1878), V. 299

Conscientious Constable (McDonald, B. P., 1897), V. 468

Conscious Lovers (Steele, Sir R., 1722), II. 1, 2, 17, 29, 34, 135, 136, 137, 138, 143, 183, 192–3, 196, 357; III. 178

Conscript (Clive, W., 1889), V. 315

— (Oxberry, W. H., 1834), IV. 366, 602

— (Raymond, R. J. and Barrymore, W., 1830), IV. 444, 570, 622

— (1839), IV. 444

— = Foster Brothers

Conscript Bride = Jeannette et Jeannot

Conscript Mother (1861), V. 661

Conscript's Bride (1830), IV. 444

Conscript's Jealousy = Soldier's Dream

Conscripts of Austerlitz = Dashing White Sergeant

Conscript's Sister (1832), IV. 444

Consequence of Industry and Idleness (1748), II. 368

Consequences (Eyre, E. J., 1794), III. 259

— (Hook, T. E., 1809) = Safe and Sound, IV. 444, 622

Consequential Landlord and his Customers = Public House

Conspiracy (Gordon, G. L., 1882), V. 385

— (Jephson, R., 1796), III. 95, 277

— (Mulholland, J. B., 1888), V. 499

— (Whitaker, W., 1680), I. 39, 156, 437

— (1826), IV. 444

Conspiracy = (1) Cromwell; (2) Richelieu

Conspiracy against Peter the Great = Natalia and Menzikof

Conspiracy Discovered (1746), II. 368

Conspiracy of Copenhagen = Bertrand and Burkenstaff

Conspiracy of Genoa = Fiesco

Conspiracy of Gowrie (Roscoe, W., 1800), III. 323; IV. 609

Conspiracy of Kamtschatka = Count Benyowsky

Conspiracy of Querini (1837), IV. 622

Conspirator in spite of himself (Coape, H. C., 1852), V. 315

Conspirators (1749), II. 368

— = Bravo and the Venetian Conspirators

Constable Jack (Rodney, S., 1889), V. 548

Constance (Robertson, T. W., 1865), V. 546

Constance Frere (Gough, H. and Edwards, M., 1887), V. 386

Constancy (Barnard, C., 1892), V. 249

— (Hallward, C., 1898), V. 401

Constancy unto Death = Warning Dream

Constant Couple (Carter, J., 1788), III. 242

— (Farquhar, G., 1699), I. 12, 246, 338, 411; II. 147

Constant Couple Rewarded = Emperor of China Grand Volgi

Constant Follower (1866), V. 661

Constantia (Hughes, Mrs A., 1790), III. 274

— (Neale, F., 1852), V. 501

Constantine (Francis, P., 1754), III. 208, 261

— (1898), V. 661

Constantine and Valeria (Dibdin, T. J., 1817), IV. 159, 300

Constantine Paleologus (Baillie, J., 1804), IV. 159, 258

Constantine the Great (Lee, N., 1683), I. 147-8, 419

— = Constantine

Constant Lady = Generous Free-Mason

Constant Lover Rewarded = Mistake

Constant Lovers (Duncan, G., 1798), III. 258

Constant Lovers (1714), II. 368

— (1719), II. 368

— (1734), II. 451

Constant Maid (1787), III. 323

— = Love will finde out the Way

Constant Nymph (1677), I. 101, 138, 440

Constant Quaker (1748), II. 451

Constellations and Cauliflowers (1823), IV. 444

Consul in England = Britons to Arms

Consultation (1705), II. 22, 368

— = Six Physicians

Contempt of Court (Boucicault, D., 1879), V. 269

— (Matthison, A., 1877), V. 481

Contending Brothers (Brooke, H., 1778), III. 240

Contending Colombines = Beggar's Pantomime

Contending Deities (1733), II. 368

Contented Cuckold (Bourne, R., 1692), I. 392

— (1763), III. 323

— = Inconsolables

Contention for the Laurel = Battle of the Poets

Contention of York and Lancaster = Richard, Duke of York

Contested Election (Taylor, T., 1859), V. 593

Contest of Beauty and Virtue (Arne, T. A., 1772), III. 69, 234

Contest of the Aonides = Apollo's Choice

Contraband Captain (Corri, M., 1835), IV. 578

Contrabandist (1847), IV. 444

Contrabandista (Burnand, F. C., 1867), V. 289

Contract (Cobb, J., 1779), III. 243, 379

— (Francklin, T., 1775), III. 118, 261, 385

— (Hiller, H. C., 1887), V. 421

— (Houlton, R., 1782), III. 273 [The date of revival is 19/5/1784]

— (1736), II. 368

— (1899), V. 661

Contract of St Cloud (Blake, T. G., 1846), IV. 268

Contractor (Dabbs, G. H. R., 1887), V. 332

Contradictions (Leigh, A.), v. 453

Contrarieties (1817), IV. 444

Contrariety (Tomlinson, ?1792), III. 312

Contrary Winds (Wood, F., 1882), v. 630

Contrast (Hoadly, J., 1731), II. 337
— (Smith, E., ?1790), III. 308
— (Waldron, F. G., 1775), III. 313, 397
— (Wilton, 1789), III. 316
— (1752), III. 323

Contre Temps (1727), II. 14, 233, 266, 368

Contrivances (Carey, H., 1715), II. 241, 246, 301, 432
— (Lancaster, E. R.), IV. 593

Conundrums (1827), IV. 444

Convenient Distance! = Omnibus!

Convenient Son-in-law (1877), v. 661

Convent (Rannie, J., 1806), III. 300
— (1832), IV. 444

Convent Belle (Bayly, T. H., 1833), IV. 444, 622

Convent Belles = Carmelites

Convent Maid = Kitty

Convent of a Pleasure (Cavendish, M., 1668), I. 396

Convent of St Bartholomew = Agatha

Conversation of a Father with his Children (1792), III. 325

Conversion of England (Creswell, H., 1885), v. 330

Convert (Garnett, C., 1898), v. 376

Converted Twins = Saint Cecily

Converts = (1) Folly of Priest-Craft; (2) Pandora

Convict (Neville, H., 1868), v. 502
— (Sheil, R. L., 1822) = Huguenot, IV. 444, 622
— (Stephenson, C. H., 1868), v. 582
— (1838), IV. 444, 622

Convict Brothers (Mead, T., 1853), v. 483

Convicted = Iron True

Convict of Munich = Genevra, the Scourged One

Convict of Toulon = Prisoner of Toulon

Convict's Career = Only for Life

Convict's Child = Life as it is!

Convict's Daughter (1881), v. 661

Convict's Escape (Marchant, F., 1864), v. 805

Convict's Flight = Blood demands its Victim

Convicts 48 and 49 (1895), v. 661

Convict Ship (1826), IV. 444

Convict's Return (1859), v. 661

Convict Steward = Lisle Wilton

Convict's Vengeance = (1) Chain Gang; (2) Harold Hawk

Convict's Vow = Lawless Witness

Convict's Wife = (1) Marah; (2) On the Track

Convict 33 (1894), v. 661

Cook (1824), IV. 444

Cook and the Secretary (1833), IV. 444

Cooke's Folly (Featherstone, J., 1840), IV. 312

Cookettish Cook (Scarlett, W., 1895), v. 557

Cook in a Stew = Out of his Element

Cooking and Copying = Cupboard and the Cabinet

Cook of Kennington (1846), IV. 444

Cool as a Cucumber (Jerrold, M. W. B., 1851), v. 436

Cooleen Drawn (Dutnall, M. and Johnstone, J. B., 1861), v. 352

Cooper (Arne, T. A., 1772), III. 121, 199, 377, 234

Cooper and Brass (1850), v. 661

Co-operative Movement (Lemon, H., 1868), v. 454

Cooper Deceiv'd (1748), II. 369

Copper and Brass (1850) v. 661

Coquet (Molloy, C., 1718), II. 146, 157, 173, 345, 419, 441; III. 116
— (Storace, S., 1771), III. 310, 396

Coquet at her Wit's End = Impertinent Lovers

Coquet's Surrender (1732), II. 369

Coquette (Dam, H. J. W. and Bingham, G. C., 1899), v. 335, 787
— (Hitchcock, R., 1776), III. 269
— (Mead, T., 1867), v. 483
— (Pattinson, R. E., 1892), v. 515
— (Poel, W., 1892), v. 529
— (Smart, H., 1885), v. 571
— (1761), III. 323
— (1792), III. 323

Coquette Cured = Annie of Edenside

Coquette et les Jaloux (1734), II. 369

Coquettes (Houston, Lady), III. 273

Coquilla (1848), IV. 444

Corsican "Bothers" (Byron, H. J., 1869), v. 297

Corsican Brother-babes-in-the-wood (Sims, G. R., 1881), v. 568

Corsican Brothers (Almar, G., 1852), v. 240

— (Boucicault, D., 1852), v. 84, 86, 267

— (Bradberry, C. S., 1888), v. 272

— (O'Neill, J. R.), v. 808

— (1852), v. 661

— = Vendetta

Corsican Brothers and Co., Limited (Burnand, F. C. and Stephens, H. P., 1880), v. 291

Corsican Conscript = Theodore the Brigand

Corsican Maid (1849), IV. 445

— = Laelia, the Queen of the Hills

Corsican Pirate (Cross, J. C., 1803), IV. 286

Corsicans (Leftly, C.), IV. 343

— (Sala, 1853), v. 555

— (1796), III. 65, 122, 323, 399

Corsican's Revenge = Vendetta

Corsican Vendetta (1897), v. 661

Cortez (Burges, Sir J. B., 1817), IV. 277

— (Helme, E., 1800), IV. 324

— (Planché, J. R., 1823) = Hernando Cortez, IV. 377, 478, 605

— (Wallace, Lady E.), III. 314

Corydon and Cochrania (Pennecuik, A., 1732), II. 348

Cosaque (Grundy, S., 1884), v. 396, 795

Così fan tutte (Browne, M. E., 1890), v. 781

Cosimo (1838), IV. 445, 623

Cosmo de' Medici (Horne, R. H., 1837), IV. 205, 328

Cosmo, Duke of Tuscany (Bird, J., 1822), IV. 199–200, 267

Cossack and No Cossack = Irish Girl

Cossacks (1854), v. 661

Coster Baron (Pleon, H., 1897), v. 528

Coster Girl = Lucky Walker

Coster's Christmas Eve (1897), v. 661

Coster's Holiday = 'Endon Way

Coster's Son (1895), v. 661

Coster Twin Brothers (Hall, F., 1880), v. 399

Cottage (Smith, J., 1796), III. 308

Cottage and the Court (1839), IV. 445

Cottage Festival (Macnally, L., 1796), III. 285

Cottage Foundling (Kean, 1811), IV. 591

Cottage in the Holly (1872), v. 661

Cottage Maid (Sicklemore, R., 1798), III. 307

— (1791), III. 323

Cottage of Love (Oxenford, J., 1845), IV. 367

Cottage of Roses = Gipsy Girl

Cottage of the Cliffs (Rannie, J., 1806), III. 300

Cottage of the Lake (1820), IV. 445

Cottage on the Cliff = Marriage Bells

Cottagers (Brunton, A., i.e. Ross, A., 1788), III. 240, 303

— (Carey, G. S., 1766), III. 197, 242

— (Goodenough, R. J., 1768), III. 265

Cotton Famine (1869), v. 661

Cotton King (Vane, S., 1894), v. 606

Could the Murder? (Dibdin, T. J., 1825) = Black Caesar, IV. 445, 623

Council of Constance = Jewess

Council of Ten (Dibdin, C. I. M., 1811), IV. 292

— (Milner, H. M., 1829), IV. 445, 623

— = Venetian

Council of Three = Red Mask

Counsel for the Defense (1895), v. 661

Counsel's Opinion (Bingham, F., 1898), v. 261

Count Alarcos (Disraeli, B., 1839), IV. 307

Count and his Companions = Lone Chateau

+Count and the Secretary (*French*)

Count Arezzi (Landor, R. E., 1824), IV. 199, 341

Count Basil (Bailie, J., 1798), III. 224–6, 235; IV. 157

Count Benyowsky (Render, W., 1798), III. 65, 301, 394

— (Thompson, B., 1800), IV. 412

Count Bertram (1823), IV. 445

Count Clermont (Bell, A., 1841), IV. 264

Count d'Alren = Honour

Count de Denia (Hoskins, W. H., IV. 328

Count de Foix (Powell, T., 1842), IV. 387

Count de Villeroi (Haggitt, J., 1794), III. 32, 54, 323, 386

Count Egmont (1848), IV. 445

Counter Attraction (Tilbury, W. H., 1851), v. 600

Counter Charm (Danvers, G. J. B., 1826), IV. 579

Counterfeit (Fisher, D., 1865), v. 661, 792, 830

— (Francklin, A., 1804), III. 261; IV. 318

— = Conscript

Counterfeit Bridegroom (?Behn, A. or Betterton, T., 1677), I. 259, 390, 392, 440

Counterfeit Captain (1781), III. 323

Counterfeit Heiress (1762), III. 114, 323

Counterfeits (Leanerd, J., 1678), I. 264, 269, 349, 419

— (1764), III. 323

+— (Crow Street, Dublin, 4/5/1773)

— (1828) = Touch and Take, IV. 445, 544

Counterplot (Goodall, T., ?1787), III. 265

Counterplots and Countermines = Try Again

Countess (Monckton, Lady, 1882), v. 490

— (Schiff, E., 1870), v. 557

Countess and the Dancer (Reade, C., 1883), v. 536

Countess Cathleen (Yeats, W. B., 1899), v. 635

Countess d'Argentine (Stalman, A., 1862), v. 662, 830

Countess for an Hour = Lola Montes

Countess Gucki (Daly, A., 1896), v. 334

Countess in Difficulties = Leonie the Sutler Girl

Countess Joan = Jewel Hunters

Countess of Castille (1886), v. 662

Countess of Essex (Shepherd, H., 1834), IV. 610

— = Elizabeth and Essex

Countess of Fergon (1886), v. 662

Countess of Lilliput (1828), IV. 445

Countess of Salisbury (Hartson, H., 1765), III. 72, 85, 267

Count Fremolio's Wedding = Geraldine

Count Julian (Landor, W. S., 1812), IV. 198, 341

Count Koenigsmark (Thompson, B., 1800), IV. 412

Count of Anjou (1816), IV. 445

Count of Burgundy (Plumptre, A., 1798), III. 65, 298, 393

Count of Burgundy (Pope, A., 1799), III. 65, 298

Count of Marolles (1869), v. 662

Count of Monte Christo (1861), v. 662

Count of Narbonne (Jephson, R., 1781), III. 14, 72, 95, 277, 389

Count of Quodlibet = Rumfustian Innamorato

Count Tremolio (Wyatt, E., 1887), v. 633

Countrey Revell (Aubrey, J., ?1671), I. 388

Countrey Wit (Crowne, J., 1676), I. 201, 270, 348, 399

Country Actors (Barrymore, W., 1821), IV. 262

— (1827), IV. 445

Country Actress = Seven in One

Country Attorney (Cumberland, R., 1787), III. 127, 252, 381

Country Ball = Girl I left behind me

Country Beau = Devil upon Two Sticks

Country Bumpkins = Betty

Country Burial = Silvia

Country Captaine (Cavendish, W., 1649), I. 27, 344, 396

Country Coquet (1755), III. 323

Country Courtship (1773), III. 323

Country Cousins (Smith, J., 1820), IV. 353, 597

Country Cricket Match (Nichols, G. B., 1898), v. 504

Country Dance (Elton, E., 1896), v. 358

Country Election (Trusler, J., 1768), III. 313

Country Fair (1775), III. 323

Country Farmer (1738), II. 369

Country Farmer Deceived (1751), III. 323

Country Gentleman (Howard, Sir R. and Villiers, G., 1669), I. 415

— (Woty, W., 1770), III. 317

Country Girl (Garrick, D., 1766), III. 45, 114, 163, 169, 263

— (1812), IV. 445

Country House (Vanbrugh, Sir J., 1698), I. 338, 436; II. xi, 135, 137, 145, 152, 362, 445

— (1897), v. 662

Country Housewife = Wedding

Country Inn (Baillie, J., 1804), IV. 258

Country Innocence (Leanerd, J., 1677), I. 264, 269, 410

Country Knight (1675), I. 440
— = Countrey Wit

Country Lass = Mountebank

Country Lasses (Johnson, C., 1715), II. 16, 136, 139–40, 196–7, 211, 339; III. 115–16, 188, 389

Country Mad-Cap in London (1770), III. 323

Country Miss with her Furbeloe = Old Mode & the New

Country Painters (1788), III. 323

Country Poet = Young Hypocrite

Country Quarters (Pocock, I., 1831), IV. 385

Country Revel = Countrey Revell

Country Revels (1732), II. 369
— = (1) Harlequin Restored; (2) Maid of the Mill

Country Squire (Dance, C., 1837), IV. 288, 445 [The play acted at the Olym. is identical with that given at C.G.]
— (Gwinnet, R., 1732), II. 178, 334
— (1859), v. 662
— = Love in a Wood

Country Squire Outwitted = Harlequin turn'd Philosopher

Country-Wake (Doggett, T., 1696), I. 261, 403; II, 434
— (Underwood, T., 1782), III. 313
— = (1) Flora; (2) Hob

Country Wedding (1740), II. 369
— (1749), II. 369
— (1750), III. 323
— = (1) Acis and Galatea; (2) Roger and Joan; (3) Wedding

Country-Wedding and Skimmington = Wedding

Country Wife (Lee, J., 1765), III. 114, 280
— (Wycherley, W., 1675), I. 2, 13, 187, 188, 201, 238, 345, 346, 439; II. 142; III. 45, 114, 163, 170, 205

Country Wit = Countrey Wit

Count's Treasure = Clarice de Clermont

County (Burney, E. and Benham, A., 1892), v. 293

County Concert = Sharps, Flats and Naturals

County Councillor (Graham, H., 1891), v. 386

County Fair (Bernard, C., 1897), v. 259

Coup de combat (1889), v. 662

Coup de Main (McLaren, A., 1783, 1816), III. 284; IV. 351

Coupe Gorge (1836), IV. 445

Couple of Thieves (1865), v. 662

Courage (Gascoigne, H., 1886), v. 376

Courage and Constancy (1766), III. 399

Courage and Liberty = Britannia Rediviva

Courage Rewarded (1798), III. 19, 323

Courier (1851), v. 662

Courier of Lyons (Reade, C., 1854), v. 536
— (Webster, B. N., 1851), v. 618
+ — (acted at Stand. 10/3/1851; printed by French)
— (1854), v. 662
— (1891), v 662

Courier of Strasbourg (1861), v. 662

Courier of the Czar (Marston, H., 1877), v. 478
— (Osborne, C., 1877), v. 508

Course of Comic Lectures = Orators

+ Course of True Love (Emson, F. E., 8°, ?1877)

Court and Camp = Fan-Fan the Tulip

Court and City (Peake, R. B., 1841), IV. 371

Court and Cottage (Taylor, T., 1861), v. 593

Court and Country (1743), II. 369

C[ourt] and Country (1735), II. 262, 369

Court and No Country (1753), III. 323

Court Ball in 1740 (1845), IV. 445

Court Beauties (Planché, J. R., 1835), IV. 380

Court Cards (Simpson, J. P., 1861), v. 567

Court Delinquent (Trueba, J. T. de, 1834), IV. 615

Courtesans (Townley, C., 1760), III. 312

Court Favour (Planché, J. R., 1836), IV. 380

Court Favourites (1847), IV. 445

Court Fool (Burton, W. E., 1833), IV. 80, 277, 575

Court Gallantry = Comical Lovers

Court Gallants (Selby, C., 1863), v. 560

Court Guide (+ Selby, C., 1848), IV. 446; v. 815

Covenanters (Dibdin, T. J., 1835), IV.
305
— (1825), IV. 623
— = (1) Battle of Bothwell Brig; (2)
Drumclog
Covent Garden Ball (1894), V. 662
Covent Garden Theatre (Macklin, C.,
1752), III. 284, 391
Covent-Garden Tragedy (Fielding, H.,
1732), II. 265, 325, 436
Coventry Act (Plumptre, J., 1792), III.
298
Covers for Three (1854), V. 662
Coward Conscience (Byrne, C. A. and
Wallack, A., 1888), V. 295
Cowardly Foe (Miller, W. F., 1892), V.
489
Cowardy, Cowardy Custard (1836), IV.
446
Cowardy Cowardy Custard ate his
Father's Mustard (Thorne, R. L.,
1851), V. 599
Cowboy and the Lady (Fitch, C., 1899),
V. 367
Cow Doctor (1810), IV. 446
Cox and Box (Burnand, F. C. and
Morton, J. M., 1867), V. 289
Coxcombs (Gentleman, F., 1771), III.
112, 264
Coy Shepherdess (Aston, A., 1709), II.
4, 224–5, 295
Cozened Cousins (1850), V. 662
Cozeners (Foote, S., 1774), III. 175, 260
Cozening (Beazley, S., Jr., 1819), IV. 263
Cozy Couple (Lewes, G. H., 1854), V.
106, 458
Cracked Heads (Hay, F. and Clements,
A., 1876), V. 411
Cracked Piece of China = Ching-Chow-
Hi
Cracker Bon-Bon for Christmas Parties
(Brough, R. B., 1852), V. 278
Crack Shot = Red House
Cradle (Mattos, A. T. de, 1893), V. 481
Cradle of Crime = True till Death
Cradle of Steam = Marion Delorme
Craft (Sketchley, A., 1882), V. 571
Craftsman (Mottley, J., 1728), II. 346
Cramond Brig (Murray, W. H., 1826),
IV. 365
— (1831), IV. 446
Crank the Clockmaker (1846), IV. 446

Crazed (Phillips, A. R., 1887), V. 522,
810
Crazy Jane (Somerset, C. A., 1827), IV.
304
— (1805), IV. 446
Crazy Old Slippers (1828), IV. 446
Crazy Old Slippers of Bagdad = Bakarak,
the Miser
Cream White Woman (Chapman, S. H.,
1825), IV. 576
Creatures of Impulse (Gilbert, W. S.,
1871), V. 136–7, 379
Credit (À Beckett, G. A., 1844), IV. 250
Credulity (McLaren, A., 1823), IV. 352
Credulous Cuckold = Debauchee
Credulous Don = Impostors
Credulous Husband (1747), II. 369
— (1766), III. 323
Credulous Knight (Millett, 1800), IV.
599
Credulous Man = Quacks
Creeping Shadows (Stanhope, B.,
1887), V. 579
Cremation (Height, R., 1879), V. 416
Cremorne (Palmer, T. A., 1876), V.
512
Creole (Brooks, C. W. S., 1847), IV. 105,
271, 574
— (Farnie, H. B. and Reece, R., 1877),
V. 362, 813
Creole of St Louis (1862), V. 662
Creole's Daughter = Heart that can feel
for another
Creon, the Patriot (Smith, J., 1828), IV.
446, 623
Crëusa, Queen of Athens (Whitehead,
W., 1754), III. 71, 315, 398
Crew of the Bright Blue Wave = Union
Jack
Crichton (?Ducrow, A. or ?Wilks, T. E.,
1837), IV. 308, 446, 623 [There is
some doubt about the authorship of
this piece: the correct date is 3/7/
1837]
— (Edgar, R. H., 1871), V. 354
— (1839), IV. 446
Crichton of Clunie (Wilks, T. E.), IV.
421 [where the title is given wrongly
as Chrichton]
Cricket Match (+Anderson, J. R.,
1850), V. 662
— (Leslie, A., 1870), V. 456

Cricket on our own Hearth (Blanchard,
E. L., 1846), IV. 96, 98, 268
Cricket on the Hearth (Archer, T.,
1846), IV. 96, 98, 255
— (Barnett, C. Z., 1846), IV. 96, 98, 260
— (Halford, J., 1855), V. 662, 795, 830
— (Lucas, W. J., 1846), IV. 96, 98, 446,
623
— (Rayner, B. F., 1846), IV. 96, 98, 389
— (Smith, A. R., 1845), IV. 96, 98, 402,
611
— (Stirling, E., 1845), IV. 96, 98, 408
— (Townsend, W. T., 1846), IV. 96, 98,
414
— (Webster, B. N., 1846), IV. 96, 98,
418
— (1846), IV. 96, 98, 623
— (1865), V. 662
— (1867), V. 662
Cries of London (Suter, W. E., 1865),
V. 662, 818, 830
Cries of London in a new Style =
St Giles's Scrutiny
Crime (Kean, L. G., 1877), V. 442
Crime and Ambition = Paul Clifford,
the Highwayman of 1770
Crime and Christening (Henry, R.,
1891), V. 418
Crime and its Atonement (Colona, E.,
1875), V. 318
Crime and Justice (Delannoy, B. and
Harvey, N., 1892), V. 341
Crime and Remorse (1855), V. 662
Crime and the Criminal = Human
Spider
Crime and the Vision = Crime and
Remorse
Crime and Virtue (Stanhope, B., 1879),
V. 578
Crime beneath the Waves = Diver's
Luck
Crime Discovered = Haunted Chamber
Crime from Ambition (Geisweiler, M.,
1799), III. 63, 68, 264, 385
Crime in the Clouds = War Balloon
Crimeless Criminal (Becher, M., 1874),
V. 254
Crime's Atonement = Crime and its
Atonement
Crimes in High Life = Returned Out-
cast
Crime Slumbers = Emma Wingrove

Crimes of Paris (Meritt, P. and Con-
quest, G., 1883), V. 486
Crimes of Twenty Years (Travers, W.,
1862), V. 822
Crime-stained Bandit and the Bleeding
Buzzum = Raiment and Agonies of
that most Amiable Pair, Raimond and
Agnes
Criminal (1839), IV. 446
— (1884), V. 662
Criminal Couple (Herbert, F. H., 1871),
V. 418
Criminals (Clinch, J. H., 1885), V. 315
Crimson Cloud (1897), V. 662
Crimson Crimes (1832), IV. 446
Crimson Cross (Scott, C. W. and
Manuel, E., 1879), V. 558
Crimson Mask = In the King's Name
Crimson Rock (Cross, J., 1879), V.
330
Crimson Scarf (Farnie, H. B., 1873), V.
361
Crinoline (Brough, R. B., 1856), V. 278
Cripple of the Clink (1850), V. 662
Crisis (Albery, J., 1878), V. 156, 238
— (Holcroft, T., 1778), III. 270
— (1775), III. 399
Crispin and Crispianus (1702), II. 451
Crispus (Smith, H. G., 1891), V. 572
Critic (?Cumberland, R., 1779), III. 381
— (Sheridan, R. B., 1779), III. 12, 196,
214–17, 306, 373, 395–6; IV. 147
— (1780), III. 323
Critical Day (1880), V. 662
Critical Hour = Fire and Water
Critical Minute = Maiden Whim
Critical Position (1852), V. 662
Critic anticipated (1779), III. 323
Critick of Taste = Marforio
Critic upon Critic (Macnally, L., 1788),
III. 285
Croaking (1810), IV. 446
Crockery's Misfortunes (Ebsworth, J.,
1821), IV. 308 [The date of acting was
11/7/1821]
Crock of Gold (Fitzball, E., 1848), IV.
317
Crocodile (Lowe, W., 1882), V. 464
Crocodile's Tears (1889), V. 662
Croesus, King of Lydia (Richards,
A. B., 1845), IV. 394
Crohoove-na-Bilhoge (1833), IV. 446

Crom-a-boo' (Dibdin, C. I. M., 1825), IV. 296

Cromwell (Duckworth, W., 1870), v. 351

— (Leigh, J. M., 1838), IV. 343

— (Phillips, F. L., 1859), v. 522

— (Richards, A. B., 1847), IV. 394

Cromwell in Scotland = Miller of Fife

Cromwell's Conspiracy (1660), I. 440

Cromwell's Own = Greatest Puritan

Croohove of the Bill-Hook (1828), IV. 446

Crooked Brothers of Damascus = Three Crumps

Crooked Mile (Lemore, C., 1885), v. 455

Crooked Paths (Dawson, L., 1888), v. 339

Crooked Ways (1866), v. 662

— (1875), v. 662

— (1882), v. 662

Croquet (Le Clercq, P., 1868), v. 452

— (Shenton, J., 1877), v. 562

Crosby Ravensworth (Pitt, G. D., 1846), IV. 374

— (1861), v. 662

Cross and the Crescent (Bandmann, D. E., 1876), v. 248

Cross-bow Letter (1854), v. 662

— = (1) Duchess of —!; (2) Miller of Whetstone

Crossed in Love (1880), v. 662

Cross for Valour = Bunch of Shamrocks

Crossing Sweeper (Hood, B., 1893), v. 425

Crossing the Frontier = Flying Colours

Crossing the Line (Almar, G., 1833), IV. 252

Cross of Blood = Armourer of Paris

Cross of Death (Neale, F., 1848), IV. 365

Cross of Gold = Veteran of the Old Guard

Cross of Honour = False Witness

Cross of Olga (Castleton, R. and Gurney, G., 1896), v. 306

+ Cross of St John's (Lucas, W. T., French)

Cross on the Boot = Snow Drift

Cross Partners (1792), III. 118, 323, 386, 388, 399

Cross Purposes (O'Brien, W., 1772), III. 119, 291, 393

— (Parselle, J., 1865), v. 515

Cross Purposes (1878), v. 662

— (1891), v. 662

Cross Roads (Sargent, J., 1885), v. 556

Cross Roads of Life = Scamps of London

Cross Strokes (Niel, C., 1894), v. 504

Crotchet Hall (1852), v. 662

Crotchet Lodge (Hurlstone, T., 1795), III. 275

Crotchets (Hay, F., 1876), v. 411

Crowded House (1877), v. 663

Crowded Houses = Crossing the Line

Crowded Villa (1841), IV. 623

Crown Brilliants (Long, C., 1846), IV. 83, 346

Crown Diamonds (Reynoldson, T. H., 1844), IV. 83, 393

— (1847), IV. 83, 446

Crown for Love (Evelyn, J., 1874), v. 359

Crown Jewels (Fitzball, E., 1846), IV. 83, 317

— = (1) Blood Royal; (2) Catarina; (3) Nigel

Crown of Thorns = Love King

Crown Prince (Wilks, T. E., 1838), IV. 420

— (1848), IV. 466

Cruel Alternative = Woman's Vengeance

Cruel Brother (Travers, W., 1864), v. 663, 830

Cruel Carmen (Jones, J. W., 1880), v. 440

Cruel City (Warden, G. and Jones, J. W., 1896), v. 613

Cruel Corsair and the Marble Maid = Zampa

Cruel Destiny (Carr, W., 1899), v. 304

Cruel Father (Reading, E., 1885), v. 536

Cruel Gift (Centlivre, Mrs S., 1716), II. 74, 80-1, 305

Cruel Heritage = Flash in the Pan

Cruel Husband = Injur'd Love

Cruel Kindness (Crowe, C., 1853), v. 330

Cruel Law (Craven, W. S., 1895), v. 329

Cruel London (Harvey, F., 1887), v. 408

Cruel Test (Hall, R. W., 1881), v. 400

Cruelties of the Dutch = Amboyna

Cruel to be kind (Williams, T. J. and Harris, A. G., 1860), v. 625

Cruelty of the Spaniards in Peru (D'Avenant, Sir W., 1658), I. 29, 60, 286, 401

Cyril's Success (Byron, H. J., 1868), v.
    111–12, 121, 297
Cyrus (Hoole, J., 1768), III. 83, 197, 272
Cyrus the Great (Banks, J., 1695), I. 10,
    66, 79, 83, 96, 156, 165, 166, 168, 389
Cytherea (Smith, J., 1677), I. 260, 432
Czar (Cradock, J., 1776), III. 249
— (O'Keeffe, J., 1790), III. 294
— (Planché, J. R., 1819), IV. 376
— (1856), v. 663
Czar and the Minister = Congress
Czarina (Barnett, M. and Reach, A. B.,
    1851), v. 250
Czar of Muscovy (Pix, Mrs M., 1701),
    II. 97, 181, 349
— (1822), IV. 447
Czartoriska (Kemble, J. P., 1794) =
    Lodoiska, III. 324, 389, 399

Dab at Anything = John Dobbs
Dacre of the South (Gore, Mrs C. G. F.,
    1840), IV. 320
Dad = Presence of Mind
Dadds (1888), v. 663
Daddy Grey (Halliday, A., 1868), v. 401
Daddy Hardacre (Simpson, J. P., 1857),
    v. 103, 567
Daddy Long Legs (Bowyer, F., 1885),
    v. 271
Daddy O'Dowd = O'Dowd
Daddy the Outlaw (1888), v. 663
Dad, the Lad, the Lord and the Lass =
    Alonzo and Imogene
Daemon of Daneswall (1802), IV. 447
Daemon of the Drachenfalls (Pitt, G. D.,
    1847), IV. 375
Daemon Owl (1831), IV. 447
Daemons Tribunal (1801) = Demon's
    Tribunal, IV. 446, 450, 623
Daft Dora (1852), v. 663
Daft Meg of the Cliff (1824), IV. 447
Dagger and the Cross (Hill, B., 1867),
    v. 421
Daggers Drawn (Seaton, P., 1890), v. 559
Daggerwoods at Dunstable = Eleventh
    of June
Dagobert (Sellman, R. and Green,
    F. W., 1875), v. 561, 816
Dagobert, King of the Franks
    (Thompson, B., 1800), IV. 412
Dairy Maids (Byrne, J., 1802), IV. 447,
    623

Daisy (Hughes, T. B., 1883), v. 430
— (Manuel, E., 1878), v. 475
— (Palmer, F. G., 1890), v. 511
— (1887), v. 663
— = Freda
Daisy Farm (Byron, H. J., 1871), v. 115,
    297
Daisy Land (Graham, H., 1890), v. 386
Daisy's Escape (Pinero, Sir A. W.,
    1879), v. 524
Dalesman (1836), IV. 623
Dalham Forge (Stephens, W., 1874), v.
    581
Dalila (1872), v. 663
Dalmaviva and Rosina (1814), IV. 447
Dalrymple versus Tubbs (1854), v. 663
Dama di Spirito in Napoli (1810), IV.
    447
Dame Blanche (Rafter, 1848), IV. 388
— (1845), IV. 447
Dame de St Tropez (Barber, J., 1845),
    IV. 259
Dame Dobson (Ravenscroft, E., 1683),
    I. 74, 255–6, 264, 272, 426; II. 142
Dame Durden (Douglass, J. T., 1864),
    v. 663, 788
Dame Durden and her Five Servant
    Maids = Dame Durden
Dame of Spades = Queen of Spades
Dame Trot (George, G. H., 1870), v. 377
Dame Trot and her Cat (Lee, N., 1842),
    IV. 594
Damnation (Stuart, C., 1781), III. 310
Damnation of Faust (Friend, T. H.,
    1894), v. 373
Damoiselles a la Mode (Flecknoe, R.,
    1667), I. 27, 35, 49, 186, 188, 344, 411
Damon and Daphne (1733), II. 369
Damon and Phillida (Cibber, C., 1729),
    II. 16, 136, 137, 138, 237, 250, 313, 434
— (Dibdin, C., 1768), III. 202, 254
Damon and Phebe (Horde, T., 1774),
    III. 273
Damon and Phyllis = Nachtigal und der
    Rabe
Damon and Pythias (Banim, J. and
    Sheil, R. L., 1821) = Force of Friend-
    ship, IV. 258, 462
— (Buckstone, J. B., 1831), IV. 274
— (Burnet, W., 1860), v. 292
Damon the Dauntless and Phyllis the
    Fair (Dryden, C., 1869), v. 351

Damp Beds (Parry, T., 1832), IV. 368

Damp Fire (1842), IV. 448

Danaides (Hoguet, 1845), IV. 447, 623

— = Hypermnestra, the Girl of the Period

Dan and Dick (Gough, H. and Edwards, M., 1887), V. 386

Dance of the Shirt (Morton, T., Jr., 1848), IV. 364

Dancing Barber (Selby, C., 1838), IV. 398

Dancing Dervish (Peile, F. K., 1894), V. 518

Dancing Dolls (D'Arcy, G., 1872), V. 787

Dancing Europeans = Difference of Nations

Dancing for Life (Kenney, J., 1834), IV. 337

— = Halt of the Ballet

Dancing Girl (Jones, H. A., 1891), V. 169–70, 187, 440

Dancing Mad = (1) Diable à Quatre; (2) Magic Pipe

Dancing Master (Pemberton, M. and Wellings, M., 1889), V. 518

— (1815), IV. 447

Dancing Master's Ball = Tigers of Paris

Dancing-Master's Lesson (1855), V. 663

Dancing Scotchman (1855), V. 663

Dandelion's Dodges (Williams, T. J., 1867), V. 625

Dandolo (Stirling, E., 1838), IV. 406

Dandy Dan, the Lifeguardsman (Hood, B., 1897), V. 425

Dandy Dick (Pinero, Sir A. W., 1887), V. 175–6, 525

Dandy Dick Turpin (Thorne, G., 1889), V. 598

Dandy Dick Whittington (Sims, G. R., 1895), V. 569

Dandy Drenched = Bride and Bridegroom

Dandy Family and the Ascot Jockies (Moncrieff, W. T., 1818), IV. 358

Dandy Fifth (Sims, G. R., 1898), V. 570

Dane's Dyke (Bright, Mrs A., 1881), V. 275

Danes in the Dumps = Breeze in the Baltic

Danger (Davis, A., 1873), V. 338

Danger (Horncastle, 1879), V. 426

— (Rayner, A., 1868), V. 535

Danger Ahead (1888), V. 663

Danger and Fatality = Alone in the Pirate's Lair

Dangerfield '95 (Dowling, M. T., 1898), V. 349

Danger of Being Wise in a Commonwealth of Fools = Socrates Triumphant

Danger of Presumption = Frankenstein

Danger on the Line (1884), V. 663

— = Railroad of Life

Dangerous (Osborne, C., 1873), V. 508

Dangerous Complaint = I'd be a Butterfly

Dangerous Curiosity and Justifiable Homicide = Bluebeard

Dangerous Friend (Oxenford, J., 1866), V. 510

Dangerous Game (Roberts, Sir R., 1885), V. 545

Dangerous Neighbourhood (1806), IV. 447

Dangerous Path (Reade, C.), V. 812

Dangerous Playthings (1862), V. 663

Dangerous Ruffian (Howells, W. D., 1895), V. 429

Dangerous Women (Scudamore, F. A., 1898), V. 559

Danger Signal (Bryant, E., 1867), V. 284

— = For Life

Dangers of London (Scudamore, F. A., 1890), V. 559

Dangers of Science (Courtney, G. F., 1896), V. 326

Dangers of the Express (1876), V. 663

Dangers of the Gin Palace = Glass

Danicheffs (Shirley, A., 1883), V. 563

Daniel (More, Mrs H., 1782), III. 288

— (Scott, J., 1873), V. 558

Daniel Bartlett (1881), V. 663

— = Deputy Sheriff

Daniel Daisytop's Delight = Dan'l's Delight

Daniel Day and the Faust Child (Johnstone, J. B., 1848), IV. 333

Daniel in the Lion's Den (1793), III. 324

Daniel O'Connell (Levey, J. C., 1880), V. 458

— (Robertson, J., 1882), V. 545

Daniel O'Rourke (1826), IV. 447

Danischeffs (Newry, Lord, 1877), V. 503

Danish Invasion = (1) Alfred the Great; (2) Osburga; (3) Streanshall Abbey

Danish Pirates = Ethelwolf

Danish Wife (Macfarren, G., 1831), IV. 350

Danites (?Howard, B., 1880), V. 664, 830

— (Miller, J., 1877), V. 488

Dan'l Bruce, Blacksmith (Gilbert, W. S. 1876), V. 380

Dan'l's Delight (Armstrong, A., 1893), V. 243

Dan'l Tra-Duced (Clements, A., 1876), V. 314

Dante (Dabbs, G. H. R. and Righton, E., 1890), V. 332

Dan the Outlaw (Robertson, J., 1888), V. 545

Daphne (Huntley, F., 1895), V. 431

Daphne and Amintor (Bickerstaffe, I., 1765), III. 40, 198, 237, 377

Daphne and Apollo (Rich, J., 1726), II. 253, 443

Daphnis (1892), V. 664

Daphnis and Amaryllis (Harris, J., 1762) = Spring, III. 213, 266, 324, 386

Daraxes (Hill, A., 1760), II. 438; III. 268

Darby and Joan (Bellingham, H. and Best, W., 1885), V. 257

— (Rogers, W., 1851), V. 664, 814, 830

— (1801), IV. 447

— (1802), IV. 447

— (1827), IV. 447

Darby Captain = Eunuch

Darby in America (1792), III. 400

Darby Kelly (1843), IV. 623

Darby's Return (Dunlop, 1789), III. 258

Dare-devil (Campbell, A. V., 1835), IV. 278

— (Shirley, A. and Leonard, H., 1894), V. 564

Dare-Devil Dick (1861), V. 664

Dare Devil Max (Brabner, W. A., 1899), V. 272

Daring Brigands = Perilous Cavern

Daring Device (Dancy, A. T., 1879), V. 336

Darius (1784), III. 324

Darius, King of Persia (Crowne, J., 1688), I. 14, 124, 151, 332, 356, 400

Darius, King of Persia = Noble Englishman

Dark Assassin = Maniac

Dark before Dawn (1871), V. 664

— (1875), V. 664

Dark Blue Waters (1862), V. 664

+ Dark Bungalow; or, 'Is his Appointment Pucka?' (Trevelyan, G. O.: 8°, 1869 (in *Ladies in Parliament and other Pieces*: acted privately at the residence of the Lieutenant-Governor of Bengal))

Dark Cloud (Sketchley, A., 1863), V. 570, 816

Dark Continent (Mouillot, F. and Morell, H. H., 1891), V. 498

Dark Days (Carr, J. W. C. and Conway, H., 1885), V. 304

— (1884), V. 664

Dark Deed in the Woods = Jasper Roseblade

Dark Deeds (Fairbairn, Mrs R., 1881), V. 359

Dark Deeds and Doings in London = Shoals and Quicksands

Dark Deeds of a Coal Pit = Collier's Wife

Dark Deeds of Bluegate Fields = Bob Lumley's Secret

Dark Deeds of London (1882), V. 664

Dark Deeds of Night = Ivan the Terrible

Dark Deeds of Old London = Adam Winter, the Fiend of Private Life

Dark Deeds of the Devil's Grip = Fred Frolic

Dark Dens of the City = Red Lamp

Dark Diamond (1832), IV. 448

Dark Doings in the Closet by the Knotting 'em Brothers (Coyne, J. S., 1864), v. 328

Dark Donald, the Idiot of the Cliff (Atkyns, S., 1848), IV. 257

Dark Duel in the Wood = Aurora Floyd

Darkest Hour (Adams-Acton, Mrs, 1895), V. 235

— (1897), V. 664

Darkest London (Stanhope, B., 1891), V. 579

— = My Maggie

Dark Events (1839), IV. 448

Dark Falcon (1846), IV. 448

Dark Glen of Bally Foihl (Stirling, E., 1871), V. 584

Dark Gondola = Tower of Nesle

Dark Hearts = Night Porter

Dark Horse (Garston, C., 1868), v. 376

Dark Hour (St Aubyn, D., 1877), v. 554

— = Break of Morn

Dark Hour before Dawn = Sister's Wrongs

Dark House (1859), v. 664

Darkie that walked in her Sleep = Nigger's Opera

Dark King of the Black Mountains (Hazlewood, C. H., 1866), v. 664, 796, 830

Dark Knight and the Fair Lady = Ah! what a Pity!!!

Dark Lady of Doona (Almar, G., 1840), IV. 568

Darkness Visible (Hook, T. E., 1811) = Four in hand, IV. 328, 463, 589

Dark Night's Bridal (Buchanan, R., 1887), v. 285

Dark Night's Work (Marchant, F., 1865), v. 664, 805, 830

— = Giralda

Dark Page (Breare, W. H., 1885), v. 274

Dark Pandour (1828), IV. 448

Dark Past (Price, F., 1890), v. 530

Dark Secret (Willing, J. and Douglass, J., 1886), v. 626

Dark Shadows and Sunshine = Wild Gipsy Girl

Dark Shadows and Sunshine of Life (Donald, J., 1857), v. 664, 788, 830

Dark Side of London Life = Toilers of the Thames

Dark Side of our Great City = London by Night

Dark Side of the Great Metropolis (Travers, W., 1868), v. 603

Dark Spirit of the Dismal Swamp = Nick of the Woods

Dark's the Hour before the Dawn = Eileen Oge

Dark Turnings in Life = Redemption

Dark Woman (Young, Mrs H., 1861), v. 664, 825, 830

Darnley (Graham, D., 1900), v. 386

Darnley, the Knight of Burgundy (1830), IV. 448

Darthula (Mylne, J., 1790), III. 290

Dash (Lathom, F., 1804), IV. 342

Dash for Freedom (Roy, G., 1884), v. 552

Dashing Dick Turpin (Stanhope, B., 1892), v. 579

Dashing White Sergeant (Barber, J., 1847), IV. 569

Dash of the Day (Lathom, F., 1799), III. 280; IV. 341

Daughter (Bayly, T. H., 1835), IV. 263, 571

— (Knowles, J. S., 1836), IV. 173, 339

— (Pocock, I., 1815) = Magpie or the Maid, IV. 448, 623

— = Sighs

+ Daughter in Law (Seymour, M., French)

— = Vicissitudes

Daughter of Air (1800), IV. 448

Daughter of England (Dundas, H. and Shelley, H., 1896), v. 352

Daughter of Erin = Biddy O'Neal

Daughter of Eve (Meritt, P., 1877), v. 486

Daughter of Fire (Barnett, C. Z., 1845), IV. 260

— = Alina

Daughter of Ghent = Witch of the White Hoods

Daughter of Ishmael = Miriam Gray

Daughter of Midnight (Marchant, F., 1863), v. 664, 830

Daughter of Night (Seaman, W., 1856), v. 664, 815, 830

Daughter of St Mark (Bunn, A., 1844), IV. 276

Daughter of the Air (1831), IV. 448

Daughter of the Danube (Osman, W. R., 1873), v. 508

— (1837), IV. 448

— (1868), v. 664

Daughter of the Deep = Black Fisherman

Daughter of the Million (1899), v. 664

Daughter of the People (Harvey, F., 1891), v. 408

— (1860), v. 664

— (1898), v. 664

Daughter of the Regiment (Archer, T., 1848), IV. 255

— (Davenport, 1848), IV. 448, 623

— (Fitzball, E., 1843), IV. 316, 584

— (Fitzball, E., 1847), IV. 317

Daughter of the Regiment (Weil, O., 1890), v. 619
— (Wigan, H., 1859), v. 622
— (1855), v. 664
— =Fille du Regiment
Daughter of the Stars (Brooks, C. W. S., 1850), v. 277
Daughter of the Tumbrils (Grogan, W. E., 1897), v. 395
Daughter of the Wolf (Travers, W., 1865), v. 822
Daughter of Truth=Truth
Daughters (Warren, T. G. and Edouin, W., 1890), v. 615
Daughter's Courage=Heroine
Daughter's Devotion=Chain of Gold
Daughter's Error=Pride and Patience
Daughter's Honour (Landeck, B. and Shirley, A., 1894), v. 447
Daughters of Babylon (Barrett, W., 1897), v. 251
Daughters of Danaus (Dibdin, T. J., 1821), IV. 303
Daughters of Robert Macaire=Illustrious Chief
Daughters of the Guadalquiver (1858), v. 664
Daughter's Sacrifice (Doone, N., 1888), v. 347
— =(1) Clara Charette; (2) Love's Sacrifice; (3) Riches and Poverty
Daughter's Secret (Peel, G., 1874), v. 518
Daughter's Trial=Henry Dunbar
Daughter's Vow=Nymph of the Grotto
Daughter to Marry (Planché, J. R., 1828), IV. 84, 378
— (1827), IV. 448
— (1837), IV. 448
— =My Daughter, Sir
Dauntless Boy of the Lake=White Spirit
Dauntless Decius, the Doubtful Decemvir=Julius See-Saw
Davenport Brothers & Co. (Pemberton, T. E., 1879), v. 519
Davenport Done (Colomb, 1867), v. 318
Davey Crockett (Dizance, F., 1873), v. 346
David (Parker, L. N. and Carson, S. M., 1892), v. 513

David and Goliath (More, Mrs H., 1782), III. 288
David and his Wives (1894), v. 664
David Copperfield (1870), v. 664
— (1892), v. 664
David Copperfield the Younger of Blunderstone Rookery (1850), v. 664
David e Bersabea (1734), II. 392
David Garrick (Colnaghi, C. P. and Ponsonby, E., 1888), v. 318
— (Robertson, T. W., 1864), v. 123-4, 126, 127, 546
David Hunt (Pitt, G. D., 1845), IV. 374
David Morgan, the Jacobite (1872), v. 664
David Rizzio (Hamilton, R., 1820), IV. 324
David's Lamentation over Saul and Jonathan (Lockman, J., 1736), II. 392, 440
— (1740), II. 392
Davis and Sally Dear (Bruton, J., 1842), IV. 272, 574
Davy Crockett (Murdoch, F. H., 1872), v. 499
— (1875), v. 664
Davy Garrick (1898), v. 664
Davy Jones (Barrymore, W., 1830), IV. 448, 623
Davy Jones's Locker (1812), IV. 448
— (1825), IV. 448
— =Ocean Sylph
Davy Jones, the Merman of the Sea (Dorrington, W., 1858), v. 788
Dawn (Thomas, G. and Oswald, F., 1887), v. 596
Dawning of Peace=Female Volunteer
Dawn of Christianity=For the Cross
Dawn of Hope (Burnette, C. and Cooper, H. B., 1896), v. 293
Dawn of Love (Ross, R., 1885), v. 551
Day after the Fair (Somerset, C. A., 1829), IV. 16, 132, 404
— (1826), IV. 448
Day after the Wedding (Kemble, M. T., 1808), IV. 145, 335
Day after Tomorrow=Old Bachelor
Day and Night (1815), IV. 448
— =Shadowed
Day and Night Adventures of Logic, Tom and Jerry=Life in London

Day and Night Scenes of Tom and Jerry = Life in Dublin

Day at an Inn (Hook, T. E., 1823), IV. 328, 589

Day at Boulogne (1860), v. 664
— = Master's Rival

Day at Donnybrook (1865), v. 664

Day at Coney Island = Surprises

Day at Dover (1845), IV. 448

Day at Gretna Green = Blacksmith

Day at Rome (Smith, C., 1798), III. 308

Daybreak (Willing, J., 1884), v. 626
— (1895), v. 664

Day by Day = Judgment

Day Dream (Courtney, J., 1846), IV. 283

Day Dreams (Hawthorn, M., 1888), v. 410
— (Leighton, Sir B., 1875), v. 454, 803
— (Swears, H., 1894), v. 589

Daye and Knight (Parke, W., 1895), v. 512

Dayes of Olde (Jarman, F., 1892), v. 434

Day in Algiers = Medicus Borealis

Day in Boulogne (Grain, R. C., 1882), v. 387
— (Law, A.), v. 450
— (1899), v. 664

Day in France = Master's Rival

Day in High Life (1860), v. 664

Day in Kingsbury Castle (Ashdown, C. H., 1899), v. 244

Day in London (Cherry, A., 1807), IV. 280

Day in Paris (Selby, C., 1832), IV. 397
— = Lost, Stolen or Strayed

Day in Spain = Masquerade

Day in the Country (1817), IV. 448

Day in the Dockyards = Czar

Day in Turkey (Cowley, Mrs H., 1791), III. 249

Day in Wales = Cottage Festival

Day near Turin (Maberley, Mrs, 1841), IV. 349

Day of Atonement (1899), v. 664

Day of Disasters (1860), v. 664, 790

Day of Dupes = Quid pro Quo

Day of Economy = Locked Up

Day of Numa Pompilius = Golden Shield

Day of Reckoning (Planché, J. R., 1850), v. 527

Day of Reckoning (1891), v. 664
— (1894), v. 664

Day of Taste (1760), III. 324

Day of Tribute = Kamtchatka

Day's Adventure at Little Snuggleton = Who's your Hatter?

Days and Knights of the Round Table = King Arthur

Day's Courtship = Tunbridge-Wells

Day's Fishing (Morton, J. M., 1869), v. 496

Day's Fun (1828), IV. 448

Days of Athens (Ducrow, A., 1831), IV. 307

Days of Charlemagne = Four Sons of Aymon

Days of Charles II = Whitefriars

Days of Chivalry (1841), IV. 448

Days of Cromwell (Rogers, C. and Livesey, C., 1896), v. 548
— = Regicide

Days of Edward IV (1835), IV. 448

Days of Ferdinand Cortez = Conquest of Mexico

Days of Good Queen Bess = Kenilworth

Days of Hogarth (1857), v. 664

Days of Jezebel (Bayne, P., 1872), v. 253

Days of Louis XV (1863), v. 665
— = (1) Armand; (2) Fan-Fan the Tulip

Days of Old (1797), III. 400
— (1812), IV. 448

Days of Oliver Cromwell (1847), IV. 623

Days of Prince Rupert = Siege of Liverpool

Days of Queen Bess = (1) Earl of Essex; (2) Elizabeth and Essex; (3) Kenilworth Castle; (4) Mysterious Freebooter

Days of Terror (Clarke, C. A., 1891), v. 312
— (1896), v. 665
— = (1) Chevalier de Maison Rouge and Marie Antoinette; (2) Chevalier of the Moulin Rouge

Days of the Commonwealth = Oliver Cromwell

Days of the Curfew Bell = William the Conqueror

Days of the French Revolution = Life's Revenge

Dead Shot (Buckstone, J. B., 1827), IV. 273

Dead Take In (Wigan, A. S., 1850), V. 621

Dead to the World (Conquest, G. and Pettitt, H., 1875), V. 321

Dead Wife (1838), IV. 448

Dead Witness (Reeve, W., 1863), V. 150, 540

— (1889), V. 665

— = Frozen Stream

Dead Woman's Secret (1861), V. 665, 830

— = (1) Gunsmith of Orleans; (2) Love's Victory

Deadwood Dick (Korrell, P., 1894), V. 446

Deaf and Dumb (Holcroft, T., 1801), IV. 326

— (Thompson, B., 1800), IV. 412

— (1801), IV. 448

Deaf and Dumb Boy = Dumb Boy

Deaf and Dumb Orphan = Julio of Harancour

Deaf as a Post (Poole, J., 1823), IV. 386

Deaf Doctor = Device

Deaf Indeed (Topham, E., 1780), III. 312

Deaf Lover (Pilon, F., 1780), III. 187, 297

Deal Boatman (Burnand, F. C., 1863), V. 288

Dealings with the Firm of Gasup and Harris (1846), IV. 448

Dean of Hazeldene (Dryden, J. P., 1889), V. 351

Dean's Daughter (Grundy, S. and Philips, F. C., 1888), V. 160, 205, 397

Dear Departed (Parke, W., 1890), V. 512

Dearer than Life (Byron, H. J., 1867), V. 297

Dearest Anna Maria (Hatch, P. H., 1851), V. 409

Dearest Elizabeth (Oxenford, J., 1848), IV. 449, 602, 623

Dearest Mama, my Mother-in-Law (Gordon, W., 1860), V. 385

Dear Girls = Lilies

Dear Jack (Giraud, Mrs, 1892), V. 382

Dear Neighbours (Blouet, P., 1885), V. 266

Dear Old Flag (1896), V. 665

Death and Glory = (1) England and Glory; (2) Idle Words

Death and Liberty = Charter

Death and Rachel (Graves, C., 1890) = Rachel, V. 665, 794

Death and the Doctor (Peake, R. B., 1835), IV. 370

Death and the Lady (1851), V. 665

Death at the Stake (James, C. S., 1849), IV. 330

Death by the Law (Towers, E., 1876), V. 601

Death Dealer (1840), IV. 449

Death Doom (1843), IV. 449

Death Fetch (Buckstone, J. B., 1826), IV. 272

— (Milner, H. M., 1826), IV. 449, 623

— (1832), IV. 449

— = Bertha Gray, the Pauper's Child

Death Hand (Taylor, T. P., 1842), IV. 411, 614

Death in the Streets (1864), V. 665

Death Kiss (Seaman, W.), V. 815

Death Light (Almar, G.), IV. 253

Death of Abel (Shoberl, F., 1806), IV. 610

Death of Abercromby (Astley, P., Jr., 1801), IV. 256

Death of Achilles = Rival Father

Death of Adam (Lloyd, R., 1763), III. 61, 282, 390

Death of Alexander the Great = Rival Queens

Death of Bucephalus (Schomberg, R., 1765), III. 304, 395

— = Alexander and Statira

Death of Bucephalus the Great = Rival Favourites

Death of Caesar (1823), IV. 449

Death of Captain Cook (1789), III. 324

Death of Captain Faulknor (1795), III. 324

Death of Christophe, King of Haiti (Amherst, J. H., 1821), IV. 253

+ Death of Darnley (Sotheby, W. in Tragedies, 1814)

Death of David Rizzio (Dibdin, T. J. ? 1795), III. 382

Death of Dido (Booth, B., 1716), II. 259, 299

Death of Dion (Harwood, T., 1787), III. 267

Death of Eva (1857), v. 665

Death of Fair Eleanor = Banks of Allan Water

Death of Fair Rosamond (Amherst, J. H., 1828), IV. 254

+ Death of General Abercrombie (Dibdin, C. I. M.; S.W. 1801)

Death of General Gordon = Fall of Khartoum

Death of General Mortier (1835), IV. 449

Death of General Wolfe (1790), III. 324

Death of General Woolfe (1833), IV. 449

Death of Giovanni (1823), IV. 449

Death of Haman = Esther, the Royal Jewess

Death of Harlequin (1716), II. 369

Death of Harold = William the Conqueror's Invasion of England

Death of Hero and Leander = Heroic Love

Death of Ingomar = Indian Captive

Death of Iturbide, Ex-Emperor of Mexico (1821), IV. 449

Death of Jane Shore = King's Mistress

Death of King Edmund (Hopkinson, A. F., 1889), v. 426

Death of Life in London (Greenwood, T., 1823), IV. 321

Death of Marc Antony = Beauty the Conqueror

Death of Marlowe (Horne, R. H., 1837), IV. 328

Death of Mary, Queen of Scotland = Island Queens = Albion Queens

Death of Mary Queen of Scots (1823), IV. 449

Death of Napoleon (1840), IV. 623

Death of Nelson = Battle of Trafalgar

Death of Richard III = English Princess

Death of Riego = Spanish Martyrs

Death of Rolla (1821), IV. 449

— = (1) Pizarro; (2) Pizarro in Peru; (3) Spaniards in Peru

Death of Sir John Moore and the Defeat at Corunna (1834), IV. 449

Death of Socrates (Harrison, E., 1756), III. 266

— = Heathen Martyr

Death of the Elephant at Exeter Change = Chuneelah

Death of the Lady Jane Grey = Innocent Usurper

Death of the Queen of France (1804), IV. 449

— = Maid of Normandy

Death of the Race-Horse (1828), IV. 449

Death of the Red King = Grim Will, the Collier of Croydon

Death of the Stag = Amorous Sportsman

Death of Tom Moody (1830), IV. 449

Death of Virginia (1829), IV. 449

Death of Wallenstein (Coleridge, S. T., 1800), III. 63, 245; IV. 281

Death of White Surrey (1858), v. 665

Death of Xavier = Prussian Brothers

Death Omen (Greenwood, T., 1840), IV. 321

Death Omen and the Fate of Lady Jane Grey = Tower of London

Death on the Tavern Stairs = "Old Blue Lion" in Gray's Inn Lane

Death or Glory (Mill, J., 1896), v. 488

Death or Glory Boys (1897), v. 665

Death or Victory (Mill, J. and Mountford, H., 1898), v. 488

Death Plank (Lucas, W. J., 1832), IV. 347

Death's Bridal (Osborne, C., 1878), v. 508

Death Secret (1849), IV. 449

Death's Head Dick, the Skeleton Pirate (Totten, R. C., 1870), v. 600

Death Shot and the Dog of the Prairie = Winona, the Sioux Queen

Death's Jest Book (Beddoes, T. L., 1850), IV. 201–2, 264

Death Signal = Midnight Watch

Death Spell = Adolph Arnal

Death Summons (Wimberley, W. C., 1832), IV. 618

Death's Waiting Room (1851), v. 830

Death Token (Wilks, T. E., 1837), IV. 420

— (1858), v. 665

Death Trap (Ware, J. R., 1870), v. 614

Death Warrant (Grattan, H. P., 1879), v. 389

Death Wedding (Mildenhall, T., 1845), IV. 355

De Bassenvelt (1845), IV. 449

Debating Club (McLaren, A., 1816), IV. 351

Debauch'd Hypocrite = Trick for Trick

Debauchee (Behn, A., 1677), I. 222, 390

Debauchees = Old Debauchees

Debo-Lear (Hazlewood, C. H., 1864), v. 665, 830

Deborah (Cheltnam, C. S., 1864), v. 309

— (Conquest, G., 1864), v. 665, 830

— (Fielding, H., 1733), II. 326

— (Humphreys, S., 1733), II. 392, 439

— (Mitchell, L. E., 1893), v. 490

Debt (De Pass, E. A., 1872), v. 342

— (1873), v. 665

Debt and the Duel = Husbands and Wives

Debt of Honour (Broughton, F. W., 1879), v. 281

— (Colnaghi, G. P., 1891), v. 318

— (Ryves, E.), III. 304

Debtor and Creditor (Kenney, J., 1814) = City Rivals, IV. 336, 443, 592

Debts of Honour (Poel, W., 1893), v. 665, 811, 830

Debutante (1867), v. 665

— (1893), v. 665

— = First Night

Debutante's Test = Come here

Deceit (Norris, H., 1723), II. 347

Deceitful Steward (1807), IV. 449

Deceived (1882), v. 665

Deceived One = Mary May

Deceiver (McLaren, A., 1816), IV. 351

Deceiver Deceived (Pix, Mrs M., 1697), I. 225, 266, 424

— (1826), IV. 449

— = Maid or Wife

Deceivers Ever (Salaman, M. C., 1883), v. 555

December and May (Dimond, W., 1818), IV. 307

Deception (De Frece, M., 1871), v. 341

— (Longmuir, A., 1889), v. 463, 804

— (?Vaughan, T., 1784), III. 313 [In The Oracle, 13/2/1796, Vaughan has a letter disavowing the authorship of this play]

— (1788), III. 324

— (1835), IV. 449

Deceptions (Cornelys, Mrs T., 1781), III. 248 [The authoress' Christian name should be Margaret, not Teresa]

+De Chatillon (Hemans, Felicia: in Works, 8° 1844, vol. IV)

Decided Fix (1860), v. 665

Decision of the Court (1893), v. 665

Decius and Paulina (Theobald, L., 1718), II. 259–60, 359

Decorum (Bayly, T. H., 1831), IV. 449, 623

Decoy (Eastwood, F., 1883), v. 353

— (Potter, H., 1733), II. 350

Decoy Bird (1892), v. 665

Decoy Duck (1898), v. 665

Decree Nisi (1892), v. 665

Decree of Java = Poison Tree

Deed in the Wood = Aurora Floyd

Deed of Separation (1883), v. 665

Deeds (Freake, Mrs, 1879), v. 372

Deeds and Doings of the Dark House (1841), IV. 623

Deeds, not Words (Courtney, J., 1855), v. 326

Deeds of Darkness (1860), v. 665

Deeds of Dreadful Note (Dubois, 1841) IV. 307

Deed Without a Name (Soutar, R., 1853), v. 575

— (1824), IV. 449

Deeming (1892), v. 665

Deene Farm (Bateman, A., 1894), v. 253

Deep Deep Sea (Planché, J. R. and Dance, C., 1833), IV. 380

Deep Shadows (1894), v. 665

Deep Waters (Grundy, S. 1889), v. 397

— (1897), v. 665

Deerfoot (Burnand, F. C., 1861), v. 288

Deer Slayers (Pitt, W. H. and Pitt, C., 1870), v. 527, 811

Deer Stalker (Lemon, M., 1841), IV. 449, 623

Deer Stealer of 1623 = Waltham Blacks

Defeated (Clay, F., 1881), v. 313

Defeated Widow = Counterfeit Bridegroom

Defeat of Apollo (1737), II. 370

— = Mirrour

Defeat of Junot = British Heroes

Defeat of the Amazons = Apollo and the Flying Pegasus

Defeat of the Dutch Fleet by the gallant Admiral Duncan, on the memorable Eleventh of October = England's Glory

Demon of the Drachenfels = Faust

Demon of the Flood = Nerestan, Prince of Persia

Demon of the Ganges (Almar, G., 1834), IV. 253

Demon of the Mystic Dart (1834), IV. 450

Demon of the Night = Nachtteufel

Demon of the Rock = Lazuli

Demon of the Wolf's Glen = Freischutz

Demon of the Woods = Wood Daemon

Demon Oof Bird (Addison, J., 1895), v. 236

Demon Pilot = Phantom Ship

Demon's Bride (Byron, H. J., 1874), v. 298

Demon's Calendar (1844), IV. 450

Demon's Compact = Fairy Page

Demon's Gift (Lemon, M.) [The play cited IV. 595 is apparently The Demon Gift, listed IV. 271]

Demon Seaman = Flying Dutchman

Demon Spider (Simpson, E. G., 1895), v. 567

Demon Statue = Skeleton Hand

Demon's Tribunal (1800), IV. 450

Demon's Trumpet and the Magic Ring (1826), IV. 450

Demon's Victim = Faustus

Demophoon (Hoole, J., 1767), III. 387

Dempster's Doom = Last Key

Denes Rest (Delannoy, B., 1897), v. 341

D'Enghien (Greene, W. A., 1842), IV. 321

Denhams = Crisis

Denham's Folly (Besley, H., 1894), v. 260

Denise (Scott, C. W. and Harris, Sir A., 1895), v. 558

Dennis (Nantz, F. C., 1833), IV. 365

Denouement = Dash

Denounced (Gascoigne, H. and Jefferson, F., 1883), v. 376

Denouncer (1848), IV. 623

— (1860), v. 666

Dentist's Identity = Filumbonum

Deoch and Durass (Dodson, R., 1877), v. 346

Departed not Defunct = Usurer

Dependant (Cumberland, R., 1795), III. 252

Deposing and Death of Queen Gin (1736), II. 370

Depredators = Bravo turn'd Bully

Deputy (Arliss, G., 1897), v. 243

— (Campbell, J. M., 1888), v. 301

— = Roma

Deputy Registrar (Lumley, R. R., 1888), v. 464

Deputy Sheriff (1892), v. 666

De Rayo (1833), IV. 623

Derby Day (Lee, N., Jr., 1867), v. 453, 803

Derby Lost and the Leger Won = Flying Jib by Snapdragon

Derby Winner (Harris, Sir A. H. G., Raleigh, C. and Hamilton, H., 1894), v. 406

Dermot and Kathlane (Byrne, J., 1793), III. 241

Dermot O'Donoghue (Fraser, J. A., 1872), v. 372

Derry Driscoll (Mackenna, S. J. and Aylmer, B., 1877), v. 471

Dervise and the Peri = Black Hand

Descart, the French Buccaneer (Jerrold, D. W., 1828), IV. 331

Descendants of Hugh Myddelton = Student of Blackfriars

Descent of Orpheus into Hell (1661), I. 41, 44, 133, 252

Descent of the Balloon = Mogul Tale

Descent of the Deities = (1) Olympus in an Uproar; (2) Widow of Delphi

Descent of the Heathen Gods (1749), II. 451

Desert (Fitzball, E., 1847), IV. 317

Deserted (Coles, C., 1894), v. 317

— (1879), v. 666

Deserted and Deceived = Cast on the Mercy of the World

Deserted Child = Rosalie

Deserted Daughter (Holcroft, T., 1795) = Tis a Strange World, III. 137, 271; IV. 571

Deserted Mill (1855), v. 666

— = Soldier's Widow

Deserted Mine = Blacksmith's Daughter and the Red Hand

Deserted Mother = Marguerite

Deserted Priory = Malediction

Deserted Tower (Rannie, J., 1806), III. 300

Deserted Village (Cooper, F. F., 1833), IV. 283

— (Saville, Mrs E. F., 1835), IV. 609

Deserted Wife (Faucquez, A., 1873), V. 666, 791, 830

Deserted Wife in Search of a Husband (1849), IV. 450

Deserted Wife of Didcot = Ramblers

Deserter (Dibdin, C., 1773), III. 120, 202, 254, 381

— (1789), III. 324

— (1801), IV. 450

— (1849), IV. 450

Deserter and his Dog = Napoleon Buonaparte

Deserter from Orleans = German Jew

Deserter in a Fix (Soane-Roby, B., 1879), V. 573

Deserter of Dresden = Maid of the Black Rock

Deserter of Moscow = Emperor of Russia

Deserter of Naples (1788), III. 120, 324

— (1789), III. 324

— (1817), IV. 450

Deserteur (1818), IV. 450

Déserteur malgré lui = Carl et Lisbeth

Desert Fiend = Shamacda

Desert Flower (Harris, A. G. and Williams, T. J., 1863), V. 405

Desert Island (Murphy, A., 1760), III. 51, 61, 70, 71, 222, 289

Deserts of Arabia (Reynolds, F., 1806), IV. 391

Deserts of Siberia = Exile

Desmore (1866), V. 666

Desmoro (Archer, W. J., 1866), V. 777

Desolate Island = (1) De la Perouse; (2) Perouse

Desolation (Towers, E., 1865), V. 666, 821, 830

Desperate Adventures of the Baby (Ross, C. H., 1878), V. 551

Desperate Deed (Delannoy, B., 1893), V. 341

Desperate Game (Morton, J. M., 1853), V. 495

Desperate Man (Pond, A. P., 1891), V. 529

Desperate Remedy (Bruce, H. P., 1892), V. 283

— = My Heart's Idol

Desperate Women = Fair Sinners

Desperation (Roy, G. and Reid, B., 1887), V. 552

Despite the World = Voltaire's Wager

Desrues the Deceiver (1833), IV. 450

Destiny (Conquest, G., 1860), V. 666 785, 830

— (Lyon, W. F., 1881), V. 465

— (Towers, E., 1860), V. 666

— (Towers, E., 1869), V. 601, 821

— (1894), V. 666, 830

Destroyed by Drink (Lacy, J. W., 1879), V. 446

Destroyer (1868), V. 666

Destroying Angel (Scudamore, F. A., 1896), V. 559

Destruction of Jerusalem = Titus Caesar

Destruction of Jerusalem by Titus Vespasian (Crowne, J., 1677), I. 40, 83, 124, 151, 346, 350, 399

Destruction of the Bastille (Taylor, T. P., 1844), IV. 411, 614

— (Webster, B. N., 1842), IV. 105–6, 418

— = (1) Paris in an Uproar; (2) Triumph of Liberty

Destruction of the Dockyard = Jack the Painter

Destruction of the Spanish Armada = Golden Days of Good Queen Bess

Destruction of the Turko-Egyptian Fleet = Britons at Navarino

Destruction of the World = Noah's Flood

Destruction of Troy (Banks, J., 1678), I. 54, 66, 67, 120, 125, 165, 389

Detection (1780), III. 324

— (1805), IV. 450

Detective (Hazlewood, C. H., 1863), V. 413, 797

— (Scott, C. W. and Manuel, E., 1875), V. 557

— = Wolves and Waifs

Deuce is in Her (Planché, J. R., 1820), IV. 376

— (Raymond, R. J., 1830), IV. 388

Deuce is in Him (Colman, G., 1763), III. 120, 182, 183, 245, 373

Deuce is in it = Three and the Ace

Deux âges (1817), IV. 450

Deux aveugles (Farnie, H. B., 1871), V. 790

Devils in the Wood (1747), II. 370

Devil's Luck (Conquest, G. and Tinsley, L., 1885), v. 322

— (1888), v. 666

Devil's Mine (Darcy, F., 1894), v. 336

Devil's Mount (Higgie, T. H., 1847), IV. 325

Devil's Opera (Macfarren, G., 1838), IV. 350, 597

Devil's Pills = Pilule du Diable

Devil's Pool (1871), v. 666

Devil's Punch Bowl (1834), IV. 450

— = King's Mail

Devil's Ride to London = More Visitors in Town

Devil's Ring (Rodwell, G. H., 1850), v. 548

Devil's Share (Raymond, C. F. M., 1843), IV. 388

— = (1) Asmodeus; (2) Asmodeus, the Little Demon

Devil's Ship (1832), IV. 450

Devil's Ship and the Pirates of the Charmed Life = Money Diggers

Devil's Son = Robert le Diable

Devil's Three-decker (1853), v. 666

Devil's Violin and the Revolt of the Flowers (Webster, B. N., 1849), IV. 418, 616

Devil's Walk (Moncrieff, W. T., 1830), IV. 450, 623

Devil's Wood = Fratricide

+Devil to Do (Crow Street, Dublin, 18/3/1779)

Devil to Do about Her = Man's Bewitched

Devil to Pay (Coffey, C. and Mottley, J., 1731), II. 136, 137, 138, 142, 237, 243-4, 315; III. 28, 38

+— (12°, 1763, Belfast)

— (1845), IV. 450

— = Merry Cobler

Devil turn'd Humourist = Nuns turn'd Libertines

Devil upon Two Sticks (Coffey, C. 1729), II. 134, 244, 315

— (Foote, S., 1768), III. 174-5, 260

Devoted Daughter = Jew and the German

Devoted Son = Murderer

Devotee = Seraphine

Devotion (Boucicault, D. G., 1884), v. 270

— (Cheatham, F. G., 1870), v. 308

— (Lane, Mrs S., 1881), v. 448

— (1884), v. 666

Devotion and Prejudice (Brough, R. B. and Bridgeman, J. V., 1874), v. 278

Dewdrop and Rosebud = Riquet with the Tuft

Dey and a Knight (Somerset, C. A., 1838), IV. 404

— (1843), IV. 450

Dey and the Knight = Zanone

Dhrame (Nugent, J. F., 1876), v. 506

Dhu Blanche = Blanche Dhu

Dhu Colleen of Ballyfoyle = Liberty

Diable à la Chasse = Asgard, the Demon Hunter

Diable à Quatre (1845), IV. 450

— (1846), IV. 450

Diabolus amans (1885), v. 666

Diadeste (Fitzball, E., 1838), IV. 315

Dial of Death (1899), v. 666

Dialogue between a Mother and a Daughter = Female Angler

Diamond and Granle (1894), v. 666

Diamond and the Pearl = Working Man

Diamond and the Snowdrop = Light of Love

Diamond Arrow (Moncrieff, W. T., 1815), IV. 358

Diamond Cavern (1850), v. 666

Diamond cut Diamond (Drayton, H., 1859), v. 666, 789, 830

— (Hook, J. or T. E., 1797), III. 272, 405

— (Murray, W. H., 1838), IV. 365

— (Wallace, Lady E., 1787), III. 121, 314

— = Swindlers

Diamond Deane (Dam, H. J. W., 1891), v. 334

Diamond Gang (Darbey, E., 1892), v. 336

Diamond in the Rough (1895), v. 666

Diamond King (Dawson, F., 1892), v. 339

Diamond Necklace (1891), v. 666

— = Number Ninety Nine

Diamond Queen (Edwards, A., 1889), v. 355

Diamond Ring (Wild, W. J., 1885), v. 622

Dick Whittington and his Cat (Greenwood, T. L., 1852), v. 393, 794
— (Lemon, M., 1842), IV. 344
— (McLelland, H. F., 1894), v. 468
— (Melville, A. and Jones, J. W., 1893), v. 485
— (Milner, H. W., 1823), IV. 451, 623
— (O'Halloran, G. B., 1878), v. 506
— (Richards, J., 1870), v. 542
— (Thorne, G., 1889), v. 598
— (Virgo, J. T. and M°Cabe, C. W., 1894), v. 609
— (1874, 1875, 1877, 1878, 1881, 1884, 1885, 1891, 1893), v. 668

Dick Whittington and his Cat-astrophe (Horner, J., 1884), v. 427

Dick Whittington and his Good Cat (Green, F. W., 1881), v. 391

Dick Whittington and his King of Pussy Cats (Green, F. W., 1883), v. 391

Dick Whittington and his Wonderful Cat (Lemon, H., 1869), v. 454
— (Marchant, F., 1863), v. 668, 830

Dick Whittington Returned (1881), v. 668

Dick Whittington the Second (1885), v. 668

Dick Wilder (Musgrave, Mrs H., 1891), v. 500

Diddlecombe Farm (Fuller, C. F., 1886), v. 374

Did He Steal It? (Trollope, A., 1869), v. 604

Did I dream it? (Wooler, J. P., 1860), v. 632, 824

Dido (Bridges, T., 1771), III. 240
— (Hoole, J., 1800), III. 387
— (Reed, J., 1767), III. 300

Dido and Aeneas (?D'Urfey, T., 1727), II. 256, 257–8, 320
— (Gildon, C., 1700), II. 332
— (Tate, N., 1689), I. 95, 434
— (1893), v. 668
— = Death of Dido

Dido Done = Æneas

Dido, Queen of Carthage (Hoare, P., 1792), III. 69, 269, 387

Dido, the Celebrated Widow (Burnand, F. C., 1860), v. 288, 781

Did she mean it? (Rennell, C. R., 1871), v. 541

Did You Ever? (Addison, H. R., 1848), IV. 251

Did you ever send your Wife to Camberwell? (Coyne, J. S., 1846), IV. 287

Did you ever take your Wife to Broughty Ferry? (1846), IV. 451

Did you ring? (Houghton, J. W. and Mabson, J. W., 1892), v. 427

Difference of Nations (1733), II. 370

Difference of Opinion (1898), v. 668

Different Husbands = Universal Gallant

Different Widows (Pix, Mrs M., 1703), II. 155, 171, 350

Difficulties of identifying an Irishman = O'Flahertys

Digger's Bride (1859), v. 831

Diggings (1877), v. 668

Dilettanti (Peacock, T. L.), IV. 369

Dillosk Gatherer (Fitzball, E., 1832), IV. 451, 623

Dimity's Dilemma (Salaman, M. C., 1887), v. 555

Dinas Bran (1830), IV. 451

Dine at my Villa (Hoare, P., 1804) = Paragraph, IV. 451, 623

Ding Dong Bell, Pussy's in the Well (Lee, N., Jr., 1866), v. 453
— (Soutar, R., 1866), v. 575
— (1834), IV. 451

Ding Dong Will (1857), v. 666

Dinky Doo (1894), v. 668

Dinner for Nothing (Cheltnam, C. S., 1865), v. 309

Dinner for Six = Who stole the Pocketbook

Dinner for Two (Carton, R. C., 1893), v. 305

Dinner of Madelon (1816), IV. 451 [See also under Sportsman and the Shepherd]
— (1828), IV. 451

Dinner Party (Brewer, G., 1794), III. 239

Dinners and Diners (Grain, R. C., 1891), v. 388

Dinorah (Chorley, H. F., 1859), v. 310, 783
— (Travers, W., 1860), v. 821
— = Little Devil's Share

Dinorah under Difficulties (Brough, W., 1859), v. 279

Dioclesian = Prophetess

Diogenes and his Lantern (Taylor, T., 1849), IV. 411; V. 592

Diogenes in Search of a Contented Man (Pitt, G. D., 1857), V. 668, 810

Dion (Rhodes, G. A., 1806), IV. 393, 608

Dione (Gay, J., 1720), II. 146, 225, 275, 331

— (1733), II. 370

— (1895), V. 668

— (1897), V. 668

Dionysius (1825), IV. 451

Diphilo and Granida (Kirkman, F., 1673), I. 418

Diplomacy (Scott, C. W. and Stephenson, B. C., 1878), V. 557

— (1836), IV. 451

Diplomacy = Dora and Diplunacy

Dirce (1821), IV. 451

Director (Greenbank, H., 1891), V. 392

Directors no Conjurors = Modern Poetasters

Dirty Dick (?Hazlewood, C. H., 1860), V. 668, 796, 831

— (Mildenhall, T., 1842), IV. 598

Disagreeable Surprise (Daniel, G., 1819), IV. 289

— (1798) ? = Saltimbanco, III. 324, 400

— — = Saltimbanco

Disappointed Authoress (Wilson, T., 1821), IV. 618

Disappointed Bachelor (Evans, 1812), IV. 583

Disappointed Country Lass = Livery Rake and Country Lass

Disappointed Coxcomb (1765), III. 324

Disappointed Gallant (Thomson, A., 1738), II. 360

Disappointed Marriage = Luckey Chance

Disappointed Villainy (Horde, T., 1775), III. 273

Disappointment (Randal, J., 1732), II. x, 351, 432

— (Southerne, T., 1684), I. 153–4, 240, 264, 350, 432–3

— — = Serenade

Disappointments (1810), IV. 451

Disaster (1779), III. 400

Disbanded Officer (Johnstone, J., 1786), III. 50, 61, 122, 277, 389

Discarded Daughter (Raymond, R. J., 1847), IV. 389

Discarded Secretary (Eyre, E. J., 1799), III. 259

Discarded Son (Webster, B. N., 1853), V. 618

Discharge your Tiger (1849), IV. 451

Discontented Man (1804), IV. 451

Discounting a Life (1844), IV. 451

Discovery (Sheridan, Mrs F., 1763), III. 139, 141, 305

— (1810), IV. 451

— = (1) Marciano; (2) Midnight

Discovery of Joseph (Hoole, J., 1800), III. 388

Discreet Princess (Planché, J. R., 1855), V. 527

— (1848), IV. 451

Disengaged (James, H., 1894), V. 433

Disestablishment (1886), V. 668

Disguis'd Lovers = Love's Metamorphosis

Disguise (Jodrell, R. P., 1787), III. 277

Disguised (1897), V. 668

Disguised Nobleman = Romance of a Poor Young Man

Disguises (Haworth, R., 1824), IV. 324

— (Webster, A., 1879), V. 823

— (1817), IV. 451

— = All-Plot

Dish of All Sorts (McLaren, A., 1806), IV. 351

Dish of the Auctioneer's Own Chocolate = Tit for Tat

Dishonourable Affair = Affair of Honour

Dishonour'd Bill = Wildfire Dick

Dishonoured (St John, A., 1896), V. 554

— (1895), V. 668

Dishonoured Bill = House Room

Dishonour's Due = Drummond

Disintegration of Bonaparte = Magic of British Liberty

Disinterested Friend = Patron

Disinterested Love (Hull, T., 1798), III. 113, 274

Disloyal Lover = He's Much to Blame

Dismal Squire = Plotting Lovers

Dismal Swamp = Dominique the Deserter

Disowned (Parry, T., 1851), V. 515

— = Conspiracy

Disputants (1780), III. 324

Disputed Marriage = Wings of Wealth

Disputed Title (1860), v. 668

— = Robert Richbourne

Disputes in China (1822), IV. 451

Dissembled Wanton (Welsted, L., 1726), II. 10, 173, 174, 233, 363

Dissipation (Andrews, M. P., 1781), III. 43, 52, 134, 233

Dissipation, Desperation and Starvation = Rope Ladder

Dissolving Views (Selby, C., 1844), IV. 399

Distant Cousins = On the Bench

Distinguished Connections (1897), v. 668

Distracted Bachelor (Hollingsworth, J., 1871), v. 798

Distraction (Bradley, C., 1885), v. 273

Distraining for Rent (1832), IV. 451

Distress'd Baronet (Stuart, C., 1787), III. 310

Distress'd Bride = Love and Duty

Distress'd Innocence (Settle, E., 1690), I. 101, 150, 429

— = Fatal Falshood

Distress'd Love = Polidus

Distress'd Princess = Rotherick O'Connor, King of Connaught

Distress'd Wife (?Colman, G., 1777), III. 324, 379, 400

— (Gay, J., 1734), II. 198, 332, 437

Distressed Beauty (1722), II. 370

Distressed Family (1787), III. 120, 227, 324

Distressed Knight (1791), III. 324

Distressed Ladies = Roman Generalls

Distressed Lovers = (1) Banished General; (2) Edwin and Catherine; (3) Fall of Tarquin; (4) Mad Tom of Bedlam; (5) Tempest

Distressed Peasants = Stolen Sheep

Distressed Princess = Thamas Kouli Kan, the Persian Hero

Distressed Virgin (Maxwell, J., 1761), II. 344; III. 287

Distress upon Distress (Stevens, G. A., 1752), III. 309

Distrest Lovers = Double Falshood

Distrest Mother (Philips, A., 1712), II. 57, 58, 59, 72, 86–7, 96, 106, 265, 348, 442

Diver and the Ocean Fiend = Fifty Years below the Sea

Diversions of the Morning (Foote, S., 1747, 1758), II. 329; III. 384

Diver's Luck (Cooke, F. and Waldron, W. R., 1887), v. 323

— (1892), v. 668

Divertisement (Cross, J. C., 1790), III. 249

Dives and Lazarus (?1682), I. 446

Dives's Doom (Lesley, G., 1684), I. 420

Divided Duty (Dauncey, S., 1885), v. 337

Divided Way (Esmond, H. V., 1895), v. 359

Divine Comedian = Souls Warfare

Diving Bell (1805), IV. 451

Divorce (Beazley, S., Jr., 1832), IV. 264

— (Bertin, W. 1859), v. 668, 778, 831

— (Daly, A., 1871), v. 333

— (Dubois, Lady D., 1771), III. 258

— (Jackman, I., 1781), III. 186, 276

— (R—d, G. M., 1810), IV. 624

— (Reece, R., 1881), v. 539

— (Towers, E., 1873), v. 601

— (1866), v. 668

Divorced (Rutter, R. P., 1898), v. 553

— (1852), v. 668

Djamileh (Bennett, J., 1892), v. 258, 778

Doating Lovers (Hamilton, N., 1715), II. 334

Dobbin's House (1883), v. 668

Dobson and Company (Coyne, J. S., 1842), IV. 284

Doctor (Burnand, F. C., 1887), v. 291

— (1891), v. 669

— (1897), v. 669

Doctor Ambrosias—his Secret (B., H., 1868), v. 669

Doctor and No Doctor (1828), IV. 451

Doctor and the Apothecary (Cobb, J., 1788), III. 244, 379

Doctor Bolus (Daniel, G., 1818), IV. 289, 579

— (1831), IV. 451

Doctor D. (Colnaghi, C. P., 1885), v. 318

Doctor Davy (Albery, J., Vezin H. and Wills, W. G., 1865) = How to Act, v. 237, 694, 777, 788

Doctor Deceived = Modern Pimp

Doctor Dilworth (Oxenford, J., 1839), IV. 367

Doctor Faustus (1662), I. 441

— = Life and Death of Doctor Faustus

Doctor Faustus and the Black Demon (1823), IV. 451

Doctor Hocus Pocus (Colman, G., 1814), IV. 282

Doctor in spite of himself (Dixon, G., 1877), V. 346

— (1871), V. 669

Doctor in the Dumps (1798), III. 400

Doctor Johnson (Trevor, L., 1896), V. 604

Doctor Last in his Chariot (Bickerstaffe, I. and Foote, S., 1769), III. 117, 237

Doctor Last's Examination (Foote, S., 1787) = Devil upon Two Sticks, III. 324, 400

Doctor Miracle (1882), V. 669

Doctor of Alcantara = Alcantara

Doctor of Music (1893), V. 669

Doctor Paddy (1884), V. 669

Doctor Poker (1816) = Each for Himself, IV. 451, 624

Doctor Porter (1887), V. 669

Doctor Sangrado (D'Egville, 1814), IV. 451, 624

Doctors Beware (1897), V. 669

Doctor's Boy (Grant, R., 1877), V. 388

Doctor's Brougham (Manuel, E., 1875), V. 475

Doctor's Dilemma (Ford, D. M., 1899), V. 370

— (1893), V. 669

Doctors of Dull-head College (Kirkman, F., 1662), I. 418

Doctor's Secret (1888), V. 669

Doctor's Shadow (Saintsbury, H. A., 1896), V. 554

Doctor's Story (Mills, A., 1894), V. 489

Doctor's Ward (Wilton, H., 1899), V. 629

Doctor Syntax and another Doctor (Dibdin, C. I. M., 1823), IV. 295

Doctor Syntax in London (1823), IV. 451

Doctor the Disease = Mother-in-Law

Doctor, the Miser and the Butcher = Opiate

Dodge for a Dinner (Palmer, T. A., 1872), V. 512

Dodges of Cupid (1863), V. 669

Does he love me? (Falconer, E., 1860), V. 121, 360

Dog and the Duck (Dibdin, T. J., 1816), IV. 300

Dog and the Shadow = Miss Michaelmass

Dog Days in Bond Street (Dimond, W., 1820), IV. 307

Dog Detectives (1879), V. 669

Doge of Duralto (Brough, R. B., 1857), V. 278

Doge of Venice (Bernard, W. B., 1867), V. 259

Doge's Daughter = Bianca Contarini

Dog Friend = Victor Hugh

Dog in the Manger = P.U.P.

Dog of Montargis (Barrymore, W., 1814) = Murder will out, IV. 82, 261, 508, 634

— (Dibdin, T. J., 1814), IV. 82, 299

Dog of the Convent (1831), IV. 451

Dog of the Desert = Avalanche

Dog of the Pyrenees (1845), IV. 451

Dog of the Quarry = Pride of Kildare

Dogs of Australia (1863), V. 669

Dogs of Loch Lomond = Dark Donald, the Idiot of the Cliff

Dogs of St Bernard (Scott, C. W., 1875), V. 557

Dogs of the Dark Blue Waters (1859), V. 831

Dogs of the Grange (James, C. S., 1850), V. 432

Dogs of the Revenue Cutter (1862), V. 669

Dogs of the Wreck = Cherokee Chief

Dogs of Tipple's Farm = Hoxton a Hundred Years Ago

Doing Banting (Brough, W. and Halliday, A., 1864), V. 279

Doing for the Best (Lacy, M. R., 1861), V. 446

Doing my Uncle (Lacy, M. R., 1866), V. 446

Doings in Bond Street (1842), IV. 624

Doings near Delgany = Mr Smith

Doing the "Hansome" (Harris, A. G., 1856), V. 405

Doing the Shah (Robinson, N., 1873), V. 547

Doldrum (O'Keeffe, J., 1796), III. 295

Dollars and Sense (Daly, A., 1883), v.
   333
Dolls (Norman, G. T., 1892), v. 505
Doll's House (Archer, W., 1889), v. 187,
   242
— (1892), v. 669
Dollusions (Muskerry, W., 1896), v. 501
Dolly (Bannister, J., 1890), v. 248
— (Clarke, H. S., 1892), v. 313
— (1860), v. 669, 831
Dolly and the Rat (Jerrold, D. W.,
   1823) = Brisket Family, IV. 331, 436,
   590
Dolly's Delusion = May
Dolly's Dilemma (Millward, H., 1887),
   v. 489
Dolly's Follies (1884), v. 669
Dolly Varden (Cympson, E., 1889), v.
   332
— (Wood, M., 1872), v. 631
Dolores (Lane, Mrs S., 1874), v. 448
Dolph Heyliger = Miser's Will
+ Dombey and Son (Brougham, J.)
   [Printed in *Dicks'* series and *French's
   American Drama*]
— (Sidney, W., 1849), IV. 611
— (Taylor, T. P., 1847), IV. 98, 411
Domenica (Ellerton, J. H., 1838), IV.
   309
Domenico the Vile 'un (Thomas, L.,
   1872), v. 596
Domestic Arrangements (1835), IV. 452
Domestic Bliss (1848), IV. 452
— (1869) v. 669
Domestic Diplomacy (Redmond, J.,
   1872), v. 537
Domestic Discipline (1855), v. 669
Domestic Economy (Burnand, F. C.,
   1890), v. 291
— (Lemon, M., 1849), IV. 345
Domestic Experiment = Mr and Mrs
   Muffett
Domestic Hercules (Becher, M., 1870),
   v. 254
Domestick Tyrant = Spirit of Contra-
   diction
Domestic Mash = Mashing Mamma
Domestic Medicine (Smith, L., 1887),
   v. 573
Domestic Tyrant = Temper
Dominicans (Wilson, R. K., 1894), v.
   628

Dominique (1831), IV. 452
Dominique the Deserter (Murray, W. H.,
   1833), IV. 365
— (1857), v. 669
— (1865), v. 669
Dominique the Possessed (Barnett,
   C. Z., 1831), IV. 259
Dominique, the Resolute (1831), IV. 452
Domino (Clarance, L., 1879), v. 310
Domino Noir (1848), IV. 83, 452
Domino of Death = Devilshoof
Domitian, the Roman Actor (1722), II.
   370
Don (Merivale, H. C. and Merivale,
   Mrs H., 1888), v. 487
— (1854), v. 669
Dona Constanza (Gollmick, A., 1875),
   v. 384
Donagh (Rowe, G. F., 1884), v. 552
Donagh's Romance (1883), v. 669
Dona Ignez de Castro (Adamson, J.,
   1808), IV. 251
Donald and Peggy (1812), IV. 452
Donald McClean, the Highland Robber
   (1820), IV. 452
Don Caesar de Bazan (À Beckett, G. A.
   and Lemon, M., 1844), IV. 250
— (Archer, T., 1844), IV. 254
— (Barnett, C. Z., 1844), IV. 260
— (Boucicault, D. and Webster, B.,
   1844), IV. 270
— (Saintsbury, H. A., 1899), v. 554
Don Carlos (Bruce, J. W., 1837), IV. 86,
   272
— (Cottrell, C. H., 1843), IV. 86, 283
— (Edwardes, C. T. M., 1869), v. 354
— (Noehden, G. H. and Stoddart, J.,
   1798), III. 62-3, 291, 392
— (Otway, T., 1676), I. 120, 348, 422
— (Russell, Lord J., 1822), IV. 86, 396
+ — (Symonds, J., 8°, 1898)
— (Thompson, B., 1798), III. 63, 311,
   397; IV. 86, 412
— (Towler, J., 1843), IV. 86, 414
— (1798), III. 62, 68, 324
Don Carlos, Prince of Spain (1734), II.
   370
Don Cossack in London (1814), IV. 452
— = Hyde Park in an Uproar
Done Brown (Craven, H. T., 1845), IV.
   285
Donellan (Innes, P. R., 1899), v. 432

Don Quixote in England (1752), III. 325

Don Quixote Junior (Goodman, J. C., and Howson, J., 1879), v. 384

Don Quixote, the Knight of the Wonderful Countenance (1833), IV. 452

Don Quixotte and his Man Sancho Panza (1831), IV. 452

Don Rafaelle (Campbell, A. V., 1845), IV. 278

Don Raymond (1797) = Raymond and Agnes, III. 325, 400

Don Roderic (O'Neil, J. R., 1852), v. 507

Don Sancho (Boyd, Mrs E., 1739), II. 67, 246–7, 299

Don Saverio (Arne, T. A., 1750), II. 236, 295; III. 199, 233

Don Sebastian (Dryden, J., 1689), I. 24, 68, 144–5, 149, 337, 352, 406; III. 58, 199

Don Sebastian, King of Portugal (1823), IV. 452

Don't be Frightened (Morton, J. M., 1839), IV. 452, 624

Don't deceive your Wife (Wilstach, P., 1897), v. 629

Don, the Duck, the Drake and the Invisible Armada = E-liz-abeth

Don't judge by appearances (Morton, J. M., 1855), v. 495

Don't Jump at Conclusions (1895), v. 669

Don't lend your Umbrella (Buckingham, L. S., 1857), v. 286

Don't Mind Me (1872), v. 669

Don't Swear (1853), v. 669

Don't Tell Her Husband (1895), v. 669

Don't you wish you may get it? (Mowbray, 1856), v. 669, 807, 831

Donzella's Oath (1854), v. 669

Doo, Brown and Co. (Rae, C. M., 1886), v. 532

Doom at Midnight = Halvei, the Unknown

Doom'd Child (1832), IV. 452

Doomed (Hodgson, A. H. and Hodgson, A. C., 1890), v. 423

Doomed at Last = Deeming

Doomed Bridge (1856), v. 669

Doomed, Drugged and Drowned at Datchet = Gentle Gertrude

Doomed Entombed = Curiosity

Doomed House (1839), IV. 452

Doomed Knight = Hag of the Storm

Doomed of Dyneley Chase = Will o' the Wisp

Doomed of the Fiend Ship = Black Buccaneer

Doomed One of the Hulk = Phantom Voice

Doomed Son = Black and Red Galleys

Doomed to Darkness (1876), v. 670

Doomed to die = Too late to save

Doomed to Siberia (1897), v. 670

Doomed to Slavery = Wrongs of Twenty Years

Doom Kiss (Pocock, I., 1832), IV. 385

— = Demon Knight

Doom Light (Townsend, W. T., 1845), IV. 414

Doom of Barostein = Ancestress

Doom of Devorgoil (Scott, Sir W., 1830), IV. 194, 397

Doom of Morana (Buckstone, J. B., 1836), IV. 275

Doom of the Daemon Knight = Walpurghi's Eve

Dora (Parker, W. S., 1893), v. 514

— (Reade, C., 1867), v. 536

Dora and Diplunacy (Burnand, F. C., 1878), v. 291

Dora Ingram (Murdoch, J. M., 1885), v. 499

Dora Mayfield (Newbound, E., 1878), v. 502

Dora O'Donovan (Pitt, G. D., 1850), v. 526

Dora's Device (Reece, R., 1871), v. 537

Dora's Dream (Cecil, A., 1873), v. 306

Dora's Love (Chamberlaine, C. W., 1872), v. 307

— (1873), v. 670

Dorastus and Fawnia (1703), II. 370

Dorcas (Paulton, H. and Paulton, E., 1898), v. 517

Do-Re-Mi-Fa (Taylor, J. G., 1873), v. 820

Dorias (Strettle, 1835), IV. 613

Doris (Stephenson, B. C. and Scott, C. W., 1889), v. 582

Dream of Fate (Barnett, C. Z., 1838), IV. 260

Dream of Life (Watts, W., 1849), IV. 417

— (1861), v. 670

— = Right and Wrong

Dream of Love (Oxenford, J., 1872), v. 510

Dream of Retribution = Paul Zegers

Dream of St Cloud (1797), III. 325

Dream of Scipio (Hoole, J., 1800), III. 387

— (Olivari, F., 1797), III. 295

Dream of the Future (Dance, C., 1837), IV. 288

Dream of the Irish Emigrant (1853), v. 670

Dream of the Past, Present and Future = Christmas Carol

Dream of the Reveller = Whiskey Dream

Dream of the White Boy (1868), v. 670

Dream of Venice = Francesca

Dream of Whitaker's Almanack (1899), v. 670

Dreams = My Lady Clara

Dreams of Delusion (Simpson, J. P., 1862), v. 567

Dreams of the Heart (Reynoldson, T. H., 1847), IV. 393

Dream Spectre (Wilks, T. E., 1843), IV. 421

Dred (Banks, W., 1872), v. 248

— (Phillips, F. L. and Colman, J., 1856), v. 522

— (Suter, W. E., 1856), v. 587, 819

— (1856), v. 670

— (1864), v. 670

— = Dominique the Deserter

Dred, a Tale of the Great Dismal Swamp (1856), v. 670

Dregs (Aveling, E. B., 1889), v. 246

Drenched and Dried (Kerr, J., 1820), IV. 338

Dresden China (Chapin, A. and Oliphant, E. H. C., 1892), v. 308

Dress Coat (Green, F. W., 1876), v. 390

Dress Rehearsal = Opera Buffers

Dr Faust and Miss Marguerite (Martin, R. J. and Hobday, E. A. P., 1885), v. 479

Dr Frankenstein and Hobgoblin of Hoxton = Humgumption

Drifted Apart (Young, Sir C. L., 1882), v. 636

Drifting Clouds (1894), v. 670

Drifting Spar (Gordon, S., 1893), v. 385

Drifting to Seaward = Storm Signal

Drink (Reade, C. and Warner, C., 1879), v. 536, 812

— = Man's Folly

Drink, Poverty and Crime = London Mechanic

Drip, drop, Drip drop (Young, Mrs H., 1863), v. 670, 831

Drive in June (Jones, H. A., 1879), v. 439

Drive Love out at the Door (Rochfort, 1815), IV. 452, 624

Driven from Home (Macdermott, G. H., 1871), v. 468

— (1884), v. 670

— = Fate

Driver and his Dog = Caravan

Dr Jekyll and Mr Hyde (Bandmann, D. E., 1888), v. 248

— (Sullivan, T. R., 1887), v. 586

— (1888), v. 669

Dromio the Drinker (1835), IV. 453

Drones Demolished = Bickerstaff's Unburied Dead

Drooping Flower = Deeds, not Words

Drooping Lily = Amy the Golden

Drop a Tear to her Memory = Richard and Betty

Drop by Drop (Walton, K. A., 1884), v. 612

Dropped In (Boyd, W., 1893), v. 272

Dropping Well of Gedar = Feodora

Dropping Well of Knaresborough = Charcoal Burner

Drop the Curtain (1849), IV. 453

Dross (Braddon, M. E., 1882), v. 273

Drover Boy (1848), IV. 624

Drover's Dog = Cattle-stealers of the Mountain

Drowned Crew = Carlmilham

Drowned for Love (1897), v. 670

Drowned Man's Legacy (Seaman, W., 1872), v. 559

Dr Palgrave (Bryce, L., 1894), v. 284

Dr Quisby (1888), v. 669

Dr Syntax (Creeman, C., 1895), v. 373

Dr Syntax (Planché, J. R., 1820), IV. 376, 604

Dr Syntax the Hypnotist (Busch, W., 1894), v. 294

Drudge, the Prince and the Plated Glass Slipper = Done-to-a-Cinderella

Druid (Capes, J. M., 1879), v. 302

— (Cromwell, T., 1832), IV. 286

— (1815), IV. 624

Druids (1774), III. 325

Druid's Curse = Owen Ivan King of Manko

Druids Elect (1899), v. 670

Druid's Oak (1851), v. 671

Drumclog (1871), v. 671

Drummed Out (1897), v. 671

Drummer (Addison, J., 1716), II. 11, 17, 27, 135, 183, 199, 295, 431

Drummer and the Babies = Military Nurse

Drummond (Poole, S. W., 1870), v. 811

Drum of the Olden Time = Watchmaker of Clerkenwell

Drunkard (Webster, B., the Younger, 1879), v. 618

— (1805), IV. 453

— (1890), v. 671

Drunkard Reclaim'd = Lottery Chance

Drunkard's Children (Johnstone, J. B., 1848), IV. 333

— (Reynoldson, T. H., 1848), IV. 393

— (Taylor, T. P., 1848), IV. 411

— (1848), IV. 453

— (1859), v. 671

— = Life

Drunkard's Doom (Pitt, G. D., 1832), IV. 372

— (1879), v. 671

— = Last Nail

Drunkard's Fate = Bottle Bane

Drunkard's Glass (Morton, T., Jr., 1845), IV. 364, 601

— (1860), v. 671

Drunkard's List (1872), v. 671

Drunkard's Progress = (1) Bottle and the Glass; (2) Our Bottle

Drunkard's Sin = Intemperance

Drunken Cobbler (1819), IV. 453

Drunken News-Writer (1771), III. 325

Drunken Recruit (1821), IV. 453

Drunken Swiss (1793), III. 325

Drury Lane and Park Lane (1879), v. 671

Dryad (1892), v. 671

D.S. = Jack Robinson and his Monkey

D.T. (Callender, E. R., 1879), v. 300

Dublin Adventure = Bashful Irishman

Dublin Bay (Robertson, T. W., 1869), v. 546

Dublin Boy = Andy Blake

Duc d'Olonne (Reynoldson, T. H., 1845), IV. 393, 608

Duchess de la Vaubaliere (Buckstone, J. B., 1837), IV. 275

Duchesse de Guise (1845), IV. 453

Duchesse de la Vallière (Lytton, Lord, 1837), IV. 80, 173, 349

Duchess Eleanour (Chorley, H. F., 1854), v. 310

Duchess of —! (Wilks, T. E., 1842), IV. 617

Duchess of Bayswater and Co. (Heathcote, A. M., 1888), v. 415

Duchess of Coolgardie (Leigh, E. and Clare, C., 1896), v. 454

Duchess of Dijon = French Maid

Duchess of Malfi (Horne, R. H., 1850), v. 426

+ Duchess of Mansfeldt (*French*)

Duchess of Ormond (Banim, J., 1836), IV. 258

Duchess of Padua (Wilde, O. F. O'F.W., 1883), v. 190, 622

Duchess or Nothing (Gordon, W., 1860), v. 385

Duck Hunting (Coyne, J. S., 1862), v. 328

Ducks and Green Pease (Lund, J., 1785), III. 283

Dude and the Dancing Girl (Steele, C. D. and Forward, C. W., 1893), v. 580

Dudley Castle in the Olden Time = King's Secret

Duel (O'Brien, W., 1772), III. 119, 291, 393

— (Peake, R. B., 1823) = My Two Nephews, IV. 369, 509, 603, 634

— (1837), IV. 453

— = Man in the Red Coat

Duel and the Valet = Mysteries of the Wall

Duel d'amour = Battle of Woman

Dumb Boy of Toulon = Ship Launch

Dumb Boy of Vienna = Theodore of Ritzberg

Dumb Brigand (Bernard, W. B., 1832), IV. 453, 624

Dumb Brother = Rock of Arpennaz

Dumb Cake (1787), III. 325

Dumb Carrier Boy and his Pony = Iron Hand

Dumb Conscript (Grattan, H. P., 1835), IV. 320

Dumb Driver (Blake, T. G., 1846), IV. 268

— (1849), IV. 453

Dumb Farce (Thurmond, J., 1719), II. 132, 253, 360

Dumb Girl of Genoa = Maid of Genoa

Dumb Girl of Portici = Masaniello

Dumb Girl of the Inn (1847), IV. 624

— = Mountain Bandit

Dumb Guide of the Tyrol (Blake, T. G., 1837), IV. 267

Dumb Henchman of the Isles = Ivan of the Mask

Dumb Lady (Lacy, J., ?1669), I. 40, 57, 188, 213, 418

Dumb Lady Cured = (1) Irish Doctor; (2) Mock Doctor

Dumb Man of Manchester = Factory Assassin

Dumb Minstrel Boy = Father's Curse

Dumb Norwegian and his Pony of Iceland (1842), IV. 453

Dumb Philosopher = Tipplers

Dumb Princess (Wilde, W. C. K., 1894), V. 623

Dumb Recruit (1840), IV. 453

Dumb Sailor (1854), V. 671

Dumb Sailor Boy = (1) Death Plank; (2) Inchcape Bell

Dumb Savoyard and his Monkey (Thompson, C. P., 1830), IV. 413

Dummerline Castle = Midnight Bell

Dun a Day (1823), IV. 453

Dunbar (Waddie, C., 1899), V. 610

Dundreary a Father (1866), V. 671

Dundreary by Special Train (1862), V. 671

Dundreary in Difficulties = My American Aunt

Dungeon of Death = Prisoner

Dunmow Festival = Spirit of the Haunted Room

Dunoir the Base (Dibdin, C. I. M., 1823), IV. 295

Dunois in the Dark = Giant

Dunstable Actor = Acting Run Mad

Dupe (Sheridan, Mrs F., 1763), III. 305

Dupes of Fancy (Carey, G. S., 1792), III. 242

Duplicate Keys = Prisoner of Lyons

Duplicity (Clift, R., 1871), V. 315

— (Holcroft, T. 1781), III. 134, 141, 270

— (Saker, M. E., 1883), V. 554

— (Turvey, G. F., ?1870), V. 822

— (1893), V. 671

Duprez (1843), IV. 453

Durazzo (Haynes, J., 1838), IV. 324

Durie in Durance = Willie Armstrong

During Her Majesty's Pleasure (Conquest, G. and Pettitt, H., 1877), V. 321

During Supper = Catchwork

During Temporary Sanity (1899), V. 671

During the Dance (Doone, N., 1889), V. 347

Duskie (Thompson, Mrs G. and Sinclair, K., 1893), V. 597

Dust (Grundy, S., 1881), V. 396

Dust in the Eyes (1879), V. 671

Dustman's Belle (Dance, C., 1846), IV. 289

Dustman's Treasure (1866), V. 671

Dutch Alliance (1759), III. 325

Dutch and Scotch Contention (1729), II. 370

Dutch Anna (1864), V. 671

Dutch Cruelties at Amboyna (1672), I. 405, 446

Dutch Girl's Troubles = Christine

Dutch Justice (Pleon, H., 1888), V. 183, 528

Dutch Law (1835), IV. 453

Dutch Lover (Behn, A., 1673), I. 24, 39, 140, 221, 222, 275, 347, 390

Dutch-Man (Bridges, T., 1775), III. 31, 240

Dutchman Outwitted (1746), II. 451

Dutchman's Dream (1835), IV. 453

Dutchmen Tricked (1784), III. 400

Dutch Pirate (1822), IV. 453

Dutch Tea Garden (1788), III. 325

Dutch the Diver (1878), V. 671

Dutiful Deception (1778), III. 325

Duty (Albery, J., 1879), v. 238
— (Bruce, H. P., 1889), v. 283
Duty and Honour = Fugitive
Dux Redux (Rhoades, J., 1887), v. 542
Dwarf (1832), IV. 453
— = Darby and Joan
Dwarf of Naples (Soane, G., 1819), IV. 403
D'ye know me now? (Braham, W. and Wellsey, N., 1872), v. 273
Dying Flower (Rogers, W., 1871), v. 814
Dying for a Kiss (1847), IV. 453
Dying for Love (Morton, J. M., 1858), v. 496
Dying Gift (Phillips, F. L., 1860) = Tramp's Adventure, v. 522, 671, 810, 831
— = (1) Gold Seekers; (2) Minerali
Dying to Live (1859), v. 671
Dyke House (Folkard, H., 1877), v. 370

Each for Himself (1816) = Doctor Poker, IV. 124–5, 453, 624
Each Man his Bird = First of September
Eagle and the Child (1856), v. 671
Eagle Joe (Herman, H., 1892), v. 419
Eagle's Cliff = Mabel Grey
Eagle's Flight = Man in the Moon
Eagle's Haunt (Fitzball, E., 1837), IV. 315
Eagle's Nest = (1) Dillosk Gatherer; (2) Eagle's Haunt
Eagle's Wing (Rimington, C., 1892), v. 543
Earl and the Baron = Bad Neighbours
Earl Goodwin (Yearsley, A., 1789), III. 317, 398
Earl Harold (1837), IV. 454
Earlier Days of Wallace = Marian
Earl of Brecon (Landor, R. E., 1841), IV. 199, 341
Earl of Douglas (1760), III. 325
Earl of Essex (Brooke, H., 1750), III. 85, 240
— (Jones, H., 1751), III. 18, 53, 84–5, 277
— = Unhappy Favourite
Earl of Essex, the Unhappy Favourite (1825), IV. 454
Earl of Gowrie (White, J., 1845), IV. 419
— = James VI

Earl of Leicester (Heath, S., 1843), IV. 324
Earl of Mar Marr'd (Philips, J., 1715), II. 262, 348, 442
Earl of Mulligatawny (Spurr, M. B. and Mayne, W., 1898), v. 577
Earl of Poverty (Almar, G., 1838), IV. 253
Earl of Ross (Munro, C. F., 1823), IV. 454, 624
Earl of Somerset (Lucas, H., 1779), III. 283
Earl of Warwick (Francklin, T., 1766), III. 61, 84, 261, 384
— (Hiffernan, P., 1764), III. 268, 387
— (Tolson, F., 1719), II. 360
Earl of Westmoreland (Brooke, H., 1742), II. 300 [At Smock Alley, Dublin, 13/5/1745, this was acted as "A New Play"]
Earl Olaf's Vow = White Pilgrim
Earl's Daughter (Russell, E. H., 1890), v. 553
Earl's Housekeeper (Seaman, W., 1872), v. 559
Earls of Hammersmith (Poole, J. and Lawler, D., 1811), IV. 386, 594
Earl's Son and the Citizen's Daughter = Curse of Mammon
Early Bird (1892), v. 671
Early Closing (Reach, A. B. and Hamilton, H., 1847), IV. 454, 624
Early Days of King Hal = King Hal's Early Days
Early Days of Richard III = Peerless Pool
Earnest Appeal (Hay, F., 1875), v. 411
Ear-ring (1872), v. 671
Earth, Air, Fire and Water (1848), IV. 454
Earthly Twins (Lewis, T. H., 1896), v. 459
Earthquake (Fitzball, E., 1828), IV. 313, 584
— (1828), IV. 454
Earthquake of Jamaica = Admiral Benbow
Easter Egg (Maynard, W., 1893), v. 483
Easter Fair (1830), IV. 454
Easter Hunting (1821), IV. 454
Easter Monday (1777), III. 325
— (1781), III. 325

Eastern Diplomacy = New Endimion

Eastern Fête = Bashaw

Eastern Treasure = Black and White

Easter Offering (1824), IV. 454

Easter Pastimes (1790), III. 325

East Indian (Lewis, M. G., 1799), III. 117, 122, 152, 281, 390

— (Thomson, A., 1799), III. 122, 312

— (1782), III. 325, 400

— (1812), IV. 454 [By error, this is wrongly equated with Rich and Poor in IV. 595 and 624]

East Lynne (Hardacre, J. P., 1898), V. 403

— (Oxenford, J., 1866), V. 510

— (Palmer, T. A., 1874), V. 148, 512

— (Paulton, J., 1889), V. 517

— (Shelley, H., 1899), V. 562

— (Wilde, L., 1898), V. 622

— (1866, 1869, 1870, 1875, 1883, 1884, 1893, 1896, 1899), V. 671

Eastward Ho = Black Cat

Eastward Hoe (1751), III. 325

Easy Shaving (Burnand, F. C. and Williams, M., 1863), V. 288

Ebb and Flow (Field, W. F., 1888), V. 366

Ebb and Flow of Fortune = High- and Low-Water Bell

Ebon Wand (1832), IV. 454

Ebony Casket (Speight, T. W., 1872), V. 576

Ebu Bekr (1840), IV. 624

Écarté (Newry, Lord, 1870), V. 503

— (1844), IV. 454

Eccentric Guardian (Zimmerman, H., 1885), V. 637

Eccentricities (1814), IV. 454

Eccentricity (McLaren, A., 1826), IV. 352

Eccentric Lover (Cumberland, R., 1798), III. 252

Eccentric Will (1899), V. 671

Echo (Heathcote, A. M., 1893), V. 415

Echo and Narcissus (Graves, R., 1776), III. 265

Echoes of the Night (Grattan, H. P. and Eldred, J., 1884), V. 389

Echoes of the Opera (Grain, R. C., 1893), V. 388

Echo of a Crime = Mighty Hand

Echo of Westminster Bridge (1835), IV. 454

Eclipse (Cross, J. C., 1801), IV. 286

Eclipsing the Son (Hartopp, W. W., 1860), V. 408

Edda (Fitzball, E., 1820), IV. 312

Eddication and Rights = Faith

Eddystone Elf = Monster of the Eddystone

Edelweiss (Broughton, F. W., 1893), V. 282

Edendale (Cheltnam, C. S., 1869), V. 102, 309

Edgar (Hallam, H., 1834), IV. 454, 624

— (Manners, G., 1806), IV. 353

— (Rymer, T., 1877), I. 142, 427

Edgar and Effie (1819), IV. 454

Edgar and Elfrida (Powell, T., ?1792), III. 394

Edgar and Emmeline (Hawkesworth, J., 1761), III. 267

Edgar Harissue (Malcolm, C. H. and Grahame, A., 1898), V. 472

Edgar the Socialist (Bonawitz, J. H., 1892), V. 267

Edict of Charlemagne = Free Knights

Edict of Spain (1859), V. 671

Edict of the Secret Council (Rayner, B. F., 1845), IV. 389

Edinburga (Buchanan, R., 1868), V. 284

Edith (Sidney, W., 1870), V. 566

Editha (Downman, H., 1784), III. 83, 257

Editha's Burglar (Burnett, Mrs F. H. and Townsend, S., 1890), V. 292

— (Clery, E., 1887), V. 313

Edith Lester the Wronged = Old Finsbury

Edith of the Marsh (Blake, T. G., 1840), IV. 268, 573

Edith's Flight (1875), V. 671

Edith the Captive (Towers, E., 1861), V. 671, 821

Edith West (1875), V. 671

Edmond, Orphan of the Castle (1799), III. 72, 325

Edmund Atherton (1853), V. 671

Edmund Kean (Pemberton, T. E., 1895), V. 519

— (Tamplin, H., 1893), V. 590

— (1864), V. 671

— (1871) V. 671

Edmund, surnamed Ironside (West, Mrs J., 1791), III. 315

Edric the Forester (Cross, T., 1842), IV. 578

Education (Morton, T., 1813), IV. 184, 363

Education of Achilles = Achille et Deidamia

Edward I (Macpherson, J., 1845), IV. 352

Edward II (1809), IV. 454

Edward III (Blake, W., 1783), III. 238
— (1814), IV. 454

Edward VI (Barnard, E., 1757), III. 235

Edward and Caroline = Dead Alive

Edward and Egwina (1776), III. 325

Edward and Eleonora (Hull, T., 1775), III. 86, 274
— (Thomson, J., 1739), II. 23, 93, 360, 445

Edward and Susan (Dibdin, C. I. M., 1803), IV. 291

Edward the Black Prince (Fenton, C., 1854), V. 365, 672
— (Hoper, Mrs, 1747), II. 337
— (Macfarren, G., 1822), IV. 349
— (Reynolds, F., 1828), IV. 392
— (Shirley, W., 1749), II. 70, 71, 113, 355, 414, 444; III. 306
— (1805, 1807), IV. 454
— (1860), V. 672

Edwin (Fitzball, E., 1817), IV. 312
— (Jeffreys, G., 1724), II. 48, 62, 116, 338
— (1822), IV. 454

Edwin and Angelina (Walford, H. L., 1871), V. 611

Edwin and Catherine (Scott, T., 1793), III. 304

Edwin and Emma (Long, C., 1847), IV. 347

Edwin and Ethelburga (Wyon, F. W., 1860), V. 634

Edwin and Morcar (1838), IV. 624

Edwin and Rosalie = Maid of the Glen

Edwin, Heir of Cressingham = Edwin

Edwin of the Green (1807), IV. 454

Edwin, the Banished Prince (Douglas, 1784), III. 257

Edwin the Fair (Taylor, H., 1845), IV. 410

Edwy (Warwick, T., 1784), III. 315

Edwy and Elgiva (D'Arblay, F., 1795), III. 253

Effects of a West India Ramble = Mistress Doggrell in her Altitudes

Effects of Drink = (1) Assommoir; (2) Nation's Curse

Effects of Passion = Tempter

Effie and Jeanie Deans (Hamilton, G., 1877), V. 401

Effie Deans (1863), V. 672
— (1865), V. 672

Effie's Angel (1871), V. 672

Egbert (Dibdin, C. I. M., 1815), IV. 293

Egmont (1848), IV. 454

Egoist (Bennett, H. L., 1895), V. 258

Egrirophadron (1815), IV. 454

Egyptian (Wilkins, J. H., 1853), V. 623

Egyptian Babies (1881), v. 672

Egyptian Beauty = Wizard of the Nile

Egyptian Boy (1802), IV. 454

Egyptian Festival (Franklin, A., 1800), III. 261; IV. 318

Egyptian Idol (Saunders, R. and Bandmann, M., 1895), v. 556
— = Raphael's Dream

Egyptian Laurels (Dibdin, C. I. M., 1801), IV. 290

Egyptian Oracle (1804), IV. 454

Egyptian War (Stanhope, B., 1882), v. 578

Egyptorica (1879), v. 672

Egypt Three Thousand Years Ago (Rogers, W., 1854), v. 672, 831

Eider-down Quilt (Wotton, T. S., 1896), v. 632
— (1894), v. 672

Eigenwillig (1870), v. 831

Eighteen Carat Soup = Prince Sohobazar

1870 (Vye, B., 1896), v. 609
— (1870), v. 672
— (1884), v. 672

1874 (Elphinstone, J., 1874), v. 358

1863 (Byron, H. J., 1863), v. 110, 117, 296

1803 = Doldrum

Eighteen Years in One Hour (Layton, G. M., 1875), v. 451

Eight Hours at the Seaside (Sawyer, W., 1857), v. 557 [A play of this title is credited by French to J. M. Morton]

Eighth Wonder of the World (1855), v. 672

Eight Miles an Hour = Hooking Walker

Eight Pages (1859), v. 672

"£8. 10. 1, if Quite Convenient" (1823), IV. 454

Eighty Years of a Woman's Life = Phoebe Hersel

Eileen Dhu (Gordon, W., 1882), v. 385

Eileen Oge (Falconer, E., 1871), v. 360

Eily O'Connor (Haines, J. T., 1831), IV. 322

— (Wilks, T. E., 1860), v. 623, 823

Eily the Banshee (1835), IV. 454

Eitha and Aidallo (1801), IV. 454

Elaine (Keith, R., 1890), v. 442

Elbow Shakers (Cooper, F. F., 1827), IV. 283

Elder Brother (Anderson, J. R., 1850) v. 777

— (1844), IV. 454

Elder Brutus = Sybil

Elder Miss Blossom (Hendrie, E. and Wood, M., 1897), v. 417

Elders (Man, H., 1780), III. 286

Eldorado (Farnie, H. B., 1874), v. 361

Eldred (Jackson, J., 1773), III. 86, 276

Eleanor's Victory (Johnstone, J. B., 1864), v. 672, 831

— (Oxenford, J., 1865), v. 510

Eleanor the Accursed = Giant's Tomb

Eleanor the Amazon (Rodwell, G. H., 1851), v. 548

Election (Andrews, M. P., 1774), III. 204, 233

— (Baillie, J., 1817), IV. 208, 258

— (Cumberland, R., 1778), III. 251, 381

— (Dibdin, C. I. M., 1826), IV. 296

— (1749), II. 370

— (1784), III. 325

— (1790), III. 325

— (1803), IV. 454

— (1813), IV. 454

— (1818), IV. 454

— = Pasquin

Election at Rottenburgh = Nomination Day

Electioneering (Moncrieff, W. T. 1830), IV. 454, 624

Election Notes (Grain, R. C., 1885), v. 387

Election of the Managers (Colman, G., 1784), III. 247

Election under Difficulties (1865), v. 672

Electra (Francklin, T., 1774), III. 71, 261

— (Shirley, W., 1765), III. 71, 306

— (Theobald, L., 1714), II. 359, 444

— (1714), II. 370, 447

Electra, in a New Electric Light (Talfourd, F., 1859), v. 590

Electric Spark (Bessle, E., 1889), v. 260

— (Pidgin, C. and Blake, C., 1884), v. 524

Electric Telegraph (Somerset, C. A., 1853), v. 574

Electrophobia (Dixon, H. J., 1898), v. 346

Elements (Dibdin, C. I. M., 1818), IV. 294, 454, 580

Elements—Earth, Air, Fire, Water (1837), IV. 455

Elena Uberti (1842), IV. 455

Elephant of Siam (Beazley, S., Jr., 1829), IV. 264

— (1829), IV. 455

Elephants of the Pagoda (1846), IV. 455

— = Rajah of Nagpore

El Escribano (1897), v. 672

Eleven Knots an Hour = Outside Passenger

Eleventh Commandment (Castleton, R., 1899), v. 306

Eleventh Day (1835), IV. 455

Eleventh Hour (Mildenhall, T., 1844), IV. 455, 624

— (Raymond, R. J., 1826), IV. 455, 624

— (Saintsbury, H. A. and Macdonald, R., 1896), v. 554

Eleventh of June (O'Keeffe, J., 1798), III. 295

Elfiana (Simpson, K., 1895), v. 568

Elfie (Boucicault, D., 1871), v. 269

Elfies' Son (1832), IV. 455

Elfinella (Neil, R., 1875), v. 501

Elfin Queen (1835), IV. 455

Elfins of the Ice (1836), IV. 455

Elfin Sprite (1833), IV. 455

Elfin Sprite of the Norwegian Seas = Lord of the Maelstrom

Elfin Tree (Wray, P., 1875), v. 633

Elf-King's Oath = Oberon

Elf of the Flame = Fire Fiend

Elfrid (Dibdin, T. J., 1822), IV. 303, 455, 580, 624

Elfrid (Hill, A., 1710), II. 53, 108-9, 335, 438

Elfrida (Mason, W., 1752, 1772), III. 286
— (1808), IV. 455
— (1834), IV. 455

Elfrida of Olmutz (Dibdin, C. I. M., 1825), IV. 295

El Gambusino (1856), v. 672

El Heyder, the Chief of the Mountains (1857), v. 672

El Hyder (1836), IV. 455

El Hyder, the Chief of the Ghaut Mountains (Barrymore, W., 1818), IV. 262

Eliduke, Count of Yeoloc (Roscoe, W. C., 1846), IV. 609

Elie and Elode (1854), v. 672

Eligible Bachelor (1871), v. 672

Eligible Villa (1869), v. 672, 831

Elijah (Dupuis, T. S., 1789), III. 354, 383

Elise (1862), v. 672

Elisha (Hull, T., 1801), IV. 589

Elisina (Klanert, C. M., 1824), IV. 338

Elisir d'amore (1836), IV. 455

Elixir of Life (Conquest, G., 1873), v. 321
— (Phillips, F. L., 1846), IV. 372
— (1870), v. 672

Elixir of Love (Reynoldson, T. H., 1839), IV. 393, 608
— = Adina

Elixir of Youth (Sims, G. R. and Merrick, L., 1899), v. 570

Eliza (Rolt, R., 1754), III. 303

Eliza and Uncle Tom = Uncle Tom

Elizabeth (1824), IV. 624
— (1828), IV. 455

E-liz-abeth (Burnand, F. C., 1870), v. 289

Elizabeth and Essex (Dibdin, T. J., 1821), IV. 94, 303

Elizabeth Lazarus (Haines, J. T., 1842), IV. 323

Elizabeth of England (Rayner, B. F., 1846), IV. 389

Elizabeth, Queen of England (Williams, T., 1882), v. 625
— (1869), v. 672

Elizabeth Storey (Davis, S., 1868), v. 339

Eliza Fenning (1857), v. 672

Eliza Fenning, the Victim of Circumstances (1855), v. 672

Eliza Holmes (Neale, F., 1845), IV. 365
— (1862), v. 672

Ellaline (1890), v. 672

Ella Rosenberg (Kenney, J., 1807), IV. 117-18, 336

Ella's Love = Midnight Mail

Ellen (Sotheby, W., 1816), IV. 405
— (Wills, W. G., 1879), v. 627

Ellen and Alberto (1812), IV. 455

Ellen and Susan (Pitt, G. D., 1845), IV. 373
— (1863), v. 672

Ellen Mavourneen (Pitt, G. D., 1845), IV. 373

Ellen Porter (Marchant, F., 1864), v. 475

Ellen Ray (1833), IV. 455

Ellen the Bride of Young Lochinvar = Galloping Lover

Ellen Trent (1840), IV. 624

Ellen Wareham (Buckstone, J. B., 1833), IV. 274
— (Burton, W. E., 1834), IV. 277

Ellie Brandon (Price, M., 1868), v. 531

Ellie Forester (Johnstone, J. B., 1857), v. 672, 800, 831

Ellinda (Robertson, Mrs, 1800), III. 302; IV. 394

El Mahdi (1885), v. 672

Elmerick (Lillo, G., 1740), II. 41, 111-12, 342, 440

Elmine (Jones, A. C., 1883), v. 439

Elmira (Stanley, E., 1790), III. 308
— (1781), III. 325

Elmira, the Female Pirate (1865), v. 672

Elodie, the Virgin of the Monastery = Angel of Peace and Pardon

Eloisa (Reynolds, F., 1786), III. 11, 120, 301

Eloise (1839), IV. 455

Eloped = Babes in the Wood

Elopement (Havard, W., 1763), II. 334; III. 267
— (Jones, H. A., 1879), v. 162, 439
— (McLaren, A., 1811), IV. 351
— (1768), III. 325
— (1784), III. 326
— (1826), IV. 455
— = Amateurs and Actors

Elopement Extraordinary (1814), IV. 455

Elopement from the Seraglio = Belmont and Constance

Elopements in High Life (Sullivan R., 1853), v. 586

Elopement to Rheims = Five Minutes too Late

Eloquence of Silence (1899), v. 672

Elphi Bey (Hamilton, R., 1817), IV. 323

Elsa Dene (Calmour, A. C., 1886), v. 300

Elsa's Hand (May, V., 1893), v. 482

Elsa's Lover: an Idyll of Rheingau (1892), v. 672

Elsdale Hall (Oswin, C. H., 1842), IV. 456, 602, 624 [cited wrongly as Esdale Hall]

Elshie (Gott, H., 1823), IV. 455, 585, 624

Elshie of the Moor = Recluse

Elsie (Broughton, F. W., 1883), v. 281

Elsie Glendinning (Haines, J. T., 1825), IV. 586

Elsie's Rival (Greet, D. A., 1888), v. 393

El Toreador (1855), v. 672

Elves (Selby, C., 1856), v. 560

Elvira (Digby, G., 1662–5), I. 192, 402–3; II. 142; III. 114

— (Mallet, D., 1762), II. 343; III. 286

Elwina (Fitzgerald, M., 1792), III. 259

Elysium (1789), III. 326

Embaras des Richesses (Ozell, J., 1735), II. 347, 442

Embarcation (Franklin, A., 1799), III. 261

Embarcation for Holland = Orange Boven

Embarassed Husband (1785), III. 326

Embarrassed Man (1863), v. 672

Embassy (Planché, J. R. 1841) IV. 381

Emblematical Tribute in Honour of Her Majesty's Nuptials (Macfarren, G., 1840), IV. 350

Emerald Isle (1861), v. 672

Emerald Queen (Travers, W., 1870), v. 603

Emigrant Family (1864), v. 672

Emigrant in London (1795), III. 326

Emigrant Murderer = Martin Rivers

Emigrant Prevented = Live and Hope

Emigrants = Adelaide

Emigrant's Daughter (Raymond, R. J., 1838), IV. 389

Emigrant's Progress (1852), v. 672

Emigrants, the Smuggler and the Bushranger = Life of a Labourer

Emigration (Connor, B., 1880), v. 320

— (O'Grady, H., 1883), v. 506

— (1835), IV. 455, 624

— (1836), IV. 455

— (1855), v. 672

Emigration—the Remedy (Stocqueler, J. H., 1848), IV. 455, 624

Emigré's Daughter (1850), v. 672

Emilia (Meilan, M. A., 1771), III. 287

— (1672), I. 441

Emilia Galotti (Holcroft, F., 1805), IV. 326

— (Maty, H., 1786), III. 64, 286

— (Thompson, B., 1800), IV. 412

— (1794), III. 64, 326

Emilie de la Roche (1834), IV. 455

Emily (D'Egville, 1807), IV. 455, 624

— (Hamilton, G., 1877), v. 80, 401

Emily Fitzormond (Denvil, Mrs, 1841), IV. 579

Emir's Edict = Ebu Bekr

Emissary (Dance, G., 1831), IV. 455, 624

Em'ly (1884), v. 672

Emma (Richards, G., 1804), IV. 394

— (1893), v. 672

Emma Hardy (1851), v. 672

Emma the Prude! Ellen the Romp! Eliza the Idiot! = Tria juncta in uno

Emma von Falkenstein = Crusaders

Emma Wingrove (1844), IV. 455

Emmeline (Suter, W. E., 1861), v. 673, 818, 831

— (1816), v. 445

Emmeline of Hungary (Dibdin, T. J., 1826), IV. 304

Emmeline the Female Parricide = Love and Error

Emperor and Galilean (Ray, C., 1876), v. 812

Emperor and his Three Sons = Chinese Sorcerer

Emperor and the Exile = Joseph II

Emperor and the Exiles (1857), v. 673

Emperor and the Page = Night after the Battle

Emperor and the Soldier = Napoleon

Emperor of China Grand Volgi (Chetwood, W., 1731), II. 306

Enchanted Ring (1836), IV. 456

Enchanted Spell = Mountain Cataract

Enchanted Standard = Alfred the Great

Enchanted Tower (Selby, C., 1848), IV. 399

Enchanted Veil = Fairy Lake

Enchanted Wives (Rice, C., 1853), V. 542

Enchanted Wood (Byron, H. J., 1870), V. 297

— (Francis, 1792), III. 261, 384

— (1785), III. 384

Enchanted Woodman = Fays of the Forest

Enchanter (Garrick, D., 1760), III. 262

— (1828), IV. 456

Enchanter of Stonehenge = Merlin

Enchanters (1806), IV. 456

Enchanter's Slave (Knowles, J., 1850), V. 446

Enchantment (Law, A., 1878), V. 449

— (1812), IV. 140, 456

Enchantress (Bunn, A., 1845), IV. 276, 575

— (Edwards, A. M., 1783), III. 258

Encounter (Kirkman, F., 1662), I. 417

Encounter and Carousal of the Wild Indian (1854), V. 673

End of a Day (Burnett, H., 1891), V. 292

End of June (1846), IV. 456

End of the Tether (Baddeley, G. C.), V. 247

'Endon Way (Brand, O. and Calvert, C., 1898), V. 274

Endora (1871), V. 673

End will come = Step by Step

Endymion (Brough, W., 1860), V. 279

— (1881), V. 673

Enemies (Coghlan, C. F., 1886), V. 316

Enemy (Neville, H., 1879), V. 502

Enemy Note Book (1857), V. 673

Enemy of Man (1899), V. 673

Enemy of the People (Archer, W., 1890), V. 61, 242

Enemy's Camp (Leonard, H., 1894), V. 456

Energy and Force of Love = Beautiful Armenia

Enfant prodigue (1815), IV. 456

Engaged (Gilbert, W. S., 1877), V. 140–1, 380

Engaged to Appear (1879), V. 673

Engagement (Stephenson, B. C., 1890), V. 582

Engelbert (Barnes, J., 1680?), I. 389

Engineer (Bolton, C., 1863), V. 673, 779, 831

Engineering (Matthison, A., 1878), V. 481

England against Italy (1787), III. 326

England and Australia = Give a Dog a Bad Name

England and France in the Days of Chivalry (Stocqueler, J. H., 1855), V. 585

England and Glory (Grafton, S., 1888), V. 386

England expects every Man to do his Duty = Rule Britannia

England Ho! (1878), V. 673

England, Home and Beauty (Bracewell, J., 1882), V. 272

England in 1450 = Sanctuary

England in the Days of Charles II (Wills, W. G., 1877), V. 627

England Invaded = Alfred the Great

England Preserved (Watson, G., 1795), III. 87, 315, 397

England run mad; with particulars of the Stratford Jubilee = Garrick's Vagary

England's Ally = Ransom of Manilla

England's Charter (Barnett, C. Z., 1848), IV. 261

England's Dark Ages = Tower of London

England's Darling (Austin, A., 1896), V. 245

England's Defenders (1895), V. 673

England's Flag (Whyte, H., 1895), V. 621

England's Glory (1706), II. 370

— (1795), III. 326

— (1797), III. 326

— (1894), V. 673

England's Golden Days = Kenilworth

England's Harvest Home and National Steeplechase (1856), V. 673

England's Joy (1795), III. 326

England's King (1827), IV. 456

England's Monarch (1843), IV. 456

England's Pride = Firm as Oak

England's Pride and Glory = Engineer

England, the Anchor and Hope of the World (1828), IV. 456

England, the Home of the Free (Campbell, A., 1874), V. 783

England the Land of Freedom = Dulce Domum

English at Paris (1821), IV. 456

English Born and Scottish Bred (1889), V. 673

English Britons (1763), III. 326

English Chevalier = Coquet

English Etiquette (Oxenford, J., 1840), IV. 367

English Fleet, in 1342 (Dibdin, T. J., 1803), IV. 142, 297

English Frier (Crowne, J., 1690), I. 10, 271, 400

English Gentleman (Byron, H. J., 1870), V. 297

English Hawks and Irish Pigeons (1860), V. 673

English Hearts (Hall, M. and Green, H. 1892), V. 399

English Hearts and Homes = Sons of Toil

English Hermit = Philip Quarll

English Hero and the American Boy = Champion of the World

English in Algeria = Britons Abroad

English, Irish and Scotch = Tricks and Blunders

English King = Harold

English Lawyer (Ravenscroft, E., 1677), I. 255, 426

— = Ignoramus

Englishman from Paris (Murphy, A., 1756), III. 180, 289

Englishman in Germany (1792), III. 326

Englishman in Paris (Foote, S., 1753), III. 172, 259, 383

Englishman in Spain = Hebrew Family

Englishman out of Paris = Reapers

Englishman returned from Paris (Foote, S., 1756), III. 115, 172, 259

Englishman's Fireside = John Bull

Englishman's House is his Castle (Morton, J. M., 1857), V. 496

Englishmen Abroad = Golden Fruit

Englishmen in Bordeaux (1764), III. 326, 400

Englishmen in Corsica = Conscript's Bride

Englishmen in India (Dimond, W., 1827), IV. 307

English Merchant (Colman, G., 1767), III. 12, 119, 140–1, 145, 246, 379

English Monarch = Edgar

English Monsieur (Howard, J., 1663). I. 215, 232, 344, 414

English Nihilist (1883), V. 673

— (1887), V. 673

English Plum-Pudding (1824), IV. 456

English Prince = Edward the Black Prince

English Princess (Caryll, J., 1667), I. 55, 116, 346, 395

English Readings (Cobb, J., 1787), III. 244

English Rogue (Thomson, T., 1668), I. 435

English Rose (Sims, G. R. and Buchanan, R., 1890), V. 569

English Sailors in America (1760), III. 326

English Stage Italianiz'd = Dido and Æneas

English Tar and the Indian Princess = Poccahontas

English Tavern at Berlin (1789), III. 326

English Violet = Mighty Hand

English Volunteer = Courage Rewarded

Englishwoman (Miller, St A., 1894), V. 488

Enjoyment (Selby, C., 1841), IV. 456, 624

Enlisted (1885), V. 673

— (1892), V. 673

— = Chain Gang

Enlisted Shepherds (Hawkins W., 1786), III. 267

Enoch Arden (Matthison, A., 1876), V. 481

Enquire Within (Boucicault, D., 1845), IV. 270

— (Burnand, F. C., 1868), V. 289

Enraged Musician (Colman, G., 1789) = Ut Pictura Poesis, III. 326, 379, 400

— (Raymond, R. J., 1828), IV. 456, 624

En Route (Grain, R. C., 1882), V. 387

— = Bombay to Henley

Ensign (Thompson, B., 1800), III. 122; IV. 412

Ensign of Freedom = Senekos the Greek

Ensnared (Frith, W., 1883), V. 373

En-tail and Ren-tail = Law's Two Tails

Entertainment of His Most Excellent Majestie (Ogilby, J., 1662), I. 422

Enthusiasm (Baillie, J., 1836), IV. 258

Enthusiast (Brougham, J., 1842), IV. 272

— (Lowe, W., 1884), V. 464

— (1892), V. 673

Entrances and Exits (Spencer, G., 1868), V. 576

Entrapped (Newbound, E., 1880), V. 502

Envious Statesman (1732), II. 370

Envoi (1890), V. 673

En Voyage (Coen, L., 1883), V. 316

Envoy who stole the King's Daughter = Princess Springtime

Eola (Rice, C., 1853), V. 542

Epaulette (1825), IV. 456

Ephesian Duke (1743), II. 140, 370

Ephesian Matron (Bickerstaffe, I., 1769), III. 199, 237, 378

— (Johnson, C., 1732), II. 340

Epicharis (Lister, T. H., 1829), IV. 346

Epicoene (Colman, G., 1776), III. 112, 246

Epidicus (Echard, E., 1693), I. 410

Episode (Stewart, K., 1895), V. 584

Episode of Eva (1857), V. 673

Episodic Sketch (1885), V. 673

Épouse persane (1810), IV. 456

Epoux de Tempe (1793), III. 326

Epponina (Carr, J., 1765), III. 242

Épreuve réciproque = Amintas et Sylvie

Epsom Downs (1818), IV. 456

Epsom-Wells (Shadwell, T., 1672), I. 2, 66, 67, 75, 205, 347, 348, 350, 430; III. 114

Equestrian Tuition = Hops without Malt

Equality Jack (Poel, W., 1891), V. 529

Equall Match (Kirkman, F., 1662), I. 417

Equal Match (1861), V. 673

Equals (Rose, E., 1883), V. 550

Equipage of Lovers = (1) Fine Lady's Airs; (2) Widow's Wish

Equivocal Appearances = Reformation

Eric of the Hills = War with the Waves

Eric's Good Angel (Bird, F. and Crofton, C., 1894), V. 261

Erin Delivered = Fingal

Erin-go-Brach (Hazlewood, C. H., 1870), V. 414

Erin-go-Brach (Travis, W. J., 1873), V. 603

— (1871), V. 673

Erl King's Daughter (Cleaver, M., 1851), V. 314

Ermingarde (Brodie-Innes, J. W., 1891), V. 276

Erminia (Flecknoe, R., 1661), I. 411

Erminie (Bellamy, C. and Paulton, H., 1885), V. 256

Ermyngarde in Fairyland = Ermingarde

Ernani (Brough, W., 1865), V. 280

— (1851), V. 673

Ernestine (Robertson, T. W., 1846), V. 546, 814 [This play is entered also under T. H. Reynoldson, IV. 393; but it appears to have been by Robertson]

— (1840), IV. 456

Ernestine and Georgette (Long, C., 1846), IV. 346

Ernest Maltravers (Medina, R., 1874), V. 483

Ernest Mountjoy (Stuart-Wortley, Lady Emmeline, 1844), IV. 613

Erotometer (1896), V. 673

Erratic Evangeline (1884), V. 673

Erring Sister (Kilpatrick, J. A., 1892), V. 444

Erroneous Fortune-tellers (1810), IV. 456

Error = Eva

Errore di Solomone (1744), II. 393

Errors and Repentance of Mr Ralfus Stucko = Newcastle in an Uproar

Errors Excepted (Dibdin, T. J., 1807), IV. 298

Errors of a Night = Which is the Uncle? + Errors of Ecstasie (Darley, G., 8°, 1822)

Escape (1798), III. 326

Escaped (Travers, W., 1870), V. 603

Escaped from Brixton = Two Gallows Slaves

Escaped from Portland (1869), V. 673

— = Black Flag

Escape from France = British Fortitude and Hibernian Friendship

Escape from Loch Leven = Mary, Queen of Scots

Escape into Prison (Cross, J. C., 1797) = Hue and Cry, III. 250, 380

Escape of Harlequin (1797), III. 326

Escape of Latude (1835), IV. 456
— = Horrors of the Bastile
Escapes (Holcroft, T., 1801), IV. 297,
326, 580, 588
Escapes of Harlequin = Tipplers
Escapes of Harlequin by Sea and Land
(Thurmond, J., 1722), II. 360
Escape upon the Common = Comic
Robbers
Escarte (1870), V. 673
Esmeralda (Barnett, C. Z.), IV. 570
— (Byron, H. J., 1861), V. 296
— (Fitzball, E., 1834), IV. 314
— (Randegger, A. and Marzials, T.,
1883), V. 806
— (Smith, A. R., 1850), V. 572
— (1879), V. 673
— (1883), V. 673
— = Young Folks' Ways
Esmerelda (Jeffereys, C., 1856), V. 435,
800
Esmond (Wills, W. G., 1893), V. 628
Esmonds of Virginia (Cazauran, A. R.,
1886), V. 306
Esop (1778), III. 115, 326
Esop in the Shades = Lethe
Esperance (1859), V. 673
Esperance, the French Foundling =
Child of Chance
Esperanza (Conquest, G., 1864), V. 674,
831
Essex Rover (1831), IV. 456
Estella (Cohen, J., 1880), V. 316
Estelle (1829), IV. 456
— (1835), IV. 456
— (1870), V. 674
Estelle Dumas (1842), IV. 457
Esther (Brereton, N., 1715), II. 299,
432
— (Humphreys, S., 1732), II. 393, 439
— = Life of King Ahasuerus
Esther Sandrez (Grundy, S., 1889), V.
397
Esther, the Royal Jewess (Polack, E.,
1835), IV. 385
Estranged (Williamson, H. W., 1881),
V. 626
Estrella (Parke, W., 1883), V. 512
Etchings and Sketchings (1836), IV. 457
Etearco (1711), II. 32, 35, 229–30, 393
Etelka (1899), V. 674
Eternal Justice = Hard as Iron

Eternal Masculine (Newte, H. C. W.,
1898), V. 503
Ethel (Webster, B., the Younger, 1866),
V. 618
Etheldrida Princess of Norwich (1837),
IV. 457
Ethelinda (West, M., 1769), III. 315
Ethelred (Richardson, S., 1810), IV. 394
Ethelreda (Poole, R., 1829), IV. 606
Ethel's Revenge (Stephens, W., 1876),
V. 581
Ethelstan (Darley, G., 1841), IV. 289
Ethel's Test (Williamson, H. W., 1883),
V. 626
Ethelwolf (Rennie, J. F., 1821, 1827), IV.
457, 607, 624
Ethiop (Dibdin, C. I. M., 1801), IV. 290
Ethiop's Revenge = Nitocris
Ethwald (Baillie, J., 1802), IV. 158–9,
258
Etiquette (Howells, C. E., 1880), V. 429
— (Power, T., 1836), IV. 387
Etiquette Run Mad (Power, T., 1830),
V. 457, 624
Étoile (1856), V. 831
Eton Boy (Morton, T., Jr., 1842), IV.
364, 601
Eton versus Harrow (Grain, R. C.,
1885), V. 387
Étrangère (1876), V. 674
Etymologist (1785), III. 326
Eudora (Hayley, W., 1790), III. 267
Eugene and Maria = Inquisition of 1650
Eugene Aram (Faucquez, A., 1879), V.
364
— (Moncrieff, W. T., 1832), IV. 97, 360
— (Wills, W. G., 1873), V. 627
— (1832), IV. 97, 457
— (1855), V. 674
Eugene Onegin (Edwards, H. S., 1892),
V. 789
Eugenia (Carr, R. and Hayes, S., 1766),
III. 242, 267
— (Francis, P., 1752), III. 61, 261, 384
— (1819), IV. 457
— (1832), IV. 457
Eugenia Claircille (Parry, T., 1846), IV.
368
Eugénie (Boucicault, D., 1855), V. 268
— (De Vere, F., 1857), V. 343
— (1885), V. 674
Eugenio (1823), IV. 457

Eulalie (Fryers, A., 1890), v. 374

Eulalie and Vermilion (Wooler, J. P., 1852), v. 632

Eunice (Towers, E., 1882), v. 601

Eunuch (Cooke, T., 1737), II. 143, 215, 316

Eunuchus (Echard, E., 1693), I. 410

Euphemia (Young, C. M., 1836), IV. 457, 618, 624

Euphemia's Flights = Maniac Maid

Euphrosyne (Graves, R., 1776), III. 265

Euranthe (1840), IV. 457

Europe's Revels for the Peace (Motteux, P. A., 1697), I. 421

Eurydice (Byron, H. J., 1871), v. 117–18, 297

— (Fielding, H., 1737), II. 265, 328

— (Mallet, D., 1731), II. 49, 82–3, 264, 343

Eurydice Hiss'd (Fielding, H., 1737), II. 328, 423, 436

Eurypilus, King of Sicily (Paynter, D. W., 1817), IV. 369, 457, 603, 624

Eustache Baudin (Courtney, J., 1854), v. 326

Euston Hotel (Bloomfield, H., 1845), IV. 269

Eva (Stuart-Wortley, Lady Emmeline, 1840), IV. 613

— (1855), v. 674

Evadne (Sheil, R. L., 1819), IV. 400

Evander (Smyth, J., 1847), IV. 612

Evangeline (1883), v. 674

Eva's Bridal = Celestia

Eva's Home (1860), v. 674

— (1880), v. 674

Eva's Inheritance (Cowper, A., 1870), v. 327

Eve (Webster, B., the Younger, 1869), v. 618

Eveleen, the Rose of the Vale (Birch, W. H., 1869), v. 261

Eveline (Archer, T., 1843), IV. 457, 569, 624

Eveline of the Hall = Michaelmas Day

Evening Adventure (?1680), I. 441

Evening at Richmond = Figure of Fun

Evening Fête (1857), v. 831

Evening Revels (Barrymore, Mrs W., 1823), IV. 262

Evening's Adventures (Stevens, Capt. J., 1707), II. 358

Evening's Exhibition = Cabinet of Fancy

Evening Shadows (Bowen, C., 1878), v. 270

Evening's Intrigue = Masquerade

Evening's Love (Dryden, J., 1668), I. 55, 56, 67, 188, 191, 228–9, 344, 350, 351, 404

Evening with Puff = Drama at Home

Eventful Reign of King John = Magna Charta

Eventide (Chrichton, W., 1895), v. 310

Events in 1821 = English at Paris

Events of a Day (Edmead, Elizabeth, 1795), III. 258

Events of a Year = Kohal Cave

Events of Time (Drake, 1809), IV. 582

Eve of Battle (Faucit, J. S., 1844), IV. 311

Eve of Marriage = Great Temptation

Eve of St Hippolyte (Manson, Dr and Mrs, 1821), IV. 597

Eve of St John (1859), v. 674

Eve of St Mark = Betrothed

Eve of the Wedding (1889), v. 674

Eve of Waterloo (Wilkins, J. H.), IV. 420

— = Vivandière [This may = the above]

Everel (1884), v. 674

Ever Faithful (Darbey, E., 1885), v. 336

Evergreen (Pollock, W. H., 1884), v. 529

Eversleigh House (Newbound, E., 1879), v. 502

+Ever-so-little Bear; or, The Pole-faces and the Put-em-in-the-Cauldron Indians (Byron, H. J.: *Dicks* (in *Sensation Dramas*))

Every Body Mistaken (Taverner, W., 1716), II. 140, 260, 358

Everybody's Business = Rejection

Everybody's Cousin (Dibdin, T. J., 1820), IV. 302

Everybody's Friend (Coyne, J. S., 1859), v. 328

Everybody's Husband (Ryan, R., 1831), IV. 396

Everybody's Relation (1840), IV. 457

Everybody's Widow (Beazley, S., Jr., 1836), IV. 264

Everybody to their own Liking (Green, Mrs, 1756), III. 386

Every Coat has a Hole in it = Helping Hand

Fair Bargain (Harley, G., 1894), v. 404

Fair Bigamist (Burford, U., 1888), v. 287

Fair Brigands = Female Mascaroni

Fair Caledonian = Love and Money

Fair Captive (Haywood, Mrs E., 1721), II. 17, 26, 31, 83-4, 335

Fair Cheating (1814), IV. 457

Fair Circassian (Croxall, S., 1720), II. 223, 317

— (Hazlewood, C. H., 1872), v. 414

— (Pratt, S. J., 1781) = Circassian, III. 299, 393

— = Almoran and Hamet

Fair Conquest (Drinkwater, A. E., 1887), v. 351

Fair Crusader (1815), IV. 457, 636

Fair Deceivers (Church, C., 1893), v. 310

Fair Deserter (1816), IV. 457

Fair Encounter (Rae, C. M., 1875), v. 532

Fair Equestrienne (Russell, E. H., 1890), v. 553

Fair Example (Estcourt, R., 1703), II. 133, 145, 183, 194-5, 320, 435

Fair Exchange (Williams, M., 1860), v. 624, 824

— (1865), v. 674

Fairfair the Tulip and the Camp at Coen = Days of Louis XV

Fair Fame (Day, J. T., 1884), v. 340

Fair Foundling = Patie and Peggie

Fair France (Digges, W., 1874), v. 345

Fair Fugitive = Coffee-House

Fair Fugitives (Porter, A. M., 1803), IV. 387, 666

Fair Gabrielle (Planché, J. R., 1822) = Henri Quatre, IV. 377, 477, 604, 628

Fair Game (Dudley, Sir H. B., 1813), IV. 308

Fair Geraldine = Count Tremolio [By error on IV. 628 The Fair Geraldine is given for The Fair Gabrielle]

Fair Greek = Irene

Fair Helen (Amcotts, V.), v. 240

Fair Hypocrite (1745), II. 451

— = Maiden Queen

Fairies (?Garrick, D., 1755), III. 111, 262, 385

— = Falls of Clyde

Fairies' Festival on Shakespeare's Birthday (Falconer, E., 1864), v. 360

Fairies' Frolic (Shield, H., 1863), v. 816

Fairies' Haunt (1856), v. 674

Fairies' Home (1840), IV. 625

Fairies of the Rhine = Alva

Fairies of the Silver Mine = Demon Arab

Fairies' Revels (Fawcett, J., 1802), IV. 311

Fair Inconstant = Elfrid

Fair Intriguers (1835), IV. 457

Fair Lady (1807), IV. 457

Fairleigh's Birthright (Peel, G., 1878), v. 518

Fair Libertine = Rival Widows

Fair Lilias (Young, Mrs H., 1865), v. 674, 825, 831

Fairlop Fair (Dibdin, C. I. M., 1812), IV. 293

Fair Lunatick (1749), II. 451

Fairly Caught (Day, G. D., 1892), v. 339

Fairly Foiled (Allen, O., 1871), v. 239

Fairly Hit and Fairly Missed (Martin, J.), IV. 597

Fairly in for't = Plants and Planets

Fairly Puzzled (Brand, O., 1884), v. 273

Fairly Taken In = Personation

Fairly Won (1873), v. 674

Fair Maid of Clifton (Goodyer, F. R., 1872), v. 384

Fair Maid of Islington = Canonburg Tower

Fair Maid of Kent = Windsor Castle [The plays listed III. 297 and 400 are probably identical]

Fair Maid of Perth (Webb, C., 1845), IV. 95, 417

— (1828), IV. 95, 457

— = St Valentine's Eve

Fair Maid of the West = Unnatural Parents

Fair Maid of Tottenham Court (1840), IV. 457

Fair Maid of York = Ivanhoe

Fair Mendicant and the Spirit of the Rock = Fatherless Fanny

Fair of Saint-Germain (Ozell, J., 1718), II. 347, 420, 442

Fair Old Maid of 1725 = Countess of Lilliput

Fair One with the Golden Locks (Conquest, G. and Spry, H., 1891), v. 322

— (Millward, C., 1877), v. 674, 807, 831

— (Planché, J. R., 1843), IV. 382, 605

— (1867, 1879, 1887, 1894), v. 674

Fair One with the Locks of Gold (Conquest, G. and Spry, H., 1861), v. 674, 817, 831

Fair on the Ice = Yahrmanka nal Dhu

Fair Orphan (Stevens, G. A., 1771), III. 326, 396, 400

Fair Parricide (1752), III. 326

Fair Penitent (Kemble, J. P., 1814), IV. 335

— (Rowe, N., 1703), II. 57, 58, 59, 70, 99–100, 352, 443

— (1813), IV. 457

Fair Persian = Noureddin

Fair Peruvian (1786) = Peruvian, III. 326, 400, 403

Fair Play (Reynolds, F., 1808) = Begone Dull Care, IV. 457, 625

— = Scarlet Sins

Fair Play's a Jewel = Heart of Hearts

Fair Pretender (Simpson, J. P., 1865), v. 567

Fair Princess (Bernard, F., 1886), v. 259

Fair Quaker (Thompson, E., 1773), III. 116, 311, 397

— (1812), IV. 140, 457

Fair Quaker of Deal (Shadwell, C., 1710), II. 9, 42, 53, 132, 133, 136, 176, 354; III. 116, 397; IV. 140

Fair Refugee (1784), III. 327, 400

Fair Rivals (Hewitt, J., 1729), II. 335

Fair Rosamond (Akhurst, W. M., 1873), v. 237

— (Burnand, F. C., 1862), v. 288

— (Ellis, B., 1893), v. 357

— (Faucit, J. S., 1821), IV. 311

— (Field, M., 1884), v. 366

— (Godwin, E. W., 1886), v. 383

— (James, C. S., 1847), IV. 330

— (Lee, N., Jr., 1860), v. 803

— (Upton, 1801), IV. 415

— (1734), II. 371

— (1813), IV. 457

Fair Rosamond (1860), v. 675

Fair Rosamond, according to the History of England (Taylor, T. P., 1838), IV. 411

Fair Rosamond's Bower (Langbridge, F.), v. 448

Fair Rosamund (Barnett, C. Z., 1837), IV. 260

Fair Sicilian (Albert, 1834), IV. 567

Fair Sinner (Appleton, G. W., 1885), v. 241

Fair Sinners (Paget, 1881), v. 511

Fair Slave (1806), IV. 457

Fair Star (Smith, A. R. and Oxenford, J., 1844), IV. 402

Fair Sylvia (1869), v. 675

Fair Take-in = Martha

Fair Venetian (1776), III. 327

Fair Winds for Foul Ways = Captain John Luck

Fair Women and Brave Men (Tharp, T. A., 1897), v. 595

Fair Words and Foul Deeds (Travers, W., 1868), v. 603

Fairy (1801), IV. 457

— (1804), IV. 457

— (1861), v. 675

Fairy and the Fawn (Rice, C., 1852), v. 542

Fairy and the Golden Dove (Stirling, E., 1858), v. 818

Fairy Ball = Milliners

Fairy Benison (Bishop, S., 1796), III. 238

Fairy Birds of the Forest = Children of the Wood

Fairy Blue and Fairy Red (Dibdin, T. J., 1825), IV. 304

Fairy Call = Appel des Fées

Fairy Circle (Grattan, H. P., 1857), v. 675, 794, 831

Fairy Court (Gentleman, F., 1761), III. 264

Fairy Elves of the Fourth Estate (Frost, F., 1856) = Tit, Tat Toe, v. 675, 793, 831, 835

Fairy Favour (Hull, T., 1766), III. 274

— (1790), III. 327

Fairy Favours (1797) = Fairy Festival, III. 327, 400

Fairy Fawn (1872), v. 831

Fairy Fern Flower (1856), v. 675

Faithful Shepherd (Grove, W., 1782), III. 70, 266, 327, 386

+— (Sheridan, T., Smock Alley, Dublin, 31/1/1740) [This is probably a revised version of the following: if so, that was by T. Sheridan]

— (1736), II. 224, 37¹, 447

— =Pastor Fido

Faithful to the End=Denounced

Faithful under Peril=Faith under Peril

Faithful unto Death (Newbound, E., 1876), V. 502

— (Robson, E. M. and Compton, E., 1881), V. 547

Faithful Virgins (?1663), I. 441

Faith, Hope and Charity (Blanchard, E. L., 1845), IV. 268

— (Hazlewood, C. H., 1863)=Widow and Orphans, V. 675, 768, 796, 832, 850

Faith in Love (1862), V. 675

Faithless Cosen german=Jugurtha

Faithless Favourites=Elfrida

Faithless Friend (Amherst, J. H., 1821), IV. 253

Faithless Wife (Lane, Mrs S., 1876), V. 448

Faith's Fraud (Landor, R. E., 1841), IV. 199, 341

Faith's Reward (1885), V. 675

Faith Triumphant=Esther

Faith under Peril (Abel, W. H., 1873), V. 1, 235

Falcon (Tennyson, Alfred Lord, 1879), V. 594

Falka (Farnie, H. B., 1883), V. 363

Falka's Baby=Brother Pelican

Fallen among Thieves (Harvey, F., 1890), V. 408

— (Morton, W. E., 1888), V. 497

Fallen Spirit (1836), IV. 458

Fallen Star (Lee, N., Jr., 1859), V. 675, 802, 832

— (Young, Mrs H., 1864), V. 675, 832

Fall from the Cliff=Minna

Falling out of Lovers is the Renewing of Love (1710), II. 371

Falling Star (1855), V. 675

Fall of Algiers (Walker, C. E., 1825), IV. 145, 416

Fall of Angels=State of Innocence

Fall of Arabi=Egyptian War

Fall of a Shattered Flower=Old Old Story

Fall of Badajoz (1812), IV. 458

Fall of Bob (Kelly, J., 1736), II. 340, 440

Fall of Bob, alias Gin=Fall of Bob

Fall of Caius Martius Coriolanus= Ingratitude of a Common-Wealth

Fall of Carthage (Joshua, J., 1810), IV. 334

— (Watkins, W., 1801), IV. 417

Fall of Clyde (1858), V. 675

Fall of Constantina=Victoire

Fall of Delhi (1857), V. 675

— =Veemah Kareeda

Fall of Desmond=Rebellion Defeated

Fall of Egypt (Hawkesworth, J., 1774), III. 355, 386

Fall of Essex (Warmington, G., 1842), IV. 616

— =Envious Statesman

Fall of Fair Rosamond (1821), IV. 458

— (1832), IV. 458

Fall of Gollo=Sophy of Brabant

Fall of Jerusalem (Milman, H. H., 1820), IV. 167, 336

— =Wars of the Jews

Fall of Khartoum (Stanley, H. J., 1885), V. 579

— (1885), V. 675

Fall of Man=State of Innocence

Fall of Martinico (1794), III. 327

Fall of Missolonghi (Amherst, J. H.), IV. 254

— =Greek Renegade [This, listed at IV. 469, may=the above]

Fall of Monsieur St Ruth=Battle of Aughrim

Fall of Montevideo (1807), IV. 458

Fall of Mortimer (Robinson-Morris, M., 1806), IV. 394

— (1731), II. 371

Fall of Otranto=Corsair's Son

Fall of Palmyra=Zenobia

Fall of Pantomime=Harlequin Student

Fall of Phaeton (Pritchard, 1736), II. 136, 256, 350

— (1733), II. 371

Fall of Portugal (Wolcot, J., 1808), III. 316; IV. 458

Fall of Pride=(1) Downfall of Pride; (2) Edith

Fall of Public Spirit (1757), III. 327

Fall of Rizzio (1795), III. 327

Fall of Robespierre (Coleridge, S. T. and Southey, R., 1794), III. 54, 245

Fall of Rosamond = Henry II

Fall of Saguntum (Frowde, P., 1727), II. 21, 28, 29, 31, 92, 329

Fall of Sebastopol (1855), V. 675

Fall of Siam = Fatal Vision

Fall of Tarquin (Hunt, W., 1713), II. 338

— = Brutus

Fall of the Avalanche (Conquest, G. and Suter, W. E., 1865), V. 675, 785, 818, 832

Fall of the Curtain = Domino

Fall of the Decemvirs = (1) Virginia; (2) Virginius

Fall of the Earl of Essex (Ralph, J., 1731), II. 350

Fall of the French Monarchy (Bartholomew, J., 1794), III. 54, 235

Fall of the Inquisition = Fatal Brand

Fall of the Leaf (Carlton, R. C., 1893), V. 305

— (1852), V. 675

Fall of the Mogul (Maurice, T., 1806), III. 286; IV. 354

Fall of Theodore = Conquest of Magdala

Fall of the Sea Robbers = French Expedition

Fall of Tunis = Bellamira

Falls of Clyde (Black, J., 1806), IV. 458, 625

— (Soane, G., 1817), IV. 403

— (1827), IV. 458

Falsacappa (Leigh, H. S., 1871), V. 454, 803

False Accusation (Fuller, F., 1874), V. 374

— (1818), IV. 458

— (1828), IV. 458

— = (1) Flirt; (2) Home once more; (3) Monte d'Or

False Accusations (1874), V. 675

— = False Accusation

False Alarm (Young, A. W., 1872), V. 635

— (1871), V. 675

False Alarms (Kenney, J., 1807), IV. 336

— = Love gives the Alarm

False Alarum = British Peasant

False and Constant (Lunn, J., 1829), IV. 348

False and Fair = Captain Gerald

False and True (Moultru, 1798), III. 289

— (1806), IV. 458

— (1864), V. 675

— = Love

False and True Heir and the Brigand of Palermo = Disputed Title

False Appearances (Conway, H. S., 1788), III. 121, 248, 380

— (1807), IV. 458

False Beacon = Sea Devil

False Bride = Merchant of Paisley

False Cards (Creamer, A., 1873), V. 329

False Colours (Fitzball, E., 1837), IV. 315

— (Morris, E., 1793), III. 21, 138, 288

— (Pass, G. F., 1881), V. 515

— = Little Laundress

False Conclusions (Long, C., 1845), IV. 346

False Concord (Townley, J., 1764), III. 169, 312

False Count (Behn, A., 1681), I. 188, 191, 261–2, 391; III. 114

False Delicacies (1803), IV. 458

False Delicacy (Kelly, H. and Garrick, D., 1768), III. 45, 130, 155, 157, 278, 389

— (Thompson, B., 1800), IV. 412

False Demetrius (Cumberland, R., 1813), IV. 287

False Dervise (Dibdin, C.), IV. 290

False Earl (1863), V. 675

False Evidence (Miller, W. F., 1891), V. 489

— (1889), V. 675

— = Honest Criminal

False Friend (Cross, J. C., 1806), IV. 287

— (Howlett, S., 1893), V. 429

— (Kemble, J. P., 1789), III. 115, 278

— (Pix, Mrs M., 1699), I. 424; II. 96–7

— (Vanbrugh, Sir J., 1702), II. 135, 136, 150–1, 221, 361, 419, 445; III. 115

— (1720), II. 451

— (1803), IV. 458

— = Constant Lovers

False Friendship (1829), IV. 458

False Glitter (Harvey, F., 1875), V. 408

False Guardians Outwitted (Goodall, W., 1740), II. 333

False Hands and Faithful Hearts (Towers, E., 1867), V. 600

False Hearts (Carter, A., 1886), V. 305

False Heire and Formal Curate (Kirkman, F., 1662), I. 417

False Impressions (Cumberland, R., 1797), III. 51, 129, 252

False Jewels = Catarina

False Key (Almar, G., 1831), IV. 252

False Knight = Woodman's Horse

False Light (Blake, T. G., 1847), IV. 268

False Lights (Bannister, T. B., 1886), V. 248

Falsely Accused (Carlyle, R., 1897), V. 303

— (Griffiths, J. C., 1876), V. 394

— = Waiting for the Verdict

Falsely Judged (Granville, H. S., 1880), V. 388

False Marriage (1828), IV. 458

False Mother (Hazlewood, C. H., 1865), V. 413, 797

False Mother and the Parent Guardian = Violet's Perils

False Mr Pope (Peake, R. B., 1845), IV. 371

False One Fitted = Female Fop

False Penitent (1805), IV. 458

False Position = (1) Patronage; (2) Trevanion

False Pride (Fairbairn, Mrs R., 1883), V. 359

— = Victor and Hortense

False Prophet of the Sudan = El Mahdi

False Relique = Excommunicated Prince

False Report = Mistakes

False Shame (Marshall, F., 1872), V. 478

— (1799), III. 65, 327, 400

— (1801), IV. 458

False Step (Matthison, A., 1878), V. 481

— (1859), V. 675

False Steps (Vanneck, F., 1886), V. 607

False Tiberinus = Agrippa King of Alba

False Triumph (1712), II. 371

False Visions (Parry, J., 1846), IV. 368, 458, 625

False Witness (Shirley, A. and Gally, M., 1890), V. 564

Falstaff (Kingston, W. B., 1896), V. 801

— = Purse

Falstaff in Pantomime = Shakespeare's Choice Spirits

Falstaff's Wedding (Kenrick, W., 1766), III. 279, 389

Fame (Osborn, H., 1850), IV. 602; V. 808

— (Rae, C. M., 1877), V. 532

— (1737), II. 371

Familiar Friend (Lemon, M., 1840), IV. 343

Families Supplied (Cuthbert, E., 1882), V. 331

Famille Laffarge = Accusation

Family Arrangements (Long, C., 1846), IV. 347

Family Compact (Rose, J., 1792), III. 303

Family Concert = Students of Jena

Family Distress (1799), III. 400

— = Self-Immolation

Family Failing (Oxenford, J., 1856), V. 509, 809

— (1896), V. 675

Family Fast (1866), V. 675

Family Feud = Vendetta

Family Feuds = Sons

Family Fix (Shelley, H., 1897), V. 562

Family Fool (Melford, M., 1882), V. 484

Family Friends (1872), V. 675

Family Genius's = London out of Town

Family Ghost (Brunton, A., 1881), V. 284

Family Honour (Marshall, F., 1878), V. 478

Family Jars (Lunn, J., 1822), IV. 348

Family Jars Mended (1839), IV. 458

Family Legend (Baillie, J., 1810), IV. 159–61, 258

Family Likeness (1839), IV. 458

Family Man (1842), IV. 458

Family Masquerading = March of Intelleck

Family Matter (Compton, C. G. and Hockley, A. G., 1894), V. 319

Family Novelette (Nesbit, E. and Barron, O., 1894), V. 502

Family of Anglade = (1) Accusation; (2) Portfolio

Family of Genius (1826), IV. 458

Family Party (Davidge, W. P., 1842), IV. 289

Family Party (Grain, R. C., 1889), v. 387

— (Oxenford, J., 1849), IV. 367

— (1789), III. 189, 327

— (1835), IV. 458

Family Peculiarities (1835), IV. 458

Family Picture (1781), III. 120, 327

— (1822), IV. 458

— = Sailor's Chest

Family Pictures (Stirling, E., 1849), IV. 409

Family Politics (1814), IV. 458, 635

Family Pride (Murray, G., 1862), v. 500

— (Sullivan, R., 1847), IV. 409

Family Propensities = Master's Rival

Family Punch-Bowl = Jack in the Green

Family Quarrel = Nobleman

Family Quarrels (Dibdin, T. J., 1802), IV. 52, 297

Family Relations (1850), v. 675

Family Secret (Falconer, E., 1860), v. 360

— (Leslie, H. T., 1861), v. 457

— = Troubled Waters

Family Secrets (Brough, W., 1853) = How to make Home happy, v. 279, 675, 832

Family Ties (Burnand, F. C., 1877), v. 290

— (1856), v. 832

Family Treacheries (Muir, J. F., 1846), IV. 365

Family Treason (1861), v. 675

Family Troubles = Old Phil Hardy

Family Tutor = Trip to the Ball

Family Will (1888), v. 675

Famine (O'Grady, H., 1886), v. 506

Famous Beauty (Stanley, H. J., 1892), v. 579

Famous Trojan Horse = Siege of Troy

Fanatic (Day, J. T., 1897), v. 340

Fanatic of Aleppo = Klebir in Egypt

Fanchette (Levey, W. C., 1864), v. 675, 832

— (Bateman, Mrs H. L., 1871), v. 253

— (Weil, O., 1894), v. 619

Fanchonette the Cricket (1871), v. 676

Fanchon the Cricket (Schuler, F., 1863), v. 815

— (1862), v. 676

Fanchon the Grasshopper (1867), v. 676

Fancourt's Folly (Findon, B. W., 1894), v. 366

Fancy Ball (Wardroper, H., 1889), v. 614

— (1832), IV. 625

Fancy'd Queen (Drury, R., 1733), II. 319

Fancy Dress Ball (Grain, R. C., 1892), v. 388

Fancy Fair (Lumley, R. R., 1892), v. 464

Fancy Land (Fuller, C. F., 1884), v. 374

Fancy's Friends = World as it Runs

Fancy's Opera (1823), IV. 458

Fancy's Sketch (Planché, J. R., 1819), IV. 376

Fan-Fan the Tulip (Suter, W. E., 1863), v. 588

Fannette (Johnstone, J. B., 1868), v. 438

Fanny (Sims, G. R. and Raleigh, C., 1895), v. 569

Fanny Lear (1885), v. 676

Fanny's Flirtations (Miller, W. F. and Havard, P., 1887), v. 489

Fanny Sims, Mistress of Arts (Coyne, J. S., 1838), IV. 458, 625

Fanny Wild, the Thief-taker's Daughter (Blake, T. G., 1851), v. 262

Fanny Wyndham (1862), v. 676

Fans and Fandangas (1865), v. 676

Fans and Fandangoes = Spanish Dancers

Fantisticuff (1871), v. 676

Far Away = Hawthorne

Far away where Angels dwell (Hazlewood, C. H., 1869), v. 414

Farce upon Segmoor Fight = Battle

Farce Writer (Pocock, I., 1815), IV. 384, 606

Farewel Folly (Motteux, P. A., 1705), II. x, 5, 38, 45, 50, 129, 209–10, 346, 441

Farewell and Return (?1739), II. 371

Farewell of the Fairies (Reece, R., 1867), v. 812

Farfadets (1881), v. 676

Farfaletta (1866), v. 676

Far, far at Sea = Mary's Dream

Far from the madding Crowd (Hardy, T. and Carr, J. W. C., 1882), v. 404

Farinelli (Barnett, C. Z., 1839), IV. 260

Farinelli in Madrid = Queen of Spain

Farm by the Sea (Wedmore, F., 1889), v. 619

Farmer (O'Keeffe, J., 1787) = Ups and Downs, III. 200, 293, 393

Farmer and his Wife = Village Story

Farmer and Pheasant (Thompson, C. P., 1836) = Poachers and Petticoats = Pheasant Shooting, IV. 614, 458, 625

Farmer Deceived (1779), III. 400

Farmer Disappointed = Harlequin Executed

Farmer Emigrant (1847), IV. 459

Farmer Hayseed (Pleon, H., 1889), v. 528

Farmer in Distress = Disaster

Farmer of Inglefield Forest (Hazlewood, C. H., 1859), v. 676, 796, 832

Farmer of Inglewood Forest (Rogers, W., 1846), IV. 396

Farmer of Labian (1825), IV. 459

Farmer of Lyons (1858), v. 676

Farmer on the Coast = Ship-Wreck

Farmer's Boy (Dibdin, C. I. M., 1809), IV. 292

— (1808), IV. 459

Farmer's Bride (1840), IV. 625

Farmer's Daughter (Pitt, G. D., 1845), IV. 374

— (1837), IV. 459

— = (1) Flitting Day; (2) Ring

Farmer's Daughter of the Severnside (Raymond, R. J., 1831), IV. 389

— = Broken Heart

Farmer's Dream = Mark Lawrence

Farmer's Gun (1834), IV. 459

Farmer's Journey to London (1769), III. 327

Farmer's Knife (1827), IV. 459

Farmer's Return from London (Garrick, D., 1762), III. 263

Farmer's Son (1733), II. 371

— (1835), IV. 459

— = Golden Glove

Farmer's Sons = Veteran Soldier

Farmer's Story (Bernard, W. B., 1836), IV. 266

Farmer's Wife (Dibdin, C. I. M., 1814), IV. 293, 580

Farm House (Kemble, J. P., 1789), III. 51, 116, 188, 278, 389

Farmhouse Story (1803), IV. 459

Farm of Senange = Henriette

Farm of Sterwick (1823), IV. 459

Farnley (Davies, B., 1894), v. 338

Far Off (Moncrieff, W. T., 1842), IV. 361

Faro Table (Tobin, J., 1816), IV. 164, 413

— (1789), III. 115, 327, 400

Farrago (1882), v. 676

Farriar Made Physician = Dumb Lady

Farrier Nicked (1734), II. 371

Farthing Rushlight (Oulton, W. C., 1810), IV. 366

Fascinating Fellows (Palmer, T. A., 1876), v. 512

Fascinating Individual (Danvers, H., 1856), v. 336, 787

Fascination (Jay, H. and Buchanan, R., 1888), v. 435

— (Merion, C., 1871), v. 806

Fashion (McLaren, A., 1802), IV. 350

— (Mowatt, A. C. O., 1850), v. 498

— (Stephens, W., 1869), v. 581

— (1884), v. 676

Fashionable Amusement = Sailor and Soldier

Fashionable Arrivals (Lemon, M., 1840), IV. 344, 595

Fashionable Beauty (Moore, G. and Glover, J. M., 1885), v. 492

Fashionable Crop quizzed (1792), III. 327

Fashionable Fallacy (1865), v. 676

Fashionable Friends (Walpole, H., 1802), III. 314; IV. 416

Fashionable Intelligence (Fendall, P., 1894), v. 364

— = World of Fashion

Fashionable Lady (Ralph, J., 1730), II. 267, 350

Fashionable Levities (Macnally, L., 1785), III. 14, 31, 49, 170, 285

Fashionable Life (Murray, A., 1845), IV. 365

Fashionable Lover (Cumberland, R., 1772), III. 126, 251

— (1706), II. 141, 177, 371

Fashionable Playfolks = Marriage by Comedy

Fashionable Recluse = Labyrinth Farm

Fashionable Wife (1782), III. 400 [A play of the same name was acted at the Haymarket, 6/5/1782]

Fashion and Famine (1855), v. 676

— (1857), v. 676

Fashion and Feeling = Steward

Fashion and Passion = Frou-Frou

Fashion Displayed (Burton, P., 1770), III. 241

Fashion's Fools (Dibdin, C. I. M., 1809), IV. 292

Fast and Slow (Lunn, J., 1827), IV, 348

Fast Asleep (Abbott, C. H., 1892) = Opiate, V. 233

— (Birch, S., 1797), III. 238, 378

Fast Coach (Soutar, J., Jr. and Claridge, C. J., Jr., 1851), V. 574, 817

— (Soutar, R., 1873), V. 575

Fast Family (Webster, B., the Younger, 1866), V. 618

Fast Friend (Herbert, F. H., 1877), V. 418

Fast Friends (Barrett, F., 1884), V. 250

— (Henry, R., 1878), V. 417

Fast Friends up a Tree (Anderson, J. R., 1864), V. 676, 777, 832

Fast Life (O'Grady, H., 1896), V. 506

— = Follies of the Day

Fast Life and Noble Life = Pace that Kills

Fast Mail (Carter, L. J., 1891), V. 305

Fast Man (1848), IV. 459

Fast Married Men (1863), V. 676

Fast Train! (Maddox, J. M., 1853), V. 472

Fatal Accusation (1825), IV. 459

— = Italians

Fatal Armour = Dark Pandour

Fatal Attachment (1831), IV. 459

Fatal Beauty (Fysher, G., 1892), V. 375

Fatal Birth-Day = Valentia

Fatal Brand (Pitt, G. D., 1850), V. 526

— = Prisoner of France

Fatal Bridge = Blood-red Knight

Fatal Card (Chambers, C. H. and Stephenson, B. C., 1894), V. 307

Fatal Chest = Mistletoe Bough

Fatal Choice = St Valentine's Day

Fatal Clock = Wood Demon

Fatal Conquest = Florazene

Fatal Constancy (Jacob, Sir H., 1723), II. 53, 91, 338

— (Whitehead, W., 1754), III. 80, 315

Fatal Coral Bank = Wreck of the Leander Frigate

Fatal Curiosity (Colman, G., 1782), III. 59, 247, 379

— (Lillo, G., 1736), II. 64, 115, 121-4, 342, 440; III. 59

— = (1) Blue Beard; (2) Shipwreck

Fatal Deed = Midnight Spectre

Fatal Discovery (Home, J., 1769), III. 18, 28, 72, 93, 272

— (1698), I. 24, 66, 170, 441

Fatal Divorce = Phæton

Fatal Dowry (Knowles, J. S., 1825), IV. 339

— (Sheil, R. L., 1840), IV. 610

Fatal Duel of the Glacis (1832), IV. 459

Fatal Elopement (1799), III. 327

Fatal Embarrassment = Labyrinth

Fatal Error (Victor, B., 1776), III. 58, 90, 313

— (1833), IV. 459

— = Florence

Fatal Experiment (Dibdin, T. J., 1826), IV. 305

Fatal Extravagance (Hill, A., 1721), II. 53, 70, 109, 115, 118-19, 120, 123, 336, 438; III. 59

Fatal Falsehood (More, Mrs H., 1779), III. 91, 97, 288

Fatal Falshood (Hewitt, J., 1734), II. 26, 115, 122, 335

Fatal Fire Damp = Life of a Miner

Fatal Floodgate (1834), IV. 459

— = Xaia of China

Fatal Friendship (Trotter, C., 1698), I. 57, 435

Fatal Gift (1876), V. 676

Fatal Glen = Meg Murnock

Fatal Gridiron = Jewess

Fatal Inconstancy (Phillips, R., 1701), II. 349

Fatal Interview (Hull, T., 1782), III. 72, 86, 90, 274

Fatal Island (Dibdin, T. J., 1817), IV. 300

Fatal Island and the Hour of Four (1824), IV. 459

Fatality (Boaden, C., 1829), IV. 269

— (Cameron, K., 1898), V. 301

— (1859), V. 676

— (1887), V. 676

Fatal Jealousie (Payne, H. N., 1672), I. 69, 83, 136, 347, 423

Fatal Keepsake = Military Execution

Fatal Land Breeze = Loss of the Royal George

Fatal Legacy (Robe, Mrs J., 1723), II. 351, 443

Fatal Letter (Suter, W. E., 1868), V. 588

Fatal Likeness (1863), V. 676

Fatal Love (Settle, E., 1680), I. 37, 149, 429

— (Wandesford, O., 1730), II. 71, 119–20, 363

— = Barnwell, the London Apprentice

Fatal Marksman (Almar, G., 1824), IV. 459, 625

Fatal Marriage (Southerne, T., 1694), I. 154, 240, 433; II. 71, 142; III. 58; V. 95

— (Towers, E., 1870), V. 601

— = (1) Fatal Friendship; (2) Isabella

Fatal Marriage Morn = John Anderson my Jo

Fatal Mistake (Haynes, J., 1692), I. 413

Fatal Necessity (Morris, R., 1742), II. 345

Fatal Oath = Robbers

Fatal Offspring = Barmecide

Fatal Pass (1830), IV. 459

Fatal Passion (1834), IV. 459

— = Love and Crime

Fatal Peanut = Jacobi

Fatal Peas = Barbazon

Fatal Penny Whistle = Handsome Hernani

Fatal Pile (1804), IV. 459

Fatal Precept (Dibdin, C. I. M., 1825), IV. 295

— = Man of Mystery [This may be a revised title for the above]

Fatal Prediction (Cross, J. C., 1802), IV. 286

Fatal Prophecy (Langhorne, J., 1766), III. 280

— = Norah O'Donnell

Fatal Purchase = Fiend of the Watch

Fatal Raft = Shipwreck of the Medusa

Fatal Ravine (1828), IV. 459

— = Bear-Hunters

Fatal Relapse = Antiochus the Great

Fatal Resemblance = (1) Convict's Escape; (2) Courier of Lyons

Fatal Resentment = Invader of his Country

Fatal Retirement (Brown, A., 1739), II. 123, 300

Fatal Retribution = St Gothard's Mount

Fatal Return = Julia

Fatal Revenge = Spaniard

Fatal Ring (Cliffe, F. H., 1893), V. 314

— = Sacontala

Fatal Rock (Barrymore, W., 1828) = Jack Robinson and his Monkey, IV. 262, 459, 625

Fatal Sandbank = Wreck of the Leander Frigate

Fatal Secret (Theobald, L., 1733), II. 359

— (1838), IV. 459

— = (1) Branded Race; (2) O'Shaughan; (3) Rival Brothers

Fatal Seduction = (1) Adelaide; (2) Clarissa

Fatal Shadow (Young, Mrs H., 1861), V. 676, 825, 832

Fatal Shaft (1836), IV. 459

Fatal Sisters (Eyre, E. J., 1797), III. 259

Fatal Snowdrift (1860), V. 676

Fatal Snowstorm (Barrymore, W.), IV. 262

— = (1) Lowina of Tobolskoi; (2) Russian Tyranny

Fatal Spoon = Maid and the Magpie

Fatal Thicket = (1) Black Cæsar; (2) Could the Murder?

Fatal Treasure = Golden Nugget

Fatal Triumph (Featherstone, J. L. and Hurd, J. C., 1886), V. 364

Fatal Urn = Dirce

Fatal Vision (Hill, A., 1716), II. 50, 81–2, 109, 336

— (1859), V. 676

Fatal Wager (1859), V. 676

— = Injured Princess

Fatal Warning = Death Fetch

Fatal Wedding Day (Townsend, W. T. 1852), V. 602

Fate (Campbell, B., 1874), V. 301

— (Gregory, H. G., 1874), V. 394

— (1865), V. 676

Fate and Fortune (Blood, J. J., 1891), V. 266

Fate and its Victims = Rosalie Mortimer

Fate and its Wonders (Rayner, A., 1856), V. 676, 812, 832

Fated Ship (1849), IV. 459

Fate of a Coquette (1863), V. 676

— = Camille

Father's Curse (1833), IV. 460
— (1836), IV. 460
— = Note Forger
Father's Dream = Old Adam
Father's Grave = Rescue of the Orphans
Father's Guilt (1823), IV. 460
Father's Legacy = Wild Flower of the Prairie
Father's Love = (1) Home; (2) Story of the Heart
Father's Love and a Mother's Care = Beggar's Petition
Father's Oath (Gould, F., 1892), V. 386
Father's Plea (Mayhew, E., 1834), IV. 460, 625
Father's Ransom and the False Key = Pilot's Son
Father's Revenge (Howard, F., 1783), III. 273
— = Stolen Birthright
Father's Sacrifice (Selby, C., 1837), IV. 398
— (Varty, W. R., 1887), V. 607
Father's Sin (Smith, H. B., 1886), V. 572
— (1896), V. 676
Father's Tragedy (Field, M., 1885), V. 366
Fathoms Deep (Cleve, J. B., 1883), V. 314
Fatinitza (Leigh, H. S., 1876), V. 454, 803
Faubourg St Germain (Reade, C., 1859), V. 536
Faugh a Ballagh = '99
Faulkner (Godwin, W., 1807), IV. 19, 319
Faults on Both Sides = Compromise
Faust (Bernard, W. B., 1866), V. 259
— (Bernays, L. J., 1839), IV. 86, 266
— ('Beta', 1895), V. 779
— (Birch, J., 1839), IV. 86, 267
— (Birds, J. A., 1880, 1889), V. 779
— (Blackie, J. S., 1834), IV. 86, 267
— (Bowen, C. H., 1878), V. 779
— (Brooks, C. T., 1856, 1857), V. 780
— (Chorley, H. F., 1864), V. 310, 784
— (Clarke, W. B., 1865), V. 784
— (Colquhoun, W. H., 1878), V. 785
— (Duckett, Sir G. F., 1845), IV. 86, 307
— (Filmore, L., 1841), IV. 86, 312
— (Galvan, J., 1860), V. 793
Faust (Gower, Lord F. L., 1823), IV. 86, 320
— (Grant, J. W., 1867), V. 794
— (Grattan, H. P., 1842), IV. 86, 320

— (Gurney, A. T., 1842), IV. 86, 322, 397
— (Hayward, A., 1833), IV. 86, 324
— (Hazlewood, C. H., 1867), V. 413
— (Hills, J., 1840), IV. 86, 325
— (Huth, A. H., 1889), V. 799
— (James, C. S., 1849), IV. 330
— (Knox, C. H., 1847), IV. 86, 340
— (Lefevre, Sir G., 1841), IV. 86, 343
— (Macdonald, W. B., 1838), IV. 86, 349, 596
— (Martin, Sir T., 1865, 1886), V. 806
— (Paul, C. K., 1873), V. 809
— (Swanwick, A., 1850), V. 819
— (Syme, D., 1834), IV. 86, 410
— (Talbot, R., 1835), IV. 86, 410
+ — (Taylor, Arthur, 8° 1838)
— (Taylor, R., 1871, 1872), V. 820
— Webb, T. E. 1880), V. 823
— (Wills, W. G., 1885), V. 627, 824
— (1838), IV. 86, 460
— (1861, 1863, 1886, 1891, 1894) V. 676
Faust and Co. (Gordon, G. L., 1886), V. 385
Faust and Loose (Burnand, F. C., 1886), V. 291
Faust and Margaret (Boucicault, D., 1854), V. 268, 779
— (Markwell, W. R.), V. 477
Faust and Marguerite (Burnand, F. C., 1864), V. 288
— (Daly, B. and Somerset, C. W., 1899), V. 334
— (Halford, J., 1854), V. 398 [The entry in IV. 323 should be deleted]
— (Halford, J., 1866), V. 398
— (Robertson, T. W., 1854), V. 546
— (1854, 1855, 1866, 1881), V. 676
Faust and Mephistopheles (1854), V. 676
Faust and the Fair Imogene = Alonzo the Brave
Faust in a Fog (Reece, R., 1870), V. 537
Faustine (Young, Sir C. L., 1880), V. 636
— (1887), V. 676
Faustine's Love (Stanhope, W., 1889), V. 579
Faust in Forty Minutes (Locke, F., 1885), V. 462
Faust in Three Flashes (Blood, J. J., 1884), V. 265
Faust Reversed (Bruce, H. P., 1888), V. 283

Faust up-to-date (Sims, G. R. and
· Pettitt, H., 1888), v. 569
Faust up too Late (Flexmore, F., 1889),
v. 369
Faustus (Auster, J., 1835), IV. 86, 254
+ — (Davies, Warburton, 12°, 1834)
— (Soane, G., 1820), IV. 86, 403
— (Soane, G. and Terry, D., 1825), IV.
86, 403
— (1824), IV. 86, 460
— (1882), IV. 86, 460
Faustus' Trip to the Jubilee (1712), II. 371
Fauvette (Rae, A., 1891), v. 532
Favette (Tresahar, J., 1885), v. 603
Favorita (Fitzball, E., 1843), IV. 316, 584
Favourite (Coe, Captain, 1893), v. 315
— (1770), III. 58, 327
— (1851), v. 676
— (1889), v. 676
— (1899), v. 676
Favourite of the Derby (Moncrieff,
W. T., 1844) = Royal Foxhunt, IV.
460, 625
Favourite of the King (Boas, F. S. and
Brandon, J., 1890), v. 266
Favourite of Fortune (Marston, J. W.,
1866), v. 479
Favourites in Town (Moncrieff, W. T.,
1831), IV. 460
Faw, Fee, Fo, Fum (Blanchard, E. L.,
1867), v. 264
Fawn in the Forest = Prince of Happy
Land
Fay o' Fire (Herman, H., 1885), v. 419
Fay o' the Fern (Legge, R. G., 1893), v.
453
Fayre Rosamund (Burnand, F. C.,
1868), v. 289
— (Cother, T., 1869), v. 325
— (1846), IV. 460
— (1885), v. 677
Fayre Rosamond, Henry II, Robin
Hood and the Merry Men of Sher-
wood (Soutar, R., 1865), v. 677, 817
Fays of the Forest (1850), v. 832
— = Prince Love
Fazio (Milman, H. H., 1816), IV. 167,
356, 484
— (Moncrieff, W. T., 1823), IV. 359
Fearful Fog (Hay, F., 1871), v. 411
Fearful Penance and the Fatal Penny
Roll = Jane Shore

Fearful Tragedy in the Seven Dials
(Selby, C., 1857), v. 560
Fearless Fred, the Fireman (Patterson,
G., 1874), v. 515
Fear of Robert Clive (Grand, S. and
McFall, H., 1896), v. 388
Feast for the Churchwardens = Bastard
Child
Feast of Anacreon (1789), III. 327
Feast of Apollo (1829), IV. 460
Feast of Bacchus (Bridges, R. S., 1889),
v. 275
— (1758), III. 327
Feast of Ceres = Edward and Egwina
Feast of Hymen (1736), II. 393
Feast of Lanterns = Chinese Exhibition
Feast of Saragossa (1859), v. 677
Feast of Thalia (1781), III. 327
— = Muse's Chaplet
Feast of the Statue (1817), IV. 460
Featherbrain (Albery, J., 1884), v. 238
Fédora (Merivale, H. C., 1883), v. 487
Fee-fi-fo-fum (Douglass, J. T. and
Marshall, F., 1887), v. 349
Feen (Reuss, T.), v. 813
Fée Urgele (1818), IV. 460
Feign'd Astrologer (1668), I. 441
Feign'd Curtizans (Behn, A., 1679), I.
14, 23, 223–4, 249, 350, 390
Feign'd Friendship (1699), I. 441
Feign'd Innocence = Sir Martin Mar-all
Feign'd Shipwreck (1742), II. 384
Felicidad (1887), v. 677
Felix (Oxenford, J., 1865), v. 510
Felix Heron (1865), v. 677
Felix Porter (1891), v. 677
Fellow Servants (Craven, H. T., 1846),
IV. 285
Felo de Se = Up the Flue
Felon Father and the Gipsey Child =
Miss Eliza Cook
Felon of Bruges (1854), v. 677
Felon of New York (Fitzball, E., 1833),
IV. 460, 625
Felon's Bond (Suter, W. E., 1859). v.
587
Felon's Hate (1825), IV. 460
Felon's Son (1848), IV. 460
Felon's Wife = Strange but True
Felon's Wrongs = Spring-heeled Jack
Female Academy (Cavendish, M., 1662),
I. 396

Female Adventurer (1790), III. 118, 327

Female Advocates (Taverner, W., 1713), II. 210, 358

Female Angler (Houlton, R., 1783), III. 273

Female Archer (1767), III. 327

Female Archers = Kenneth, King of Scots

Female Bandit = Fillebrande

Female Barbarism (Hancock, E. L., 1890), V. 402

Female Bluebeard (Dillon, C., 1845), IV. 305

— (1845), IV. 460

— (1862), V. 677

— = Devil's Mount

Female Buccaniers = Pauline the Pirate

Female Captain = (1) Black Eagle; (2) Contract

Female Cavaliers (Dunlop, Mrs, 1834), IV. 460, 625

Female Chevalier (Colman, G., 1778), III. 116, 246

Female Constancy = Laugh when you can

Female Contest = Rose

Female Courage (1809), IV. 460

Female Crusoe = Hannah Hewitt

Female Curiosity = (1) Blue-Beard; (2) Clock-Case

Female Detective (1865), V. 677

Female Dramatist (Colman, G., the Younger, 1782), III. 262, 379 [It would appear that this play definitely belongs to Colman and not to Mrs Gardner]

Female Duellist (1793), III. 112, 327

Female Enthusiast (1744), II. 372

Female Fop (Sandford, 1723), II. 353

Female Fortune Hunters = (1) Belle's Stratagem; (2) Imitation

Female Fortune-Teller (Johnson, C., 1726), II. 51, 142, 157, 339

Female Freebooter (Dibdin, C. I. M., 1823), IV. 295

Female Freemason (1831), IV. 460

Female Gamester (Howard, G. E., 1782), III. 273

Female Government (Dibdin, T. J., 1834), IV. 305

Female Heroism (West, M., 1804), IV. 418

— = (1) North Briton; (2) Russian Daughter

Female Hussar (1802), IV. 460

Female Iago (Goldsmith, W. H., 1872), V. 383

Female Innocence (1732), II. 372

Female Intrepidity = Heroic Sergeant

Female Jacobin-Club (Siber, J. C., 1801), IV. 87, 401

Female Jockey (Dimond, W.), IV. 581

Female Judas = Lady Satan

Female Lancers (1833), IV. 460

Female Macbeth = Elfrida

Female Mascaroni (Somerset, C. A., 1831), IV. 404

Female Matchmakers = Sharpers

Female Officer (Brooke, H., 1740), III. 240

— (Kemble, J. P., 1778), III. 278

Female Orators (1780), III. 327

— = Belles' Association

Female Parliament (1754), III. 327

Female Parricide (Crane, E., 1761), III. 249

Female Parson (Coffey, C., 1730), II. 237, 243, 315

Female Patriots = Spanish Heroine

Female Pedant (Horde, T., 1782), III. 273

Female Pirate (Stewart, D., 1870), V. 583

Female Politician = (1) Fate of Corsica; (2) Rival Priests

Female Politics (1841), IV. 460

Female Prelate (Settle, E., 1679), I. 37, 40, 79, 148–9, 428–9

Female Pursuit (1790), III. 328

Female Rake (Dorman, J., 1736), II. 160, 247, 372, 435

Female Rebellion (?Burkhead, H., ?1660), I. 394

Female Robinson Crusoes of America = Three Fast Men

Females Beware! (McLaren, A., 1820), IV. 352

Female Sentinel (1829), IV. 460

Female Serenaders = Buffalo Girls

Female Society = Baronet

Female Soldier (1789), III. 328

Female Spy and the Chief of Ten = Master Passion

Female Tournament (1849), IV. 460

Female Travellers = Colonel

Female Travelling Companion = Mutual Expense

Female Vertuoso's (Wright, T., 1693), I. 12, 13, 188, 260, 438

— = No Fools like Wits

Female Victor = Witty Combat

Female Volunteer (Halloran, L. H., 1801), IV. 323

— (Oxberry, W. H., 1833), IV. 460, 602, 625

Female Volunteers (1859), V. 677

— = Saw ye Bony coming?

Female Warriour = Friendship Improv'd

Female Waterman's Society (Worrell, 1840), IV. 460 [This is the same as The Ran-Dan Club, see IV. 618]

Female Wits (?1697), I. 250, 441

Feminine Strategy (Adams, C., 1893), V. 235

Femme Sentinelle (Barnett, Miss, 1832), IV. 460, 625

Femme Soldat = Colonel's Come

Fencing Master (Smith, H. B., 1892), V. 572

Fénelon (Merry, R., 1795), III. 287

Fenian (O'Grady, H., 1888), V. 506

Feniza (?1660–1700), I. 441

Fennel (Jerome, J. K., 1888), V. 436

Feodora (Pitt, G. D., 1845), IV. 373

Ferdinand, Count Fathom (Dibdin, T. J., 1818), IV. 96, 301

Ferdinand Lassalle (1893), V. 677

Ferdinando (Parke, W., 1886), V. 512

Ferdinand of Spain (1813), IV. 460

Ferguson (1837), IV. 460

Fernande (Edwardes, H. S., 1870), V. 43, 355

Fern Light = Wreck at Sea

Ferry and the Mill (Pocock, I., 1833), IV. 385

Ferry Girl (Downshire, Dowager Marchioness of, 1890), V. 350

Ferryman (Landor, R. E., 1841), IV. 199, 341

Ferryman of the Lone Hut (Taylor, T. P., 1843), IV. 411, 614

Ferryman's Daughter (Johnson, H. T. and Cordingley, C., 1891), V. 437

— = Old Father Thames

Ferry of the Guiers (1823), IV. 460

Festa di Ballo (1864), V. 677

Festival (1733), II. 372

Festival of Bacchus (Byrne, J., 1802), IV. 460, 625

Festival of Fancy (1805), IV. 460

Festival of Peace (1856) = Triumph of Peace, V. 677, 760, 848

Festival of Roses = Felix

Festival of the Fauns = Sylvan Statue

Festival of the Rose = Who kissed Jeannette

Festive Cottagers (1823), IV. 460

Fetches (Falconer, E., 1861), V. 360

Fête à Lisbon (1856), V. 832

Fête at Rosherville = Out on the Sly

Fête at Seville (1865), V. 677

Fête au serail = Marchand d'esclaves

Fête Champêtre (1843), IV. 460

— = Carron Side

Fête dansante (1856), V. 832

Fete-day and the Fall = Robespierre

Fête du Village (Hullin, 1820), IV. 589

Fête in Andalusia (1855), V. 677

Fête Napolitaine (1852), V. 677

Fête of Nations (1855), V. 677

Fête of Terpsichore (Albert, 1844), IV. 567

Fête of the Hermitage = Lestocq

Fête orientale (1853), V. 832

Fêtes de Memphis = Enfant prodigue

Fettered (Phillips, W., 1869), V. 523

Fettered at Last (1881), V. 677

Fettered Freedom (Kenne, M. and Stephenson, C. H., 1887), V. 442

Fettered Lives (Whyte, H., 1893), V. 621

— (1893), V. 677

Fetters (Burnley, J., 1875), V. 293

Fetters of Passion (Warwick, H. S. and Holderness, C. T., 1894), V. 615

Feudal Lady (1831), IV. 460

Feudal Times (Colman, G., the Younger, 1799), III. 248

— (White, J., 1847), IV. 419

Feuds of Loch Lomond = Ratheil Sullivan

Few More Passages in the Life of the Renowned and Illustrious Robert Macaire = Jacques Strop

F.F.F. (Bracewell, J., 1882), v. 272

Fiammina (1872), v. 677

Fiat of the Gods (Outram, L. S., 1891), v. 509

Fibbing for a Friend = Peter Jenkyns

Fibs (Tylar, W., 1882), v. 605

Fickle Fair One = Fortune's Task

Fickle Fatima (Robertson, W. G., 1892), v. 547

Fickle Fortune (Steele, C. D., 1890), v. 580

Fickle Shepherdess (1703), II. 141, 224, 372

Fiction and Reality = Tea-Room

Fiddler's Wife = O'Jupiter

Fidelio (Browne, M. E., 1891), v. 781

— (Phillips, M., 1837), IV. 372

— (1845), IV. 461

Fidelity (1884), v. 677

Fidget's First Floor = F.F.F.

Field against the Favourite (1855), v. 677

— = Derby Day

Field of Death = Sacred Trust

Field of Forty Footsteps (Farren, W., 1830), IV. 311

— (1858), v. 677

Field of Terror (Fitzball, E., 1852), v. 368

— = Black Spider

Field of the Cloth of Gold (Brough, W., 1868), v. 117, 280

— (Scott, S., 1869), v. 558

— (1831), IV. 461

— = Darnley, the Knight of Burgundy

Fiend (1842), IV. 461

Fiend at Fault (Edwards, H. S. and Taylor, W., 1894), v. 355

Fiend Father (Lacy, M. R., 1832), IV. 83, 461, 625

Fiend King (1838), IV. 461

Fiend of Ferrara = Lucrece Borgia

Fiend of Fleet Street = String of Pearls

Fiend of the Drachenfels (1852), v. 677

Fiend of the Fated Valley = Land of Enchantment

Fiend of the Fountain = Student's Dream

Fiend of the Volcano = Faust

Fiend of the Watch (1830), IV. 461

Fiend of the Whirlpool = Kerim the Pearl Diver

Fiend's Mountain (1855) = Adventurer, v. 638, 677, 832

Fiery Coursers of the Sun = Jupiter's Decree and the Fall of Phaethon

Fiery Furnace = Fiery Ordeal

Fiery Ordeal (Hazleton, F., 1862), v. 677, 796, 832

— (1894), v. 677

Fiery Parisienne (1898), v. 677

Fiesco (Anderson, J. R., 1850), v. 740

— (Noehden, G. H. and Stoddart, J., 1796), III. 63, 291, 392

— (Planché, J. R., 1850), v. 527

— (1841), IV. 86, 461

Fiesko (Daguilar, Sir G. C., 1832), IV. 86, 287

Fif (McArdle, J. F., 1882), v. 467

Fi, Fi (1845), IV. 461

1588 (Upton, 1804), IV. 415

Fifteen Minutes Grace (Goodman, W., 1894), v. 384

Fifteenth Carbineers (1834), IV. 461

Fifteenth Century (Fuller, C. F., 1883), v. 374

Fifteenth of October (Leterrier, E. and Vanloo, A., 1875), v. 457

Fifteen Years of a British Seaman's Life (1830), IV. 461

— (1859), v. 677

Fifteen Years of a Drunkard's Life! (Jerrold, D. W., 1828), IV. 331

Fifteen Years of a Soldier's Life (1848), IV. 461

Fifteen Years of Labour Lost (Amherst, J. H.), IV. 254

Fifteen Years of Prosperity and Adversity = London Tradesman's Life

Fifth of November (Bridel, E. P., 1807), IV. 574

— (Cox, R. D., 1854), v. 327

— (Rhodes, G. A., 1830), IV. 393

— = Guy Fawkes

Fifty Fafty, the Tyneside Mystery (Freeman, C., 1882), v. 373

Fifty Millions of Money = All for Gold

50 to 1 against him = Betting Boy's Career, from the Counting House to the Hulks

Fifty Weddings = Daughters of Danaus

Fire and Frost (Pratt, S. J., 1805), IV. 388

Fire and Spirit (Dibdin, C. I. M., 1803), IV. 290, 461, 580, 625

Fire and Water (Andrews, M. P., 1780), III. 204, 233

— (Beazley, S., Jr., 1817), IV. 263

Fire Banner = Knights of St John

Firedrake and the Fairy of the Silver Flame (Grady, T. J., 1843), IV. 320

Fire Eater (Ashton, J. T., 1874), V. 245

— (Selby, C., 1851), V. 560

Fire Fiend (1830), IV. 461

— = Elephant of Siam

Fire, Fire, burn Stick (1854), V. 677

Firefly (Sandford, E., 1869), V. 555

Fire Goblin (1818), IV. 461

Fire King (Cross, J. C., 1801), IV. 286

— (1830), IV. 461

— (1885), V. 677

— = Albert and Rosalie

Fire King, Harlequin, and the Water Queen (1819), IV. 461

Fireman and the Volunteer (Douglass, J. T., 1861), V. 677, 788, 832

Fireman of Glasgow (Dwyer, J., 1875), V. 353

Firematch the Trooper = Striking· the Hour

Fire of Life = She

Fire of London (Atkyns, S., 1849), IV. 257

— (Fullerton, Lady G., 1882), V. 375

Fire-Raiser (Almar, G., 1831), IV. 252

— (1831), IV. 461

Fireside Hamlet (Carr, J. W. C., 1884), V. 304

Fireside Story = Smuggler's Haunt

+Fireside Tragedy (Douglas, Sir G., 8°, 1887)

Fire, Water, Earth and Air = Devil's Ring

Fireworks (Philips, F. C. and Fendall, P., 1893), V. 522

Fire Worshippers (Fitzball, E., 1824), IV. 312

— = (1) Gheber; (2) Hafed the Gheber

Firm as Oak (Peel, G., 1873), V. 518

Firm Changed = New Brooms

Firmilian (Aytoun, W. E., 1854), V. 247

First Act of Taste (Foote, S., 1761) = Lindamira, III. 260, 384

First Affections (Simpson, J. P., 1860), V. 567

First and Last Love = Spanish Husband

First and Second Floor (1857), V. 677

— = Actor of All Work

First and Second Love = Red Rob the Coiner

First and Second Marriage = Aurora Floyd

First-Born (Harness, W., 1844), IV. 587

— (Powers, F., 1897), V. 530

First Breeze (Denny, W. H., 1891), V. 342

— (1882), V. 678

First Champaigne (1845), IV. 461

First Claim (1835), IV. 461

First Class (Scudamore, F. A., 1885), V. 559

First Come, First Served (Carr, Sir J., 1808), IV. 279

— (1797), III. 328

First Cousins (1879), V. 678.

First Crime (1856), V. 678

— = Weaver's Wife

First Day after the Trial (1858), V. 678

First days Entertainment (D'Avenant, Sir W., 1656), I. 285, 400

First Experiment (Jones, J. W., 1882), V. 441

First Faults (Kemble, Mrs M-T., 1799), III. 279

First Favourite (Hazlewood, C. H., 1873), V. 414

First Floor (Cobb, J., 1787), III. 156, 189, 244

— (1818), IV. 461

First Floor, Second Floor and Attics (1863), V. 678

First Floor to Let (1851), V. 678

First Friendship (Pitt, G. D., 1848), IV. 375

First Impressions (Smith, H., 1813), IV. 402

— (1831), IV. 461

First Impression's Everything (Douglass, J. T., 1861), V. 678, 788, 832

First in the Field (Rae, C. M., 1881), V. 532

— = Suit of Tweeds

First Love (Cumberland, R., 1795), III.
128-9, 252

— (Edwardes, C., 1841), IV. 582

— (Phillips, E. and Wigan, A. S., 1839),
IV. 604

— (Pocock, I., 1828), IV. 461

— (Suter, W. E., 1863), V. 588

— (Travers, W., 1859), V. 821

— (1866), V. 678

— = Bourbons and Bonapartists

First Love and False Hearts (1856), V.
678

First Mate (Henry, R., 1888), V. 418

First Night (Maddox, J. M., 1853), V.
472

— (Parry, T., 1834), IV. 368

— (Saintsbury, H. A., 1899), V. 554

— (Wigan, A. S., 1849), IV. 419, 461,
617, 625

— (1888), V. 678

First Night of a New Piece = Broad but
not Long

First Night of my Wedding (1848), IV.
461

First Night's Lodging (McLaren, A.,
?1800), III. 284; IV. 350

First of April (Boaden, C., 1830), IV.
369

— (McLaren, A., 1802), IV. 350

— = (1) My Beaux; (2) My Uncle's
Card

First of August = Waterman

First of May (Hill, I., 1829), IV. 325

— (Young, A., 1849), IV. 423

First of October (1899), V. 678

— = Fair Game

First of November = Our Town

First of September (Oliphant, R., 1789),
III. 328, 393, 401

— (Oxberry, W. H. and Phillips, F. L.,
1839), IV. 366

— = Shooter's Hill

First Printer (Taylor, T. and Reade, C.,
1856), V. 592

First Rehearsal (Cottell, L., 1892), V.
325

First Step (Heinemann, W., 1895), V.
416

First Violin (Bowkett, S., 1899), V. 271

Fish and the Ring (Amherst, J. H.),
IV. 254

Fisher Girl (Hannan, C., 1890), V. 402

Fisherman (Tobin, J., 1819) = Fisherman's Hut, IV. 413, 461, 614, 625

Fisherman and the Genie (Blanchard,
E. L., 1856), V. 263, 779

— = Enchanted Lake

Fisherman a Prince = Rise and Fall of
Massaniello

Fisherman caught = Bathing Machine

Fisherman of Algiers = Abdellac the
Terrible

Fisherman of the Lake = Lost Child

Fisherman of the Thames = Queen of
the Thames

Fisherman's Daughter (Garvice, C.,
1881), V. 376

— (Ward, M. A., 1892), V. 613

— (1843), IV. 461

— = Found at Sea

Fisherman's Hut (Tobin, J., 1819) =
Fisherman, IV. 413, 461, 614, 625

— = Knight of the Black Plume

Fishermen (Stanfield, J. F., 1786), III.
308

Fisher's Prize = Maxey's Money

Fisher's Story = Dead Calm

Fishguard in an Uproar = Cambro-
Britons

Fish in the Ring (Neale, F., 1848), IV.
366

Fish-o'-Man of Naples = Masaniello

Fish out of Water (Lunn, J., 1823), IV.
348

— = Changed at Nurse

Fists (1895), V. 678

Fit of Heroics (1880), V. 678

Fit of the Blues (1873), V. 678

Fits and Starts (Jones, J. W. and
Browne, G. W., 1885), V. 441

Fitzpatricks (Moncrieff, W. T., 1838),
IV. 462, 625

FitzSmythe of FitzSmythe Hall (Morton, J. M., 1860), V. 496

Five Brothers = Wolf Rock

Five Days Fête of Pekin = Chinese
Wonders

Five Degrees of Crime (Rede, W. L.,
1833), IV. 389

Five Hours at Brighton = (1) Boarding
House; (2) My New Boarding House

Five Hundred Francs (Browne, E. M.,
1885), V. 283

Five Hundred Pounds (1821), IV. 462

Floating Kingdom (Faucit, J. S., 1838), IV. 311

Flodden Field (Kemble, S., 1818), IV. 92, 336

Flora (Hippisley, J., 1729), II. 135, 136, 137, 138, 237, 250, 311, 336, 438–9

Flora, and Hob in the Well = Hob

Flora and Zephyr (Conquest, Mrs G., 1852), V. 678, 785, 832

Flora, Sequel to the Opera of (Hippisley, J., 1732), II. 250, 337, 439

Flora's Holiday (1736), II. 372

Flora's Sports (1810), IV. 462

Flora's Vagaries (Rhodes, R., 1663), I. 258, 343, 427

Florazene (Goodhall, J., 1754), III. 265

Flor de la Marcarena (1854), V. 678

Flor de Sevilla (1866), V. 678

Floreat Etona (À Beckett, G. A., 1844), IV. 250

Florence (Palmer, T. A., 1872), V. 512

— (1857), V. 678

Florence Macarthy (Bryant, M., 1823), IV. 574

— (Dibdin, T. J., 1819), IV. 301

Florence Montaubon (1855), V. 678

Florenski and Nina (1819), IV. 462

Florentines (Berwick, E. L. A., 1845), IV. 462, 625

Florentine Wooing (Graves, C., 1898), V. 389

Floretta (Farjeon, E., 1899), V. 361

Florian (Latham, G., 1886), V. 449

Florien (Merivale, H. C., 1884), V. 487

Florinda (1851), V. 678

Florinda Salviati, the White Devil (1828), IV. 462

Florist (1802), IV. 462

Florists' Feast (1765), III. 401

Florizel and Perdita (Garrick, D., 1756), III. 111, 213, 262

— = Sheep-Shearing

Florodora (Hall, O., 1899), V. 400

Flo's First Frolic (Williams, T. J., 1868), V. 626

Flossie the Frivolous = A.B.C.

Flower Girl (Macivay, 1870), V. 469

— (1855), V. 678

Flower Girl and the Convict Marquis (Townsend, W. T., 1855), V. 602

Flower Girl of Ghent (1856), V. 678

Flower Girl of the Innocents = Bronze Medal

Flower Girl of the Temple = Royalists of Paris

Flower Makers and Heart Breakers (Hazlewood, C. H., 1869), V. 414

Flower Makers of Finsbury = Flower Makers and Heart Breakers

Flower of Castille = King, Queen and Knave

Flower of Ellerslie = Auld Lang Syne

Flower of Erin = Shamrock of Ireland

Flower of Llandovery = Heiress of Maes-y-Felin

Flower of Lucerne (Soane, G., 1843), IV. 462

— = Woman's Trust

Flower of the Farm (1862), V. 678

— (1896), V. 678

Flower of the Flock (Melford, M., 1880), V. 484

— (1858), V. 678

Flower of the Mill (1836), IV. 462

Flower of the Port (1854), V. 678

Flower of Waterloo = Forget me not!

Flower of Woolwich = Bound 'Prentice to a Waterman

Flower of Yarrow (Warde, G. A., 1846), IV. 615

Flowers of Joy and Flowers of Sorrow = Lady Lillian

Flowers of Loveliness (1835), IV. 462

Flowers of Progress = Utopia (Limited)

Flowers of the Forest (Buckstone, J. B., 1847), IV. 275

Flowery Land = Celestials

Fluff (McArdle, J. F., 1881), V. 466

Flutters (1886), V. 678

Fly and the Web (Troughton, A. C., 1866), V. 604

Fly-away's Race (Whitehouse, S., 1892), V. 621

Flying Colours (Coape, H. C., 1851), V. 678, 784, 832

— (Cofe, 1847), IV. 462, 625

Flying Dutchman (Brough, W., 1869), V. 280

— (Conquest, G. and Spry, H., 1868), V. 320

— (Fitzball, E., 1827), IV. 25, 113–15, 313

— (Jackson, J. P., 1876), V. 432, 799

Flying Dutchman (Jerrold, D. W., 1839), IV. 332
— (Reece, R., 1883), V. 539
— (1869), V. 678
— (1877), V. 678
Flying Dutchwoman (1827), IV. 462
Flying Fish (1835), IV. 462
Flying from Justice (Melford, M., 1890), V. 484
Flying Indians = Peter Wilkins
Flying Island of Laputa (1806), IV. 462
Flying Jib by Snapdragon (1867), V. 678
Flying Scud (Boucicault, D., 1866), V. 269
Flying Visit (Grain, R. C. and Law, A., 1880), V. 387
— (Greet, D. V., 1889), V. 393
Fly in the Honey = Happy Pair
F.M. Julius Caesar (Burnand, F. C., 1870), V. 289
Foam of the Sea (1899), V. 678
Fog Family = Boarding School Miss
Fog Fiend and the Fairy Fanakin = Bargemaster's Daughter
Fogged (1882), V. 679
Foggerty's Fairy (Gilbert, W. S., 1881), V. 380
Foiled (Alberton, J. R., 1891), V. 237
— (Buckland, W., 1890), V. 286
— (Williamson, H. W., 1882), V. 626
— = Mate
Foiled at Last = Aileen
Foire de Batavia (1803), IV. 462
Foire de Smirne (D'Auberval, 1792), III. 253
Folded Page (Greet, D. V., 1891), V. 393
Folds of the Flag (1896), V. 679
Folle Farine (Avondale, W., 1884), V. 246
Follet (1725), II. 372
Follies of a Day (Holcroft, T., 1784), III. 119, 270-1, 387; IV. 140
— (Kemble, J. P., 1811), IV. 335
— (1812), IV. 140, 462
— = Bloomerism
Follies of a Night (Planché, J. R., 1842), IV. 382
— (1787), III. 328
— = April Fool
Follies of Fashion (Butler, R., 1829), IV. 277
— = Ton

Follies of the Day (Grattan, H. P. and Eldred, J., 1882), V. 389
Follower of the Family = Katty O'Shiel
Following the Ladies (1855), V. 679
Follow my Leader (Maxwell, H. B., 1899), V. 482
— (Thomson, J., 1843), IV. 413
— = Playing First Fiddle
Follow the Drum (Challis, R., 1888), V. 307
Follow the Leader (Rae, C. M., 1873), V. 153, 532
— (1868), V. 679
Folly (1862), V. 679
Folly and Friendship (Planché, Mrs J. R., 1837), IV. 462, 625
Folly as it Flies (Reynolds, F., 1801), IV. 391
— (1828), IV. 462
Folly Exposed (McLaren, A., 1820), IV. 352
— = How to grow wise
Folly Fête (Galer, E. J. N., 1865), V. 679, 793, 832
— = May Queen
Folly, Love and Marriage = Rake and his Pupil
Folly of Age (Ingram, A., 1894), V. 431
— (1797), III. 328
Folly of Priest-Craft (1690), I. 441
Folly Reclaim'd = City Lady
Folly's Fortunes (1899), V. 679
Fond Cuckold = (1) Fair Hypocrite; (2) Maiden Queen
Fond Hearts (Evanson, F., 1889), V. 359
Fond Hearts Blighted = Dying Flower
Fond Husband (D'Urfey, T., 1677), I. 26, 273, 308, 349, 351, 408
— (?1723), I. 408
Fond Lady = Amorous Old-woman
Fondlewife and Letitia (1767), III. 114, 328
Fond Uncle (Miller, H., 1843), IV. 356
Fontainebleau (O'Keeffe, J., 1784), III. 293
— (1814), IV. 462
Fontainville Abbey (1824), IV. 462
Fontainville Forest (Boaden, J., 1794), III. 18, 33, 60, 72, 98, 103-4, 238
Food for Gossip (1855), V. 679
Food for Mirth (McLaren, A., 1821), IV. 352

Fool (Topham, E., 1785), III. 40, 47; 186, 312

Fool and his Money (Byron, H. J., 1878), v. 298

Fooled by Fortune (Walton, H., 1874), v. 612

Fool in Fashion = Love's Last Shift

Fool Made Wise (Johnson, S., 1741), II. 340, 439–40

Fool of Finsbury (Pitt, G. D., 1842), IV. 604

Fool of Fortune = King's Favourite

Fool of the Family (Hume, F., 1896), v. 430

— (1860), v. 679

— (1876), v. 679

Fools (McCord, T. D., 1885), v. 468

+ Fool's Cap (Dibdin, C. I. M., R.A., 1798)

Fool's Errand = First of April

Fool's Expectation (1698), I. 441

Fool's Fidelity (Capel, G., 1887), v. 302

Fools Have Fortune (?1680), I. 441

Fool's Mate (Broughton, F. W., 1889), v. 281

Fools of Fashion (Lathom, F., 1802), IV. 462, 625

Fool's Opera (Aston, A., 1731), II. 246, 296

Fool's Paradise (Grundy, S., 1887), v. 205, 396

— (Meritt, P. and Maltby, A.), v. 486

Fool's Preferment (D'Urfey, T., 1688), I. 275, 409

Fool's Revenge (Taylor, T., 1859), v. 98, 593, 820

Fool's Tragedy = Death's Jest Book

Fool's Trick (Votieri, A., 1891), v. 609

Fool Turn'd Critick (D'Urfey, T., 1676), I. 16, 17, 43, 273, 346, 408

Football (1886), v. 679

Football King (Gray, G., 1896), v. 390

Foote, Shuter and Weston in the Shades = Peep into Elysium

Footlights (Shenton, J., 1872), v. 562

— (1880), v. 679

Footman (1732), II. 372

Footman turn'd Gentleman (1717), II. 372

Footmarks in the Snow (Towers, E., 1867), v. 600

Footprints in the Sand = Pyramids

Fop's Fortune = Love Makes a Man

For a Child's Sake (Herman, H. and Turner, M., 1899), v. 419, 797

For a Life (McCloskey, J., 1886), v. 468

For an Old Debt (Buckley, F. R. and Panting, J. H., 1895), v. 286

For a Woman's Honour (Herbert, F. H., 1899), v. 418

For Better, for Worse (Braddon, M. E., 1890), v. 273

— (Farren, F., 1891), v. 363

— (Maltby, A., 1870), v. 473

Forbidden Fruit (Abbotts, F. M., 1869), v. 233

— (Boucicault, D., 1876), v. 269

— (1850) = What will my Aunt say? v. 679, 766, 832, 849

Forbidden Love (Digges, W., 1877), v. 345

For Bonnie Prince Charlie (Clarke, J. J., 1897), v. 313

For Bonnie Scotland (Stevens, E., 1897), v. 583

Forc'd Inconstancy = Fatal Love

Forc'd Marriage (Behn, A., 1670), I. 55, 101, 140, 267, 390

Forc'd Vallour (Kirkman, F., 1662), I. 417

Forced from Home (Wills, W. G., 1880), v. 627

— (1882), v. 679

Forced Marriage (Armstrong, J., 1770), III. 233

— (Cooke, Mrs T. P., 1842), IV. 282

— (Faucquez, A., 1861) = Willow Marsh, v. 679, 791, 832, 850

— (Foote, S., 1762), III. 384

+ — (8°, 1834)

— = (1) Dona Costanza; (2) Exiled

Forced to Crime = Travers' Secret

Force of Calumny (Plumptre, A., 1799), III. 65, 298, 393

Force of Conscience (Dibdin, T. J., 1819), IV. 302

— = Ravens

Force of Credulity = Fortunate Youth

Force of Fashion (Mackenzie, H., 1789), III. 284

Force of Friendship (Johnson, C., 1710), II. 105, 116, 339, 439

— (Sheil, R. L., 1821) = Damon and Pythias, IV. 462

Force of Friendship = Dionysius

Force of Love (Tighe, E., 1786), III. 59, 312

— = (1) Perjur'd Devotee; (2) Theodosius

Force of Nature (Thackeray, T. J., 1830), IV. 412

— = (1) Thirteen Years' Labour Lost; (2) Wild Boy of Bohemia

Force of Ridicule (Holcroft, T., 1796), III. 271

Force of Superstition = Credulity

For Charity's Sake (Bowyer, F. and Hedgecock, W. H., 1893), V. 271

— (Fawcett, C. S., 1891), V. 364

For Claudia's Sake (Lloyd, M. F., 1891), V. 461

For Country's Sake (1894), V. 679

For Cuba's Freedom (1898), V. 679

For Dear Life (Muskerry, W., 1873), V. 501

Ford Frivolous (Wyke, E. B., 1880), V. 633

Forecastle Fun (1798), III. 328

Foreign Affairs (Webster, B. N., 1841), IV. 418

Foreign Airs and Native Graces (Moncrieff, W. T., 1839), IV. 361

Foreign Policy (Doyle, Sir A. C., 1893), V. 350

Foreign Prince (1839), IV. 462

— = Irish Nigger

Foreman of the Works (Fenn, G. M., 1886), V. 365

For England (Vane, S., 1893), V. 606

— = Send her Victorious

For England, Ho! (Pocock, I., 1813), IV. 115, 384

— (1818), IV. 462

For England's Glory (1898), V. 679

For England's Sake (Lindley, H., 1889), V. 459

Forest Bandit = Anchorite

Forest Bride (1890), V. 679

Forester (Bayley, J., 1798), III. 111, 236

Forester King (Howard, J., 1892), V. 428

Forester of Savoy (1829), IV. 462

Foresters (Atkyns, S., 1849), IV. 257

— (Dibdin, C. I. M., 1826), IV. 296

— (Plumptre, B., 1799), III. 63, 298, 394

— (Serle, T. J., 1838), IV. 400

Forester's Daughter (Masters, W. C., 1867), V. 480

— = Aloyse

Forester's Fate = Robin Hood

Foresters, Robin Hood and Maid Marian (Tennyson, Alfred Lord, 1892), V. 595

Forest Fiend = Kapschou

Forest Flower = Sylvia

Forest Foundling = Maniac Mother

Forest Keeper (Holl, H., 1860), V. 424

Forest Knight (Scott, J. M., 1813), IV. 462, 625

— (1824), IV. 462

Forest Maiden and the Moorish Page (Tully, J. H., 1847), IV. 414

Forest of Ardennes (Wade, T., 1833), IV. 415

Forest of Blarney = Cat of Kilkenny

Forest of Bondy = Dog of Montargis

Forest of Cercotte = Ravens of Orleans

Forest of Friuli = Serbelloni

Forest of Hermanstadt (Dibdin, T. J., 1808), IV. 298

Forest of Monte-Scarpini = Bobinet the Bandit

Forest of Palms = Sacred Standard and the Chinese Prince

Forest of Picardy = Child of Concealment

Forest of Rosenwald = Travellers Benighted

Forest of St Ange = Convict

Forest of Saint Euphemia = Brigands of Calabria

Forest of St Vallier = Two Farmers

Forest of Segovia = Pedro the Devil

Forest of Unterwald = Laurette

Forest Oracle (Campbell, A. V., 1829), IV. 76, 101, 103, 112, 278

Forest Princess (Barnes, C. M. S., 1844), IV. 259

Forest Queen = Una and the Lions

Forest Rose and the Yankee Ploughboy (Woodworth, S., 1851), V. 631

Forest Savage (1825), IV. 462

Forest Tangle = Dux Redux

Forêt aux aventures = Zelis

Forêt Enchantée (1802), IV. 462

Forêt noire (1792), III. 328

For Ever (Meritt, P. and Conquest, G., 1882), V. 486

For Ever and Ever = Prodigal Parson

For Ever Mine (Stevens and Logan, 1889), v. 583

Forewarned is Forearmed = Won by a Head

For Family Fame (McDonald, B. P., 1895), v. 468

For Further Particulars Enquire Within = Bill of Fare

Forged Cheques (Darbey, E., 1882), v. 336

Forge in the Forest = Robber's Sister

Forge Master (Wood, G. W., 1884), v. 630

Forger (Roberts, G., 1886), v. 544
— (1884), v. 679

Forger and his Victim (Pitt, C., 1856), v. 679, 810, 832

Forgery (Buckstone, J. B., 1832), IV. 274
— (Carne-Ross, J., 1888), v. 303
— (Self, C. S., 1899), v. 560
— (1814), IV. 463, 635
— (1824), IV. 463
— (1828), IV. 463
— = Billet-Master

Forgery in Love = Twin Sisters

Forges of Kanzell = Illustrious Traveller

Forget and Forgive (Besemeres, J., 1874), v. 260
— (Conquest, G., 1861), v. 679, 785, 832
— (Kenney, J., 1827), IV. 337
— (Lindoe, 1794), III. 390; IV. 346
— (McLaren, A., 1814), IV. 351
— = Reapers

Forget me not! (Dibdin, C. I. M., 1817), IV. 294
— (Merivale, H. C. and Grove, F. C., 1879), v. 487

Forget-me-not (1876), v. 679
— = (1) Man's Talisman—Gold; (2) Three to One

Forgive and Forget (Dance, C., 1838), IV. 463
— (1835), IV. 463

Forgiven (Albery, J., 1872), v. 237
— (Cave, R. H., 1873), v. 306
— (1878), v. 679
— (1899), v. 679

Forgiveness (Carr, J. W. C., 1891), v. 304

Forgive us our Trespasses (Hope, N., 1896), v. 426

For Gold (Galer, E. J. N., 1882), v. 375

For Good or Evil (Macdonnell, Mrs A. J., 1894), v. 468

Forgotten (Moore, F. F., 1889), v. 492

Forgotten Trust = Wind and Wave

For Hearts and Home (1888), v. 679

For Her Child's Sake (Young, Sir C. L., 1880), v. 636

For Her Sake (Aveling, E. B., 1888), v. 246
— (1886), v. 679

For Himself Alone (Kingston, H., 1888), v. 444

For His Life = His Natural Life

For Honour's Sake (Hazlewood, C. H., 1873), v. 414

For King and Country (Leathes, E., 1883), v. 451

For Lack of Gold ("Maia", 1880), v. 472

For Life (Coghlan, C. F., 1880), v. 316
— (1871), v. 679
— (1878), v. 679

For Life through Thick and Thin (Taylor, J. G., 1868), v. 591

Forlorn Hope (Hazlewood, C. H., 1871), v. 414
— (Scott, C. W. and Coward, J. M., 1896), v. 558

For Love (Robertson, T. W., 1867), v. 546

For Love and Liberty (1888), v. 679

For Love of Prim (Phillpotts, E., 1899), v. 524

For Love or Money (Halliday, A., 1870), v. 401
+ — (Nichol, C. J. S., 8°, Bedford, n.d.)

For Love's Sake (Stephens, L. E. B., 1882), v. 581

For Mildred's Sake (Steele, C. D., 1895), v. 580

Formosa (Boucicault, D., 1869), v. 269

For Old Sake's Sake (Grange, A. D., 1898), v. 388

For Old Virginia (Herman, H., 1891), v. 419

For Papa's Sake (Spurr, M. B., 1896), v. 577

For Queen and Country (Ashley, Mrs J. B., 1890), v. 245
— = Absent-minded Beggar

Forsaken (Marchant, F., 1869), v. 475

Forsaken Daughter = Selima de Gray

For Sale (Douglass, J. T., 1869), v. 348

Forte Thieves, played piano (Smith, B., 1889), v. 572

For the Benefit of the Playful Crocodile (Buckingham, L. S., 1854), v. 679, 781, 832

For the Cause (1895), v. 679

For the Colours (Brabner, W. A., 1899), v. 272

For the Cross (Soden, J. E., 1898), v. 573

For the Crown (Davidson, J., 1896), v. 338

For the Czar (Sykes, P. H. T., 1896), v. 589

For the Honour of the Family (1897), v. 679

For the Honour of the House (1894), v. 679

— (1895), v. 679

For the King (Howard, W. and Pease, S., 1899), v. 428

For the King's Sake (Hale, Mrs C., 1897), v. 398

For the Old Love's Sake (Rogers, T. S. and Kimm, H., 1884), v. 549

For the People = Lady Godiva

For the Queen (1883), v. 679

For the Sake of a Name (Pilmore, F. and Holland, J., 1888), v. 524

For the Sake of a Woman (1895), v. 679

For the Sake of the Duchess (Dawson, F., 1899), v. 339

Fortress (Hook, T. E., 1807), iv. 82, 327

— (Stocqueler, J. H., 1848), iv. 409

Fortress and the Mine = Zamoski

Fortress of Astracan = Almazaide

Fortress of Ganzbrough (1845), iv. 463

Fortress of Kingratz = Signal Fire

Fortress of Magdeburg = Baron Trenck

Fortress of Paluzzi (1822), iv. 463

Fortress of Pressburg (1822), iv. 463

Fortress of Rotzberg (Bounden, J., 1818), iv. 573

Fortress of St Jacques = Fidelio

Fortunate Departure (1810), iv. 463

Fortunate Isles (Planché, J. R., 1840), iv. 381, 605

Fortunate Irishman = Ups and Downs of Life

Fortunate Peasant (Victor, B., 1776), iii. 118, 313

Fortunate Prince (1734), ii. 372

Fortunate Sailor (Morison, D.), iii. 288

Fortunate Slave = Paul

Fortunate Tar = Thomas and Susan

Fortunate Tars (Oulton, W. C., 1810), v. 356

Fortunate Youth (1818), iv. 463

Fortunatus (1866), v. 832

Fortunatus and his Sons (1819), iv. 463

Fortune (Albery, J., 1873), v. 777

Fortune Hunter (Bernard, W. B., 1846), iv. 463, 625

— (Gilbert, W. S., 1897), v. 381

— = Noble Pedlar

Fortune-Hunters (Carlisle, J., 1689), i. 218, 279, 395

— (Dibdin, C., 1789), iii. 256

— (Hewlett, 1812) = Love and Impudence, iv. 325, 495, 588, 631

— (Macklin, C., 1750), ii. 342

— = Double Disappointment

Fortune-Hunters rightly served = Match Maker Fitted

Fortune in her Wits (Johnson, C., 1705), ii. 339, 439

Fortune Mends (Holcroft, F., 1805), iv. 326

Fortune of War (Kenney, J., 1815), iv. 336

— (Philips, F. C., 1896), v. 522

— = (1) Farewell and Return; (2) Josephine

Fortunes and Vicissitudes of a Bohemian Girl = Arline

Fortune's Changes = Beggar's Haunt

Fortune's Favourite (1813), iv. 463

Fortune's Fool (Hamilton, H., 1895), v. 402

— (Harbury, C., 1890), v. 403

— (Reynolds, F., 1796), iii. 133, 301

Fortune's Frolic (Allingham, J. T., 1799), iii. 188, 232; iv. 140

— (1812), iv. 140, 463

— = Frolics of Fortune

Fortune's Frolics (1806), iv. 463

Fortune's Gift (1810), iv. 463

Fortunes of an Irish Peasant = Ballanasloe Boy

Foul Weather (Somerset, C. W., 1881), v. 574

Foul Weather Jack=(1) Life Boat; (2) Mary Marsden

Found (Haywell, F., 1869), v. 412

— (Stein, F. J., 1888), v. 580

Found at Last (Wise, A. B., 1899), v. 629

Found at Sea (Chetham, T. G., 1863), v. 680, 833

Found Brummy (Maltby, A., 1874), v. 473

Found Dead in the Streets (Waldron, W. R., 1869), v. 611

Found Drowned (Rowe, G. F., 1870), v. 552

— (Townsend, W. T., 1865), v. 680, 821, 833

Found Dying (Wardhaugh, M., 1877), v. 614

Found Dying in the Streets (Wardhaugh, M., 1870), v. 614

Foundered Fortune (Morton, W. E., 1890), v. 497

Found in a Four-wheeler (Williams, T. J., 1866), v. 625

Found in Exile (Galer, E. J. N., 1888), v. 375

Found in London (Baldie, D., 1879), v. 247

Foundling (Lestocq, W. and Robson, E. M., 1894), v. 457

— (Moore, E., 1748), II. 137, 184, 206–7, 345, 423, 441

— (1881), v. 680

— =(1) Tom Jones; (2) Walter

Foundling of Fortune (Cheatham, F. G., 1867), v. 308

Foundling of Notre Dame (Banks, W., 1876), v. 248

Foundling of the Forest (Dimond, W., 1809), IV. 306, 581

Foundling of the Sea (Rayner, A., 1859)=Ben Lighterware, v. 812

Foundling of the Streets=Female Detective

Foundling Prince and the Vizier's Daughter=Beauty in a Box

Foundlings (Buckstone, J. B., 1852), v. 287

— (Lewis, L. D., 1881), v. 459

Foundlings of Notre Dame=Julie de Launay

Found £100 (1847), IV. 463

Found Out (Hewson, J. J., 1888), v. 420

Found out at home=Peter Piper

Foundry of Kanzel=Hoorn, the Scourge of Norway

Fountain of Beauty (Kingdom, J. M., 1853), v. 444

Fountain of Life (1886), v. 680

Fountain of Zea (Coyne, J. S., 1848), IV. 285

Four and Twenty Hours in Algiers= Dey and a Knight

Four Brothers=Castle of Aymon

Four by Honours (1879), v. 680

— =Reprobate

Four Cousins (Mayhew, A. and Edwards, H. S., 1871), v. 483

Four Gates (1813), IV. 463

Four Hunchbacks (Gott, H., 1825), IV. 585

£452. 12. 6. (1874), v. 680

Four in Hand (Hook, T. E., 1811)= Darkness Visible, IV. 463

Four Inside (1824), IV. 463

Four Kings (Hazlewood, C. H., 1873), v. 414

Four Knaves and the Pack (Towers, E., 1865), v. 680, 821, 833

Four-leaved Shamrock (Travers, W., 1863), v. 680, 833

— =Rogue Riley

Four Legged Fortune=Flying Scud

Four Legs and Two Legs (Dibdin, T. J., 1826), IV. 304

Four Legs better than Two=Bears not Beasts

Four Little Girls (Craven, W. S., 1897), v. 329

Four Lovers (Coyne, J. S., 1836), IV. 284

Four Mowbrays (1851), v. 680

Four O'Clock Tea (1887), v. 680

Four Phantoms=Ye Legende

Four Quarters of the Globe (1850), v. 680

Four Quarters of the World (1791), III. 328, 381, 401

Four Score Years Ago=London Actor

Four Seasons (Motteux, P. A., 1699), I. 421; II. 345

— (1859), v. 680

Four Sisters (Bernard, W. B., 1832), IV. 265

— (1833), IV. 463

Four Sons of Aymon (Fitzball, E., 1850), v. 367

— (1844) = Castle of Aymon, IV. 463

Four Stages of Life (1862), v. 680

Fourteen Days (Byron, H. J., 1882), v. 299

Four Thieves = Pestilence of Marseilles

Fourth of June (1792), III. 328

— = British Sailor

Four Valiant Brothers = Quatres Fils d'Hemons

Four Wishes = Bee and the Orange Tree

Fowl Play (Burnand, F. C., 1868), v. 289

Fox and Geese (Dibdin, C. I. M., 1802), IV. 290

— (1823), IV. 464

Fox and the Goose (Webster, B. N. and Boucicault, D., 1844), IV. 418, 616

Fox and the Grapes (Lee, N., 1855), v. 681, 802, 833

Fox and the Wolf (1839), IV. 464

Fox and Wolf (1898), v. 681

Fox Chase (Boucicault, D., 1853), v. 268

Fox Glove (Dyall, C., 1883), v. 353

Fox Hunt = Fox Chase

Foxonian Charity = Bankrupt

Fox trap't = Raree Show

Fox Uncas'd (1733), II. 372

Fox versus Goose (Brough, W. and Stockton, J. D., 1869), v. 280

Fra Angelo (Russell, W. C., 1865), v. 553

Fra Diavolo (Lacy, M. R., 1831), IV. 340, 592

— (1830), IV. 464

— (1831), IV. 464

— (1857), v. 681

Fra Diavolo the Second (Denny, J. T., 1882), v. 342

Fra Diavolo Travestie (Byron, H. J., 1858), v. 295

Fragment (Hannan, C., 1894), v. 402

Frailty (Harris, Sir A. H. G. and Merritt, P., 1893), v. 406

France (1822), IV. 464

— = Paris

France and Algeria = Veteran and his Son

France and Austria (1859), v. 681

France as it was (1795), III. 328

France in an Uproar = Royal Fugitives

Francesca (Falconer, E., 1859), v. 360

Francesca da Rimini = Francesca

Francesca Doria (Morris, V., 1849), IV. 464, 625

Francesco di Rimini (Williams, T. J.), v. 824

Francillon (1897), v. 681

Francis Beaumont (Kennedy, C. R., 1860), v. 443

Francis I (Kemble, F. A., 1832), IV. 335

— (McKinlan, 1838), IV. 464, 625

— (Slous, F. L., 1843), IV. 402

Francois the Radical (McCarthy, J. H., 1885), v. 467, 804

Franco-Prussian War (Elphinstone, J., 1872), v. 358

Frank Charington's Return (Norman, G. T., 1897), v. 505

Frankenstein (Brough, W. and Brough, R. B., 1849), IV. 96, 271

— (Henry, R., 1887), v. 417

— (Milner, H. M., 1823), IV. 96, 356

— (1823), IV. 96, 464

Frankfort Lottery = Barber Baron

Frank Fox Phipps, Esq. (Selby, C., 1834), IV. 397

Frank Heartwell (Taylor, T. P., 1848), IV. 411

— (1854), v. 681

Frank-in-Steam (1824), IV. 464

Franklin (Brougham, J., 1868), v. 281

Frankly Feminine (1897), v. 681

Frank the Fool (Wilks, T. E., 1843), IV. 617

Frank the Ploughman (Rogers, W., 1849, 1859), IV. 396; v. 681, 814, 833

Frank Wildeye (1848), IV. 464

— (1861), v. 681

Frantick Stock-Jobber = Female Advocates

Fra Rupert (Landor, W. S., 1841), IV. 199, 341

Frasquita (1893), v. 681

Fraternal Friendship = Step-mother

Fraternization (1855), v. 681

Fratricide (1840), IV. 464

— = Murder will out

Fraud and its Victims (Coyne, J. S., 1857) = Victims of Fraud, v. 327

Freaks and Follies (Rodwell, G. H., 1827), IV. 395

Freaks at Aboukir Bay = Petticoat Service

Freaks in an Attic (Webb, C., 1841), IV. 464, 625

Freaks of Fortune = Y.Y.

Freaks of Love = Men and Women

Freaks of the Passions = Arcadia

Freda (Bussy, B. F. and Blackmore, W. T., 1887), v. 294

Freddy's Client (1896), v. 681

Frederick and Voltaire (Dibdin, T. J., 1821), IV. 303

Frederick, Duke of Brunswick-Lunenburgh (Haywood, Mrs E., 1729), II. 58, 74, 104, 335, 438

Frederick of Bavaria (Milner, H. M., 1822), IV. 464, 625

— (1822), IV. 464

Frederick of Prussia (Selby, C., 1837), IV. 398, 464, 610, 625

Frederick the Great (Arnold, S. J., 1814), IV. 256

— (Maddox, F. M., 1824), IV. 353

Frederick the Great and the Deserter (1821), IV. 464

Fred Frolic, his Life and Adventures (Pitt, C., 1868), v. 526

Fredolfo (Maturin, C. R., 1819), IV. 167, 354

Fred Walters, a Grimsby Fishing Apprentice (Stuart, B., 1877), v. 585

Free and Easy (Arnold, S. J., 1816), IV. 256

— = Arbitration

Free Archers of the New Forest = Deer Slayers

Freebooter = Buonaparte

Freebooters (Napier, H., 1827), IV. 464, 601, 625

Freebooter's Boy = Sea Devil

Freebooters of the Desert = Arab

Freebooters of Vienna (Milner, H. M., 1824), IV. 464, 625

Freedom (Rowe, G. F. and Harris, Sir A., 1883), v. 552

Freedom and Slavery (Morton, T., 1816) = Slave, IV. 464, 626

Freeholder (Moser, J., 1810), IV. 364

Free Judges = Herman and Halstein

Free Knights (Reynolds, F., 1810), IV. 52, 391

Free Labour = Put Yourself in his Place

Free Lance (Horsman, C., 1869), v. 427

Freemason (Hart, J. P., 1839), IV. 324

— (Smith, J. F., 1843), IV. 611

— (1854), v. 681

Freemen and Slaves (Ball, W., 1838), IV. 258

Free Nigger of New York (1840), IV. 464

Free Pardon (Philips, F. C. and Merrick, L., 1897), v. 522

— (1893), v. 681

Free Trader = False Colours

Free-traders of Piedmont = Strozzi

Freezing a Mother-in-Law (Pemberton, T. E., 1879), v. 519

— (1887), v. 681

Freischutz (Almar, G.), IV. 253

— (Amherst, J. H., 1824), IV. 87, 254, 568

— (Burnand, F. C., 1866), v. 289

— (Byron, H. J., 1866), v. 296

— (Douglass, J. T., 1866), v. 348

— (Fitzball, E., 1824), IV. 87, 312

— (Kerr, J., 1824), IV. 592

— (Logan, W. M., 1824), IV. 367, 596, 603

— (Oxenford, J., 1866), v. 681, 809, 833

— (Planché, J. R. + with Washington Irving), 1824), IV. 87, 377

— (Soane, G., 1824), IV. 87, 403

— (1824), IV. 87, 88, 464

— (1828), IV. 464

Freischutz Travestie (1824) = Fryshot, IV. 88, 464, 626

French Beau = Deceiver Deceived

French Company (À Beckett, G. A., 1835), IV. 249

French Conjurer (Porter, T., 1677), I. 253, 425

French Coronation = Ramsbottoms at Rheims

French Doctor Outwitted (1743), II. 372

French Exhibition (Hay, F., 1867), v. 411

French Expedition (1830), IV. 464

French Faith (1786), III. 328

French Flogged (Stevens, G. A., 1760), III. 309

French Forest (1803), IV. 464

French Gallantry = Italian Jealousy
French Gardeners (1763), III. 328
French Girl's Love (Hazlewood, C. H., 1872), V. 414
French Grenadier's Coat = Murat
Frenchified Lady Never in Paris (Dell, H., 1756), III. 253
French in Algiers (Somerset, C. W., 1857), V. 681, 817, 833
— = Lion of the Desert
French in Egypt and the Siege of Acre = Passage of the Deserts
French Ingratitude = Shipwreck
French Invasion (1783), III. 401
French Jezebel = London Arab
French Jubilee (1790), III. 54, 328
French Law (Barry, P., 1893), V. 252
French Libertine (Payne, J. H., 1826), IV. 464, 626
French Maid (Hood, B., 1896), V. 425
Frenchman at Florence = Adventures in Italy
Frenchman Bit = Harlequin Englishman
Frenchman in India = Gallic Gratitude
Frenchman in London (Stafford, J. J., 1834), IV. 405
— (1755), III. 119, 328, 401
Frenchman Puzzled = Fire King
French Milliners (1802), IV. 464
French Polish (Lunn, J., 1840), IV. 348
— (Wilde, W. C. K., 1895), V. 623
French Prison = British Lion
French Puritan = Tartuffe
French Refugee (Hall, Mrs A. M., 1837), IV. 323
French Regicides = Infernal Machine
French Revolution (1830), IV. 464
— = Charlotte Corday
French Revolution of 1830 = "Vive la Liberté"
French Robber = Cartouche
French Spy (Haines, J. T., 1831), IV. 464, 626
— (Haines, J. T., 1837), IV. 322
— (Hill-Mitchelson, E., 1899), V. 422
— = Arab of the Desert
French Vallet = Mock-Duellist
French Village surrender'd (1794), III. 328
French War (1832), IV. 464
French Zealot = Tartuffe
Freshman (Ellis, H., 1899), V. 681, 833

Fresh Start (1896), V. 681
Freshwater Man = Little Tom Tug
Fretful Porcupine (Buckingham, L. S., 1867), V. 286
Freya's Gift (Oxenford, J., 1863), V. 510
Friar (Carr, J. W. C., 1886), V. 304
Friar Bacon (O'Keeffe, J., 1783), III. 293
— (Smith, E. T., 1863), V. 572
— (?1670), I. 446
— (1720), II. 451
Friar Rush (Crowquill, A. and Smith, A. R., 1847), IV. 287
Fricandeau (Payne, J. H., 1831), IV. 464, 626
Fridolin (Lemon, M., 1840), IV. 464, 626
Fried Mackerel for Supper = Nicholas Dunks
Friend and Foe = Boccagh
Friend at a Pinch = (1) True British Tar; (2) Up to Snuff
+ Friend at Court (Amherst, J. H.; Pav. 10/11/1828)
— (Douglas, T., 1811), IV. 307
— (Planché, J. R., 1831), IV. 379
— (1830), IV. 465
Friend Felix (1875), V. 681
Friend Indeed (Dibdin, C. I. M., 1817), IV. 294
— (1846), IV. 465
— = Much too clever
Friend in Need (French, S. and Sorrell, W. J., 1860), V. 373, 793
— (Runciman, F., 1897), V. 553
— (1832), IV. 465
— (1834), IV. 465
— (1894), V. 681
Friend in Need, a Friend indeed (Capper, H. W., 1889), V. 303
Friend in Need is a Friend Indeed (Hoare, P., 1797), III. 121, 270, 387
— (O'Bryan, D., 1783), III. 291, 393
Friend in Need when others fail = Good as Gold
Friendly Foe (Mills, A., 1895), V. 489
Friendly Friend = Manslaughter by Moonlight
Friendly Hints (Bingham, F., 1889), V. 261
Friendly Impertinents (1734), II. 447
Friendly Rivals (1752), III. 328
Friendly Tars (1788), III. 328

Friend of the Family (Dixon, B. H., 1894), v. 346
— (Siddons, H., 1810), IV. 401, 611
— = (1) Atlantic Jack; (2) Swamp Hall
Friend of the People (Rowsell, M. C. and Saintsbury, H. A., 1893), v. 552
Friend or Foe (Wright, F., 1891), v. 633
Friends (Meilan, M. A., 1771), III. 287
— (Parker, A. D., 1887), v. 513
+ — (Seymour, M., *French*)
— (1872), v. 681
— (1884), v. 681
— = Benevolent Planters
Friends and Foes (Roberts, T., 1858), v. 545
Friends and Neighbours (Bayly, T. H., 1839), IV. 263
Friends and their Shadows = Man with the Red Beard
Friends at Court (Taylor, T., 1845), IV. 465; v. 820
— = Cattarina
Friends at Sea and Foes on Shore = Sailor's Sheet-Anchor
Friendship (Reece, R., 1873), v. 537
Friendship à la Mode (1766), III. 115, 328
Friendship Improv'd (Hopkins, C., 1699), I. 413
Friendship in Fashion (Otway, T., 1678), I. 258, 349, 422
— (1829), IV. 465
Friendship, Love and Duty (Siddons, H., 1813), IV. 465, 611, 626
Friendship, Love and Truth (Leslie, H. T., 1868), v. 457
Friendship's Test (Dibdin, C. I. M., 1826), IV. 296
Friends in Need = Pedlar
Friends, Lovers and Enemies = Blanche and Brunette
Friends or Foes (Wigan, H., 1862), v. 622
— (1886), v. 681
Friend Waggles (Morton, J. M., 1850), v. 495
Frightened Ghost (1835), IV. 465
Frightened to Death (Oulton, W. C., 1817), IV. 366
Frightful Accident (Higgie, T. H., 1860), v. 421
Frightful Frost (1879), v. 681

Frightful Hair (Burnand, F. C., 1868), v. 289, 781
Frightful Murder in Hoxton (1857), v. 681
Frightful Tragedy in Willow Walk (1859), v. 681
Frilled Petticoats (Lyne, L. C., 1871), v. 465
Fringe of Society (Wyndham, Sir C. and Moore, J., 1892), v. 681, 807, 825, 833
Fritz, Our German Cousin (Halliday, A., 1872), v. 401
Fritz's Folly (Starr, H., 1896), v. 579
Fritz's Wager (1888), v. 681
Fritz the Outlaw (1813), IV. 465
— (1838), IV. 465
Frivoli (Beatty-Kingston, W., 1886), v. 254
Frivolity (Leopolds, 1895), v. 456
— (Melford, M., 1883), v. 484
Frog (Aveling, E. B., 1893), v. 246
Froggie goes to Eaton (Ambient, M., 1892), v. 240
Froggy would a-wooing go (Green, F. W., 1874), v. 681, 794, 833
Frog he would a-wooing go (Allen, O., 1875), v. 239
— (Cave, J. A., 1877), v. 306
— (Hall, F., 1884), v. 399
— (1876), v. 681
— (1880), v. 681
Frogs (Dunster, C., 1785), III. 258
Frogs and Bulls (Wilmot, Mrs B., 1838), IV. 618
Frog that would a-wooing go (1876), v. 681
Frog, the Tortoise and the Sapajou = King of the Hills
Frog who would a-wooing go (Muskerry, W., 1887), v. 501
Frolic (Brown, J., 1783), III. 240
— (Dibdin, C., 1804), IV. 290
Frolic in Bagdad = Little Hunch-Back
Frolick (Polwhele, E., 1671), I. 424
— (1786), III. 328, 401
Frolicks in France (Kenney, J., 1828), IV. 337
Frolicksome Lasses (1747), II. 372
Frolics in Bagdad = Hunchback
Frolics in "Forty-Five" (?Peake, R. B., 1836), IV. 465, 626

Frolics in France (1856), v. 681

Frolics of an Hour (1795), III. 328

Frolics of Fancy = Match for a Widow

Frolics of Fortune (1835), IV. 465

Frolics of Puck = Robin Goodfellow

Frolics of the Fairies (?À Beckett, G. A., 1834), IV. 465, 626

— (Rede, W. L., 1841), IV. 390

Frolicsome Fanny (Calmour, A. C., 1897), v. 300

Frolique (Farnie, H. B. and Byron, H. J., 1882), v. 363

From Bad to Worse (Holcroft, F., 1805), IV. 326

From Beneath the Deep (Abel, W. H., 1876). v. 235

From Cross to Crown = Christian's Cross

From Fatherland to the Far West = Heinrich

From Father to Son (À Beckett, A. W. and Simpson, J. P., 1882), v. 233

From Grave to Gay (Webster, B., the Younger, 1867), v. 618

From Gulf to Gulf (Smith, H. J., 1892), v. 572

From Information Received = John Wopps

From Life to Death (1875), v. 681

From London to Paris (Raleigh, C. and Harris, Sir A., 1892), v. 533

From Nine till Ten = Ninth Hour

From Scotland Yard (Douglass, J. T. and Bateman, F., 1897), v. 349

— (1897), v. 681

From Shore to Shore (Edwin, P., 1891), v. 356

— (England, A. and Noble, C. R., 1892), v. 358

From Start to Finish = Kildare

From Stem to Stern (Hay, F., 1876), v. 411

From the Jaws of Death (Patmore, W. J., 1893), v. 515

From the Vanished Past (Holton, F., 1888), v. 424

From Village to Court (Morton, J. M., 1854), v. 495

+ Frontello and Dorinda (Lumley, George, 4°, 1737 (Newcastle))

Frontier Life (1895), v. 681

Frost and Thaw (Holman, J. G., 1812) = Adolphus Count Zelmar, IV. 327, 424, 589

Frost at the Heart = Two Winters

Frost Fair (1814), IV. 465

Frost of Life (Wilkins, J. H., 1856), v. 623

Frou-Frou (Achurch, J. and Charrington, C., 1886), v. 235

— (Carr, J. W. C., 1881), v. 304

— (Daly, A., 1870), v. 333

— (Edwards, H. S., 1870), v. 355

— (Webster, B., the Younger, 1870), v. 618

— (1870), v. 681

— (1887), v. 681

— (1894), v. 681

Frozen Cliff (1827), IV. 465

Frozen Deep (Collins, W. W., 1857), v. 318, 785

Frozen Gift = Kolaf

Frozen Hand = Ice Witch

Frozen Hands (1831), IV. 465

Frozen Lake (Planché, J. R., 1824), IV. 84, 377

— (1824), IV. 84, 465

Frozen Mountain (1809), IV. 465

Frozen Regions (1822), IV. 465

Frozen Ships and the Hermit of the Sea-bound Bay = Sea Lion

Frozen Stream (Coates, A., 1872), v. 315

Fruitless Precaution = Spanish Barber

Fruitless Revenge = Unhappy Kindness

Fruits of a Single Error = Adelgitha

Fruits of a Single Lie = Victim of Falsehood

Fruits of Bad Advice = Ten Years of a Woman's Life

Fruits of Geneva = Teresa Tomkins

Fryer Bacon and Fryer Bungay (1711), II. 372

Fryshot (1825) = Freischutz Travestie, IV. 88, 465

Fugitive (Craven, T., 1887), v. 329

— (O'Keeffe, J., 1790), III. 294

— (Richardson, J., 1792), III. 13, 112, 139–40, 196, 302

— (Shapter, T. 1790), III. 305, 307 [The author's name is Shapter, not Shrapter]

— (1850), v. 681

Fugitive Baron = Love and Agility

Fugitives (Conquest, G., 1858), v. 681, 785, 833

— (Roberts, W., 1791), III. 302

— (1778), III. 328

Fugitives and their Faithful Steed = Revolt in the East

Fugitive Slave = Uncle Tom's Cabin

Fugitives of Derrinane = Poor Parisheen

Fugitive's Pearls = Volcano of Italy

Fugitives' Wedding = Forgery

Fugitive Tree (1857), v. 681

Fulham Waterman Defeated = Country Wedding

Full Moon (1891), v. 681

Full Particulars of that Affair at Finchley (1861), v. 681

+ Full Private Perkins; or, He Wiped away a Tear (Byron, H. J.: *Dicks* (in *Sensation Dramas*))

Fulvius Valens (Serle, T. J., 1823), IV. 399

Fun (Kenrick, W., 1752), III. 279

Fun Alive = St Bartholomew

Fun and Fright (?Rodwell, T. G., 1819), IV. 465, 626

Fun and Frolic (1799), III. 328

Fun and Harmony = Board of Conviviality

Funeral (Steele, Sir R., 1701), II. 35, 129, 130, 131, 134, 137, 140, 183, 191, 230, 356

Funeral a la Mode = Funeral

Funeral Pile (1821), IV. 465

— = (1) Gallic Gratitude; (2) Orlando and Seraphina

Fun for the Gallery = Scraps

Fun in a Fog (1871), v. 681

Fun in a Japanese Tea House (1898), v. 682

Funnibone's Fix (Williams, A., 1880), v. 624

+ Funny Facts and Foolish Fancies (Paxton, A., *French*)

Funny World (Grain, R. C., 1894), v. 388

Fun on an Island (1895), v. 682

Fun on the Bristol (1882), v. 682

Fun on the Rhine = Our Goblins

Furibond (1807), IV. 465, 626

Furioso (1836), IV. 465

Furioso the Terrible (1862), v. 682

Furnished Apartments (Hay, F., 1860), v. 411

Furor of Friendship (Dibdin, C. I. M., 1822) = Manslaughter by Moonlight, IV. 295, 500

Fuss about Nothing (1862), v. 682

Future Mrs Ransome (1894), v. 682

Future Mrs Skillimore (Craven, S., 1897), v. 329

Gaberlunzie (Black, L., 1839), IV. 572

Gaberlunzie Man (Ballantyne, J., 1858), v. 247

— (Rede, W. L., 1836), IV. 390

Gabriel Grub the Sexton (Furtado, C., 1880), v. 375

Gabriella (Byrne, C. A., 1893), v. 295, 782

Gabrielle (Hodges, F. S., 1884), v. 423

— (1835), IV. 465

Gabrielle de Belleisle (1840), IV. 465

Gabrielle the Girondist (1854), v. 682

Gabrielli (Peake, R. B., 1847), IV. 371

Gabriel's Plot (1871), v. 682

Gabriel's Trust (Calmour, A. C., 1891), v. 300

Gadfly (Shaw, G. B., 1898), v. 562

+ Gaffer Grey's Legacy (*French*)

Gaffer Jarge (Ramsay, A., 1896), v. 534

Gaffer's Mistake (Dibdin, T. J., 1795), III. 328, 382, 401; IV. 297, 580

Gaia = Léonore

Gaiété (Eldred, J. and Aylen, H., 1874), v. 356

Gaiety Girl (Hall, O., 1893), v. 11, 399

Gain (Sargent, H., 1880), v. 556

— (1885), v. 682

Galatea (Schwab, F. A., 1887), v. 682, 833

— (Stephens, H. P., 1883), v. 580

— (1831), IV. 465

Galatea of Oregon (1895), v. 682

Gale Breezeley (Johnstone, J. B., 1845), IV. 333

Galician Fête (1855), v. 682

Gallantee Showman (Jerrold, D. W., 1837), IV. 333, 590

Gallant in the Closet = Coquettes

Gallant Moriscoes (1795), III. 328

Gallant Peasants (1767), III. 328

Gallantry (Penley, S., 1820), IV. 465, 626

Garde Nationale (Boucicault, D., 1850), v. 267
— = International Visits
Gardener of Versailles (1854), v. 682
Gardener's Wedding (1740), II. 372
Garden of Life = Weeds and Flowers
Garden Party (Jones, H. A., 1880), v. 439
— (Morton, J. M., 1877), v. 496
Garibaldi (Cooper, F. F., 1860), v. 682, 786, 833
— (Taylor, T., 1859), v. 593
Garibaldi Excursionists (Byron, H. J., 1860), v. 111, 296
Garibaldi in Sicily (Sawyer, W., 1867), v. 557, 815
Garibaldi's Englishmen (1859), v. 682
Garibaldi the Italian Liberator = Garibaldi
Garland (Hook, T. E., 1805) = Soldier's Return, IV. 466
— (1765), III. 329
Garland of Love (1815), IV. 466
Garland of Truth = Integrity
Garnet King = Corporal's Daughter
Garret Angel (Webb, C., 1867), v. 617
— (1860), v. 682
Garrick (Daly, A., 1874), v. 333
— (Muskerry, W., 1886), v. 501
Garrick and his Double (Dibdin, T. J., 1825), IV. 304
Garrick Fever (Planché, J. R., 1839), IV. 381
Garrick in the Shades (1779), III. 329
Garrick's Sacrifice (Lindo, F. and Young, Sir C. L., 1897), v. 460
Garrick's Vagary (1769), III. 329
Garrick the Actor (1890), v. 682
Garry Owen (Levey, J. C., 1877), v. 458
Gasconado the Great (Worsdale, J., 1759), III. 317
Gascon Adventurer = Fiend's Mountain
Gascons (Muskerry, W., 1876), v. 501
Gas in Burlesque Meter = Oxygen
Gasman (Bradford, H., 1873), v. 273
Gaspard Hauser (1838), IV. 466
Gaspardo the Gondolier (Almar, G., 1838), IV. 253
Gaston Boissier (Courtney, W. L., 1893), v. 326
+ Gaston de Foix (Mitford, E. L. in Poems, 1869)

Gaston Phoebus (Buchanan, R., 1868), v. 284
Gathering = Lord of the Isles
Gathering of the Clans (Dibdin, C. I. M., 1818), IV. 294
— (1895), v. 682
— = (1) Bonnie Dundee; (2) Lord of the Isles; (3) Montrose
Gaul, King of Ragah (Hawkes, W. R., 1813), IV. 466
Gaul versus Lavater = Knobs and Noses
Gauntlet (Braekstad, H. L., 1890), v. 780
— (Edwards, O. and Hawtrey, G. P., 1894), v. 355, 789
— (1799), III. 62, 329
Gavotte (Bell, M., 1890), v. 256
Gawyim Honor (Jones, M. E. M., 1844), IV. 591
Gay Boulogne = J.P.
Gay Cavalier (Cuthbert, E., 1879), v. 331
Gay Chaperon (Howlett, S., 1894), v. 429
Gay City (Sims, G. R., 1881), v. 568
— (1871), v. 682
Gay Deceiver (Mortimer, J., 1879), v. 494
Gay Deceivers (Colman, G., the Younger, 1804), IV. 282, 577
Gay Goddess = Juno
Gay Gracer of Three Wives (1845), IV. 466
Gay Grisette (Dance, G., 1898), v. 335
Gay Husband (Allerton, 1886), v. 239
Gay Lord Quex (Pinero, Sir A. W., 1899), v. 525, 810
Gay Lothario (Calmour, A. C., 1891), v. 300
Gay Musketeers (Eldred, J. and Paulton, H., 1870), v. 356
Gay Parisienne (Dance, G., 1894), v. 335
Gay Photographer (1896), v. 682
Gay Widow (Burnand, F. C., 1894), v. 292
Gay Widower (Mayer, S., 1892), v. 482
Gay Young Fellow = Billy Taylor
Gazette Extraordinary (Holman, J. G., 1811), IV. 327
Gazza Ladra (1835), IV. 466
Geisha (Hall, O., 1896), v. 400
Gelert (Balsilio, D., 1896), v. 247

Genius of Glasgow (1792), III. 329

Genius of Ireland (Macaulay, J., 1784), III. 283

Genius of Liverpool (Harpley, T., 1789), III. 266

Genius of Nonsense (Colman, G., 1780), III. 210, 247, 379

Genius of the Ring = Bride of Golconda

Genius Wanted (1831), IV. 466

Genoese Conspiracy = Fiesco

Genoese Pirate (Cross, J. C., 1798) = Black Beard, III. 250, 380

Genoveva (Vance, L., 1893), V. 606

Gentle Amy Robsart = Kenilworth

Gentle Gertrude (Pemberton, T. E., 1881, +4°, 1880 (Birmingham) as Gentle Gertrude of the Infamous Red Lyon Inn, or Drugged and Drowned in Digbeth), V. 519

Gentle Ivy (Fryers, A., 1894), V. 374

Gentle Juliet = Modern Juliet

Gentleman (Steele, Sir R.), II. 444

Gentleman and the Upstart (Ranger, E., 1848), IV. 606

Gentleman Citizen (Foote, S., 1762), III. 384

Gentleman-Cully (Johnson, C., 1701), II. 21, 169, 339, 422

Gentleman Dancing-Master (Wycherley, W., 1672), I. 13, 75, 188, 192, 238, 438; III. 114, 198

Gentleman Gardener (Wilder, J., 1751), III. 316

— (1749), II. 138, 372

Gentleman in Black (Gilbert, W. S., 1870), V. 379

— (Lemon, M., 1840), IV. 344

— (Rede, W. L., 1842), IV. 607

— = (1) Dominique the Deserter; (2) Grave Subject

Gentleman in Difficulties (Bayly, T. H., 1835), IV. 262, 571

Gentleman in Paris = Discounting a Life

Gentleman in White (1866), V. 682

Gentleman Jack (Mouillot, F., 1888), V. 498

— (Vincent, C. T. and Brady, W., 1894) V. 609

— (1850), V. 682

Gentleman Jim (Walkes, W. R., 1893), V. 611

Gentleman Joe (Wilks, T. E., 1838), IV. 420

— (1838), IV. 466

Gentleman Joe, the Hansom Cabby (Hood, B., 1895), V. 425

Gentleman Opposite (Buckingham, L. S., 1854), V. 682, 781, 833

Gentleman Quack = Justice Busy

Gentleman Rover (1827), IV. 466

Gentleman's Son = Lancers

Gentleman Whip (Paull, H. M., 1894), V. 516

Gentleman with a Bee in his Bonnet = Slightly Touched

Gentlemen of the Night = Under the Lamps

Gentlemen, we can do without you = Ladies at Home

Gentle Nelly (1871), V. 682

Gentle Revenge = Treble Lover

Gentle Savage = Pocahontas

Gentle Shepherd (Bethune, G., 1817), IV. 267

— (McLaren, A., 1811), IV. 351

— (Ramsay, A., 1725), II. 250, 350, 443; III. 117

— (Tickell, R., 1781), III. 117, 312

— (Turner, Mrs M., 1790), III. 117, 313

— (Vanderstop, C., 1777), III. 117, 313

— (Wood, W., ?1785), III. 117, 317

— = Patie and Roger

Gentle Thieves (1877), V. 682

Gentoo's Daughter = Brahman's Curse

Genuine Grub-Street Opera = Welsh Opera

Geoffrey Dunstan (1828), IV. 466

Geoffrey Kurdistan (Pitt, G. D., 1845), IV. 373

George (James, W., 1895), V. 434

George III, the Father of his People (Macfarren, G., 1824) = Life and Reign of George III, IV. 349, 492, 597, 631

George a Green (1775), III. 113, 329

George and the Crocodile (1834), IV. 466

George Barnwell (1811), IV. 466

— (1844), IV. 466

— = London Merchant

George Barrington (Taylor, T. P., 1844), IV. 19, 411

— = Night Birds

George Cameron (Mitchell, L. E., 1891), V. 490

George Dandin (1747), III. 145, 372, 447
George Darville (Boucicault, D., 1857), v. 268
George de Barnwell (Byron, H. J., 1862), v. 296
George Geith (Reeve, W., 1877), v. 540
George Heriot (Murray, W. H., 1823), IV. 93, 365, 601
— (Ryder, C., 1823), IV. 93, 396
— = Fortunes of Nigel
George's Natal Day (1780), III. 329
Georgette (1854), v. 682
George Vernet (Conquest, G., 1855), v. 682
Georgey Barnwell (1833), IV. 466
Georgey Porgey Pudding and Pie (Douglass, J., 1857), v. 348
Georgian Princess (Craven, E., 1799) = Princess of Georgia, III. 329, 380, 401
Georgians (Wilson, C. J. S., 1875), v. 628
Gerald (Marston, J. W., 1842), IV. 353
Geralda = British Heroine [This appears in the newspapers also as Gerilda]
Geraldi Duval, the Bandit of Bohemia (Walker, C. E., 1821), IV. 416
Geraldine (À Beckett, G. A., 1843), IV. 466, 567, 626
— (Bateman, Mrs H. L., 1865), v. 253
— (1887), v. 682
Geraldine's Ordeal (Bannister, T. B., 1871), v. 248
+ Gerald of Kildare (Bibby, T., 12°, 1854, Dublin)
Gerard the Pedlar = Leontine
Gerilda = Geralda
German Baron (1784), III. 401
German Blunder (Greffulhe, 1809) = Is He a Prince? IV. 467, 626
German Forest = Natural Son
German Hotel (Holcroft, T., 1790), III. 7, 122, 134–5, 271, 387
Germanicus (Bernel, G., 1817), IV. 266
— (1775), III. 329
— (1817), IV. 467
German Jew (Tilbury, W. H., 1830), IV. 467, 626
German Patrol (1830), IV. 467
German Princess (Holden, J., 1664), I. 220, 413
Germans and French (Douglass, J. T., 1871), v. 348
German Silver (1895), v. 682

German Silvery King (Burnot, W., 1883), v. 293
Gertie's Garter (Southern, E. H., 1883), v. 574
Gertrude (Collins, M. T., 1848), IV. 577
— (Richardson, S., 1810), IV. 394
Gertrude and Beatrice (Stephens, G., 1839), IV. 406
Gertrude of Elsinore (1836), IV. 467
Gertrude's Cherries (Jerrold, D. W., 1842), IV. 129, 333
Gertrude's Money Box (Lemon, H., 1869), v. 454
Gerty (1881), v. 683
Gervaise Skinner (Jerrold, D. W., 1830), IV. 332
Gervase Skinner (1831), IV. 467
G.G. = Mistake
Gheber (Dibdin, C. I. M., 1818), IV. 294
Ghebirs of the Desert = Lalla Rookh
Ghetto (Fernald, C. B., 1899), v. 683, 792, 833
Ghillie Callum (1895), v. 683
Ghost (James, H. and others, 1899), v. 799
— (1767), III. 115, 329
— (1892), v. 683
Ghost Hunter (Banim, J., 1833), IV. 258
— (Conquest, G., 1862), v. 683, 785, 833
— (1856), v. 683
Ghost in Spite of Himself (1866), v. 683
— = Spectre Bridegroom
Ghost no Conjurer = All up at Stockwell
Ghost of a Hamper of Wine = (1) Manslaughter by Moonlight; (2) Furor of Friendship
Ghost of an Idea (Heathcote, A. M., 1892), v. 415
Ghost of an old Fiddle = Music hath Charms
Ghost of Cock Lane (1862), v. 683
Ghost of the Back Drawing Room = Jane Jenkins
Ghost of the Past (Darrell, C., 1899), v. 337
Ghosts (Archer, W., 1891), v. 187, 242
— (Holden, J., 1665), I. 413
— (1886), v. 683
Ghost's Advice = Leave the House
Ghosts and Apprehensions = All a Fetch
Ghost's Bargain = Haunted Man

Ghost Seer = Bannockburn

Ghosts of Tom and Jerry (Dibdin, C. I. M., 1823), IV. 295

Ghost Story (Serle, T. J., 1836), IV. 400

Ghost's Tower = Seven Maids of Munich

Ghost! The Ghost! = Awful Rise in Spirits

Ghost with the Golden Casket = Wreckers of the Craig Foot

Gian Ben Gian and the Elixir = Loadstone of the Earth

Giant (Webb, C., 1839), IV. 467, 626

Giant and the Dwarf (Addison, J., 1896), V. 236

Giant Defeated (1789), III. 329

Giant Horse (1833), IV. 467

Giant of Palestine (1838), IV. 467

Giant of the Mountains (Addison, J., 1894), V. 236

— (Marchant, F., 1869), V. 476

Giant's Castle (1839), IV. 467

Giant's Causeway (1829), IV. 467

— (1844), IV. 467

Giant Spectre = Prophecy

Giant Staircase = Council of Ten

Giant's Tomb (1858), V. 683

Giaour (1897), V. 683

Gibbet and the Rampart = Just in Time

Gibbet Law of Halifax = Dennis

Gibbet of Hounslow = Young Highwayman

Gibbet of Mont Faucon = Dagger and the Cross

Gibraltar (Dennis, J., 1705), II. 16, 129, 210, 318

— (Houlton, R., 1783), III. 273

— (Murray, A., 1881), V. 499

Giddy Galatea (Edlin, H., 1895), V. 354

Giddy Girl (1899), V. 683

Giddy Godiva (Newton, H. C., 1883), V. 503

Giddy Major General (1898), V. 683

Giddy Miss Carmen (Lester, S., 1894), V. 457

Gideon Giles the Roper (Pitt, G. D., 1845), IV. 374

Gideon's Ghost (1860), V. 683

Gifted Lady (Buchanan, R., 1891), V. 285

Gift of Mammon = Devil's Ducat

Gift of Venus (1895), V. 683

Gifts of Immortality = Tempter

Gilbert the Idiot (1859), V. 683

Gil Blas (Bates, 1788), III. 329, 377

— (Moore, E., 1751), III. 7, 288, 392

— (1823), IV. 467

— = Boy of Santillane

Gil Blas and the Robbers of Asturia = Boy of Santillane

Gil Blas at 17, 25, 52 (Macfarren, G., 1822), IV. 349 [There is doubt about the authorship of this play. It is attributed as well to R. B. Peake, while Thomas Hood's daughter said it was by her father and J. H. Reynolds, see *University of Texas Studies in English* (1951), p. 187]

Gil Blas de Santillane (1821), IV. 467

Gilded Age = Colonel Sellers

Gilded Crime (1884), V. 683

Gilded Love (Yeldham, Major, 1888), V. 635

Gilded Youth (Young, Sir C. L., 1872), V. 149, 635

Gilderoy (Murray, W. H., 1827), IV. 365

Gilderoy, the Bonnie Boy (Barrymore, W., 1822), IV. 262

Gillette (Clarke, H. S., 1883), V. 313, 784

Gillian the Gipsey (Blake, T. G., 1846), IV. 268

Gin (Roberts, G., 1880), V. 544

Gin and Water (1854), V. 683

Gingerbread Nut (1790), III. 329

Gin versus Water (1854), V. 683

Giorno Felice (Scott, J. M., 1812), IV. 609

Giovanna of Naples (Landor, W. S., 1839), IV. 199, 341

Giovanni in Botany (1822), IV. 467

Giovanni in Ireland (Moncrieff, W. T., 1821), IV. 467, 626

— (1821), IV. 467

Giovanni in London (Moncrieff, W. T., 1817), IV. 358, 600

Giovanni in the Country (1820), IV. 467

Giovanni Redivivus (Cooper, F. F., 1864), V. 786

Giovanni, the Vampire (Planché, J. R., 1821), IV. 376

Gipsey and the Gentle Goat = Esmeralda

Gipsey and the Stolen Child = Justice

Girls of Chelsea Reach = Boys of Horsley Down

Girls of the Period (Burnand, F. C., 1869), v. 289

Girl's Romance = Rescued

Girl that was sent to Coventry = Giddy Godiva

Giroflé Giroflá (O'Neil, C. and Clarke, C., 1874), v. 507

Girouette (Reece, R., 1889), v. 539, 813

Gisela (Holroyd, J. J., 1839), IV. 327

Giselle (Byron, H. J., 1871), v. 298

— (Moncrieff, W. T., 1841), IV. 101, 103, 113, 361

— (1843), IV. 467

— (1846), IV. 467

— = Wilis

Giselle and the Phantom Night Dancers (Fenton, F. and Osman, W. R., 1863), v. 683, 833

Gisippus (Griffin, G., 1842), IV. 321

Gismonda (1895), v. 683

Gis, the Armourer of Tyre (Selby, C., 1859), v. 560

Gitana (Moreton, F. L., 1895), v. 493

— (Towers, E., 1876), v. 601

Gitama's Love = Manola

Gitanilla (Wilson, J. C., 1860), v. 628

Gitano Boy (Reynoldson, T. H., 1866) = True at Last, v. 683, 813, 833

Gitta la ballerina (1865), v. 683

Give a Dog a Bad Name (Lewes, G. H., 1854), v. 458

— (Lewis, L. D., 1876), v. 459

— (1866), v. 683

Give a Man Luck = New Way to get Married

Give and Take (Pryce-Jenkins, T. J., 1894), v. 531

Give me my Wife (Suter, W. E., 1859), v. 587

Give Them their Way = Children

Gladiator (Bird, R. M., 1836), IV. 267

— (1786), III. 401

Gladiator of Ravenna (Charlton, W. H., 1861), v. 783

— (Martin, Sir T., 1885), v. 806

— (Vericour, de, 1859), v. 608

Gladiators (Bannister, T. B., 1893), v. 248 [The entry in IV. 258 is in error and should be deleted]

Glad Tidings (Willing, J. and Stainforth, F., 1883), v. 626

Gladys (Law, A., 1886), v. 450

Glamour (Farnie, H. B. and Murray, A., 1886), v. 363

Glance at a Court = Madame du Barry

Glasgow in 1300 (1855), v. 683

Glashen Glora (Dodson, R., 1875), v. 346

Glass (1847), IV. 467

Glass Door (Ebsworth, J., 1837), IV. 308

Glass Houses (Broughton, F. W., 1881), v. 281

Glass of Fashion (Grundy, S. and Sims, G. R., 1883), v. 396

Glass of Water (Suter, W. E., 1863), v. 588

Glass too much = (1) Challenge; (2) Truth

Glaucus (Traill, F. T., 1865), v. 602, 821

Glazier (Dibdin, T. J., ?1796), III. 383

Glazier's Conspiracy = Illumination

Gleam in the Darkness (1899), v. 683

Gleam of Hope (1866), v. 683

Gleam of Sunshine = Wanderer

Gleaner (Moser, J., 1809), IV. 364

Gleaners (1809), IV. 467

— (1811), IV. 467

— (1857), v. 683

Glenarvon (1819), IV. 467

Glencoe (Talfourd, T. N., 1840), IV. 48, 64, 79, 177–8, 410

Glendelough (Gurney, E., 1891), v. 398

Glendwyr of Snowdon (1849), IV. 467

Glen Girl (Blake, T. G.), IV. 573

Glider (1895), v. 683

Glimpse of Paradise (Dilley, J. J., 1887), v. 345

Glimpse of the World (Howlett, S., 1895), v. 429

Glin Gath (Meritt, P., 1872), v. 148, 485

Glitter (À Beckett, G. A., 1868), v. 233

Glittering Gem (Rennell, C. R., 1874), v. 541

Gloaming and the Mirk (1869), v. 684

Globe (1881), v. 684

Gloriana (Lee, N., 1676), I. 14, 67, 96, 123–4, 126, 128, 129, 148, 419

— (Mortimer, J., 1891), v. 494

Glorie Aston (Dawson, F., 1898), v. 339

Glories of England in 1356 = Edward the Black Prince

Glorious Bit of Fun (1857), v. 684

Glorious First of August = (1) Aboukir Bay; (2) Mouth of the Nile

Glorious First of June (Sheridan, R. B. and Cobb, J., 1794), III. 306

Glorious Princess (1747), II. 372

Glorious Queen of Hungary (1743), II. 372, 452

Glorious Revolution, 5th November, 1688 (Lee, F., 1821), IV. 342

Glory (Grattan, H. P., 1873), v. 389

Glory's Resurrection (Settle, E., 1698), v. 429

Glo'stershire Squire = Country 'Squire

Gloucestershire Story = Lock and Key

Glove and Fan (1857), v. 684

Glow-worm (Isla, Count de la, 1884), v. 432

Gnome (Wewitzer, R., 1788), III. 315

Gnome Fly (Conquest, G. and Spry, H., 1869), v. 320

— (1838), IV. 467

Gnome King (Brough, W., 1868), v. 280

— (Reynolds, F., 1819), IV. 468, 607, 626

— (1823), IV. 467

— (1838), IV. 467

Gnome Lamp = Field of Terror

Gnome of the Gold Mines = (1) Mirror of Fate; (2) Slave of Wealth

Gnome of the Hartsberg = Berta

Gnomes and Fairies (Dibdin, C. I. M., 1816), IV. 298

+ Goal (Jones, H. A., 8°, 1898 (priv.))

Goatherd of the Mountain = Octavian

Goat-herd's Oath = Worga

Go Bang (Ross, A., 1894), v. 551

Goblin Bat (Bowyer, F., 1886), v. 271

Goblin Mine = Fairy Fern Flower

Goblin of the Chest = Trooper's Horn

Goblin Tale = Chimes

God-daughter = Atonement

Goddess of El Dorado = Naida

Goddess of Morni = Aurora

Goddess of the Moon = Diana

Godefroi and Yolande (Irving, L. S. B., 1894), v. 684, 799, 833

Godfather's Legacy = Two Sisters

Godfrida (+ J. Davidson, 8°, 1898), v. 684

Godiva (Hale, W. P. and Talfourd, F., 1851), v. 398

God of War (Whitlock, C., 1898), v. 621

Godolphin (Hope, 1843), IV. 589

Godolphin Arabian (1845), IV. 468

Godolphins (1860), v. 684

Godolphin, the Lion of the North (Thompson, B., 1813), IV. 413

Godpapa (Philips, F. C. and Brookfield, C. H. E., 1891), v. 522

Gods as they were and not as they ought to have been = Venus

God save the Queen (Palgrave, R. and Gover, F., 1886), v. 511

Gods grown old = Thespis

Goetz of Berlichingen, With the Iron Hand (Scott, Sir W., 1799), III. 63, 304; IV. 193

Gog and Magog (Dibdin, T. J., 1822), IV. 303

— = Pindar of Wakefield

Goggin's Gingham (Wigan, H., 1863), v. 622

Going it (Morton, J. M. and Vicars, W. A., 1885), v. 497

Going on the Stage (Henry, Mrs R., 1895), v. 417

Going out a-shooting = First of September

Going over to Rome = Innocents Abroad

Going the Pace (Shirley, A. and Landeck, B., 1898), v. 565

Going to Chobham (Hazlewood, C. H., 1853), v. 412

Going to Cremorne (Courtney, J., 1852), v. 326

Going to Execution (1822), IV. 468

Going to my Uncle's (1833), IV. 468

Going to see the Fireworks (1856), v. 684

Going to the Bad (Taylor, T., 1858), v. 593

Going to the Derby (Morton, J. M., 1848), IV. 363

Going to the Dogs (Brough, W. and Halliday, A., 1865), v. 280

Gold (Reade, C., 1853), v. 535

— (1851), v. 684

— (1880), v. 684

+ Gold and Guilt; or, The True Ring of the Genuine Metal (Byron, H. J.: *Dicks* (in *Sensation Dramas*))

Golden Plume (Howells, C. E., 1880), v. 429

Golden Ring (Sims, G. R., 1883), v. 569

— (1883), v. 684

Golden Serpent (Walter, T. N., 1897), v. 612

Golden Shield (1836), IV. 468

Golden Sorrow (Drinkwater, A. E., 1891), v. 351

Golden Test (1887), v. 684

Golden Web (Stephenson, B. C. and Corder, F., 1893), v. 582

Golden Wedding (Cole, J. P., 1899), v. 316

— (Groves, C. and Phillpotts, E., 1898), v. 810

— (Sketchley, A., 1885), v. 684, 816, 833

Golden Witness (Pitt, G. D., 1850), v. 526

Golden Wreath (Albery, J., 1878), v. 684, 777, 833

Gold Fields of Australia (1853), v. 684

Gold Fiend (Townsend, W. T., 1850), v. 602

Gold Fiend of Australia = Gold Fiend

Gold Fiend of the Black Forest (1859), v. 684

Goldfinch (Hoskins, F. R., 1851), v. 427

Gold Finders of Australia (1853), v. 684

Goldfish (Mattos, A. T. de, 1892), v. 481

Gold Goblin = Heart of Old Ireland and the Lepreghaun

Gold Guitar (Wilks, T. E., 1843), IV. 617

Golding's Debt = Friendship

Gold is Nothing—Happiness is All (Levey, J. C., 1868), v. 458

Gold Mine (Matthews, B. and Jessop, G. H., 1889), v. 480

— (Stirling, E., 1854), v. 584

Gold Regions of Australia (Johnstone, J. B., 1853), v. 438

Gold Seekers (Grattan, H. P., 1839), IV. 320

— (1838), IV. 468

Gold Seekers of Alasca (1842), IV. 468

Gold Seekers of Carpentara = New Fortune

Gold Slave (Barclay, T. G., 1886), v. 248

Goldsmith (Holcroft, F., 1827), IV. 326

Goldsmith of Frankfort (Haines, J. T.), IV. 587

Goldsmith of Grenoble = Mount St Bernard

Goldsmith's Daughter = Julie Ledru

Goldsmiths Jubilee (Jordan, T., 1674), I. 416

Goldsmiths of Clerkenwell = Pledge

Goldsmith's Wife (1889), v. 684

Gombeen's Gold (1891), v. 684

Gommoch (O'Grady, H., 1877), v. 506

Gondibert and Birtha (Thompson, W., 1751), III. 312

Gondolier (1815), IV. 636

Gondoliers (Gilbert, W. S., 1889), v. 145, 380

— (1751), III. 329

Gone Away (Righton, E. and Stow, D., 1886), v. 543

Gone to Texas (Oxenford, J., 1844), IV. 468, 626

Gonsalve de Cordoue (1816), IV. 468

Gonsalvo (1822), IV. 626

Gonsalvo de Cordova (Cross, J. C., 1802), IV. 286

Gonzaga (Solly, H., 1877), v. 574

— (1814), IV. 468, 636

Gonzalo (Fortescue, 1821), IV. 317

Gonzalo, the Traitor (Roscoe, T., 1820), IV. 609

+ Gonzalvo of Cordova (Wilmot, Mrs B., 8°, 1821)

Good and Bad (1792), III. 329

— = Hearts, Hearts, Hearts

Good and Evil = Forger

Good as Gold (Hazlewood, C. H., 1869), v. 413

— (Monk, M., 1883), v. 491

— (1877), v. 684

Good Business (Hervey, R. K., 1887), v. 420

Good-bye (Bourchier, A., 1889), v. 270

— (Hicks, Sir S., 1893), v. 420

— (Johnson, H. T., 1896), v. 437

Goodbye Sweetheart (1894), v. 684

Good Cast for a Piece = Freischutz

Good Conduct Prize = Jane Annie

Good Fairy of St Helen's (Brockbank, J., 1872), v. 276

Good for Both (Kennedy, J., 1887), v. 443

Good for Evil=(1) Home Truths; (2) Little Bidette; (3) Reconciled
Good for Nothing (Buckstone, J. B., 1851), V. 107, 287
— (Lemon, M., 1841), IV. 344
— (Yates, E. and Harrington, N. H., 1858), V. 635
Good Fortune (Coghlan, C. F., 1880), V. 316
Good Friday that came on Saturday=Jack Robinson Crusoe
Good Gracious! (Hawtrey, G. P., 1885), V. 410
Good Hearts (1858), V. 684
Good Husbands make Good Wives (Buckstone, J. B., 1835), IV. 274
Good King Arthur=Merry Mr Merlin
Good-looking Fellow (Almar, G., 1834), IV. 253
— (Kenney, J. and Bunn, A., 1834), IV. 337
Good Luck (Burnett, J. P., 1885), V. 292
— (1878), V. 684
— =Glorie Aston
Good Luck at Last=(1) Richmond Wells; (2) Virtue's Escape; (3) Virtuous Wife
Goodman's Fields in the Olden Time (1831), IV. 468
Good Morning, Mr Smith (1861), V. 684
Good Name (Stocqueler, J. H., 1845), IV. 468, 626
Good Natur'd Man (Goldsmith, O., 1768), III. 45, 130, 157-9, 162, 265, 386
— =Fathers
Good News (Byron, H. J., 1872), V. 298
Good News for British Tars (1790), III. 329
Good News! Good News! (McLaren, A., 1814), IV. 351
Good Night, Signor Pantalon (Somerset, C. A., 1852), V. 574
— (1851), V. 684
Good Night's Rest (Gore, Mrs C. G. F., 1837), IV. 319
Good Old Barnes of New York (Burnot, W., 1888), V. 293
Good Old Cause=Roundheads
Good Old Queen Bess (Lewin, W., 1891), V. 459

Good Old Times (Caine, H. and Barrett, W., 1889), V. 299
Good or Evil (1885), V. 684
Good out of Evil=(1) Vagabonds; (2) Sid
Good Queen Bess (Collins, C. J., 1856), V. 684, 785, 833
— (Trevor, H. and Trevor, L., 1895), V. 603
— (1861), V. 684
Good Run for it (Bridgeman, J. V., 1854), V. 274
Good Samaritan (1892), V. 685
Good Shepherd (1898), V. 685
Good Sovereign and the Bad Yellow Boy=Yellow Dwarf
Good Time=Shipped by the Light of the Moon
Good Time Coming (1851), V. 685
Good Times of Queen Bess=Northern Inn
Good Turn (Broughton, F. W., 1880), V. 281
Good Woman in the Wood (Planché, J. R., 1852), V. 527
Goody Goose (Hazlewood, C. H., 1858), V. 412
Goody Two Shoes (Blanchard, E. L., 1862), V. 263
— (Clarance, L., 1877), V. 310
— (Dibdin, C. I. M., 1803), IV. 291
— (Dibdin, T. J., 1820), IV. 302
— (1878, 1879, 1884, 1887, 1889, 1890, 1891, 1895, 1899), V. 685
Goody Two Shoes and her Queen Anne's Farthing (Strachan, J. S., 1872), V. 585
Goose and the Golden Eggs (Draper, J. F., 1869), V. 350
Goose Chase=Fox versus Goose
Goose Fair (Goodyer, F. R., 1874), V. 384
Goose Green=Pop!
Goose with the Golden Eggs (Mayhew, A. and Edwards, H. S., 1859), V. 482
Goosey Goosey Gander (Hazlewood, C. H., 1860), V. 685, 796, 833
— (1832), IV. 468
Gordian Knot Unty'd (1690), I. 442
Gordon Gray (1811), IV. 468
Gordon Highlanders=Our British Empire

Gordons to the Front = Ladder of Life

Gordon the Gypsey (Peake, R. B., 1822), IV. 468, 626

Gore (1889), v. 685

Gorilla Hunt in the Forest of Gabon (Hazlewood, C. H., 1863), v. 685, 796, 833

Gorillas (Marchant, F., 1869), v. 805

Gorilla Warfare = Sugar and Spice

Gortz of Berlingen, with the Iron Hand (Lawrence, R., 1799), III. 63, 280, 390

Gosling the Great (Keating, Miss, 1860), v. 685, 800

Gospel Shop (Hill, R., ?1770), III. 269

Gossip (Fitch, C. and Dietrichstein, L., 1895), v. 367

— (Harris, A. G. and Williams, T. J., 1859), v. 405

— (1831), IV. 468

Go straight (Outram, L. S., 1894), v. 509

Gotham Election (Centlivre, Mrs S., 1715), II. 20, 211, 305

Gotham in Alarm ("Odd Fellow", 1816), IV. 602

Gothmund the Cruel (Dibdin, C. I. M., 1804), IV. 291

Go-to-bed Tom (Morton, T., Jr., 1852), v. 497

Go to Putney (Lemon, H., 1868), v. 454

Gout = Tragopodagra

Governess (Belot, A., 1886), v. 257

— (1785), III. 329

— = Duenna

Governor (1793), III. 329

Governor of Barcelona (1711), II. 373

Governor of Kentucky (1896), v. 685

Governor's Wife (Mildenhall, T., 1845), IV. 355, 598

Governour of Cyprus (Oldmixon, J., 1703), II. 26, 30, 53, 105–6, 160, 347, 442

Gowrie Conspiracy (Wilson, J. M., 1828), IV. 618

Gowrie Plot = James VI

Go Wyn Wyn Wyn = Taffy's Triumph

Grace (Dutch, J. S., 1880), v. 352

Grace Challoner (Barnett, C. Z., 1845), IV. 260

Grace Clairville (Lewis, A., 1843), IV. 345

Grace Darling (Bosworth, J., 1838), IV. 573

Grace Darling = Wreck at Sea

Grace Darrell (James, R., 1896), v. 433

Grace Gayton (1846), IV. 468

Grace Holden (Cheltnam, C. S., 1869), v. 309

Grace Huntley (Holl, H., 1833), IV. 326

Grace Mary (Jones, H. A., 1895), v. 440

— (1899), v. 685

Grace Rivers (Lee, N., 1844), IV. 468, 626

Grace Royal (Meritt, P., 1876), v. 486

Graces (Dibdin, C., 1782), III. 256

Graciosa and Percinet (Planché, J. R., 1844), IV. 382

Graciosa the Fair (Roberts, J. F., 1807), IV. 394

Graeme (1824), IV. 468

Gra-Gal-Machree (Connor, B., 1876), v. 320

Graham, the Regent of Scotland (1827), IV. 468

Gramachree Molly (1844), IV. 468

Granada taken and done for = Court of Lions

Granby Enticed from Elysium (Watson, W., 1782), III. 315

Grandad's Darling (Gurney, E.), v. 398

Grand Army (1838), IV. 468

Grand Baby Show (1856), v. 685

Grand Caravan and the Saddler of Cairo = Peacock's Feather

Grand Duchess (Brookfield, C. H. E., 1897), v. 277

Grand Duchess of Gerolstein (Kenney, C. L., 1867), v. 443, 801

— (1871), v. 685

Grand Duke (Gilbert, W. S., 1896), v. 381

— (Gordon, G. L., 1886), v. 385

— = Prima Donna

Grand Duke of Camberwell (Akhurst, W. M., 1876), v. 237

Grande Doctresse = Lucrezia Borgia, M.D.

Grandfather's Clock (Baron, J., 1883), v. 250

— (Bertrand, E. C., 1879), v. 260

Grandfather's Little Nell (1870), v. 685

Grandfather's Secret (1885), v. 685

+ Grandfather's Story (French)

Grandfather Whitehead (Lemon, M., 1842), IV. 344

Grand Junction Canal (Dibdin, C. I. M., 1801), IV. 290

Grand Master of Malta = Corsican Pirate

Grand Mogul (Farnie, H. B., 1884), v. 363, 791

Grandmother Browning (À Beckett, G. A., 1844), IV. 250

Grandmother Grizzle (Buckstone, J. B., 1851), v. 287

Grandmother's Gown = Lord Dolly

Grandmother's Pet (1844), IV. 468

Grand National (Elphinstone, J., 1869), v. 358

Grandpapa (1825), IV. 468

Grandpapa's Promise (Corcoran, L., 1887), v. 325

Grandpa's Birthday (1895), v. 685

Grand Sabre, the Traitor (1829), IV. 468

Grand Secret; A Tale of 1642 = Lord Mayor's Fool

Grandsire (Woodhouse, W. A., 1889), v. 631

Grand Tour (1821), IV. 468

Grand Venetian Carnival (1821), IV. 469

Granna Waile and the Bridal Eve (Archer, W. J., 1874), v. 242

Grape Girl of Madrid (1850), v. 685

Grapeshot (Field, W. F., 1889), v. 366

Grasping a Shadow (Craven, T., 1885), v. 329

Grasshopper (Hollingshead, J., 1877), v. 424

— (Webster, B., the Younger, 1867), v. 618

Grass Widow (Fane, F., 1898), v. 361

Grass Widows (Whittaker, J. H. G., 1879), v. 621

Grateful (Towers, F., 1877), v. 602

Grateful Fair (Smart, C., ?1747), II. 355

Grateful Father (Pemberton, T. E., 1878), v. 519

Grateful Lion (1793), III. 401

Gratitude (Hazlewood, C. H., 1859), v. 685, 796, 833

— (Pitt, W. H., 1869), v. 527

Grau-a-Aille (1891), v. 685

Grave (1802), IV. 469

Grave Charge (1896), v. 685

Grave-makers (Kirkman, F., 1662), I. 417

Graven Image (Cheatham, T., 1862), v. 685, 783, 833

Grave of the Forsaken = Adeline

Grave on the Sands = Eyes in the Dark

Grave Subject (1828), IV. 469

Gray Ladye of Fernlea (Towers, E., 1867), v. 600

Gray Lady of Fernlea (Hazlewood, C. H., 1867), v. 413

Gray Mare (Webster, B., the Younger, 1863), v. 618

Great Alexander (1828), IV. 469

Great Bank Robbery (Darbey, E., 1896), v. 336

Great Bastard = Royal Cuckold

Great Bear and the Two Kings = Toolooloo and Woolooloo

Great Bed of Ware (Glover, E., 1852), v. 382

Great Caesar (Grossmith, G., Jr. and Rubens, P., 1899), v. 395

Great Casimir (Leigh, H. S., 1879), v. 454, 803

Great Catch (Aidé, H., 1883), v. 236

Great Cigar = Page 21

Great City (Halliday, A., 1867), v. 400

Great Comet (Dick, C., 1896), v. 344

Great Demonstration (Zangwill, I. and Cowen, L., 1892), v. 637

Great Devil (Dibdin, C. I. M., 1801), IV. 290

Great Diamond Robbery (Alfriend, E. M. and Wheeler, A. C., 1898) = Heart of Fire, v. 238, 691

— (Delannoy, B. and Waldron, W. R., 1892), v. 341

Great Dismal Swamp = Dred

Great Divorce Case (Scott, C. W., 1876), v. 557

Greatest Puritan (1899), v. 685

Great Exhibition of 1851 (Webb, C., 1851), v. 617

Great Expectations (Gilbert, W. S., 1871), v. 379

— (1892), v. 685

Great Favourite (Howard, Sir R., 1668), I. 137–8, 415

Great Felicidad (Paull, H. M., 1887), v. 516

Great Fire of London (Pitt, G. D., 1861), v. 810

Great Gentleman in the Little Parlour (Dibdin, T. J., 1825), IV. 304

Great Globe (Stewart, J. O., 1889), v. 584

Great Gun Trick (Le Ross, C., 1855), v. 456

Great Horse of Greece = Siege of Troy

Great Illusion (Bell, Mrs H., 1895), v. 256

Great Metropolis (Burnand, F. C., 1874), v. 290

— (Terriss, W., 1892), v. 595

— (1845), IV. 469

Great Mogul (Oxenford, E., 1881), v. 509

Great Muddleborough Election = Blue and Buff

Great News from France = Whimsicality

Great Night (1860), v. 685

Great Pearl Case (Courte, S. X., 1894), v. 325

Great Percentage = Upstairs and Downstairs

+ Great Pickwick Case (Pollitt, R., 8°, 1884, Manchester)

Great Pink Pearl (Carton, R. C. and Raleigh, C., 1885), v. 305

Great Ruby (Raleigh, C. and Hamilton, H., 1898), v. 534

Great Russian Bear (Morton, T., Jr., 1859), v. 497

Great Secret (1885), v. 685

Great Sensation (Lee, S., 1862), v. 685, 803, 833

Great Sensation Trial (Brough, W., 1863), v. 279

Great Separation (1876), v. 685

Great Steeplechase (1844), IV. 469

Great Strike (1866), v. 685

— = Work and Wages

Great Success (Hewson, J. J., 1884), v. 420

Great Taykin (Law, A., 1885), v. 450

Great Temptation (Shirley, A., 1899), v. 565

— (1874), v. 685

Great Temptations = Great Temptation

Great Tichborne Case (Mackay, W., 1872), v. 471

Great Tom-Tom (Stanhope, B., 1886), v. 578

Great Tyrant (1861), v. 685

Great Unknown (Daly, A., 1889), v. 333

— (Stirling, E., 1840), IV. 469, 626

Great Unknown (1823), IV. 469

Great Unpaid (Horner, F., 1893), v. 427

Great Wall of China (1876), v. 685

Great Wealth (1885), v. 685

Great World of London (Lander, G. and Melville, W., 1898), v. 448

— (1893), v. 686

Grecian Amazon = Massacre of Cyprus

Grecian Daughter (Kemble, J. P., 1815), IV. 335

— (Murphy, A., 1772), III. 29, 31, 52, 53, 76, 290

— (1813), IV. 469

Grecian Heroine (D'Urfey, T., 1718), II. 320

— = Tyrant of Syracuse

Gredel (1884), v. 686

Greed for Gold = Mystery

Greed of Gold (Silva, H. R., 1894), v. 566

Greek Amazon (1833), IV. 469

Greek Boy (Lover, S., 1840), IV. 347

Greek Brigands (Meadows, L., 1870), v. 483

Greek Brothers (Pitt, G. D., 1844), IV. 373

Greek Captive (1844), IV. 469

Greek Family (Raymond, R. J., 1829), IV. 388

— = Suliote

Greek Girl (1862), v. 686

Greek Hero and the Jewish Maid = Hebrew Tribe of Rome

Greek Pirates of the Gulph = Corsair

Greek Renegade (1845), IV. 469

Greeks and the Turks (1821), IV. 469

Greeks at Brixton = Treadmill

Greek Slave (Fitzball, E., 1851), v. 368

— (Hall, O., 1898), v. 400

— (1791), III. 112–13, 329

Greek Soprano (1897), v. 686

Green Bushes (Buckstone, J. B., 1845), IV. 275

Green Business = Stock Exchange

Green Dragon (Moncrieff, W. T., 1819), IV. 358

— (1828), IV. 469

Green Enchantress (Sharp, E., 1898), v. 561

Greene's Tu Quoque (D'Avenant, Sir W., 1667), I. 401

Green-eyed = Jealous of the Past

Green-eyed Monster (Planché, J. R., 1828), IV. 378
— (Pocock, I., 1811), IV. 383
Green Gosling (1828), IV. 469
+ Green Grow the Rushes, Oh! or, The Squireen, the Informer and the Illicit Distiller (Byron, H. J.: *Dicks* (in *Sensation Dramas*))
Green Hills of Shannon = My Poor Dog Tray
Green Hills of Surrey (Courtney, J., 1849), IV. 284
Green Hills of the Far West (Wilkins, J. H.), IV. 420
Green in France (1823), IV. 469
Green Isle of the Sea (1874), V. 686
Green Lanes and Blue Waters (1861), V. 686
Green Lanes of England (Conquest, G. and Pettitt, H., 1878), V. 321
Greenleaf and Redburg, the Forest Twins = Gold Finders of Australia
Greenleaf the Graceful (Osman, W. R., 1872), V. 508
Green Man (Jones, R., 1818), IV. 334
Green Mantle (1837), IV. 469
Green Old Age (Reece, R., 1874), V. 538
Green Rider = De Bassenvelt
Green Room (Finney, 1783), III. 259
— (Kenney, J., 1826), IV. 337
— (1821), IV. 626
— (1825), IV. 459
Green-Room Controversy = Rivals
Green Room Scene (Monro, T., 1795), III. 392
Greenwich Fair (1831), IV. 469
Greenwich Park (Mountfort, W., 1691), I. 38, 69, 279, 421
Greenwich Pensioner (Cheltnam, C. S., 1869), V. 309
— (1830), IV. 469
— (1832), IV. 469
Greenwich Railway (1835), IV. 469
Gregarach, the Highland Watchword (Barrymore, W., 1821), IV. 93, 469, 626
Gregory VII (Horne, R. H., 1840), IV. 328
Grelley's Money (Ross, E., 1882), V. 551
Grenadier (Bayly, H., 1831), IV. 469, 626
— (O'Keeffe, J.), III. 294

Grenadier (1788), III. 329
— = Brigadier
Grenadier Guard = Holstein Hussar
Gr[envi]lle Agonistes (Hale, 1807), IV. 587
Greshamite = Harlequin-Hydaspes
Gretchen (Gilbert, W. S., 1879), V. 380
Gretna Blacksmith = Scotch Lovers
Gretna Green (Beazley, S., Jr., 1822), IV. 264
— (Ford, T. M., 1889), V. 370
— (Stuart, C., 1783) = New Gretna Green, III. 310, 403
— = Trip to Gretna
Grey Doublet (Lemon, M., 1838), IV. 343
Grey Man of Tottenham Cross = Seven Sisters
Grey Mare (Sims, G. R. and Raleigh, C., 1892), V. 569
Grey Mare's Better Horse (1795), III. 329
Grey Mare the Better Horse = Welsh Opera
Grey Parrot (Jacobs, W. W. and Rock, C., 1899), V. 432, 799
Grey the Collier (Soane, G., 1820), IV. 469, 626
Grief A-la-mode = Funeral
Grierson's Way (Esmond, H. V., 1899), V. 358
Grieving's a Folly (Leigh, R., 1809), IV. 343
Grif (Lestocq, W., 1891), V. 457
— (Towers, F., 1877), V. 602
Griffith Gaunt (Reade, C., 1871), V. 536
Griffith Murdoch (Spier, M. H., 1893), V. 576
Grimaldi (Bailey, W., 1822), IV. 257
— (Murray, G. and Hipkins, T. H., 1861), V. 422
— = Life of an Actress
Grimalkin (Rodwell, G. H., 1828), IV. 395
Grimalkin the Great (Blanchard, E. L., 1868), V. 264
— (Buckstone, J. B., 1830), IV. 469, 626
Grim Goblin (Conquest, G. and Spry, H., 1876), V. 321
Grim Grey Woman = Elfin Sprite
Grim Griffin Hotel (Oxenford, J., 1867), V. 510
Grim Look Out (1877), V. 686

Grimshaw, Bagshaw and Bradshaw (Morton, J. M., 1851), v. 495

Grimstone Grange (À Beckett, G. A., 1879), v. 234, 777

Grimthorpe Case (1894), v. 686

Grim Will, the Collier of Croydon (1825), IV. 469

"Grin" Bushes (Byron, H. J., 1864), v. 296

Gringoire (Bessle, E. and Basing, S. H., 1890), v. 260

— (Stephenson, B. C., 1899), v. 582

— (Wills, W. G., 1885), v. 627

— (1879), v. 686

— (1892), v. 686

Gringoire the Ballad Monger = Pity

Grip (1871), v. 686

Gripe in the Wrong Box (1831), IV. 469

Grip of Iron = Stranglers of Paris

Griselda (Anstruther, R. A., 1841), IV. 254

— (Arnold, Sir E., 1856), v. 243

— (Braddon, M. E., 1873), v. 273

— (1844), IV. 469

Griseldis (Sieg, W., 1871), v. 816

Griselides (1893), v. 686

Grist to the Mill (Planché, J. R., 1844), IV. 382

Grizzel Jamphray (Ellenden, 1846), IV. 309

Grove (Oldmixon, J., 1700), II. 233, 347

Groves of Blarney (Hall, Mrs A. M., 1838), IV. 323

Grub-Street Opera = Welsh Opera

Grumbler (Goldsmith, O., 1773), III. 265, 386

— (Sedley, Sir C., 1719), I. 428; III. 114

— (1754), III. 114, 330

Grump's Menage (1876), v. 686

Grunt and Gaby = Mrs Mullins

Guarded by Honour (Stanley, H. J., 1885), v. 579

Guard House (Dance, G., 1835), IV. 469, 626

Guardian (Cowley, A., 1650), I. 398

— (Garrick, D. 1759), III. 119, 262, 385

Guardian Angel (Brooks, C. W. S., 1849), IV. 271

Guardian Out-witted (Arne, T. A., 1764), III. 199, 233

— = Venetial Nuptials

Guardians (1808), IV. 469

— = (1) Faro Table; (2) Man of Taste

Guardians off their Guard (1840), IV. 469

Guardians Outwitted (1823) = Assumptions, IV. 469, 626

Guardians overreached in their own Humour (1742), II. 384

Guardian Spirit (O'Neil, J. R., 1853), v. 507

Guardian Storks = Ida

Guardian Sylph (Selby, C., 1835), IV. 397

Guardroom Slave (1841), IV. 469

Guards = Mirabel

Guardsman (Sims, G. R. and Raleigh, C., 1892), v. 569

Gubbins stands for the Council (1889), v. 686

Gude Man of Ballangeich (1849), IV. 469

Gudeman of Ballangrich = Cramond Brig

Gudgeons (Carson, S. M. and Parker, L. N., 1893), v. 304

Gudgeons and Sharks (Poole, J., 1827), IV. 386

Guerilla Boy and the Spectre Sister = Zitella

Guerilla Chief (1826), IV. 469

Guerilla Chief and his Daughters (1827), IV. 470

Guerillas (Atkyns, S., 1848), IV. 257

Guide of the Tyrol (?Blake, T. G., 1838), IV. 470, 626

Guiding Star (Elkington, C., 1899), v. 356

— (Suter, W. E., 1868), v. 588

Guiding Star of Virtue = Lamplighter

Guido and Imilda (Moore, R., 1869), v. 492

Guido Fawkes (Stirling, E., 1840), IV. 407

Guido Ferrandi = Duchess of Padua

Guidone (Smith, W., 1846), IV. 612

Guillaume Tell (Bunn, A., 1838), IV. 276

Guilt (Frye, W. E., 1819), IV. 318

— (Gillies, R. P., 1819), IV. 319

Guilt Discovered = Father's Curse

Guilt its own Punishment = Fatal Curiosity

Hān Koong Tsew (Davis, Sir J. F., 1829), IV. 579

Hannah (Smart, C., 1764), III. 356, 396

Hannah Hewitt (Dibdin, C., 1798), III. 256, 382

Hannele (Archer, W., 1894), V. 242

Hannibal (Nichol, J., 1873), V. 504
— (Shore, L., 1898), V. 565
— (1861), V. 687

Hannibal in Bithynia (Knight, H. G., 1839), IV. 592

Hannibal's Overthrow = Sophonisba

Hans, an Alsatian (1880), V. 687

Hans Anderson's Fairy Tales (Hood, B., 1897), V. 798

Hansel and Gretel (Bache, C., 1894), V. 687, 778, 833

Hans Ketzler's Close Shave = Enchanted Barber

Hans of Iceland (Fitzball, E., 1825, 1841), IV. 316, 470, 627

Hans of the Iron Hand (1832), IV. 470

Hansom Cab (1888), V. 687

Hans the Boatman (Greene, C. M., 1887), V. 392

Hans von Stein (Fitzball, E., 1851), V. 367

Hap (1882), V. 687

Happier Days (Scotti, S., 1886), V. 558

Happiest Day of my Life (Buckstone, J. B., 1829), IV. 273

Happiest Man Alive (Bernard, W. B., 1840), IV. 266

Happiness (1880), V. 687

Happiness at Home (Hazlewood, C. H., 1871), V. 414

Happiness at Last = Rover

Happiness of Colombine = Harlequin's Distress

Happy African = Irishman in London

Happy Africans (1796), III. 391

Happy Arcadia (Gilbert, W. S., 1872), V. 379

Happy at Last (1805), IV. 470

Happy Bungalow (Law, A., 1877), V. 449

Happy Captive (Theobald, L., 1741), II. 359, 399, 445

Happy Change = Late Revolution

Happy Constancy (Jacob, H., 1738), II. 205, 338

Happy Converts = Pilgrims

Happy Counterplot = Celadon and Florimel

Happy Cruise (Cuthbert, E., 1873), V. 331

Happy Day (Henry, R., 1886), V. 417
— = Giorno Felice

Happy Disguise (Oulton, W. C., 1784), III. 295

Happy Fair One = Love's Triumph

Happy Family (Dance, C., 1848), IV. 289
— (Taylor, J. G., 1873), V. 687, 820, 834
— (Thompson, B., 1799), III. 311, 397; IV. 412

Happy-go-lucky (Hazleton, F., 1875), V. 412
— (Pemberton, T. E., 1884), V. 519

Happy-go-lucky, True-love and Forget-me-not (Spry, H., 1882), V. 577

Happy Hamstead (Desprez, F., 1876), V. 343

Happy Hero (1746), II. 373

Happy Hours (1862), V. 687

Happy Island = Enchantress

Happy Land (Gilbert, W. S. and À. Beckett, G. A., 1873), V. 379

Happy Life (Parker, L. N., 1897), V. 513

Happy Lovers (Ward, H., 1736), II. 363, 446

Happy Man (Lover, S., 1839), IV. 347

Happy Manager (O'Neil, J. R., 1852), V. 507

Happy Marriage (1727), II. 373
— = Orphan

Happy Medium (Pemberton, T. E., 1875), V. 519
— = Planchette

Happy Miller just arriv'd = All Alive and Merry

Happy New Year (Law, A., 1882) = Strange Host, V. 450, 687, 802

Happy Nuptials (1733), II. 373

Happy Pair (Smith, S. T., 1868), V. 152-3, 573
— = Indian Merchant

Happy Prescription (Hayley, W., 1784), III. 226-7, 267, 386

Happy Recess = Fugitive

Happy Relief = Soldier's Widow

Happy Resentment = Mistakes

Happy Result (1865), V. 687

Harlequin and Riddle me, Riddle me Ree (Lee, N., 1841), IV. 472, 594

Harlequin and Robin Redbreast (1859), V. 687

Harlequin and St Crispin's Day (1833), IV. 472

Harlequin and St George and the Dragon (1846), IV. 472

— (1855), V. 687

Harlequin and Sinbad the Sailor (Douglass, J. T., 1881), V. 348

Harlequin and the Astrologer of Stepney (1827), IV. 472

Harlequin and the Babes in the Wood (1859), V. 834

Harlequin and the Book of Life (1839), IV. 472

Harlequin and the Child of Hale (1850), V. 834

Harlequin and the Crystal Palace of 1851 (1850), V. 687

Harlequin and the Cygnet (1822), IV. 472

Harlequin and the Dandy Club (1818), IV. 472

Harlequin and the Dragon of Wantley (Barrymore, W., 1824), IV. 262

— (Greenwood, T., 1849), IV. 472, 627

— (1824), IV. 472

Harlequin and the Eagle (1826), IV. 472

Harlequin and the Elfin Sprite (Vining, W., 1838), IV. 472, 627

Harlequin and the Enchanted Figs (1838), IV. 472

Harlequin and the Enchanted Fish (Reynolds, F., 1840), IV. 392

Harlequin and the Enchanted Prince (Townsend, W. T., 1862), V. 821

Harlequin and the Enchanter of the Coral Cavern (1843), IV. 473

Harlequin and the Fairy Queen of the Magic Teapot (1849), IV. 473

Harlequin and the Five Senses (1855), V. 687

Harlequin and the Flying Chest (1823), IV. 473

Harlequin and the Forty Thieves (1858), V. 687

— = Forty Thieves

Harlequin and the Giant Helmet (Planché, J. R., 1840), IV. 381

Harlequin and the Giant King (1832), IV. 473

Harlequin and the Golden Alphabet (Douglass, J., 1852), V. 348

Harlequin and the Golden Branch (1845), IV. 473

Harlequin and the Golden Peacock (1848), IV. 473

Harlequin and the Happy New Year = Harlequin and a Happy New Year

Harlequin and the House that Jack built (Blanchard, E. L., 1861), V. 263

Harlequin and the House that Jack built in 1851 (Greenwood, T. L., 1850) = House that Jack built in 1851, V. 393, 687, 794, 834

Harlequin and the King of the Ruby Mine (1824), IV. 473

Harlequin and the Knave of Clubs (1832), IV. 473

Harlequin and the Kohinoor (1851), V. 687

Harlequin and the Little Black Hen (1860), V. 834

Harlequin and the Little Mouse who built his House in a Christmas Cake (Hazlewood, C. H., 1859) = Little Mouse, V. 687, 796, 834, 839

Harlequin and the Lord Mayor of London (1847), IV. 473

Harlequin and the Loves of Cupid and Psyche (Selby, C., 1857), V. 687, 815, 834

Harlequin and the Magic Axe = Magic Axe

Harlequin and the Magic Wreath (1863), V. 834

Harlequin and the Magic Marrowbone (1828), IV. 473

Harlequin and the Magic Rose (1825), IV. 473

Harlequin and the Magic Sirloin (Barnett, C. Z., 1845), IV. 260

Harlequin and the Maid and the Magpie (Morton, J. M., 1855), V. 687, 807, 834

Harlequin and the Merry Devil of Edmonton (1839), IV. 473

Harlequin and the Miller and his Men (Morton, J. M., 1853), V. 495

Harlequin and the Ogress (1822), IV. 473, 627

Harlequin in the Oven (1779), III. 401

Harlequin in the Stocks (Cherry, A., 1793), III. 243

Harlequin Invader (1746), II. 373

Harlequin Invincible (1795), III. 330

Harlequin Invisible (1724), II. 373

Harlequin Jack-a-Lantern (Reynolds, F., 1837), IV. 392

Harlequin Jack and the Beanstalk (Soutar, R., 1869), v. 575

Harlequin Jack in the Box (Green, F. W., 1877), v. 391

— (1886), v. 689

Harlequin Jack of All Trades (Farrell, J., 1844), IV. 311

— (1825), IV. 474

Harlequin Jack Sheppard (1839), IV. 474

Harlequin Jack Sprat (Blanchard, E. L. and Greenwood, T. L., 1864)＝Jack Sprat, v. 689, 699, 779, 794, 835, 837

Harlequin Jack the Giant Killer (Lee, N., 1843), IV. 474, 627

— (1853), v. 689

Harlequin Junior (1784), III. 330

Harlequin Kafoozalum (1866), v. 689

Harlequin King Aboulifar (Mowbray, T., 1857), v. 498

Harlequin King Atlas (Faucit, H. S., 1864), v. 791

Harlequin King Candle and the Empress Rushlight (1856), v. 689

Harlequin King Crystal (Towers, E., 1863), v. 689, 835

Harlequin King Frolic (Pettitt, H., 1880), v. 521

Harlequin King Holliday (Higgie, T. H., 1859), v. 689, 798, 835

Harlequin King Humpty Dumpty (Townsend, W. T., 1862)＝Harlequin Humpty Dumpty, v. 689, 821, 835

— (1864), v. 689

Harlequin King Muffin (Forrester, A. W. and Shepherd, T., 1853), v. 371

Harlequin King Nutcracker (Halford, J. and Planché, J. R., 1853), v. 398

Harlequin King of Carbuncles (James, C. S., 1852), v. 433

Harlequin King of Spades (1808), IV. 475

Harlequin King One Eye and Davy Jones's Locker (1856), v. 689

Harlequin King Peewit and his Merry Little Men (Towers, E., 1865), v. 689, 821, 835

Harlequin King Pumpkin (Dutnall, M., 1864), v. 689, 789, 835

Harlequin King Richard III (James, C. S., 1853), v. 433

Harlequin King Rufus (1858), v. 835

Harlequin King Ugly Mug (Lee, N., 1853), v. 452

Harlequin Libertine (1817), IV. 627

Harlequin Lincoln Lucky of Lambeth (1843), IV. 475

Harlequin Little Bo Peep (1878), v. 689

Harlequin Little Bo Peep and Tom Tucker (Branson, W. S., 1874), v. 274

Harlequin Little Boy Blue (Arnold, H. T. and Greenwood, T. L., 1868), v. 243

Harlequin Little Goody Two Shoes and the Fairies of the Chrystal Lake (1861), v. 835

Harlequin Little Jack Horner (Soutar, R., 1864), v. 689, 817, 835

Harlequin Little Red Riding Hood (Rae, L. and Walden, W., 1880), v. 533

Harlequin Little Tom Tucker and the Fine Lady of Banbury Cross and the Old Lady who lived in a Shoe and had so many Children she didn't know what to do (1863), v. 689

Harlequin Lord Lovell (Blanchard, E. L., 1848), IV. 269

Harlequin Mamaluke (1801), IV. 475

Harlequin Mariner (1788, 1797), III. 330, 401

Harlequin Married＝Amorous Goddess

Harlequin Master Walter (Mowbray, T., 1858), v. 689, 807, 835

Harlequin Mercury＝Apollo and Daphne

Harlequin Molly Coddle (1862), v. 689

Harlequin Mountebank (1756), III. 330

Harlequin Munchausen (Farley, C., 1818), IV. 475, 627

— (1843), IV. 627

Harlequin Mungo (Bates, 1788), III. 236

Harlequin Negro (1795), III. 401

Harlequin Nimble Nip (Marchant, F., 1871), v. 476

Harlequin's Whim = (1) As You Like It; (2) Tithonus and Aurora

Harlequin Tam o' Shanter (1851), v. 690

Harlequin Tam o'Shanter and his Steed Meg (Lee, N., 1843), IV. 476, 627

Harlequin Teague (O'Keeffe, J., 1782), III. 210, 292

Harlequin Tee-to-Tum (1847), IV. 627

Harlequin the Knight of the Silver Shield (1863), v. 690

Harlequin the Man in the Moon (1741), II. 374

Harlequin the Phantom of a Day (Dibdin, C., 1783), III. 256

Harlequin the Queen of Spades and the Fairy the Fawn (1852), v. 690

Harlequin Tit, Tat, Toe (Frost, F., 1856) = Fairy Elves of the Fourth Estate = Tit, Tat, Toe, v. 374, 675, 690, 793, 835

Harlequin Tom Moody (Lee, N., Jr., 1859), v. 690, 835

Harlequin Tom the Piper's Son Stole a Pig (1820), IV. 476

Harlequin Tom the Piper's Son who stole the Pig and away he run (George, G. H., 1869), v. 377

Harlequin Tom, Tom, the Piper's Son, Pope Joan and Little Bo-Peep (Greenwood, T. L., 1865), v. 690, 794, 835

Harlequin Tom Tucker (Blanchard, E. L. and Greenwood, T. L., 1863), v. 263

Harlequin Touchstone (1789), III. 331

Harlequin Toy Horse (1858), v. 690

Harlequin trapped by Colombine = Robbers

Harlequin Traveller (1782), III. 401
— (1832), IV. 476

Harlequin Triumphant = (1) Defeat of Apollo; (2) Mirrour; (3) Punch's Defeat

Harlequin True Blue and Queen Britannia (1858), v. 690

Harlequin turn'd Cook (1746), II. 374

Harlequin turn'd Dancing-Master (1730), II. 374

Harlequin turn'd Enchanter by Magic Art = Fairy Queen

Harlequin turn'd Fryar = Ship Launching

Harlequin turn'd Judge (Weaver, J., 1717), II. 132, 252, 374, 446
— = Columbine

Harlequin turn'd Philosopher (1739), II. 374

Harlequin turn'd Tapster = Guinguette

Harlequin Uncle Tom (Neale, F., 1852), v. 501

Harlequin Valentine and Orson (Conquest, G. and Spry, H., 1859), v. 690, 785, 817, 835
— (1861, 1866), v. 690

Harlequin Vulcan and Venus (1829), IV. 476

Harlequin Warrior (1801), IV. 476

Harlequin White Cat (Morton, J. M., 1857), v. 496

Harlequin Whittington (1814), IV. 476

Harlequin Whittington and his Cat (Douglass, J. T., 1885), v. 349

Harlequin Wild Man (Dibdin, C. I. M., 1814), IV. 293 [This is the same as Rival Genii, see IV. 527]

Harlequin William the Conqueror and King Vice of the Silent City (1856), v. 690

Harlequin Worm Doctor = Chymical Counterfeits

Harlequin Yorkshireman (1833), IV. 476

Harlequin Zambullo (Farley, C., 1810) = Harlequin and Asmodeus, IV. 476, 627

Harlot's Progress (Cibber, T., 1733), II. 28, 136, 254, 314
— (1730), II. 451
— = Decoy

Harmonious Discords (1873), v. 690

Harmony = Harmony Restored

Harmony Hall (Lunn, J., 1836), IV. 476, 627

Harmony Restored (Jones, H. A., 1879), v. 162, 439, 800

Harold (Boyce, T., 1786), III. 239
— (Bussy, F. M., 1892), v. 294
— (Dew, D., 1820), IV. 290
— (Hopkins, T., 1843), IV. 589
— (Malet, Sir E., 1895), v. 472, 805
— (Nance, A., 1875), v. 501
— (Tennyson, Alfred Lord, 1877), v. 208, 594

Harold Hawk (Selby, C., 1858), v. 560

Harold the Renegade (1823), IV. 476

Harold the Saxon (Boulding, J. W., 1897), V. 270
Haroun Alompra (1824), IV. 627
Haroun Alraschid (Dibdin, T. J., 1813), IV. 299, 580
Harper's Daughter (Lewis, M. G., 1803), IV. 345
Harper's Son and the Duke's Daughter (Dibdin, T. J., 1810), IV. 298
Harp of Altenberg (1833), IV. 476
Harpooner (1833), IV. 476
Harpooner of Fish Hook Bay = Gwinett Bremmel
Harry Bluff (1840), IV. 627
Harry Carley (1862), V. 690
Harry Hawser (1858), V. 690
Harry le Roi (1834), IV. 476
— = Forest Knight
Harry le Roy (Pocock, I., 1813), IV. 383, 606
Harry of England (Greenwood, T., 1842), IV. 476, 627
Harry's Disguise (1868), V. 690
Harsh Step-Father = Taking the Veil
Hartford-Bridge (Pearce, W., 1792), III. 26, 29, 297
Hartley Manor (Farmer, E., 1849), IV. 311
Harvest (Hamilton, H., 1886), V. 401
Harvest Frolic = Gleaners
Harvest Home (Bennett, G., 1808), IV. 476, 627
— (Dibdin, C., 1787), III. 203, 256
— (Parry, T., 1848), IV. 368
— (1801), IV. 476
— (1811), IV. 476
— = (1) Autumn Sheaves; (2) Generous Father; (3) Great Steeplechase
Harvest of Crime (Randford, M., 1897), V. 534
— (1897), V. 690
Harvest of Hate (Withers, F. and Eglington, H., 1899), V. 630
Harvest of Sin (1891), V. 690
Harvest of Wild Oats (Bartlett, H., 1897), V. 252
Harvest Queen (1838), IV. 476
Harvest Storm (Hazlewood, C. H., 1862), V. 796
Harvey's Portrait—Twelve for One Shilling (Sorrell, W. J., 1869), V. 574

Has anybody seen Mr Brown? (Legg, J., 1860), V. 690, 803, 835
Haska (Spicer, H., 1877), V. 576
Hassan and Lara (1829), IV. 476
Hassan Pacha (1837), IV. 476
Haste (Wood, C., 1879), V. 630
Haste to the Wedding (Gilbert, W. S., 1892), V. 381
— (Sorrell, W. J., 1873), V. 574
— (1804), IV. 476
Hasty Conclusion (Planché, Mrs J. R., 1838), IV. 383
Hasty Conclusions (Dance, C., 1844), IV. 289
— (1891), V. 690
Hasty Wedding (Shadwell, C., 1717), II. 354
Hate (West, B., 1824), IV. 476, 627
Hate and Love (1836), IV. 476
Hated Race = Alfonso and Claudina
Hatred (1880), V. 690
Haunted Abbey Ruin = Owl Sisters
Haunted Castle (Oulton, W. C., 1783), III. 295
Haunted Chamber (1821), IV. 476
— (1823), IV. 476
— = (1) Barney the Baron; (2) Black Spirits and White
Haunted for Ever (Howe, J. B., 1880), V. 428
Haunted Glen (Webber, H. and Davis, M., 1888), V. 617
Haunted Grange = Heart and the Key
Haunted Grove (Dubois, Lady D., 1773), III. 258
Haunted Hall (Pitt, G. D., 1847), IV. 375
Haunted Head (1836), IV. 476
Haunted House (1847), IV. 627
— = (1) Drummer; (2) Stolen Will
Haunted House at Lodore (Jefferys, C. A., 1895), V. 435
Haunted Houses (Byron, H. J., 1872), V. 298
Haunted Hulk (Fitzball, E., 1831), IV. 313
— (Haines, J. T., 1824), IV. 322
— (1832), IV. 476
Haunted Hut = Rival Brothers
Haunted Inn (Peake, R. B., 1828), IV. 370
— (1832), IV. 476

Haunted Lives (Jones, J. W., 1884), v. 441

Haunted Man (Dircks, R., 1863), v. 345

— (Robertson, T. W., 1849), IV. 608; v. 546

— (Stirling, E., 1848), IV. 98, 476, 627

— (1848), IV. 98, 477

— (1849), IV. 98, 477

Haunted Manor = Incendiaries

Haunted Mill (Wooler, J. P., 1865), v. 632

Haunted Priory = De Raye

Haunted Tower (Cobb, J., 1789), III. 244

— = Fire Raiser

Haunted Village (Young, 1800), III. 318; IV. 423

— (1792), III. 331

— (1809), IV. 477

— (1811), IV. 477

Haunts of the Hunted Down = Night and Day

Have at All (Williams, J., 1694), I. 437

Haven of Content (Watson, T. M., 1896), v. 616

Haven of Rest (Walker, M., 1868), v. 611

Have you seen my Sister? = Where is Eliza?

Hawaia (Thompson, A., 1880), v. 597

Hawkes Nest (Mackay, J., 1878), v. 470

Hawk's Grip (Don, L., 1887), v. 347

Hawk's Nest = Wheel of Fortune

Hawkwood Hall (Royd, L., 1895), v. 552

Hawser Trunnion on Horseback = Peregrine Pickle

Hawthorne (1882), v. 690

Haydee (Soane, G., 1848), IV. 84, 404

— (1848), IV. 84, 477

Haymakers (James, C. S., 1849), IV. 330

Haymaking (Allwood, 1877), v. 239

Hazard (Burnett, H., 1891), v. 292

Hazard of the Die (Jerrold, D. W., 1835), IV. 332

— = Blue Beard

Hazel Kirke (Mackaye, J. S., 1880), v. 471

Hazelwood Hall (Bloomfield, R., 1823), IV. 269

"H.B." (Peake, R. B., 1839), IV. 371

Headless Horseman (Hazlewood, C. H., 1868), v. 413

Headless Man (Burnand, F. C., 1889), v. 291

— (1857), v. 691

+ Headless Woman (Serle, T. J., ?1837)

Head of a Clan (Horne, F. L., 1875), v. 691, 798, 835

Head of a Lawyer = Marianne, the Child of Charity

Head of the Family (Emden, W. S., 1859), v. 358, 790

Head of the Pole (Law, A., 1882), 450

Head or Heart (Chapman, A., 1890), v. 308

Head Professor (1871), v. 691

Head Quarters (1853), v. 835

Heads and Blockheads (1819), IV. 477

Heads and Hearts (Burslem, C., 1877), v. 293

Heads and Tails (1843), IV. 477

Heads and Tales = Our Family Legend

Heads, Hands and Hearts = Strike

Head's in Peril (1851), v. 691

Headsman (Almar, G., 1831) = Headsman of Vienna, IV. 477, 627

— (Smith, A. R., 1849), IV. 402

— = Mount St Bernard

Headsman of Vienna (Almar, G.) = Headsman, IV. 253, 477, 627

Headsman's Axe (Macdermott, G. H., 1870), v. 468

Headsman's Bond = Hinko

Heads or Tails (Simpson, J. P., 1854), v. 567

Heads versus Pockets (1826), IV. 477

Health to the Rich and Work to the Poor (McLaren, A., 1817), IV. 351

Hear Both Sides (Holcroft, T., 1803), IV. 326

Hear Him Out = Hear It Out

Hearing is Believing (1835), IV. 477

Hear It Out (Reynolds, F., 1804) = Blind Bargain, IV. 391, 477 [By error, this appears in the text as Hear Him Out]

Heart (1848), IV. 477

Heart and the Key (1848), IV. 477

— = Death Secret

Heart and the World (Marston, J. W., 1847), IV. 353

— (1858), v. 691

Heart for Heart = Cagot

Heartless = Puck

Heart of a Brother (1871), v. 691

Heart of a Father = Jew of Lubeck

Heart of a Hero = Saved from the Scaffold

Heart of an Irishman (1854), v. 691

Heart of a Queen = Mary Tudor

Heart of a Sailor (1861), v. 691

Heart of a Soldier = Frederick the Great

Heart of a True Blue = White Nun

Heart of a Woman = Ups and Downs

Heart of Fire (Alfriend, E. M. and Wheeler, A. C., 1897), v. 238, 691

Heart of Gold (Jerrold, D., 1854), v. 69, 800

Heart of Hearts (Jones, H. A., 1887), v. 439

Heart of Hours = Esperance

Heart of London! (Moncrieff, W. T., 1830), IV. 360

Heart of Maryland (Belasco, D., 1895), v. 255

Heart of Midlothian (Dibdin, T. J., 1819), IV. 39, 93, 301, 477, 580

— (Dimond, W., 1819), IV. 93, 307

— (Montague and Jervis, 1819), IV. 93, 361

— (Murray, W. H., 1824), IV. 93, 365

— (Osman, W. R., 1863), v. 691, 835

— (Rafter, 1849), IV. 93, 388

— (Terry, D., 1819), IV. 93, 412

— (1862), v. 691

— = (1) Filial Duty; (2) Trial of Effie Deans

Heart of Old Ireland and the Lepreghaun (Litchfield, C., 1859), v. 691, 804, 835

Heart Repose (Irvine, Mrs M. C., 1867), v. 432

Hearts (Bertie, J. C., 1874), v. 259

— (Bruce, H. P., 1891), v. 283

— = Sailor and his Lass

Hearts against Diamonds and the Struggle of Life = Frost of Life

Hearts and Actresses = Lilies

Hearts and Diamonds (Jerrold, D. W., 1835), IV. 332

Hearts and Hampers (Clarke, M., 1881), v. 313

Hearts and Hands (Taylor, T., 1865), v. 593

Hearts and Homes (Barnett, C. Z., 1848), IV. 261

Hearts and Homes (Browne, G. W., 1876), v. 282

— (1886), v. 691

— = Life's Seasons

Hearts are Trumps (Lawrence, W., 1879), v. 451

— (Lemon, M., 1849), IV. 345

— (Raleigh, C., 1899), v. 534

— (1857), v. 691

— (1889), v. 691

Hearts at Fault (Courtney, J., 1850), IV. 284

Heart's Delight (Halliday, A., 1873), v. 401

Heart's Devotion = First Love

Heartsease (Mortimer, J., 1875), v. 494, 807

Hearts, Hearts, Hearts (Hazlewood, C. H., 1868), v. 413

Hearts of Gold (Darbey, E., 1888), v. 336

— (1892), v. 691

Hearts of Iron (Almar, G., 1845), IV. 253

Hearts of Oak (Allingham, J. T., 1803), IV. 252

— (Jones, H. A., 1879), v. 162-3, 439

— (Stevens, G. A., 1762), III. 309

Hearts of the West (Cassidy, J. R., 1896), v. 305

Heart's Ordeal (Courtney, J., 1863), v. 691

— = Day Dream

Hearts or Diamonds (Cassilis, I. L., 1891), v. 306

Heart's Secret = Deserted Wife

Hearts that Love us (Archer, W. J., 1862), v. 691, 778, 835

Heart's Trials (1849), IV. 477

Heart Strings and Fiddle Strings (Fisher, D., 1865), v. 367

Heart's Victory (Mead, T., 1858), v. 691, 806, 835

Heart Test = Heart

Heart that can feel for another (Rogers, W., 1836), IV. 396

— (1850), v. 691

Heart Wreck = (1) Alvarez; (2) Signet Ring

Heathen Goddess (1894), v. 691

Heathen Martyr (Adams, G., 1746), II. 294

Heather Field (Martyn, E., 1899), v. 479

Heir of Vironi (Pocock, I., 1817), IV.
384

Heirship of Roselva = Mysterious Marriage

Heirs of Rabourdin (Mattos, A. T. de,
1894), v. 481, 806

Held Asunder (Watson, J. S. W., 1888),
v. 616

Held at Bay (1879), v. 691

Held by the Enemy (Gillette, W., 1886),
v. 381

Held in Harness (Clarke, C. A., 1890),
v. 312

Held in Judgement (Campbell, N. S.,
1891), v. 301

Held in Slavery (Haydon, M., 1894), v.
411

Held in Terror (Dix, F., 1897), v. 345

Helen (Burnand, F. C., 1866), v. 289,
781

Helena in Troas (Todhunter, J. and
Godwin, E. W., 1886), v. 600

Helen Douglas (1870), v. 691

Helen Fortescue (1847), IV. 477

Helen in Egypt (Lavallin, J. P., 1882),
v. 802

Helen Oakleigh (Coyne, J. S., 1840), IV.
284

Helen of the Hurst = Disowned

Helen of Troy up-to-date (Jones, J. W.,
1893), v. 441

Helen Porter (1864), v. 691

Helen's Babies (Walch, G., 1878), v.
610

— (1895), v. 691

Helen's Love = Helen Douglas

Helga (1812), IV. 477

He "lies like Truth" (Kimpton, F.,
1828), IV. 338

Hellas (Shelley, P. B., 1822), IV. 401

Hell's Belles = Devil's Daughters

Hells Higher Court of Justice (D., J.,
1661), I. 442

Helmsman of the Spirit Crew = Rip van
Winkle

Helots (Boyd, H., 1793), III. 239

"He loves me, he loves me not"
(Greville, E. E., 1891), v. 394

Help (1891), v. 691

Helping a Friend (Denny, W. H., 1899),
v. 342

Helping Hand (1859), v. 691

Helping Hands (Taylor, T., 1855), v.
592

Help in Time (Rennell, C. R., 1879), v.
541

Helpless Animals (Parry, J., 1819), IV.
368, 603

Helps (Robbins, A. F., 1878), v. 544

Helter Skelter (Browne, G. W., 1886),
v. 283

Helvard Solness (1892), v. 691

Helvellyn (Oxenford, J., 1864), v. 510

Helvetic Liberty (1792), III. 331

Hemlock Draught (Oxenford, J., 1849),
IV. 477, 628

Hempen Cravat = Only a Head

He must be Married (1815), IV. 477, 636

He must have her = Perseverance

Hen and Chickens (Webster, B., the
Younger, 1864), v. 618

Henault Forest (1839) = Hainault
Forest, IV. 477, 628

Hengist (1816), IV. 628

Hengist, Saxon King of Kent (1700), II.
374

Henley Regatta (Grain, R. C., 1886), v.
387

Hen-Peck'd Captain (Cross, R., 1749),
II. 138, 316, 434

Henri de Rochemaine (Roberts, H. B.,
1844), IV. 477, 628

Henrietta (Howard, B., 1887), v. 428,
798

Henriette (1821), IV. 477

Henriette the Forsaken (Buckstone,
J. B., 1832), IV. 274

Henri Quatre (Morton, T., 1820), IV.
364

— (Planché, J. R., 1822) = Fair Geraldine, IV. 477, 628

— (1825), IV. 477

Henri Quatre and the Fair Gabrielle =
Fair Gabrielle

Henrique (Haines, J. T., 1839), IV. 323

Henrique, Prince of Sicily (Greenfield,
A., 1790), III. 266

Henriquez (Baillie, J., 1836), IV. 162,
258

Henry I (1821) = Owen Prince of
Powys, IV. 477, 628

Henry II (Bancroft, J., 1693), I. 168,
352, 388

— (Hull, T., 1773), III. 85-6, 274, 388

Henry II (Ireland, S. W. H., 1799), III. 276
— (Whightwick, G., 1851), V. 823
Henry III (1840), IV. 628
Henry III of France (Shipman, T., 1672), I. 116, 432
Henry IV (Kemble, J. P., 1815), IV. 335
Henry IV, Sequel of (Betterton, T., 1707), II. 298
Henry V (Boyle, R., 1664), I. 9, 66, 107–8, 393
— (Kemble, J. P., 1806), IV. 335
— (Macready, W. C., 1839), IV. 352
— (1830), IV. 477
Henry VI, the First Part (Crowne, J., 1681), I. 10, 79, 173, 399
Henry VI, the Second Part = Misery of Civil War
Henry VII (Chenevix, R., 1812), IV. 279
Henry VIII and Anne Bullen (1732), II. 374
Henry VIII and Francis I = Field of the Cloth of Gold
Henry and Almeria (Birrell, A., 1802), IV. 195, 267
Henry and Edwy = Secret Castle
Henry and Emma (Arne, T. A., 1749), II. 138, 374, 431, 447
— (Bate, H., 1774), III. 235
Henry and Louisa (1797), III. 331
Henry and Mary (1817), IV. 477
Henry and Rosa (1819), IV. 478
Henry and Rosamond (Hawkins, W., 1749), II. 335, 438
Henry de Fleurville (1820), IV. 478
Henry Dunbar (Taylor, T., 1865), V. 593
Henry Esmond (Pemberton, T. E., 1897), V. 519
Henry, Lord Darnley (Brown, R., 1823), IV. 574
Henry of Richmond (Edison, J. S., 1857), V. 354
Henry of Transtamare (1805), IV. 478
Henry's Entertainment (1828), IV. 478
Henry's Table-Talk (1825), IV. 478
— (1826), IV. 478
Henwitchers (Fitzgerald, P., 1878), V. 369
He of the Red Hand = Red Hand
Heraclius (1664), I. 98, 442

Heraclius, Emperor of the East (Carlell, L., 1664), I. 50, 98, 395
Her Advocate (Frith, W., 1895), V. 374
Her Apron Strings (Hood, B., 1897), V. 425
Her Atonement (1885), V. 691
Her Birthday (Young, Sir C. L., 1884), V. 636
— (Young, G., 1899), V. 636
Her Cousin Frank (Capel, G., 1879), V. 302
Hercules (Motteux, P. A., 1697), I. 263, 421
— (1749), II. 394
Hercules and Omphale (Brough, W., 1864), V. 280
— (1746), II. 374
— (1794), III. 331
Hercules, King of Clubs (Cooper, F. F., 1836), IV. 283
Hercules's Choice of Pleasure and Virtue (1753), III. 399
Her Dearest Foe (Lindley, H., 1894), V. 459
Hereditary Honours (Lancaster, E. R. and Oxberry, W. H.), IV. 593
Heredity = Gifted Lady
Here He Is Again = Pedro Lobo
Here's Another Guy Mannering (Burnand, F. C., 1874), V. 290
Here, There and Everywhere (1785), III. 331
— = Tourist
Here we are (Dibdin, T. J., 1825), IV. 304
Her Father (Rose, E. and Douglass, J. T., 1889), V. 550
Her Father's Friend (Rudall, H. A., 1896), V. 553
Her Father's Sin (1889), V. 691
Her First Appearance (Russell, E. H., 1890), V. 553
Her First Ball (Cutler, J., 1899), V. 332
Her First Engagement (Swan, M., 1894), V. 588
Her First Night = (1) Debutante; (2) First Night
Her Guardian (Brown, J. R., 1895), V. 282
Her Hero = Sensualist
Her Ladyship (Fenn, G. M., 1889), V. 365

Her Ladyship's Guardian (Wyndham, Sir C., 1865), v. 691, 825, 835

Her Level Best (Melford, M., 1894), v. 484

Her Living Image (1884), v. 691

Her Majesty's Service = Bluejackets

Herman and Halstein (Dibdin, C. I. M., 1819), IV. 294

Hermann (1834), IV. 478

Hermesianax (1869), v. 692

Hermetic Seal (1822), IV. 478

Hermine (Thomas, C., 1888), v. 596

Herminius and Espasia (Hart, C., 1754), III. 56, 87, 267

Hermione (Dibdin, T. J., 1800), IV. 297

Hermit (Love, J., 1766), III. 210, 283

— (Whitlock, C., 1892), v. 621

— (1792), III. 331

Hermit Converted (Cooke, A. M. E., 1771), III. 248

Hermit of Mount Pausilippo (Dibdin, T. J., 1819), IV. 301

Hermit of St Kilda = Love's Perils

Hermit of Saxallan = Patriot

Hermit of the Alps (1797), III. 331

Hermit of the Rock = Knights of Villeroy

Hermit of the Tweed = Noble Foundling

Hermit of Warkworth = Edda

Hermit Robber = Barsissa

Hermit's Altar (1810), IV. 478

Hermit's Prophecy = Knights of the Cross

Hermit Wanted (1828), IV. 478

Hermon, Prince of Choroea (Clancy, M., 1740), II. 112, 314

Her Mother's Ransom (Marchant, P., 1891), v. 476

Hernando Cortez (Planché, J. R., 1823) = Cortez, IV. 478, 628

Hernani (Crosland, Mrs N., 1867), v. 787

— (Gower, Lord F. L., 1831), IV. 80, 320

— (Osborne, C., 1868), v. 508

— (Sharpe, R. F., 1898), v. 816

— (1847), IV. 478

— (1879), v. 692

Herne's Oak (Parke, W., 1887), v. 512

— (1834), IV. 478

Herne the Hunter (Conquest, G. and Spry, H., 1870), v. 320

Herne the Hunter (Reece, R. and Yardley, W., 1881), v. 539

— (Taylor, T. P., 1843), IV. 411

— (1857), v. 692

— (1862), v. 692

— (1881), v. 692

Herne the Hunter and his Demon Band (1866), v. 692

Herne the Hunter, Anne Boleyn and the Fair Maid of the River Dee = King, the Ring and the Giddy Young Thing

Her New Dressmaker (Walkes, W. R., 1891), v. 611

Hero and Error Win = Pa's Odd Trick

Hero and Leander (Bellew, H. K., 1892), v. 256

— (Jackman, I., 1787), III. 276

— (Rede, W. L., 1838), IV. 478, 628

— (Stapylton, Sir R., 1668), I. 101, 433

— (1728), II. 374

— (1891), v. 692

Her Oath (Wylde, Mrs H., 1891), v. 634

Herod and Mariamne (Pordage, S., 1673), I. 50, 119, 348, 424

— (1723), III. 374

Herod the Great (Boyle, R., 1694), I. 55, 107, 152–3, 393

— (Peck, F., 1740), II. 348

Herod the Tetrarch (Wardhaugh, M., 1874), v. 614

Heroes (Edwardes, C. T. M., 1876), v. 354

— (1887), v. 692

Heroes of the Fleet (1894), v. 692

Heroes of the Frozen Land = Elfins of the Ice

Heroic Daughter = (1) Cid; (2) Siberian Exile

Heroick Daughter = Ximena

Heroick Footman (1736), II. 374

Heroick Friendship (1719), I. 423; II. 374

Heroick Jew = Beltshazzar

Heroick Love (Granville, G., 1697), I. 92, 141, 157, 412

Heroick-Lover (Cartwright, G., 1661), I. 104–6, 107, 395

Heroic Love (1712), II. 374

Heroic Sergeant (1820), IV. 478

Heroic Serjeant = Female Hussar

Heroic Soldier's Wife = Maniac of the Pyrenees

Heroine (Phillips, R., 1819), IV. 372

Heroine of Cambria (Hayley, W., 1811), IV. 588

Heroine of China = Zingina

Heroine of Glencoe (Marsh, C. H., 1899), V. 477

Heroine of Love (Robertson, 1778), III. 302

Heroine of Padua = Montrezar

Heroine of the Cave (Hiffernan, P., 1774), III. 268

Heroine of Yucatan = Aggression

Heroines of Switzerland = Sisters

Her Only Failing (1864), V. 692

Hero of an Hour (Summers, K., 1869), V. 587

Hero of England = Edward the Black Prince

Hero of Heroes (Whitbread, J. W., 1889), V. 620

Hero of Jerusalem (Fineman, S. H., 1896), V. 367

Hero of Romance (Marston, J. W., 1868), V. 479

Hero of Switzerland = William Tell

Hero of the Arctic Regions = Captain Ross

Hero of the Drama (1860), V. 692

Hero of the North (Dimond, W., 1803), IV. 306

Hero, the Champion and the Murderer = Mountain Monarch

Her Own Enemy = Only a Woman

Her Own Rival (Broughton, F. W. and Lawrence, S. B., 1889), V. 281

Her Own Witness (Dabbs, G. H. R., 1889), V. 332

Her Release (Edlin, H., 1892), V. 354

Her Retaliation (Vorzanzer, C., 1889), V. 609

Her Royal Highness (Hood, B., 1898), V. 425

— (1852), V. 692

Her Second Love = Passion's Power

Her Secret (Courtney, G. F., 1897), V. 326

Her Sin = My Partner

Her Talisman (Scott, F., 1896), V. 558

Hertford (Eastwood, F., 1880), V. 353

Hertfordshire Tragedy (Milner, H. M., 1824), IV. 478, 628

Her True Colours (Brabner, W. A., 1891), V. 272

Her Trustee (Blood, J. J., 1887), V. 266

Her Uncle (1886), V. 692

Her Vengeance (1895), V. 692

Her Wedding Day (De Banzie, E. T., 1895), V. 340

Her World against a Lie (Marryat, F. and Neville, G. F., 1880), V. 477

He's a Lunatic (Dale, F., 1867), V. 332

He's coming via Slumborough (Burnand, F. C., 1874), V. 290

He's Here Again (1828), IV. 478

He's Much to Blame (Holcroft, T., 1798), III. 120, 121, 271, 387

He's no Conjuror (Harding, C. T., 1829), IV. 478, 628

— = Legerdemain

He's not a-miss (Dance, C., 1832), IV. 478, 628

He's so nervous (De Frece, M., 1872), V. 341

Hester (1893), V. 692

Hester Gray (Reece, R. and Farnie, H. B., 1877), V. 538

Hester Prynne (Hatton, J., 1876), V. 409

Hester's Legacy (1892), V. 692

Hester's Mystery (Pinero, Sir A. W., 1880), V. 524

He stoops to win (Bridgman, C., 1891), V. 275

+ He that will not when he may (Gardner, H., *French*)

Heureuse ruse = Lindorf et Rosalie

Hewie the Witless (1854), V. 692

He Wiped away a Tear = Full Private Perkins

He with the Hump (1846), IV. 478

He would be a Bohemian (Garton, W. R., 1870), V. 376

He would be an Actor (Mathews, C. J., 1836), IV. 354, 478, 598, 628

He Would Be a Player (1810), IV. 478

— That's the Manager

He would be a Sailor (Hazlewood, C. H., 1868), V. 413

— = Coming Up, Sir!

He Would be a Soldier (Pilon, F., 1786), III. 40, 43, 298

+ He Would be in Love (Crow Street, Dublin, 1/5/1795)

He Wou'd if he Cou'd (Bickerstaffe, I., 1771), III. 199, 237, 378

Hewson Reduc'd (1661), I. 442

Hexen am Rhein (Stirling, E., 1841), IV. 613

Hey Diddle Diddle (Blanchard, E. L., 1855), V. 263

Hezekiah, King of Judah (Allen, 1798), III. 54, 232

Hibernia Freed (Phillips, W., 1722), II. 26, 107, 349

Hibernian Hag and the Chief of Kildare = O'Donnell the Red

Hibernia's Triumph (1748), II. 374

Hic et Ubique (Head, R., 1663), I. 413

Hickedy Pickedy my Black Hen (1857), v. 692

Hickerty Pickerty (1833), IV. 478

Hickety Pickety, the Black Hen (1834), IV. 478

Hickory Dickory Dock (Hazlewood, C. H., 1863), V. 692, 835

Hidden (Wyke, E. B., 1888), v. 634

Hidden Crime (Pitt, C., 1871), V. 692, 810, 835

Hidden Enemy (Gray, A., 1887), V. 390

Hidden Foe (Cassilis, I. L., 1892), V. 306

Hidden Gold (Bertrand, E. C. and Gould, F., 1882), v. 260

Hidden Hand (Taylor, T., 1864), V. 98, 593

— = Masked Mother

Hidden Light (Conquest, G., 1861), v. 692, 785, 835

Hidden Past (Edmonds, E. V., 1896), v. 354

Hidden Terror (Melford, M., 1891), v. 484

Hidden Treasure (Parry, T. and Oxenford, J., 1871), v. 515

— = (1) Hedge Carpenter; (2) Hollow Way; (3) Idiot of the Mill; (4) Marietta; (5) Past and Present; (6) Rock of Sculls

Hidden Worth (Sedger, H., 1886), v. 560

Hide and Seek (Lunn, J., 1824), IV. 348, 596

— (?Lunn, J., 1830), IV. 478, 628

— (1789), III. 331 [This is attributed to William Walter in *The Town and Country Magazine*, Feb. 1789]

Hide and Seek (1833), IV. 478

High and Low, Rich and Poor = 1874

High- and Low-Water Bell (1855), v. 692

High Art (1883), v. 692

High Crime and Low Crime = (1) Money and Misery; (2) Starved to Death

Highdays and Holidays = Ingratitude

Highdays and Holydays from Tyburn to Whitechapel = London

Highest Bidder (1898), v. 692

Highgate Mystery = Over the Garden Wall

Highgate Tunnel (Smith, T., 1812), IV. 403

High Jinks (1886), v. 692

Highland Cateran (Murray, W. H., 1837), IV. 478, 628

Highland Chiefs (McLaren, A., 1815), IV. 351

Highland Drover (McLaren, A., 1795), III. 284, 391

— (McLaren, A., 1805), IV. 351

Highlander Bit = Harlequin turn'd Dancing-Master

Highlanders (Bruce, E., 1872), v. 283

Highlander's Return = Caledonian Laurels

Highland Fair (Mitchell, J., 1731), II. 250, 345

Highland Fling (Dilley, J. J., 1879), v. 345

Highland Funeral (McLaren, A., 1819), IV. 352

— = Private Theatre

Highland Hearts (Gordon, H. C., 1889), v. 385

Highland Jessie Brown (1858), v. 692

Highland Laddie = Hooley and Fairly

Highland Lassie = Lowland Lassie in London

Highland Legacy (Thomas, B., 1888), v. 596

Highland Reel (O'Keeffe, J., 1788), III. 294

Highland Revenge = Kelpie's Cave

Highland Rivals (1822), IV. 478

Highland Robbers (McLaren, A., 1817), IV. 351

— = Edgar and Effie

Highland Wedding (McLaren, A., 1819), IV. 352

Highland Widow (Marston, H., 1837), IV. 95, 478

— (Wilson, J. M., 1828), IV. 618

High Life (1801), IV. 478

High Life Above Stairs = Bon Ton

High Life Below Stairs (Townley, J., 1759), III. 8, 312, 397

High Life in London (1826), IV. 478

High Life in the City (Eyre, E. J., 1810), IV. 310

High, Low, Jack, and the Game (Planché, J. R. and Dance, C., 1833), IV. 55, 136–7, 380, 605

Highly Improbable (Gilbert, W. S., 1867), V. 379

Highly Improper = I'll tell your Wife

High-mettled Racer (Dibdin, T. J., 1813) = Life, Death and Restoration of the High Mettled Racer, IV. 299

— (1872), V. 692

High Notions (Parry, J., 1819), IV. 368, 603

— (1843), IV. 628

High Road of Life (Kingdom, J. M., 1857), V. 801

High Road to Marriage (Skeffington, L. St G., 1803), IV. 402

— (1820), IV. 478

— = Love in Full Gallop

High Street Mystery (Machale, L., 1885), V. 469

High-toned Soprano and the Villain Base = Tra-la-la Tosca

Highwayman (McCarthy, J. H., 1891), V. 467

— (Morton, J. M., 1843), IV. 362

— (1892), V. 692

Highwayman for the Ladies = Claude Duval

Highwayman Knight (Hedmondt, E. C. and Neilson, F., 1898), V. 416

Highwayman of Life = Paul Clifford

Highwayman of 1764 = Paul Clifford

Highwayman's Holiday (Suter, W. E., 1863), V. 588

Highwayman's Revenge = Captain Gerald

Highway Robbery = Two Bonnycastles

Highways and Byways (Webster, B. N., 1831), IV. 417, 616

— = Night's Adventure

High Ways and By Ways of Life (Suter, W. E., 1861), V. 692, 818, 835

Hilda (Halliday, A., 1872), V. 401

— (1892), V. 692

Hilda's Inheritance (Muskerry, W., 1871), V. 500

Hindoo Prince = Idolaters

Hindoo Robber (Fitzball, E., 1836), IV. 315

Hindoo Widow = Law of Brahma

Hind's Disease = Village Doctor

Hinko (Wills, W. G., 1871), V. 627, 824

Hint for Bachelors = Out-generalled

Hint for Duelling = Wife Hunting

Hints for 1851 = Novelty Fair

Hints for Husbands (Beazley, S., Jr., 1835), IV. 264

Hints for Painters (1803), IV. 478

Hints on Etiquette = Jack on the Green

Hints to the Curious (1853), V. 835

Hints to Wives (1845), IV. 478

Hint to a Cross Husband = Two Wives!

Hint to Husbands (Cumberland, R., 1806), IV. 287

— = (1) Cabinet and Two Wives; (2) Two Wives

Hint to the Theatres (1736), II. 374

Hippolytus (Wodhull, M., 1786), III. 316

Hippopotamus (1850), V. 692

His Club Friend (1893), V. 692

His Directions = City Friends

His Double = As in a Glass

His Evening Out (Tarpey, W. B., 1899), V. 591

His Excellency (Gilbert, W. S., 1894), V. 381

— (Mathews, C. J., 1860), V. 480

His Excellency the Governor (Marshall, R., 1898), V. 478

His First Campaign (Planché, J. R., 1832), IV. 379

His First Champagne (Rede, W. L., 1833), IV. 390, 628

— (1848), IV. 479

His First Peccadillo (1848), IV. 478

His Future Wife (Francks, F. H., 1890), V. 372

His Grace the Duke = Out of Luck

His Hidden Revenge (Holton, F., 1887), V. 424

— (1890), V. 692

His Highness (Houghton, J. W. and Tate, A., 1893), v. 427

His Highness (Hurst, B., 1894), v. 431

— (1832), IV. 479

His Holiday (1894), v. 692

His Hydropathic Highness = Belle of the Bath

His Journey to London = Robin Bullcalf's Readings

His Landlady (Mudie, G., 1892), v. 498

His Last Chance (Harraden, H., 1890), v. 404

— (1896), v. 692

His Last Cruise (Gunton, R. T., 1893), v. 397

His Last Legs (Bernard, W. B., 1839), IV. 266

His Last Stake (Webster, J. P., 1888), v. 618

His Last Victory (Phillips, W., 1862), v. 523

His Little Dodge (McCarthy, J. H., 1896), v. 467

His Little Mania (1890), v. 692

His Lordship (Barczinski,A.,1890),v.249

His Lordship's Birthday (Raphael, F. and Lauri, E., 1894), v. 535

His Majestie's Entertainment (Ogilby, J., 1661), I. 422

His Majesty (Burnand, F. C. and Lehmann, R. C., 1897), v. 292

His Majesty's Musketeers = Three Musketeers

His Masterpiece (Vane, S., 1898), v. 606

His Mother (Day, G. D., 1891), v. 339

His Mother's Ransom (1891), v. 692

His Natural Life (1886), v. 692

— (1896), v. 692

His Nephew (1896), v. 693

His New French Cook (1899), v. 693

His Novice (Spicer, H., 1878), v. 576

His Only Coat (1882), v. 693

His other I (Outram, L. S. and Brown, W. H., 1898), v. 509

His Own Enemy (Dillon, C., 1898), v. 345

— (Meadow, A., 1873), v. 483

His Own Guest (Ayres, A. and Blake, P., 1883), v. 247

His Own Wife (1894), v. 693

His Relations (Saintsbury, H. A., 1896), v. 554

His Romance (Milton, M., 1888), v. 490

His Satanic Majesty (Marlow, F. and Barron, H., 1899), v. 477

His Second Wife (Hope, V., 1892), v. 425

His Son-in-Law (Giveen, R. F., 1896), v. 382

— (Watson, W. G. and Rodman, A., 1890), v. 616

His Success (Grogan, W. E., 1895), v. 395

His Toast (Heathcote, A. M., 1889), v. 415

Historical Register, For the Year 1736 (Fielding, H., 1737), II. 7, 18, 68, 126–7, 261, 328, 434, 436; III. 116; v. 142–3

History and Her-story in a Modern Milo-metre = Antony and Cleopatra

History of a Crime = Dead Man's Gold

History of a Flag (1860), v. 693

History of a Rough Gem = King of Diamonds

History of Bacon in Virginia = Widdow Ranter

His Treasures (Kingsley, E., 1897), v. 444

His Wife (Jones, H. A., 1881), v. 162, 439

His Wife's Little Bill (Henning, A., 1894), v. 417

His Wives (Cleveland, E. A., 1894), v. 314

— (Warren, T. G., 1888), v. 615

His Word, his Bond = Winning Defeat

His Worship the Cully = Braggadochio

Hit him, he has no friends (Yates, E. and Harrington, N. H., 1860), v. 635

Hit if you like it = Success

Hit or Miss (Burnand, F. C., 1868), v. 289, 781

— (Milton, A., 1883), v. 490

— (Pocock, I., 1810), IV. 144, 383

Hive of Life: Its Drones and Workers (Calvert, C., 1862), v. 693, 783, 836

H.M.S. Missfire (Drury, W. O., 1894), v. 351

H.M.S. Pinafore (Gilbert, W. S., 1878), v. 143–4, 380

Hoax (1810), IV. 479

— (1826), IV. 479

Hoaxer (1814), IV. 479

Hoaxing (1824), IV. 479

Hob (Cibber, C., 1711), II. 132, 133, 250, 311, 434
— = Flora
Hobbies (Stephens, H. P. and Yardley, W., 1885), v. 580
Hobbs, Dodds and Stubbs (Webster, B. N., 1840), IV. 417
Hobby-Horse (Pinero, Sir A. W., 1888), v. 176, 177, 525
— (Thompson, E., 1766), III. 311
Hobby Horses (1789), III. 331
Hob in the Well = Flora
Hobson's Choice (Oulton, W. C., 1787), III. 296
— (Summers, K., 1895), v. 587
Hob's Wedding (Leigh, J., 1720), II. 341
Hocus Pocus, IV. 479
Hoddy Toddy, all Head and no Body (1851), v. 693
Hodge Podge (1781), III. 331
Hofer (Fitzball, E., 1830) = Andreas Hofer, IV. 584
— (Planché, J. R., 1830), IV. 379
Hogarth's Apprentices (1821), IV. 479
— (1848), IV. 479
Hogarth's Mirror (1847), IV. 628
Hogmanay (Sidney, F. W., 1896), v. 565
Hokee Pokee (Conquest, G. and Spry, H., 1878), v. 321
Hokey Pokey Wankey Fum (1836), IV. 479
Hold Fast (1885), v. 693
Holding the Mirror (Howell-Poole, W., 1885), v. 429
Hold your Tongue (Planché, J. R., 1849), IV. 129, 383
Hole in the Wall (Poole, J., 1813), IV. 386
— = Secret
Holidays (Eyre, E. J., 1813), IV. 479, 628
— = Juvenile Friendship
Holiday Time (Lathom, F., 1799), III. 280; IV. 341, 342
Hollow Tree = Raykisnah the Outcast
Hollow under the Hill = Saul the Servant
Hollow Way (Moncrieff, W. T., 1828), IV. 479, 628
Holly Branch (Thomas, C., 1891), v. 596
Holly Bush Hall (Mordaunt, J., 1860), v. 693, 807, 836

Holly Bush Hall (Seaman, W., 1860), v. 693, 815, 836
— (Suter, W. E., 1860), v. 587, 819
— (1866), v. 693
Holly Lodge (1855), v. 693
Holly Tree Inn (Beringer, Mrs O., 1891), v. 259
— (Johnstone, J. B., 1856), v. 693, 800, 836
Holofernes (?1664), I. 446
Holyrood (Bell, S., 1896), v. 256
Holstein Hussar (Pitt, G. D., 1838), IV. 373
Homage to Flora (1860), v. 693, 836
Homburg (Hatton, J., 1893), v. 409
Home (Robertson, T. W., 1869), v. 546
— (1880), v. 693
Home Affairs (1879), v. 693
Home Again (Fitzball, E., 1844), IV. 316
— (Jones, H. A., 1881), v. 162, 439
— (Marston, H., 1877), v. 478
Home and Happiness = Paris and Pleasure
Home and the Homeless = Alone in the World
Home and the Love of Yore = Home Chimes
Home Chimes (Arthur, A., 1888), v. 244
Home Circle (1850), v. 693
Home Circuit (Mathews, C. J., 1827), IV. 354
Home Coming (Cosham, E., 1892), v. 325
Home Diplomacy (1867), v. 693
Home Feud (Frith, W., 1890), v. 374
Home for a Holiday (Gordon, W., 1860), v. 385, 794
Home for Home (Lee, R., 1879), v. 453
Home for the Holidays (Moncrieff, W. T., 1828), IV. 359 [This was printed 8°, 1828 as Old Heads on Young Shoulders, and evidently is an earlier version of the play listed under that title IV. 360]
Home from War (1855), v. 693
Home in the Heart (Conquest, G., 1861), v. 693, 785, 836
Home in the Mountains = Indian Queen
Home in the West (1853), v. 693
Home is Home After All = King's Coin
Homeless (Murray, J. K. and Comer, G., 1893), v. 500

Home of our Adoption (1892), v. 693

Home of the Brave (1832), IV. 479

Home once more (Crauford, A. L., 1885), v. 328

Home, Out and Home (Squires, J., 1862), v. 817

Home Phantasies (1879), v. 693

Home Plays (Blake, T. G.), v. 262

Home Rule (Brady, E. J., 1880), v. 273

— (Taylor, J. G., 1877), v. 591

Home Rule Bill (1893), v. 693

Home Ruler = Tight Rein

Home Secretary (Carton, R. C., 1895), v. 305

Home Service = Nice Young Ladies

Homespun (Calmour, A. C., 1884), v. 300

Homestead Story (1861), v. 693

Home Sweet Home (Farjeon, E., 1876), v. 361

— (Somerset, C. A., 1829), IV. 404

— (Swears, H., 1895), v. 589

— = Swiss Family

Home Truths (Reynoldson, T. H., 1852) = Barrister, v. 542, 693, 813, 836

— (1858), v. 693

Homeward Bound (Bertie, J. C., 1874), v. 259

— (1833), IV. 479

— (1838), IV. 479

— (1882), v. 693

— (1885), v. 693

Homewreck (Coyne, J. S. and Denis, J., 1869), v. 328

— (1851), v. 693

Homicide (Baillie, J., 1836), IV. 258

— (1824), IV. 479

Homme blasé = Used Up

Homme Noir (1839), IV. 479

Homoeopathy (1837), IV. 479

Honest Attorney (Emden, W. S., 1855), v. 693, 790, 836

Honest Cheats (Coyne, J. S., 1836), IV. 284

Honest Criminal (Astley, P., Jr., 1808), IV. 257

— (1778), III. 331

Honest Electors (1733), II. 375

Honest Farmer (Berguin, M., 1791), III. 236

Honest Frauds (Lunn, J., 1830), IV. 348

Honest Hearts = Go Straight

Honest Irishman = Brave Irishman

Honest Israelite = Little Aaron

Honest Jew of Frankfort = Rise of the Rothschilds

Honest John (Hazlewood, C. H., 1875), v. 415

Honest Labour (Marchant, F., 1870), v. 476

Honest Lawyer = Honest Attorney

Honest Living (Lawrence, W., 1891), v. 451

Honest Man (Pettitt, H., 1878), v. 521

— = John of the Forge

Honest Man's Fortune (1849), IV. 479

Honest Men of Taunton = Downfal of Bribery

Honest Munsterman = Connaught Wife

Honest Soldier (Colls, J. H., 1805), III. 245; IV. 281

Honest Tar and the Wicked First Luff = H.M.S. Missfire

Honest Thieves (Knight, T., 1797), III. 114, 280; IV. 479, 592, 628

Honest Welchman (Dibdin, T. J., 1827), IV. 305

— = Journey to Bristol

Honest Welshman = St David's Day

Honest Wife = Intriguing Widow

Honesty (Spicer, H., 1845), IV. 405

— (Young, M., 1897), v. 636

— (1872), v. 693

Honesty in Distress (Ward, E., 1708), II. 363

Honesty is the Best Policy (1791), III. 331

— = Good Hearts

Honest Yorkshire-Man (Carey, H., 1735), II. 43, 137, 233, 302, 432-3

Honesty the Best Policy (Lemon, M., 1849), IV. 345

— (1815) = Cady, IV. 479, 628

— (1865), v. 693

— (1879), v. 693

— (1898), v. 693

— = (1) Heir of Vironi; (2) Power of Gold; (3) Tantara-Rara, Rogues All; (4) Tricks of London; (5) World as it goes

Honeydove's Troubles (Reece, R., 1867), v. 537, 812

Honey Moon (Linley, W., 1796), III. 281, 390

Hop o' my Thumb (Green, F. W., 1880), v. 391
— (Green, F. W., 1881), v. 391
— (Smith, A. R., 1846), IV. 402, 611
— (1854, 1877), v. 693
Hop o' my Thumb and his Brothers (1831), IV. 479
Hop o' my Thumb and his Eleven Brothers (Blanchard, E. L., 1864), v. 263, 779
Hop o' my Thumb and the Giant Ogre of the Seven Leagued Boots (1863), v. 694
Hop Pickers (1849), IV. 479
— (1861), v. 694
Hop Pickers and Gipsies (Hazlewood, C. H., 1869), v. 413
Hops! and Steps! (1811), IV. 479
Hops without Malt (1823), IV. 479
Horace (Cotton, C., 1671), I. 98, 398
— (Philips, K. and Denham, Sir J., 1668), I. 98, 344, 423
+ Horace at the University of Athens (Trevelyan, G. O.: 8°, 1869 (in *Ladies in Parliament and other Pieces*; apparently acted privately at Cambridge))
Horatia (1845), IV. 479
Horatii (1846), IV. 628
Horatii and Curatii (Macfarren, G., 1820), IV. 349
Hornet's Nest (Byron, H. J., 1878), v. 299
— (Gordon, G. L., 1876), v. 384
Horn of Plenty (Ascher, G., 1897), v. 244
Horns and Hounds = Is it a Wedding?
Horns of a Dilemma = Ernani
Horoscope = Pong Wong
Horrid Barbarian = Our Geordie
Horrification (Dibdin, C. I. M., 1825), IV. 295
Horrors (1885), v. 694
Horrors of an Assault = Victim of St Vincent
Horrors of Extravagance = Prodigal
Horrors of Intemperance = Profligates
Horrors of 1720 = Plague of Marseilles
Horrors of Slavery = Uncle Tom's Cabin
Horrors of the Bastile (1835), IV. 479
Horrors of the Bastille = Tale of Two Cities

Horrors of the Forest = Stop Thief!
Horrors of the French Revolution = Reign of Terror
Horrors of the Press-gang = Paul Periwinkle
Horrors of War (1827), IV. 480
— (1831), IV. 479
— = (1) Siege of Sebastopol; (2) Soldier's Progress
Horse and Foot (1834), IV. 480
— = Gallopade
Horse and the Murderer = (1) Black Legend; (2) Kentucky Rifle
Horse and the Ostler = Black Legend of Rotherhithe
Horse and the Widow (Dibdin, T. J., 1799), III. 122, 189, 256, 383
Horse Banditti = (1) Gil Blas de Santillane; (2) Voorn the Tiger
Horse Banditti and their Forty Steeds (1830), IV. 480
Horse Dealer of Vienna (1860), v. 694
Horseman (1893), v. 694
Horsemonger-lane Joe (Travers, W., 1861) = Poor Joe of Horsemonger-lane, v. 734, 843
Horse of the Arab Chief = Moors of Spain
Horse of the Cavern (1856) = Carlo Brunari, v. 655, 694, 836
Horse of the Disinherited = Battle of Blenheim
Horse of the Elements = Prince of Cyprus
Horse Poisoner = James Lawson
Horseshoe (1860), v. 694
— (1898), v. 694
Horse to be Sold (1861), v. 694
Hortensia (1815), IV. 480, 636
Horton Towers (1895), v. 694
Hospital for Fools (Miller, J., 1739), II. 13, 145, 237, 344, 437, 441
Hot and Cold (Dibdin, T. J., 1826), IV. 304
— (1850), v. 694
Hot Boiled Beans and the Very Good Butter (1834), IV. 480
Hot Codlings (1822), IV. 480
Hotel (Jephson, R., 1783), III. 122, 277, 389
— (Vaughan, T., 1776), III. 185–6, 313
Hotel Charges (Selby, C., 1853), v. 560

Hot Night = Kindred Souls

Hot Potatoe (1885), v. 694

Hot Potatoes = Cousin Johnny

Hottentot Venus (1810), IV. 480

Hot Water (Farnie, H. B., 1876), v. 362

Hot Weather (1846), IV. 480

Houp-la! (Warren, T. G., 1891), v. 615

— (1885), v. 694

Houp La! Tra, la, la! (Dunstan, H. M., 1886), v. 352

Hour and a Half in Paris = Retaliation

Hour at Ipswich Station (Harvey, F., 1874), v. 408

Hour at Rugby Junction (1873), v. 694

Hour at the Carnival = Hour in Venice

Hour at Weybridge = Spirit of the Grotto

Hour before Marriage (1772), III. 332

— = Man of Two Thousand

Hour in Seville (Selby, C., 1858), v. 560

Hour in Venice (1859), v. 694

Hour of Midnight = Deception

Hour of One = Amazon's Oath

Hour of Retribution, see St Aubert

Hour of Retribution (1821), IV. 480

— (1846), IV. 480

— = St Aubert

Hour of Triumph (1896), v. 694

Hour of Twelve (1836), IV. 480

Hour's Romance = Where's Brown?

Hour with Napoleon (Webb, C., 1844) = One Hour with Napoleon, IV. 480, 628

House Besieged = Mad Monarch

House Boat (Williamson, H. W., 1886), v. 626

Housebreaker (Rogers, T. S., 1892), v. 549

— (1897), v. 694

Housebreaker of the Last Century = Jack Sheppard

House Burners = Incendiary

House Divided (Haines, J. T., 1836), IV. 322, 586

— = (1) Lord Marple's Daughter; (2) Uncle Oliver

House Dog (Higgie, T. H., 1845), IV. 325

Housefull of Rebels (1895), v. 694

Household Fairy (Talfourd, F., 1859), v. 590

Household Gods = Junius Brutus

Household Picture under Two Lights = Wife's Portrait

Household Words (Bourne, W., 1884), v. 270

— (1858), v. 694

Household Words, All the Year Round (1859), v. 694

House in a Hurry = All Bedevil'd

House in Thames Street (Dorrell, A., 1885), v. 347

House in the Forest = Old Heads on Young Shoulders

House in the Valley (Conquest, G., 1860), v. 694, 785, 836

Housekeeper (Jerrold, D. W., 1833), IV. 332

Housekeeper's Elopement = Marriage by Licence

House of Aspen (Scott, Sir W., 1829), IV. 194, 397

House of Atreus and the House of Laius (Smith, J., 1818), IV. 611

House of Cards (Grundy, S., 1891), v. 397

House of Colberg (Serle, T. J., 1832), IV. 399

House of Commons = Westminster

House of Darnley (Lytton, Baron, 1877), v. 466

House of Dives (1893), v. 694

House of Ladies (Lemon, M., 1840), IV. 344

House of Lies (Hannan, C., 1892), v. 402

House of Lords (Greenbank, H., 1894), v. 392

House of McOuld = Life's Mistakes

House of Morville (Lake, J., 1812), IV. 341

House of Mystery (Harvey, F., 1898), v. 409

House of Sleep (Warwick, H. S., 1897), v. 615

House on the Bridge (Johnstone, J. B., 1852), v. 438

House on the Bridge of Notre Dame (Douglass, J. T., 1861), v. 694, 788, 836

— (Hazlewood, C. H., 1861), v. 412

— (Lacy, M. R., 1861), v. 694, 801

— = Gipsy Twins

House on the Cliff = Royal Pardon

House on the Heath (1857), v. 694

House on the Marsh (Warden, F., 1885), v. 613

— (Willoughby, H., 1885), v. 626

— (Wood, G. M., 1885), v. 630

House or the Home? (Taylor, T., 1859), v. 185, 593

House out at Windows (Kenney, J., 1817), IV. 337

House out of Windows (Brough, W., 1852), v. 278

House Room (Peake, R. B., 1836), IV. 370

Houses of Campbell and Maclean = John of Lorne and Helen of Argyle

Houses of York and Lancaster = Days of Old

House that Jack built (Chambers, T., 1862), v. 783

— (Fox, G., 1821), IV. 317

— (Keating, Miss, 1859), v. 801

— (Mackay, J., 1878), v. 470

— (Newton, H. C., 1894), v. 503

— (1859), v. 694

— (1860), v. 836

— (1864), v. 694

— (1871), v. 836

— (1877, 1878, 1880, 1881, 1889, 1890), v. 694

— (1897), v. 836

— (1898), v. 694

House that Jack built in 1851 (Greenwood, T. L., 1850) = Harlequin and the House that Jack built in 1851, v. 393, 687, 794, 834

House to be Sold (Baylis, J., 1804), IV. 262

— (Cobb, J., 1802), IV. 145, 281

House to Let (1859), v. 694

House Tyrant = Spirit of Contradiction

House upon the Heath = All in One Night

House versus the Home = House or the Home?

House-warming (Dibdin, T. J., 1816), IV. 300, 480, 580, 628

Hovel (1797), III. 332

Howard Howard (Arthur, A., 1888), v. 244

How does he love me? (1876), v. 694

How do you manage? (Bayly, T. H., 1835), IV. 262, 571

How Dreams come true (Todhunter, J., 1890), v. 600

How Fair the World Is! (1843), IV. 480

How happy could I be with either! (Dibdin, T. J., 1807) = Two Faces under a Hood, IV. 480

How I found Crusoe (Thompson, A., 1872), v. 597

How I tamed Mrs Cruiser (1858), v. 694

How it's to be done (Buckingham, L. S., 1857), v. 694, 781, 836

Howlet's Haunt (1832), IV. 480

How London lives (Field, M. and Shirley, A., 1897), v. 365

How Many More Wives? = Family Man

How many were Bavarians = "Buy a Broom?"

How many Wives has he? (1832), IV. 480

How Money's Made (Warren, F. B., 1899), v. 615

How Remarkable! = Whang Fong

Howse the Informer (1897), v. 694

How shall we get rid of him? = Giovanni, the Vampire

How she loves him! (Boucicault, D., 1863), v. 268

How Silver was tricked (1899), v. 694

How's that, Umpire? (Bidwell, H., 1880), v. 261

How stout you're getting (Morton, J. M., 1855), v. 495

How's your poor Feet? (1862), v. 694

How's your Uncle? (Wilks, T. E., 1855), v. 623, 823

How the Average became the Abnormal = Average Man

How the Duchess convinced the Princess (1899), v. 694

How Time Flies (Elphinstone, J., 1869), v. 358

How to Act (Albery, J., Vezin, H. and Wills, W. G., 1865) = Doctor Davy, v. 237, 694

How to be happy though married = Woman Tamer

How to Buy a Horse without Money = Speculation

How to choose a Husband = Lottie's Love

How to come at Her = Comet

How to Cook a Biffin = Hotel Charges

+Hugger Mugger (Clarke, H. S., French)

Hugh the Gipsey (Barnett, C. Z., 1844), IV. 260

Hugh Weston's Mill (1880), V. 695

Hugo Bambino (1824), IV. 480

Hugo the Dane (Lighterness, W. B.), IV. 595

Huguenot (Sheil, R. L., 1822) = Convict, IV. 401, 444, 610

Huguenots (Howe, J. B., 1873), V. 428

— (Russell, H., 1849), IV. 83, 480, 628

— (Wilkins, J. H., 1851), V. 695, 823, 836

— (1832), IV. 83, 480

— (1836), IV. 83, 480

— (1857), V. 695

Huguenots under Louis XV = Paul Rabaut

Hull Fair (1774), III. 402

Human Hearts = Stolen from Home

Humanity (Locksley, C., 1881), V. 462

— (Marston, H. and Rae, L., 1882), V. 478

Human Nature (Harris, A. G. and Williams, T. J., 1867), V. 405

— (Pettitt, H. and Harris, Sir A., 1885), V. 185, 521

Human Spider (Lyle, K., 1898), V. 465

Human Sport (Fryers, A., 1895), V. 374

Humble Origin = Victim of Delusion

Humbug (Burnand, F. C., 1867), V. 289

— (Jones, H. A., 1881), V. 439

— (Silvester, H., 1845), IV. 480, 628

— (1827), IV. 480

— (1885), V. 695

Humbugs of the Hour (À Beckett, G. A., 1844), IV. 250

Humfrey, Duke of Gloucester (Philips, A., 1723), II. 54, 106, 348

Humgumption (1823), IV. 480

Humorists (Shadwell, T., 1670), I. 24, 204, 236, 430

Humorous Cuckold = Merry Masqueraders

Humorous Lieutenant (Reynolds, F., 1817), IV. 392, 607

Humorous Lovers (Cavendish, W., 1667), I. 215, 346, 396

Humorous Quarrel (Pottinger, I., 1761), III. 299

Humourist (Cobb, J., 1784), III. 244

Humourists (1754), III. 332

Humour of Bumpkin (Kirkman, F., 1662), I. 417

Humour of Hobbinal (Kirkman, F., 1662), I. 417

Humour of John Swabber (Kirkman, F., 1662), I. 417

Humour of Simpleton (Kirkman, F., 1662), I. 417

Humour of the Age (Baker, T., 1701), II. 174-5, 181, 296, 432

Humours and Passions = School of Shakespeare

Humours of an Election (Coyne, J. S., 1837), IV. 480, 628

— (Pilon, F., 1780), III. 298

Humours of an Inn = Rider

Humours of an Irish Court of Justice (1750), III. 332

Humours of Bluff King Hal = Beggar of Cripplegate

Humours of Brighton (Cross, J. C., 1792), III. 249

Humours of Covent-Garden = Rival Milliners

Humours of Dublin = Hic et Ubique

Humours of Dugald = Bonny Lass of Leith

Humours of Elections = Gotham Election

Humours of Exchange Alley = (1) It should have come sooner; (2) Stock-Jobbers

Humours of Gil Blas (1788), III. 332

Humours of Greenock Fair (McLaren, A., 1788), III. 284

Humours of Harlequin (1729), II. 375

Humours of Harry Humbug = Intriguing Footman

Humours of John Bull (Oswald, J., 1789), III. 295

Humours of King Henry VIII and the Merry Cobler (1797), III. 332

Humours of May Day (1787), III. 332

Humours of Monsieur Galliard (Kirkman, F., 1662), I. 417-18

Humours of Oxford (Miller, J., 1730), II. 177, 203, 344

Humours of Portsmouth (1760), III. 332

Humours of Purgatory (Griffin, B., 1716), II. 142, 212, 333, 375, 447

Humours of St Andrews = Students

Humours of Sancho Panza = Don
Quixote, the Knight of the Wonderful
Countenance

Humours of Teague = Irish Evidence

Humours of the Army (Shadwell, C.,
1713), II. 53, 145, 176, 354, 444; III.
116

Humours of the Compter (1717), II. 375

— = City Ramble

Humours of the Court (Bridges, R. S.,
1893), v. 275

— (1732), II. 18–19, 251, 375

Humours of the Fair = Mountebank

Humours of the Forc'd Physician (1732),
II. 375

Humours of the Forth = Easter Monday

Humours of the Green Room = Critic
anticipated

Humours of the Militia = Hen-Peck'd
Captain

Humours of the Navy (1830), IV. 480

— = (1) Fair Quaker; (2) Fair Quaker
of Deal

Humours of the Road (1738), II. 375

Humours of the Times (McLaren, A.,
1799), III. 284

Humours of the Town (1748), II. 375

Humours of the Turf = Newmarket

Humours of Wapping (1703), II. 375

— = (1) Constant Quaker; (2) Sailor's
Wedding

Humours of Whist (1743), II. 262,
375

— = Polite Gamester

Humours of York = Northern Heiress

Humpback (Rede, W. L., 1832), IV.
480, 628

— (1843), IV. 480

Hump-backed Lover (Mathews, C. J.,
1835), IV. 354, 597

Humphrey Clinker (Dibdin, T. J.,
1818), IV. 96, 301

Humpty Dumpty (Harris, Sir A. H. G.
and Nichols, H., 1891), v. 406

— (Jones, J. W., 1890), v. 801

— (Seaman, W., 1864), v. 815

— (1832), IV. 480

— (1875, 1876, 1882, 1883), v. 695

— (1892), v. 836

— (1898), v. 695

Humpty Dumpty Crook-a-back Dick
and Jane Shore (1857), v. 836

Hunchback (Knowles, J. S., 1832), IV.
172, 339

— (1820), IV. 481

— (1831), IV. 481

Hunchback and his Horse Beelzebub
(1832), IV. 481

Hunchback and the Sutler (Lewis, A.),
IV. 595

Hunchback back again (Burnand, F. C.,
1878), v. 291

Hunchback Doctor (1866), v. 695

Hunchbacked Brothers of Bagdad
(1826), IV. 481

Hunchback of Notre Dame = (1) Bell-
ringer; (2) Esmerelda

Hunchback of Paris = Duke's Daughter

Hunchback's Love = Bell-Ringer of
Notre Dame

Hundred Days of Buonaparte = Champ
de Mai

Hundred Eyes (1820), IV. 481

Hundred Thousand Pounds (Byron,
H. J., 1866), v. 297

Hundredth Victim of the Shark's Cliff =
Sightless Tyrant of Persia

Hundred Years Ago (Aveling, E. B.,
1892), v. 246

— = (1) Barrington; (2) Green Bushes;
(3) Life and Adventures of George
Barrington

Hungarian Cottage (Kemble, C., 1813),
IV. 334 [The entry on IV. 481 refers to
the same play]

Hunger (Raymond, W., 1869), v. 535

— (1858), v. 695

— (1860), v. 696

Huniades (Brand, H., 1791), III. 239
[This was acted Norwich, 7/4/1791]

Hunt after Happiness = Abou Hassan

Hunted by the Law = Iron Maiden

Hunted Down (Bennett, G. W., 1881),
v. 258

— (1883), v. 695

— = Two Lives of Mary Leigh

Hunted Down by Fate (1883), v. 695

Hunted Tailor's Journey to Brentford
(1813), IV. 481

Hunted to Death (Cooper, H., 1867), v.
324

— = Convict

Hunted to Death by a Woman = Old
Sarum

Hut of the Danube = Fortress of Press-
burg
Hut of the Red Mountains (Milner,
H. M., 1827), IV. 357
Hut of Valais (1843), IV. 481
Huzza for Lisbon = Spain and Portugal
Huzza for Old England (1782), III. 332
— = Little Ben and Little Bob
Hydaspes = Idaspe Fedele
Hyde Park in an Uproar (Eyre, E. J.,
1813), IV. 310
Hyder Ali (Buckstone, J. B., 1831), IV.
26, 481, 628
— (Bunn, A., 1831), IV. 481, 628
— (1832), IV. 481
Hydra, the Moon and the Daffodil
(1830), IV. 481
Hydropathics (1898), V. 695
Hydropathy (Boyce, W., 1892), V. 272
Hydrophobia (Herbert, J., 1820), IV. 325
+ Hyldemoer, the Witch of the Elder-
Tree (Rose, E.; R. Polytechnic, 1878;
8° [1878])
Hymen (Allen, 1764), III. 232
Hymeneal Party (1789), III. 332
Hymen's Muster Roll (Long, C., 1847),
IV. 347
— (1860), V. 695
Hymen's Triumph (1737), II. 375
Hymen wins (Field, W. F., 1890), V. 366
Hypatia (Ogilvie, G. S., 1893), V. 506
Hypermnestra (Owen, R., 1703), II. 347,
442
Hypermnestra, the Girl of the Period
(Sikes, F., 1869), V. 566
Hypnotist (McCullough, B., 1895), V. 468
— = Suggestion
Hypochondriac (Mathews, C. J., 1821),
IV. 354, 597
— (1718), II, 133, 375, 447; III. 188
— (1825), IV. 481
— = Robust Invalid
Hypocondriac (Franklin, A., 1785), III.
261 [This was first acted Smock
Alley, Dublin, 28/12/1784]
— (1771), III. 402
Hypocrisie Alamode = Stage-Beaux
toss'd in a Blanket
Hypocrite (Bickerstaffe, I., 1768), III.
115, 237
— (Shadwell, T., ?1670), I. 430
— (1819), IV. 481, 628

Hypolita, Queen of the Amazons (1819),
IV. 481
Hyram Balthazar (1856), V. 695

I am here = Blache of Nevers
I and my Double (Oxenford, J., 1835),
IV. 367
I beg you wouldn't mention it (Suter,
W. E., 1857), V. 695, 818, 836
I believe you, my busy = Red Rover
Ibrahim (Pix, M., 1696), I. 75, 424
Ibrahim the Illustrious Bassa (Settle,
E., 1676), I. 86, 96, 118, 129, 428
Ibsen Christmas (Gibson, H., 1897), V.
378
Ibsen's Ghost (Barrie, J. M., 1891), V.
211, 251, 778
Icebound (Cooke, F., 1892), V. 324
Ice Fiend of the Alps = Mont Blanc
Ice King (1843), IV. 481
Iceland King (1835), IV. 481
Ice Sea and the Monster Whale of
Greenland = Harpooner
Ice Witch (Buckstone, J. B., 1831), IV.
273
— (1860), V. 836
Içi on (ne) parle (pas) français (1891), V.
695
Ici on parle français (Williams, T. J.,
1859), V. 625
I couldn't help it (Oxenford, J., 1862),
V. 510, 809
Ida (Simpson, J. P., 1865), V. 567
Ida and Carelia = Sisters
+ Ida de Galis; a Tragedy of Powis
Castle (Morgan, R. W., 8°, 1851)
Ida Lee (Young, Mrs H., 1863), V. 695,
836
Idalia (Roberts, G., 1867), V. 544
Ida May (Young, H., 1855), V. 695,
825, 836
Ida May, the Kidnapped Child (1857),
V. 695
Ida of the Cottage (Soane, G., 1819) =
Self-Sacrifice, IV. 481, 628
Idaspe Fedele (1710), II. 32, 34, 229, 394
I'd be a Butterfly (1868), V. 695
Ideal Husband (Wilde, O. F. O'F. W.,
1895), V. 190, 192, 622
Idealist (1897), V. 695
Ideal King = Fancy Land
Idela (Simeon, Y. F., 1802), IV. 401

I did it for the best = Our Cousin German

I Dine with my Mother (Levey, R. M., 1871), v. 458

— (McLachlan, C., 1886), v. 471

Idiot and the Twin Brother = Fate and its Wonders

Idiot Boy (Oxenford, J., 1838), IV. 367

Idiot Heir (1819), IV. 481

Idiot of One-Tree Lane = Jared Swool

Idiot of the Island = Sea Lion's Den

Idiot of the Mill (Stirling, E., 1848), IV. 409

— (1859), v. 836

Idiot of the Mountain (Lee, N., Jr. and Travers, W., 1862), v. 695, 802, 836

— (Suter, W. E., 1861), v. 588

Idiot Queen (Milner, H. M., 1835), IV. 357

Idiot Son = Tower of Lochlain

Idiot, the Roue and the Miser = Lost Inheritance

Idiot Witness (Haines, J. T., 1823), IV. 322

Idle Apprentice (Marchant, F., 1865), v. 695, 805, 836

— = Jack Sheppard

Idle Jack (1883), v. 695

Idleness the Root of Evil (Suter, W. E., 1864), v. 819

Idle 'Prentice (Farnie, H. B., 1870), v. 361

Idler (Chambers, C. H., 1890), v. 187, 307

Idle Words (Fraser, J. A., 1896), v. 372

Idol (Wyndham, Sir C., 1878), v. 634

Idolaters (Hazlewood, C. H., 1862), v. 695, 796, 836

Idol of an Hour (Collingham, G. G., 1899) = Sappho, v. 317, 746, 785, 846

Idol of the King = Launcelot the Lovely

Idol's Birthday (Oxenford, J., 1838), IV. 481, 628

Idol's Eye = Indian Mutiny

Idols of the Heart (Steer, J., 1890), v. 580

Iduna (Conway, H., 1889), v. 323

— (Wilkinson, T. F., 1846), IV. 617

Idyll of New Year's Eve (Filippi, R., 1890), v. 366

Idyll of Seven Dials = Idyll of New Year's Eve

Idyll of the Closing Century (Burney, E., 1896), v. 293

If I had a Thousand a Year (Morton, J. M., 1867), v. 496

If it takes Place = When it takes Place

If I were rich (Stainforth, F., 1881), v. 578

If the Cap fits (Harrington, N. H. and Yates, E., 1859), v. 404

If the Cap fits ye, wear it = Latin, Love and War

If you don't— = Pay me

Ignacio (Maes, F., 1845), IV. 353

Ignatius (1781), III. 332

Ignes de Castro (Musgrave, T. M., 1825), IV. 365

— (Thompson, B., 1800), IV. 412

Ignoramus (Codrington, R., 1662), I. 354, 397

— (Parkhurst, F., 1662), I. 423

— (1736), II. 375

I hope I don't intrude = Mr Paul Pry

Iky le Noir (1877), v. 695

Ildamor and Zulem (1811), IV. 481

Iliad = Siege of Troy

I'll be your Second (Rodwell, G. H., 1831), IV. 395

Ill-gotten Gains (1898), v. 695

+ Ill-Natured Man (8°, 1773)

I'll not have a Wife (Selby, C., 1838), IV. 398

I'll see you right (Crauford, J. R., 1878), v. 328

"I'll sleep on it" = (1) Victor Dene; (2) Victorine

I'll Stay where I am (1823) = "I won't go!", IV. 481

I'll tell your Wife (Webster, N. S., 1855), v. 619

— (1855), v. 695

I'll tell you What (Inchbald, Mrs E., 1785), III. 145, 148, 150, 165, 275

Ill-treated Il Trovatore (Byron, H. J., 1863), v. 296

Illuminated Lake = Prince

Illumination (Pilon, F., 1779), III. 297

Illuminé = Urania

Illusion (Arnold, S. J., 1813), IV. 481, 628

— (Le Clercq, P., 1890), v. 452

Illusions (Dilley, J. J., 1870), v. 345
Illustration in Discord (Brough, W., 1861), v. 279
Illustrious Chief (1836), IV. 481
Illustrious Sclaves (1672), I. 442
Illustrious Stranger (Kenney, J. and Millingen, J., 1827), IV. 146, 337
— (1837), IV. 481
Illustrious Traveller (Reynolds, F., 1818), IV. 392
I'll write to the Times (Wooler, J. P., 1856), v. 632
I Love You! (Reeve, W., 1872), v. 540
Imaginary Cuckold (1733), II. 375, 447
Imaginary Evils = Woman's Word
Imaginary Heir = Feign'd Shipwreck
Imaginary Obstacle (Foote, S., 1762), III. 384
Imann's Daughter = Desert
Imelda (Barrez, Mme, 1846), IV. 570
Imitation (Waldron, F. G., 1783), III. 314
Imitation Tea (McLaren, A., 1818), IV. 352
Immitator = One, Two, Three, Four, Five, by Advertisement
Immolation = Norma
I'm not myself at all (Maltby, A., 1869), v. 473
Imogen's New Cook (Mead, M. S., 1898), v. 483
Im-patience (Browne, G. W., 1884), v. 283
Impeached (Walford, H. L., 1873), v. 611
Imperial Captives (Mottley, J., 1720), II. 110, 160, 346
Imperial Conspirator Overthrown (Edwards, P. H., 1808), IV. 309
Imperial Guard (Hazlewood, C. H., 1872), v. 414
— (1850), IV. 628
Imperial Tragedy (Killigrew, Sir W., 1669), I. 137, 417
Imperial Victims (1819), IV. 481
Imperick (Kirkman, F., 1662), I. 418
Impertinent Lovers (Hawling, F., 1723), II. 44, 173, 335
Impertinents = Sullen Lovers
Imp of the Brazen Spell (1846), IV. 628

Importance of Being Earnest (Wilde, O. F. O'F. W., 1895), v. 190, 192, 622
Impostor (Brooke, H., 1778), III. 240
— (1734), II. 451
Impostor Detected, II. 375
Impostors (Cumberland, R., 1789), III. 115, 127, 176, 252
— (Reed, J., 1776), III. 118, 300
Impostor Unmasked = Rival Captains
Imposture Defeated (Powell, G., 1697), I. 261, 425
Impresario (Grist, W., 1877), v. 395, 795
Imprisoned (1898), v. 695
Imprisonment of Harlequin (1746), II. 375
— (1750), III. 333
Imprisonment, Release, Adventures and Marriage of Harlequin (1740), II. 375
Improved Edition of the Songs in the Burletta of Midas, adapted to the Times (1789), III. 336
Improvisatore = Twine the Plaidon
Imprudence (Pinero, Sir A. W., 1881), v. 173, 525
+ Imprudent Counsel (8°, 1796)
Impudence versus the World (1862), v. 695
Impudent Intruder = Supper Gratis
Impudent Puppy (Buckingham, L. S., 1855), v. 695, 781, 836
Impulse (Stephenson, B. C., 1882), v. 582
I'm Puzzled (Abbot, W., 1819), IV. 249
Ina (Wilmot, Mrs B., 1815), IV. 422, 618
In a Day (Webster, A., 1882), v. 617
In Advance of the Times (Jones, J. W., 1875), v. 440
In a Fit of Abstraction (Malyon, E. J. and James, C., 1897) = Lady Burglar, v. 473, 695, 805
In a Locket = World of Trouble in a Locket
In an Afternoon (Norman, G. T., 1898), v. 505
In an Attic (Jones, J. W., 1895), v. 441
In and Out (Stirling, E., 1845), IV. 481, 628
— (1821), IV. 481
In and Out and Round About (Hall, F., 1863), v. 795

In and out of a Punt (Esmond, H. V.,
1896), v. 359
In and out of Place (Johnson, G. D.,
1857), v. 695, 800, 836
In and out of Service (Douglass, J. T.,
1869), v. 348
In and Out of Tune (Lawler, D., 1808),
IV. 280, 342
In Another Man's Castle (Lundin, C.,
1898), v. 465
Ina of Sigiswold = Ina
In a Telegraph Office (Bell, Mrs H.,
1893), v. 256
In a Terrible Storm (1897), v. 695
In Black and White (Bertrand, W. C.,
1880), v. 260
Inca (1819), IV. 481
In Camp (Vokes, V., 1883), v. 609
Incarcerated Victim of the Bastille =
Tale of Two Cities
In Carnival Time (1890), v. 695
Incas (Thelwall, J.), III. 101, 311
Incas of Peru (1790), III. 332
Incendiaries (1859), v. 695
Incendiary (1834), IV. 481
Incestuous Marriage = Arsinoe
In Chancery (Pinero, Sir A. W., 1884),
v. 525
In Charge (Cassel, H. and Duckworth,
H. C., 1888), v. 305
— (1885), v. 695
Inchavogue (Cahill, W. B., 1873), v. 299
Inchcape Bell (Fitzball, E., 1828), IV.
313
In Chrysanthemum Land (Moore,
H. T., 1899), v. 492
Inch Verra = Verdict of the World
Incidents of the War of 1871 = Germans
and French
Incog. (?Lennox, Lord W. or Keep,
W. A., 1817), IV. 345, 428, 591, 595
— = (1) Gabrielle; (2) Tom, Dick and
Harry
Incognita (Burnand, F. C., 1892), v. 292
— (Rose, E., 1879), v. 550
Incognito (Aidé, H., 1888), v. 236
— (Antonini, Mlle, 1881), v. 241
"Incog!" What's in a Name (1829), IV.
481
Incompatibility of Temper (Suter,
W. E.), v. 588
Inconsolables (1738), II. 375

Inconstant (Farquhar, G., 1702), I. 183;
II. 135, 140, 148, 321, 435
Inconstant Villager (1814), IV. 481
Incorrigibles (1882), v. 696
Incorruptible = Citizen Robespierre
In Cupid's Court (Watson, T. M.,
1885), v. 616
In Danger (Lestocq, W. and Creswell,
H., 1887), v. 457
In Darker London (1894), v. 696
In Days of Old (Rose, E., 1899), v. 211,
550
In Deadly Peril (Collier, H., 1890), v.
317
Indécis (Bell, Mrs H., 1887), v. 255
Independence (Allingham, J. T., 1809)
= Trustee, IV. 252, 545, 568, 641
— = Uncle Jonathan
Independent Patriot (Lynch, F., 1737),
II. 68, 205, 233, 342
India in 1857 (1857), v. 696
Indian (Fenwick, J., 1800), IV. 312
Indiana (Farnie, H. B., 1886), v. 363
Indian Captive (1796), III. 332
Indian Chief (Williams, J.), III. 316
Indian Chief's Revenge = Magawiska
Indian Emperour (Dryden, J., 1665), I.
26, 36, 96, 99, 111–13, 126, 227, 234,
315, 343, 344, 345, 404; IV. 102
Indian Empress (1731), II. 375
Indian Exiles (Thompson, B., 1800), IV.
412
Indian Father (1822), IV. 481
Indian Girl (1837), IV. 482
Indian Hunters = Inscription
Indian Lovers = Nabob
Indian Maid (1823), IV. 482
— (1850), v. 696
Indian Merchant (1748), II. 451–2
Indian Mutiny (Daventry, G., 1887), v.
338
Indian Nuptials (Rochfort, 1815), IV.
482, 629
Indian Pirate's Vessel = Koeuba
Indian Prince (Perry, T. G., 1897), v.
520
Indian Princess = Pocahontas
Indian Puzzle (À Beckett, G. A.) v. 234
Indian Queen (Howard, Sir R. and
Dryden, J., 1664), I. 35, 36, 39, 49, 50,
81, 83, 96, 107, 110–12, 125, 337, 354,
414

Intrigue (1876), v. 696
Intrigue All-A-Mode = Different
  Widows
Intrigue in a Cloyster (Horde, T., 1783),
  III. 273
Intrigue, Love, Honour and Obey
  (1812), IV. 482
Intrigue on the House-Top = Enraged
  Musician
Intrigues and Disasters = Green Room
Intrigues at Versailles (D'Urfey, T.,
  1697), I. 277, 409
Intrigues of a Day (1814), IV. 482, 635
Intrigues of a Morning (Parsons, Mrs E.,
  1792), III. 296
Intrigues of Harlequin = Jupiter and
  Europa
Intriguing Chambermaid (Fielding, H.,
  1734), II. 136, 138, 145, 245-6, 326,
  419, 436; III. 116
— (1790), III. 332
Intriguing Columbine (1747), II. 375
Intriguing Courtiers (1732), II. 376
Intriguing Dame = Jealous Doctor
Intriguing Footman (Whiteley, J.,
  1791), III. 315
— (1742), II. 376
Intriguing Harlequin (1734), II. 452
Intriguing Milliners and Attornies
  Clerks (Robinson, W., 1738), II. 351
Intriguing Servant = Livery Rake and
  Country Lass
Intriguing Squire = Hasty Wedding
Intriguing Valet = Jealous Taylor
Intriguing Widow (1705), II. 376
Intruder (1892), v. 696
Intruders (Day, J. T., 1898), v. 340
Intruding Widow = Wife's Trial
In Two Minds (Heathcote, A. M.,
  1894), v. 415
Inundation (Archer, T., 1847), IV. 255
— = (1) Saved; (2) Siege of Antwerp
Inundation of the Nile (1846), IV. 482
— = Spirit of the Moon
Invader of his Country (Dennis, J.,
  1719), II. 43, 48, 86, 318, 435
Invaders Vanquished = Armed Briton
Invasion (Grant, J. M., 1803), IV. 320
— (Pilon, F., 1778), III. 297
— (Roche, E., 1808), IV. 395
— (1759), III. 332
— (1803), IV. 482

Invasion Defeated = Loyalty
Invasion of England (1803), IV. 482
Invasion of England by William the
  Conqueror (Courtney, J., 1844) =
  William the Conqueror's Invasion of
  England, IV. 482, 555, 629, 643
Invasion of Holland = Sans Culottes and
  the Grand Culottes
Invasion of Naples by the French =
  Charles the Eighth of France
Invention of Powder = (1) Barber Bravo;
  (2) Barber's Secret
Inventories (Clarke, H. S., 1885), v. 313
Invincibles (Morton, T., 1828), IV. 363
Invisible Avengers (1809), IV. 482
Invisible Bridegroom (Jameson, R. F.,
  1813), IV. 330
Invisible Brothers = Salvator
Invisible Client (Blanchard, E. L.,
  1844), IV. 268, 482, 573, 629
— (Blanchard, E. L., 1875), v. 264
Invisible Girl (Hook, T. E., 1806), IV.
  327
— (1800), IV. 629
— (1823), IV. 482
Invisible Green (Oxenford, J., 1848),
  IV. 482, 629
Invisible Husband (Haines, J. T., 1833),
  IV. 322
— = Giralda
Invisible Lover = Magician
Invisible Mistress (1788), III. 116, 332,
  402
— = Wrangling Lovers
Invisible Prince (Maitland, F., 1862), v.
  805
— (Planché, J. R., 1846), IV. 42, 382,
  605
— (1878), v. 696
Invisible Ring (Dibdin, C. I. M., 1806),
  IV. 291
Invisible Tribunal (Milner, H. M.,
  1826), IV. 482, 629
Invisible Witness (Dibdin, T. J., 1818),
  IV. 82, 301
— (1839), IV. 482
Invissible Smirk (Kirkman, F., 1662), I.
  417
Invitation (1787), III. 332
— (1823), IV. 482
Invitation à la Fête (Barnett, M. B.,
  1848), IV. 570

Irish Fidelity = (1) Aileen Asthore; (2) Round Tower

Irish Fine Lady (Macklin, C., 1767), III. 284

Irish Footman (Clements, A., 1872), v. 314

Irish Gentleman (Murray, D. C. and Shine, J. L., 1897), v. 500

— (Raymond, R. J., 1834), IV. 483, 629

Irish Girl (M°Laren, A., 1813), IV. 351

— (Ryan, R., 1830), IV. 483, 629

— (1819), IV. 483

Irish Heiress (Boucicault, D., 1842), IV. 269

— (1832), IV. 483

Irish Hospitality (Shadwell, C., 1717), II. 183, 354 [This was acted Smock Alley, Dublin, late in 1717]

— (1766), III. 332

Irish Immigrant (Brougham, J., 1854), v. 280

Irish Intrigue (Doyle, T. F., 1873), v. 350

Irish Legacy (Arnold, S. J., 1797) = Legacy, III. 234, 377

Irish Life (Creamer, A. and Downey, L. T., 1888), v. 330

Irish Lion (Buckstone, J. B., 1838), IV. 275, 575

Irish Loyalty (1821), IV. 483

Irishman (Whitbread, J. W., 1889), v. 620

Irishman Bothered = Mistake upon Mistake

Irishman in all his Glory = Sprig of Shillelah

Irishman in Bagdad = Ninth Statue

Irishman in Distress = Committee

Irishman in England = Phantoms

Irishman in France = British Carpenter

Irishman in India = Surooz Seeing

Irishman in Italy (1813), IV. 483

— = False and True

Irishman in London (Macready, W., 1792), III. 285, 391

Irishman in Naples (1822), IV. 483

Irishman in Spain (Stuart, C., 1791), III. 310, 396

Irishman in Turkey = Middle Dish

Irishman in Windsor (1826), IV. 483

Irishman's Dream (1839), IV. 483

Irishman's Fortune (1830), IV. 483

Irishman's Fortune = Born to Good Luck

Irishman's Frolics = Money at a Pinch

Irishman's Heart (Levey, J. C., 1879), v. 458

Irishman's Home (1833), IV. 483

— (1875), v. 697

Irishman's Love = Teddy O'Connor

Irishman's Policy (Richardson, H., 1875), v. 543

Irish Mimic (O'Keeffe, J., 1795) = Lounge at Brighton, III. 294, 393

Irish Minstrel (Court, F. H., 1867), v. 697, 786, 836

— (1889), v. 697

Irish Molly (+Pitt, G. D., 1845), IV. 483 [This is the same as The Primrose of Ireland, see IV. 374]

Irish Nieces = All at Home

Irish Nigger (Rede, W. L., 1841), IV. 483, 629

Irish Patriot = Pike O'Callaghan

Irish Poleander (1823), IV. 483

Irish Post (Planché, J. R., 1846), IV. 382

Irish Priest (Ellis, B., 1890), v. 357

Irish Promotion (1791), III. 332 [A newspaper notice declares this was by "Counsellor Shannon"]

Irish Reapers (1818), IV. 483

Irish Sharebroker = Railway Mania

Irish Tar (Oulton, W. C., 1797), III. 296

Irish Taylors (1791), III. 332

Irish Tiger (Morton, J. M., 1846), IV. 362

Irish Traveller = False Friendship

Irish Tutor (Butler, R., 1822), IV. 277, 575

Irish Valet = More Blunders than One

Irish Wedding = Dermot and Kathlane

Irish Widow (Garrick, D., 1772), III. 117, 263

— (1821), IV. 483

Irish Wife (1832), IV. 483

Irish Witch (Amherst, J. H.), IV. 254

Irishwoman (Clarke, Lady O., 1819), IV. 280

Irma (Bonawitz, J. H., 1885), v. 267, 779

Irmengarda (Beatty-Kingston, W., 1892), v. 254

Iron Arm (Suter, W. E., 1857), v. 697, 818, 836

Iron before Gold (Osborne, C., 1872), v. 508

Iron Casket (1868), v. 697

— = Hans of Iceland

Iron Chain (1895), v. 697

Iron Chest (Colman, G., the Younger, 1796), III. 41, 43, 72, 104–5, 247–8, 367

— (1811), IV. 483

Ironclad Warriors and the Little Tug of War = Ulysses

Iron Clasp (Townsend, W. T., 1862), v. 697, 821

Iron Collar (Amherst, J. H., 1832), IV. 254

— = Death by the Law

Iron Gates (Henderson, J., 1883), v. 416

Iron Grave = Waiting for Death

Iron Grip (James, C. S., 1849), IV. 330

Iron Hand (Haines, J. T., 1841), IV. 323, 483, 629

Iron Hand and Velvet Glove = Secret Society

Iron Hands (Pitt, H. M., 1873), v. 526

Iron Heart (1830), IV. 483

Iron Latch Farm (Mackay, H., 1865), v. 697, 805, 836

Iron Maiden (Wilkinson, M. and Hallatt, W. H., 1896), v. 623

Iron Mask = Queen's Secret

Iron Masque = Island of St Marguerite

Iron Master (Pinero, Sir A. W., 1884), v. 525

Iron Master of Samarkand by Oxus = Timour the Tartar

Iron Road (1899), v. 697

Iron Statue (1868), v. 697

Iron Tower (Astley, P., Jr., 1801), IV. 256

Iron True (Sennett, T., 1886), v. 561

Iroquis (1820), IV. 483

— (1823), IV. 483

Irregular Rum 'un = F.M. Julius Caesar

Irresistibles (Moncrieff, W. T., 1828), IV. 359

— (1857), v. 697

Irvingmania (1877), v. 697

Isaac Abroad (Plowman, T. F., 1878), v. 528

Isaac Comnenus (Taylor, H., 1827), IV. 410

Isaac of York (Plowman, T. F., 1871), v. 528

— = (1) Isaac Abroad; (2) Ivanhoe

Isaac the Jew of York = Ivanhoe

Isabel (Cape, F., 1874), v. 302

Isabel Bertrand (1846), IV. 483

Isabel D'Arville (1895), v. 697

Isabella (Garrick, D., 1757), III. 58, 262

— (Kemble, J. P., 1814), IV. 335

Isabelle (Buckstone, J. B., 1834), IV. 274

Isabelle de Montral (1834), IV. 483

Isabel that was a Belle = East Lynne

Isalda (Horner, F., 1890), v. 427

Isaure (Webster, B. N., 1832), IV. 483, 616, 629

— (1833), IV. 483

Is Brown at Home? (De Frece, M., 1873), v. 341

Is he a Christian? (Connynghame, F. L. and Price, F., 1898), v. 320

Is He Alive? (1818), IV. 483

Is He a Prince? (Greffulhe, 1809) = German Blunder, IV. 321, 467, 586, 626

Is He Dead? (1847), IV. 629

Is He Jealous? (Beazley, S., Jr., 1816), IV. 263, 571

— (1820), IV. 483

Is his Appointment Pucka? = Dark Bungalow

Ishnabrogue (1891), v. 697

Isidore and Merida (Dimond, W., 1827), IV. 483, 629

Is it a Spectre? = Dunoir the Base

Is it a Wedding? (1800), IV. 483

Is it a Woman? (Abbott, W., 1833), IV. 483, 629

Is it He or his Brother = Twins

Is it the King? (Greenwood, T. L., 1861), v. 697, 836

Island (Jerrold, D. W., 1823), IV. 331, 483, 590, 629

Island Ape = (1) Bibboo; (2) Juan Fernandez

Islanders (Byrne, O., 1816), IV. 483, 629

— (Dibdin, C., 1780), III. 119, 255, 381

Island Home (Calvert, C., 1861), v. 697, 783, 837

Island Nymph (Barrez, 1846), IV. 483

Island of Bachelors (Reece, R., 1874), v. 538, 812

Island of Calypso = Telemachus

Island of Darkness (1815), IV. 484

Island of Jewels (Planché, J. R., 1849), IV. 383, 605

Island of Nowpartickeler Folley = Girls of the Period

Island of Owhyhee = Captain Cook

Island of St Marguerite (St John, J., 1789), III. 304, 395

Island of Silver Store (1858), V. 697

Island of Slaves (Clive, C., 1761), III. 118, 243, 379

Island of Trances and the Land of Flowers (1852), V. 697

Island of Tranquil Delights = Invisible Prince

Island Princess (Motteux, P. A., 1699), I. 55, 426; II. 29–30, 132, 134, 345

— (Tate, N., 1687), I. 338, 434

— (1669), I. 40, 344, 345, 351, 442

Island Queens (Banks, J., 1684), I. 53, 79, 166–7, 389

Is Law Justice? = Iron Maiden

Isle of Love = St Helena

Isle of Mull (McLaren, A., 1820), IV. 352

Isle of Palms (Wilson, 1812), IV. 422

Isle of St Tropez (Williams, M. and Burnand, F. C., 1860), V. 624, 824

Isle of the Genii = Storm

Isle of Utopia (St Clare, G., 1892), V. 554

Is Life worth living? (Scudamore, F. A., 1887), V. 559

Islington (Osman, W. R., 1867), V. 508

Islington in Olden Time = Clerke's Well

Islington in the Olden Time = St John's Priory

Islington Spa = Spleen

Islington Stage = Double X.X.

Is Madame at Home? (Bell, M., 1887), V. 256

Is Marriage a Failure? (Collier, H. and Dudley, F. H., 1888), V. 317

Isn't it a Duck? (Barnett, M., 1849), IV. 484, 629

Isofel (Lawrence, E., 1887), V. 451

Isolate and the Ape (Dibdin, C. I. M., 1826), IV. 296

Isolda (Richards, A. B., 1848), IV. 394

Isoline of Bavaria = Bavarian Girl

Israel in Egypt (1739), II. 394

Israelites (Smollett, T. G., 1785), III. 308

Israelites in Egypt (Lacy, M. R., 1833), IV. 484, 629

Is she a Woman? (Collier, W., 1835), IV. 281

Is she guilty? (Faucquez, A., 1877), V. 364

Is she his Daughter? (Murray, G. and Hipkins, T. H., 1861), V. 798, 808

Is She his Wife? (Dickens, C., 1837), IV. 146–7, 305

Is She Mad? = Delusion

Italian Boys (1833), IV. 484

Italian Bravo (1861), V. 697

Italian Brigand = Nameless

Italian Captain (1847), IV. 629

Italian Conspiracy = Patriot

Italian Flower Girl (1817), IV. 484

Italian Foresters = Minstrel

Italian Gamester (Barrett, C. F., 1810), IV. 484

— = Wife and Mistress

Italian Husband (Eyre, E. J., 1812) = Look at Home, IV. 484, 629

— (Lewis, E., 1754), III. 281

— (Ravenscroft, E., 1697), I. 169–70, 426

— (1795), III. 332

Italian Jealousy (1729), II. 376

Italian Love = Ravenna

Italian Lover (Phillips, F. L., 1846), IV. 372

— = Julia

Italian Monk (Boaden, J., 1797), III. 72, 238

Italian Nuptials = Corsair

Italian Patriot = Patriot

Italian Romance (Darwin, P., 1889), V. 337

Italians (Bucke, C., 1819), IV. 68, 78, 200, 272

Italian Shadows (1720), II. 376

Italians in Algiers (1844), IV. 484, 629

Italian Sister (1829), IV. 484

Italian's Revenge = Hunted Down

Italian Traitors (1830), IV. 484

Italian Villagers (Hoare, P., 1797), III. 197, 270

Italian Wanderers = Minstrel Boy

17

Italian Wife (Dibdin, T. J., 1816), IV. 300
— (Doubleday, T., 1823), IV. 582
— (1817), IV. 484
— (1855), V. 697
— (1858), V. 697
— = Fazio
It Cannot Be = Sir Courtly Nice
It is all a Farce = Modern Comedy
It is a long lane that has no turning = Released Convict
It is Fate = Sensualist
It is Justice (Zech, M., 1890), V. 637
It is never too late to learn (1864), V. 697
It is the Devil! = Dominique
It might have been worse = My Lord and my Lady
It must be true, 'twas in the papers (1862), V. 697
It never rains but it pours (Meritt, P., 1877), V. 486
— (1862), V. 697
It runs in the Family (1855), V. 697
It's All a Mistake (Farrell, J., 1819), IV. 311
— = (1) Newspaper Blunders; (2) Q.E.D.
It's all through the Lad (1885), V. 697
It's All Very Well Mr Ferguson, But You Don't Sleep Here (Suter, W., 1837), IV. 613
It's a Long Lane that has no Turning (Suter, W. E., 1860), V. 819 [This is presumably the original form of The Test of Truth, see V. 588]
It's an Ill Wind that blows Nobody Good (Oxenford, J., 1860), V. 697, 809, 837
It's better late than never = Better late than never
It's Fifty Years Since = Irish Attorney
It Should have come Sooner (Hawling, F., 1723), II. 335
Its Mother's Pet (1848), IV. 629
It's never too late to mend (Reade, C., 1864), V. 110, 536
— (Young, H., 1860), V. 825
— (1861), V. 837
It's never too late to repent (Lewis, G., 1875), V. 459

It's only my Aunt (Bartholomew, Mrs A. C. V., 1849), IV. 484, 571
It's Only Round the Corner = Harmony Restored
It's Two to One = No Misses
It's Well if it Takes = More Ways than One
It was a Dream (Field, J., 1890), V. 697, 792, 837
It was Right at the Last (Horde, T., 1787), III. 115, 273
Ivan (Sotheby, W., 1816), IV. 405
Ivan Daniloff (Planché, Mrs J. R., 1835), IV. 383
Ivan de Bessenvelt (Phillips, F. L., 1845), IV. 372
Ivanhoe (Beazley, S., Jr., 1820), IV. 93, 264
— (Bunn, A., 1820), IV. 93, 484, 629
— (Calcraft, J. W., 1823), IV. 93, 278
— (Cooper, F. F., 1859) = Lists of Ashby, V. 80, 697, 786, 837
— (Cowie, R., 1875), V. 80, 327
— (Dibdin, T. J., 1820), IV. 93, 302
— (Edgar, R. H., 1871), V. 80, 354
— (Jones, R.), IV. 93, 591
— (Moncrieff, W. T., 1820), IV. 93, 358, 484, 600, 629
— (Murray, W. H., 1824), IV. 93, 345
— (Stevens, E., 1896), V. 80, 583
— (Sturgis, J., 1891), V. 80, 586
— (Suter, W. E., 1863), V. 80, 697, 837
— (1820) IV. 93, 484
— (1872), V. 80, 697
Ivanhoe in accordance with the Spirit of the Times (Byron, H. J., 1862), V. 80, 296
Ivanhoe settled and Rebecca righted = Isaac Abroad
Ivan of the Mask (Lynch, T. J., 1826), IV. 484, 629
Ivan the Armourer = Czarina
Ivan the Terrible (1866), V. 697
Ivar (1785), III. 332
I've beat all three (Douglass, J. T., 1861), V. 697, 788, 837
I've been roaming = Scapegrace
I've eaten my Friend (Bridgeman, J. V., 1851), V. 274
I've left my Place = I've lost my Place
I've lost my Place (1833), IV. 484
I've quite forgot = Green Dragon

Iver and Hengo (Rees, T. D., 1795), III. 301

Ivers Dean (Young, Sir C. L. and Howard, B., 1877), v. 635

I've seen a Harem = Morocco Bound

I've taken a House (Grain, R. C., 1889), v. 387

I've written to Browne (Williams, T. J., 1859), v. 625

Ivor (Hitchener, W. H., 1808), IV. 325

Ivory Tablets (1898), v. 697

Ivy (Melford, M., 1887), v. 484

— (1894), v. 697

Ivy Hall (Oxenford, J., 1859), v. 509

+ Ivy Hall, Richmond (Emson, F. E., 8°, 1873)

Iwan (Fitzball, E., 1823), IV. 484, 629

Iwanowna (Dibdin, C. I. M., 1816), IV. 294

"I want my Ma" = Sham Captain

I will be a Duchess (Buckstone, J. B., 1839), IV. 275

I will have an Uncle (Dance, C., 1836), IV. 484, 629

I will have a Wife! (Planché, J. R., 1823), IV. 377

I will if you will (Bruton, J., 1860), v. 284

I wish you may get it (1825), IV. 484

I won't go! (1823) = I'll stay where I am, IV. 484, 629

Ixion (Burnand, F. C., 1863), v. 69, 288

— (Ravenscroft, E., 1697), I. 426

Ixion Rewheeled (Burnand, F. C., 1874), v. 290

Izaak Walton (Dance, C., 1839), IV. 289

Jabez North = Dark Deeds

Jacintha (1821), IV. 484

Jack (Beckett, Mrs H., 1886), v. 254

— (Rogerson, H., 1898), v. 549

— (1879), v. 697

— (1882), v. 697

— (1884), v. 697

Jackal (Aveling, E. B., 1889), v. 246

— = Only Way

Jack and his Nine Wives (1840), IV. 484

Jack and Jack's Brother (Johnstone, J. B., 1855), v. 438

— = Gipsey Farmer

Jack and Jill (Blanchard, E. L., 1854), v. 263, 779

Jack and Jill (Blanchard, E. L., 1872), v. 264

— (Clements, A. and Soutar, R., 1874), v. 314

— (Conquest, G. and Spry, H., 1898), v. 323

— (Green, F. W., 1876), v. 390

— (Green, F. W., 1879), v. 391

— ("Marcus", 1882), v. 476

— (Wade, W., 1893), v. 698, 822, 837

— (1812), IV. 484

— (1854), v. 698

— (1876, 1878), v. 697

— (1878, 1879, 1883, 1884, 1889, 1893, 1897), v. 698

— = (1) Seaweed Hall; (2) Toto and Sata

Jack and Jill and the Sleeping Beauty (Soutar, R., 1868), v. 575

Jack and Jill and the Well on the Hill (Conquest, G. and Spry, H., 1883), v. 322

Jack and Jill Up-to-date (1899), v. 698

Jack and the Beanstalk (Blanchard, E. L., 1844), IV. 268

— (Blanchard, E. L., 1859), v. 698, 779, 837

— (Conquest, G. and Spry, H., 1886), v. 322

— (Dibdin, C. I. M. 1819), IV. 294

— (Green, F. W., 1873), v. 390

— (Green, F. W., 1875), v. 390

— (Green, F. W., 1878), v. 391

— (Green, F. W., 1884), v. 391

— (Green, F. W. and Clay, T. L., 1880), v. 391

— (Hersee, H. and Lennard, H., 1887), v. 420

+ — (Hodson, W., printed in *Juvenile Plays for Home Performance* (*French*))

— (Lennard, H., 1884), v. 455

— (Lennard, H., 1893), v. 456

— (McLelland, H. F., 1893), v. 468

— (McLelland, H. F., 1897), v. 468

— (Millward, C., 1872), v. 489

— (Millward, C., 1877), v. 489

— (Nichols, H. and Harris, Sir A., 1889), v. 504

— (Thorne, G., 1893), v. 599

— (Thorne, G. and Palmer, F. G., 1886), v. 598

Jack and the Beanstalk (1847), IV. 629
— (1855), v. 698
— (1857), v. 837
— (1859, 1874, 1875, 1876, 1877, 1878, 1879, 1880, 1882, 1883), v. 698
— (1884), v. 837
— (1884, 1885, 1886, 1888, 1889), v. 698
— (1890), v. 837
— (1892, 1893, 1894, 1895, 1896, 1898), v. 698
Jack Ashore (Blake, T. G.), IV. 573
— = Girl o' my Heart
Jack Brag (À Beckett, G. A., 1837), IV. 249
Jack Cade, the Captain of the Commons (Conrad, R. T., 1861), v. 323
Jack Crawford (1877), v. 698
+ Jack Dolphin (Jerrold, D.; provinces, 1833)
Jacket of Blue (Wilks, T. E., 1838), IV. 420
Jacket of Green = Neale O'Neale
Jackeydora (Melford, M., 1890), v. 484
Jack Frock (Courtney, J., 1848), IV. 284
Jack Grapplehard (1810), IV. 484
Jack Horner (1876), v. 698
Jack in a Box (Simpson, J. P., 1866), v. 567
Jack in the Box (Blanchard, E. L., 1873), v. 264
— (Green, F. W., 1876), v. 698, 794, 837
— (Green, F. W. and Hall, F., 1886), v. 391
— (Sims, G. R. and Scott, C. W., 1885), v. 569
— (Towers, E., 1881), v. 601
Jack in the Box, And Harlequin and the Princess (Barrymore, W., 1829), IV. 484, 629
Jack in the Green (Dibdin, T. J., 1821), IV. 303
— (Lemon, M., 1850), v. 455
Jack in the Water (Rede, W. L., 1842), IV. 390, 607
Jack in Wonderland (Blanchard, E. L., 1875), v. 264
Jack Junk (1842), IV. 484
Jack Ketch (Almar, G., 1841), IV. 253, 568
Jack Long of Texas (Johnstone, J. B., 1847), IV. 333

Jack Long of Texas (1858), v. 698
Jack Mingo, the London Street-Boy (Roberts, V., 1866), v. 698, 814, 837
Jack Noakes and Tom Styles (Blanchard, E. L., 1842), IV. 268
Jack o' both Sides (Reynoldson, T. H., 1845), IV. 393
Jack of All Trades (Gibney, S., 1896), v. 378
— (Neville, H. and Haydon, F., 1861), v. 699, 796, 807, 837
— = Throw Physic to the Dogs!
Jack of Newbury (Hook, J., 1795), III. 272
Jack of Paddington (1844), IV. 484
Jack o' Hearts (Vereker, S. and Dearlove, W. H., 1894), v. 608
Jack o' Lantern (Hazlewood, C. H., 1867), v. 413
— (1828), IV. 484
Jacko, the Brazilian Ape (1861), v. 699
Jack o' the Hedge (Suter, W. E., 1862), v. 588
Jack on the Green (1850), v. 699
Jack Rag out of Place = Unfinished Gentleman
Jack Ram (1848), IV. 484
Jack Robinson and his Monkey (Barrymore, W., 1828) = Fatal Rock, IV. 262, 459, 570
— (Thompson, C. P., 1828), IV. 413
Jack Robinson Crusoe (Jones, J. W., 1876), v. 440
Jack Royal (1850), v. 699
Jack's Alive (Soane, G., 1837), IV. 484, 629
Jacks and Jills (Albery, J., 1880), v. 238
Jack's Arrival from Canton (1864), v. 699
Jack's Delight (Williams, T. J., 1862), v. 625, 824
Jack's Delight in his Lovely Nan (1835), IV. 484
Jack Sheppard (Buckstone, J. B., 1839), IV. 97, 265
— (Greenwood, T., 1839), IV. 311, 586
— (Haines, J. T., 1839), IV. 97, 323, 587
— (Hatton, J., 1898), IV. 409
— (Murray, W. H., 1840), IV. 97, 365
— (1839), IV. 18, 97, 484
— (1855), v. 699

John and Angelina (Lathair, H., 1890),
v. 449

John Anderson my Jo (1839), IV. 486
— = Old Church Porch

John and Jeannette (Machale, L., 1885),
v. 469

John Aylmer's Dream (Burbey, E. J.,
1886), v. 287

John Baliol (Tennant, W., 1828), IV. 411

John Brown (1823), IV. 486
— (1826), IV. 486

John Bull (Boucicault, D., 1872), v. 269
— (Colman, G., the Younger, 1803),
IV. 52, 184, 282
— (Lacy, T. H., 1854), v. 802

John Bull Abroad (Grain, R. C., 1888),
v. 387

John Bull and Buonaparte (Cross,
J. C., 1803), IV. 286

John Bull and the Rural Police = Prometheus Britannicus

John Bull and the Wet Quaker = Irishman in Windsor

John Bull in France (1811), IV. 486

John Bull in his Dotage = Jubilee

John Bull's Dilemma (1885), v. 700

John Bull Triumphant = Reform

John Buzzby (Kenney, J., 1822), IV. 337

John Cade of Asliford (1850), v. 700

John Chetwynd's Wife = Dr Chetwynd

John Churchill, Duke of Marlborough
(1820), IV. 630

John Darrell's Dream (France, E. S.),
v. 792

John Dobbs (Morton, J. M., 1849), IV.
363

John du Bart (Pocock, I., 1815), IV.
384

John Duddlestone, the Breeches Maker
of Bristol (1837), IV. 486

John, Earl of Gowrie (Brown, R., 1825),
IV. 574

John Felton (1850), v. 700

John Gabriel Borkman (Archer, W.,
1897), v. 242
— (1896), v. 700

John Gilpin (1815), IV. 486, 630
— (1817), IV. 486, 630

John Grant's Daughter and the Flaming
Hand = Blacksmith's Daughter and
the Red Hand

John Heriot, Yeoman (1887), v. 700

John Howard, the Philanthropist =
Convict Ship

John Jasper's Wife (Harvey, F., 1876),
v. 408

John Johnson (Pitt, G. D., 1835), IV. 373

John Jones (Buckstone, J. B., 1831), IV.
274

John Lester, Parson (Knight, R. and
Foster, L., 1892), v. 445

John Marchmont's Legacy (1866), v.
700

John Martin's Secret (Vane, S., 1895),
v. 606

Johnnie Armstrong (Cross, J. C., 1803),
IV. 486, 630
— (1822), IV. 486

Johnnie Fa (1842), IV. 630

Johnny Gilpin (1823), IV. 486

Johnny Gilpin's Ride to Edmonton
(Lee, N., Jr., 1861), v. 700, 802, 837

Johnny Newcomes at Epping = Easter
Hunting

John o' Armhall (1828), IV. 630

John of Calais (Dibdin, T. J., ?1796),
III. 382

John of Leyden (1849), IV. 486

John of Lorne and Helen of Argyle
(1824), IV. 486

John of Paris (Pocock, I., 1814), IV. 144,
384

John of Procida (Knowles, J. S., 1840),
IV. 339

John of the Forge (1850), v. 700

John Overy, the Miser (Jerrold, D. W.,
1829), IV. 331

John Savile of Haysted (White, J.,
1847), IV. 419

John Smith (Hancock, W., 1862), v. 402
— (Law, A., 1889), v. 450

John Stafford (Townsend, W. T. or
Bosworth, J., 1835), IV. 414, 573

John Thurgood, Farmer (Byatt, H.,
1893), v. 295

John Wharton (Fielding, H., 1868), v.
366

John Wilson (1865), v. 700

John Woodvil (Lamb, C., 1802), IV.
194-5, 341

John Wopps (Suter, W. E., 1860), v. 588

Joint Household (Bell, Mrs H., 1891),
v. 255

Joke = Sixty-third Letter

Joker (Tennyson, M. H., 1894), v. 595

Joke's a Joke (Hook, T. E., 1830), IV. 486, 630

Joking Girl = Aunt Chimpanzee

Jolie Parfumeuse (Kenny, C. L., 1875), v. 801

Jolliboy's Woes (Fawcett, C. S., 1878), v. 364

Jolly Beggars (Burns, R., 1823), IV. 277

Jolly Boy Blue (1893), v. 701

Jolly Crew (1799), III. 333

Jolly Dick the Lamplighter = Life's a Lottery

Jolly Dogs of London (Hazlewood, C. H., 1866), v. 701, 796, 837

Jolly Jack (1850), v. 701

Jolly Jock (1899), v. 837

Jolly Joe (Hazlewood, C. H., 1868), v. 413

Jolly King Christmas (Marchant, F., 1863), v. 701, 837

Jolly Miller (1861), v. 701

Jolly Miller of Stratford (Giovanelli, A., 1869), v. 382

Jolly Miller of the Dee (Millward, C., 1864), v. 807

Jolly Young Waterman = Alice Lowrie

Jonathan (Barber, J., 1845), IV. 259

Jonathan Bradford (Fitzball, E., 1833), IV. 36, 120, 314

— (1835), IV. 486

Jonathan Dobson, the Congress Trooper (1831), IV. 486

Jonathan in England (Peake, R. B., 1824), IV. 369

Jonathan Oldakre (Wilson, J. C.), v. 824

Jonathan Wild (James, C. S., 1848), IV. 330

— (Young, H., 1886), v. 636

— (Young, Mrs H., 1868), v. 636

Jonathan without a David (Foster, L., 1894), v. 371

Jones (Shirley, A. and Landeck, B., 1891), v. 564

Jones and Co. (Burleigh, F., 1893), v. 781

Jones and Co., Matrimonial Agents (Bingham, F., 1893), v. 261

Jones's Aunt = Prodigal Father

Jones's Notes (Tabrar, J., 1886), v. 589

Jones the Avenger (Talfourd, F., 1856), v. 701, 819, 837

Jonnie Armstrong (Dibdin, C. I. M., 1812), IV. 292

Jonny Gilpin (1808), IV. 486

Joseph (1745), II. 395

Joseph II (1830), IV. 486

Joseph and his Brethren (Howard, H. L., 1824), IV. 589

— (Miller, J., 1744), II. 395

— (Wells, C. J., 1824), IV. 202-3, 418

Joseph Andrews (Pratt, S. J., 1778), III. 299

Joseph Chavigny (Phillips, W., 1856), v. 523

Joseph Gombert (1860), v. 701

Josephine (Buckstone, J. B., 1844), IV. 275

Josephine, the Child of the Regiment (Buckstone, J. B., 1858), v. 287

Joseph's Luck (1897), v. 701

Joseph sold by his Brethren (1789), III. 333

Joseph's Sweetheart (Buchanan, R., 1888), v. 285

Joshua (Morell, T., 1747), II. 395, 441

Joshua Haggard (Young, J., 1879), v. 636

Josiah's Dream (Rogers, C., 1896), v. 548

Jo, the Waif (1881), v. 701

Jour de Fête (1856), v. 837

Journey of Adventure = I've lost my Place

Journey of Love = Knight of the Eagle Crest

Journey's End (Newte, H. C. W., 1891), v. 503

Journeys End in Lovers Meeting (Hobbes, J. O., 1894), v. 422

Journey to Bristol (Hippisley, J., ?1730), II. 337

Journey to London (Vanbrugh, Sir J., 1728), II. 15, 152, 190, 363

— = Provok'd Husband

Journey to Paris (1860), v. 701

Jo versus Jo (Green, F. W. and Allen, O., 1876), v. 390

Jovial Coopers (1759), III. 402

Jovial Crew (Concanen, M., Rooke, E. and Yonge, Sir W., 1731), II. 142, 237, 247, 376, 434, 446

Julie (1898), v. 701

Julie de Launay (1860), v. 701

Julie de Moin (Barnett, C. Z., 1849), IV. 261

Julie Ledru (1846), IV. 486

Juliet by Proxy (1899), v. 701

Juliette (1860), v. 701

Julio of Harancour (1819), IV. 486

Julio Romano (Bucke, C., 1830), IV. 272

Julius Caesar (D'Avenant, Sir W. and Dryden, J., ?1676), I. 173, 402

— (Kemble, J. P., 1812), IV. 335

— (Sheffield, J., 1722), II. 355

— (1818), IV. 90, 486

+ Julius Caesar, The Rum Un (Emson, F. E., 8°, ?1877)

Julius See-Saw (Pitt, H. M., 1869), v. 526

Julius Sterne = Old Jew

Jumbo Jim (1838), IV. 486

Jump a Little Wagtail (Johnstone, J. B., 1868), v. 438

Jumper = Sam Patch

Jumping at Conclusions (Homrigh, A. Von, 1892), v. 425

Jungle Death = Lion Conqueror

Junior Partner (Naden, A. T., 1890), v. 501

— (Russ, S., 1887), v. 553

— = Fate and Fortune

Juniper Jack (Hallett, Mrs, 1845), IV. 587 [see also 323, where the play is entered wrongly under Mrs A. M. Hall]

Junius Brutus (Lytton, Baron, 1885), v. 466

Juno (1896), v. 701

Juno, by Jove! = Caught Courting

Junto (1778), III. 333

Jupiter and Alcmena (Dibdin, C., 1781), III. 113, 255

— (1750), III. 333

Jupiter and Europa (Rich, J., 1723), II. 253, 376, 443

Jupiter and Io (1735), II. 376

Jupiter and Juno (Rede, W. L., 1835), IV. 607

Jupiter Chuff (1865), v. 701

Jupiter, Juno and Mercury (Fielding, H., 1743), II. 328

Jupiter L.L.D. (1894), v. 701

Jupiter's Decree and the Fall of Phaethon (Suter, W. E., 1853), v. 587

Jura (1868), v. 701

Juror (1718), II. 376

Juror Murderer = Cry of Blood

Just as Well (+ Manners, J. Hartley, Kensington Town Hall, 20/1/1899, *French*), v. 701

Just Broke Up = Holidays

Justice (Dening, Mrs C., 1893), v. 342

— (Doran, J., 1824), IV. 581

— (Faucit, J. S., 1820), IV. 311

— (1853), v. 701

— (1892), v. 701

— (1893), v. 701

— = Law, not Justice

Justice and Quackery (1822), IV. 486

Justice at Fault = Guilty or Not Guilty

Justice at Last (Roberts, G., 1894), v. 545

— (1884), v. 701

Justice Busy (Crowne, J., 1699), I. 400

Justice Caught in his Own Trap = Rape upon Rape

Justice Nell (Soutar, J. F. and Harwood, R., 1899), v. 575

Justice Triumphant (1747), II. 376

— = Elmerick

Justifiable Homicide (1884), v. 701

Justina (McCarthy, D. F., 1848), IV. 596

Justinio (1820), IV. 487

Just in Time (Anderson, C., 1897), v. 240

— (Burnand, F. C., 1884), v. 291

— (Hurlstone, T., 1792), III. 274

— (1862), v. 701

— = One too many

Justizia (Bennett, G. J., 1848), IV. 265

Just like a Woman (Dubourg, A. W., 1879), v. 351

Just like Roger (Webster, B., the Younger, 1872), v. 618

Just my Luck (Maltby, A., 1852), v. 473

— (Maltby, A., 1877), v. 473

Just One Word (1873), v. 701

Just Retribution (Bayne, R., 1893), v. 253

Juvenile Dramatist (1801), IV. 487

Juvenile Friendship (McLaren, A., 1822), IV. 352

— (1802), IV. 487

Juvenile Indiscretion = Emily

Juvenile Party (1852), v. 701

Kaffir War (Browne, G. W., 1879), v. 282

— (James, C. S., 1851), v. 433

Kaffir Warfare = Amakosa

Kafrali Karabush, Chief of the Eagle Tribe (1852), v. 701

Kais (Brandon, I., 1808), IV. 270

Kaleidoscope (1818), IV. 487

Kaloc (Dibdin, C. I. M., 1813), IV. 293

Kamtchatka (Kemble, C., 1811), IV. 87, 334

Kangaroo Girl (1897), v. 702

Kapschou (1809), IV. 630

Karackoo (1834), IV. 487

Karfa the Slave (Murray, W. H., 1834), IV. 601

Karin (Bell, Mrs H., 1892), v. 255

Karl (Mooney, H., 1884), v. 491

Karl Pietrehl = Dutchman's Dream

Kasil Irmark (1829), IV. 487

Katawompas (Summers, K., 1896), v. 587

Kate Carroway (1842), IV. 487

Kate Coventry = Day Dreams

Kate Kearney (Collier, W., 1836), IV. 281

— (1864), v. 702

+ Kate of Brockmoor; or, The Watchful Mother Duped (Stourbridge, 5/8/1811)

Kate of Colerane (Wilkins, J. H.), IV. 420

Kate of Coventry = Day Dreams

Kate of Dover (1858), v. 702

Kate of Killarney (1864), v. 702

Kate Peyton = Jealousy

Kate Peyton's Lovers (Reade, C., 1873), v. 536

— = Jealousy

Kate's Assignation (1863), v. 702

Kate Wynsley (1849), IV. 487

— (1856), v. 702

Kate Wynsley, the Cottage Girl = Woman's Love

Katharine and Petruchio = Taming of the Shrew

Katharine Kavanagh (Graves, C., 1891), v. 702, 794, 838

Kathleen (1848), IV. 487

— (1861), v. 702

— (1893), v. 702

Kathleen Mavourneen (Travers, W., 1862), v. 602

Kathleen O'Neill (Balfour, M., 1814), IV. 258

Katie's Birthday (Shield, H., 1873), v. 563

Katitzka (1848), IV. 487

Katrina (1893), IV. 702

Katti, the Family Help (Fawcett, C. S., 1887), v. 364

Katty from Connaught (Phillips, E., 1849), IV. 372

Katty O'Shiel (1841), IV. 487

Kedeth, the Hag of Poland (Dibdin, T. J., 1821), IV. 303

Keeley Worried by Buckstone (Lemon, M. and Webster, B. H., 1852), v. 455, 803

Keen Blades (Cross, A. F. and Elliston, J. F., 1893), v. 330

Keeper of the Castle Hill = Lord Darnley

Keeping a Place (Reynoldson, T. H., 1846), IV. 393

Keeping up Appearances (Ebsworth, J., 1816), IV. 308

— = Exit by Mistake

Keep of Castle Hill = King and the Freebooter

Keep to the Right (Reynolds, W., 1899), v. 541

— (Scudamore, F. A., 1884) = Oakdell Mystery, v. 559, 702

Keep your Door Locked (Matthison, A., 1866), v. 702, 806, 838

Keep your Eye on her (Williams, T. J., 1876), v. 626

Keep your own Counsel (Bellingham, H. and Best, W., 1895), v. 257

Keep your own Secret (1807), IV. 487

Keep your Places (Reece, R., 1886), v. 539

Keep your Temper (Wooler, J. P., 1862), v. 632

— (1829), IV. 487

Keereda and Nana Sahib (Young, H., 1857) = Veemah Kareeda, v. 702, 763, 825, 838

Kelaun and Guzzarah (Roberts, J. F., 1808?), IV. 608

Kelpie's Cave (1830), IV. 487

Kenilworth (Archer, C. J. and Aubert, A. E., 1893), v. 242

— (Blythe, J. S., 1899), v. 266

Kenilworth (Bunn, A., 1821), IV. 94, 276, 575
— (Deshayes, 1831), IV. 579
— (Dimond, W., 1821), IV. 94, 307
— (Goldberg, M., 1895), V. 383
— (Halliday, A. and Lawrence, F., 1858), V. 400
— (Oxberry, W., 1824), IV. 94, 487, 602, 630
— (Reece, R. and Farnie, H. B., 1885), V. 539
— (1822), IV. 94, 487
— (1824), IV. 94, 487
— (1825), IV. 94, 487
— (1832), IV. 94, 487
— (1833), IV. 94, 487
— (1847), IV. 94, 487
— (1858), V. 702
— (1859), V. 838
— (1862), V. 702
— (1866), V. 702
— (1870), V. 702
— (1871), V. 702
— = Elizabeth and Essex
Kenilworth Castle (Planché, J. R., 1821), IV. 94, 376
— (1821), IV. 94, 487
Kenneth Dunbar (Brabner, W. A., 1893), V. 272
Kenneth, King of Scots (McLaren, A., 1807), IV. 351
Kennyngton Crosse (Wilks, T. E., 1848), IV. 421
Kensington Gardens (Brough, R. B., 1851), V. 278
— (Cobb, J., 1781), III. 244
— (Leigh, J., 1719), II. 6, 53, 177, 341
Kentish Barons (North, F., 1790), III. 291
Kentish Election (1735), II. 376
Kentish Smuggler = (1) Coast Blockade; (2) Will Brockman
Kentuckian (Bernard, W. B., 1833), IV. 265
Kentucky in 1782 = Nick of the Woods
Kentucky Rifle (1832), IV. 487
Këolanthè (Fitzball, E., 1841), IV. 316
Kept In (Ambient, M., 1895), V. 240
Kept Mistress (1756) = Mock Orators, III. 333, 402
Kerim the Pearl Diver (Pitt, G. D., 1847, 1859), IV. 487, 630; V. 702, 838

Kerry = Night and Morning
Kerry's Pride and Munster's Glory = Daniel O'Connell
Kettle-drum of the Surrey (Parselle, J., 1858), V. 702, 809, 838
Kevin's Choice (Hazlewood, Miss, 1867), V. 415
Key of the Garden (Young, 1801), IV. 422
Key of the Kingdom (1845), IV. 487
Key of the Streets (1866), V. 702
Keys of the Castle (1894), V. 702
Key to King Solomon's Riches Limited (St Maur, H., 1896) V. 554
Key to the Lock (1788), III. 119, 333
Key under the Doormat (1859), V. 702
Khan's Daughter = Secret Pass
Khartoum (Muskerry, W. and Jourdain, J., 1885), V. 501
Kicks and Halfpence (Brough, W. and Franck, 1858), V. 702, 780, 793, 838
Kick-up in Kerry = Snap Apple Night
Kiddie (1898), V. 702
Kiddle-a-wink (Hill, B., 1864), V. 702, 838
— (Travers, W., 1864), V. 702, 838
Kidnapper (Graham, H., 1888), V. 386
Kidnappers (Osman, W. R. and Fenton, F., 1865), V. 702, 792, 808, 838
Ki-ki-ko-ko-oh-ki-key (Lauri, E. and McCormack, B., 1871), V. 802
Kildare (1890), V. 702
Killarney (Falconer, E., 1862), V. 360
— (George, C. H., 1872), V. 377
Killiecrumper (Watson, T. M., 1891), V. 616
Killigrew (1825), IV. 487
Killing No Murder (Hook, T. E., 1809), IV. 17, 327
Killing Time (Morton, J. M., 1863), V. 496
Kill or Cure (Dance, C., 1832), IV. 288
Kimberley Mail (Longden, C. H., 1892), V. 462
Kind Heart with a Rough Covering (Pitt, W. H., 1875), V. 527
Kind Imposter (1821), IV. 487
Kind Impostor = She Wou'd and She Wou'd Not
Kind Intentions (1831), IV. 487
Kind Keeper (Dryden, J., 1678), I. 78, 90, 222, 230, 349, 406

King Christmas (Planché, J. R., 1871), v. 528

King Coal and his Merry Men = Good Fairy of St Helen's

King Coffee (Elphinstone, J., 1874), v. 358

— (1873), v. 702

King Comet and Prince Quicksilver (Lee, N., Jr., 1858), v. 702, 802, 838

King Crib (1856), v. 702

King Diamond (Young, E., 1864), v. 825

Kingdom of the Birds = Wonders in the Sun

King Dreams (1894), v. 702

King Edgar and Alfreda (Ravenscroft, E., 1677), I. 54, 101, 255, 426

+King Edward II (Grindrod, C., 8°, 1883)

King Edward III (Bancroft, J., 1690), I. 168, 352, 357, 388

King Edward VI (Gregg, T. D., 1857), v. 394

King Egbert, King of Kent and Monarch of England (1719), II. 370

King Emerald (Lee, N., 1852), v. 452

+King Eric and the Outlaws (Chapman, J. F., 12°, 1843) [Translated from a play by B. S. Ingemann]

King Flame and Queen Pearly-drop (Lee, N., Jr., 1865), v. 452

King Foo (Adams, E., 1873), v. 235

King for a Day (Smith, V., 1893), v. 573, 817

King Galistan (1898), v. 703

King George's Shilling (Stirling, E., 1879), v. 584

King Glumpus (Barrow, J., 1837), IV. 570

King Hal and Herne the Hunter = Rose of Windsor

King Hal's Early Days (1837), IV. 488

King Hal the Bluff (Lee, N., Jr., 1862), v. 803

King Harold (Haines, J. T., 1839), IV. 323

+King Henry I (Grindrod, C., 8°, 1883)

+King Henry II (Grindrod, C., 8°, 1883)

King Henry III (Edison, J. S., 1840), IV. 582

+— (Grindrod, C., 8°, 1883)

King Henry III (Helps, Sir A., 1843), IV. 588

— = England Preserved

King Henry IV (Betterton, T., 1700), II. 297

— (Valpy, R., 1801), IV. 415

King Henry IV of France (Beckingham, C., 1719), II. 27-8, 90, 297

King Henry V (Hill, A., 1723), II. 30, 109, 336, 438

— (Kemble, J. P., 1789), III. 278, 389

King Henry VI = Roses

King Henry VII (Macklin, C., 1746), II. 342, 440

King Henry VIII (Kemble, J. P., 1804), IV. 335

King Henry VIII and the Cobbler (1812), IV. 488, 630

King Incog. (À Beckett, G. A., 1834), IV. 249, 567

King Indigo (Burnand, F. C., 1877), v. 290, 782

King in Dublin = Irish Loyalty

King in the Country (Waldron, F. G., 1789), III. 314

— = Loyal Salopian

King James I (Buchanan, R., 1868), v. 284

King James I and his Times = Fortunes of Nigel

+King James I of Scotland (Erskine, D.; 12°, 1827 (Kelso))

+— (Grindrod, C., 8°, 1883)

King James II (Whitehead, J. C., 1828), IV. 419

King James and the Piper (Duggan, J., 1847), IV. 308

King Jamie (1849), IV. 488

— (1879), v. 703

King Jamie's Frolic = Lancashire Witches

King John (Kemble, J. P., 1800), IV. 335

— (Valpy, R., 1800), III. 313; IV. 415

— (1749), II. 452

— (1823), IV. 488

King John with the Benefit of the Act (À Beckett, G. A., 1837), IV. 249, 567

King Jupiter and the Freaks of the Graces (1856), v. 703

King Klondyke (Addison, J., 1898), v. 236

King Pepin's Campaign (Shirley, W., 1745), II. 355; III. 306

King Philip and Queen Mary (1739), II. 381

King Pluto (Talfourd, F. 1858) = Pluto and Proserpine, v. 590, 703, 819, 838

King, Queen and Knave (Towers, E., 1862), v. 600

— (1829), IV. 488

King, Queen and Maid = Muleteer of Toledo

King Queer and his Daughters Three (Halford, J. and Collins, C. J., 1855), v. 703, 785, 795, 838

King René's Daughter (Chapman, J., 1845), IV. 576 ˉ

— (Martin, Sir T., 1849), IV. 318, 585, 597; v. 479

— (Phipps, E., 1849), IV. 372

— (Weatherley, F. E., 1872), v. 617

— (1849), IV. 483

King Richard II (Goodhall, J., 1772), III. 265

— (Tate, N., 1680), I. 10, 79, 173, 434

King Richard III (Cibber, C., 1700), I. 397; II. x, 102, 307, 433

— (1743), II. 382

— (1812), IV. 88, 140, 488

King Richard III according to Act of Parliament (Malone, 1854), v. 805

King Richard III Travestie (1816), IV. 488

— (1823), IV. 488

King Richard Cœur de Lion (Brough, W., 1853), v. 278

King Richard ye Third (Selby, C., 1844), IV. 91, 399

King's Advocate (1866), v. 703

— = Dunbar

King's Amusement = Court Fool

King Saul (?Boyle, R. or Trapp, J., 1703), I. 100, 394; II. 361, 445

King's Avenger = Bellamonde

King's Banner (Cresswell, Mrs G., 1872), v. 330

King's Barber (Webster, B. N., 1841), IV. 417

King's Beggar (1873), v. 703

King's Bench = Abroad and at Home

King's Butterfly (Bellew, 1864), v. 703, 838

— = Fan-Fan the Tulip

King's Captive (1861), v. 703

King's Casket = Voice from the Sea

King's Choice (Phillips, E., 1848), IV. 372

King's Coin (1823), IV. 488

King's Command (Summers, K., 1893), v. 587

— (Thompson, C. P., 1835), IV. 413

King's Cure (Turner, J. H., 1892), v. 605

King's Death Trap (Hazlewood, C. H., 1867), v. 413

King's Diversion (Slous, A. R., 1887), v. 816

King's Dragoons (Jones, J. W., 1880), v. 440

King's Edict (Fairclough, B., 1872), v. 790

King's Evidence = Skeleton Witness

King's Faith and the Fisher's Fealty (1837), IV. 488

King's Favourite (1873), v. 703

— = Jane Shore

King's Favourites (1844), IV. 488

King's Fireside (Morton, T., 1830), IV. 488, 630

King's First Lesson (1849), IV. 488

+ King's Fool (Hayley, W. T.: printed in The Romanticist, v. 1841)

— (Millingen, J. G., 1833), IV. 356, 599

King's Friend (?Sullivan, R., 1845), IV. 488, 630

King's Frolic = Three Wishes

King's Gardener (Selby, C. 1839), IV. 398

King's Guardsmen (1876), v. 703

King's Highway (1843), IV. 488

— = Rookwood

King Sillyninny who sold his Wife for Half-a-Guinea (Cheatham, F. G., 1862), v. 703, 783, 838

King's Mail (Townsend, W. T., 1866), v. 703, 821, 838

King's Milliner = Milliner to the King

King's Mistress (1824), IV. 488

King's Musketeers (1855), v. 703

— (1856), v. 703

Kings of Mercia and East Anglia and the Wild Woman of Mosswold Heath = Etheldrida Princess of Norwich

King Solomon (1865), v. 703

Klebir in Egypt (Dibdin, C. I. M., 1825), IV. 295

Klepht of the Evil Eye = Demetri the Outcast

Kleptomania (Melford, M., 1888), v. 484

Klondyke Nugget (Cody, S. J., 1898), v. 315

Klondyke Rush (Fielding, H., 1898), v. 366

Klondyke the Golden (1897), v. 704

Knapsack (1884), v. 704

Knave of Clubs = Card-Drawing

Knave of Diamonds (Henry, S. C., 1896), v. 418

Knave of Hearts = Baccarat

Knave of Hearts and the Companions of Crime = Rocambole

Knave of Spades (1895), v. 704

Knave or Not? (Holcroft, T., 1798), III. 99, 122, 137, 271, 387

Knavery in all Trades (1664), I. 442

Knaves and Fools (Reynolds, W., 1899), v. 541

Knaves of Knaves Acre = Sixteen String Jack

Knaves Overtrumped = Heads versus Pockets

Knife, Fork and Spoon (Lee, N., 1850), v. 452

Knight against Rook (Dove, O. and Lefebre, J. G., 1893), v. 349

Knight and his Page (Dibdin, C. I. M., 1826), IV. 296

Knight and the Naiads = Nymph of the Lurleyburg

Knight and the Sprite (À Beckett, G. A. and Lemon, G., 1844), IV. 250

Knight and the Water-Lily (1854), v. 704

Knight and the Wood Daemon = One O'Clock!

Knight Errant (Barrington, R., 1894), v. 251

Knight for a Day = Patrick the Foreigner

(K)night in Armour (Burnot, W. and Bruce, H. P., 1895), v. 293

+ Knight in a Wood (Smock Alley, Dublin, 5/5/1772)

Knight of Arva (Boucicault, D., 1848), IV. 270

Knight of Burgundy = Field of the Cloth of Gold

Knight of Malta (1783), III. 113, 333

Knight of Rhodes (Burges, Sir J. B., 1817), IV. 276

Knight of Snowdoun (Morton, T., 1811), IV. 92, 363

— (1823), IV. 92, 489

Knight of the Black Plume (1814), IV. 489

Knight of the Bloody Hand = Valvoni

Knight of the Boots (1817), IV. 489

Knight of the Couch Leopard = King Richard Cœur de Lion

Knight of the Doleful Countenance = Dox Quixote

Knight of the Dragon and the Queen of Beauty (Stirling, E., 1839), IV. 406

Knight of the Eagle Crest (1849), IV. 489

Knight of the Garter (Wilson, S., 1882), v. 628

Knight of the Hermitage = Bonifacio and Bridgetina

Knight of the Road (French, W. P., 1891), v. 373

— (Russell, E. H., 1892), v. 553

Knight of the Sepulchre (Almar, G., 1840), IV. 568

Knight of Wharley = Husband's Vengeance

Knights (Foote, S., 1749), III. 172 259, 403

Knight's Lodging (1898), v. 704

Knights of Castile = Poisoned Goblet

Knights of Knavery (1895), v. 704

Knights of Merry England = Ivanhoe

Knights of Rhodes (Dibdin, T. J., 1820), IV. 302

Knights of St Albans (Taylor, T. P., 1837), IV. 411

Knights of St George (1805), IV. 489

Knights of St John (Almar, G., 1833), IV. 252

Knights of Sicily = Ocean Fiend

Knights of the Cross (Beazley, S., Jr., 1826), IV. 95, 264

Knights of the Garter (1805), IV. 489

Knights of the Green Baize = Way of the Wicked

Knights of the Last = Daisy

Knights of the Lion (Dibdin, T. J., 1818), IV. 301

Knights of the Oven = Royal Baker

Knights of the Post (1797), III. 118, 333

— = System of Lavater

Knights of the Road (Travers, W., 1868), v. 603

Knights of the Round Table (Planché, J. R., 1854), v. 527

— = King Arthur

Knights of the Sun (1802), IV. 489

Knights of Villeroy (1817), IV. 489

Knights Templar = Ivanhoe

Knights Templars = Maid of Judah

Knight Templar = Ivanhoe

Knight, the Giant and the Castle of Manchester = Lancashire Witches

Knight, the Lady and the Lake = Mountain Dhu

Knobs and Noses (1820), IV. 489

Knotting 'em Brothers = Dark Doings in the Closet by the Knotting 'em Brothers, v. 328

Knowing ones taken in (1797), III. 333

Knowledge (Ogilvie, G. S., 1883), v. 704, 808, 838

Known to the Police (Douglass, J. T., 1897), v. 349

Know Whom you Marry = Keep your Temper

Know Your Own Mind (Murphy, A., 1777), III. 118, 164, 290

Ko and Zoa (Dibdin, C. I. M., 1802), IV. 290

Koeuba (Fitzball, E., 1824), IV. 489, 630

Koffee Kan Brothers (1897), v. 704

Kohal Cave (Rede, W. L., 1838), IV. 390

Koh-i-noor (Rice, C.), v. 813

Kolaf (Akhurst, W. M., 1876), v. 237

Kompact, the Kick and the Kombat = New Edition of the Corsican Brothers

Kongo Kolo (1811), IV. 489

Koranzo's Feast (Hayes, 1811), IV. 324

Korastikam Prince of Assassins (1821), IV. 489

Koromantyns (1808), IV. 489

Kosciusko (1840), IV. 489

Kouli Khan (Dibdin, T. J., 1818), IV. 301

Ku-Klux-Klan (Macdermott, G. H. and Major, H. A., 1873), v. 468

Kynge Lear and Hys Faythefull Foole (Marchant, F., 1860), v. 704, 805

La Ba Kan (Roe, J. E., 1869), v. 548

Labour Leader (1895), v. 704

Labour of Love (Broughton, F. W., 1875), v. 281

Labour of Love (Newte, H. C. W., 1897), v. 503

Labour Question (1861), v. 704

Labyrinth (Stratford, A., 1795), III. 333, 396, 402

— (1664), I. 442

— (1797), III. 333

Labyrinth Farm (1812), IV. 489

Labyrinth of Crete = Theseus and Ariadne

Labyrinth of Death = Wreck and Rescue

Labyrinth of Love = Trip to Marseilles

Labyrinths of Life = Haunted Houses

Lacemakers of Lisle = Lessons of Life

Ladder across the Street (1848), IV. 489

Ladder of Life (Rogers, C. and Boyne, W., 1898), v. 548

— (1884), v. 704

— = (1) Jack in the Water; (2) Pride shall have a Fall; (3) Ups and Downs

Ladder of Love (Bayly, T. H., 1837), IV. 263

Ladder of Wealth (Orchard, J. R., 1899), v. 507

Lad from the Country (Morton, J. M., 1863), v. 496

Ladies a la Mode = Damoiselles a la Mode

Ladies among themselves = Belles without Beaux

Ladies at Court (1832), IV. 630

Ladies at Home (Millingen, J. G., 1819), IV. 356, 599

Ladies' Battle (Reade, C., 1851), v. 535

— (Robertson, T. W., 1851), v. 546

— (1891), v. 704

Ladies Beware (1847), IV. 489

— (1858), v. 704

Ladies' Champion (Gwindon, H., 1868), v. 398

Ladies' Chance (1894), v. 704

Ladies' Club (Lemon, M., 1840), IV. 343, 595

Ladies Distress = Banditti

Ladies Doctor = Self-Enamoured

Ladies Friendship = Lying Lover

Ladies Frolick (Love, J., 1770), III. 113, 283, 391

Ladies Idol (Law, A., 1895), v. 450

+ Ladies in Parliament (Trevelyan, G. O., 8°, 1869 (apparently acted privately at Cambridge))

Ladies' Matrimonial Club (1840), IV. 489

Ladies of St Cyr (1869), v. 704

Ladies of the Convent (Suter, W. E., 1853), v. 587

Ladies of the Court = How's your Uncle

Ladies of the Palace (1735), II. 377

Ladies' Pet = Paul Clifford

Ladies Philosophy = Refusal

Ladies' Privilege = Leap Year

Ladies Ridiculed = Two Pence

Ladies Seminary (Wilks, T. E., 1841), IV. 421

Ladies' Stratagem (Hitchcock, R., 1775), III. 269

Ladies' Subscription (Cleland, J., 1755), III. 243

Ladies' Temperance Club (1869), v. 704

Ladies Visiting-Day (Burnaby, W., 1701), II. 50, 142, 153, 162, 301

Ladle (Dibdin, C., 1773), III. 254

Lad of the Hills = Wicklow Gold Mines

Lad of the Village (Burton, E. G., 1850), v. 294

Ladrone's Daughter = Paula Lazaro

Lads of the Hills = Wicklow Gold Mines

Lads of the Village = Jemmy for Ever

Lady and Gentleman in a peculiarly perplexing Predicament (Selby, C., 1841), IV. 398

Lady and the Convict (1841), IV. 489

Lady and the Devil (Dimond, W., 1820), IV. 307

Lady and the Lawyer = Irish Poleander

Lady and the Lawyers (De Vere, F., 1857), v. 343

Lady and the Magistrate (Sharp, T., 1897), v. 561

Lady Anne's Well (Travers, W., 1868), v. 603

Lady at Dover (1848), IV. 489

Lady Audley's Secret (Hazlewood, C. H., 1863), v. 415, 797

— (Roberts, G., 1863), v. 544

— (Suter, W. E., 1863), v. 588

Lady Aurora (Woodward, F. W. and Woodward, J. W., 1894), v. 631

Lady Barbara's Birthday (Barker, 1872), v. 249

Lady Barter (Coghlan, C. F., 1891), v. 316

Lady Belle Belle (Byron, H. J., 1863), v. 296, 782

Lady Bird (Boucicault, D., 1862), v. 268

Lady-Bird Bower (Webb, C.), IV. 616

Lady Bookie (Hallward, C., 1898), v. 401

Lady Bountiful (Pinero, Sir A. W., 1891), v. 179, 187, 525

Lady Browne's Diary (Bell, M., 1892), v. 256

Lady Burglar (Malyon, E. J. and James, C., 1897) = In a Fit of Abstraction, v. 473, 695, 805

Lady by Birth (Smythies, W. G., 1893), v. 573

Lady Cameleon = Traviata

Lady Caprice (Jones, H. A., 1880), v. 439

Lady Clancarty (Taylor, T., 1874), v. 98, 594

Lady Clara Vere de Vere (1888), v. 704

Lady Clare (Buchanan, R., 1883), v. 284

Lady Clerk (Hurst, C., 1899), v. 431

Lady Contemplation (Cavendish, M., 1662), I. 396

Lady Cyclist (Miller, St A., 1897), v. 488

Lady Daisy (Dent, B., 1896), v. 342

Lady D'Arcy (Hilton, B. H., 1870), v. 422

Lady Deadlock's Secret (Simpson, J. P., 1874), v. 568

Lady Deane (Wilmot, A. A., 1887), v. 628

Lady Delmar (1891), v. 704

Lady Detective = Bilbery of Tilbury

Lady Di's Visit (Thursby, C., 1897), v. 600

Lady Dorothy's Scheme (Walton, T., 1895), v. 613

Ladye Bird Bower (Somerset, C. A., 1858), v. 574

Ladye-Bird, fly away home (Neale, F., 1853), v. 501

Lady Elizabeth = 'Twixt Axe and Crown

Ladye of Lambethe (Wilks, T. E., 1839), IV. 421

Lady Flora (Coghlan, C. F., 1875), v. 316

Lady Fortune (Thomas, C., 1887), v. 596

Lady from the Sea (Aveling, E. M., 1891), v. 187, 246

Lady Gladys (Buchanan, R., 1894), v. 285

Lady Godiva (Akhurst, W. M., 1871), v. 236

— (Grattan, H. P., 1885), v. 389

— (Muskerry, W., 1889), v. 501

— (Robson, F., 1873), v. 547

— (1851), v. 704

— (1877), v. 704

— (1894), v. 704

Lady Godiva and Peeping Tom (Ridgway, J., 1846), IV. 394

— (Spry, H., 1875), v. 576

Lady Godiva and Peeping Tom of Coventry (Lee, N., 1848), IV. 343

— (1846, 1848), IV. 489

Lady Godiva, the Bare-back Rider (1896), v. 704

Lady Guide (1891), v. 704

Lady Hatton (Pitt, G. D., 1850), v. 704, 810, 838

— (1883), v. 704

Lady Hatton and the Mystery of the Bleeding Heart = Suicide's Tree

Lady Henrietta (St George and Mazilier, 1844), IV. 489, 630

Lady in Black (Somerset, C. A., 1848), IV. 405

— (Young, H., 1860), v. 825

— (1859), v. 704

Lady in Difficulties (Planché, J. R., 1849), IV. 383

— (1835), IV. 489

Lady in Fashion = Woman's Wit

Lady in her Sleep (Dibdin, T. J., 1828), IV. 305

Lady in Search of an Heiress (Leigh, A.), v. 453

Lady Interviewer (Swears, H., 1896), v. 589

Lady Isabel (Kempe, A., 1873), v. 442

Lady Jane Gray (Rowe, N., 1715), II. 18, 58, 101–2, 353, 443; III. 85

Lady Jane Grey (Hazlewood, C. H., 1874), v. 415

— (Neil, R., 1871), v. 501

— (Poel, W., 1885), v. 529, 811

— (1875), v. 704

Lady Jemima (Grant, N., 1888), v. 388

Lady Journalist (Zangwill, I., 1893), v. 637

Lady Judge (1894), v. 704

Lady Killer (Chevalier, A. and Mackintosh, W., 1885), v. 309

— (Fawcett, C. S., 1893), v. 364

— (Jerrold, D., 1831), IV. 489, 630

— = Gay Lothario

Lady Lady's Maid = Military Manœuvre

Lady Laura's Arcadia (Broughton, F. W., 1897), v. 282

Lady Lawyer (Lynch, G. D., 1897), v. 465

Lady Legislators = Mrs Speaker

Lady Lillian (Towers, E., 1880), v. 601

— (1885), v. 704

Lady Lovington (Villars, G., 1888), v. 608

Lady Macbeth (Galt, J., 1812), IV. 585

Lady Mary Wortley Montague (1839), IV. 489

"Lady May" = Dream of an Irish Emigrant

Lady of Bayonne (Macgowan, W. S., 1897), v. 469

Lady of Belleisle (Gully, J. M., 1839), IV. 321

Lady of Buccleuch = Border Feuds

Lady of Kildare (1872), v. 704

Lady of Lions (Dowling, M. G., 1838), IV. 489, 630

Lady of Longford (Harris, Sir A. H. G. and Weatherley, F. E., 1894), v. 406

Lady of Lyons (Byron, H. S., 1858), IV. 175; v. 295

— (Lytton, Lord, 1838), IV. 63, 173–5, 349, 596

— (Younge, W., 1879), v. 637

Lady of Lyons Married and Claude Unsettled (Reece, R., 1884), IV. 175; v. 539

Lady of Lyons married and settled (Merivale, H. C., 1878), IV. 175; v. 487

Lady of Munster (1860), v. 704

— = Perfection

Lady of Nuremberg = Broken Chain

Lady of Ostend (Burnand, F. C., 1899), v. 292

Lady of Quality (Burnett, Mrs F. H. and Townsend, S., 1896), v. 292

Lady of St Tropez (1845), IV. 489

— (1846), IV. 489

— (1857), v. 704

— = Privateer

Lalla Rookh (O'Sullivan, M., 1818), IV.
366

— (Rayner, B. F., 1836), IV. 389

Lalli Tollendal (1839), IV. 490

Lambeth in Olden Times = Edith of the
Marsh

Lambeth in the Olden Time = Old
House on the Thames

Lambton Worm (Roxby, S., 1848), IV.
396

— (1877), V. 705

Lame Common-wealth (Kirkman, F.,
1662), I. 417

Lamed for Life (Marston, J. W., 1871),
V. 479

Lame Excuse (Hay, F., 1869), V. 411

Lame Lover (Foote, S., 1770), III. 174,
260

Lamp and the Scamp = Aladdin

Lamplighter (Davis, S., 1855), V. 787

— (Dickens, C., 1879), IV. 209–10, 305

— (1854), V. 705

Lancashire Lass (Byron, H. J., 1867), V.
114, 297

Lancashire Life (Towers, E., 1875), V.
601

Lancashire Sailor (Thomas, B., 1891), V.
596

Lancashire Weaver Lad (Brierley, B.,
1877), V. 275

Lancashire Witches (Dibdin, C., 1783),
III. 256

— (Fitzball, E., 1848), IV. 317

— (Fitzball, E., 1858), V. 368

— (Gunton, R. T., 1879), V. 397, 795

— (Pitt, G. D., 1847), IV. 375

— (Shadwell, T., 1681), I. 8, 10, 79, 90,
132, 207, 337, 431

— (1810), IV. 490

Lancelot the Lovely (Henry, R., 1889),
V. 418

Lancer = Long Cloth

Lancers (Payne, J. H., 1827), IV. 369

— (Vernon, L., 1853), V. 107, 608

Land Ahead (Fenn, G. M., 1878), V.
365

Land and Love (Dubourg, A. W.,
1884), V. 351

Land and Sea (Blake, T. G.), IV. 573

Land and the People (Moss, A. B. and
Patmore, W. J., 1893), V. 497

Land and Wave = Life of the Brave

Landed from China = My Wife's Lodgings

Landgartha (Barnes, J., 1683), I. 389

Landgrave's Leap (1819), IV. 490

Landlady (Aveling, E. B., 1889), V. 246

— (Kirkman, F., 1662), I. 418

— (1888), V. 705

— = Pothooks

Landlord (Hall, W. J. C., 1886), V. 400

Landlord and Tenant (1847), IV. 490

Landlord Bit = Merry Sailors

Landlord in Jeopardy! = Jealous on All
Sides

Landlord outwitted = Who pays the
Rent?

Landlord's Dilemma (1895), V. 705

Land of Diamonds (Coen, L., 1884), V.
316

Land of Enchantment (1846), IV. 490

Land of Gold (Lander, G., 1888), V. 448

Land of Heart's Desire (Yeats, W. B.,
1894), V. 635

Land of Khem = Snefern the Second

Land of Luna = Celestia

Land of Nod (Chevalier, A., 1897), V.
309

Land of Pie (Bunner, H. C., 1899), V.
287

Land of Promise = Christian's Crime

Land of Simplicity (Dibdin, C.), IV. 290

Land of the Living (Harvey, F., 1889),
V. 408

Land Rats and Water Rats (Phillips,
W., 1868), V. 523

Land Sharks and Sea Gulls (Edwards,
1841), IV. 309

Land Storm (1819), IV. 490

Land we live in (Holt, F. L., 1804), IV.
30, 327

— (1791), III. 333

— = Hall of Augusta

Langamo's Cave (1844), IV. 490

Language of Flowers (Wooler, J. P.,
1852), V. 705, 824

— = Bouquet

Lansdown Castle (Cunningham, A. C.,
1893), V. 331

Lantern Light (D'Arcy, G. and Ross,
C. H., 1873), V. 336

Laoeudaimonos (1789), III. 333

Laon-Seng-Urh (Davis, J. F., 1817), VI.
579

La-Peyrouse (Plumptre, A., 1799), III. 65, 298, 393

— (Thompson, B., 1799), III. 65, 311, 397

— (1781), III. 333

Lapidary of Leyden (1840), IV. 490

+Laplander (Smock Alley, Dublin, 21/3/1772)

Laplanders (1788), III. 333

Lapland Fairy (1812), IV. 490

Lapland Witch (Lancaster, E. R.), IV. 593

Lapse of 20 Years = Gambler's Fate

Lara (Bass, C., 1827), IV. 262

— (Oxenford, J., 1865), V. 705, 809, 838

Larboard Fin (1837), IV. 490

Large as Life (1890), V. 705

Larkin's Love Letters (Williams, T. J., 1866), V. 625

Lark in the Temple (1866), V. 705

Larks (Jones, J. W., 1886), V. 441

Larks in a Cage (1863), V. 705

Larks in London = Larks

Larks of Logic, Tom and Jerry = Life in London

Larks with a Libretto = Trovatore

Lashed to the Helm (Hazlewood, C. H., 1864), V. 705, 838

La! Somnambula! (Byron, H. J., 1865), V. 297

Lasses of Leixlip = Irish Courtship

Lass of Gowrie (1839), IV. 490

— (1853), V. 705

— = Rose Graham

Lass of Richmond Hill (Trevor, H., 1893), V. 603

Lass of the Lakes = Helvetic Liberty

Lass o' Moorside = Puck

Lass that Loved a Carpenter (1879), V. 705

Lass that loved a Sailor (Clarance, L., 1883), V. 310

— (Doone, N., 1893), V. 347

— = H.M.S. Pinafore

Lass that Loves a Sailor = Ruth

Last Act (Leigh, E. M., 1899), V. 453

— (1814), IV. 490, 635

Last Appeal (1859), V. 705

— = Alice May

Last Call (Charles, H. and Greigg, H. J. S., 1895), V. 308

Last Cause (1868), V. 705

Last Century = Great Metropolis

Last Chance (Sims, G. R., 1885), V. 185, 569

Last Chapter (Broadhurst, G. H., 1899), V. 276

Last Chime of Midnight (France, E. S.), V. 792

Last Chord (1879), V. 705

Last Command = My Comrade

Last Crime = Golden Farmer

Last Cruise of the Vampire = Coast-guard

Last Crusade (Vyse, B., 1850), V. 609

Last Day (Godwin, G., Jr., 1840), IV. 490, 585, 630

Last Days of Napoleon Buonaparte (1828), IV. 490

Last Days of Nelson = Trafalgar

Last Days of Pompeii (Buckstone, J. B., 1834), IV. 97, 274

— (Fitzball, E., 1835), IV. 97, 314

— (Oxenford, J., 1872), V. 510

Last Deed of Garboni = Maid of Velitri

Last Dread Penalty (1897), V. 705

Last Edition of Ivanhoe (Brough, R. B. and Brough, W., 1850), V. 277

Last Express (Abel, W. H., 1871), V. 234

Last Glass (1851), V. 705

Last Guerilla Chief (1826), IV. 490

Last Hope (Abel, W. H., 1873), V. 235

— (Oxenford, J., 1859), V. 509

Last Hour (1811), IV. 630

— = (1) Love's Rescue; (2) Midnight Bell

Lasting Love (Newbound, E., 1878), V. 502

Last Key (1834), IV. 490

Last Kiss (Stirling, E., 1846), IV. 408

Last Leaf of the Tree = Light of Other Days

Last Life (Palmer, T. A., 1874), V. 512

Last Lily (Scott, C. W., 1886), V. 558

Last Link in the Chain = (1) Babbi's Son; (2) Wager

Last Link of Love (Hazlewood, C. H., 1867), V. 413

— (1845), IV. 490

Last Link of the Chain = (1) Whitsun Eve; (2) Whitsuntide

Last Mail (1836), IV. 490

Last Man (Pitt, G. D., 1833), IV. 373, 604

Last Man (1845), IV. 490
— = Miser of Eltham Green
Last Man on Earth (Stephens, V., 1897), v. 581
Last Moment (Travers, W., 1867), v. 602
— (1875), v. 705
Last Nail (Pitt, G. D., 1833), IV. 372, 604
Last New Year's Gift = Artificial Flower Maker
Last Night and the Last Morning (1860), v. 705
Last of his Race = (1) Gamester's Son; (2) King Maker
Last of Lord Nelson's Agamemnon = Ben Brace
Last of the Barons (Du Terreaux, L. H., 1872), v. 352
— (1845), IV. 490
— = (1) Hit or Miss; (2) Battle of Barnet
Last of the Bravoes (Oxenford, J., 1845), IV. 367
Last of the Burnings = Two Fishermen of Lynn
Last of the Caesars = Constantine and Valeria
Last of the Cavaliers = Bonnie Dundee
Last of the Cobbler = Rienzi Reinstated
Last of the Decemviri = Death of Virginia
Last of the Doges = Dandolo
Last of the Doomed Race = Kiddle-a-wink
Last of the Fairies (Fitzball, E., 1852), v. 368
Last of the Family (Cumberland, R., 1797), III. 252
Last of the Greeks (Howard, F., 1828), IV. 329
Last of the Latouches (Ellis, Mrs R. and Rennell, C. R., 1877), v. 357
Last of the Legends (À Beckett, G. A., 1873), v. 147–8, 234
Last of the Lotteries (1847), IV. 630
Last of the Mohicans = Uncas
Last of the Moors of Granada = Mendicant's Revenge
Last of the Murdakes (1830), IV. 490
Last of the Paladins (Reece, R., 1868), v. 537

Last of the Pigtails (Selby, C., 1858), v. 560
Last of the Race (Sanger, G., 1871), v. 555
Last of the Romans (1830), IV. 490
Last of the Stuarts = Prince Charlie
Last of the Vendeans = Carline
Last of the Wampanoags = Metamora
Last of the Welsh Bards (1873), v. 705
Last on the Programme (Ganthony, N., 1892), v. 375
Last Overture (1892), v. 705
Last Prince of Abyssinia and the True British Seaman = Blind Child of Africa
Last Resource (1886), v. 705
Last Sacrifice (1874), v. 705
Last Shift (McLaren, A., 1814), IV. 351
Last Shilling (Faucit, J. S., 1844) = Lost Shilling, IV. 311, 495, 631
— = Spendthrift
Last Slave (1867), v. 705
Last Straw (Dickinson, C. H., 1888), v. 344
— (1892), v. 705
Last Stroke of Midnight (Guiver, J., 1879), v. 397
Last Temptation (Sykes, P. H. T., 1897), v. 589
Last Train (Forshaw, F., 1898), v. 371
Last Voyage of Captain Cook = Floating Kingdom
Last Whistle (Addison, H. R., 1835), IV. 490, 630
Last Witch = Jackeydora
Last Witness (1840), IV. 630
Last Word (Daly, A., 1890), v. 333
Last Words = Conrad
Latch Key (Stirling, E., 1855), v. 705, 818, 838
Late Lamented (Horner, F., 1891), v. 427
— (Taylor, T., 1859), v. 593
Late Love (Outram, L. S., 1886), v. 509
Late Mr Castello (Grundy, S., 1895), v. 206, 397
Late Mr M. = Procrastination
Late Ralph Johnson (Edwards, H. S., 1872), v. 355
Late Revolution (1690), I. 442
Late Sir Benjamin (Young, Sir C. L., 1882), v. 636

Legacy Love (Cuthbert, E., 1872), v.
331
Legacy of Honour (Stirling, E., 1853),
v. 584
Legacy of Wrong = Better Angel
Legal Friend (1845), IV. 491
Legal Impediment (Oxenford, J., 1861),
v. 510, 809
Legal Wreck (Gillette, W., 1888), v.
381
Legatees (Ebsworth, J.), IV. 309
Leg Bail (1899), v. 706
Legend of a Lawyer = Tufelhausen
Legend of a Soul (1897), v. 706
Legend of Bleeding Heart Yard = Lady
Hatton
Legend of Castille = Catalina
Legend of Florence (Hunt, L., 1840),
IV. 180-1, 329
Legend of Glendalough = King
O'Toole's Goose
Legend of Lisbon = Maiden's Fame
Legend of Llandarff = Whitefriars
Legend of Mab's Cross (1883), v. 706
Legend of Montrose = Children of the
Mist
Legend of Mount Blanc = Lone Hut
Legend of Notre Dame (Smith, J. C.,
1871), v. 572
Legend of Ravenstone = Red Man
Legend of Sleepy Hollow = Rip Van
Winkle
Legend of Spring (1872), v. 706
Legend of the Black Rock = Carynthia
Legend of the Devil's Dyke (Bouci-
cault, D., 1838), IV. 188, 269
Legend of the Fairy Dell = Four-leaved
Shamrock
Legend of the Headless Man (Webster,
B. J., 1857), v. 706, 823, 838
Legend of the Kaatskill Mountains =
Rip van Winkle
Legend of the Lake = Spirits of the
Night
Legend of the Old Lime Tree = Rook-
wood!
Legend of the Thames = Kirkauld's
Point
Legend of Vandale (Drinkwater, A. E.,
1890), v. 351
Legend of Walworth = Richard Planta-
genet

Legend of Wehrendorf (Newbound, E.,
1878), v. 502
Legerdemain (Oxenford, J., 1842), IV.
367, 491, 630
Leghorn Bonnet (Oxenford, J., 1852),
v. 509
— (1852), v. 706
Legion of Honour (Planché, J. R.,
1831), IV. 379
Leida (Mattos, A. T. de, 1893), v. 481
Leila, the Maid of the Alhambra (1838),
IV. 491
Leilia (Bosworth, J., 1838), IV. 573
Leisure to Laugh = Big O and Sir Glory
Lekinda, the Sleepless Woman (1833),
IV. 491
Lelamine (Krusard, E., 1889), v. 446
Lela's Love Letters (Soden, J. E. and
Ganthony, A., 1888), v. 573
Lelia's Lamp (1833), IV. 491
Lelia the Betrothed (Coleman, H.,
1852), v. 316
Lelio (D'Arcy, G., 1885), v. 336
— (1875), v. 706
Lena (Van de Velde, Mme, 1889), v. 606
Lena Despard (1887), v. 706
Lending a Hand (À Beckett, G. A.,
1866), v. 233
— = More Free than Welcome
Lending your Name (1833), IV. 491
Lend me Five Shillings (Morton, J. M.,
1846), IV. 362
Lenza the Child of the Wanderer =
Halfpenny Club
Leo (Knowles, J. S., 1810), IV. 170, 338
Leocadea (1825), IV. 491, 630
Leoline (1846), IV. 492, 630
— (1848), IV. 491, 630
Leona = Love and Stratagem
Leonard (Dodson, R., 1876), v. 346
Leonard's Love = Minnie
Leon de Val (1850), v. 706
Leonie, the Sutler Girl (Rhys, H.,
1863), v. 706, 813
Leon of Arragon (1857), v. 706
Leon of Marana = Fallen Spirit
Leon of the Iron Mask (Bernard,
W. B., 1855), v. 259
Leonora (Dibdin, T. J., 1821), IV. 303
Leonore (Ashworth, J. H. E., 1894), v.
245
— (Newte, H. C. W., 1892), v. 503

Life and Death of Sweeny Tod = String of Pearls

Life and Death of Tom Moody = Royal Foxhunt

Life and Death of Tom Thumb = Tom Thumb

Life and Death of Uncle Tom = Christian Slave

Life and Honour = Blanche Farreau

Life and Love in These Times = Under the Gaslight

Life and Reign of George III = George III, IV. 359, 492, 631

Life and Struggles of a Working Man (1853), V. 706

Life as it is (Blake, T. G., 1839), IV. 268, 573

— (Blake, T. G., 1852), V. 262

Life as we find it in 1850 = Tricks and Trials

Life at the East End of London (Lee, N., Jr., 1864), V. 803

Life below the Earth = Coal Mine

Life Boat (Blake, T. G., 1850), V. 707, 779, 838

— (1887), V. 707

Life Buoy (Hoskins, F. R., 1869), V. 427

Life Chase (Courtney, J., 1852) = Marriage Day, V. 326, 716, 786, 840

— (Oxenford, J. and Wigan, H., 1869), V. 510

Life, Death, and Renovation of Tom Thumb (1785), III. 334

Life, Death and Restoration of the High Mettled Racer (Dibdin, T. J., 1815) = High Mettled Racer, IV. 492, 631

Life down South (Cantwell, R. F., 1874), V. 302

Life Epitomised = Lyric Novelist

Life for a Life (Baring, S. and Beaumont, W., 1899), V. 249

— (Hazlewood, C. H., 1860), V. 412

— (Travers, W., 1860) = Reprieve, V. 707, 740, 821, 838, 845

Life for Life (Marston, J. W., 1869), V. 479

— = (1) Comrades and Friends; (2) Humanity

Life for Love = Bolivar

Life for the Czar (1888), V. 707

Lifeguardsman (1849) = Little Guardsman, IV. 492, 631

Life in All Shapes (1857), V. 707

Life in America (1836), IV. 492

Life in a Mirror = Dash of the Day

Life in an Hotel (1823), IV. 492

Life in Australia, from Our Own Correspondent (Phillips, Mrs A., 1853), V. 522

Life in Death = Innocent

Life in Dublin (Egan, P., 1839), IV. 492, 582, 631

Life in Edinburgh = Writer's Clerk

Life in England and California = Land of Gold

Life in Galway = O'Dowd

Life in Glasgow = Speculation

Life in Ireland = Florence Macarthy

Life in Lambeth (Osman, W. R., 1864), V. 707, 808, 838

Life in Little = Yorkshire School

Life in London (Dibdin, C. I. M., 1821), IV. 96, 295

— (1821), IV. 492

— = (1) Diamond King; (2) Hunger; (3) Key of the Streets; (4) Tom and Jerry; (5) Tom, Jerry and Logic

Life in London as it was and is = What will become of him?

Life in Louisiana = Octoroon

Life in New Orleans = Slave Hunter and the Half Caste

Life in New York (1848), IV. 492

— = Fashion

Life in Olympus (Mowbray, T., 1860), V. 807

Life in Oxford = Peter Priggins

Life in Paris (1822), IV. 492

Life in Russia = Living Death

Life in Santa Lucia = Elise

Life in 1796 = Incorrigibles

Life in the Black Country = Old Grimey

Life in the Clouds (Brougham, J., 1840), IV. 272

Life in the Coal Pits (Levey, J. C., 1867), V. 458

Life in the Cotton Fields = Down South

Life in the Diggings = In for a Dig

Life in the Far Wild West = Mexican Bill

Life in the Golden Gulch = Danites

Life in the Merry Greenwood = Gipsey Norris

Life in the Mine = Pit's Mouth

Life in the Rail = Hooker and Snooker

Life in the Ranks = Whipping Post

Life in the Streets = Islington

Life in the Sunny South (1857), v. 707

Life in the Temple = Chamber Practice

Life in the Trenches (1855), v. 707

Life in the Wild West = Buffalo Bill

Life, its Morn and Sunset (Hazlewood, C. H., 1872), v. 414

Life Lost = Lost Life

Life, Love and Fortune = London Vice and London Virtue

Life of a Beggar (Travers, W., 1857), v. 707, 821, 838

Life of a Betting Boy (1852), v. 707

Life of a Cabman = George Pernet

Life of a Gamester = Thirty Years

Life of a Labourer (Atkyns, S., 1848), IV. 257

Life of a Member of Parliament = Blight of Ambition

Life of a Mill Girl (1884), v. 707

Life of a Miner (Faucquez, A., 1862), v. 707, 839

Life of an Actor (Peake, R. B., 1824), IV. 370

Life of an Actress (Boucicault, D., 1855), v. 268

— (Suter, W. E., 1853) = Violette la Grande, v. 587, 764, 819, 849

Life of an Ape = Brazilian Jack

Life of an Emigrant = (1) Gold Diggings of Australia; (2) New World

Life of a Pickpocket = George Barrington

Life of a Policeman = Willie the Wanderer

Life of a Pottery Lass (Walters, F., 1869), v. 612

Life of a Sailor = Nelson

Life of a Shingler (Hall, C. I., 1870), v. 399

Life of a Ship from her Cradle to her Grave (Townsend, W. T., 1847), IV. 414

Life of a Slaver = Under the Line

Life of a Soldier (Pitt, G. D., 1848), IV. 604

— (1861), v. 707

Life of a Soldier = (1) Horrors of War; (2) Standard of England

Life of a Street Boy = London

Life of a Thames Waterman = Jacob Faithful

Life of a Tradesman's Daughter = Two Homes

Life of a Vagrant = Moneylender

Life of a Weaver (Hazlewood, C. H., 1859), v. 412

Life of a Woman (Haines, J. T., 1840), IV. 323, 587

Life of Guilt (1851), v. 707

Life of James Dawson (1841), IV. 631

Life of King Ahasuerus (1719), II. 376

Life of King Henry VIII = Queen Catherine and Cardinal Wolsey

Life of Man and Horse = Favourite of the Derby

Life of Ned Cantor (1855), v. 707

Life of Pleasure (Harris, Sir A. H. G. and Pettitt, H., 1893), v. 406

Life of Spritsail Jack = Blue Anchor

Life of the Brave (1844), IV. 492

Life of William Shakespeare = Shakespeare's Early Days

Life on the Board = Gentleman Jack

Life on the Mississippi = Conrad and Lizette

Life on the Ocean (1868), v. 707

Life on the Ocean and the Land = Boy Pirate

Life on the Ocean Wave (1849), IV. 492

Life on the Road = Captain Macheath

Life on the Turf = Chase

Life on the Western Border = Si Slocum

Life or Death (Harvey, F., 1886), v. 408

Life Policy (Davis, H., 1894), v. 339

Life Preserver (1876), v. 707

Life Race (Evelyn, J., 1872), v. 359

Life Raft (Townsend, W. T.), v. 707, 821, 839

— (1845), IV. 492

Life's a Dream = Such Stuff as Dreams are made of

Life's a Jest = Ridicule

Life's a Lottery (Rede, W. L., 1842), IV. 390

Life's Battle (Comer, G., 1891), v. 319

— (Faucit, H. S., 1878), v. 363

Life's Battle for Gold = Gratitude

Light o' Day (McCullough, B., 1888), v. 468

Light of Asia (Beatty-Kingston, W., 1892), v. 254

Light of his Eyes (Bellingham, H. and Best, W., 1895), v. 257

Light of Love (Young, Mrs H., 1867), v. 636

— =(1) Angel's Visit; (2) Blanche

Light of Other Days (Meller, R., 1889), v. 485

— (Taylor, T. P., 1837), IV. 411

Light of Pengarth (Cassilis, I. L., 1891), v. 306

Light of the Isles (Allen, O., 1876), v. 239

Lights and Shades of Virtue and Vice = Mechanic

Lights and Shadows = Road of Life

Lights and Shadows in a Young Girl's Path = Nearly Lost

Lights and Shadows of Life = Dissolving Views

Lights and Shadows of London Life = Guinea Gold

Lights and Shadows of Pit Life = Black Diamonds

Lights and Shadows of the World we live in = Maximums and Speciments of William Muggins

Lights of Home (Buchanan, R. and Sims, G. R., 1892), v. 285

Lights of Liberty = Power of the Press

Lights of the Age (1899), v. 707

Lights o' London (Sims, G. R., 1881), v. 568

Light that failed (Thorpe, C., 1891), v. 599

Light Troop of St James's (1847), IV. 492

Like and Unlike (Langford, and Sorrell, W. J., 1856), v. 448

Like Father, like Son (Behn, A., 1682), I. 391

— (Raymond, R. J. or Kenney, J., 1840), IV. 389, 592, 606

— (1801), IV. 492

— (1876), v. 707

Like Master, Like Man (Ryder, T., 1766), III. 115, 303

— =(1) Jacintha; (2) Lover's Quarrels; (3) Wrangling Lovers

Likeness (1849), IV. 492

Like to Like (1701), II. 377

Lilia (1886), v. 707

Lilian Gervais (Barnett, M., 1853), v. 250

Lilian Locke, the Widow of the Mill = Last Glass

Lilian, the Show Girl (Soane, G., 1836), IV. 404

Lilies (Paulton, H., 1884), v. 517

+ Lilies that Fester (Poel, W.: St George's Hall, 9/7/1897; N.Y. 1906. Adapted from *Arden of Feversham*)

Liline and Valentin (Layton, G. M., 1875), v. 451, 802

Lilla (Planché, J. R., 1825), IV. 378

Lilla the Lost One (Hazlewood, C. H.), v. 797

Lillian Trafford (Bronson, W. S., 1864), v. 707, 780, 839

Lilliput (Fisher, F. G., 1817), IV. 492, 583, 631

— (Garrick, D., 1756), III. 262

Lilliputian Camp (1767), III. 334

Lilliputian Sports (1802), IV. 492

Lilliput Island (1810), IV. 492

Lilly Dawson (Atkyns, S., 1847), IV. 257

— (Stirling, E., 1847), IV. 408

Lilly Laburnem (Pitt, G. D., 1848), IV. 375

Lilly of the Valley (1844), IV. 493

Lily (Darbey, E., 1878), v. 336

— (Delille, H. A., 1888), v. 342

Lily and the Rose = Protector at Houghall

Lily Dale (Delafield, J. H., 1869), v. 341

Lily Lyle = Workman

Lily of Devon = Amy the Skipper's Daughter

Lily of Killarney (Oxenford, J. and Boucicault, D., 1862), v. 510, 809

Lily of Léoville (Rémo, F. and Murray, A., 1886), v. 541

Lily of Limerick = Dora O'Donovan

Lily of Lismore = Row of Ballynavogue

Lily of Pontsarn (1893), v. 707

Lily of St Clarens = Laurette

Lily of St Leonard's = (1) Effie Deans; (2) Heart of Midlothian; (3) Jeannie Deans

Lily of Snowdon = Welsh Wolf

Lily of the Desert (Stirling, E., 1849), IV. 409

Lily of the Field (Hannan, C., 1896), v. 403

Lily of the Village = Blue-eyed Mary

Lily's Love (Abel, W. H., 1872), v. 234

Limbs of the Law (1879), v. 707

Limerick Boy (Pilgrim, J., 1865), v. 524

Lime Tree Chateau (1857), v. 707

Limited = Skittles Limited

Limited Liability (Naden, A. T., 1888), v. 501

+ Lina and Gertrude (*French*)

Linco's Travels (Garrick, D., 1767), III. 263

Linda di Chamouni (Edwardes, C. T. M., 1869), v. 354

— (Linley, G., 1851), v. 460

Linda Grey (Young, Sir C. L., 1885), v. 636

Lindamira (Foote, S., 1805) = First Act of Taste, III. 260, 384

— (1821), IV. 493

Linda of Chamouni (Thompson, A., 1869), v. 597, 820

Linda of Chamouny (Ryan, M. D., 1848), IV. 493, 631

Lindlove's Abbey (1877), v. 707

Lindor and Clara (Fennell, J., 1790), III. 259

Lindorf et Rosalie (1813), IV. 493

Linen Draper (Brown, J. R. and Thornthwaite, J. F., 1890), v. 282

Linen-draper's Tour — Jonny Gilpin

Line of Fate (Hewson, J. J., 1894), v. 420

Line of March = Bagshot-Heath Camp

Lines to an Old Ban-ditty = Utter Perversion of the Brigand

Lingo in a New School = Fig Hall

Lingo's Opinions on Men and Manners (Edwin, J., 1787), III. 383

Lingo's Wedding (1784), III. 334

Line of Life (Sidney, W. and Grattan, H. P., 1871), v. 566

Linishee Lovel (1828), IV. 493

Link by Link (Hay, F. and Fenton, F., 1870), v. 411

Linked by Love = Thad

Link of Love (Colville, W. F., 1882), v. 319

Link o' Gold (Capel, G., 1882), v. 302;

Linnet's Lark (Hay, F., 1878), v. 411

Lion and the Mouse = (1) Only a Waif; (2) Stolen Kisses

Lion and the Tiger = Mr Pep

Lion and the Unicorn (Higgie, T. H., 1851), v. 421

Lion and the Unicorn were fighting for the Crown (Byron, H. J., 1864), v. 296, 782

Lion at Bay (Phillips, W., 1869), v. 523

Lion Brothers of the Burning Zaara = Aslar and Ozines

+ Lion Chief; or, The African Horseman (Farrell, J.; Roy. 10/1820)

Lion Conqueror (Townsend, W. T., 1860), v. 707, 821, 839

Lionel and Clarissa (Bickerstaffe, I., 1768), III. 198–9, 237

Lionel Prince of Saxony = White Eagle

Lioness of the North (Selby, C., 1845), v. 389

Lioness of the Sea = Female Pirate

Lion Hunters of the Burning Zaara = Aslar and Ozines

Lion King (1840), IV. 493

— (1842), IV. 493

— (1851), v. 707

Lion Limb (Pitt, C., 1867), v. 525

Lion of England (Clifton, 1825), IV. 576

Lion of England and the Eagle of France (1855) = United Service, v. 707, 762, 839

Lion of the Desert (1840), IV. 493

Lion of the Jungle (Johnstone, J. B., 1844), IV. 333

Lion Queen (1852), v. 707

Lion Queen and the Lawyer's Clerk = Mysteries of Old Father Thames

Lion's Den (1871), v. 708

— (1882), v. 708

Lions for a Lark (1838), IV. 493

Lion's Heart (Shirley, A. and Landeck, B., 1892), v. 564

Lion Slayer (Williams, T. J., 1860), v. 625

Lion's Love (Conquest, G., 1866), v. 707, 839

Lion's Mouth (Thompson, A., 1867), v. 597

Lions of Mysore = Hyder Ali

Lion's Tail and the Naughty Boy who wagged it (Reece, R., 1877), v. 538

Lirenda's Misery = Cola's Fury
Lisbeth of the Tyrol (1845), IV. 493
Lisbon (1811), IV. 493
Lischen and Fritzchen (1869), V. 839
Lisette (1831), IV. 493
— (1873), V. 708
Lisle Wilton (1849), IV. 493
Listeners hear no good of themselves =
    Figure of Fun
Lists of Ashby (Cooper, F. F., 1837) =
    Ivanhoe, IV. 94, 493, 631, 697, 837
Lita (Conway, A. G., 1888), V. 323
Literary Dustman (Rogers, W., 1840),
    IV. 609
Literary Nephew (Seed, H., 1868), V.
    560
Litigants (Ozell, J., 1715), II. 347, 442
Litigious Suitor Defeated (1742), II.
    172, 384
Little Aaron (1810), IV. 493
Little Alexander the Great = Rival
    Queens
Little Amy Robsart (1887), V. 708
Little Amy Robsart from a Comic Point
    of View (1872), V. 708
Little and Good = Quite Out of the
    Common
Little Back Parlour (Stirling, E., 1839),
    IV. 406
Little Baronet (Hoffman, M. H., 1897),
    V. 423
Little Beauty and the Great Beast =
    Bella Donna
Little Ben and Little Bob (1795) = Poor
    Sailor, III. 334, 402, 403
Little Ben Bolt (Keene, E., 1879), V. 442
— (1876), V. 708
Little Bidette (Pitt, G. D., 1850), V.
    526
Little Billie Carlyle (Harbon, W. J.,
    1881), V. 403
Little Bill that was taken up = Latest
    Edition of Black-eyed Susan
Little Blind Earl (1898), V. 708
Little Blue Bottle (Baddeley, G. C.,
    1873), V. 247
Little Bob and Little Ben = Poor Sailor
Little Bo-Peep (Buckstone, J. B., 1854),
    V. 287, 781
— (Glover, E., 1854), V. 382
— (Henderson, J., 1892), V. 416
— (Locke, F., 1892), V. 708, 804, 839

Little Bo-peep (Paulton, H. and Paul-
    ton, J., 1875), V. 516
— (Woolfe, J. H., 1894), V. 708, 839
— (1857, 1860), V. 839
— (1865), V. 708
— (1873), V. 839
— (1875, 1876, 1877, 1878, 1879, 1880,
    1881), V. 708
— (1881), V. 839
— (1882, 1883, 1884, 1887, 1890, 1891),
    V. 708
— (1892), V. 839
— (1892, 1894, 1896, 1898), V. 708
Little Bo-Peep! Boy Blue! (Stainforth,
    F., 1880), V. 578
Little Bo-Peep, Little Boy Blue and the
    Little Old Woman that lived in a
    Shoe (Younge, W., 1881), V. 637,
    825
Little Bo-Peep, Little Red Riding Hood
    and Hop o' my Thumb (Harris,
    Sir A. H. G. and Jones, J. W., 1892),
    V. 406
Little Bo-Peep who lost her Sheep
    (McCabe, F., 1867), V. 467
— (Marchant, F., 1875), V. 476
Little Bo Peep, who lost her Sheep, and
    Humpty Dumpty (Marchant, F.,
    1871), V. 476
Little Boy Blue (Watts, F. J., 1875), V.
    616
— (1863), V. 839
— (1877, 1880), V. 708
Little Boy Blue and Red Riding Hood
    (1894), V. 708
Little Boy Blue, come blow your Horn
    (Merion, C., 1874), V. 485
Little Bright Eyes (1860), V. 708
Little Buonaparte and his Warhorse =
    King of Rome
Little Busy Bee (Hazlewood, C. H.,
    1864), V. 708, 839
Little Captive (1828), IV. 493
Little Captive King (1852), V. 708
Little Carmen (Murray, A., 1884), V.
    499
Little Chang (Burnand, F. C., 1872), V.
    290
Little Change (Grundy, S., 1872), V.
    205, 396
Little Chap, Curly and Brown (Rix,
    W. J. and Gillett, F. J., 1895), V. 544

Little Christopher Columbus (Sims, G. R. and Raleigh, C., 1893), v. 569

Little Cinderella (Jones, J. W., 1887), v. 441

Little Claude and the Big Lady of Lyons (Field, W. F., 1892), v. 366

Little Claus and Big Claus (Hood, B., 1897), v. 425

Little Comedies (Sturgis, J., 1882), v. 818

Little Coquette (Barry, J. L., 1899), v. 252

Little Corporal (Buckstone, J. B., 1831), IV. 493, 631

Little Cricket (Mortimer, J., 1878), v. 494

Little Culprit (Atwood, A. and Vaun, R., 1897), v. 245

Little Daisy (Williams, T. J., 1863), v. 625

Little Dawson (1847), IV. 493

Little Demon (Halford, J., 1855), v. 708, 795, 839

Little Demon's Treasure = Little Devil's Share

Little Devil (Webster, B. N., 1843), IV. 418

Little Devil's Share (1860), v. 708

— = Asmodeus, the Little Demon

Little Dick Whittington (Byron, H. J., 1866), v. 782

— (1894), v. 708

Little Dicky Dilver with his Stick of Silver (Blanchard, E. L. and Greenwood, T. L., 1871), v. 264

Little Dinner (Grain, R. C., 1884), v. 387

Little Doctor Faust (Byron, H. J., 1877), v. 298

Little Don Caesar de Bazan (Byron, H. J., 1876), v. 298

Little Don Giovanni (Byron, H. J., 1865), v. 297

Little Don Quixote (1882), v. 708

Little Dorothy (Thorne, R., 1863), v. 709, 839

Little Dorrit (Cooper, F. F., 1856), v. 709, 786, 839

Little Duchess (Marshall, F. W. and Mouillot, F., 1898), v. 478

— (1861), v. 708

Little Duck and the Great Quack = Dulcamara

Little Duke (Scott, C. W. and Stephenson, B. C., 1878), v. 557

— (1841), IV. 493

Little 18-Carat (Dawtrey, R. A., 1885), v. 339

Little Emily (Halliday, A., 1869), v. 80, 401

— =(1) Emily; (2) Poor Em'ly

Little Em'ly's Trials (Brooke, E. H., 1871), v. 80, 276

Little Eyolf (Archer, W., 1896), v. 242

Little Fanny's Love = Scotch Ghost

Little Fibs (Berrie, E., 1869), v. 259

Little Flirting = I will be a Duchess

Little Flutter (Clarke, H. S., 1892), v. 313

Little Foster Brother (1877), v. 709

Little Fra Diavolo (1881), v. 709

— = Young Fra Diavolo

Little Freeholder (Hailes, Lord, 1790), III. 185, 266

Little French Doctor = Morgue

Little French Lawyer (Booth, Mrs, 1778), III. 113, 239

— (1749), II. 140, 377, 447

Little Game of Nap = Rip Van Winkle

Little Genius (Harris, Sir A. H. G. and Sturgess, A., 1896), v. 406

Little Gentleman (1867), v. 709

Little Gerty = Uncle True

Little Gil Blas (Farnie, H. B., 1870), v. 361

Little Gipsies (Dibdin, C. I. M., 1804), IV. 291

Little Gipsy (Lemon, M., 1841), IV. 344

— (1888), v. 709

— = May-Day

+ Little Girl who Tells Fibs (*French*)

Little Giselle, the Dancing Belle (Hazlewood, H. C., Jr., 1867), v. 415

Little Glass Man and the Fiend of the "Pinkiknoll" = Peter Monk's Dream of the Marble Heart

Little Goody Two Shoes (Blanchard, E. L. and Greenwood, T. L., 1872), v. 264

— (Blanchard, E. L., 1876), v. 264

— (Filippi, R., 1888), v. 366

— (Green, F. W., 1871), v. 794

— (1829), IV. 493

— (1875, 1877, 1878, 1899), v. 709

Little Guardsman (1849) = Lifeguards-
man, IV. 493, 631
Little Gulliver's Travels to the North
Pole (1876), v. 709
Little Hand and Muckle Gold (1889),
v. 709
Little Hermit (Trimmer, Mrs S., 1788),
III. 313
Little Hunch-Back (O'Keeffe, J., 1789),
III. 294
— (1839), IV. 493
— = Hunchback
Little Innocent (Townsend, W. T.,
1843), IV. 493, 631
Little Intruder = Shadows on the Blind
Little Jack and the Big Beanstalk
(Lloyd, A., 1887), v. 461
Little Jack Carpenter (1875), v. 709
Little Jack Frost (1883), v. 709
Little Jack Horner (Allen, O., 1876), v.
239
— (Blanchard, E. L., 1857), v. 263, 779
— (Clay, T. L. and Allen, O., 1881), v.
313
— (Stainforth, F., 1879), v. 578
— (1870, 1880, 1893), v. 709
Little Jack Horner and his Christmas
Pie (1858), v. 839
Little Jack Shepherd (Stephens, H. P.
and Yardley, W.), v. 580
Little Jack the Giant Killer (1871,
1875), v. 709
Little Jessie (Darâle, F., 1891), v. 336
— (1892), v. 709
Little Jim, the Collier's Son = Black
Country
Little Jockey (Dimond, W., 1831), IV.
307
Little Joey (1845), IV. 493
Little John and the Giants = Jack the
Gyant Queller
Little Johnny Horner (1896), v. 709
Little King (1861), v. 709
Little King Charles (1883), v. 709
Little King Pippin (Blanchard, E. L.,
1865), v. 264
Little Lady Loo = Jealousy
Little Lalla Rookh (Denny, J. T., 1885),
v. 342
Little Laundress (Peake, R. B., 1837),
IV. 493, 631
— (1856), v. 709

Little Lohengrin (Bowyer, F., 1884), v.
271
Little Lord Fauntleroy (Seebohm,
E. V., 1888), v. 560
Little Madcap (Cheltnam, C. S., 1846),
IV. 279
— (1884), v. 709
Little Man in Green = Young Man in
Green
Little Mary Plowden (1896), v. 709
Little Milliner = Mam'zelle
Little Minister (Barrie, J. M., 1897), v.
211, 251
Little Misery and a Little Mischief =
Cheap Bargain
Little Miss Beauty (1884), v. 709
Little Miss Cute (Vincent, C. T., 1894),
v. 609
Little Miss Muffet = Mulberry Bush
Little Miss Muffett and Little Boy Blue
(Buckstone, J. B., 1861), v. 287
Little Miss Nobody (Graham, H.,
1898), v. 386
Little Miss Wallflower (1895), v. 709
Little Mistake (1894), v. 709
Little Mother (Morton, J. M., 1870), v.
496
Little Mouse who built a House in a
Christmas Cake (Hazlewood, C. H.,
1860) = Harlequin and the Little
Mouse, v. 709, 834, 839
Little Mr Faust (Leslie, A., 1894), v. 456
Little Ned (1844), IV. 493
Little Nell = Nell
Little Nelly (Wood, M., 1872), v. 631
Little Nobody (Righton, M., 1890), v.
543
Little Nun (Craven, H. T., 1847), IV.
285
Little of Everything = Dead and the
Living
Little Offspring (1843), IV. 493
Little Offsprings (Peake, R. B. or
Percy, T. 1828), IV. 371, 603, 604
Little Old Man (1897), v. 709
Little Old Woman and her Pig (Lee,
N., 1841), IV. 493, 631
Little One (Ayres, A., 1885), v. 247
Little Orphan of the House of Chao
(Percy, T., 1763), III. 297
Little Orpheus and his Lute = (1)
Eurydice; (2) Pluto

Little Sunbeam (Wylde, Mrs H., 1892), v. 634

Little Sutler (1858), v. 710

Little Thumb and the Ogre (1807), IV. 493, 631

Little Tiger (Blake, T. G.), IV. 573

Little Toddlekins (Mathews, C. J., 1852), v. 480

Little Tom Bowling (Simpson, F., 1889), v. 567

Little Tommy Tucker (1845), IV. 493

Little Tom Tittlemouse and the Eleven Dancing Princesses (Greenwood, P. and Arnold, H. T., 1870), v. 393

Little Tom Tucker (Akhurst, W. M., 1876), v. 237

— (Clarance, L., 1877), v. 310

— (Ward, 1864), v. 822

— (1878), v. 710

Little Tom Tucker sang for his Supper (1859), v. 710

Little Tom Tucker, who sang for his Supper (Green, F. W. and Allen, O., 1877), v. 391

Little Tom Tug (Burnand, F. C., 1873), v. 290

Little too Late = Too Late for Dinner

Littletop's Christmas Party (1866), v. 710

Little Trader = Prize

Little Treasure (Buckstone, J. B., 1862), v. 287

— (Harris, A. G., 1855), v. 405

Little Vagrant (Moule, F. and Avery, E. W., 1897), v. 498

Little Viscount (Vezin, H., 1884), v. 608

Little Vixen (Capel, G., 1884), v. 302

Little Vixens (Neville, G. F., 1878), v. 502

Little Widow (Jarman, F., 1891), v. 434

Little Wonder (Jones, J. W., 1874), v. 440

— = Pizarro, the Great Tyrant

Little Youth (1881), v. 710

Live and Hope (McLaren, A., 1817), IV. 351

Live Lumber (1796), III. 334

Lively Boy (1895), v. 710

Lively Hal (Yabsley, A. G., 1893), v. 634

Lively Honeymoon (Stuart-Smith, E., 1897), v. 586

Lively Nancy (Taylor, T. P., 1838), IV. 614

Liverpool in 1796 (1812), IV. 494

Liverpool in the Olden Time = Bride of Everton

Liverpool Merchant = (1) Gold Curse; (2) Two Friends

Liverpool Prize (Pilon, F., 1779), III. 297

Liverpool Welcome = Elopement

Livery Rake = Livery Rake and Country Lass

Livery Rake and Country Lass (Phillips, E., 1733), II. 247–8, 349

Livery Rake Trapped = Livery Rake and Country Lass

Living at Ease (Sketchley, A., 1870), v. 571

Living Dead = Miriam Gray

Living Death (1891), v. 710

Living for Appearances = London Pride

Living for Love (1849), IV. 494

Living in Glass Houses (Courtney, J., 1851), v. 326

Living in London (Jameson, R. F., 1815), IV. 183, 330

Living Lie (Dickens, F., 1883), v. 344

— = Won by a Neck

Living Models (Walton, G., 1898), v. 612

Living or Dead (Stephens, W., 1886), v. 581

Living Skeleton (Jerrold, D. W., 1825), IV. 332

Livingstone's Son = Hilda's Inheritance

Living too fast (Troughton, A. C., 1854), v. 604

Living Will = Dead

Liz (Matthison, A. and Hatton, J., 1877), v. 481

Lizer's New Lodger (Kingsley, E., 1897), v. 444

Lizzie Leigh (Waldron, W. R., 1863), v. 610

Lizzie Lyle = Flower Makers and Heart Breakers

Lizzie Shrie, the Brave Lass o' Haltwistle (1868), v. 711

Lizzie Stone (1868), v. 711

Llewellyn, Prince of Wales (Cherry, A., and Dibdin, T. J., 1813), IV. 280

Llewelyn the Great = Cambrian Hero

London Barber (1875), V. 711

London Beaux and Bath Belles (1848), IV. 631

London, Birmingham and Bristol = Railroad Trip

London Bridge a Hundred and Fifty Years Ago (McNab, J., 1873), V. 471

London by Day and Night = (1) Bootblack; (2) Jessie Ashton

London by Gaslight (Hazlewood, Miss, 1868), V. 415

London by Night (Selby, C., 1845), IV. 399

— (Selby, C., 1868), V. 560

— (1899), V. 711

— = Cruel City

London Carrier (1835), IV. 494

London Characters (Jerrold, D. W., 1825), IV. 331

London Chimes (1897), V. 711

London Cuckolds (Ravencroft, E., 1681), I. 74, 79, 188, 255, 308, 349, 426

London Day by Day (Sims, G. R. and Pettitt, H., 1889), V. 569

+ Londoner in Dublin (Crow Street, Dublin, 10/5/1779)

London Fog (Lemon, M., 1851), V. 455

London Frolics in 1638 = Merchant's Wedding

London Gentleman (Howard, E., 1667), I. 414

London Hermit (O'Keeffe, J., 1793), III. 294

— (1810), IV. 494

— (1822), IV. 494

London Highways and Byways (1864), V. 711

London in 1840 = Cripple of the Clink

London in 1814 = Hard Frost

London in Exhibition Time = Good Time Coming

London in 1444 = Widow of Cornhill

London in its Splendor (Jordan, T., 1673), I. 416

London in Luster (Jordan, T., 1679), I. 416

London in 1724 = Jack Sheppard, the Housebreaker

London in 1664 = Queen of Bohemia

London in the Days of Charles II = Queen of Bohemia

London in the Last Century = Law of the Land

London in the Reign of George II = Felix Heron

London in 1370 = Dick Whittington and his Cat

London Labour and London Poor (Elphinstone, J., 1854), V. 711, 790, 840

London Lady (1848), IV. 494

London Life (Clark, T. G., 1881), V. 311

London Lions (1838), IV. 494

London, Liverpool and Bristol = Wanted, a Wife

London Love = £20,000

London Manners at a Country Mansion (1823), IV. 494

London Mechanic (1859), V. 840

London Merchant (Lillo, G., 1731), II. 2, 59, 61, 115, 119, 120–2, 124, 248, 341, 418, 440; III. 88

— = George Barnwell

London Merchant Tailor = George Barnwell

London Mystery (Bourne, W., 1895), V. 270

London out of Town (McLaren, A., 1809), IV. 351

London 'Prentice (?Clive, C., 1754), III. 334, 378, 402

— = Distressed Beauty

London Prentice's Glory = Amurath, the Great Emperor of the Turks

London Pride (Gordon, G. L. and Mackay, J., 1882), V. 385

— (Kenney, J., 1859), V. 443

London Raree Show = Day of Taste

London's Anniversary Festival (Taubman, M., 1688), I. 435

London's Annual Triumph (Taubman, M., 1685), I. 435

London Scamps = Modern Bohemians

London Sensation = Stolen Bonds

London's Glory (Jordan, T., 1680), I. 416

— (Tatham, J., 1660), I. 434

London's Great Jubilee (Taubman, M., 1689), I. 435

London's Joy (Jordan, T., 1681), I. 416

London's Light o' Love = Power and the Glory

London's Poor (1899), V. 711

Lord and Lady Algy (Carton, R. C., 1898), v. 305

Lord and Lady Guilderoy (Aidé, H., 1896), v. 236

Lord and the Lout (Pitt, W. H., 1859), v. 711, 811, 840

Lord and the Peasant (1860), v. 711

Lord Anerley (Quinton, M. and Hamilton, H., 1891), v. 532

Lord Bateman (Byron, H. J., 1869), v. 297

— (Daly, C., 1876), v. 334

— (French, S., 1875), v. 373

— (Stephens, H. P., 1882), v. 580

Lord Bateman and the Fair Sophia (Dibdin, T. C., 1858), v. 788

Lord Bateman's Overland Journey (1854), v. 711

Lord Blunder's Confession (1733), II. 377

Lord Burleigh = Reaping the Whirlwind

Lord Byron in Athens (1832), IV. 494

Lord Darcy (Greene, A. E., 1896), v. 392

Lord Darnley (Wilks, T. E., 1837), IV. 420

Lord Dolly (Anderson, C., 1898), v. 240

Lord Dundreary married and done for (Byron, H. J., 1864), v. 296

Lord Dunnohoo (Redgrave, R., 1897), v. 537

Lord Edward (Whitbread, J. W., 1894), v. 620

Lord Fitzharris (Walford, H. L., 1873), v. 611

Lord Halifax (Wardhaugh, M., 1878), v. 614

Lord Harry (Jones, H. A. and Barrett, W., 1886), v. 59, 439

Lord-in-Waiting (Bartholeyns, A. O'D., 1893), v. 252

Lord Lovel and Lady Nancy Bell (Burnand, F. C., 1856), v. 287

Lord Lovington (Villars, G., 1888), v. 608

Lordly Husband (1737), II. 447

Lordly Ploughman = Frolics of Fortune

Lord Macninney (1886), v. 711

Lord Mansfield's Wig (1823), IV. 494

Lord Marple's Daughter (Harvey, F., 1886), v. 408

Lord Mayor (Bradley, W. E., Paulton, H. and Paulton, E. A., 1895), v. 273

Lord Mayor of London = Wat Tyler

Lord Mayor's Daughter = Cedar Chest

Lord Mayor's Day (O'Keeffe, J., 1782), III. 293

— (1830), IV. 494

— (1879), v. 711

Lord Mayor's Fool (1834), IV. 495

Lord Mayor's Fool of 1642 (1837), IV. 495

Lord Mayor's Show (Jordan, T., 1682), I. 416

Lord of the Castle (1817), IV. 495

Lord of the Isles (Fitzball, E., 1834), IV. 314, 495, 584

— (1815), IV. 495

Lord of the Ladrones = Contrabandista

Lord of the Maelstrom (1829), IV. 495

Lord of the Manor (Burgoyne, J., 1780), III. 120, 201, 241, 378

— (Dibdin, C. I. M., 1812), IV. 293

— (Merivale, H. C., 1880), v. 487

— (1795), III. 336

— (1837), IV. 495

Lord of the Storm = Algernon the Blind Guide

Lord Peebles' Secret (1896), v. 711

Lord Russell (Hayley, W., 1784), III. 267

— (Stratford, T., 1784), III. 310

Lords and Commons (Gore, Mrs C. G. F., 1831), IV. 319

— (Pinero, Sir A. W., 1883), v. 525

Lords of Creation (Drinkwater, A. E., 1895), v. 351

Lords of Ellingham (Spicer, H., 1848), IV. 405

Lord Tom Noddy (Dance, G., 1896), v. 335

Lord Ullin's Daughter (1844), IV. 495

Lord William Russell (Chapman, J., 1858), v. 783

Lord Wyndhamere's Fan = Babble Shop

Lorenzino di Medici (Rough, W., 1797), III. 303

Lorenzo (Haynes, J., 1821) = Conscience, IV. 495

— (Hopkinson, A. F., 1889), v. 426

— (Merry, R., 1791), III. 287

Lorenzo, the Outcast Son (Gandy, E., 1823), IV. 318 [The entry on IV. 397 under Sandy is in error]

Love and Liberty = (1) American Slaves; (2) Bondman; (3) Scanderbeg

Love and Life (Taylor, T. and Merritt, P., 1878), v. 594

Love and Lottery = Rival Serjeants

Love and Love's Vision = Agnes of Bavaria

Love and Loyalty (McDonald, A., 1791), III. 283

— (Robson, W. J., 1854), v. 547

— (1795), III. 334

— = (1) Captive Prince; (2) Fate of Villany; (3) Gascons; (4) Irish Poleander

Love and Lucre (1860), v. 712

Love and Madness (Waldron, F. G., 1795), III. 113, 314, 397

— (1811), IV. 495

— = (1) Amy; (2) Charlotte and Werther

Love and Magic (1802), IV. 495

— = Enchanter

Love and Mercy = (1) Hussar; (2) Young Huzzar

Love and Money (Benson, 1795), III. 207, 236

— (Reade, C. and Pettitt, H., 1882), v. 536

— (1795), III. 334

Love and Murder (Barnett, M., 1851), v. 250

— (Brougham, J., 1861), v. 280

— (Buckstone, J. B., 1837), IV. 275

Love and Mystery (Haines, J. T., 1832) = Mystification, IV. 322, 509, 587, 634

— = Strolling Players

Love and Nature (Berkeley, G. M., 1789), III. 236

Love and Passion = Cora

Love and Politics (Johnson, H. T., 1888), v. 437

Love and Poverty (1817), IV. 495

Love and Pride = Lady of Lyons

Love and Reason (Lacy, M. R., 1827), IV. 340

Love and Revenge (Settle, E., 1674), I. 40, 205, 348, 428

— (1729), II. 377

Love and Riches Reconcil'd (1699), I. 412

Love and Stratagem (Brand, O. and Linging, E. W., 1886), v. 273

Love and the Chase (1819), IV. 495

Love and the Lancet (1817), IV. 495

Love and the Law (Millward, H., 1886), v. 489

Love and the Slave-Trade (1828), IV. 495

Love and the Toothache (1816), IV. 495

Love and Transformation = Soldier's Stratagem

Love and Treason = Sailor and his Lass

Love and Valour (1779), III. 113, 334

Love and Wambles = My Old Woman

Love and War (Jephson, R., 1787), III. 277

— (Lemon, M., 1842), IV. 344

— (Olde, B. and Young Sir W. L., 1895), v. 507

— (1897), v. 712

— = Estelle Dumas

Love and War in Yankyland = Coup-de-Main

Love and Wine (1754), III. 334

Love Apple (1874), v. 712

Love at a Loss (Trotter, Mrs C., 1700), II. 176–7, 361

Love at a Venture (Centlivre, Mrs S., 1706), II. 4, 142, 145, 162, 186, 304

— (1782), III. 334

Love at Fault = Widow Bewitched

Love at First Sight (Crauford, D., 1704), II. 154, 316, 434

— (Jocelyn, J. K. J., 1889), v. 437

— (King, T., 1763), III. 279

— (Yarrow, J., 1742), II. 364

— = Princesse

Love at Home (Dauncey, S., 1891), v. 337

Love, Avarice and Repentance = Orphans

Love Awake and the Guard Asleep = Patrick's Return

Love Betray'd (Burnaby, W., 1703), II. 27, 50, 140, 153, 195, 301, 432

Love beyond Price = Cupid from Jewry

Love Bird (Edwardes, C. T. M., 1872), v. 354

Love Birds (1844), IV. 496

— (1883), v. 712

Love brooks no jesting (Whitaker, John, Jr., 1882), v. 620

Love by Lantern Light (Barnett, M., 1862), v. 250

Love in a Tub (1866), v. 712
— = (1) Comical Revenge; (2) Wives of Whitechapel
Love in a Veil (Savage, R., 1718), II. 172, 353
Love in a Village (Bickerstaffe, I., 1762), III. 114, 116, 118, 198, 237
— (1837), IV. 496
Love in a Wheelbarrow = Night before the Wedding
Love in a Wood (Jacob, G., 1714), II. 338
— (Wycherley, W., 1671), I. 68, 237–8 438; III. 161
Love in Castile = Disappointments
Love in Disguise (Lucas, H., 1766), III. 283
— = In Search of a Wife
Love in Distress = (1) Mutineer; (2) Noble Soldier; (3) Parthian Hero
Love in Every Age = Four Seasons
Love in Fashion = Amorous Orontus
Love in Full Gallop (Dibdin, T. J., 1816), IV. 300
— = High Road to Marriage
Love in Germany = One and Twenty
Love in his Dotage (1773), III. 334
Love in Humble Life (Payne, J. H., 1822), IV. 84, 368
— (1862), v. 712
Love in Idleness (Parker, L. N. and Goodman, E. J., 1896), v. 513
Love in Limbo (1815), IV. 496
Love in Livery (Wooler, J. P., 1845), IV. 496, 631
— (1857), v. 712
Love in Low Life = (1) Nancy; (2) Press Gang
Love in Many Masks (Kemble, J. P. 1790), III. 114, 278
Love in Mexico = New Spain
Love in Miniature = Infant Soldier
Love in New York = Down East Bargain
Love in Ruines = Fatal Discovery
Love in Scotland = Cunning against Art
Love in Several Masques (Fielding, H., 1728), II. 10, 158, 160, 323
Love in Tandem (Daly, A., 1892), v. 334
Love in Tears = Hypermnestra
Love in the City (Bickerstaffe, I., 1767), III. 198, 207, 237

Love in the City (1813), IV. 496
Love in the Country (Thompson, W. G., 1830), IV. 614
— = Primrose Green
Love in the Cupboard (1821), IV. 496
Love in the Dark (Fane, Sir F., 1675), I. 37, 191, 258, 410
Love in the Desarts = Kais
Love in the Desert (Hitchener, W. H., 1802), IV. 325
Love in the East (Cobb, J., 1788), III. 244, 379, 399
Love in the East Indies = Campaign
Love in the Grove (1814), IV. 496
Love in the Highlands = (1) Bessie Bell and Mary Gray; (2) Donald and Peggy; (3) Fairies' Revels
Love in the Moon = Luna
Love in the Nursery Grounds = Kiss and the Rose
Love in the Vineyards = Peter and Paul
Love in the Vintage (1815), IV. 496
Love in Tripoli = Peggy Larkins
Love in Wrinkles (Lacy, M. R., 1828), IV. 340, 592
Love is Blind (À Beckett, G. A., 1837), IV. 249
Love is the Best Doctor (1771), III. 402
Love is the Doctor (1734), II. 377, 447
Love King (Elliott, G., 1893), v. 356
Love Knot (Coyne, J. S., 1858), v. 328
— (Parker, L. N., 1892), v. 513
Love Ladder = Ladder of Love
Love Laughs at Bailiffs (1829), IV. 496
Love Laughs at Law = Guinevere
Love Laughs at Locksmiths (Colman, G., the Younger, 1803), IV. 282, 577
— (Fogerty, E., 1899), v. 369
— (1803), IV. 496
— (1811), IV. 496
Love, Law and Physic (Kenney, J., 1812), IV. 336
Love, Law and Pugilism (1824), IV. 496
Love Letter (Argent Lonergau, E., 1894), v. 242
Love Letters (Dibdin, T. J., 1822), IV. 303
— (1822), IV. 496
— (1885), v. 712
Love levels all = Serf
Love lies a-bleeding = Philaster
Love, Lies and Literature = White Lion

Lovers' Quarrels (King, T., 1790), III. 115, 334, 390

+ — (Lovers' Quarrels; or, Like Master like Man (D.L. 1816; Vic. 1864) *French*)

+ Lover's Resolution (Gilbert-Cooper, J., 1767) [MS. in Nottingham Central Library. See A. D. Guest in *Theatre Notebook*, XI. 1957, pp. 135–41]

Lovers' Resolutions (Cumberland, R., 1802), IV. 287

Lover's Ruse (Burslem, C., 1873), V. 293

Lover's Signal = Alive or Dead

Lovers' Signals = Turret Clock

Lovers' Stratagem (?1660–1770), I. 442

— = Fugitives

Lover's Trial (Dibdin, T. J., ?1796), III. 382

Lovers' Vows (Inchbald, Mrs E., 1798), III. 49, 65, 145, 147, 275, 388

— (Porter, S., 1798), III. 65, 299, 394

— (Thompson, B., 1800), IV. 412

Lover's Well = (1) Geraldine; (2) Glashen Glora

Lover, the Lugger and the Lacquey = Ruy Blas Righted

Lover turn'd Philosopher = Fame

Love Rules = Sybil

Love Rules the World = Pity the Sorrows of a Poor Old Man

Love Runs all Dangers (1733), II. 377

Love Sacrifice = Factory Boy

Love's Adventures (Cavendish, M., 1662), I. 396

Love's a Jest (Motteux, P. A., 1696), I. 12, 263, 420

Love's Alarms (Fitzwilliam, E. F., 1853), V. 369

— (Rae, C. M., 1878), V. 532

Love's Alarum (Planché, J. R., 1821), IV. 377

Love's a Lottery (Harris, J., 1699), I. 412

Loves and Gloves (Wyke, E. B., 1878), V. 633

Love's Anguish (Schon, O. H., 1882), V. 557

Love's Artifice (Wignell, J., 1762), III. 116, 316

— (1827), IV. 496

Love's Awakening = Meroflède

Love's Blind They Say (1849), IV. 496

Love's Compact (1852), V. 713

Love's Conflict = Broken Vows

Love's Constancy = King and the Countess

Love's Contrivance (Centlivre, Mrs S., 1703), II. 34, 52, 129, 144, 166, 303, 433

Love's Contrivances (1825), IV. 496

Love's Crosses (Day, J. T., 1881), V. 340

Love's Cunning = Ellen

Love's Device = Cupid in Camp

Love's Devotion (Dearlove, W. H. and Franklin, J., 1890), V. 340

— (1854), V. 713

Love's Dilemma (1881), V. 713

Love's Disguises = (1) Tallow-chandler Bewitched; (2) Mob Cap; (3) Woman's Wit

Love's Doctor (Halliday, A., 1870), V. 401

Love's Dream (Beazley, S., Jr., 1820), IV. 84, 264

— (Spry, H., 1880), V. 577

Love's Enchantment = Laura

Love's Error (Manby, F. H., 1870), V. 474

Love's Errors (Kemble, C., 1812) = Child of Chance, IV. 496, 631

Love's Eyes (Levy, E. L., 1891), V. 458

Love's Fetters (1847), IV. 496

— = Creole

Love's Fidelity = Louisa

Love's Frailties (Holcroft, T., 1794), III. 17, 51, 136–7, 271

— (Stafford, J. J., 1828), IV. 405, 496, 631

Love's Jealousy = Dutch and Scotch Contention

Love's Kingdom (Flecknoe, R., 1664), I. 34, 132, 138, 264, 411

Love's Labour Lost...Regained (Brown, Major, 1841), IV. 574

Love's Labour's Lost (Thompson, E., ?1760), III. 397

Love's Labyrinth (Emden, W. S., 1843), IV. 310

— (Forde, T., 1660), I. 138, 412

— (Thomson, J., 1819) = Cure for Romance, IV. 496, 631

— (1865), V. 713

Love's Last Shift (Cibber, C., 1696), I. 263, 278, 337, 397; II. 126

Love's Test (Edwards, J., 1874), v. 355
Love's the Physician = Quacks
Love's Trial (Moore, H. W., 1882), v. 492
— (1846), IV. 631
— (1857), v. 713
Love's Trials (Pratt, S. J., 1805), IV. 388
Love's Trickery (Bridgman, C., 1889), v. 275
Love's Triumph (Cooke, E., 1678), I. 125, 398
— (Motteux, P. A., 1708), II. 229, 395
— (Planché, J. R., 1862), v. 528
— (1718), II. 377
— (1866), v. 713
— = Fleurs de Lys
Love Suits = Lawyers and their Clients
Love's Vagaries (Vaughan, T., 1776, 1791), III. 313
— (1823), IV. 497
— = Tho' Strange 'Tis True
Love's Victim (Gildon, C., 1701), II. 28, 30, 31, 67, 76, 116, 332
— = Charlotte and Werther
Love's Victory (Chamberlayne, W., 1658), I. 396
— (Hyde, G., 1825), IV. 329
— (1846), IV. 497
Love's Weathercock = Way of the Wind
Love's Young Dream (Bright, E., 1891), v. 276
— (Buckingham, L. S., 1864), v. 286
— = Moreen and Sham Van Voght
Love Test (Johnstone, J. B., 1859), v. 713, 800, 840
— (Lisle, W., 1872), v. 152, 460
— = Amilie
Love Tests (Amcotts, V.), v. 240
Love that blooms for ever = Marriage not Divorce
Love that Kills (Brandon, J., 1888), v. 274
— (1868), v. 713
— = Jewess and Christian
Love that lasts (Harvey, F., 1881), v. 408
Love that wins = Karl
Love the best Contriver = Friendly Rivals
Love the Cause and Cure of Grief (Cooke, T., 1743), II. 115, 123, 316
Love the Cure of all Woes = Mournful Nuptials

Love the Leveller (1704), II. 188, 221, 377
— = Dora Mayfield
Love the Magician (Rae, J. and Sidney, T., 1892), v. 533
Love Trap (Moss, H., 1883), v. 498
Love Triumphant (Bellamy, D., 1722), II. 235, 297
— (Dryden, J., 1694), I. 83, 93, 145, 407
— (1788), III. 334
Love under a Lamppost = Wooing a Widow
Love unto Death = Sacrifice
Love versus Science (Lonergan, Mrs E. A., 1896), v. 462
Love, War and Victory = King of the Assassins
Love, War, Physic and Latin = Student
Love will finde out the Way (1661), I. 443
Love will find out the Way = Rencontre
Love wins (Clarke, H. S. and Du Terreaux, L. H. F., 1873), v. 312
Love wins the Day (Finlayson, 1865), v. 713, 792, 840
— (Towers, E., 1879), v. 601
Love Wisely = Setting of the Sun
Love without Interest (Pinkethman, W., 1699), I. 424; II. 377
Love, Youth and Folly = Youth, Love and Folly
Loving and Scheming (Walker, G. R., 1874), v. 611
Loving Cup (Halliday, A., 1868), v. 401
Loving Enemies (Maidwell, L., 1680), I. 217, 420
Loving Hearts and Buried Diamonds (Neville, G. F., 1870), v. 502
Loving Legacy (Sidney, F. W., 1895), v. 565
Loving not wisely but too well = Cast Aside
Loving Woman (Peake, R. B., 1849), IV. 497, 631
Lowina of Tobolskoi (1817), IV. 497
Lowland Lassie (Rannie, J., 1806) = Lowland Lassie in London, III. 300; IV. 388
Lowland Lassie in London (Rannie, J., 1803) = Lowland Lassie, III. 300; IV. 388
Lowland Romp (1810), IV. 497

Lurline (Reece, R. and Farnie, H. B.,
   1886), v. 539
— (1874), v. 713
— (1881), v. 713
Lyar (Foote, S., 1762), iii. 117, 173–4,
   260, 384
— (1763), iii. 334
— = Mistaken Beauty
Lycidas (Jackson, W., 1767), iii. 276
— (1762), iii. 334
Lyddy Beale (Hazlewood, C. H., 1861),
   v. 713, 796, 840
Lying Dutchman (Green, F. W. and
   Swanborough, W. H., 1876), v. 390
Lying in Ordinary (Peake, R. B., 1838),
   iv. 371
Lying Lover (Steele, Sir R., 1703), i.
   263; ii. 129, 183, 191–2, 193, 356, 444
Lying made Easy (1826), iv. 497
Lying Valet (Garrick, D., 1741), ii. 138,
   329, 437
Lynce and Pollidore (1781), iii. 334
Lynch Law (Pettitt, H., 1874), v. 520
— (1854), v. 713
— (1881), v. 713
Lynn Wives (1838), iv. 497
Lyons Mail = Courier of Lyons
Lyrical Lover (Clarke, H. S. 1881), v.
   313
Lyric Novelist (Cherry, A., 1804), iv.
   279

Mabel (Fox, G. D., 1891), v. 371
— (Hay, F., 1880), v. 411
— (Reynoldson, T. H., 1840), iv. 497,
   632
Mabel Connell (1845), iv. 497
Mabel Gray (1844), iv. 497
Mabel Lake (Hazlewood, C. H., 1873),
   v. 414
Mabel's Curse (Hall, Mrs A. M., 1837),
   iv. 323
Mabel's Life (Byron, H. J., 1872), v. 298
Mabel's Secret (Ferneyhaugh, G. F.,
   1870), v. 365
Mabel's Twins = Those Terrible Twins
Mabel's Two Birthdays = Ebony Casket
Mabel the Forsaken (Lloyd, H., 1869),
   v. 461
Mabel the Maniac = Whitefeet
Mabel Whyte, the Maid of Stratford
   (1851), v. 713

Mab's Mangle (1883), v. 713
Macaire (Fox, G. D., 1887), v. 371
— (Henley, W. E. and Stevenson, R. L.,
   1885), v. 417
+ McAllister McVitty McNab; or, The
   Laird, the Daftie and the Highland
   Maiden (Byron, H. J.: *Dicks* (in
   Sensation Dramas))
Macaroni (Hitchcock, R., 1773), iii.
   269
Macbeth (D'Avenant, Sir W., 1673), i.
   37, 59, 133, 134, 172, 401–2
— (Kemble, J. P., 1794), iii. 278, 389
— (Lee, J., 1753), iii. 57, 280
— (Macready, W. C., 1837), iv. 352
— (Rowe, H., 1799), iii. 395
— (1857), v. 713
— (1889), v. 713
Macbeth according to Act of Parliament
   (Hodson, G., 1853), v. 423
Macbeth Modernized (Bell, R., 1838),
   iv. 91, 264
Macbeth Mystified (Mason, W. H. and
   Rae, J. E., 1869), v. 480
Macbeth Travestie (Malone, 1853), v.
   805
— (Talfourd, F., 1850), iv. 91, 410
— (1813), iv. 91, 497
— (1842), iv. 91, 497
MacCarthy More (Lover, S., 1861), v.
   463
Macfarlane's Will (Mackay, J., 1881), v.
   470
McGreggors (1825), iv. 632
MacHaggis (Jerome, J. K. and Phill-
   potts, E., 1897), v. 436
Macheath in the Shades (1735), ii. 377
Macheath turn'd Pyrate (1737), ii. 447
Macintosh and Co. (Kenney, J., 1838),
   iv. 338
McKenna's Flirtation (Selden, E.,
   1892), v. 560
McTavish (1896), v. 713
Mad (Dearlove, W. H., 1893), v. 340
— (Rose, E., 1880), v. 550
Mad Actor (1825), iv. 497
Madame (Coghlan, C. F.), v. 316
— (Tanner, J. T., 1895), v. 590
Madame Angot (Desprez, F., 1875), v.
   343, 788
Madame Berliot's Ball (Burnand, F. C.,
   1863), v. 288

Madame Cartouche (Edwards, H. S., 1891), v. 335, 789

Madame de Moray's Secret = Guiltless

Madame de Raimont (Henry, R., 1883), v. 417

Madame du Barry (Poole, J., 1831), IV. 497, 632

Madame Favart (Farnie, H. B., 1879), v. 362, 791

Madame l'Archiduc (Farnie, H. B., 1876), v. 362, 790

Madame Midas, the Gold Queen (Beck, P. and Hume, F., 1888), v. 254

Madame Morensky (1896), v. 713

Madame Pompadour's Pearl (Wilks, T. E., 1840), IV. 617

Madame Rose = Gibraltar

Madame Sans-Gene (Carr, J. W. C., 1897), v. 304

Madam Fickle (D'Urfey, T., 1676), I. 24, 43, 273, 348, 408

Madam Laffarge (1841), IV. 497

Madam Scaite in the Seraglio = Odd Fish

Mad as a Hatter (Marshall, F., 1863), v. 478

— (Thorp, A. C., 1872), v. 599

Mad as a March Hare (1837), IV. 479

— (1857), v. 713

— (1879), v. 713

Madcap (Aveling, E. B., 1890), v. 246

— (Reece, R. and Farnie, H. B., 1878), v. 538

— = Lowland Romp

Madcap Madge (Stephens, L. E. B., 1895), v. 581

Madcap Midge (Fawcett, C. S., 1889), v. 364

Madcap Prince (Allen, A. M., 1894), v. 238

— (Buchanan, R., 1874), v. 284

— (1884), v. 713

Mad Captain (Drury, R., 1733), II. 247, 319

— (Stevens, G. A., 1769), III. 334, 396

Madcap Violet (Stockton, E., 1882), v. 584

Mad Couple = All Mistaken

Mad Crime (1895), v. 713

Maddalen (Galt, J., 1812), IV. 585

Madeira (Adams, H., 1875), v. 235

Madelaine (1843), IV. 498

Madelaine = Daughter of the Regiment

Madeleine (Mortimer, J., 1873), v. 494

— (1841), IV. 632

— (1851), v. 713

Madeleine Dumas (1856), v. 714

Madeline (Bedingfield, R., 1847), IV. 264

— (Cooke, C., 1874), v. 323

— (Kingdom, J. M.), v. 444

— (1837), IV. 498

Madeline Martel (Harvey, F., 1882), v. 408

Madeline Morel (Bandmann, D. E., 1878), v. 248

Madelon (Peake, R. B., 1844), IV. 371

Mademoiselle de Belle Isle (Kemble, F. A., 1864), v. 442

Mademoiselle de Lira (Thompson, Mrs G. and Sinclair, K., 1890), v. 597

Mademoiselle Fifi (1898), v. 714

+ Mademoiselle Squallino (Featherstone, J. L., *French*)

Mad for Love = Maypole

Mad-Fred (Dutnall, M., 1863), v. 714, 840

Madge (Rogers, F., 1888), v. 548

— (Wade, F. and Austin, H., 1890), v. 610

Madge's Adventure (1874), v. 714

Madge Wildfire (Stirling, E., 1868), v. 584

Mad Girl of St Martin's = Pirate Smuggler

Mad Guardian (Dibdin, T. J., 1794), III. 256, 382

Mad House (Baker, R., 1737), II. 296

— (Oulton, W. C., 1784), III. 296 [The date of production should be 1/5/ 1784]

Mad Inventor (1895), v. 714

Mad Lover (1701), II. 447

Mad Lovers (1738), II. 378

— = Blazing Comet

Madman (Walker, G. R., 1881), v. 611

— (1770), III. 334

Mad, Marred and Married = Our M.D.

Mad Marriage (Harvey, F., 1884), v. 408

Mad Match (Moss, H., 1887), v. 498

Mad Meg (Burnette, C., 1885), v. 293

Mad Monarch (1834), IV. 498

Mad Mother and her Lost Son (1884), v. 714

Magic Minstrel (Dibdin, C. I. M., 1808), IV. 292
— = Oberon
Magic Mirror (À Beckett, G. A., 1843), IV. 250, 567
— = Ninth Statue
Magic Mistletoe (Buckingham, L. S., 1856) = Harlequin Humbug, V. 689, 714, 781, 834, 840
Magic Moonstone (1899), V. 714
Magic Mule (Marchant, F., 1878), V. 476
Magic Oak (Bennett, J., 1793), III. 377
— (Farley, C. and Dibdin, T. J., 1799), III. 335, 383, 402; IV. 310, 583
Magic of British Liberty (Cherry, A., 1803), IV. 498, 632
Magic of Life (Courtney, J., 1851), V. 326
Magic of Orosmanes (1785), III. 335
Magic Opal (Law, A., 1893), V. 450
Magic Pagoda (Astley, P., Jr., 1808), IV. 257
Magic Pearl (Fitzball, E., 1873), V. 368
Magic Picture (Bate, H., 1783), III. 32, 33, 113, 236
Magic Pipe (1810), IV. 498
— (1833), IV. 498
— = Harlequin Orpheus
Magic Pipe and the Fatal I.O.U. = Innocentinez
Magic Purse and Wishing Cap = Fortunatus and his Sons
Magic Ring (Brand, O., 1886), V. 274
— = Magic Opal
Magic Rose (1871), V. 714
— = (1) Azor and Zemira; (2) Beauty and the Beast; (3) Cloud King; (4) Enchanter's Slave; (5) Guardian Sylph; (6) Man in the Moon
Magic Shield (1896), V. 714
Magic Star (1807), IV. 632
Magic Sword (1807), IV. 498
Magic Thimble = Cymbra
Magic Toys (Oxenford, J., 1859), V. 509
Magic Urn (1808), IV. 498
Magic Veil = Fairy Lake
Magic Well (1804), IV. 498
Magic Whisper (Hazlewood, C. H., 1870), V. 414
Magic Wishing Cap (Hazlewood, C. H., 1865), V. 714, 796, 840

Magic Wishing Cap = Fortunatus
Magic Witch = Rothomago
Magic World (1787), III. 335
— (1807), IV. 498
— (1810), IV. 498
Magic Zone = Olympic Frailties
Magistrate (Pinero, Sir A. W., 1885), V. 174–5, 525
— (1808), IV. 498
Magloire = Jocrisse the Juggler
Magna Charta (Faucit, J. S., 1840), IV. 498, 583, 632
— (1823), IV. 498
— (1888), V. 714
— = Runnymede
Magnet (Dalton, L., 1893), V. 333
— (Dubois, Lady D., 1771), III. 258
Mago and Dado (Lonsdale, M., 1794), III. 282, 401
Magpie (Dibdin, T. J., 1815), IV. 299, 580
Magpie and Thimble (Smelt, T., 1877), V. 571
Magpie or the Maid (Pocock, I., 1815) = Daughter, IV. 33, 115, 148, 384, 448, 606, 623
Mahatma (Montague, L. A. D., 1894), V. 491
Mahdi (1894), V. 714
Mahmoud (Hoare, P., 1796), III. 270
Mahogany Polka = Spirit Rappings and Table Moving
Mahomet and Irene = Irene
Mahomet the Impostor (Miller, J., 1744), II. 66, 72–3, 111, 345, 441
Maid and the Magpie (Byron, H. J., 1858), V. 295
— (James, S., 1848), IV. 330
— (Lee, N., 1844), IV. 342
— (1846), IV. 498
— (1852), V. 714
Maid and the Magpye (Arnold, S. J., 1815), IV. 256
Maid and the Mandarin = Chinese Junk
Maid and the Mirror (Pitt, G. D., 1847), IV. 375
Maid and the Monarch = Priscella
Maid and the Monk (1840), IV. 632
Maid and the Monkey = Miss Esmeralda
Maid and the Monster = Perseus and Andromeda

Maiden Aunt (Knowles, R. B., 1845), IV. 339

Maiden Lane Murder (1833), IV. 632

Maiden of Myrtlewood Manor = Tawno's Bride

Maiden of the Black Rock (1834), IV. 498

Maiden Queen (1745), II. 378
— = Secret-Love

Maidens, Beware! (Haines, J. T., 1836), IV. 322, 586

Maiden's Dream = Lighthouse

Maiden's Fame (Bernard, W. B., 1838), IV. 266

Maiden's Second Slip = Farmer's Son

Maiden that perished of a Pain in the Chest = Mistletoe Bough

Maiden, the Masher and the Monarch = Bluff King Hal

Maiden Whim (Hill, Sir J., 1756), III. 269

Maiden Wife (1886), V. 714

Maid Marian (Planché, J. R., 1822), IV. 377

Maid Marian and Robin Hood (Smith, H. B., 1890), V. 572, 816

Maid of All-he-uns = Joan of Arc

Maid of All Work (1861), V. 714
— = Wanted, an Errand Boy

Maid of Altona = Iceland King

Maid of Antwerp = Quentin Matrys

Maid of Aosta = Perilous Pass

Maid of Artemis (Dillon, A., 1895), V. 345

Maid of Artois (Bunn, A., 1836), IV. 276

Maid of Athens (Edmund, C. and Newton, H. C., 1897), V. 354, 789
— = Revolt of the Greeks

Maid of Bagdad = Vizier's Son, the Merchant's Daughter and the Ugly Woman

Maid of Bath (Foote, S., 1771), III. 42, 174, 260

Maid of Bath Married = Hermit Converted

Maid of Biggar = Maid of St Aubin's

Maid of Bonfleur (1855), V. 714

Maid of Bristol (Boaden, J., 1803), III. 239; IV. 179, 269

Maid of Brittany = Likeness

Maid of Canada (1838), IV. 498

Maid of Cashmere (Fitzball, E., 1833), IV. 314, 584

Maid of Castile (1835), IV. 498
— = Peter the Cruel

Maid of Cefn Ydfa (O'Dowd, J. C., 1870), V. 506

Maid of Croissey (Gore, Mrs C. G. F., 1835), V. 319

Maid of Croxdale (Richley, R., 1877), V. 543

Maid of Erin = Brian Boroihme

Maid of Erin and the Griffin of the Thames = John Felton

Maid of Geneva = (1) Judith; (2) Therese

Maid of Genoa (Farrell, J., 1820), IV. 15, 311

Maid of Glendalough = Kevin's Choice

Maid of Grenada (1832), IV. 498

Maid of Honour (Fitzball, E., 1847), IV. 317
— (Kemble, J. P., 1785), III. 113, 278, 389
— (Waters, J., 1899), V. 615
— (Wooler, J. P., 1864), V. 632
— (1841), IV. 498

Maid of Jersey (1854), V. 714

Maid of Judah (Lacy, M. R., 1829), IV. 94, 340, 592
— = Cœur de Lion

Maid of Kars = Ayesha

Maid of Kent (Stirling, E., 1843), IV. 613
— (Waldron, F. G., 1773), III. 313

Maid of Leyden (1898), V. 714

Maid of Liverpool (1799), III. 335

Maid of Lochlin (Richardson, W., 1801), III. 302; IV. 394
— = Mysteries of the North

Maid of Lorn (McLaren, A., 1815), IV. 351

Maid of Madrid (1841), IV. 632

Maid of Mandalay (1896), V. 714

Maid of Marienburg (1798), III. 63, 335, 402

Maid of Mariendorpt (Knowles, J. S., 1838), IV. 339 [Presumably this is the play listed IV. 498 as acted at Perth in 1839]

Maid of Mexico (1859), V. 714

Maid of Milan = Clari

Maid of Moffat Dale (1825), IV. 499

Maid the Mistress (Taverner, W., 1708), III. 141, 170–1, 232, 358; III. 116
— = (1) He Wou'd if He Cou'd; (2) Serva Padrona
Maid, the Murder and the Mystery = Gamekeeper's Gun
Maid, Wife and Widow = (1) Paradox; (2) Ruth of Rosedale; (3) 'Tis She
Maid with the Milking Pail (Buckstone, J. B., 1846), IV. 275
Maid with the Parasol = Cat in the Larder
Mail-Coach Passengers (Jameson, R. F., 1816), IV. 330
Main Chance (Farnie, H. B., 1873), V. 361
Maine Liquor Law = Teetotal Family
Main Hope (Comer, G., 1885), V. 319
Main-top Night Watch = Homeward Bound
Maintop Watch (1868), V. 714
Maison à Vendre (1840), IV. 499
Maison de Santé (Pitt, C., 1860), V. 810
Maison Rouge (1849), IV. 499
Maison Rustique = Country House
Maitre de chapelle (1845), IV. 499
Majesty Misled (1734), II. 378
Major (Jones, J. McL., 1890), V. 440
— (Melford, M., 1882), V. 484
— (1893), V. 714
Major and Miner (Ellis, W., 1881), V. 357
Major and Minor (Dance, G., 1835), IV. 499, 632
— = White Lies
Major Baggs (Lloyd, A., 1878), V. 461
Major Domo (1844), IV. 499
Major Hope = Hope
Major Marie Annie (Newbound, E., 1880), V. 502
Major Proposes (Milner, H. T., 1884), V. 490
Major Raymond (Havard, P., 1896), V. 410
Majors and Minors = Dramatic Committee
Major's Daughter (Bridgeman, J. V., 1849), IV. 499 [+ L.C.]; V. 780
Major's Dilemma (1894), V. 714
Major, the Miner and the Cock-a-doodle-do = Olympic Games
Make a Noise Tom (1718), II. 378

Makebeliefs (Grein, J. T., 1892), V. 394
Make the best of it (Oxenford, J., 1851), V. 509
Make yourself at home (Maltby, A., 1875), V. 473
Make your Wills (Mayhew, E. and Smith, G., 1836), IV. 354
Making it pleasant (Clement, W., 1887), V. 314
Malade imaginaire (Wright, J.), I. 438
Maladetta (1863), V. 714
Malaeska (1866), V. 714
Malak the Jew (1830), IV. 499
Malala (1871), V. 714, 840
Malcolm (Roberts, R., 1779), III. 302
Male and Female Serenaders (Wilson, G., 1847), IV. 422
Male Coquette (Garrick, D., 1757) = Modern Fine Gentleman, III. 262
Male Curiosity = Sir Peter Pry
Malediction (1830), IV. 499
— = Rigoletti
Malediction of the Dead = Moyra
Malice (1898), V. 714
Maliel the Avenger = Retributive Justice
Mall (?Dover, J., 1674), I. 233, 241, 262, 403
Malt and Hops = Brewer of Preston
Maltster's Daughter = Rye House Plot!
Malvesi the Deformed = Dwarf
Malvina (Macfarren, G., 1826), IV. 349
— (1786), III. 335
Malvina and Calmar = Chieftains of Scotia
Malvoli (1849), IV. 499
Mamamouchi = Citizen turn'd Gentleman
Ma mie Rosette (Dance, G., 1892), V. 335
Mamma (Chippendale, Mrs M. J., 1876), V. 310
— (Grundy, S., 1888), V. 397
Mamma's Opinions (Poel, W., 1893), V. 714, 811, 840
Mammon (Grundy, S., 1877), V. 396
Mammon and Gammon (Talfourd, F., 1848), IV. 499, 632
Mam'zelle (Gill, W., 1894), V. 381
Mam'zelle Nitouche (1884), V. 714
Man (Glyn, H. A., 1874), V. 382
— (Pettitt, H., 1873), V. 520
— (1856), V. 715

Man about Town (Bernard, W. B., 1836), IV. 265
— (Mee, H., 1897), V. 483
— (Stange, S., 1899), V. 578
Management (Lunn, J., 1828), IV. 348
— (Reynolds, F., 1799), III. 301
Manager (Burnand, F. C., 1882), V. 291
— (1834), IV. 499
— = Impresario
Manager an Actor in spite of himself (Bonnor, C., 1784), III. 121, 239, 378
— = Transformation
Manager and his Friends = Mr Buckstone at Home
Manager at a Nonplus = Wanted an Actor
Manager at Home (1852), V. 715
Manageress in a Fix = Please to Remember the Grotto
Manager Hoax'd = Opening Night
Manager in Affliction (1795), III. 335
Manager in Distress (Colman, G., 1780), III. 210–11, 247
Manager in his Slippers = Rejected Addresses Received
Manager in Love (1870), V. 715
Manager in Perplexities (1862), V. 715
Manager in Prosperity (1820), IV. 499
Managers (1768), III. 335
Manager's Daughter (Lancaster, E. R., 1837), IV. 499, 593, 632
Manager's Last Kick = Quadrupeds
Managers Manag'd = Author's Triumph
Manager's Night = Spoiled Children
Manager's Room (1852), V. 715
Manager's Son = Country Actors
Manager Worried = Smock Alley Secrets
Managing Director = No. 13
Managing Mama = New Men and Old Acres
Man and a Brother = Worcester Sauce
Man and her Master = Jack Ram
Man and his Brother (1872), V. 715
Man and his Makers (Barrett, W. and Parker, L. N., 1899), V. 251
Man and his Master (1883), V. 715
— (1894), V. 715
Man and Metal (1894), V. 715
Man and Money (1860), V. 715
Man and the Maid = Trick for Trick

Man and the Marquis (Dibdin, T. J., 1825), IV. 304
Man and the Monkey (1815), IV. 148, 499
— = Animal Sympathy
Man and the Monster (Milner, H. M., 1827), IV. 499, 632
— = Frankenstein
Man and the Shadow (1866) V. 715
Man and the Spirit (Hazlewood, C. H., 1881), V. 415
Man and the Tiger = P.P.
Man and the Woman (Buchanan, R., 1889), V. 285
Man and Wife (Arnold, S. J., 1809), IV. 255
— (Collins, W. W., 1873), V. 318
— (Colman, G., 1769), III. 45, 118, 183, 246
— (James, D. S., 1885), V. 433
— (Stephenson, C. H., 1870), V. 582
Man and Wife before Marriage = Who's at Home?
Man and Woman (De Mille, H. C. and Belasco, D., 1893), V. 342
— (1883), V. 715
Man at the Wheel = Ixion
Man Cat (1871), V. 715
Manchester Friends = Love in his Dotage
Manchester Girl = False Glitter
Manchester Man's Million = Grelley's Money
Manchester Marriage (Cheatham, F. G., 1859), V. 715, 783, 840
Mandarin (1789), III. 335
— (1811), IV. 499
— (1896), V. 715
Mandarin's Daughter = Willow-Pattern Plate
Mandarin's Ghost (1897), V. 715
Mandingo Warriors = Kongo Kolo
Mandrill (1830), IV. 499
Mandrin (Mathews, C. J., 1835), IV. 354
— (1864), V. 715
Manette (Reynoldson, T. H., 1846), IV. 393, 537 [Manette and A Speaking Likeness are identical]
Man for the Ladies (Jerrold, D. W., 1836), IV. 333
— = Peter the Beauty

Man Milliner (1821), IV. 500
Manners and Customs of America (1857), V. 715
Manners make the Man = Love is Blind
Man o' Airlie (Wills, W. G., 1867), V. 627
Manoeuvre = Blind Man
Manoeuvres of Jane (Jones, H. A., 1898), V. 440
Manoeuvring (Planché, J. R. and Dance, C., 1829), IV. 84, 378, 605
— (1814), IV. 635
— = Two make a Pair
Man of Business (Cobb, J., 1809) = Sudden Arrivals, IV. 500, 632
— (Colman, G., 1774), III. 119, 123, 141, 246
— (Olaf, W. and Chapman, W., 1887), 507
Man of Bus'ness = Love in the Dark
Man of Crime = Quadroona
Man of Destiny (Shaw, G. B., 1897), V. 189, 195, 203–4, 562
Man of Enterprise (Shillito, C., 1789), III. 188–9, 306
Man of Family (Jenner, C., 1771), III. 120, 276, 388
Man of Few Words = Joe Miller
Man of Forty (Frith, W., 1898), V. 374
— (Poel, W., 1880), V. 529, 811
Man of Genius = William March
Man of Honour (Davies, W., 1786), III. 253
— (Lynch, F.), II. 342
— = Brittanicus
Man of Iron (1885), V. 715
Man of Law (Webster, B. N., 1851), V. 618
Man of Many Friends (Coyne, J. S., 1855), V. 327
Man of Mile End (1834), IV. 500
Man of Mode (Etherege, Sir G., 1676), I. 43, 60, 188, 198, 236, 348, 410
Man of My Choice = Guardians
Man of Mystery (1826), IV. 500 [and see note under Fatal Precept]
— (1870), V. 715
Man of Newmarket (Howard, E., 1678), I. 52, 214, 414
Man of No Principle (Brownson, J. H., 1895), V. 283

Man of Parts (Jackman, I., 1785), III. 276 [This was acted as A Trip to London, Smock Alley, Dublin, 2/12/1785]
Man of Quality (Hollingshead, J., 1870), V. 424
— (Lee, J., 1773), III. 280
Man of Reason (Kelly, H., 1776) = Reasonable Lover, III. 131, 278, 389
Man of Stratagems = Clinton
Man of Straw = My Grandfather's Will
Man of Taste (Miller, J., 1735), II. 135, 144, 164–5, 203, 344; III. 116
— (1752), III. 116, 335
Man of Ten Thousand (Holcroft, T., 1795), III. 271
Man of the Black Forest (1820), IV. 500
Man of the Day = Well-born Workman
Man of the Family (Jenner, C., 1771), III. 276
Man of the Mill (1765), III. 335
Man of the People (Branson, W. S., 1879), V. 274
Man of the Red Chateau = Chevalier of the Moulin Rouge
Man of the Red Mansion (Rice, C., 1851), V. 715, 813, 840
Man of the Wood, the Fair Maniac and the Dumb Brother and Sister (1823), IV. 500
Man of the World (Goldman, L. B., 1894), V. 383
— (Macklin, C., 1781), III. 19, 140, 284, 391
Man of Two Lives (Bernard, W. B., 1869), V. 259
— (Thompson, L., 1879), V. 598
Man of Two Masters (1858), V. 715
— = Jonathan
Man of Two Thousand (1821), IV. 500
Man of War (Bosworth, J., 1838), IV. 573
Manola (Farnie, H. B., 1882), V. 362, 791
— (Lucas, Sergeant, 1872), V. 464
Manon (Bennett, J., 1885), V. 258
Man on the Rock = Prometheus
Manor House of Mont Louvier = Marie
Man or Wife = Castle of Limburg
Man-o'-War's Man (Dellow, H. and Livesey, C., 1894), V. 342

313

Ma Part (Horncastle, J. H., 1846), IV. 328

Mara (Sapte, Walter, Jr., 1889), V. 556

Marble Arch (Rose, E. and Garroway, A. J., 1881), V. 550

Marble Bride (Hazlewood, C. H., 1857), V. 412

Marble Heart (Selby, C., 1854), V. 97, 560

Marble King (James, C. S., 1851), V. 433

Marble Lover (1854), V. 715

Marble Maiden (Layton, G. M., 1873), V. 451

— (Stocqueler, J. H., 1846), IV. 500, 632

— (1845), IV. 500, 632

— (1866), V. 715

Marble Statue (1856), V. 715

— (1883), V. 715

Marcelia (Boothby, F., 1669), I. 140, 392

Marcella (Hayley, W., 1789), III. 227, 267, 386

Marcelle (1879), V. 715

Marcelline (Selby, C., 1839), IV. 398

+ Marcellus and Julia (8°, 1788)

Marchand d'esclaves (1819), IV. 500

Marches Day (Finlayson, J., 1814), IV. 583

— (1771), III. 335

March Hare Hunt (Moore, F. F., 1877), V. 492

Marchioness de Brinvilliers (1846), IV. 500

Marchioness of Brinvillion (1862), V. 715

March of Crime = Oscar the Bandit

March of Intelleck (Macfarren, G., 1827), IV. 350

March of Intellect = Adelphi Academy

March on Magdala (Warrington, F., 1870), V. 615

March Winds and April Showers (1860), V. 715

Marciano (Clark, W., 1662), I. 397

Marcoretti (Kingdom, J. M., 1853), V. 444

Marco Schiarra (1860), V. 715

Marco Sciarro (Dillon, C., 1844), IV. 581

— (1840), IV. 632

Marco Spada (Simpson, J. P., 1853), V. 567

Marcus Brutus (Sheffield, J., 1722), II. 355

Marcus Manlius (Colombine, D. E., 1837), IV. 577

Marcus Tullius Cicero (Patsall), III. 296

Marden Grange (1869), V. 715

Mardo (Frayne, F. J., 1883), V. 372

Mareschal de Logis = Veteran

Mare's Nest (Hamilton, H., 1887), V. 401

— (Mouillot, F., 1889), V. 498

Marforio (1736), II. 378

Margaret Byng (Philips, F. C. and Fendall, P., 1891), V. 522

Margaret Catchpole (Stirling, E., 1845), IV. 407

— (1845), IV. 500

Margaret Catchpole, the Female Horse-stealer (1845), IV. 500

Margaret Maddison (Pitt, G. D., 1846), IV. 374

Margaret of Anjou (Jerningham, E., 1777), III. 84, 277

— (Wilson, J. M., 1829), IV. 500, 618, 632

Margaret of Regensburg (1837), IV. 500

Margaret's Ghost (Fitzball, E., 1833), IV. 500, 584

Margate (White, B., 1895), V. 620

Margate Milkmaid = Pyramus and Thisbe

Margate Sands (Hancock, W., 1864), V. 402

— = New Brighton Sands

Margery (Carey, H., 1738), II. 137, 266-7, 303, 433

Margery Daw (Morton, J. M., 1861), V. 496

— = Ballad Singer

Margery's Lovers (Matthews, B., 1884), V. 480

Margot (Manuel, E., 1875), V. 475

— (1879), V. 715

Marguerite (Halford, J., 1856), V. 398

— (Pede, T., 1873), V. 518

— (Reade, C.), V. 812

— (1821), IV. 500

Marguerite's Colours (Archer, T., 1847), IV. 190, 255

Marguerite's Mangle = Faust

Maria (Davidson, A., III. 253, 381

Maria (Meighan, J., 1890), v. 483
Mariage Night (Cary, H., 1663), I. 136, 395
Mariamne (Fenton, E., 1723), II. 6, 43, 58, 72, 110, 264, 323, 436; III. 78
— (Waller, W., 1839), IV. 615
Marian (Arnold, W. N., 1825), IV. 569
— (Brooke, F., 1788), III. 240
— (Cooke, C., 1870), v. 323
Mariana (Graham, J., 1897), v. 387
Marian and the Knight Templar = Marian
Marianne de Lancy (1854), v. 840
Marianne Duval the Vivandière (Phillips, L., 1851), v. 523, 810
Marianne, the Child of Charity (Pitt, G. D., 1844), IV. 373
Marian of the Grange = Marian
Maria Padilla (Barnett, C. Z., 1841), IV. 260
Maria Stuarda (Williams, T. J.), v. 824
Marie (Addison, H. R., 1836), IV. 251
— (Barnett, C. Z., 1843), IV. 260
— (Carte, R. D., 1871), v. 305
— (1855), v. 715
Marie Antoinette (Simpson, J. P., 1868), v. 568
— (Yarnold, E., 1835), IV. 422
— (1858), v. 716
Marie de Chamouni (Wilton, F., 1848), IV. 618
— (1843) = Marie, the Pearl of Chamouni, IV. 632
Marie de Courcelles (Holford, Mrs, 1878), v. 424
Marie de Meranie (1864), v. 716
Marie de Rohan (1862), v. 716
Marie de Roux (1860), v. 716
Marie de Rudney = Nun
Marie Ducange (Bernard, W. B., 1841), IV. 266
Marie Jeanne (Bandmann, D. E., 1879), v. 248
Marie Mignot = Ambition
Marie Stuart (1876), v. 716
Marie, the Foundling of the Lake (1849), IV. 500
Marie, the Pearl of Chamouni (1843) = Marie de Chamouni, IV. 500, 632
Marietta (?Raymond, E. M. or C. F. M., 1843), IV. 500, 632 [There is some

doubt about this play: it is attributed to E. M. Raymond, but a Mariette of the same year is given to C. F. M. Raymond]
Marietta = Mariette's Wedding
Mariette (?Raymond, C. F. M., 1843), IV. 388 [see also under Marietta]
— (1821), v. 490
Mariette Duval (Barnett, C. Z., 1839), IV. 260
Mariette's Wedding (Morton, W. E. and Millars, H., 1882), v. 497
Marigold (Matthison, A., 1879), v. 481
Marigold Farm (Sapte, Walter, Jr., 1893), v. 556
Marina (Coleman, J., 1888), v. 316
— (Lillo, G., 1738), II. 70, 141, 223, 342, 440
Mariner and his Monkey = Phillip IV
Mariner and the Delowar (1854), v. 716
Mariners (Birch, S., 1793), III. 238
Mariner's Compass (Leslie, H. T., 1865), v. 457
Mariner's Daughter (1866), v. 716
— = White Squall
Mariner's Dream (Barnett, C. Z., 1838), IV. 260
Mariners of England (Buchanan, R. and Jay, H., 1897), v. 285
Mariner's Sister = Minute Gun at Sea
Marinette (Stonehouse, J., 1843), IV. 409
— (1853), v. 716
Marino Faliero (Byron, Lord G. G., 1821), IV. 169, 220, 278
— (Swinburne, A. C., 1885), v. 589
Marion (Ellis, W. and Greenwood, P., 1898), v. 357
Marion Delorme (Davey, R., 1887), v. 338, 787
— (1859), v. 716
Marionettes (Reece, R. and McArdle, J. F., 1879), v. 539
— (1876), v. 716
Marion Hazleton (Courtney, J., 1848), IV. 284
— (1854), v. 716
Marishka (Zalewska, W., 1891), v. 637
Maritana (Fitzball, E., 1845), IV. 316
Maritta (1899), v. 716
Marjolaine (Edwards, H. S., 1877), v. 355

Marjorie (Clifton, L. and Dilley, J. J., 1889), v. 315, 784

Marjorie's Cousin (Major, A. F., 1886), v. 472

Marjory Gilzean (Gower, J., 1888), v. 386

Mark Drummond (1849), IV. 500

Marked Man (Hewson, J. J., 1893), v. 420

Market Cross (Douglass, J. T., 1864), v. 348

Mark Fresland (1842), IV. 500

Markham and Greenwood (1846), IV. 500

Mark Jarrett's Diary (1872), v. 716

Mark Lawrence (Lighterness, W. B., 1837), IV. 595

Mark of Cain (Jarman, F., 1887), v. 434

Mark of the Beast (1893), v. 716

Mark Ringwood (1862), v. 716

Mark the End On't (Siddons, H., 1807) = Time's a Tell-tale, IV. 500, 632

Mark the Mulatto (Jefferini, 1836), IV. 331

Mark the Smuggler (1849), IV. 500

Mark Winslow (Douglass, J. T., 1864), v. 716, 788, 840

Marlborough (Phillips, W., 1870), v. 523

Marleyvale (Searle, C., 1886), v. 559

Marmaduke Snooks (Leslie, B., 1879), v. 456

Marmaduke the Smuggler = Dead Wife

Marmion (Buchanan, R., 1891), v. 285

— (Fitzball, E., 1848), IV. 92, 317

— (Grosett, H. W.), IV. 586

— (Macready, W. C., 1814), IV. 92, 352

— (1810), IV. 92, 500

— (1811), IV. 92, 500

Maroon (Reid, M., 1865), v. 716, 813, 840

Mar-Plot (Centlivre, Mrs S., 1710), I. 39; II. 167, 305

Marplot in Lisbon (Woodward, H., 1755), III. 317

Marplot in Spain (Planché, J. R., 1821) = Too Curious by Half, IV. 500

Marquesa (Uniacke, J., 1889), v. 605

Marquis and the Cobbler = Marriage of Pride

Marquis de Carabas (1818), IV. 501

Marquis de St Valéry (Edwards, J., 1876), v. 355

Marquis of Carabos (1892), v. 716

Marquis of·Montrose (1829), IV. 632

Marriage (Bell, R., 1842), IV. 30, 264

— (Thomas, B. and Keeling, H., 1892), v. 596

— = Bridal Tour

Marriage Act (Dibdin, C., 1781), III. 255

— (1822), IV. 501

— = Ripe Fruit

Marriage à la mode (Dick, C., 1895), v. 344

— (Dryden, J., 1672), I. 75, 140, 188, 229–30, 274, 337, 345, 404–5; II. 142

— (1760), III. 335

— (1875), v. 716

— = (1) Comical Lovers; (2) Days of Hogarth; (3) Prodigal

Marriage a Lottery (Dance, C., 1858), v. 335

— = False and True

Marriage and Murder (1822), v. 491

Marriage at any Price (Wooler, J. P., 1862), v. 632, 824

Marriage at Last = Fortunate Prince

Marriage at the Drum Head = Hymen's Muster Roll

Marriage Bells (Archer, W. J., 1864), v. 716, 840

— (Gough, H., 1881), v. 386

Marriage by Candlelight (1861), v. 716, 840

Marriage by Comedy (1796), III. 335

Marriage by Licence (1858), v. 716

Marriage by Stratagem (1789), III. 335

Marriage Certificate (Hazlewood, C. H., 1867), v. 413

— (Mildenhall, T., 1843), IV. 501, 632

Marriage Contract (Brooke, H., 1778), III. 240

— (1803), IV. 501

— (1837), IV. 501

— (1842), IV. 501

Marriage Day (Courtney, J., 1852) = Life Chase, v. 326, 716, 786, 840

— (1805), IV. 501

Marriage Dowry (1800), IV. 501

Marriage, 1892 (Fitch, C., 1892), v. 367

Marriage Eve (1891), v. 716

Marriage-Hater Match'd (D'Urfey, T., 1692), I. 12, 276, 338, 409

Marriage in Miniature (1835), IV. 501

Marriage in Sicily = Traveller

Marriage in the East = Illustrious Stranger

Marriage Knot (Jarman, F., 1894), v. 434

Marriage Lines (Besemeres, J., 1873), v. 260

Marriage Night = Mariage Night

Marriage not Divorce (Levey, J. C., 1870), v. 458

Marriage of Bacchus = Theseus and Ariadne

Marriage of Convenience (Grundy, S., 1897), v. 397

Marriage Office = Device

Marriage of Figaro (Holcroft, T., 1819), IV. 326, 588

— (Mould, J. W., 1848), IV. 501, 601, 632

— (Planché, J. R., 1842), IV. 381

— (1878), v. 716

— = Follies of a Day

Marriage of Gamacho (1818), IV. 501

Marriage of Georgette (Harrison, W., 1860), v. 407, 796

Marriage of Interest = Mary Melvyn

Marriage of Love = Bridal of Beauty

Marriage of Pride (1854), v. 716

Marriage of Reason (1844), IV. 84, 501

Marriage of Sir Gawaine (Seally, J., 1782), III. 305

Marriage of the Devil = Belphegor

Marriage Portion = Haste to the Wedding

Marriage Projects (Ebsworth, J.), IV. 309

— = Matchmaking

Marriage Promise (Allingham, J. T., 1803), IV. 252

Marriage Prospects = Widow to Let

Married (Albery, J., 1873), v. 237

Married and Buried = Illustrious Stranger

Married and Single (Poole, J., 1824), IV. 386

Married and Unmarried = The Way to get Un-Married

Married another (Dixon, G., 1877), v. 346

Married Bachelor (O'Callaghan, P. P., 1821), IV. 366

— (1855), v. 716

Married Bachelors (1859), v. 716

Married Beau (Crowne, J., 1694), I. 271–2, 400

Married beneath him (Braddon, M. E., 1882), v. 273

Married by Force = (1) Danicheffs; (2) Danischeffs

Married by Proxy (Yuill, A. W., 1894), v. 637

Married Coquet (Baillie, J., 1746), II. 165, 296

Married Daughters and Young Husbands = Young Husbands

Married Flirt = Conjugal Lesson

Married for Hate = Delilah

Married for Money (Buckstone, J. B., 1857), v. 287

— (Mathews, G., 1855), v. 480

— (Towers, E., 1873), v. 601

Married from School (Brown, W., 1876), v. 282

Married General = Perjured Prince

Married in Haste (Byron, H. J., 1875), v. 116, 121, 298

— = Camilla's Husband

Married in Mistake = Lady of Kildare

Married in Spite of Himself (1865), v. 716

Married Libertine (Macklin, C., 1761) = School for Husbands, III. 284, 391

Married Life (Buckstone, J. B., 1834), IV. 274

Married Lovers (Power, T., 1831), IV. 387

Married Man (Inchbald, Mrs E., 1789), III. 118, 144, 275, 388

— (1786), III. 335

— (1890), v. 716

Married Moths (1881), v. 716

Married, not Mated (Harvey, F., 1877), v. 408

Married or Not? (Amherst, J. H., 1822), IV. 253

— = Married Bachelor

Married Philosopher (Kelly, J., 1732), II. 145, 184, 202, 340, 440

Married Rake (Selby, C., 1835), IV. 397

Married Tomorrow (1898), v. 716

Married Unmarried (Barnett, M., 1854), v. 250

Married Woman (1899), v. 716

Marrowbones and Cleavers (Lee, N., 1838), IV. 594
— = Music has Charms
Marrying for Money (Rogers, W., 1850), V. 549
Marry in Haste and Repent at Leisure = Found Drowned
Marry, or Do Worse (Walker, W., 1703), II. 171, 363
Marry, or Not to Marry (Inchbald, Mrs E., 1805), III. 275
Marry yourselves (Prior, H., 1873), V. 531
Marsac of Gascony (Vroom, E., 1899), V. 609
Mars and Venus (Weaver, J., 1717), II. 132, 136, 378, 446
Mars et l'Amour (1815), IV. 501
Mars' Holiday (1792), III. 335
Marston Brothers (Duncan, G., 1867), V. 352
Marston Moor (Lacy, T. H.,), IV. 593
Martelli (Brewer, G., 1844), IV. 501, 632
Martha (Reece, R., 1873), V. 537
— (Reynoldson, T. H., 1858), V. 813
— (1824), IV. 501
— (1855), V. 716
— (1859), V. 716
— = Bishop
Martha of Mile End = White Cross Knight
Martha's Double (Wright-Matron, G. E., 1896), V. 633
Martha, the Factory Girl (1851), V. 716
Martha the Gipsy (1824), IV. 501
Martha Willis, the Servant Maid (Jerrold, D. W., 1831), IV. 332
Martial Achievements of Sir William Wallace (Anderson, D., 1821), IV. 568
Martial Law (Mayhew, E., 1834), IV. 501, 632
— (1822), IV. 501
— = Wreckers
Martial Queen (Carleton, R., 1675), I. 395
Martin and James (Pitt, G. D., 1847), IV. 375
Martin Chuzzlewit (Higgie, T. H. and Lacy, T. H., 1844), IV. 98, 325

Martin Chuzzlewit (Stirling, E., 1844), IV. 98, 407
— (Webb, C., 1844), IV. 98, 616
— (Wigan, H., 1868), V. 622
Martin Faber (White, G., 1839), IV. 501, 632
Martin Family = Old Joe and Young Joe
Martin Guerre (Pearl, E. M., 1873), V. 518
Martin Hayward (P t, G. D., 1849), IV. 375
Martin Luther (Moore, G., 1879), V. 492
Martin Rivers (1835), IV. 501
Martin the Foundling (Pitt, G. D., 1847), IV. 374
Martinuzzi (Stephens, G., 1841), IV. 406, 612
Martyn Langton (1852), V. 716
Martyr (Baillie, J., 1826), IV. 258
— (Norton, Mrs E., 1848), IV. 602
— = Browne, the Martyr
Martyrdom of Ignatius (Gambold, J., 1740, 1773), III. 261
Martyrdom of Michael = Message of Mercy
Martyr of Antioch (Milman, H. H., 1822), IV. 167, 356
— (1898), V. 716
Martyr of Freedom (1882), V. 716
+ Martyr to Science (Weston, F., French)
Marvels of Electricity (1868), V. 716
Mary (Wynter, H. J., 1897), V. 634
Mary Barton (Townsend, W. T., 1861), V. 716, 821, 840
— (1850), V. 716
Mary Blane (1859), V. 716
Mary Campbell (1845), IV. 501
Mary Clifford (1841), IV. 501
— (1862), V. 716
Mary Edmonstone (Hazlewood, C. H., 1862), V. 412
Mary Fenwick (1845), IV. 501
Mary Glastonbury (Fitzball, E., 1833), IV. 314, 584
Mary Graham (1844), IV. 501
— (1862), V. 716
Mary Jones (1868), V. 716
Mary le More! (Hart, J. P., 1838), IV. 324
Mary Lester (1845), IV. 501
Mary Lister (1844), IV. 501

Mary Livingstone (Pitt, G. D., 1846), IV. 374

Mary, Mary Quite Contrary (1845), IV. 501

— (1860), v. 839

Mary, Mary, Quite Contrary, how does your Garden grow? (1859), v. 717

Mary May (1856), v. 717

Mary Melvyn (Fitzball, E., 1843), IV. 316

Mary of Manchester (Stirling, E., 1847), IV. 408

Mary of Scotland = Abbot

Mary of the Lighthouse (1861), v. 717

Mary Pennington, Spinster (Walkes, W. R., 1896), v. 612

Mary Price (Hazlewood, C. H., 1853), v. 717, 796, 840

— (1852), v. 717

Mary Queen of Scots (Boulding, J. W., 1873), v. 270

— (Deverell, Mrs M., 1792), III. 85, 254

— (Francklin, T., 1737), III. 261

— (Murray, W. H., 1825), IV. 94, 365

— (St John, J., 1789), III. 85, 304

— (Thompson, R. H., 1894), v. 598

— (Wills, W. G., 1874), v. 627

Mary's Bower (Brown, R., 1811), IV. 574

Mary's Devotion (Frere, C., 1898), v. 373

Mary's Dream (Townsend, W. T., 1837), IV. 414

Mary's Holiday (Vandervell, W. F., 1879), v. 606

Mary's Secret (Matthison, A., 1876), v. 481

Mary Stewart, Queen of Scots (Grahame, J., 1801), IV. 195, 501, 633

Mary Stuart (Gibbons, Mrs A., 1838), IV. 585

— (Haynes, J., 1840), IV. 324

— (Macaulay, Miss, 1823), IV. 596

— (Mellish, J. C., 1801), IV. 86, 355

— (Percival, E. L., 1839), IV. 86, 371

— (Peter, W., 1841), IV. 86, 371

— (Salvin, H., 1824), IV. 86, 396

— (Swinburne, A. C., 1881), v. 589

— (Trelawney, A., 1838), IV. 86, 414

— (Wingfield, L., 1880), v. 629

— (1833), IV. 86, 501

— (1839), IV. 82, 501

— (1850), v. 717

Mary Stuart (1866), v. 717

— = Mary, Queen of Scots

Mary Stuart, Queen of Scotland (1819), IV. 501

Mary Stuart, the Child of Misfortune (1893), v. 717

Mary, the Maid of the Inn (Scott, J. M., 1809), IV. 501, 633

— (1857), v. 717

Mary Tudor (Dickinson, A., 1876), v. 344

— (Gregg, T. D., 1858), v. 394

— (Stirling, E., 1849), IV. 613

— (Vere, A. de, 1847), IV. 415

— (1835), IV. 501

+ Mary Tudor (Duvard, P., 8°, 1844 (Northallerton))

Mary Turner (Burnand, F. C., 1867), v. 289

Mary Warner (Taylor, T., 1869), v. 593

Mary White (1842) = Mary White, the Charity Girl, IV. 501, 633

Mary White, the Charity Girl (1840) = Mary White, IV. 501, 633

Marzovan, the Apostate (1830), IV. 501

Masaniello (Brough, R. B., 1857), v. 278

— (Kenney, J., 1829), IV. 83, 337, 592

— (Levius, B., 1829), IV. 83, 345

— (Milner, H. M., 1829), IV. 83, 357, 599

— (1829) IV. 83, 501

— (1886), v. 717

Masaniello, the Fisherman of Naples (Soane, G., 1825), IV. 403, 612

— (1826), IV. 501

Mascotte (Farnie, H. B. and Reece, R., 1881), v. 362, 791

Mashing Highwayman = Dandy Dick Turpin

Mashing Mamma (Park, T., 1888), v. 512

Mask and the Surgeon = Huguenots

Mask'd Friend (1796), III. 135, 335

Masked (1870), v. 717

Masked Ball (Fitch, C., 1892), v. 367

— (1850), v. 717

— = (1) Black Domino; (2) Gustavus III; (3) Gustavus of Sweden; (4) Woman's the Devil

Masked Battery (1834), IV. 502

Masked Man (1866), v. 717

Masked Mother (Calvert, C., 1859), v. 783

Masked Mother and the Hidden Hand = Capitola

Masked Rider = Wife's Revenge

Mask of Bronze (1860), v. 717

Mask of Death (Ford, H., 1897), v. 370

Mask of Guilt (Vane, S., 1894), v. 606

Mask of Love (Osborne, C., 1877), v. 508

Masks and Faces (Taylor, T. and Reade, C., 1852), v. 68, 105, 150, 592, 820

— (1856), v. 717

Ma's Mistake (Parker, W., 1895), v. 514

Ma's Old Bean (Hill, H., 1888), v. 421

Mason (1899), v. 717

Mason and the Locksmith (1879), v. 717

Mason of Buda (Planché, J. R., 1828), IV. 378

Masonry (Dibdin, T. J., 1821), IV. 303

Masque for the Marriage of the Prince of Wales (Gretton, J., 1795), III. 386

Masque for Valentinian (Fane, Sir F., 1684), I. 410

Masque of Hymen = Royal Nuptials

Masque of the Deities (Thurmond, J., 1723), II. 360

Masquerade (Galt, J., 1814), IV. 318, 635

— (Griffin, B., 1717), II. 212, 333

— (Johnson, C., 1719), II. 132, 142, 144, 156–7, 175, 183, 339

— (1795), III. 335, 402

— (1820), IV. 502

— = Cent per Cent

Masquerade Ball (Ward, H. R., 1846), IV. 416

Masquerade Frolic = Fair Intriguers

Masqueraders (Jones, H. A., 1894), v. 166–7, 189, 440

— = (1) Love a Bo-Peep; (2) Oh! this Love

Massacre of Abergavenny (Furness, J. R., 1897), v. 375

Massacre of Cyprus (Milner, H. M., 1823), IV. 502, 633

Massacre of English Tourists by the Aravaniteakai = Greek Brigands

Massacre of Glencoe (1856), v. 717

Massacre of Jerusalem = Warrior Kings

Massacre of Paris (Lee, N., 1689), I. 148, 352, 420

— = Paris

Massacre of Paris on the 27th, 28th and 29th of July = French Revolution

Massacre of Rajahpoor (Milner, H. M., 1826), IV. 502, 633

Massacre of St Bartholomew = (1) Carpenter of Rouen; (2) Huguenots; (3) Jean Hennuyer, Bishop of Lisieux

Massacre of the Greeks = Siege of Missolonghi

Massacre of the Huguenots = Lady of the Louvre

Massacre of the 28th = Paris

Massacres of 1576 = Huguenots

Massaniello = Rise and Fall of Massaniello

Massaroni (Moreton, F. L., 1894), v. 493

Masse-en-yell-oh (Paulton, H. and Tedde, M., 1886), v. 517

Mass Unmask'd = Antichristian Opera

Mast and the Ploughshare (1804) = Ship and the Plough, IV. 502, 633

Master (Ogilvie, G. S., 1898), v. 506

Master Alfred (Combe, J., 1876), v. 319

Master and Man (Sims, G. R. and Pettitt, H., 1889), v. 569

— = Married Bachelor

Master Bell Blue (1860), v. 717

Master Builder (Archer, W. and Gosse, E., 1893), v. 242

Master Clarke (Serle, T. J., 1840), IV. 400, 610

Master Humphrey and His Clock = Tables Turned

Master Humphrey's Clock (Cooper, F. F., 1840), IV. 283

Master Jones's Birthday (Morton, J. M., 1868), v. 496

Master Key (1821) = Two Wives!, IV. 502

— = Love among the Roses

Master of Hope (Hawkins, L., 1898), v. 410

Master of Ravenswood (Simpson, J. P., 1865), v. 567

Master of the Forge (Bernard, C., 1884), v. 778

Master of the Situation (Hannan, C., 1899), v. 403

Master Passion (Falconer, E., 1859), v. 360

— (Phillips, Mrs A., 1852), v. 522

Matrimonial Masquerading = Snapping Turtles

Matrimonial Noose (Spier, M. H., 1885), v. 576

— = (1) Next-door Neighbours; (2) Queen Ellinor

Matrimonial Perplexity = What a Corporation!

Matrimonial Prospectuses (Simpson, J. P., 1852), v. 567

Matrimonial Trouble (Cavendish, M., 1662), I. 396

Matrimonio segreto (Grist, W., 1877), v. 795

Matrimony (Cameron, C., 1886), v. 300

— (Derby, C., 1844), IV. 290

— (Kenney, J., 1804) = Two Prisoners, IV. 144, 336, 547, 592, 641

— (Norman, G. P., 1893), v. 505

— (1798), III. 335

— (1812), IV. 502

— (1883), v. 717

Matrimony and Magic = Taming a Tartar

+ Matrimony by Advertisement (Emson, F. E., 8°, n.d.)

+ Matrimony Displayed (Smock Alley, Dublin, 24/4/1740)

Matron of Palermo = Sicilian Mother

Matteo Falcone (Oxberry, W. H., 1836), IV. 366

Matteo Falconi (Mayhew, E., 1834), IV. 502, 633

Matter of Doubt (Rodwell, G. H., 1823), IV. 502, 633

Matter of Right (1849), IV. 502

Matthew Hopkins (1829), IV. 502

Maud = Maud's Peril

Maude Muller (1883), v. 717

Maudlin, the Merchant's Daughter of Bristol (1729), II. 378

Maud's Peril (Phillips, W., 1867), v. 70–1, 523

Maum Guinea (1862), v. 717

Maureen na Laveen (Cooke, F., 1873), v. 323

Maurice (Dibdin, C. I. M., 1822), IV. 295

— (Dibdin, C. I. M., 1825), IV. 296

Maurice the Outcast (1834), IV. 502

Maurice the Woodcutter (Somerset, C. A., 1829), IV. 404, 612

Maurice the Woodcutter (?Somerset, C. A., 1835), IV. 502, 633

— (1854), v. 717

Mausoleum (Hayley, W., 1784), III. 267

Maxey's Money (1893), v. 717

Maximian (Burrell, Lady S. R., 1800), III. 60, 241; IV. 277

Maximums and Speciments of William Muggins (Selby, C., 1842), IV. 502, 633

May (Reece, R., 1874), v. 538

May and December (Grundy, S. and Mackay, J., 1882), v. 396

— (Miller, W. F., 1890), v. 489

— (1832), IV. 502

— (1835), IV. 502

— (1858), v. 840

— (1865), v. 717

— (1875), v. 717

— = Old Man's Darling

May Blossom (?Belasco, D., 1884), v. 717, 840

— = Thunderbolt

May Brierley = Six Years After

May-Day (Garrick, D., 1775), III. 202, 264

— = Fairy-Hill

May-Day Wedding = Sailor's Prize

May Dudley (Marchant, F., 1863), v. 717, 840

Mayfair (Pinero, Sir A. W., 1885), v. 185, 525

Mayfair and Ragfair (Mackay, J., 1878), v. 470

Mayflower (Moore, F. F., 1892), v. 492

— (Parker, L. N., 1899), v. 514

May Marsden (1846), IV. 502

May Meetings (Nowell, H. and Wynne, H., 1894), v. 506

May Morning (Norman, G. T., 1895), v. 505

— (1850), IV. 502

May Myrtle (1875), v. 717

Mayoralty of Trueborough = Contrast

Mayor and the Monkey (Coyne, J. S., 1838), IV. 502, 633

Mayor and the Three Coffins = Misconception

Mayor Deceived = Harvest Home

Mayor in a Hamper = Peeping Tom

Mayor of Garratt (1810), IV. 502

— (1837), IV. 502

Mayor of Garret (Foote, S., 1763), III. 114, 260

Mayor Outwitted = Hoaxing

Mayor's Dilemma = Well Played

Maypole (Wade, C. B. and Elliot, S., 1887), v. 610

May Queen (Buckstone, J. B., 1828), IV. 273

— (Buckstone, J. B., 1843), IV. 502

— (1871), v. 717

— (1874), v. 718

— (1883), v. 717

— (1893), v. 718

— (1898), v. 718

— = (1) Folly Fête; (2) Concealed Royalty; (3) Sylvia

May 17th, 1076 = Gallery of St Nicholas

May Tempest (1883), v. 718

Maze of Life (1882), v. 718

Mazeppa (Burnand, F. C., 1885), v. 291

— (Byron, H. J., 1859), v. 295

— (Milner, H. M., 1823), IV. 357, 502, 633

— (Newton, H. C., 1882), v. 718, 808, 841

— (1851), v. 718

— (1866), v. 718

— (1880), v. 718

— (1883), v. 718

— (1888), v. 718

— (1893), v. 718

Maze, the Maiden and the Monarch = Fair Rosamond

Mazourka (Byron, H. J., 1864), v. 296

— (1835), IV. 502

M.D. (Barri, O., 1879), v. 251

— (Lee, N., Jr., 1874), v. 453

— (Paulton, H. and Tedde, M., 1888), v. 517

M.E. = Post House

+Meadows of St Gervais (Ware, J. R., *Dicks*)

Meadow Sweet (Prevost, C. M., 1890), v. 530

Mean Advantage (Dircks, R., 1863), v. 345

— (Hart, F. and Herbert, G., 1897), v. 407

Me and Myself (1834), IV. 633

Measure for Measure (Gildon, C., 1700), II. 67, 71, 220, 332, 437

— (Kemble, J. P., 1803), IV. 335

Mechanic (Clair, G., 1859), v. 718, 784, 841

— (Lindo, F., 1889), v. 460

Mechanical Babes in the Wood (1882), v. 718

Mechanical Partner (Redmond, J., 1873), v. 537

Mechanical Toy (Taylor, M., 1870), v. 591

Mechanic's Wife (1883), v. 718

— = Downfall of Pride

Medæa (Johnson, C., 1730), II. 89, 264, 339

Medal of Death (Towers, E., 1866), v. 718, 821, 841

Meddle and Muddle (Bellingham, H. and Best, W., 1887), v. 257

Medea (Brough, R. B., 1856), v. 278

— (Glover, R., 1761), III. 71, 81, 265

— (Heron, M., 1861), v. 419

— (Sherburne, Sir E., 1648), I. 432

— (Stillingfleet, B., 1765), III. 309

— (Webster, A., 1867), v. 617

— (Williams, T. J., 1856), v. 625

— (1876), v. 718

— (1883), v. 718

Medea and Jason (1781), III. 336

Medea in Corinth (Heraud, J. A., 1857), v. 418

— (Wills, W. G., 1872), v. 627

Medea's Kettle (1792), III. 336

Medecine for the Million = Humbug

Medecin Malgre Lui = Love's Contrivance

Media (1853), v. 718

Mediaeval Strike = Simon the Smith

Medical Man (Gilbert, W. S., 1872), v. 379

Medical Student (Frances, B. and Laeland, H. J., 1893), v. 372

Medician Brutus = Italian Traitors

Medicine Man (Traill, H. D. and Hichens, R. S., 1891), v. 602

Medico (Lane, F., 1894), v. 448

Medicus Borealis (1816), IV. 502

Medium (Brown, J. R., 1899), v. 282

Medlars = King and Titi

Medley (1765), III. 336

— (1778), III. 336

Medley Lovers = Benevolent Man

Medley of Lovers = Miss in her Teens

324

Medley of Mirth and Sorrow = Rum Duke and the Queer Duke

Medusa (Hayes, F. W., 1882), v. 411

Meeting at Dover = John Bull and Buonaparte

Meeting of Friends = Day in the Country

Meeting of Managers = Bad Business

Meeting of the Company (Garrick, D., 1774), III. 263, 385

Meet me by Moonlight (Parry, T., 1839), IV. 368

— (1837), IV. 502

— = Barney Brallaghan

Mefistofele (Marzials, T., 1884), v. 718, 806, 841

Mefistofele II (Maltby, A., 1880), v. 473

Meg (1899), v. 718

Meg Merrilies (Leslie, H. T., 1873), v. 457

— (1832), IV. 502

Meg Murnoch (Barrymore, W., 1816), IV. 261

Meg's Diversion (Craven, H. T., 1866), v. 107–8, 329

Mehalah (Poel, W. and Palmer, W. H. G., 1886), v. 529

Meistersingers = Master Singers

Melanchollicks = Mr Turbulent

Meleager and Atalanta (1747), II. 378

Melfi (Mitford, M. R., 1823) = Julian, v. 502

Melita, the Parsee's Daughter (Kennerley, J., 1882), v. 443

Melite (1776), III. 117, 336

Melmoth the Wanderer (West, B., 1823), IV. 503, 633

Melocosmiotes (1796), III. 336

Melodrama (1899), v. 718

Melodramania (Watson, T. M., 1894), v. 616

Melo-dramatist (1819), IV. 503

Melodrame Mad! (Dibdin, T. J., 1819), IV. 148, 301

Melpomene's Overthrow (Cawdell, J., 1778), III. 242

Melting Moments (Pemberton, T. E., 1884), v. 519

Meltonians (Peake, R. B., 1838), IV. 370

Melusine the Enchantress (Layton, G. M., 1874), v. 451, 802

Member for Slocum (Sims, G. R., 1881), v. 568

Member's Wife = House or the Home?

Memoirs of an Umbrella (1846), IV. 503

Memoirs of a Servant Girl = Mary Price

Memoirs of the D—l (Barber, J., 1842), IV. 259

Memoirs of the Duchess de Berri (1834), IV. 503

Memories (Palmer, T. A., 1878), v. 512

Mem. 7 (Lisle, W., 1879), v. 460

Men and Money = Day to Day

Men and Women (Buckland, J., 1899), 286

— (Fairbairn, Mrs R., 1882), v. 359

— (Lindo, F., 1890), v. 460

— (1828), IV. 503

+ Mendacious Mariner; or, Pretty Poll of Portsea, and the Captain with his Whiskers (Byron, H. J.: *Dicks* (in *Sensation Dramas*))

Mendicant (À Beckett, G. A., 1836), IV. 249

Mendicant Heir = May Morning

Mendicant Monks = Purse of Almo

Mendicant Murderer (1830), IV. 503

Mendicant Son (Stirling, E., 1845), IV. 408; v. 841

— (?Stirling, E., 1851), v. 718, 841

Mendicant's Revenge (Townsend, W. T., 1862), v. 821

Men in Pursuit of Money = All Alive and Merry

Men in the Gap = Inisfallen

Men of Metal (Clarke, C. A. and Silva, H. R., 1890), v. 312

Men of Pleasure (De Trueba, J. T., 1832), IV. 414

Men of the Day = Extremes

Men of the Wilderness = Wigwam

Men o' Sense (Burslem, C., 1876), v. 293

Mentalist (Gentleman, F., 1759), III. 264

Mephisto (Henley, W. E., 1886), v. 417

— (1880), v. 718

Mephistopheles (Brough, R. B. and Edwards, H. S., 1852), v. 278

— (1894), v. 718

Mephistopheles in Town = Devil's in Dr Faustus

Mercenary Lover, II. 378

Mercantile Lovers (Wallis, G., 1775), III. 314

Mercedes (Wood, F., 1896), v. 630

Mercer of Ludgate (Barnett, C. Z., 1847), IV. 261

Merchant (Colman, G., 1769), III. 246

Merchant and his Clerks (Coyne, J. S., 1842), IV. 284

Merchant and the Mendicant (Rice, C., 1858), v. 542, 813

Merchant of Bruges (Kinnaird, D. J. W., 1815), IV. 338

Merchant of Brussels = Widow's Son

Merchant of Guadeloupe (Wallace, J., 1802), IV. 416

Merchant of London (Serle, T. J., 1832), IV. 399

Merchant of Paisley (1870), v. 718

Merchant of Venice (Blanchard, E. L., 1843), IV. 268

— (Kemble, J. P., 1814), IV. 335

— (Talfourd, F., 1849), IV. 410

— (Valpy, R., 1802), IV. 415

— (1896), v. 718

— = Shylock

Merchant Prince of Cornville (1896), v. 718

Merchant's Clerk (Pitt, G. D., 1847), IV. 375

Merchant's Daughter (Barnett, C. Z., 1839), IV. 260

— (1884), v. 718

— = (1) Clarisse; (2) Grace Rivers; (3) Jarvis the Honest Man

Merchant's Daughter of Toulon (Thomas, Mrs E., 1856), v. 596

Merchant's Honour (1858), v. 718, 841

Merchant's Steed of Syracuse (1840), IV. 503

Merchant's Venture (Moore, R., 1868), v. 492

Merchant's Vow = Canonburg

Merchant's Wedding (Planché, J. R., 1828), IV. 378

Merchant's Wife of Havre = Two Clerks

Merciful Soul (1899), v. 718

Merciless Marauder = Alaric and Eliza

Merciless World = Light Ahead

Mercury Harlequin (Woodward, H., 1756), III. 209, 317

Mercury Harlequin in Ireland (1763), III. 336

Mercy (Goodwin, 1879), v. 384

Mercy Dodd = Presumptive Evidence

Mercy's Choice (1871), v. 718

Mercy to the Penitent = Babes of the Castle

Mere Blind (Villiers, E., 1871), v. 822

Mere Child (Marston, J. W., 1866), v. 479

Merely Acting (Ashlyn, Q., 1898), v. 245

Merely Players (1882), v. 718

— (1898), v. 718

Mere Question of Time (Malyon, E. J. and James, C., 1897), v. 473

Mere Scratch (1883), v. 718

Merit and Justice = Scales of Justice

Merit before Money = Choice

Merit is its own Reward = Honesty

Meritorious Maiden and the Millicious Milliner = Little Ben Bolt

Merlin (Giffard, W., 1736), II. 332

— (Theobald, L., 1734), II. 359

— (1767), III. 336

Merlin in Labour = Hint to the Theatres

Merlin in Love (Hill, A., 1760), II. 254–5, 438; III. 268

Merlin's Cave (1750), III. 336

— (1788), III. 336

— (1814), IV. 503

— = Royal Chace

Merlin's Mount (Dibdin, T. J., 1825), IV. 304

Mermaid (Dibdin, C. I. M., 1815), IV. 293

— (Franklin, A., 1792), III. 268

— (Galt, J., 1814), IV. 318, 636

— (Heath, S., 1887), v. 415

— (Walter, T. N., 1898), v. 612

— (1804), IV. 503

— (1822), IV. 503

Mermaiden's Well (+Calcraft, J. W., 1828), IV. 94, 503

Mermaids (Mackay, W. G., 1897), v. 470

Mermaid's Well = Bride of Lammermuir

Meroflède (Collingham, G. G., 1892), v. 317

Merope (Arnold, M., 1858), v. 244

— (Ayre, W., 1740), II. 73, 95, 296, 432

— (Hill, A., 1749), II. 59, 73, 110, 336, 418, 438

Merry Wives of Windsor (Kemble, J.
P., 1797), III. 279, 389; IV. 335
— (Reynolds, F., 1824), IV. 392
— (1812), IV. 140, 503
— (1850), V. 718
Merry Woodcutters = Sabotiers
Merry Zingara (Gilbert, W. S., 1868), V.
379
Mervyn Clitheroe (Conquest, G., 1859),
V. 718, 785, 841
Mesmeric Mystery (Osman, W. R.,
1867), V. 508
Mesmerism (Clyde, C., 1890), V. 315
Mesmerism versus Galvanism (Beswick,
G., 1845), IV. 267
Mesmerist (Conquest, G. and Robin-
son, H., 1879), V. 321
— (Jarman, F., 1890), V. 434
Message from Mars (Ganthony, R.,
1899), V. 376
Message from the Dead = Wrath
Message from the Sea (?Collins, W. W.,
1861), V. 318, 785
— (1869), V. 718
— (1873), V. 718
Message of Mercy (1898), V. 718
Messalina (Blackburn, V., 1899), V.
262
Messene Freed (Preston, W., 1792), III.
300
Messiah (1742), II. 396
Metamora (Stone, J. A., 1845), IV. 503,
633
Metamorphoses (Dibdin, C., 1775), III.
117, 254
— (1867), V. 718
Metamorphoses of Harlequin (1740), II.
378
Metamorphosis (Corye, J., 1704), II.
141, 145, 208, 231, 316
— (Jackson, W., 1783), III. 276
— (1723), II. 378
Metamorphosis of the Beggar's Opera
(1730), II. 378
Metaphysical Muddle (Moss, H., 1882),
V. 497
Meted Out! (Vellère, Dr, 1873), V.
607
Metempsychosis (Bernard, W. B.,
1832), IV. 265
— (Fonblanque, A., 1853), V. 370
— = Puss

Meteor (Gent, 1809), IV. 319 [The
sub-title should be "but a Bright
One", not "for a Bright One"]
Methinks I see my Father (Mathews,
C. J., 1837), IV. 503, 633
— (1849), IV. 503, 633
Methodism Display'd (Este, 1744), II.
447–8
Methodist (Pottinger, I., 1761), III. 299
— (1823), IV. 503
Methodist Preachers (1775), III. 336
Mexican Bandit (Young, Mrs H., 1863),
V. 719, 841
Mexican Bill (Stanhope, B., 1887), V.
579
Mexican's Watchword = War Woolf of
Tlascala
Mexico (1895), V. 719
Mezzetin Outwitted = Restoration of
Harlequin
Miami (Hollingshead, J., 1893), V. 424
Micawber (Collette, C., 1881), V. 784
Michael and Christine (Kerr, J., 1849),
IV. 84, 503, 592, 633
Michael and his Lost Angel (Jones,
H. A., 1896), V. 162, 168–9, 172, 189,
440
Michael Cange, the Porter of the
Abbaye (1832), IV. 503
Michael Ceno (1854), V. 719
Michael Dane's Grandson (Cassilis,
I. L., 1896), V. 306
Michael Earle, the Maniac Lover
(Wilks, T. E., 1839), IV. 421
Michael Howe, the Terror of Van
Dieman's Land (1821), IV. 503
Michaelmas Day (Vaile, 1851), V. 606
Michael Scott the Wizard = Anster Fair
Michael Strogoff (Byron, H. J., 1881), V.
299
Michel Perrin (Younge, A., 1850), V.
719, 825, 841
Michigan Chief = Rifle-Shot
Midas (O'Hara, K., 1762), III. 195, 291
— (1827), IV. 503
Mid-day Murder = Red Barn
Middle Dish (Oulton, W. C., 1804), IV.
366, 602
— (1815), IV. 503
Middleman (Jones, H. A., 1889), V.439
Middle Temple (Peake, R. B., 1829), IV.
370

Mildred's Well (Burnand, F. C. and Reed, G., 1873), v. 290

Milesian (Jackman, I., 1777), III. 207, 276

— (McDermott, J., 1772), III. 283

Milesian Mother = Chains of the Heart

Milesian's Trust in Luck = Erin-go-Bragh

Miles's Boy (Pitt, G. D., 1847), IV. 375

— (1835), IV. 503

Miles the Marauder = Wreck Ashore

Militant Couple (Villiers, G., 1704), I. 436

Military Billy Taylor (Burnand, F. C., 1869), v. 289, 781

Military Execution (Selby, C.), IV. 610

Military Manoeuvre (Dilley, J. J. and Clifton, L., 1879), v. 345

— (Elmer, G., 1899), v. 358

Military Manoeuvres (Bartholeyns, A. O'D., 1893), v. 252, 778

Military Marriage = Roll of the Drum

Military Movements (1831), IV. 503

— = Military Promotion

Military Nurse (1848), IV. 504

Military Promotion (1843), IV. 504

Military Punishment (1846), IV. 95, 504

Military Tactics (Planché, J. R., 1824), IV. 377, 378, 605

Military Tournament (Jecks, A. E., 1898), v. 435

Militia Muster (Beazley, S., 1832), IV. 504, 633

Milk Maid (Dibdin, C., 1787), III. 382; IV. 290

Milky White (Craven, H. T., 1864), v. 328

Miller and his Men (Pocock, I., 1813), IV. 101, 115–16, 384

— (Talfourd, F. and Byron, H. J., 1860), v. 590

— (1883), v. 719

Miller and the Maid (1898), v. 719

Miller Bit = Harlequin Happy

Miller of Derwent Water (Fitzball, E., 1853), v. 368

Miller of Fife (Lowe, W., 1869), v. 464

Miller of Goodwood = Miles's Boy

Miller of Grenoble = Gold Mine

Miller of Hazlebury (Carnegie, W., 1890), v. 303

Miller of Milberg (Lutz, M., 1872), v. 465

Miller of the Hartz Mountains = King of the Mist

Miller of Whetstone (Wilks, T. E., 1857), v. 623, 823

Miller outwitted (1752), III. 336

— = (1) Harlequin Collector; (2) More Sacks than One

Millers (Joubert, 1802), IV. 591

— (1802), IV. 504

Miller's Apprentice (1821), IV. 504

Miller's Daughter (Suter, W. E., 1865), v. 719, 819, 841

— (1818), IV. 504

— = Click Clack

Miller's Dog (1849), IV. 504

Miller's Holiday (1730), II. 379

Miller's Maid (Faucit, J. S., 1821), IV. 311

— (Waldron, F. G., 1804), III. 314; IV. 415

Miller's Trials = Mike

Miller's Wife (Fitzball, E., 1842), IV. 316

— (1854), v. 719

— = Giralda

Miller's Wife of Charlton = Three Johns

Mill Girl (Sheridan, B., 1884), v. 563

Millicent (Williams, 1868), v. 624

Mill in an Uproar (1861), v. 719

Milliner (Wood, A. C. F., 1893), v. 630

Milliners (Harpley, T., 1790), III. 266

— (Montague, C., 1838), IV. 600

— (1828), IV. 504

Milliners and Lifesguardsmen (1849), IV. 504

— (1854), v. 719

Milliner's Holyday (Morton, J. M., 1844), IV. 362

Milliner's Shop (1789), III. 336

Milliner to the King (Mathews, C. J., 1859), v. 719, 806, 841

Millionaire (Godfrey, G. W., 1883), v. 383

— (Towers, E., 1874), v. 601

Million of Money (Pettitt, H. and Harris, Sir A., 1890), v. 521

Millions in it (Gordon, G. L., 1877), v. 385

Millions of Money (Melville, A., 1886), v. 485

Mill of Aldervon (1829), IV. 504

Mill of Austerlitz = Treasure Seeker

Mill of Bagdad (1834), IV. 504

— = Barber

Mill of Berezina (Pitt, G. D., 1835), IV. 373

Mill of Glaris = Red Riven

Mill of Keben (1831), IV. 504

— = Siege of Montgatz

Mill of Marimount = Stanislaus of Poland

Mill of St Aldervon = Two Galley Slaves

Mill of the Happy Valley (Hazlewood, C. H., 1870), v. 797

Mill of the Lake (1827), IV. 504

Mill of the Loire = Soldier's Widow

Mill of the Pyrenees (Webb, C., 1836), IV. 504, 616

Millo' Taftie Annie (1888), v. 719

Mills of God (Overton, R., 1892), v. 509

Mills of the Eternal = Master of Hope

Milly, the Collier's Wife = Lost for Ever

Milo of Brittany = Wood Wolf of the Black Mountains

Milord Sir Smith = Campano

Mimi (Boucicault, D., 1872), v. 269

Mimic Art and Attic Science = Scheming and Seeming

Mina (Linley, G., 1849), IV. 504, 633

Minc'd Pie (Moser, J., 1806), IV. 364

Mind's Magnet = Riches

Mind the Shop (Reece, R. and Righton, E., 1878), v. 538

Mind your Letters (1833), IV. 504

Mind Your Own Business (Lemon, M., 1852), v. 455

Mind your Points (1869), v. 719

— = Line of Life

Mind your Stops (1850), v. 719

Mine (Cross, J. C., 1800), IV. 286

— (Sargent, J., 1785), III. 304

— = Married for Money

Mine and Countermine = Plot and Passion

Mine Friend and the Lake Fay (1852), v. 719

Mine Girl of Kebal (1846), IV. 504

Mine Hostess (Webster, D., 1899), v. 618

Mine Host of the Flagon = Baron's Daughter

Mine of Wealth (Towers, E., 1867), v. 600

Minerali (Grattan, H. P., 1835). IV. 383

— (1835), IV. 504, 633

Miner of Mexico = Ocean Grave

Miner's Dog (1872), v. 719

Miner's Luck (Edwards, F., 1894), v. 355

Miners' Queen (Jarman, F., 1892), v. 434

Miners' Strike = Strike

Minerva and Ulysses (1746), II. 379

Minerva's Triumph = Don Sancho

Minerva's Triumphs = Words made visible

Mines of Ischinski = Iwan

Mines of Poland (1822), IV. 82, 504

Mines of Rubies = Orphan of Hindoostan

Minette's Birthday (André, R., 1889), v. 241

Miniature (1836), IV. 504

Miniature Picture (Craven, E., 1780), III. 20, 41, 170, 249

Minister (Lewis, M. G., 1797), III. 63, 281, 390

Minister and the Favourite (1856), v. 841

Minister and the Mercer (Bunn, A., 1834), IV. 19, 38, 84, 183, 276

Ministering Angel (Doone, N. and Newte, H. C. W., 1893), v. 347

Minister of Finance (1849), IV. 504

Minister of Spain (Wooler, J. P., 1863), v. 632

Minister's Call (Symons, A., 1892), v. 589

Minkalay (Leeds, A. and Reade, G., 1896), v. 453

Minna (Edwards, H. S., 1886), v. 355

Minna von Barnhelm (Holcroft, F., 1805), IV. 326

Minnie (Byron, H. J., 1869), v. 297

Minnie Grey (Davis, S., 1856), v. 787

— (Johnstone, J. B., 1852), v. 438

— (Young, H. and Roberts, G., 1886), v. 636

— (1852), v. 719

Minnie Grey (1853), v. 719
Minnie Grey, the Gipsey Girl (1852), v. 719
Minor (Foote, S., 1760), III. 172–3, 260, 384, 403
Minorca (Dell, H., 1756), III. 253
Minstrel (Ebsworth, J., 1822), IV. 308
— (West, J., 1805), IV. 418
— = Forest of Ardennes
Minstrel Boy (Pitt, G. D., 1846), IV. 374
— (1829), IV. 504
Minstrel Maid (Dibdin, T. J., 1822) = Tale of Other Times, IV. 504
Minstrel of Lochmaben (Lynch, T. J., 1827), IV. 504, 633
Minstrels of Provence (1848), IV. 633
Mint of Money (Law, A., 1884), v. 450
Minute Gun at Sea (Barnett, C. Z., 1845), IV. 260
— (1856), v. 719
Minx and the Man (Lindo, F., 1895), v. 460
Mirabel (Dering, C. E. and Holloway, J., 1883), v. 343
Miracle (Howell-Poole, W., 1883), v. 429
— (1839), IV. 504
Miracle of Love = Warrior Slaves
Miracles of the Moon = Devil on Two Sticks
Miraculous Cold Water Cure = Wonderful Water Cure
Miraculous Cure (Forde, B., 1771), III. 115, 261
— (1881), v. 719
Miraculous Doll (Wardroper, W., 1886), v. 614, 823
Mirage (Cleary, E., 1888), v. 313
Miranda (1844), IV. 504
— (1855), v. 719
Mirandola (Cornwall, B., 1821), IV. 283
Mirette (Greenbank, H., 1894), v. 392
Miriam (Park, L. J., 1849), IV. 603
Miriam Gray (Patmore, W. J., 1896), v. 515
Miriam's Crime (Craven, H. T., 1863), v. 328
Mirka the Enchantress (1895), v. 719
Mirror (Campbell, A. V., 1830), IV. 278
— (Dibdin, C., 1779), III. 255
Mirror for the Ladies (1779), III. 336
Mirror of Fate (1844), IV. 504

Mirror of Witchcraft = Silver Star
Mirrour (Dell, H., 1756), III. 253
— (1737), II. 379
Mirrour of the late Times = Rump
Mirsa and Lindor (1794), III. 336
Mirth and Harlequin (Dibdin, T. J., 1811), IV. 299
Mirth and Magic (1790, 1795), III. 336, 402
Mirza (Bryant, W., 1893), v. 284
Mis-adventures of a Night = Dark Events
Misanthrope = (1) Chaubert; (2) King of the Alps
Misanthropy and Repentance (1821), IV. 504
— = Stranger
Misapprehension (Dance, C., 1831), IV. 504, 633
Miscarriage of Justice (Roy, G., 1882), v. 552
Mischance (Dibdin, C., 1772), III. 254
Mischief (Bridgman, C., 1886), v. 275
Mischief Maker (Henderson, E., 1891), v. 416
Mischief Making (Buckstone, J. B., 1828), IV. 273
— = Gossip
Mischievous Annie (1856) = Lesson for Husbands, v. 706, 719, 838, 841
Mischievous Eyes (Bayly, J. H., 1838), IV. 504, 633
Misconception (Rose, E., 1873), v. 549
— (1831), IV. 504
Misconstructions (1862), v. 719
Miser (Boissy, C., III. 239
— (Cross, J., 1887), v. 330
— (Fielding, H., 1733), II. 28, 135, 137, 143, 144, 158–9, 165, 178, 326, 436
— (Gomm, E. H., 1884), v. 384
— (Hughes, J., 1735), II. 144, 338
— (Mitchell, S. W., 1891), v. 490
— (Shadwell, T., 1672), I. 85, 188, 204–5, 430
— (Thurmond, J., 1727) = Wagner and Abericot, II. 360
— (Wild, J., 1789), III. 316
— (1793), III. 336
— (1890), v. 719
Miser and his Daughter = Miser's Daughter
Miser Bit (1742), II. 452

Miseries of Civil War = Misery of Civil
War

Miseries of Human Life (Dibdin, T. J.,
1807), IV. 298

— (Webster, B. N., 1845), IV. 418

Miseries of Love (1732), II. 379

Miser of Bagdad = Crazy Old Slippers

Miser of Clerkenwell = Colonel Jack

Miser of Coventry = Edmund Atherton

Miser of Eltham Green (1867), v. 719

— = Last Man

Miser of Lewes (1823), IV. 633

Miser of Madrid (1831), IV. 504

Miser of Shoreditch (Prest, T. P., 1854),
V. 530, 811

Miser of Tewkesbury (1854), v. 719

Miser of the Hill Fort = Inundation

Miser of Walden = Young Courier

Miser Outwitted (1848), IV. 504

— = He must be Married

Miser Reformed (1812), IV. 504

— = Temple of Plutus

Miser's Daughter (Millingen, J. G.,
1835), IV. 356

— (Stirling, E., 1842), IV. 407

— (Taylor, T. P., 1835), IV. 411

— (1885), v. 719

— = (1) Avarice; (2) Hilda; (3) Jew's
Daughter

Miser Smoked (1823), IV. 504

Misers of Smyrna (1810), IV. 504

Miser's Resolve upon the Lowering of
Interest = Fame

Miser's Retreat = Whim

Miser's Treasure (Mortimer, J., 1878),
V. 494

Miser's Warning = Christmas Carol

Miser's Will (Craven, T., 1889), v.
329

— (Peake, R. B., 1844), IV. 504, 633

Miser, the Maid and the Mangle =
Ingomar the Idiotic

Miser Tricked = Stratagem of Harlequin

Misery of Civil-War (Crowne, J., 1680),
I. 79, 399

Misfortunes of an Exile = Charles Edward Stuart the Pretender in Scotland

Misjudged (Gilbert, E., 1884), v. 378

Misled (Wilmot, A. A., 1887), v. 628

Misogynist = Woman Hater

Misplaced Affections (1863), v. 719

Misrepresentor Represented (1755), III.
402

Miss Betty (1898), v. 719

Miss Chester (Young, Sir C. L. and
Marryatt, F., 1872), v. 635

Miss Chiquita (Sims, G. R., 1899), v.
570

Miss Cinderella (Walkes, W. R., 1890),
v. 611

Miss Decima (Burnand, F. C., 1891), v.
292, 782

Miss Eily O'Connor (Byron, H. J.,
1861), v. 296

Miss Eliza Cook (1846), IV. 505

Miss Esmeralda (Leslie, F. and Mills,
H., 1887), v. 456

Miss Formosa (1870), v. 719

Miss Forrester (1876), v. 719

Miss Francis of Yale = Leading Lady

Miss Galatea of Oregon (Cleveland,
E. A., 1894), v. 314

Miss Gwilt (Collins, W. W., 1875), v.
318

Miss Hobbs (Jerome, J. K., 1899), v.
436

Miss Hoyden's Husband (Daly, A.,
1890), v. 333

Miss Impudence (Morton, E. A., 1892),
v. 494

Missing (Gibney, S., 1894), v. 378

— (Melford, M., 1890), v. 484

— (Newbound, E., 1881), v. 503

Missing Duchess = Night in Paris

Missing Link (Collier, H., 1886), v. 317

— (Shirley, A., 1894), v. 564

— (1893), v. 719

Missing Mortgage (1883), v. 719

Missing Waterloo (1880), v. 719

Missing Witness (Braddon, M. E.,
1880), v. 273

Miss in her Breeches = Country Coquet

Miss in her Teens (Garrick, D., 1747),
II. 138, 216, 330, 419, 437

Mission from Rome into Great Britain
in the Cause of Popery and the Pretender (?1746), II. 379

Mission of Mercury (Rede, W. L.,
1841), IV. 390

— = King's Pledge

Mission to Borneo (1848), IV. 505

Missis Brown of the "Missis" sippi =
"Grin" Bushes

Modern Ireland (Sager, R. F., 1890), v.
554
Modern Judas (Guion, N. C., 1892), v.
397
Modern Juliet (1893), v. 720
Modern Life in London = Fanny
Wyndham
Modern Magician = Wonder Worker
Modern Marriage (Doone, N., 1890), v.
347
Modern Marriage Match = Marriage
(1892)
Modern Misses (Loveday, W., 1812),
IV. 347
Modern Orpheus (Webster, B. N.,
1837), IV. 417
Modern Pimp (1736), II. 379
Modern Poetasters (1725), II. 379
Modern Practice = Quack, Quack,
Quack
Modern Promise to Pay = Frank-in-
Steam
Modern Prophets (D'Urfey, T., 1709),
II. 22, 130, 176, 194, 320
Modern Receipt (1739), II. 379
Modern Semiramide (1843), IV. 505
Modern Sentiment = Sons of Erin
Modern Sentiments = Sons of Erin
Modern Shrew (1889), v. 720
Modern Sinbad the Sailor (1892), v.
720
Modern Student = Folly as it Flies
Modern Tragedy = First Act of Taste
Modern Travellers (1822), IV. 505
Modern Tutor (Field, W. F., 1892), v.
366
Modern Vittoria Bracciano (1832), IV.
505
Modern Wife (Stevens, J., 1744), II.
216, 358
— (1771), III. 336
— = Distress'd Wife
Modern Wives (Warren, E., 1887), v.
614
Modern Wizard (Henderson, J., 1895),
v. 416
Modes of the Court = Mr Taste the
Poetical Fop
Modish Citizens = Fair Example
Modish Couple (Boadens, C., 1732), II.
14, 201–2, 299, 432; III. 116
Modish Gallants = Intriguing Courtiers

Modish Husband (Burnaby, W., 1702),
II. 50, 153–4, 301
Modish Lovers = Mall
Modish Wife (Gentleman, F., 1761),
III. 264
— = Tom Essence
Moggy and Jemmy (1799), III. 336
Mogul Tale (Inchbald, Mrs E., 1784),
III. 275, 388
— (1805), IV. 505
Mohammed (1853), v. 720
Mohawk Chief = Oconesto
Mohicans of Paris (Elton, E. and
Hazlewood, C. H., 1873), v. 720, 790,
796, 841
Mohocks (Gay, J., 1712), II. 214, 240,
330
Mokana (Cooper, W., 1843), IV. 283
Mokanna (1891), v. 720
Molière (Frith, W., 1891), v. 374
Molly (1884), v. 720
Molly Malone (1862), v. 720
Molly Maydew (1865), v. 720
Molly Sullivan (Pitt, G. D., 1855), v.
720, 810, 841
Moment of Terror (Conquest, G.,
1862), v. 720, 785, 841
Momentous Question (Fitzball, E.,
1844), IV. 316
Moments of Mystery (Buckstone, J. B.,
1831), IV. 505
Momus's Gift (1795), III. 336
+ Momus's Motto; or, Harlequin in
Malabar (Dibdin, C. I. M.; R.A.,
1798)
Momus turn'd Fabulist (Forrest, E.,
1729), II. 145, 237, 244–5, 379, 436,
448
Monarch and the Mimic = Frederick of
Prussia
Monarchicall Image (Fleming, R.,
1691), I. 412
Monarch of the World (1885), v. 720
Monarch, the Maiden, the Maze and
the Mixture = Fair Rosamond's
Bower
Mona's Dream (1895), v. 720
Monastery (1820), IV. 505
Monastery of St Juste (Oxenford, J.,
1864), v. 510
Mona, the Bride of Glen Maye (Slater,
A., 1893), v. 571

Moncrieff (Millard, A., 1896), v. 488

Money (Lytton, Lord, 1840), IV. 45, 173–5, 349, 596; V. 120, 121, 126, 194

Money and Misery (Wilkins, J. H., 1855), v. 623

Money and Music = Honest Frauds

Money at a Pinch (Robson, H., 1793), III. 302

Money Bags (Pemberton, T. E. and Shannon, 1885), v. 519

Money Diggers (Milner, H. M., 1829), IV. 505, 633

Money is an Asse (Jordan, T., 1668), I. 415

Money Lender (Ford, T. M., 1888), v. 370

— (Lee, N., Jr., 1861), v. 720, 802

Money Mad (Mackaye, J. S., 1890), v. 471

Money Spider (Eliot, A., 1897), v. 356

Money Spinner (Pinero, Sir A. W., 1880), v. 173, 524

Money the Mistress (Southerne, T., 1726), II. 356

Money works Wonders = Bird in a Cage

Monica (Swarbreck, J. W., 1893), v. 589

Monk = Aurelio and Miranda

Monkeyana = Jack Robinson and his Monkey

Monkey and the Murder = Easter Fair

Monkey Island (1824), IV. 505

Monkey of the Wreck = Treacherous Black

Monkey that has seen the World (Moncrieff, W. T., 1831), IV. 505, 633

Monkey, the Mask and the Murderer = Who Owns the Head?

Monkish Warriors = Victims of Tyranny

Monk of Palluzi = False Penitent

Monks and Smugglers (1820), IV. 505

Monks' Cowl (Moncrieff, W. T., 1818), IV. 505, 633

Monks of St Nicholas = Mystery

Monks of the Great St Bernard = Julian and Agnes

Monk's Room (Lart, J., 1887), v. 449

Monk, the Friend and the Enemy = Daemon of the Drachenfalls

Monk, the Mask and the Murderer (Amherst, J. H.), v. 254

Monmouth Up-to-Date (Mackay, D., 1895), v. 469

Monomania (1838), IV. 505

Monopolizer Outwitted (McLaren, A., 1800), III. 284; IV. 350

Monopoly (1782), III. 336, 402

Monseigneur (Archer, T., 1845), IV. 255

— (Reynoldson, T. H., 1844), IV. 393

— (1845), IV. 505

Monsieur Alphonse (Vaughan, Mrs, 1875), v. 607

Monsieur de Paris = Executioner's Daughter

Monsieur de Pourceaugnac (Ozell, J., 1704), II. 144, 152, 216, 442

— = Squire Trelooby

Monsieur in the Suds = Harlequin Sclavonian

Monsieur Jacques (Barnett, M., 1836), IV. 261

Monsieur Laroche (Bellingham, H., 1878), v. 257

Monsieur La Saxe's Disappointment = Schemes of Harlequin

Monsieur le Duc (Prinsep, V., 1879), v. 531

Monsieur Malbrouk (1827), IV. 505

Monsieur Mallet (Moncrieff, W. T., 1829), IV. 183, 359

Monsieur Raggou = Old Troop

Monsieur Tonson (Moncrieff, W. T., 1821), IV. 359

Mons. Moulan = Fisher Girl

Monster (1790), III. 337

Monster and the Magician (Kerr, J., 1826), IV. 592

Monster Ballroom of 1837 = Elements— Earth, Air, Fire, Water

Monster of Mysore and the Fiend of the Whirlpool = Kerim the Pearl Diver

Monster of the Cave (1798), III. 337

Monster of the Eddystone (Pitt, G. D., 1834), IV. 372

Monster of the Glen (Dibdin, C. I. M., 1826), IV. 296

Monster of the Woods (1772), III. 337

Monstrum Horrendum (1732), II. 379

Montagu (Gemmell, R., 1868), v. 377

Montalbert (1815), IV. 505

Montaldi (1818), IV. 505

Montaleoni (Young, H., 1853), v. 636

Montalto (À Court, W., 1821), IV. 505, 567, 633

— = Guerilla Chief

Montbar (Moore, T., 1804), IV. 361

Mont Blanc (Campbell, A., 1853), V. 301

— (Mayhew, A., 1874), V. 483

— (Wilks, T. E., 1853), V. 623

Montcalm (Young, Sir C. L., 1872), V. 635

Monte Carlo (Carlton, S., 1894), V. 303

— (1887), V. 720

— (1891), V. 720

Monte Cristo (Henry, R., 1886), V. 417, 797

— (1860), V. 720

— (1868), V. 720

— (1888), V. 720

— (1899), V. 720

Monte d'Or (1828), IV. 505

Montem (Rowe, H., 1808), IV. 396

Monte the Prisoner (1856), V. 720

Montezuma (Brooke, H., 1778), III. 240

— (Sladden, D., 1838), IV. 402

— (Stephens, G., 1823), IV. 612

Month after Date = Divided Duty

Month from Home (1857), V. 720

Months and Mummery = April Fools

Montilladios (1897), V. 721

Montoni (Sheil, R. L., 1820), IV. 401, 610

Montrano, the Pirate Lord of Sicily (Atkyns, S., 1845), IV. 257

Montrezar (1840), IV. 633

Montrose (Atkinson, 1829), IV. 569

— (Dibdin, T. J., 1819), IV. 94, 302, 505, 580, 633

— (Murray, W. H., 1823), IV. 94, 365

— (Pocock, I., 1822), IV. 94, 384

— (1820), IV. 94, 505

— (1826), IV. 94, 633

— (1827), IV. 94, 505

— (1847), IV. 94, 505

Mont St Michel (Bernard, W. B., 1852), V. 259

Monument in Arcadia (Keate, G., 1773), III. 278

Mooltan and Googerat (1849), IV. 505

Moonbeams (Russell, E. H., 1891), V. 553

Moonflowers: A Cobweb (1891), V. 721

Moonlight Blossom (Fernald, C. B., 1899), V. 211, 365

Moonlight Jack (Travers, W., 1866), V. 721, 821, 841

Moonlight Knight = Sir Marigold the Dottie

Moonlight Night = Fairy Legends

Moon Maiden (1845), IV. 505

Moon Queen and King Knight (Crowquill, A., 1849), IV. 287

Moon's Age (Addison, H. R., 1835), IV. 505, 633

Moonshine (Booth, J. H., 1892), V. 267

— (Stuart-Wortley, Lady E., 1843), IV. 506, 633

Moonstone (Collins, W. W., 1877), V. 318

Moonstruck (Reece, R., 1873), V. 538

Moorish Banditti (1806), IV. 506

Moor of Sicily = Avenger

Moor of Toledo (1836), IV. 506

Moors and Africans = Fair Slave

Moors in Grenada = Alonzo the Patriot

Moors in Spain = Florinda

Moors of Spain (1841), IV. 82, 506

— = Charlemagne

Moor's Revenge = Abdelazer

Moor the Merrier = Boabdil el Chico

Morah, the Beast Tamer (1848), IV. 506

Moral Brand = Alice Grey

Morality (1882), V. 721

Moral Philosopher (Selby, C., 1843), IV. 399

Moral Quack (Bacon, P., 1757), III. 235

Moral Suasion (Palmer, T. A., 1875), V. 512

Mora's Love (D'Egville, 1809), IV. 506, 633

Morass of the Murdered = Will o' the Wisp

Morays (1884), V. 721

Mordecai (1851), V. 841

Mordecai Lyons (Harrigan, E., 1882), V. 404

Mordecai's Beard (1790), III. 337

Morden Grange (Burnand, F. C., 1869), V. 289

More Blunders = Advertisement for a Husband

More Blunders than One (Rodwell, G. H., 1824), IV. 395

Moreen and Sham Van Voght (1862), V. 721

More Ethiopians (1847), IV. 506

More Flirts than One = Belle Have at Ye All

More Free than Welcome (Suter, W. E.), v., 588

More Frightened than Hurt (Jerrold, D. W., 1821), IV. 331, 590

— (1785), III. 337

— = (1) Execution; (2) Wife's Stratagem

More Good News = Orange Boven

More Jonathans = Tarnation Strange

More Kotzebue (1799), III. 337

More Laugh than Love = Gay Deceivers

More Marriages than One = Count of Anjou

More Merry than Wise (1837), IV. 506

More Precious than Gold (Cheltnam, C. S., 1861), v. 309

More Reform! (1831), IV. 506

More Sacks than One (1817), IV. 506

More Scenes in Town = Mirror

More Secrets than One = Man and Wife

More Sinned against than Sinning (1892), v. 721

More than ever (Matthison, A., 1882), v. 481

More than meets the Eye = Laurette's Bridal

More the Merrier = Wives in Plenty

More Visitors in Town (1838), IV. 506

More Ways than Means (Colman, G., the Younger, 1786) = Ways and Means, III. 337, 379, 403

More Ways than One (Cowley, Mrs H., 1783) = New Ways to Catch Hearts, III. 167, 249

— (1819), IV. 506

— = (1) Contrivances; (2) Simon

More Ways than One for a Wife = Petticoat-Plotter

More Ways than One to Win Her (1745), II. 379

More Wives than One = Thelyphthora

Morgiana (Du Maurier, G., 1892), v. 352

Morgue (1828), IV. 506

Morilda's Wand (1821), IV. 506

Morlais Castle in the Olden Time = Lily of Pontsarn

Mormon (Calthorpe, W. D., 1887), v. 300

Mormons (1881), v. 721

Morna of the Glen (Prest, T. P.), v. 811

Morning at Margate = Fortune Hunter

Morning at Versailles in 1750 = Promotion

Morning Call (Dance, C., 1851), IV. 289; v. 335

Morning Drive (Plant, F. W., 1896), v. 528

Morning, Noon and Night (Dibdin, T. J., 1822), IV. 303

Morning of Life (1852), v. 721

Morning Post and the Morning Herald (Pocock, I., 1811), IV. 383

Morning Ramble (Payne, H. N., 1672), I. 77, 216–17, 347, 423

Morning Star and the Gipsey's Brick = Michael Ceno

Moro (Barrett, W., 1882), v. 250

Morocco Bound (Branscombe, A., 1893), v. 274

Morphia Maniac = White Devil

Mortgage Deeds (Hazlewood, C. H., 1875), v. 415

Moscow (Moncrieff, W. T., 1810), IV 358

— (1819), IV. 506

Moses and Mammon (Dibdin, C. I. M., 1800), IV. 290

Moses and Shadrac (1780), III. 337, 403

Moses and Son (Gordon, J., 1892), v. 385

Moses in the Bulrushes (More, Mrs H., 1782), III. 288

— (1793), III. 337

Moslem's Oath = Alp, the Renegade

Mossoo in London (Grain, R. C., 1888), v. 387

Moss Rose Rent (Law, A., 1883), v. 450

Most Excellent Story = Prisoner of War

Most Unwarrantable Intrusion (Morton, J. M., 1849), IV. 363

Most Votes (Dibdin, C., 1804), IV. 290

Most Votes carry it = Love at a Loss

Moth and Flame (Moore, F. F., 1878), v. 492

Mother (Harvey, F., 1879), v. 408

— (Jerrold, D. W., 1838), IV. 333

— = Domenica

Mother and Child (Morton, J. M., 1879), v. 497

Mother and Child are doing well (Morton, J. M., 1845), IV. 362

— (1855), v. 721

Mother and Daughter = Star of my Home

Mother and Son (Bell, S., 1883), v. 256

Moulds of the Mould Manor (1856), v.
721
Mountain Bandit (1824), IV. 506
Mountain Cataract (1844), IV. 506
Mountain Cataran (Barnett, C. Z.),
IV. 570
Mountain Chief (1818), IV. 506
Mountain Cottager = Mouse-traps
Mountain Devil (Reeves, G., 1879), v.
540
— (1854), v. 721
Mountain Dhu (Halliday, A., 1866), v.
400
Mountaineers (Colman, G., the
Younger, 1793), III. 104, 123, 247; IV.
32
— = Maniac of the Sierra Morena
Mountaineers' Dance (1859), v. 721
Mountain Farm = Blind Sister
Mountain Flower (Travers, W., 1864),
v. 721, 821
Mountain Guide (1895), v. 721
Mountain Haunt = Bandit of Sicily
Mountain Heiress (À Beckett, G. A.,
1883), v. 234
Mountain Home = Fall of the Avalanche
Mountain Hut (Planché, J. R., 1821),
IV. 377
Mountain King (Almar, G.), IV. 253
— (Nance, A. and Winterbottom, J.,
1875), v. 501
— = Castle Burners
Mountain Maid (1837), IV. 506
Mountain Monarch (1855), v. 721
Mountain of Miseries (1797), III. 337
Mountain Pass = (1) Alp, the Tartar
Khan; (2) Guerilla Chief
Mountain Robber = (1) Camilla the
Amazon; (2) Maid of Genoa
Mountain Robbers (1806), IV. 506
— (1863), v. 721
Mountain Smugglers = Manslayer
Mountains of Modena (1826), IV. 506
Mountains of Saxony = Adrian and
Orrila
Mountain Sylph (Thackeray, T. J.,
1834), IV. 412
Mountain Torrents (1861), v. 721
Mountebank (Motteux, P. A., 1705), II.
346
— (1715), II. 379
— (1805), IV. 506

Mountebank (1851), v. 721
Mountebank of Ravenna = Love Spell
Mountebanks (Gilbert, W. S., 1892), v.
381
Mounted Brigands of the Abruzzi =
(1) Carlo Brunari; (2) Horse of the
Cavern
Mounted Brigands of Valentia = Manuel
of Spain
Mounting Sylph (Rogers, W., 1844), IV.
396
— (1838), IV. 506
— (1839), IV. 507
Mount St Bernard (Moncrieff, W. T.,
1839), v. 507, 600, 633
— (1834), IV. 507
Mournful Nuptials (Cooke, T., 1739),
II. 123, 316
Mourning Bride (Congreve, W., 1697),
I. 69, 73, 143-4, 180, 398
— = School for Greybeards
Mouse Trap (White, J., 1853), v. 620
— (1897), v. 721
— = (1) Fool's Paradise; (2) Mars and
Venus
Mouse-traps (Dibdin, T. J., 1819), IV.
302
Mousquetaires au Couvent (Farnie,
H. B., 1880), v. 362, 791
Moustache Movement (Brough, R. B.,
1854), v. 278
Mouth of the Nile (Dibdin, T. J., 1798)
= News from the Nile, III. 256, 383
Mouth of the Pit (Miller, W. F., 1892),
v. 489
Move on (Mortimer, J., 1883), v. 494
Moving Statues (1840), IV. 634
Moving Tale (Lemon, M., 1854), v.
455
Mowbray Chase (1859), v. 721
Moyna-a-Roon (Levey, J. C., 1875), v.
458
Moyra (Pitt, G. D., 1845), IV. 374
Moyra the Doomed (1854), v. 721
M.P. (Moore, T., 1811), IV. 361
— (Robertson, T. W., 1870), v. 546
— = Love and Laugh
M.P. for Puddlepool (Summers, K.,
1868), v. 587
M.P. for the Rotten Borough (Lemon,
M., 1838), IV. 343
M.P.'s Wife (1895), v. 721

Mr Albert Smith's Ascent of Mont Blanc (Smith, A. R., 1854), v. 572

Mr Albert Smith's Ascent of Mont Blanc; Holland and up the Rhine (Smith, A. R., 1854), v. 572

Mr and Mrs Briggs (Rodwell, G. H. and Lee, N., 1851), v. 548

Mr and Mrs Grubb (1840), IV. 507

Mr and Mrs Gulliver (1870), v. 721

Mr and Mrs Muffet (Smith, L., 1892), v. 573

Mr and Mrs Pringle (De Trueba, J. T., 1832), IV. 414

Mr and Mrs Toodles = Farmer's Daughter of the Severnside

Mr and Mrs White (1854), v. 721

Mr Anthony (Boyle, R., 1672), I. 17, 69, 257, 393

Mr B— (Stafford, J. J., 1833), IV. 612

Mr Barnes of New York (Barrington, R., 1888), v. 251

Mr Bayes Practice = Prunella

Mr Bony's Wedding = Empress and No Empress

Mr Briggs (1849), IV. 507

Mr Briggs in his Pleasures of House Keeping (1854), v. 721

Mr Buckstone at Home (Coyne, J. S., 1863), v. 328

Mr Buckstone's Ascent of Mount Parnassus (Planché, J. R., 1853), v. 9, 527

Mr Buckstone's Voyage round the Globe (Planché, J. R., 1854), v. 527

Mr Busy (1832), IV. 507

Mr Chairman (Fitzball, E., 1829), IV. 313

Mr Cynic (Locke, W. J. and Roper, G., 1893), v. 462

Mr Dick's Heir (Crofton, C. and Brooke, H., 1895), v. 330

Mr Donnithorpe's Rent (Seaton, R., 1890), v. 559

Mr Fitz W—? (Newte, H. C. W., 1894), v. 503

Mr Flimsey's Family (1868), v. 721

Mr Gorilla (Addison, H. R., 1861), v. 235

Mr Greenfinch (Bayly, T. H., 1838), IV. 263

Mr Greenlea's Courtship (Mudie, G., 1891), v. 498

Mr Guffin's Elopement (Law, A. and Grossmith, G., 1882), v. 450

Mr H— (Lamb, C., 1806), IV. 123-4, 341

Mr Hughes at Home (1856), v. 721

Mr Jarley at Court (1899), v. 721

Mr Jericho (Greenbank, H., 1893), v. 392

Mr Joffin's Latchkey (Robinson, N., 1875), v. 547

Mr Jolliboy's Conjugal Woes (1878), v. 722

Mr Limberham = Kind Keeper

Mr Martin (Hawtrey, C., 1896), v. 410

Mr Midshipman Easy (Oxenford, J., 1836) = Midshipman Easy, IV. 507, 634

Mr Napie's Reception in Elba (McLaren, A., 1814), IV. 351

Mr Neville's Sheep = Follow the Leader

Mr Nightingale's Diary (Lemon, M., 1851), v. 455

Mr N'Importe (Dibdin, C. I. M., 1825), IV. 296

Mr Paul Pry (1826), IV. 507

Mr Pep (1835), IV. 634

Mr Peppercorn at Home = Gallantee Showman

Mr Pickwick's Little Mistake (1892), v. 722

Mr Potter of Texas (Stephens, W., 1888), v. 581

Mr Richards (Bourchier, A. and Blair, J., 1892), v. 270

Mr Robert Roy, Hielan Helen, his Wife and Dougald the Dodger (Lowe, W., 1880), v. 464

Mrs Annesley (Cooke, J. F., 1891), v. 324

Mrs Beflat's Blunder (Routledge, W., 1869), v. 552

Mrs Brown (Wilton, J. H., 1874), v. 629

Mrs Brown at the Play (Sketchley, A., 1863), v. 570

Mrs Bunbury's Spoons (Coyne, J. S., 1849), IV. 507, 634

Mrs Caudle (Barnett, C. Z., 1845), IV. 507, 634

Mrs Caudle Abroad and at Home (1845), IV. 507

Mrs Caudle's Adventures in France = Mrs Caudle Abroad and at Home

Mr Walker's Trunks (Ebsworth, J., 1837), IV. 308

Mr Webster's Company is requested at a photographic Soirée (Yates, E. and Harrington, N. H., 1858), V. 722, 795, 825, 841

Mr Weller's Watch (1840), IV. 97, 507

Much Ado about Nothing (Kemble, J. P., 1797), III. 279, 389; IV. 335

— = Cabinet

Much Ado about Nothing (as usual) = Competition

Much too clever (Oxenford, J. and Hatton, J., 1874), V. 510

Mudborough Election (Brough, W. and Halliday, A., 1865), V. 280

Muddled and Mixed = Sock and Buckskin

Muddler (Hill, H., 1890), V. 421

Muddles (Jessup, 1885), V. 437

Muette de Portici (1845), IV. 507, 634

Muffled Bells of Paris = Dead Duchess

Muff of the Regiment (Ganthony, R., 1898), V. 376

— = Goodbye

Mufti's Tomb (1828), IV. 507

— = Misers of Smyrna

Mugwump (1898), V. 722

Mulatto = Mathilde

Mulatto Murderer (1854), V. 722

Mulatto Nobleman = Serpent on the Hearth

Mulberry Bush (Albery, J., 1882), V. 238

Mulberry-Garden (Sedley, Sir C., 1668), I. 27, 187, 214, 234–5, 344, 427

Muldoon's Picnic (Pleon, H., 1886), V. 183, 528

Mule-driver and his Dogs (1846), IV. 507

Muleteer (Frazer, T. J., 1844), IV. 318

Muleteer and his Monkey = Napoleon's Godson

Muleteer of Toledo (Morton, J. M., 1855), V. 495

— (Robertson, T. W., 1856), V. 546

Muleteer's Vow (Haines, J. T. or Serle, T. J., 1835), IV. 507, 634

Mulic the Slave (1802), IV. 507

Mullibaloo (Green, F. W., 1874), V. 390

Multum in Parvo = Two Thumbs

Mummies and Marriage (Mackinnon, A. M. and Adderley, J. G., 1888), V. 471

Mummy (Bernard, W. B., 1833), IV. 265

— (Brand, O., 1884), V. 273

— (Day, G. D. and Bowkett, S., 1895), V. 339

Mummy and the Study of Living Pictures = Raphael's Dream

Mumps the Masher (Craven, T. and Nelson, R., 1884), V. 329

Mungo Park (Corri, M.?, 1844), IV. 578

— (1819), IV. 507

— (1824), IV. 507

— (1841), IV. 507

Mungo Parke (Bernard, B., 1840), IV. 507, 634

Murat (1843), IV. 507

Murder and Madness (Dibdin, C. I. M., 1825), IV. 295, 507, 580, 634

Murder at Sadlers Wells = Ruby Ring

Murder at the Black Farm = John Stafford

Murder at the Dead Man's Pool = Dark Night's Work

Murder at the Hall = Crock of Gold

Murder at the Mansion = Clock House

Murder at the Old Crook Farm = Silas Bruton

Murder at the Pit's Bank = Miner's Dog

Murder at the Roadside Inn = Jonathan Bradford

Murder at the Turnpike Gate 100 Years Ago = Tollcross

Murder Brought to Light = Iron Chest

Murder Cellar of Fleet Ditch = Thieves' House

Murdered Guest (Dibdin, T. J., 1818), IV. 301

— (1826), IV. 507

— = Fatal Experiment

Murdered Heir = Glenarvon

Murdered Maid (E., S. N., 1820), IV. 507, 634

Murdered Monk (1827), IV. 507

Murderer (Amherst, J. H., 1822), IV. 507, 634

— (1823) = Father and the Son, IV. 507, 634

Murderer of the Pyrenees = (1) Belphegor the Buffoon; (2) Geneviève

Murderers at the Desolate Cottage = Gamblers

Murderer's Doom = Tomb of Sigismond

Murderer's Dream (1818), IV. 507

Murderer's Dream (1830), IV. 507

Murderers of Grenoble = Two Thieves

Murderers of Massiac = Peter Bell the Waggoner

Murderer's Sacrifice = Demon of the Desert

Murder House (Pitt, G. D., 1844), IV. 19, 373

Murder in Hoxton (1859), V. 722

Murder in Leicester Square (1873), V. 722

Murder in Piper's Row in 1672 = Ruby Ring

Murder in the Mine = Damp Fire

Murder in the Oak Coppice = Amy Arlington

Murder near the Old Mill: A Story of Three Christmas Nights = Lizzie Leigh

Murder of Fualdes = Six Brigands of the Monastery de l'Annonciade

Murder of Leyburn Mill = Emma Hardy

Murder of Mary Clifford, the Foundling Apprentice Girl = Mother Brownrigg, the Painter's Wife of Fetter Lane

Murder of St George's Fields = Solitary of Lambeth

Murder of 1694 = Widow's Daughter

Murder of the Cliffs (1834), IV. 508

Murder of the Courier of Naples (1822), IV. 508

Murder of the Eskdale Hermit = Penny Hedge

Murder of the Five Fields Copse = Simon Lee

Murder of the Mine = Fatal Shaft

Murder of the Mount (1834), IV. 508

— = Skeleton Witness

Murder of the Old Oak Wood = Father's Curse

Murder of the Old Stone Quarry = Bayonet

Murders of the Old Tabbard = Mary White

Murders of the Round Tower Inn (1830), IV. 508

Murder of the Willow Marsh = Adventurer's Doom

Murder on the Heath = Farmer's Gun

Murder on the Thames (Townsend, W. T., 1847), IV. 414

Murder Vision and the Wilt and the Way = Mystery of the Abbey

Murder will out (Barrymore, W., 1814) = Dog of Montargis, IV. 261, 508, 634

— (1899), V. 722

— = (1) Dark before Dawn; (2) Is He Dead?; (3) Presumptive Evidence

Muriel (Leslie, H. T., 1870), V. 457

Murphy's Weather Almanac! (1838), IV. 508

Murtzoufle (Aird, T., 1826), IV. 200, 251

Muse and the Merchant (1840), IV. 508

Muse of Britain (1785), III. 337

Muse of New-Market (1680), I. 201, 443

Muse of Ossian (Baker, D. E., 1763), III. 222, 235

Muse's Chaplet (West, M., 1822), IV. 418

Muses in Mourning (Hill, A., 1760), II. 438; III. 268

Musette (Marsden, F., 1883), V. 477

Music (1676), I. 443

Musical Amateur = Marriage by Stratagem

Music à la mode (Grain, R. C., 1895), V. 388

— (1764), III. 337

Musical Bob (1856), V. 722

Musical Box (Burnand, F. C., 1877), V. 290

Musical Clock (Leigh, C., 1883), V. 453

Musical Discord (Greene, C. M., 1897), V. 392

Musical Family (Grain, R. C., 1880), V. 387

Musical Folly = Independent Patriot

Musical Interview with the Parish Pump (Grain, R. C., 1894), V. 388

Musical Lady (Colman, G., 1762), III. 182, 196, 245

Musical Madness in Three Fyttes = Night of Terror

Musical Marionettes (McArdle, J. F., 1876), V. 466

Musical Mummy (George, G. H., 1859), V. 793

Musical Village (Johnston, M., 1893), V. 437

Musical Whist (1896), V. 722

Music at Home (Seaton, R., 1890), V. 559

Music has Charms (McLaren, A., 1824), IV. 352

Music hath Charms (Fisher, D., 1856), V. 367

— (1823), IV. 508

Musician of Venice (1838), IV. 508

Musician's Daughter (1850), V. 722

Musician's Romance (Harvey, F., 1898), V. 409

Music Mad (Hook, T. E., 1807), IV. 327

— (1829), IV. 508

Music Master (Howard, F., 1887), V. 428

— (1892), V. 722

— = Sham Fight

Musico (Jodrell, R. P., 1787), III. 277

Music's Fascination = Travellers

Music's the Language = Operamania

Music the Food of Love = Modern Orpheus

Musketeers (Grundy, S., 1898), V. 397

Musquetaire (1834), IV. 508

Mustapha (Boyle, R., 1665), I. 38, 39, 66, 80, 107–9, 127, 305, 321, 346, 351, 393; II. 70–1

— (Mallet, D., 1739), II. 27, 58, 65, 70–1, 82, 83, 343

— (Wilkinson, T. F., 1829), IV. 617

— (1814), IV. 508

Mustard Plaster (1898), V. 722

Must he die? (1892), V. 722

Mutineer (1744), II. 379

— (1817), IV. 508

Mutineers of 1727 = Casco Bay

Mutineers of the High Seas = John Adams

Mutineer's Widow (Bosworth, J., 1838), IV. 573

Mutines, the Traitor (Downes, J. F., 1898), V. 349

Mutiny at the Nore (Jerrold, D. W., 1830), IV. 332

— = Richard Parker

Mutiny of Spithead and the Nore (1830), IV. 508

Mutiny of the Britannia (1823), IV. 508

Mutiny of the Caroline = Red Rover

Mutiny of the Dolphin = Red Rover

Mutiny of the Isis = Vin Willoughby

Mutius Scaevola (Ireland, S. W. H., 1801), III. 276; IV. 329

Mutual Deception (Atkinson, J., 1785), III. 118, 177, 234

— = Adventurers

Mutual Expense (Fitzball, E., 1836), IV. 315

Mutual Ground (Brockbank, J., 1875), V. 276

Mutual Inconstancy (1795), III. 337

Mutual Mistake (Denny, W. H., 1891) V. 342

Mutual Misunderstanding (Lee, H., 1876), V. 452

Mutual Objections = I'll not have a Wife

Mutual Separation (Compton, E., 1877), V. 319

My Absent Son (1828), IV. 508

My Album (Bayly, T. H., 1838), IV. 14, 263

My American Aunt (1864), V. 722

My Artful Valet = Gloriana

My Astral Body (Hudson, C. and Colthurst, N., 1896), V. 429

My Auld Mare Maggie = Tam o' Shanter

My Aunt (Arnold, S. J., 1815), IV. 508, 634

— (1864), V. 722

My Aunt Grumble (Johnson, E., 1877), V. 437

My Aunt's Bantam = Cockorico

+ My Aunt's Heiress (French)

My Aunt's Hobby = Juniper Jack

My Aunt's Husband (Selby, C., 1858), V. 560

My Aunt's in Town (Grain, R. C., 1889), V. 387

My Aunt's Luggage = Face to Face

My Aunt's Narcotic (Lancaster, E. R.), IV. 593

My Aunt's Secret (Burnand, F. C., 1872), V. 290

My Aunt's Tragedy = Treacle and Mustard

My Aunt, the Dowager = Winterbottoms!

My Awful Dad (Mathews, C. J., 1875), V. 480

My Awful Luck (Doone, N., 1892), V. 347

My Bachelor Days (Morton, J. M., 1883), V. 807

My Beaux (Stack, T. A., 1868), v. 578
My Benefactor (Rose, E., 1883), v. 550
My Best Friend (1827), IV. 508
My Bonny Boy = Our Tuner
My Boy (Lubimoff, A., 1886), v. 464
My Brave Little Wife (Seaton, A. M., 1882), v. 559
My Brother's Sister = Nadine
My Collaborator (Jones, K., 1892), v. 441
My Comrade (Horsman, C., 1885), v. 427
My Cook and Housekeeper (1854), v. 722
My Country Cousin (1827), IV. 508
— = Actress of All Work
My Courier (Leterrier, J., 1886), v. 457
My Cousin (Hewson, J. J., 1885), v. 420
— = (1) False Alarms; (2) False Appearances
My Cousin Peppy (1861), v. 722
My Cousin the Minister (1839), IV. 508
My Dad = Myrtle
My Darling = Light
My Daughter (Bancroft, Lady, 1892), v. 248
— (Chapman, A., 1888), v. 308
My Daughter-in-Law (1899), v. 722
+ My Daughter's Daughter (*French*)
My Daughter's Debut (Craven, H. T.), v. 786
My Daughter's Intended (Suter, W. E.), v. 819
My Daughter, Sir (Planché, J. R., 1832), IV. 379
My Daughter's Letter = Monsieur Mallet
My Daughter the Duchess (Meadow, A., 1884), v. 483
My Dearest Anna Maria (1851), v. 722
My Dear Relations = Brother Tom
My Detective (1876), v. 722
My Dress Boots (Williams, T. J., 1864), v. 625
My Eleventh Day (Bayly, T. H., 1832), IV. 262, 508, 634
— = Cupid
My Enemy (Reece, R., 1880), v. 539
My Father = Twenty per Cent
My Father did so before me (1848), IV. 508

My Father! Methinks I see my Father!
= Who's my Father?
My Fellow Clerk (Oxenford, J., 1835), IV. 367, 603
My Fetch (1858), v. 722
My First and Last Courtship (1849), IV. 508
My First Brief (1861), v. 722
My First Case (Courtice, T., 1897), v. 326
My First Client (1890), v. 722
My First Fit of the Gout (Morton, J. M., 1835), IV. 361
My First Patient (Cassel, H. and Ogden, C., 1887), v. 305
Myfisto (Montague, V. and St Clare, F., 1887), v. 491
My Friend (Long, C. 1846), IV. 346
— (Tabrar, J., 1885), v. 589
My Friend from India (1896), v. 722
— = My Friend the Prince
My Friend from Leatherhead (Harrington, N. H. and Yates, E., 1857), v. 404
My Friend from Town (Lunn, J., 1831), IV. 14, 508, 634
My Friend Gomez (Smith, L., 1896), v. 573
My Friend in the Straps (1850), v. 722
My Friend Jarlet (Goldsworthy, A. + in collaboration with Norman, E. B., 1887), v. 384
My Friend's Address (1885), v. 722
My Friend the Captain (Coyne, J. S., 1841), IV. 284
My Friend, the Governor (Planché, J. R., 1834), IV. 380, 605
My Friend the Major (Selby, C., 1854), v. 560
My Friend the Prince (McCarthy, J. H., 1897), v. 467
My Gal at Tea (1889), v. 722
My General (Forrester, S., 1890), v. 371
My Girl = Clergyman's Daughter
My Good Name (Turner, E., 1896), v. 604
My Grandfather (Bayly, T. H., 1834), IV. 508, 634
My Grandfather's Legacy = Wife well won
My Grandfather's Will (Reynolds, F., 1838), IV. 391

My Grandmother (Hoare, P., 1793), III. 197, 269; IV. 140
— (1812), IV. 140, 508
— = All about the Battle of Dorking
My Grandmother's Estate (1840), IV. 508
My Grandmother's Pet = Young Scamp
My Great Aunt (Planché, J. R., 1831), IV. 379
My Great-great-grandfather = 102
My Guardie (Trevelyan, C., 1896), v. 603
My Heart for Yours = Maids and Bachelors
My Heart's Darling (Ellis, B., 1876), v. 357
My Heart's Idol (Planché, J. R., 1850), v. 527
My Heart's in the Highlands (Brough, W. and Halliday, A., 1863), v. 279
My Home is not my Home (Peake, R. B., 1840), IV. 371
My Husband's Ghost (Morton, J. M., 1836), IV. 361
My Husband's Secret (Meadows, T., 1822), IV. 355
— (Whitty, W. D., 1874), v. 621
— (1858), v. 722
My Husband's Widow = Too late for the Train
My Husband's Wife (Perry, J., 1885), v. 520
My Husband's Will (Phillips, Mrs A., 1853), v. 522
My Idiot (1899), v. 722
My Innocent Boy (Sims, G. R. and Merrick, L., 1898), v. 570
My Jack (Coffin, E., 1887), v. 316
— (Landeck, B., 1889), v. 447
— (1895), v. 722
My Knuckleduster (Wilson, J. C., 1863), v. 628, 824 [and see under Antigarotte, v. 642]
My Lady Clara (Robertson, T. W., 1869), v. 546
My Lady Fanciful (Jenner, A., 1899), v. 436
My Lady Help (Macklin, A., 1890), v. 471
My Lady Hilda (Faucit, H. S., 1870), v. 363
My Lady, M.D. (Lynch, G. D., 1895), v. 465

My Lady of Levenmore (1894), v. 722
My Lady's Lord (Esmond, H. V., 1899), v. 722, 790
My Lady's Orchard (Beringer, Mrs O. and Hawtrey, G. P., 1897), v. 259
My Landlady's Daughter (Berton, P. M., 1893), v. 260
My Landlady's Gown (Oulton, W. C., 1816), IV. 366
My Landlady's Side Door = In and Out
My Landlord (1894), v. 722
My Last Resource (Newton, J., 1863), v. 808
My Late Friend (Dance, G., 1835), IV. 508, 634
My Latest Opera (1894), v. 722
My Life (Archer, Miss, 1882), v. 242
My Life by Myself (St Maur, H., 1876), v. 554
My Little Adopted (Bayly, T. H., 1838), IV. 263
My Little Brother (1840), IV. 508
My Little Girl (Boucicault, D. G., 1882), v. 702
My Little Red Riding Hood (Rae, J. and Sidney, T., 1895), v. 533
My Little William (McCullough, B., 1876), v. 468
My Lord (Dance, C., 1822), IV. 508, 634
— (1843), IV. 508
My Lord and my Lady (Planché, J. R., 1861), v. 527
My Lord Cardinal (Alexander, G., 1894), v. 238
My Lord in Livery (Smith, S. T., 1886), v. 573
My Lord is not my Lord (+ Dance, C., 1840), IV. 508, 578
My Love and I (Bellingham, H. and Best, W., 1886), v. 257
My Lover (1839), IV. 508
My Love the Captain (Thomson, J. E., 1852), v. 598
My Maggie (Thompson, H., 1884), v. 598
My Maiden Aunts (Sala, F., 1842), IV. 508, 634
My Man and the Barber (Martin, J.), IV. 597
My Man Tom (Lemon, M., 1842), IV. 344

My Master's in Trouble (1839), IV. 508

My Medical Man = Fascinating Fellows

My Mice (1890), v. 722

My Milliner's Bill (Godfrey, G. W., 1884), v. 383

My Miser (1886), v. 722

My Missis (Lewis, C. and Robertson, D., 1886), v. 459

My Mother (Steinberg, A., 1890), v. 580

My Mother, my Wife and my Child = Love and Duty

My Mother's Maid (1858), v. 722

My Nadine (Collier, H., 1889), v. 317

My Name is Jones (Whittaker, J. H. G., 1870), v. 621

My Name is Norval (Oxenford, J., 1860), v. 509

My Native Land (Manning, W., 1891), v. 474

My Neighbour and Myself = Neighbours

My Neighbour Brown (1884), v. 723

My Neighbour's Wife (Bunn, A., 1833), IV. 276

My New Boarding House (1839), IV. 508

My New Maid (Farnie, H. B., 1874), v. 790, 841

— (1878), v. 723, 841

My New Place (Wood, A., 1863), v. 630

My New Wife (1859), v. 723

Mynheer Jan (Paulton, H. and Tedde, M., 1887), v. 517

My Niece and my Monkey (Herman, H., 1876), v. 419

My Night-Gown and Slippers (Colman, G., the Younger, 1797), III. 337, 379, 403

My Noble Capting (1883), v. 723

My Official Wife (Gunter, A. C., 1892), v. 397

My Old Luck (1858), v. 723

My Old Woman (Buckstone, J. B., 1843), IV. 575

— (Macfarren, G., 1829), IV. 350, 597

— = May and December

My Only Coat (Dallas, J., 1882), v. 787

My Own Blue Bell (Pitt, G. D., 1831), IV. 372

My Own Familiar Friend (Maxwell, P. D., 1898), v. 482

My Own Ghost = First Night

My Own Lover (Rodwell, G. H., 1832), IV. 395

My Own Man (Peake, R. B., 1824), IV. 508, 634

My Own Pizarro = More Kotzebue

My Own Rival (1819), IV. 508

My Own Twin Brother (Hill, I., 1834), IV. 509, 634

My Partner (Campbell, B., 1879), v. 301

My Paying Guest (Crofton, M., 1895), v. 330

My Playmate (Evanson, F., 1888), v. 359

My Poll and My Partner Jo (Haines, J. T., 1835), IV. 118, 322

— = Poll and Partner Jo

My Poor Dog Tray (Blake, T. G., 1845), IV. 268, 520, 573, 637, 779 [Although sometimes acted as Poor Dog Tray, the proper title is My P.D.T.]

— (Blake, T. G., 1854), v. 723, 841

My Precious Betsy (Morton, J. M., 1850), v. 495

My Preserver (Craven, H. T., 1863), v. 328

My Queen (Poole, W. H., 1884), v. 529

— (1889), v. 723

My Queenie (Williamson, H. W., 1889), v. 626

Myra (Thompson, Mrs N., 1880), v. 598

Myrtillo (Cibber, C., 1715), II. 249–50, 311

— (1721), II. 379

Myrtle (Havard, P., 1889), v. 410

My Sin (Bogue, J. R., 1888), v. 266

My Sister and I (Hewson, J. J., 1897), v. 420

My Sister from India (Selby, C., 1852), v. 560

My Sister Kate (Lemon, M., 1838), IV. 345, 595

My Sister's Secret (1848), IV. 509

My "Soldier" Boy (Maltby, A. and Lindo, F., 1898), v. 473

My Son and I (Lancaster-Wallis, E., 1894), v. 447

My Son, Diana (Harris, A. G., 1857), v. 405

My Son Dick (Maurice, W., 1874) = Ready Money Mortiboy, v. 482, 723, 806, 841

Mysterious Waiter=Man of Mystery
Mysterious Widow (Fripp, F., 1897), v. 373
Mysterious Wife=Fritz the Outlaw
Mystery (Stephens, W., 1873), v. 581
— (1815), IV. 634
— (1863), v. 723
— =Adele
Mystery and Vengeance=Red Dwarf
Mystery Jairah (Stuart-Wortley, Lady Emmeline, 1840), IV. 613
Mystery, Love and Crime=Blue Dwarf
Mystery of a Gladstone Bag (Francks, F. H., 1889), v. 372
Mystery of a Handsome Cap (André, R., 1888), v. 241
Mystery of a Hansom Cab (Law, A. and Hume, F., 1888), v. 450
— (1888), v. 723
Mystery of Carrow Abbey=Will and the Way
Mystery of Chesney Wold=Jo, the Waif
Mystery of Cloisterham (Stephens, W., 1871)=Mystery of Edwin Drood, v. 581, 723, 817, 841
Mystery of Edwin Drood (Macdermott, G. H., 1872), v. 468
— (Stephens, W., 1871)=Mystery of Cloisterham, v. 581, 723, 817, 841
+Mystery of Muddlewitz (French)
Mystery of Rosedale Hollow=Who did it?
Mystery of the Abbey (Young, H., 1853), v. 636
Mystery of the Ruined Mill=Will o' the Wisp
Mystery of the Seven Sisters (Scudamore, F. A., 1890), v. 559
Mystical Milkman=Camberwell Brothers
Mystical Miss (Klein, C. H., 1899), v. 445
Mystic Branch (1859), v. 723
— =Demon Duke
Mystic Cavern (1803), IV. 509
Mystic Coffer (1812), IV. 509
Mystic Cypress Tree=Demon Bracelets
Mystic Mahatma (Taylor, T. M., 1892), v. 591

Mystic Number VII (1872), v. 723
Mystic Ring (Johnson, E. C., 1893), v. 437
Mystic Tomb (1819), IV. 509
Mystification (Haines, J. T., 1832)=Love and Mystery, IV. 509, 587, 634
— (1821), IV. 509
— (1826), IV. 509
My Sweetheart (Maeder, F. and Gill, W., 1883), v. 472
Mythology run Mad (Moore, T. and Runtz, E., 1893), v. 492
My Turn Next (Williams, T. J., 1866), v. 625
— =Dobson and Company
My Two Nephews (Peake, R. B., 1823)=Duel, IV. 509, 634
My Uncle (Beazley, S., Jr., 1817), IV. 263
— (James, D. S. and Stewart, W. Y., 1883), v. 433
— (Steinberg, A., 1889), v. 580
— (1811), IV. 509
My Uncle Gabriel (Parry, J., 1824), IV. 27, 358, 368
My Uncle's Card (Grattan, H. P., 1840), IV. 320
— (1855), v. 723
My Uncle's House (+Dibdin, C. I. M., 1815), IV. 509
My Uncle's Parlour (1807), IV. 509
My Uncle's Pet (Archer, T., 1846), IV. 255
— (1845), IV. 509
— (1860), v. 723
My Uncle's Will=Uncle's Will [The play by S. T. Smith, v. 573, has My Uncle's Will on the printed title page, but the running titles read Uncle's Will]
— =Widow
My Uncle Thomas=Dare-Devil
My Uncle Toby (Stafford, J. J., 1828), IV. 405, 612
My Valet and I (Wilks, T. E., 1842), IV. 421
My Vassal's Dog=Cottage of the Lake
My Very Last Proposal (Phipps, A. J., 1874), v. 524
My Villa in Italy (Rae, C. M., 1871), v. 532
My Wife (Cowell, A. E., 1892), v. 327
— (Roberts, G., 1885), v. 544

My Wife and Child (1836), IV. 509

My Wife and First Baby = Club

My Wife and my Umbrella (1857), v. 723

My Wife or my Place (Thackeray, T. J. and Shannon, C., 1831), IV. 412

My Wife Polly = Bamboozling

My Wife's Baby (Hughes, F., 1872), v. 430

— (1898), v. 723

My Wife's Bedroom (1834), IV. 509

My Wife's Bonnet (Morton, J. M., 1864), v. 496

My Wife's Come (Morton, J. M., 1843), IV. 362

My Wife's Cousin (1853), v. 723

My Wife's Daughter (Coyne, J. S., 1850), v. 327

My Wife's Dentist (Wilks, T. E., 1839), IV. 421

My Wife's Diary = Wife's Journal

My Wife's Father's Sister (Pemberton, T. E., 1878), v. 519

My Wife's First Husband (Suter, W. E., 1854), v. 723, 819, 841

My Wife's Future Husband (Mayhew, A. and Edwards, H. S., 1851), v. 482

My Wife shan't act (1850), v. 723

My Wife's Husband (1830), IV. 509

— = Going to my Uncle's

My Wife's Lodgings (1844), IV. 509

My Wife's Lover (1859), v. 723

My Wife's Lovers (1899), v. 723

My Wife's Maid (Williams, T. J., 1864), v. 625

My Wife's Mother (Mathews, C. J., 1833), IV. 354

My Wife's Out (Rodwell, G. H., 1843), IV. 395

My Wife's Party (Grain, R. C., 1892), v. 388

My Wife's Relations (Gordon, W., 1862), v. 385

My Wife's Second Floor (Morton, J. M., 1843), IV. 362

My Wife's Step Husband (Du Souchet, H. A., 1897), v. 352

My Wife! What Wife? (Barrett, E. S., 1815), IV. 261

— (Poole, J., 1829), IV. 386

My Wig and my Wife's Shawl (1855), v. 723

My Young Wife and my Old Umbrella (Webster, B. N., 1837), IV. 417

Nabal (Morell, T., 1764), III. 358, 392

Nabob (Degville, 1809), IV. 509, 634

— (Foote, S., 1772). III. 175, 260

— (1898), v. 723

Nabob for an Hour (Poole, J., 1833), IV. 84, 387

Nabob outwitted (1797), III. 337

Nabob's Fortune (Pettitt, H., 1881), v. 521

Nabob's Pickle (1883), v. 723

Nabob's Return = My Home is not my Home

Nabob, the Farmer and the Miser = Blighted Joys

Nachtigal und der Rabe (1828), IV. 509, 634

Nachtlager von Granada (1849), IV. 510

Nachtteufel (1844), IV. 510

Nadel (Lyon, W. F., 1886), v. 465

Nadeshda (Sturgis, J., 1885), v. 586

Nadeshta, the Slave Girl (1850), v. 723

Nadgy (Murray, A., 1887), v. 500

Nadia (Greville, Lady V., 1892), v. 394

Nadine (Grover, L., 1887), v. 396

— (Rogers, F., 1885), v. 548

Nadir (Wise, J., 1779), III. 316

Nadir Shah (1825), IV. 510

Nadjezda (Barrymore, M., 1886), v. 252

Naiad = Ondine

Naiad Queen (Dalrymple, J. S., 1883), v. 333

— = Reine des Naiades

Naida (1848), IV. 510

Naissance de Flore (1809), IV. 510

Naissance de Venus (Degville, 1826), IV. 579

Nameless (1845), IV. 510

— (1884), v. 723

Namesakes (Lennard, H., 1883), v. 455

— (1835), IV. 510

Name the Winner (Millingen, J. G., 1834), IV. 510, 634

Namouna (1882), v. 723

Nana Sahib (Fenton, F. and Osman, W. R., 1863), v. 723, 841

Nance (Douglass, J. T., 1893), v. 349

Nance Oldfield (Reade, C., 1883), v. 536

Natural Son (Mason, J., 1805), IV. 353
— (Plumptre, A., 1798), III. 65, 298, 393
— (1794), III. 337
— (1814), IV. 510
— =(1) Forêt noire; (2) Lovers' Vows
Nature against the World = Passions of
the Heart
Nature and Art (1840), IV. 510
Nature and Philosophy (1876), v. 723
Nature and Sentiment = Rough and
Smooth
Nature's above Art (Falconer, E., 1863),
v. 360
Nature's Nobleman (Scudamore, J. F.,
1882), v. 559
— (1882), v. 724
Nature's Three Daughters (Cavendish,
M., 1662), I. 396
Nature will Prevail (Horde, T., 1784),
III. 273
— (Walpole, H., 1778), III. 314
— (1788), III. 337
— (1824), IV. 510
— =(1) Fortunate Peasant; (2) Love
Triumphant
Naughtology (Stanford, F., 1889), v.
578
Naughty Boy who cried for the Moon =
Endymion
Naughty Boys = Chinaman
Naughty Forty Thieves (Thorne, G.,
1892), v. 599
— (1893), v. 724
Naughty Husband = Trip to Blackpool
Naughty Little Rose Pompon (1847),
IV. 510
Naughty Man = Love Letters
Naughty Men (Harvey, F., 1885), v. 408
Naughty Novel (1881), v. 724
Naughty Rosina (Montague, L. A. D.
and Atwood, A., 1898), v. 491
Naughty Titania (Rogers, T. S. and
Rushworth, J., 1893), v. 549
Naulahka (1891), v. 724
Nautch Girl (Dance, G., 1891), v. 335
Nautical Tom and Jerry (Somerset,
C. A., 1843), IV. 97, 405
Naval Cadets (1880), v. 724
Naval Engagements (Dance, C., 1838),
IV. 288
— (1865), v. 724
Naval Gratitude (1797), III. 337

Naval Pillar (Dibdin, T. J., 1799), III.
257
Naval Victory and Triumph of Lord
Nelson (1805), IV. 14, 510
Naval Volunteers (1795), III. 337
Navigators (1818), IV. 510
Navvie's Wife = Life's Luck
Nazarenes (1893), v. 724
Neale O'Neale (Sidney, W., 1874), v.
566
Neapolitan Assassins (1827), IV. 510
Neapolitan Nuptials = Shipwreck of
Policinello
Neapolitan Pirate (1807), IV. 510
Neapolitan Revenge = Almeyda
Nearly Lost (Travers, W., 1867), v. 602
Nearly Seven (Brookfield, C. H. E.,
1882), v. 276
Nearly Severed (Hurst, J. P., 1885), v.
431
Nearly Stranded (1872), v. 724
Near Relations (Sketchley, A., 1871), v.
571
Near Shave (Day, G. D., 1895), v.
339
Neck or Nothing (Conquest, H. and
Pettitt, H., 1876), v. 321
— (Garrick, D., 1766) = Narrow Escape,
III. 118, 185, 263, 385
+ — (Crow Street, Dublin, 5/3/1795)
Necromancer (Howe, J. B., 1862), v.
724, 798, 841
— (Rich, J., 1723), II. 49, 135, 137, 253,
256, 379, 425, 443
— (1809), IV. 510
Ned Dauntless (1850), v. 724
Ned Kelly (1880), v. 724
Ned Knowles (Warren, T. G., 1885), v.
615
Ned's Chum (Murray, D. C., 1890), v.
500
Needful (Craven, H. T., 1866), v. 329
Needle of Agony (1849), IV. 510
Needles and Pins (Daly, A., 1880), v.
333
— (1860), v. 724
Needless Stratagem = I've written to
Browne
Ne'er-do-Weel (Gilbert, W. S., 1878),
v. 380
Ne'er-do-well (Bowkett, S., 1894), v.
271

Neglected Child, the Vicious Youth and the Degraded Man = Wrath's Whirlwind

Neglected Home (Travers, W., 1865) = Spirit Child's Prayer, v. 724, 753, 821, 841, 847

Neglected Virtue (Horden, H., 1695), I. 413

Neglected Wives (1832), IV. 634

Negro Murderer (1831), IV. 510

Negro of Wapping (Fitzball, E., 1838), IV. 315

Negro's Curse (1825), IV. 510

Negro Slave = Uncle Tom's Cabin

Negro Slaves (McLaren, A., 1799), III. 284

— (1796), III. 65, 337, 403

— = King Caesar

Neighbourly Action (1885), v. 724

Neighbours (Oxenford, J., 1866), v. 510

Neil Jagger's Cave = Chiverton Hall

Neither's the Man (Holford, Mrs M., 1798), III. 271

Nell (Halliday, A., 1870), v. 401

— (1880), v. 724

Nell Gwyn = Peckham Frolic

Nell Gwyn (Wills, W. G., 1878), v. 627

Nell Gwynne (Arnold, H. T., 1871), v. 243

— (Farnie, H. B., 1876), v. 362

— (Farnie, H. B., 1884), v. 363

— (Jerrold, D. W., 1833), IV. 16, 185, 332

— (Lee, N., 1852), v. 452

Nell Gwynne, the Orange Girl (Walker, J., 1833), IV. 416

Nellie (Hazlewood, C. H., 1865), v. 797

Nellie's Flight (Edwards, H. S. and Thomas, B., 1886), v. 355

Nellie's Trials (Brougham, J., 1866), v. 281, 780

Nell Snooks (Russell, C., 1899), v. 553

Nelly Nightingale (1885), v. 724

Nelly's Sister (1895), v. 724

Nelly, the Rag-gatherer (1852), v. 724

Nelson (Fitzball, E., 1827), IV. 313

— (1892), v. 724

Nelson's Arrival in the Elysian Fields (1806), IV. 510

Nelson's Enchantress (Home, R., 1897), v. 798

Nelson's Funeral = National Gratitude

Nelson's Glory (Dibdin, T. J., 1805), IV. 298

Nelson's Monument (1843), IV. 510

Nelson's Ring (1843), IV. 510

Nemesis (Farnie, H. B., 1873), v. 361

Nephew and Niece (1827), IV. 510

Nephews (Lloyd, H. E., 1799), III. 282, 390

Neptune's Friendship (1787), III. 337

Neptune's Gift = (1) Burning Mountain; (2) Diving Bell

Neptune's Levee (1791), III. 337

Neptune's Love Messenger = Jack Grapplehard

Neptune the Smuggler's Friend = Blue Anchor

Nerestan, Prince of Persia (Fitzball, E., 1823), IV. 312

Nero (Bridges, R. S., 1885), v. 275

Nero, a Roman-tick Fiddler (Millingen, J. G., 1833), IV. 510, 634

Nero, Emperour of Rome (Lee, N., 1674), I. 121–2, 130, 419

Nero's Niece (Palmer, L. S., 1899), v. 511

Nerves (Carr, J. W. C., 1890), v. 304

Nervous Family = Quack

Nervous Man (Bernard, W. B., 1833), IV. 265

Nest of Beasts = Northern Election

Nest of Plays (Jacob, Sir H., 1738), II. 16–17, 205, 338, 439

Nestor (1892), v. 724

Netley Abbey (Pearce, W., 1794), III. 204, 297

— (1858), v. 841

Net-Maker and his Wife = Zembuca

Nettle (Warren, E., 1886), v. 614

Nettlewig Hall (Westmacott, C. M., 1831), IV. 418

— = Maids and Bachelors

Neuha's Cave (Peake, R. B., 1831), IV. 510, 634

Neuter (Inchbald, E., 1786) = Widow's Vow, III, 337, 388, 403

Never Again (Hall, K. E., 1873), v. 399

— (1897), v. 724

Never despair (Comer, G., 1887), v. 319

— (Drayton, H., 1859), v. 724, 789, 841

— (James, W., 1871), v. 434

— (Ranger, 1856), v. 812

— (Stephenson, C. H., 1869), v. 582

Never despair (1875), v. 724

Never Introduce your Dinah to a Pal = Cavalearyer Costercana

Never Judge by Appearances (Drayton, H., 1859), v. 724, 789, 841

— (1857), v. 724

Never Plead's Hopes of being a Lord Chancellor = Fame

Never Reckon your Chickens before they are Hatched (Reeve, W., 1871), v. 540

— (Suter, W. E., 1858), v. 724, 819, 842

Never Satisfied (1886), v. 724

Never say die = Hampshire Hog

Never taste Wine at the Docks (Soutar, R., 1854), v. 575

Never to Know (Fairfax, M., 1899), v. 360

Never too late to learn (Branson, W. S., 1874), v. 274

Never too late to mend (Conquest, G., Jr., 1858), v. 724, 785, 842

— (Hazlewood, C. H., 1859), v. 724, 796, 842

— (Johnstone, J. B., 1858), v. 800

— (1858), v. 724

Never Travel during a Revolution = Lost a Sovereign

New Actress (Drew, E., 1888), v. 350

— (1835), IV. 511

New Adam (Melford, M., 1897), v. 484

New Agent (Lindo, R. H., 1896), v. 460

New Apollo (Grey, C., 1889), v. 394

New Apple of Discord = Not for me!

New Athenian Comedy (Settle, E., 1693), I. 429

New Baby (Bourchier, A., 1896), v. 270

New Babylon (Meritt, P. and Rowe, G. F., 1878), v. 486

New Barmaid (Bowyer, F. and Edwardes-Sprange, W., 1895), v. 272

New Boy (Lumley, R. R., 1893), v. 464

— = Boy

New Brighton Sands (Harrison, W., 1881), v. 407

New Brooms (Byron, H. J., 1881), v. 299

— (Colman, G., 1776), III. 12, 112, 193, 195, 210, 246

— (Dibdin, C. I. M., 1803), IV. 290

New Case for the Lawyers = Will and No Will

Newcastle in an Uproar (?Dodds, R., 1851), v. 842

Newcastle Rider = Ducks and Green Pease

New Cinderella (Simpson J. P., 1879), v. 568

New Comedy (1704), II. 380

New Comedy of Errors = Shakespeare's Festival

New Comic Scene to the Comedy of the Minor (1761), III. 403

New Corsican Brothers (Raleigh, C. and Slaughter, W., 1889), v. 533

New Cosmetic (Pratt, S. J., 1790), III. 299

New Court Legacy = Ladies of the Palace

New Dean (Ellis, H., 1897), v. 357

New Divertisement (1794), III. 337, 403

New Don Juan (1828), IV. 511

New Don Quixote (Buchanan, R. and Jay, H., 1896), v. 285

New Drama (1792), III. 337

New East Lynne (Gurney, E., 1898), v. 398

New Edition of the Corsican Brothers (Mason, W. H., 1870), v. 480

New Edition of the Fairy Tales of Mother Goose, with many Highly Coloured Illustrations (1855), v. 724

New Endimion (1882), v. 724

Newest Woman (Newton, H. C., 1895), v. 503

New Farce (1835), IV. 511 [This has a sub-title, or, A Scene of Confusion]

New Footman (Selby, C., 1842), IV. 398

New Fortune (1853), v. 724

New Found Home = Eugenia Claircille

New Front to an Old Dicky = Rise and Fall of Richard III

Newgate Ned (1834), IV. 511

New Gretna Green (Stuart, C., 1783) = Gretna Green, III. 310, 337, 403

New Groom (Hannah, C., 1899), v. 403

New Hay at the Old Market (Colman, G., the Younger, 1795), III. 23, 156–7, 164, 212, 247

— = Sylvester Daggerwood

New Hand (1885), v. 724

New Haymarket Spring Meeting (Planché, J. R., 1855), v. 527

New Trial of Effie Deans = Heart of Midlothian

New Trick to get a Wife = Litigious Suitor Defeated

New Utopia = Six days Adventure

New Version of Uncle Tom's Cabin (1857), V. 724

New Wags of Windsor (Howard, J. and Cooper, F., 1854), V. 724, 786, 798, 842

New Way of Knowing Things = Telegraph

New Way Old Debts to pay = Sir Giles Overreach

New Way to blow up a King = Guy Fawkes

New Way to Dress an Old Dish = Harlequin turn'd Cook

New Way to get a Husband = Sexes Mismatch'd

New Way to get Married (Dibdin, T. J., 1820), IV. 302

New Way to get rid of a Wife = Bristol Tar

New Way to Keep a Place = I won't go!

New Way to Keep a Wife at Home (Oulton, W. C., 1785), III. 296

— = Letter-Writers

New Way to Obtain Consent = Florenski and Nina

New Way to pay Old Debts (Kemble, J. P., 1810), IV. 335

New Way to Pay the National Debt (1841), IV. 635

New Way to Pay your Rent = Quarter Day

New Way to play an Old Game = False Count

New Ways to Catch Hearts (Cowley, H., 1783) = More Ways than One, III. 338, 380, 403

New Wheat (1795), III. 338

New Wing (Kennedy, H. A., 1890), V. 443

New Wit for a Husband = Modern Prophets

New Woman (Grundy, S., 1894), V. 397

New Wonder (Oulton, W. C., 1784), III. 296

New World (Dawson, F., 1893), V. 339

— (France, E. S., 1880), V. 372

— (Young, H., 1861), V. 825

New World (1801), IV. 511

— = Devil's Mine

New Year (Clarence, R., 1899), V. 311

New Year's Chimes (Shirley, A., 1890), V. 564

New Year's Eve (Lindo, F., 1894), V. 460

— (1861), V. 724

— (1873), V. 724

— = Hogmanay

New Year's Gift (Barrymore, W., 1830), IV. 511, 635

— = Old Customs

New Year's Gifts = Up to Snuff

New York Divorce (Clarke, W., 1895), V. 313

New York Politics (Aikin, J., 1890), V. 236

Next Department (1899), V. 724

Next Door (Wigan, A. S., 1845), IV. 511, 635

— (1897), V. 724

Next Door Neighbours (Inchbald, Mrs E., 1791), III. 118, 144, 275, 388

— (1822), IV. 511

Next of Kin (Falconer, E., 1860), V. 121, 360, 790

— (Overton, R., 1887), V. 509

— = (1) Day of Disasters; (2) Foundling of Fortune

Next Please (1892), V. 725

Next Year's Morning (1899), V. 725

Nibelungen Treasure (1847), IV. 511

Nicandra (Vaun, R., 1898), V. 607

Nice Boy, Jim! (Drinkwater, A. E., 1893), V. 351

Nice Firm (Taylor, T., 1853), V. 592

Nice Girl (Thomas, W. M., 1873), V. 725, 820, 842

Nice Lady (Green, G. S., 1762), III. 265

Nice Mince Pie (1868), V. 725

Nice Quiet Day (Hipkins, T. H. and Murray, G., 1861), V. 422

Nicette (Rose, E., 1879), V. 550

Nice Young Ladies (Stirling, E., 1843), IV. 407

Nicholas Dunks (Lee, N., 1843), IV. 594

Nicholas Flam (Buckstone, J. B., 1833), IV. 274

Nicholas Mendoza (Bromley, F., 1829), IV, 511, 635

Nicholas Nickleby (Halliday, A., 1875),·
v. 401
— (Stirling, E., 1838), IV. 97, 406
— (1875), v. 725
— (1876), v. 725
— (1885), v. 725
Nicholas Nickleby and Poor Smike
(Moncrieff, W. T., 1839), IV. 97, 511,
635
Nicholson's Niece (Bell, Mrs H., 1892),
v. 255
Nick Carter = Hue and Cry
Nick of the Woods (Davis, A., 1855), v.
787
— (Medina, L. H. and Haines, J. T.,
1839), IV. 323, 365, 587, 598
— (1841), IV. 511
— (1844), IV. 511
Nick of Time (Colville, Sir H., 1896), v.
319
Nicksey (1880), v. 725
Nicodemus in Despair (Craven, E.,
1803), IV, 285
Nicolete (Ferris, E. and Stewart, A.,
1899), v. 365
Nicomede (Dancer, J., 1671), I. 98, 400
Niewgemaakten Adelman = New-made
Nobleman
Nigel (Pocock, I., 1823), IV. 93, 384
Nigger Life in London = Uncle Tom's
Crib
Nigger's New Place = Lost Son Found
Nigger's Opera (1861), v. 725
Nigg's Affinity (1896), v. 725
Night (Douglass, J. T., 1863), v. 725,
788, 842
Night-Adventurers = Squire Oldsapp
Night after the Battle (1823), IV. 511
— = (1) Duke's Coat; (2) Wellington
Night after Waterloo = Duke's Coat
Night and Day (1868), v. 725
Night and Morn (Falconer, E., 1864), v.
360
Night and Morning (Boucicault, D.,
1871), v. 269
— (Brougham, J., 1855), v. 280
— (Dillon, C., 1844), IV. 581
Night at an Inn = Three Beggars
Night at Dover = Twelve Precisely
Night at Notting Hill (Harrington,
N. H. and Yates, E., 1857), v. 404
Night at Sea = Fun on the Bristol

Night at the Bal Masqué (1866), v. 725
Night at the Bastille (Archer, T., 1839),
IV. 254 [This appears also as Night in
the Bastile, IV. 511]
Night at the Casino = Early Closing
Night at the Widow's (1851), v. 725
Night before the Battle = (1) Advance
Guard; (2) Duke
Night before the Wedding (1827), IV. 511
— = Deux nuits
Night Birds (Gordon, G. L. and Mackay,
J., 1878), v. 385
— (Travers, W., 1859), v. 821
Night Cometh (Grogan, W. E., 1895), v.
395
Night Dancers = Wilis
Night Errand (1834), IV. 511
Night Express (Holcroft, G., 1890), v.
424
Night Guard (Pitt, C., 1868), v. 526
— = Duke and the Policeman
Night Hag (Barrymore, W., 1820), IV.
511, 635
Night in a Churchyard (1854), v. 725
Night in Fairy Land = Shakespeare's
Dream
Nightingale (Melford, M., 1884), v. 484
— (Robertson, T. W., 1870), v. 546
— (1848), IV. 511, 635
Nightingale at Home (1880), v. 725
Nightingale of the Mountain = Rocco
Salvioni
Nightingale's Wooing (Rushton, A. and
Arlon, F., 1871), v. 553
Night in Granada (1840), IV. 511
Night in La Berlandiere = Gustave
Dubarry
Night in Paris (Klein, C. H., 1896), v.
445
— (1889), v. 725
Night in Persia (1851), v. 725
Night in Spain = Matamoros
Night in the Alhambra = Captives
Night in the Bastile = Night at the
Bastille
Night in the Bastille = Lady of Belleisle
Night in the Haunted Dell = Wishing
Gate
Night in the Tower (1849), IV. 511
Night in Town (Sherburn, H. A., 1891),
v. 563
Night in Venice = Gondolier

Night in Wales (Gardner, H., 1885), v. 376 [*See also under* Night on Snowdon]

Nightly Courier of the Air = War Balloon

Night Mail (1893), v. 725

Nightmare (1895), v. 725

Night of Excitement (1846), IV. 511

Night Off (Daly, A., 1885), v. 333

Night of Horrors (1844), IV. 511

Night of Suspense (1843), IV. 511

Night of Terror (Wyndham, Sir C. and Matthison, A., 1877), v. 634

Night of the French Revolution = Robert le Grange

+ Night on Snowdon (Gardner, H., *French*) [Apparently = Night in Wales]

Night on the Big Wheel = Ballyhooley

Night Out = Night in Paris

Night Patrol (Pocock, I., 1835), IV. 385

Night Porter (1861), v. 725

Night Rehearsal (Rede, W. L., 1835), IV. 607

Night's Adventure (Robertson, T. W., 1851), v. 546

— = (1) Black Domino; (2) Cares of Love

Night's Adventures (1819), IV. 511

Night Session (1897), v. 725

Night's Frolic (Thomas, A. and Barry, H., 1891), v. 595

— (1845), IV. 511

— = (1) Couple of Thieves; (2) Devilish Good Joke

Nightshade (Hall, K. E., 1873), v. 399

Night's Intrigue = (1) Evening Adventure; (2) Feign'd Curtizans

Night Surprise (Cromer, W. and Reed, G., 1877), v. 330

— (Law, A.), v. 450

Night's Wonders = Three Cheers for Charity

Night with Burns (1853), v. 725

Night with Punch (Peake, R. B., 1843), IV. 511, 635

Night with Shakespeare = Old House at Home

Night with the Forty Thieves = (1) Ali Baba; (2) Open Sesame

Nihilist (Towers, E. J., 1897), v. 601

Nihilists = Vera

Nihilist's Doom = Scarlet Brotherhood

Nihilists of St Petersburg = Mardo

Nimble Nymph and the Terrible Troglodyte = Xcis and Galatea

Nimble Shilling (Levey, J. C., 1877), v. 458

Nimrod (Jameson, R. W., 1848), IV. 590

Nina (Berkeley, G. M., 1787), III. 236 [By error this is said, III. 377, to have been acted at C.G.]

— (Kennion, Mrs, 1885), v. 443

— (Wolcot, J., 1787), III. 316, 398

— (1787), III. 338

+ — (8°, 1800; or, Love has turned her Head)

— (1837), IV. 511

Nina Sforza (Troughton, R. Z. S., 1841), IV. 414

Nina, the Bride of the Galley Slave (Fitzball, E., 1832), IV. 511, 635

Nincompoop (1898), v. 725

Nine Days' Queen (Buchanan, R., 1880), v. 284

Nine Days' Wonder (Aidé, H., 1875), v. 236

Nine Points of the Law (Jameson, R. F., 1818) = Poor Relations, IV. 331, 521, 590, 637

— (Taylor, T., 1859), v. 593

"1990" (Arthur, B., 1895), v. 244

Nineteenth Century (Morell, H. H. and Mouillot, F., 1894), v. 493

1934 (1834), IV. 511

Nine too many (Buckstone, J. B., 1847), v. 146, 265

Ninetta (Fitzball, E., 1830), IV. 313, 584

Ninette à la cour (1806), IV. 512

Ninety Days (1893), v. 725

'98 (Cooke, F., 1874), v. 323

— = Lord Edward

99 (Boucicault, D., 1891), v. 269

99 victims = Petites Danaïdes

92 (Macintyre, W. T., 1892), v. 469

Ninon (Wills, W. G., 1880), v. 627, 824

Ninth Hour (1847), IV. 512

Ninth Statue (Dibdin, T. J., 1814), IV. 299

— (1833), IV. 512

— (1849), IV. 512

Niobe (Cross, J. C., 1797), III. 250

Niobe (All Smiles), (Paulton, H. and Paulton, E., 1890), v. 517

Nipkins and the Spectre Steed = .
Charmed Charger

Nipped in the Bud (Hewson, J. J.,
1892), v. 420

— (Sullivan, W. C., 1883), v. 587

— = King's Gardener

Nipt in the Bud (1824), IV. 512

Nita's First (Warren, T. G., 1883), v.
615

Nitocris (Collins, C. J., 1855), v. 725,
785

— (Fitzball, E., 1855), v. 368

— (Graves, C., 1887), v. 389

Nitouche (1884), v. 725

Nixie (Burnett, Mrs F. H. and Townsend, S., 1890), v. 292

Nix, the Demon Dwarf (Conquest, G.
and Spry, H., 1872), v. 321

No (Murray, W. H., 1826), IV. 365, 601

— (Pentreath, F. G., 1881), v. 519

— (Reynolds, F., 1828), IV. 391

— (1829), IV. 512

— (1876), v. 725

No Actress (Bartlett, H., 1898), v. 252

Noah's Ark (Paulton, H., 1885), v. 517

Noah's Flood (Ecclestone, E., 1679), I.
101, 410

No Appeal (Craven, W. S., 1897), v. 329

No Assets (1898), v. 725

Noble Art (Norwood, E., 1892), v. 505

Noble Atonement (Cassilis, I. L., 1892),
v. 306

Noble Brother (Summers, W. J., 1889),
v. 587

Noble Coward (Naden, A. T., 1890), v.
501

Noble Deed (1899), v. 725

Noble Englishman (1721), II. 380, 452

Noble Englishman Rewarded = Baronet
Bit

Noble Error = Garcia

Noble Falsehood (Drew, E., 1894), v.
351

Noble Foresters (Smith, A., 1776), III.
111, 308

Noble Foundling (Trotter, T., 1813),
IV. 615

— = Seven Years' Secret

Noble Heart (Lewes, G. H., 1850), v.
458, 804

— (1848), IV. 512

Noble Hero = Heroes

Noble Ingratitude (Lower, Sir W.,
1659), I. 98, 420

Noble Lie (Geisweiler, M., 1799), III.
65, 264, 385

— (Jarman, F., 1890), v. 434

— (1799), III. 338, 403

Noble Love (Clarke, C. A. and Hewson,
J. J., 1890), v. 312

Nobleman (Cooper, Mrs E., 1736), II.
316

Noble Outlaw (1815) = Pilgrim, IV. 512,
635

Noble Peasant (Holcroft, T., 1784), III.
111, 203, 270

Noble Pedlar (Carey, G. S., 1771), III.
242

Noble Pilgrim (1791), III. 403

Noble Revenge = Debating Club

Noble Savage (Corder, F. and Corder,
Mrs F., 1885), v. 325

Noble's Daughter (1897), v. 725

Noble Shepherd = Douglas

Noble Slave (Harwood, T., 1788), III.
267

Noble Soldier (1717), II. 380

Noblesse Oblige (Bright, Mrs A., 1878),
v. 275

— = Our Family Motto

Noble Troubadour (1840), IV. 512

Noble Vagabond (Jones, H. A., 1886),
v. 439

Nobly Won (Bradley, C., 1885), v. 273

+ Nobodies at Home; Somebodies
Abroad (Hallett, Mrs, 12°, 1847)

Nobody (Robinson, M., 1794), III. 302

Nobody in London (Blanchard, E. L.,
1873), v. 264

Nobody in Town (1851), v. 725

Nobody's Child (Arnold, H. T., 1868),
v. 243

— (Phillips, W., 1867), v. 523

Nobody's Claim (Lock, E. A., 1886), v.
461

Nobody's Fault (Law, A., 1882), v. 450

Nobody's Fortune (Grattan, H. P.,
1872), v. 389

Nobody's Son (1866), v. 725

Nobs and Snobs = Honour before Titles

No Cards (Gilbert, W. S., 1869), v.
379

— (Oxenford, J., 1872), v. 510

Noce du Village (Aumer, 1823), IV. 569

Noces de Flore = Zéphyr inconstant, puni et fixé

Noces de Gamache = Don Quichotte

No Coronet (Hamilton, H., 1883), v. 401

No Credit (Coffin, E., 1892), v. 316

— (Taylor, Mrs F., 1898), v. 820

No Cross, no Crown (Williams, B. and Sorrell, H., 1896), v. 624

Noctroff's Maid Whipt = Presbyterian Lash

No Cure no Pay (Rowe, H., 1797), III. 207, 303

No Dinner Yet (Rodwell, J. T. G., 1823) = Race for a Dinner, IV. 512, 635

Noe Ainslie (Grogan, W. E. and Norman, N. V., 1897), v. 395

Noemi (1859), v. 842

— = Ernestine

Noemie (Suter, W. E., 1852), v. 587

No Escape (Davies, R. C., 1888), v. 338

No Evidence (Gordon, G. L., 1886), v. 385

No. 50 (Marshall, F., 1876), v. 478

No. 5 (1899), v. 726

No Followers (Oxenford, J., 1837), IV. 367, 603

No Followers Allowed = Cook of Kennington

No Foole like ye Old Foole (1676), I. 346, 443

No Fool like an Old One = Who's to Blame

No Fools Like Wits (1721), II. 380

No. 49 (Lawrence, F., 1860), v. 726, 802, 842

No Harm Done = Tame Tigers

No Irish need apply (1854), v. 725

No Joke like a True Joke (1732), II. 380

Nologoise, King of the Parthenes (1803), IV. 512

No Magick like Love = British Enchanters

No Man's Land (Douglass, J. T., 1890), v. 349

No Matter What (1758) = Politician, III. 338, 340, 403

No Mercy (Melford, M., 1883), v. 484

Nomination Day (1873), v. 725

No Misses (1873), v. 725

No Name (Bernard, W. B., 1863), v. 259

— (Collins, W. W., 1870), v. 318, 785

— (Reeve, W., 1877), v. 540

Nondescript (Hewlings, A., 1813), IV. 325

— (1814), IV. 635

— (1857), v. 725

None but the Brave (Vane, S. and Shirley, A., 1898), v. 607

None but the Brave deserve the Fair (Webster, B. N., 1850), v. 618

None so Blind as those who won't see (Dibdin, C., 1782) = Blind Man, III. 121, 256, 382

Non-Juror (Cibber, C., 1717), II. 14, 132, 163, 189–90, 212, 312, 434; III. 115

Non-marriables = Colonel's Belle

No, no (1846), IV. 512

Non-suited (Rhoades, W. C., 1891), v. 542

Noodledom (Marshall, E., 1877), v. 478

No. 117, Arundel Street, Strand (Addison, R. A., 1860), v. 235

No One's Enemy but His Own (Murphy, A., 1763), III. 7, 119, 181, 290, 392

Noontide Branches (Field, M., 1899), v. 366

Nootka Sound (1790), III. 338

No Pain, no Gain (Cantwell, R. F., 1872), v. 302

No Peace for the Frenchman = He's Here Again

No Play this Night (1797), III. 338

No Plot without Danger (1835), IV. 512

No Prelude (Elliston, R. W., 1803), IV. 309

Nora (Lord, F., 1885), v. 463

— (1894), v. 725

Nora Creina (Stirling, E., 1848), IV. 409

Norah (Henry, R., 1897), v. 417

— (1826), IV. 512

— = Norah's Vows

Norah Creina (1858), v. 725

Norah O'Donnell (Grattan, H. P., 1840), IV. 311

Norah O'Neille (Travers, W., 1876), v. 603

Norah's Vows (Boucicault, D., 1878), v. 269

Nordisa (Corder, F., 1887), v. 325, 786

Nore Light (1834), IV. 512

Norfolk Lass (Murray, C., 1784), III. 392

Norfolk Sharp-shooter = Sure Aim

No Risk, no Gain (1862), v. 725

Norma (Draper, J. F., 1875), v. 350

— (Mildenhall, T., 1842), IV. 598

— (Planché, J. R., 1837), IV. 381

— (Richards, A. B., 1875), v. 542

Norman Conquest = Harold

Normandy Pippins (Byron, H. J., 1874), v. 298

Normandy Sisters (1860), v. 725

Norman Fiend (1820), IV. 512

Norman Invasion (Killick, J. M., 1870), v. 444

Norma Travestie (Oxberry, W. H., 1841), v. 357

No Room to Live = Nell Snooks

No Rose without a Thorn (Melford, M., 1886), v. 484

— = Beast and the Beauty

North and South (Forrest, H., 1877), v. 370

— (Francks, F. H., 1888), v. 372

— = Belgravia

North Briton (Ridgway, J., 1810), IV. 394

Northern Castle (1667), I. 444

Northern Election (1749), II. 380

Northern Feuds = Edgar

Northern Fleet (1801), IV. 512

Northern Heiress (Davys, Mrs M., 1716), II. 163-4, 317, 422

Northern Heroes (1748), II. 380, 386, 448

Northern Imp (1855), v. 725

Northern Inn (Kemble, S., 1791), III. 113, 279

Northern Lass = Northern Inn

Northern Night = Princess Tarakanoff

Northern Star = (1) Jenny Lind; (2) Star of the North

North Pole (Dibdin, C. I. M., 1821), IV. 295

— (Haines, J. T.), IV. 587

— (1818), IV. 512

North Steamer = Death of the Race-Horse

North Tower = Plots!

Northumberland (Meilan, M. A., 1771), III. 85, 287

North West Passage (+ Dibdin, C. I. M., 1820), IV. 512

Norval (Rede, W. L., 1842), IV. 390

Norwegian Wreckers = Floating Beacon

Norwich Festival (1837), IV. 512

Norwich in 1549 = Rebellion

Norwich Lass (Lindoe, 1793), III. 390

Norwood Gipsies (1777), III. 338

Nosegay of Weeds (O'Keeffe, J., 1798), III. 295

No. 17 (Leigh, A.), v. 453

No. 728 = Hurly Burly

No. 70 (1886), v. 726

No. 72 (Patmore, W. J., 1893), v. 515

No. 16 (Mitchell, W. A., 1828), IV. 599

Nos. 1, 2 and 3 (1883), v. 726

No Song, No Supper (Hoare, Prince, 1790), III. 269; IV. 140

— (1812), IV. 140, 512

No Spy = Love Conquers

Not a Bad Judge (Planché, J. R., 1848), IV. 187, 382, 605

Nota Bene (Hookham, 1816), IV. 319

Not a Formosa = Linda of Chamouni

Not a Friend in the World = Blue-eyed Witch

Not All Smoke (McDonald, B. P., 1898), v. 468

Not Alone (Lander, G. and Weldon, Mrs, 1885), v. 448

Not at all Jealous (Robertson, T. W., 1871), v. 546

Not at Home (Aidé, H., 1886), v. 236

— (Dallas, R. C., 1809), III. 253; IV. 11, 130, 288

— = Saracen's Head

Not a Word (Dove, O., 1884), v. 349

— (Kenney, J., 1835), IV. 337

Not Dead (Rousby, A., 1874), v. 552

Not Dead Yet (1863), v. 726

Not Dined Yet = No Dinner Yet

Note at hand = I'll be your Second

Note Forger (Fitzball, E., 1835), IV. 314

Note of Hand (Cumberland, R., 1774), III. 251

— (Keith, H., 1891), v. 442

Notes and Gold (Robbins, A. F., 1885), v. 544

Not false but fickle (Bright, Mrs A., 1878), v. 275

Not for Jo = Miss Maritana

Not for me! (1828), IV. 512

Not Found (Towers, E., 1870), v. 601

No Wit like a Woman's = Sir Barnaby Whigg

No Work! No Wedding! (1824), IV. 512

Now or Never (Dance, G., 1839), IV. 512, 635

Now's your Time, Taylors!! (1794), III. 338

Now Taylors is your Time = Now's your Time, Taylors

Noyades (Peake, R. B., 1828), IV. 370

— (1829), IV. 512

Nubby the Q.C. = Fancy Ball

Nubian Captive (1857), V. 726

Nugae Antiquae et Novae = Rowley and Chatterton in the Shades

Number Fifty One (Callender, E. R., 1880), V. 300

Number Nine = Lady of Ostend

Number Ninety Nine (1882), V. 726

Number Nip (Conquest, G., 1862) = Spider and the Fly, V. 320, 753, 785, 847

— (Cross, J. C., 1803), IV. 286

Number Nip and the Spirit Bride (Brooks, C. W. S. and Lemon, M., 1853), V. 277

Number One! (Buckstone, J. B., 1831), IV. 512, 635

Number I A (Talfourd, F.), V. 819

Number One round the Corner (Brough, W., 1854), V. 279, 842

Number Six, Duke Street (Becher, M., 1871), V. 254

Number Twelve (Français, J., 1886), V. 371

Number Two (Hiller, H. C., 1890), V. 421

Number 204 (Burnand, F. C., 1877), V. 290

Number Two versus Number One (1822), IV. 512

Numpo's Courtship (1758), III. 338

Nun (1835), IV. 512

Nunkey (Wilmot, A. A., 1892), V. 628

Nunnery (Pearce, W., 1785), III. 203, 296

Nun of Florence (Sorelli, G., 1840), IV. 612

Nun of the Bank = Lady in Black

Nun of the Black Convent = Nun

Nuns' Conclave = Punch's Politics

Nuns of Cambray = Fénelon

Nuns of Glossenbury = Maids

Nuns of Minsk (Thompson, R. H., 1878), V. 598

— (1877), V. 726

Nuns of St Jago = Terrible Unknown

Nuns turn'd Libertines (1730), II. 380

Nun, the Dun and the Son of a Gun = Robert the Devil

Nuovo Figaro (1837), IV. 513

Nuptial Benison = Fairy Favours

Nuptial Masque (1734), II. 380

Nuptial Noose (Brown, W. H., 1884), V. 282

Nuptials (Christian, T. P., 1791), III. 243

— (Ramsay, A., 1723), II. 350

— (Shepherd, R., 1761), III. 305

Nurse Charity (1894), V. 726

Nurse Dorothy (1855), V. 726

Nursery Comedies (Bell, Mrs H., 1892), V. 255

Nursery Maid Mistress (1812), IV. 513

+ Nursery Pastoral (Paxton, A., French)

+ Nurseryrhymia (Paxton, A., French)

Nursey Chickweed (Williams, T. J., 1859), V. 625

Nut-brown Maid = Henry and Emma

Nutting Girls = Witch of the Wood

Nydia, the Blind Girl of Pompeii (Fox, G. D., 1892), V. 371

— (1869), V. 726

Nymph of Lurleyburg (Byron, H. J., 1859), V. 295

Nymph of Mount Helicon (1819), IV. 513

Nymph of Nozenaro = Competitors

Nymph of the Danube (Capel, G., 1882), V. 302

Nymph of the Fountain (Cross, J. C., 1797), III. 250

Nymph of the Grotto (Dimond, W., 1829), IV. 307

Nympholept = Amaranthus

Nymphs of the Forest = Marble Bride

Oak and the Bramble = Harry Carley

Oak and the Ivy (Byrne, J., 1808), IV. 575

Oakdell Mystery (Scudamore, F. A., 1884) = Keep to the Right, V. 559, 702

Oakland's Mists = Bought

Oak Leaves and Emeralds (1856), V. 726

Odd Man Out (Turner, M. and Dix, F., 1897), v. 605

Odd Pair (Watson, T. M., 1893), v. 616

Odds and Ends (Planché, J. R., 1819), IV. 376

Odds are Even (Jameson, Mrs, 1893), v. 434

Odd Sayings and Queer Doings = Henry's Table-Talk

Odds—What they were; who won; and who lost them (Parry, S., 1870), v. 515

Odd! to say the least of it (Rose, E., 1886), v. 550

Odd Trick (Muskerry, W., 1895), v. 501

Odd Tricks and Rubbers (1832), IV. 513

Odd Volume (1831), IV. 513

Odd Whims (Repton, H., 1803), IV. 391

Odette (Scott, C. W. and Stephenson, B. C., 1882), v. 726, 815, 842

— (Scott, C. W. and Stephenson, B. C., 1894), v. 558, 815

Odin (Richards, G., 1804), IV. 394

O'Donnell Abou (Stanhope, B., 1875), v. 578

O'Donnell the Red (1826), IV. 513

O'Donaghue of the Lakes (Howard, A., 1840), IV. 589

O'Donoghue and the Princess (1860), v. 726

O'Donoghue of the Lakes (Storer, S., 1858), v. 818

O'Donoghue's Warning (Falconer, E., 1878), v. 361

O'Donoughue and his White Horse (Dibdin, C. I. M., 1818), IV. 294

O'Dora (Burnand, F. C., 1885), v. 291

O'Dowd (Boucicault, D., 1873), v. 93, 269

Oedipus (Dryden, J. and Lee, N., 1678), I. 19, 24, 69, 94, 130, 144, 338, 406

— (Faucit, J. S., 1821), IV. 583

Œdipus, King of Thebes (Clarke, G. S., 1790), III. 243, 378

— (Theobald, L., 1715), II. 359, 444

Œdipus Tyrannus (Maurice, T., 1779), III. 286

— (Shelley, P. B., 1820), IV. 401

Œil crevé (Farnie, H. B., 1872), v. 361, 790

Oello's Friends (1871), v. 726

Oenone (Kirkman, F., 1673), I. 418

O'er Land and Sea (Sheen, W. P., 1899), v. 562

Of Age Tomorrow (Dibdin, T. J., 1800), IV. 142, 287, 580

— (1812), IV. 513

Offa and Ethelbert (Preston, W., 1791), III. 300

Off by the Night Coach = Four Inside

Off Chance (1899), v. 726

Off Duty (Pemberton, T. E., 1884), v. 519

Offer of Marriage = Ambition

Off for London = West Wind

Officer of Fortune (Stanley, A., 1875), v. 579

Officers' Mess = Giddy Major General

Offrande à Terpsichore (Deshayes, 1821), IV. 579

Offrande aux Gracos (Aumer, 1823), IV. 569

Off she goes = Harlequin High flyer

Offspring of Flora (Bretin, 1846), IV. 574

Off the Line (Scott, C. W. and Stephenson, B. C., 1871), v. 557

Off to Algiers (1894), v. 726

Off to the Continent (1835), IV. 513

Off to the Diggings (Courtney, J., 1852), v. 326

— (Nightingale, J. H., 1852), v. 808

— = Gold Fields of Australia

O'Flahertys (Falconer, E., 1864), v. 360

O'Flannigan and the Fairies (Boucicault, D., 1851), v. 267

— (Power, T., 1836), IV. 387

+ Of Noble Birth (Heighway, W., French)

O Gemini (À Beckett, G. A. and Lemon, M., 1852), v. 233

Og, Gog and Magog = Tower of London

Ogre and the Witch (Faraday, P. M., 1897), v. 361

Oh dear! what can the matter be? (1853), v. 726

Oh! Betsy! = Tale of the Kitchen

Oh! It's Impossible (Kemble, J. P., 1780), III. 278, 389

Oh, Liza! (Fryers, A., 1899), v. 374

Oh! my Head! (Allen, F., 1871), v. 238

Oh! my Wife! (De Rohan, D., 1897), v. 343

O'Hooligan's Holiday (Bogue, J. R., 1894), v. 266

Oh! Susannah! (Ambient, M., Atwood, A. and Vaun, R., 1897), v. 240

Oh! These Widows! (Mortimer, J., 1889), v. 494

Oh! this Love! (Kenney, J., 1810)= Love's Mysteries, iv. 336, 592

Oh! those Babes (Clement, W., 1888), v. 314

Oh! those Girls! (Soutar, R.,1882), v. 575

Oh! What a Night! (Terriss, W., 1898), v. 595

Oh, Woman! (Hardie, F., 1895), v. 403

Oil and Vinegar (Byron, H. J., 1874), v. 298

— (Hook, T. E., 1820), iv. 328

Oil Lamp in a New Light = Aladdin the Third

Oily Collins (1861), v. 726

Oithona (1768), iii. 72, 338

Ojitteway Indians = Bounce

O'Jupiter (Hall, F., 1880), v. 399

'Ωκεάνεια (Dibdin, C. I. M., 1804), iv. 42, 291

Okee Pokee Wangee Fum, how do you like your Tartar done? (Travers, W., 1861), v. 726, 821, 842

Old Abbey Ruins = England's Charter

Old Adam (Townsend, W. T., 1853), v. 602

Old Adam's Trust = Grandfather's Clock

Old Admirer (Brookfield, C. H. E., 1899), v. 277

Old and New (1892), v. 726

Old and New Regime = Love's Ordeal

Old and Young (Poole, J., 1822), iv. 386

— (1899), v. 726

Old and Young Stager (Rede, W. L., 1835), iv. 390

Old Bachelor (1830), iv. 513

— = Old Batchelour

Old Bachelor's Birthday (Harvey, F., 1873), v. 408

Old Batchelour (Congreve, W., 1693), i. 193, 199, 241–2, 357, 397; iii. 114

Old Bear (Dibdin, C. I. M., 1825), iv. 296

Old Beelzebub and Harlequin (1812), iv. 513

Old Bishop's Gate (1851), v. 726

"Old Blue Lion" in Gray's Inn Lane (Wilks, T. E., 1843), iv. 421

Old Bogie (1844), iv. 513

Old Bogie of the Sea (Addison, J., 1891), v. 236

Old Booty (Mildenhall, T., 1841), iv. 598

— (1860), v. 726

Old Booty of Bishopsgate = Old Booty

Old Boys and the New (Lewis, H. M., 1888), v. 459

Old Bridge of the Isle of Luis = Dead Guest

Old Bureau (Paull, H. M., 1891), v. 516

Old Chapel Ruins = Rose Lendin

Old Chateau (Coyne, J. S., 1854), v. 327

— (1831), iv. 513

Old Cherry Tree (Hazlewood, C. H., 1866), v. 726, 796, 842

Old Christmas Eve = Regicide

Old Chums (Byron, H. J., 1876), v. 298

— (1884), v. 726

+ Old Church Porch; or, John Anderson My Jo (Dillon, C.; C.L. 1841)

Old Church Walls (1852), v. 726

Old City Manners (Lennox, C., 1775), iii. 113, 281

Old Clay Pipe (Avondale, J. H., 1878), v. 246

— (Henderson, J., 1883), v. 416

Old Clo' (Mackay, C., 1894), v. 469

Old Clo Man (Mendez, C., 1897), v. 806

Old Clothesman (Holcroft, T., 1799), iii. 271

Old Coat (1897), v. 726

Old Coat with a New Lining = Jilted

Old Commodore (1864), v. 726

Old Corporal's Story = Soldier's Legacy

Old Cronies (Smith, S. T., 1880), v. 573

Old Curiosity Shop (Dickens, C., Jr., 1884), v. 344

+ — (Lander, G. (York, 14/5/1877), Dicks)

— (Mackay, J. and Lennard, H., 1881), v. 803

— (Sidney, W., 1871), v. 566

— (Stirling, E., 1840), iv. 97, 407

— (1892), v. 726

— = Nell

Old Customs (Beazley, S., Jr., 1816), iv. 263, 571

Old Daddy Longlegs and Sir Regent Circus (Hazlewood, C. H. and Johnson, D., 1865), v. 727, 796, 800, 842

Old Dame Trot (Allen, O., 1884), v. 239
— (1883), v. 727
Old Dame Trot and her Comical Cat (1864), v. 727
Old Debauchees (Fielding, H., 1732), II. 158, 325
Old England for Ever! (McLaren, A., 1799), III. 284
Old England's Curse = Drop by Drop
Old English Baron (1821), IV. 513
Old English Gentleman (1841), IV. 513
— = Sir Roger de Coverley
Olden Time = (1) Dacre of the South; (2) Henri Quatre
Olden Times (Bain, D., 1841), IV. 258
Oldest Inhabitant (1850), v. 727
Old Fairy of the Woods (1756), III. 403
Old Family Legend = Oliver the Outlaw
Old Farm House on the Common = Kennyngton Crosse
Old Father Thames (Pitt, G. D., 1850), v. 526
Old Father Time (Shute, E. A., 1889), v. 565
— (1847), IV. 513
Old Ferry House (Kingdom, J. M., 1850), v. 444
Old Fidelity = Mysteries of Callow Abbey
Old Figure = No. 2
Old Finsbury (Wilkins, J. H., 1860), v. 823
Old Flame (Blackmore, W. T., 1882), v. 262
Old Flames (Maltby, A., 1884), v. 473
Old Fleet Prison (Cooper, F. F., 1845), IV. 283
Old Folks (Paul, H. M., 1867), v. 516
— (1864), v. 727
Old Folks at Home = March Winds and April Showers
Old Fools (Dibdin, C. I. M., 1800), IV. 290
Old Fools will be medling = Win her and Take her
Old Fool worse than any = He wou'd if he Cou'd
Old Forge (Osborne, C., 1872), v. 508
— (1890), v. 727
Old Fox Caught at Last (1740), II. 367
Old Fox Inn (Hazlewood, C. H., 1875), v. 415

Old Friends (Atkyns, S., 1847), IV. 257
— (Greville, Lady V., 1890), v. 394
— (1890), v. 727
Old Gamul (Newbigging, T., 1892), v. 502
Old Garden (Davies, H., 1895), v. 338
Old Gentleman (Webster, B. N., 1832), IV. 417
Old Gooseberry (Williams, T. J., 1869), v. 626
Old Gossett = Going it
Old Graspall outwitted (1790), III. 338
Old Grimey (Murdoch, J. M., 1872), v. 499
Old Guard (Boucicault, D., 1843), IV. 269
— (Farnie, H. B., 1887), v. 363
Old Harlequin's Fireside (1804), IV. 513
Old Heads and Young Hearts (Boucicault, D., 1844), IV. 270
Old Heads on Young Shoulders (Moncrieff, W. T., 1830), IV. 360 [This is evidently a revised version of Home for the Holidays]
Old Home (Buchanan, R., 1889), v. 285
Old Honesty (Morton, J. M., 1848), IV. 363
Old Horse Pistol = Little Strawbonnet-maker
Old House at Home (Coyne, J. S., 1847) = This House to be Sold, IV. 285, 514
— (1860), v. 727
Old House in the City = Bill-Sticker
Old House in the West = Cead Mille Failthe
Old House of Paris = Partners
Old House on Thames Street (Kingdom, J. M., 1861), v. 444
Old House on the Bridge of Notre Dame (Suter, W. E.), v. 819
Old House on the Thames (1849), IV. 514
Old Hulk = Exiles of France
Old Husbands and Young Wives (Seed, H., 1868), v. 560
Old Interest (1753), III. 338
Old Ireland's Shamrock has not withered yet = Shingawn
Old Isaak Walton (Greenwood, T. L., 1858) = Harlequin and Old Isaac Walton, v. 727, 842

Old Mother Goose and the Golden Eggs (Burnot, W., 1882), v. 293

Old Mother Hubbard (1880), v. 727

Old Mother Hubbard and her Dog (1833), IV. 514

Old Mother Hubbard and her Wonderful Dog, Mother Shipton and her Comical Cat, Jack and Jill, and the Extraordinary Adventures of Master Tommy Tucker and Little Miss Muffet (1871), v. 727

Old Mother Hubbard (Doyle, T. F., 1889), v. 789

Old Nick (Dibdin, T. J., 1822), IV. 304, 581

Old Oak Chest (Scott, J. M., 1816), IV. 397

Old Oak Tree (Raymond, R. J., 1835), IV. 389

— = Criminal

Old Offender (Planché, J. R., 1859), v. 527

Old Old Story (Marchant, F., 1868), v. 475

Old One Caught in a Trick = Harlequin Scapin

Old One in Danger of being Dissected = French Doctor Outwitted

Old Ones and Young Ones (Dibdin, T. J., 1829), IV. 305

Old Pals (Clarance, L., 1884), v. 311

— (Mackersy, W. A.), v. 471

Old Parr (Lemon, M., 1843), IV. 344, 595

Old Parr and the Magic Pills (Pitt, G. D., 1848), IV. 375

Old Partners (1880), v. 727

Old Phil Hardy (Conquest, G., 1863), v. 727, 842

Old Phil's Birthday (Wooler, J. P., 1862), v. 632, 824

+ Old Poz (Edgeworth, Maria; printed in *Juvenile Plays for Home Performance (French)*)

Old Promise (Crozier, C., 1898), v. 331

Old Quizzes (Hall, R., 1797), III. 266

Old Ragshop (Marchant, F., 1869), v. 475

Old Regimentals (Bernard, W. B., 1831), IV. 265

Old Robin and his Niece = Deceiver

Old Roscius (McLaren, A., 1805), IV. 351

Old Rugg's Words = Billy Duck

+ Old Sadler's Ghost; or, The Wells in the Days of Queen Bess (Dibdin, C. I. M.; S.W., 1802)

Old Sailors (Byron, H. J., 1874), v. 113, 298

Old St Paul's (1841), IV. 514

— (1859), v. 727

— = Midnight, the Thirteenth Chime

Old Salt (Besemeres, J., 1868), v. 260

Old Sarah (Greenbank, H., 1897), v. 392

Old Sarum (Hough, A. J., 1868), v. 798

Old Scapegoat (Fryers, A., 1884), v. 374

Old School (1846), IV. 514

Old School and the New (1852), v. 727

Old School-fellow = All's Right

Old Score (Gilbert, W. S., 1869), v. 379

Old Servants in New Places = Nosegay of Weeds

Old Shadow (1857), v. 727

Old Sinners (Mortimer, J., 1886), v. 494

Old Soldier (Lemon, M., 1845), IV. 344

— (1810), IV. 514

— = Shepherd of Derwent Vale

Old Soldiers (Byron, H. J., 1873), v. 113, 298

Old Song (Wills, F. and King, A. F., 1894), v. 627

Old Spoons (Smale, Mrs T. E., 1899), v. 571

Old Sport (Rimington, C. and Pryce-Clairemont, J., 1893), v. 543

Old Spanish Guinea = Kate of Dover

Old Steady (Murdoch, J. M., 1881), v. 499

Old Story (Byron, H. J., 1861), v. 296

— (1881), v. 727

Old Strike a Light (1833), IV. 514

Old Swansea Castle (Jones, D. H., 1858), v. 800

Old Swiss Church (1849), IV. 514

Old Times (1878), v. 727

— (1890), v. 727

Old Times and New Times = Wig Reforms

Old Times in Virginia = Yankee Pedlar

Old Toll House (Hazlewood, C. H., 1861), v. 727, 796, 842

— (1845), IV. 514

Old Troop (Lacy, J., 1663), I. 52, 212, 418

Old Trusty (Gordon, W., 1861), v. 385

Old Turtles (1819), IV. 514

On and Off the Stage = Woodleigh

On an Island (Jones, J. W., 1879), v. 153, 440

On an old Harpsichord (1897), v. 728

On Bail (Gilbert, W. S., 1877), v. 380

On Board the Mars (1830), IV. 514

On Business (Desprez, F., 1880), v. 343

Once Again (Broughton, F. W. and Browne, G. W., 1884), v. 281

— (Cuthbert, E., 1879), v. 331

Once a Lover, Always a Lover = She-Gallants

Once a Week (Wilmot, A. A. and Harrison, 1881), v. 628

Once in a Century (À Beckett, G. A. and Bligh, V., 1877), v. 234

Once in a Hundred Years = Night's Frolic

Once too often (Glover H., 1862), v. 728, 793, 842

Once upon a Time (Goodyer, F. R., 1868), v. 384

— (Parker, L. N. and Tree, Sir H. B., 1894), v. 513

— (Russell, E. H. and Furnival, H., 1889), v. 553

Once upon a time there were two kings (Planché, J. R., 1853), v. 527

On 'Change (Lawrence, E., 1885), v. 451

— (1867), v. 728

On Chesil Beach (1894), v. 728

On Condition (Reece, R., 1882), v. 539

Ondine (Fitzball, E., 1843), IV. 83, 316

— (Stirling, E., 1843), IV. 613

— (1843), IV. 514

On Distant Shores (Burnot, W. and Bruce, H. P., 1897), v. 293

On Duty (1845), IV. 514

One and All (Jodrell, R. P., 1787), III. 277

One and Twenty (Dibdin, T. J., 1828), IV. 305

One Bird in the Hand is worth Two in the Bush (1803), IV. 514

One Black Spot (Hazlewood, C. H., 1870), v. 414

One Coat and Two Bodies = Lancers

One Crime (Townsend, W. T., 1839), IV. 414

— = Strange but True

One False Step (Mackay, W. J., 1893), v. 470

One False Step (Travers, W., 1874), v. 603

— (1873), v. 728

— = Guilty Mother

One Fault (Moncrieff, W. T., 1833), IV. 360, 600

— (Selby, C., 1831), IV. 84, 397

— (Warren, E. and Elliott, C., 1885), v. 614

One Fool makes many (1807), IV. 515

One Foot by Land and One Foot by Sea (Male, G., 1811), IV. 515, 635

One for Another = My Landlady's Gown

One for his Nob (Manuel, E., 1874), v. 475

One Good Turn deserves another (Morton, J. M., 1862), v. 496

— = (1) Rival Tars; (2) Rob the Ranter

One Half Hour (Norman, G. T., 1892), v. 505

One-handed Monk = Manfredoni

One Hour (Bayly, T. H., 1836), IV. 263, 571

One Hour from Humphrey's Clock = Old Curiosity Shop

One Hour with Napoleon (Webb, C., 1844) = Hour with Napoleon, IV. 480, 515, 635

£150,000 (Ebsworth, J., 1854), v. 353

102 (Milner, H. M., 1827), IV. 357

— (1834), IV. 515

One Hundred Battle Steeds (1836), IV. 515

One Hundred Cuirassiers (Phillips, R., 1859), v. 728, 810, 842

£100 a Side (Brown, J. R., 1881), v. 282

£100 Note (Peake, R. B., 1827), IV. 370

£100 Reward (1879). v. 728

One Hundred Pounds Reward—A Child Lost (1865), v. 728

One Hundred Years Hence = 1934

One Hundred Years Old (1875), v. 728

One Law for Man (Brookfield, C. H. E., 1899), v. 277

One More (1899), v. 729

One Night at Margate (1828), IV. 515

One O'Clock (Lewis, M. G., 1811), IV. 346

— (1848), IV. 515

One O'Clock = (1) Robber's Wife; (2) Wood Demon

One of Our Girls (Howard, B., 1885), v. 428

One of the Best (Hicks, Sir S. and Edwardes, G., 1895), v. 420

One of the Boys (Summers, W., 1896), v. 587

— = On the Move

One of the Bravest (1895), v. 728

One of the Family (Capel, G. and Benton, F., 1898), v. 302

— = Turtle Doves

One of the Girls (Darnley, J. H. and Dallas, J., 1896), v. 337

One of Them (Chambers, C. H., 1886), v. 205, 307

One of Us (Melford, M., 1884), v. 484

+ One of You Must Marry (n.d., *French*)

One Rake in a Thousand (1783), III. 338, 403

One Shade Deeper (1863), v. 728

+ One Snowy Night (Ware, J. R., *Dicks*)

One Step from the King's Highway (1885), v. 728

One Summer Afternoon (1894), v. 728

One Summer's Day (Esmond, H. V., 1897), v. 359

One Summer's Night (Broughton, F. W., 1882), v. 281

One Thousand Napoleons (Campbell, A. V., 1862), v. 728, 783, 842

£1000 Reward (Cordyce, and Roberts, G., 1892), v. 325

One Thousand Seven Hundred and Seventy Three = Charlotte

One too many (Burnand, F. C., 1874), v. 290

— (Ryan, D. L., 1836), IV. 396 [where wrongly ascribed to M. D. Ryan]

One too many for him (Williams, T. J., 1868), v. 625

One Touch of Nature (Webster, B. N., 1859), v. 618

One Tree Hill (Craven, H. T., 1865), v. 329

One Tree Square (1865), v. 728

One True Heart (1875), v. 728

One, Two, Three, Four, Five, by Advertisement (?Reeve, J. or ?Reynolds, J. H., 1819), IV. 515, 635

One Witness (Townsend, W. T., 1850), v. 728, 821, 842

One Word (1858), v. 728

On Foreign Service (1898), v. 728

On Guard (Gilbert, W. S., 1871), v. 379

On Guy Fawkes Day (Darnley, J. H. and Bruce, H. P., 1897), v. 337

On Her Majesty's Service (Hatchman, H. W. and May, H. G., 1891), v. 409

On his Oath (Aldin, C. A., 1887), v. 238

On Lease (Dick, C., 1891), v. 344

On Leave (Horner, F., 1897), v. 427

Only a Boy (1899), v. 728

Only a Clod (Simpson, J. P., 1851), v. 567

Only a Clown = Harlequinade

Only a Common Sailor (1896), v. 728

Only a Dream (Brandon, J., 1888), v. 274

— (Forde, A. C., 1885), v. 370

— (1894), v. 728

Only a Farmer's Daughter (Barnes, E. and Levick, F., 1897), v. 249

Only a Governess (Sketchley, A., 1872), v. 571

Only a Half-penny (Oxenford, J., 1855), v. 509, 809

Only a Head (Newbound, E., 1880), v. 503

+ Only a Jest (Seymour, M., *French*)

Only a Life = Ethel

Only a Model (Ramsay, C., 1892), v. 728, 812, 842

Only an Actor (1884), v. 728

— = Garrick

Only an Actress (Gratienne, Mlle, 1898), v. 388

Only a Player (Bandmann, D. E., 1873), v. 248

Only a Quaker Maid (Llewellyn, F., 1898), v. 461

Only a Scrap of Paper = Scrap of Paper

Only a Shilling and What became of it (Abel, W. H., 1872), v. 234

Only a Tramp (1880), v. 728

Only a Vagabond (1881), v. 728

Only a Waif (Clement, W., 1888), v. 314

— (1876), v. 728

Only a Woman (Daly, A., 1875), v. 333
— = Clarice
Only a Woman's Hair (Vandenhoff, H., 1873), v. 606
Only for Life (Hazlewood, C. H., 1877), v. 415
— (1874), v. 728
Only Jones (1883), v. 728
Only My Cousin (Newbound, E., 1880), v. 502
Only One (1886), v. 728
Only Six Hours More (1825), IV. 515
Only Three Years Ago (Dickinson, C. H., 1898), v. 344
Only To-night (Russell, E. H., 1888), v. 553
Only Two Common Sailors = Bill and Me
Only Way (Wills, F., 1898), v. 210, 627
On Oath = Wrexford
On Parade (Scarlett, W., 1895), v. 557
On Probation (Matthews, B. and Jessop, G. H., 1889), v. 480
On Ruin's Brink (Newbound, E., 1881), v. 503
On Service (Digges, W., 1878), v. 345
On Shannon's Shore (Cooke, F., 1895), v. 324
On Shore from the Hercules (1880), v. 728
On Strike (À Beckett, A. W., 1873), v. 233
— (Goldschmidt, A., 1894), v. 383
On the Bench (Pemberton, T. E., 1883), v. 519
On the Brain (Pleon, H., 1888), v. 528
On the Brink (Schiff, E., 1875), v. 557
[A play of this name is credited by *French* to J. T. Grein]
On the Briny (1895), v. 728
On the Cards (Thompson, A., 1868), v. 597
On the Clyde (Scott, W. S., 1875), v. 558
On the Continong (Blouet, P., 1897), v. 266
On the Frontier (Johnstone, A. L., 1891), v. 438
On the Indian Ocean (Lee, H., 1878), v. 452
On the Jury (Phillips, W., 1871), v. 523
On the March (Yardley, W., Stephenson, B. C. and Clay, C., 1896), v. 635

On the Move (Tanner, J. T., 1899), v. 591
On the Ranch (Everitt, H., 1896), v. 359
On the Rink (Burnand, F. C., 1876), v. 290
On the Road (Dowsett, E., 1894), v. 350
— = Strollers
On the Sands (Marshall, P. F., 1887), v. 478
On the Sea Shore (1891), v. 729
On the Sly (Morton, J. M., 1864), v. 496
On the Spree (1873), v. 729
On the Spur of the Moment = Spur of the Moment
On the Thames (Grain, R. C., 1883), v. 386
On the Tiles (Stirling, E., 1846), IV. 408
On the Track (Towers, E., 1877), v. 601
— (1878), v. 729
— = Vagabonds
On the Verge (France, E. S. and Dobell, F., 1888), v. 372
— (1885), v. 729
On the Wrong Tack = Anxious Time
On Thorns (Robinson, D., 1880), v. 547
On Toast (Horner, F., 1888), v. 427
On Tour (Field, W. F., 1887), v. 366
— (Mortimer, J., 1886), v. 494
— (1895), v. 729
Ony-na-Pocas (Connor, B., 1879), v. 320
On Zephyr's Wings (Hodgson, A. H. and Hodgson, A. C., 1891), v. 423
Oonagh (Falconer, E., 1866), v. 360
Oonagh of the Broken Heart = Boyne Water
Oonah of the Hills = Deoch and Durass
Oor Geordie = Our Geordie
Opal Ring (Godfrey, G. W., 1885), v. 185, 383
Open Gate (Chambers, C. H., 1887), v. 205, 307
Open House (Buckstone, J. B., 1833), IV. 274
— (Byron, H. J., 1885), v. 299
Opening Night (1814), IV. 515
Opening of London Bridge = August First
Open Sesame (À Beckett, G. A. and Lemon, M., 1844), IV. 250
— (Douglass, J. T., 1876), v. 348
— (Heathcote, A. M., 1892), v. 415

Orphans of Valneige = Sister's Sacrifice
Orphan Soldier (1821), IV. 515
Orphans Protected = Deceitful Steward
Orpheus (Galt, J., 1814), IV. 318, 636
— (Hill, Sir J., 1740), II. 336; III. 269
— (1749), II. 380
Orpheus and Eurydice (Byron, H. C.,
 1863), V. 296
— (Dennis, J., 1707), II. 318
— (Gentleman, F., 1783), III. 264
— (Houlton, R., 1784), III. 273
— (Sommer, H., 1740), II. 355
— (Theobald, L., 1740), II. 359, 445
— (Weekes, J., 1743), II. 363
— (1712), II. 380
— (1718), II. 132, 252, 380
— (1792), III. 338
— (1871), V. 729
— = Olympic Devils
Orpheus and P(Eurydice) (Rose, E. and
 "Captain Coe", 1891), V. 550
Orpheus and the Death of Eurydice
 (1740), II. 451
Orpheus in the Haymarket (Planché,
 J. R., 1865), V. 528, 811
Orra (Baillie, J., 1812), IV. 161–2, 258
Orsino (Dibdin, T. J., 1820), IV. 302
Orson (Grattan, H. P., 1876), V. 389
Orson the Great and Valentine the
 Small (1862), V. 729
O'Sahara = Black and Blue
Osbern and Ursyne (Hobbes, J. O.,
 1899), V. 422
Osbert (1846), IV. 516
Osburga (Haskin, J., 1829), IV. 324
Oscar and Malvina (1791), III. 72, 338
Oscar the Bandit (Pocock, I., 1834), IV.
 516, 636
Oscar the Dane (1852), V. 729
O'Shatter in his Glory = Wild Irishman
O'Shaughan (Thompson, M. A., 1850),
 V. 598
Osman (Arnold, C., 1757), III. 234
— (Gentleman, F., 1754), III. 264
Osmyn the Renegade (Maturin, C. R.,
 1830), IV. 598
Osorio (Coleridge, S. T., ?1798), III.
 224, 245; IV. 192–3
Osric the Dane (1845), IV. 516
Osric the Lion (Dibdin, C. I. M., 1804),
 IV. 291
— (1823), IV. 516

Ossian (1805), IV. 516
Ostler and the Robber = Innkeeper of
 Abbeville
Ostler's Vision (Rayner, A., 1860), V.
 729, 812, 843
Ostrolenka (Wetherill, and Tryon,
 1884), V. 619
Oswald and Egberta (1801), IV. 516
Oswald of Deira (Chatterton, Lady G.,
 1867), V. 783
Osway (Plumptre, J., 1795), III. 298
Oswyn and Helen = Red Roy
Othello (Kemble, J. P., 1804), IV. 335
— (Soane, G., 1844), IV. 516, 636
— (1892), V. 729
Othello (according to Act of Parliament)
 = Othello Travestie
Othello of Private Life (1849), IV. 91,
 516
Othello, the Moor and his Amour (1861),
 V. 729, 843
Othello, the Moor of Fleet-street
 (Westmacott, C. M., 1833), IV. 418
Othello Travestie (Dowling, M. G.,
 1834), IV. 91, 307, 582
— (1813), IV. 91, 516
Other Days (Robertson, T. W., 1883),
 V. 546
Other Fellow (Horner, F., 1893), V. 427
Other Lady (Horner, F., 1898), V. 427
Other Little Lord Fondleboy (Bowyer,
 F., 1888), V. 271
Other Man's Wife (Peile, F. K., 1898),
 V. 518
Other Men's Sins = Hard Hearts
Other Mr Brooks (1859), V. 729
Other Mr Smith = Facing the Music
Other Woman (Kingsley, E., 1897), V.
 444
Otho and Rutha (Edwards, Miss, 1780),
 III. 258
Otho the Great (Keats, J., 1819
 (written), 1883 (published)), IV. 197–
 8, 334
Otto, a German (Marsden, F., 1879), V.
 477
Otto of Wittelsbach (Thompson, B.,
 1800), IV. 412
Otto the Outcast (Starr, H., 1898), V.
 579
Oude Doullagh (Avondale, J. H., 1879),
 V. 246

Oughts and Crosses (Gordon, G. L., 1884), v. 385

Ought we to visit her? (Gilbert, W. S., 1874), v. 379

— (1877), v. 729

Ouida's Moths = Moths Quitoes

Our Accomplished Domestic (Dale, E., 1878), v. 332

Our Agency (Brumell, R. and Matchem, W. G., 1886), v. 284

Our Amateur Theatricals (Hilliard, H. L., 1894), v. 421

Our American Cousin (Taylor, T., 1858), v. 55, 68, 104–5, 593

Our Angels (Dabbs, G. H. R., 1891), v. 332

Ourang Outang and his Double (Oxberry, W. H., 1833), iv. 602

Our Autumn Manoeuvres (Kenney, C. L., 1871), v. 443

Our Awful Lads (Wyke, E. B., 1878), v. 633

Our Babes in the Wood (Burnand, F. C., 1877), v. 290

Our Babies (Morton, W. E., 1888), v. 497

Our Baby (1878), v. 729

Our Bachelor Friends = Tiffins

Our Bairn (Francks, F. H., 1889), v. 372

Our Beadle (1839), iv. 516

Our Bitterest Foe (Herbert, G. C., 1874), v. 148, 418, 797

Our Boarding School (Rogers, F., 1884), v. 548

Our Bonnie Prince (Chute, J. and Coleman, J., 1887), v. 310

Our Borough Election (Collier, J. W., 1847), iv. 281

Our Bottle (1847), iv. 516

Our Boys (Byron, H. J., 1875), v. 298

Our British Empire (Aldin, C. A., 1898), v. 238

Our Burlesque Baby (De Banzie, E. T., 1895), v. 340

Our Card Basket (Brooks, C. W. S., 1861), v. 277

Our Cinderella (Reece, R., 1883), v. 539

Our Clerks (Taylor, T., 1852), v. 592

Our Club (Burnand, F. C., 1878), v. 291

Our Coastguards (Worden, J., 1892), v. 632

Our Colonial Relative (1886), v. 729

Our Court (Humphrey, E. and Addison, J., 1888), v. 430

Our Cousin German (1839), iv. 516

Our Cousins (Argles, A. and Stayton, F., 1898), v. 243

— (Romer, A., 1869), v. 549

Our Daily Bread (Hazlewood, H. C., Jr., 1885), v. 415

Our Dancing Days (Byrne, J., 1801), iv. 516, 636

Our Daughters = Daughters

Our Dear Boz (1878), v. 729

Our Dear Old Home (Archer, W. J., 1868), v. 242

Our Diva (Rae, C. M., 1886), v. 532, 811

Our Doctors (Roberts, Sir R. and Mackay, J., 1891), v. 545

Our Doll's House = Our Toys

Our Domestics (Hay, F., 1867), v. 411

Our Eldorado (Scudamore, F. A., 1894), v. 559

Our Elsie (1894), v. 729

Our Emmie (Clark, M., 1892), v. 311

Our English Admirals (1854), v. 729

Our Eyes may deceive us = Mew Peerage

Our Family Dentist (1858), v. 729

Our Family Jars (1896), v. 729

Our Family Legend (Stockton, R., 1892), v. 585

— (1862), v. 729

Our Family Motto (Durant, H., 1889), v. 352

Our Farm (Rose, E., 1872), v. 549

Our Father (1897), v. 729

Our Female American Cousin (Galen, C., 1860), v. 729, 793, 843

Our First Visitors = Triple Dilemma

Our Flat (Musgrave, Mrs H., 1889), v. 500

Our Flirt (1897), v. 729

Our Flossie (Field, W. F., 1888), v. 366

Our French Lady's Maid (Morton, J. M., 1858), v. 496

Our Friends (March, M. G., 1872), v. 475

— (Righton, M., 1888), v. 543

Our Friend the Duke (Webb, C., 1848), iv. 516, 636

Our Future Fate (1823), iv. 97, 516

Our Gal (Johnson, G. D., 1856), v. 437

Our Garden (McNamara, A., 1894), v. 471

Our Geordie (Cooper, J. B., 1872), v. 324

Our Girls (Byron, H. J., 1879), v. 299
— (1898), v. 729

Our Goblins (1882), v. 729

Our Golden Wedding (1876), v. 729

Our Great Surprise (Blyth, H., 1890), v. 266

Our Greek Play (1892), v. 729

Our Guardian Angel (Burnette, C., 1895), v. 293

Our Hated Rival (Bayliff, R. L. and Bayliff, C. M. A., 1891), v. 253

Our Helen (Reece, R., 1884), v. 539

Our Hostess (Bartholeyns, A. O'D., 1897), v. 252

Our House (1842), IV. 14, 516

Our Hussars (1862), v. 729

Ourika, the Orphan of Senegal (Ebsworth, J., 1828), IV. 308

Our Irish Lodger (1840), IV. 636

Our Irish Visitors (1894), v. 729

Our Island Home (Gilbert, W. S., 1870), v. 379

Our Joan (Merivale, H. C. and Merivale, Mrs H., 1887), v. 487

Our John (Murray, P., 1899), v. 500

Our Lady of the Willow (1844), IV. 516
— (1854), v. 729

Our Lass (Stephens, W., 1886), v. 581

Our Last Rehearsal (Perry, Mrs, 1893), v. 520

Our Lodger (Blood, J. J., 1885), v. 266

Our Lodgers (Brunner, Mme, 1868), v. 284

Our Lot in Life (Hazlewood, C. H., 1862), v. 412

Our Lottie = For Charity's Sake

Our Lovers (1881), v. 729

Our Luck (Friel, C. D., 1876), v. 373

Our Mary Anne (Buckstone, J. B., 1838), IV. 275

Our M.D. (1881), v. 729

Our Mess (Grain, R. C., 1883), v. 387

Our Mutual Friend = Found Drowned

Our National Defences (?Coyne, J. S. or ?Webster, B. N., 1848), IV. 516, 577, 616
— (1852), v. 729

Our Native Home (Whitlock, C. and Sargent, J., 1892), v. 621

Our Native Land (Cross, J. C., 1803), IV. 286

Our Nelly (Craven, H. T., 1853), v. 328

Our New Governess (Brooks, C. W. S., 1845), IV. 14, 271

Our New Lady's Maid (Coape, H. C., 1852), v. 729, 784, 843

Our New Man = (1) New Groom; (2) Waiter at Cremorne

Our Nurse Dorothy (Harris, A. G., 1855), v. 729, 795, 843

Our Old House at Home (Blake, T. G., 1841), IV. 268

Our Opera (1893), v. 729

Our Own Anthony and Cleopatra (Burnand, F. C., 1873), v. 290

Our Own Correspondent (Strachan, J. S., 1871), v. 585

Our Own Hearth at Home (Wilkins, J. H., 1849), IV. 419

Our Pal (Dabbs, G. H. R., 1889), v. 332

Our Party (Lloyd, A., 1884), v. 461

Our Pet (Edwardes, C. T. M., 1873), v. 354

Our Play (Graham, R. G., 1893), v. 387

Our Pleasant Sins (Barrett, W. and Hannan, C., 1893), v. 251

Our Polly (Towers, E., 1881), v. 601

Our Private Theatricals (1894), v. 730

Our Quiet Chateau (Reece, R., 1867), v. 537

Our Regiment (Hamilton, H., 1883), v. 401

Our Relations (Jarman, F., 1891), v. 434

Our Relatives (Ellis, W., 1880), v. 357

Ours (Robertson, T. W., 1866), v. 546

Our Sailor Lad (Kirke, F. J., 1895), v. 445

Our Seamen = Scuttled Ship

Ourselves (Burnand, F. C., 1880), v. 291
— (Chambers, M., 1811), IV. 279

Our Servant Girl (Lawrence, F. and Vane, C. A., 1896), v. 451

Our Servants' Hall (Grain, R. C., 1887), v. 387

Our Silver Wedding (Willing, J., 1886), v. 626

Our Sisters (1834), IV. 516

Our Social Parlour (Lindon, E., 1892), v. 460

Our Sons and Daughters (Cooke, J. F., 1879), v. 324

Out of his Element (1831), IV. 516

Out of Luck (Stirling, E., 1839), IV. 406

Out of Place (Lemon, M., 1840), IV. 344, 516, 636

— (Reynolds, F., 1805) = Castle of Lausanne, IV. 51, 391, 439, 607

— (1826), IV. 516

— (1870), V. 730

Out of Sight (Stephenson, B. C., 1881), V. 582

Out of Sight, out of 'Erin = Conn

Out of Sight, out of Mind (Summers, K., 1894), V. 587

— (1859), V. 730

Out of Sorts (1884), V. 730

Out of Spirits = Slate Pencillings

Out of the Beaten Track (Milton, M., 1889), V. 490

Out of the Frying Pan (Graves, A. P. and Toft, P., 1872), V. 389

— (Wright, B., 1867), V. 633

Out of the Frying Pan into the Fire = Visit to the Wells

Out of the Hunt (Reece, R. and Thorpe, T., 1881), V. 539

Out of the Past (Grayle, P., 1893), V. 390

— (Nolan, H., 1898), V. 505

Out of the Rain (1847), IV. 516

Out of the Ranks (Reece, R., 1884), V. 539

Out of the Shadow-land (Stuart, M., 1899), V. 586

Out of the World (?Burnett, H. or Smith, L., 1892), V. 292, 782, 817

Out of Town (1896), V. 730

Out on the Loose (Barnett, M. and Barnett, B., 1850), V. 249

Out on the Sly (Selby, C., 1847), IV. 399

Outpost (1838), IV. 516

Outside Passenger (Brewer, G., 1811), IV. 516, 636

Outsider (Dawson, F., 1890), V. 339

Outward Bound (Ganthony, N., 1896), V. 376

— (1875), V. 730, 842, 843

Outwitted (Anderson, G., 1899), V. 240

— (Aylmer, B., 1873), V. 246

— (Praegèr, N., 1890), V. 530

— (Serle, Mrs W., 1889), V. 561

— (Smythies, W. G., 1891), V. 573

— (Vaughan, Mrs, 1871), V. 607

— (1884), V. 730

Outwitted = Woman Outwitted

Outwitted at last (Earle, 1817), IV. 308

— (1864), V. 730

Over Heads and Ears (Reece, R., 1876), V. 538

Overland Journey to Constantinople (Brough, R. B., 1854), V. 278

Overland Mail (1858), V. 730

Overland Route (Taylor, T., 1860), V. 593

Overlooker (1851), V. 730

Over-Proof (Burnand, F. C., 1878), V. 291

Over the Border (1870), V. 730

Over the Bridge = (1) Blue Baron; (2) Modern Collegians

Over the Cliff (Robbins, A. F., 1884), V. 544

Over the Garden Wall (Grundy, S., 1881), V. 396

Over the Garden Wall again (1882), V. 730

Over the Wall = Dinky Doo

Over the Water (Hook, T. E., 1820), IV. 328

Over the Way (Buckingham, L. S., 1856), V. 781

— (Meritt, P., 1878), V. 486

— (Robertson, T. W., 1893), V. 547

Overthrow of Evil Ministers = Majesty Misled

Ovingdean Grange (Cooper, F. F., 1851), V. 324

— (1863), V. 730

Owen Ivan King of Manko (1833), IV. 516

Owen, Prince of Powys (1822) = Henry I, IV. 516

Owl Sisters (Fitzball, E., 1842), IV. 316

Owner of the Works = Man of the World

Oxford Act (1733), II. 380

Oxford Agreement (Hawkins, L., 1897), V. 410

Oxford Roratory = Ragged Uproar

Oxford Scholar = (1) Brazen Nose College; (2) Frolick

Oxonian in Town (Colman, G., 1767), III. 8, 182-3, 246

Oxygen (Reece, R. and Farnie, H. B., 1877), V. 538

Ozmyn and Daraxa (Boaden, J., 1793), III. 118, 238

Paali (1823), IV. 516

Pace that Kills (Hazlewood, C. H., 1870), v. 414

Pacha = Ali Pacha

Pacha's Bridal (Lemon, M., 1836) = Pasha's Bridal, IV. 345, 517, 595

Pacha's Pets (Oxberry, W. H., 1838), IV. 367, 602, 603

Pacha's Revenge = Turkish Lovers

Packet Boat (Birch, S., 1794), III. 238

Packet from England (Tristram, W. O., 1895), v. 604

Pad (Woodbridge, R., 1793), III. 317

Paddy Bull (McLaren, A., 1811), IV. 351

Paddy Carey (1860), v. 843

Paddy Carey's Fortune = Valentine's Day

Paddy Cary, the Boy of Clogheen (Power, T., 1833), IV. 387

Paddy in the Moon = Four Kings

Paddy Miles, the Limerick Boy (Pilgrim, J., 1836), IV. 372

Paddy O'Rafferty (1811), IV. 516

— = Irishman's Fortune

Paddy's Dream = Whiskey and Water

Paddy's Ghost (1863), v. 730

Paddy shooting the Moon (1854), v. 730

Paddy's Portfolio (1854), v. 730

Paddy Whack in Italia (Lover, S., 1841), IV. 347

Padlock (Bickerstaffe, I., 1768), III. 123, 199, 237

Paetus and Arria (Burton, or Nicholson, J., 1809), IV. 277

Pagan King, the Christian Bishop and the Princely Martyrs of Eagle's Hall = Tamworth in A.D. 670

Pageant (O'Keeffe, J.), III. 294

Page from a Novel (1881), v. 730

Page from Balzac = Night Off

Page from History (1850), v. 730

Page from the Life of David Garrick (1895), v. 730

Page from Woman's History = Lady Rosabel

Page of Palermo (1837), IV. 636

Page's Escapade = Which is it?

Page's Revenge = Countess d'Argentine

Page 13 of the Black Book = Hand and Glove

Page 21 (Almar, G., 1838), IV. 253

Page 21 of an Interesting History = Page 21

Pahdre na Mouhl (1830), IV. 516

Paid in Full (Miller, St A., 1887), v. 488

— (1873), v. 730

Painless Dentistry (Becher, M., 1875), v. 254

Painter of Antwerp (1882), v. 730

Painter of Athens (Macnair, A., 1862), v. 471

Painter of Ghent (Jerrold, D. W., 1836), IV. 332

Painter of Rome (Rice, C.), v. 813

Painter of Terracina (1853), v. 730

Painter's Breakfast (Brenan, 1756), III. 239 [This was acted Smock Alley, Dublin, 2/4/1756]

Painter's Study (1841), IV. 516

— = Plots in Madrid

Paint, Poetry and Putty! = Caleb Quotem and his Wife!

Paired Off (Buckle, G., 1885), v. 286

— (Parry, J., 1833), IV. 516

Pair of Boots (1873), v. 730

Pair of Kids (Hewson, J. J., 1888), v. 420

Pair of Knickerbockers (Phillpotts, E., 1899), v. 524

Pair of Lovers (1892), v. 730

Pair of Lunatics (Walkes, W. R., 1889), v. 611

Pair of Pigeons (Stirling, E., 1857), v. 584, 818

Pair of Red Heels (1892), v. 730

Pair of Spectacles (Grundy, S., 1890), v. 206, 397

Pair of Them (Wray, P., 1879), v. 633

Pair o' Wings (Meritt, P. and Girnot, H., 1878), v. 486

Palace of Geneva (1841), IV. 516

Palace of Mirth (1778), III. 339

Palace of Mystery = Zangarotti, the Demon of the Apennines

Palace of Palermo = Heir of Villeroy

Palace of Pearl (Younge, W. and Murray, A., 1886), v. 637

Palace of Plenty = Basket-Maker

Palace of Statues = Morilda's Wand

Palace of the Silver Lake = Witch and the Owl

Palace of the Waters = Two Caliphs

Palace of Truth (Gilbert, W. S., 1870), v. 133-6, 142, 379

Paris (Croly, G., 1830), IV. 285
— (Sketchley, A., 1864), V. 570
Paris and London (Planché, J. R., 1828), IV. 36, 145, 378
Paris and Pleasure (Selby, C., 1859), V. 560, 815
Paris Drag = Delights of the Diligence
Paris Federation (1790), III. 338
Parish Beadle (1831), IV. 517
Parish Boy's Adventures = Oliver Twist
Parish Boy's Progress = (1) "Boz's" Oliver Twist; (2) Oliver Twist
Parish Clerk (Boucicault, D., 1866), V. 268
Parish Revolution (À Beckett, G. A., 1836), IV. 517, 636
Parish Waif (1866), V. 731
Parisian Romance (Cazauran, A. R., 1888), V. 731, 783, 843
Paris in an Uproar (1789), III. 54, 339
Paris in 1750 = Comfortable Lodgings
Paris in 1793 = Delicate Ground
Paris in 1792 (1856), V. 731
Paris in 1720 = Monseigneur
Paris in the Olden Time = Henri Quatre
Paris Robbers = Monseigneur
Paris's Triumph = False Triumph
Parliamentary Express = Railroad of Life
Parlour Maid (1897), V. 731
Parlours (Reece, R., 1880), V. 539
Parma Violets = Baffled
Parnasso in Festa (1734), II. 397
Parole of Honour (Serle, T. J., 1837), IV. 400, 610
Parricide (Allen, R., 1824), IV. 251, 567, 583
— (King, W., 1833), IV. 592
— (Shirley, W., 1739), II. 58, 355
— (Sterling, J., 1736), II. 357
— (1822), IV. 517
— = Battle of Agincourt
Parricide's Curse = (1) Bridge of Notre Dame; (2) Doomed Bridge
Parricide's Return = Doomed House
Parricide, the Lover and the Avenger = Swiss Girl
Parrot (1895), V. 731
Parson (Fizgerald, S. J. A., 1891), V. 369
Parson Jim (Dickinson, C. H., 1889), V. 344

Parson's Nose! (Moncrieff, W. T., 1835), IV. 143, 360, 600
Parson's Play (Battams, J. S., 1889), V. 253
Parson's Wedding (Killigrew, T., 1663), I. 299, 416
Parson Thorn (Challis, R., 1891), V. 307
Parson Wynne's Trust (Heriot, P., 1898), V. 419
Part du demon (1845), IV. 517, 636
Parted (Reeve, W., 1874), V. 540
Parted and Reunited (Hazlewood, C. H., 1872), V. 414
Parted in Crime = Vagabond
Parted on the Bridal Hour (Libby, L. J., 1888), V. 459
Parthenia (1764), III. 339
Parthian Exile (Downing, G., 1773), III. 257
Parthian Hero (Gardiner, M., 1742), II. 329 [This was acted Smock Alley, Dublin, 16/3/1742]
Partial Eclipse (1892), V. 731
Particulars of that Affair at Finchley (Coyne, J. S., 1861), V. 328
Partie de chasse d'Henri Quatre (1816), IV. 517
Parting (Fitzgerald, S. J. A., 1899), V. 369
Parting Lovers = Nancy
Parting of the Ways (Bowyer, F. and Edwardes-Sprange, W., 1890), V. 271
Partisans (Planché, J. R., 1829), IV. 378
Partition War (Pryce, R., 1889), V. 531
Partner for Life (1858), V. 731
Partners (Buchanan, R., 1888), V. 285
— (Hoare, P., 1805), IV. 326
— (1840), IV. 636
Partners for Life (Byron, H. J., 1871), V. 113–14, 298
Partners in Crime = Sons of Toil
Parts and Players (Harlowe, F., 1887), V. 404
Party at Hampton Court = Lie of the Day
Party at Montpellier = World as it Goes
Party Wall = (1) Pyramus and Thisbe; (2) Secret
Parvenu (Godfrey, G. W., 1882), V. 383
Pascal Bruno (À Beckett, G. A., 1837), IV. 250, 567
— (Fitzball, E.), IV. 317

Pascha of Pimlico (Morton, J. M., 1861), v. 496, 807

Pas de Fascination (Coyne, J. S., 1848), IV. 285

— (1855), v. 731

Pas de Pippins = Judgment of Paris

Pasha (Ellis, W. and Greenwood, P., 1899), v. 357

— (Grey, A., 1898), v. 394

Pasha of Paradise Place, Pimlico = Pascha of Pimlico

Pasha's Bridal (Lemon,. M., 1836) = Pacha's Bridal, IV. 517, 636

Pa's Odd Trick (Kennedy, J. P., 1897), v. 443

Pa's Pills (Fisher, C. A., 1894), v. 367

Pasquin (Fielding, H., 1736), II. 45–6, 65, 67, 202, 232, 265, 328, 436; III. 116

Pasquin turn'd Drawcansir, Censor of Great Britain = Covent Garden Theatre

Passage in the life of Grace Darling = Humanity

Passage of the Danube = Wallachian

Passage of the Deserts (1838), IV. 517

Passage of the Red Sea = Israelites in Egypt

Passing Cloud (Bernard, W. B., 1850), IV. 266; v. 259

Passing Clouds (1854), v. 843

Passing Fancies (1867), v. 731

Passing Hour (1873), v. 731

Passing the Frontier = Marguerite's Colours

Passing through the Fire (Mead, T., 1873), v. 483

Passion (Roberts, G., 1873), v. 544

— (Stephens, W., 1873), v. 581

Passion and Pride (1853), v. 731

Passion and Principle (Wagner, L., 1883), v. 610

— (1861), v. 731

Passion and Repentance = Love's Frailties

Passionate Mistress = Vice Reclaim'd

Passion Flower = Woman and the Law

Passion Flowers (Robertson, T. W., 1868), v. 546

Passion of Life (Fuller, H., 1899), v. 375

Passion of Sappho (1718), II. 133, 380

Passions (Dibdin, C.), IV. 290

Passions (1899), v. 731

Passion's Battleground = Passing through the Fire

Passions, Love and Jealousy (1823), IV. 517

Passions of the Heart (1876), v. 731

Passion's Paradise = Seven Sins

Passion's Penalty (1884), v. 731

Passion's Peril (Faucquez, A., 1874), v. 364

Passion's Power (Shirley, A., 1886), v. 563

Passion's Slave (Stevens, J. A., 1886), v. 583

— (Stirling, E., 1851), v. 584

Passive Husband = Word for Nature

Pass of Abruzzi = Rat-Trap

Pass of Beresina = Paulina

Pass of Rathconnell = Sylvena! the Rose of Athlone

Passport (Stephenson, B. C. and Yardley, W. 1894), v. 582

Past and Present (Poole, J., 1830), IV. 387

— (1826), IV. 517

Past Four O'Clock (1829), IV. 517

Pasticcio (Arne, T. A., 1773), III. 234

Past Master (Prescott, N., 1899), v. 530

Past Midnight (1855), v. 731

Pastora = Coy Shepherdess

Pastor Fido (Clapperton, W., 1809), IV. 517, 576, 636

— (Fanshawe, Sir R., 1647), I. 138, 410–11

— (Hill, A., 1712), II. 224, 397, 438

— (Settle, E., 1676), I. 101, 118, 428

Pastor's Daughter (Phillips, F. L., 1846), IV. 372

Pastor's Fireside (1831), IV. 517

— = Vicar of Wakefield

Past, Present and Future (Lee, N., 1847), IV. 342

— (1837), IV. 517

— = (1) Scrooge the Miser's Dream; (2) Timely Warning

Past Ten O'Clock and a Rainy Night (Dibdin, T. J., 1815), IV. 299

— (1816), IV. 517

Pat (Roberts, G., Monkhouse, H. and Erwin, H., 1891), v. 545

— (1888), v. 731

Pat a Cake, Pat a Cake, Baker's Man
(Douglass, J. T. and Wright, B.,
1865), v. 731, 788, 824, 843
— (Lee, N., 1843), IV. 517, 636
Pat and his Potatoes (1838), IV. 517
Patchwork (Paul, H. M., 1859), v. 516
Patent of Gentility (1869), v. 731
Patent Seasons (1820), IV. 517
Paternal Affection (1828), IV. 517
Pater Noster (1898), v. 731
Pa, the Ma and the Padishah = Kissi-
Kissi
Path of Life (Dearlove, W. H., 1896), v.
340
Patie and Peggie (Cibber, T., 1730), II.
250, 314, 350
Patie and Roger (1812), IV. 517
Patience (Gilbert, W. S., 1881), v. 144,
380
— (1866), v. 731
Patience the Best Remedy = Wife in the
Right
Patient Carried Off = Six Physicians
Patient Griselda (1799), III. 339
Patient Grizill (?1667), I. 446
Patient Penelope (Burnand, F. C. and
Williams, M., 1863), v. 288
Patient Wife = Griselda
Pat in Portugal (1837), IV. 517
Patricia in a Quandary (Hamilton, C.,
1899), v. 401
Patrician and Parvenu (Poole, J., 1835),
IV. 387
Patrician and Pensioners = Seaweed
Hall
Patrician's Daughter (Marston, J. W.,
1842), IV. 205, 353; V. 103
Patrick Hamilton (Johnston, T. P.,
1882), v. 437
Patrick in Prussia (O'Keeffe, J., 1786),
III. 293
Patrick's Dream (1835), IV. 517
Patrick's Return (Byrne, O., 1817), IV.
517, 636
Patrick's Vow (Franklin, J., 1873), v.
372
— (1876), v. 731
Patrick the Foreigner (1835), IV. 517
Patriot (Bain, D., 1806), IV. 517, 636
— (Code, H. B., 1811), IV. 577
— (Gildon, C., 1702), II. 22, 71, 76, 333,
437

Patriot (Hamilton, C., 1784), III. 69,
266, 386
— (Harrod, W., 1769), III. 267
— (Simpson, J., 1785), III. 31, 32, 307
— (1736), II. 380
— (1784), III. 339
— (1837), IV. 517
— (1861) v. 731
— = (1) Gustavus Vasa; (2) Martinuzzi
Patriot Father (Shoberl, F., 1830), IV.
87, 401
Patriotism! (+Baillie, 1763), III. 339
Patriot King (Bicknell, A., 1788), III.
52, 59, 87, 238
— (Dobbs, F., 1773), III. 257
— = Alfred the Great
Patriot Martyrs = Laura Dibalzo
Patriot Prince (1809), IV. 517
Patriots (1826), IV. 517
Patriot's Daughter (Stirling, E., 1872),
v. 584
Patriots of 1863 = Wrongs of Poland
Patriots of Poland = Oath of Freedom
Patriot Spy (Phillips, F. L., 1859), v.
731, 810, 843
Patron (Foote, S., 1764), III. 156, 173–4,
260
— (Odell, T., 1729), II. 161, 243, 347
— (1793), III. 339
Patronage (1848), IV. 517
— (1849), IV. 517
Patron Saint (Thomas, C., 1888), v. 596
Pat's Thanksgiving (De Frece, M.
1872), v. 341
Pat's Vagaries and the Road-side Inn
(1845), IV. 517
Patter versus Clatter (Mathews, C. J.,
1838), IV. 354
Pat, the Irish Lancer (1888), v. 731
Patty (1872), v. 731
Paul (1852), v. 731
Paula Lazaro (Lemon, M., 1854), v. 455
Paul and Virginia (Cobb, J., 1800), III.
244–5; IV. 280, 577
— (Davey, R., 1886), v. 338
— (Degville, 1810), IV. 579
— (Neil, R., 1881), v. 502
— (Wood, A., 1870), v. 630
— (1811), IV. 517
— (1818), IV. 517
+Paul Braintree, the Poacher (Jerrold,
D.; Cob. 5/7/1831)

Pay to the Bearer—a Kiss (Gordon, W., 1868), v. 385
Peace (1877), v. 731
Peace and Quiet (Williams, T. J., 1861), v. 625
Peace at any Price (Robertson, T. W., 1856), v. 546
Peaceful War (Scotti, S. and Wagner L., 1887), v. 558
Peace in Europe (1749), ii. 397
Peacemaker (1887), v. 731
Peace or War (1878), v. 731
+Peace Triumphant (Smock Alley, Dublin, 15/6/1713)
Peace with Honour = New Year
Peacock and the Crow (Parry, J., 1837), iv. 518, 636
Peacock's Feather (Dibdin, T. J., 1826), iv. 304
Peacock's Holiday (Merivale, H. C., 1874), v. 487
Peal of Belles (1863), v. 731
Pearl among Women (Leslie, H. T., 1870), v. 457
Pearl Darrell (Wilton, K., 1883), v. 629
Pearl of Chamouni (Smith, A. R., 1843), iv. 611
Pearl of Chamouny = Marie
Pearl of Cyprus (1879), v. 731
Pearl of London City = Alice Wingold
Pearl of Paris (Johnstone, J. B., 1871), v. 438
Pearl of Rouen (1852), v. 731
Pearl of Savoy = Marie de Chamouni
Pearl of Spain (1859), v. 731
Pearl of the Drowned = Madeleine
Pearl of the Harem (1842), iv. 518
Pearl of the Ocean (Selby, C., 1847), iv. 399
Pearls of the Rhine = Playing with Water
Pearl, the Peer and the Page = Good Old Queen Bess
Pearly Earl (1895), v. 732
Peasant Boy (Dimond, W., 1811), iv. 47, 306
— (1812), iv. 518
Peasant Bride (1843), iv. 518
Peasant Countess (1843), iv. 518
Peasant Girl of the Pyrenees = Valley of Andoire
Peasant Girl's Dream = Naomi

Peasant Judge (1840), iv. 518
Peasant Marchioness = Blind Father
Peasant of Lucerne (Soane, G., 1815), iv. 403
Peasant Prince = Blindness
+Peasant Queen (Keating, Miss, French)
Peasant Ruffian (1829), iv. 518
Peasant's Dream (1847), iv. 518
Peasant's Frolic (1823), iv. 518
Peasant's Pic-nic = House-warming
Peasant's Revenge = Prisoner of Toulon
Peasant's Wife = Fashionable Fallacy
Peasant Tricked = Stratagems of Harlequin
Pease Porridge Hot (1848), iv. 518
Peccadilloes = Innocent Sins
Pecheur de Portici = Masaniello
Peckham Frolic (Jerningham, E., 1799), iii. 187, 277
Peck's Bad Boy (Pleon, H., 1891), v. 183, 528
— = Shop Boy
Pecksniff (Paulton, H., 1876), v. 516
Peculiar Case (Law, A., 1884), v. 450
Peculiar Family (Reed, G., 1865), v. 540
Peculiar Julia = Hunchback back again
Peculiar Position (Planché, J. R., 1837), iv. 380
Peculiar Proposals (Lowry, J. M., 1876), v. 464
Pedantic Apothecary Quizzed (1794), iii. 339
Pedagogue Puzzled = Two Pupils
Pedigree (Bowring, C. C. and Court, F. H., 1889), v. 271
Pedlar (Davies, R. C., 1889), v. 338
Pedlar Boy (Harrington, R., 1862), v. 404, 795
Pedlar's Acre (Almar, G., 1831), iv. 252
— (Cross, J. C., 1804), iv. 286
— (Dibdin, T. J., 1816), iv. 300
Pedlar's Dream (1836), iv. 518
Pedlar's Pack (1832), iv. 518
Pedlar's Revenge = Life of a Shingler
Pedlar tricked (1763), iii. 339
Pedlar turned Merchant = Caledonia
+Pedrarias (Wilmot, Mrs B.; 8°, 1821 (in Dramas))
Pedrillo (Johnstone, J. B., 1857), v. 438
— (1837), iv. 518
Pedrillo del Campo (1829), iv. 518

Pedro Lobo (1821), IV. 518

Pedro Mendez the South American Pirate = Silver Store Island

Pedro the Cruel and Manuel the Cobbler (1838), IV. 518

Pedro the Devil (1830), IV. 518

Peebles (Chevalier, A. and Mackintosh, W., 1882), V. 309

Peek-a-boo (1886), V. 732

Peel Castle in the Olden Time (Lawson, E., 1873), V. 451

Peep at Portsmouth = Humours of the Navy

+Peep at the Danube; or, Boney Defeated (Dibdin, C. I. M.; S.W., 1809)

Peep at the Election = Paul Pry on Horseback

Peep at the Lord Mayor's Show (McLaren, A., 1821), IV. 352

Peep at the Past = Drama's Levee

Peep at the Times = All for Fame!

Peep at the Vices and Virtues of Rustic and City Life = Young Girl from the Country

Peep Behind the Curtain (Garrick, D., 1767) = New Rehearsal, III. 41, 178, 214, 263, 385

Peep behind the Scenes = CountryActors

Peep behind the Veil = Packet Boat

Peeping Tom (Dibdin, T. J., 1811), IV. 299

— (1897), V. 732

Peeping Tom of Coventry (O'Keeffe, J., 1784), III. 200, 293, 393

Peep into Elysium (1784), III. 339

— = Garrick in the Shades

Peep into the House of Correction = Trumps in the Dumps

Peep into the Forum = School for Orators

Peep into the Seraglio = (1) Greek Captive; (2) Sultan

Peep o'Day (Falconer, E., 1861), V. 360

Peep of Day by a new (Lime) Light (1863), V. 732

The Peep-show Man (Williams, T. J., 1868), V. 625

Peepshowman's Visit = Shah

Peep through the Keyhole = Curiosity

Peer and Peasant (Moncrieff, W. T., 1832), IV. 360, 600

Peer and the Peasant = (1) Armand; (2) Preux Chevalier

Peer and the Peri = Iolanthe

Peer and the Secretary (1849), IV. 518

Peer Gynt (Archer, C. and Archer, W., 1892), V. 242

Peerless Pool (Almar, G., 1833), IV. 252

— (1861), V. 732

Peer of the Realm (Broughton, F. W., 1890), V. 282

Peer or Pauper (Macdonnell-Green, A., 1885), V. 469

Peevish Man (Ludger, C., 1799), III. 283, 391

Peggy (Mackay, J., 1881), V. 470

Peggy Green (Selby, C., 1847), IV. 399

Peggy Larkins (Dibdin, T. J., 1826), IV. 304

Peggy's Little Game (Hodgson, G. S., 1868), V. 423

Peggy's Plot (Gibney, S., 1893), V. 378

Peg the Rake (Grey, A., 1897), V. 394

Peg Woffington (1845), IV. 518

Peleus and Thetis = Jew of Venice

Pelican Lodge = Our Girls

Pelléas and Mélisande (Mackail, J. W., 1898), V. 469

Pemberton (1890), V. 732

Penal Code (Daly, A., 1878), V. 333

Penal Law (Dodson, R., 1879), V. 346

Penal Servitude (Cross, F., 1893), V. 330

Penalty (Cross, J., 1890), V. 330

Penalty of Crime (Gilbert, L., 1896), V. 378

Penance of Polygamy = Chit-Chat

Pen Combatants = Invissible Smirk

Pendarvon (Watson A. E. T. and Clarke, W. S., 1874), V. 615

Penelope (Hawtrey, G. P., 1889), V. 410

— (Horner, B., 1892), V. 426

— (Mottley, J. and Cooke, T., 1728), II. 346, 434

Penmaenmawr (1794), III. 339

Pennsylvania Dutchman = Struck Oil

Penny Hedge (De Vere, F., 1883), V. 344

Penny Wise and Pound Foolish = (1) Gervaise Skinner; (2) Three Fives

Pennyworth of Wit (Dibdin, T. J., ?1795), III. 382

Pens, Ink and Paper (1849), IV. 518

Pensioner's Bride = Chelsea

Pentheus (Amcotts, V. and Anson, W. R., 1866), v. 240

Pentlands (France, E. S., 1872), v. 372

Pentrobin (1891), v. 732

People made happy = Laoeudaimonos

People's Hero (Poole, W. H., 1889), v. 529

People's Idol (Barrett, W. and Widnell, V., 1890), v. 160-1, 250

People's Lawyer (Jones, J. S., 1856), v. 440, 847

People's William (1884), v. 732

Pepita (Tedde, M., 1886), v. 594

Pepper and Salt (1894), v. 732

Pepper's Diary (Morris, A., 1890), v. 493

Percy (More, Mrs H., 1777), III. 96, 288

— (Towne, L., 1877), v. 602

Perdita, the Royal Milkmaid (Brough, W., 1856), v. 279

Peregrinations of Pickwick (Rede, W. L., 1837), IV. 97, 390, 607

Peregrine Pickle (Reade, C., 1851), v. 536

— (1818), IV. 518

Perequillo (1855), v. 732

Perfect Confidence (1854), v. 732

Perfect Crime (Sapte, Walter, Jr., 1898), v. 556

Perfection (Bayly, T. H., 1830), IV. 262

— (1839), IV. 518

Perfect Love (Reece, R., 1871), v. 537

Perfidious Brother (Mestayer, H., 1716), II. 118, 344

— (Theobald, L., 1716), II. 71, 118, 359

Perfidious Pirate, the Modest Maiden and the Trusty Tar = Lass that loved a Sailor

Perfidious Robinson (Lawrence, W., 1882), v. 451

Perfidy (Falconer, E., 1887), v. 361

Perfidy Punished = (1) Black Knight; (2) Brave Cossack

Performers and Fashionables = Tea and Turn Out

Peri (1843), IV. 518

Periander (Tracy, J., 1731), II. 82, 111, 360

Perichole (Desprez, F., 1870), v. 732, 788, 843

— (Murray, A., 1897), v. 500, 808

Perichon (Stephens, L. E. B., 1882), v. 581

Peril (Scott, C. W. and Stephenson, B. C., 1876), v. 557

Peril of the Sea = Sam Scud

Perilous Cavern (1802), IV. 518

Perilous Pass (Campbell, A. V., 1862), v. 732, 783, 843

Perilous Pass of the Cataract = Gipsy King

Perilous Picnic (Wyke, E. B., 1879), v. 633

Perils by Land and Wave (Travers, W., 1858), v. 732, 821, 843

Perils of a Beauty = One False Step

Perils of a Bride = Wedded and Lost

Perils of a Night = Remorse

Perils of a Sailor = Mutiny of the Britannia

Perils of a Seaman = Mutiny of the Britannia

Perils of a Steam Forge = Orphan and the Outcast

Perils of Certain English Prisoners and their Treasure in Women, Children, Silver and Jewels (1858), v. 732

Perils of Crinoline (Barnett, M., 1857), v. 250

Perils of Life (McGuire, T. C., 1899), v. 469

— = Thugs of Paris

Perils of Paris (Shirley, A., 1897), v. 564

Perils of Penury = Prodigal

Perils of Pippins (Jerrold, D. W., 1836), IV. 333

Perils of the Alps = Night

Perils of the Battle and the Breeze = Yellow Admiral

Perils of the Bush = Ned Kelly

Perils of the Ocean = Fifteen Years of a British Seaman's Life

Perils of the Plague = Old St Paul's

Perils of the Road = Stand and Deliver

Peril, the Pelf and the Pearl = Sylvius

Perinet Leclerc (Almar, G., 1833), IV. 252

Peri of the Mist (Cooper, J. W., 1845), IV. 283

Peri who loved the Prince = Camaralzaman and Badoura

Perizzi (1838), IV. 518

Perjur'd Devotee (Bellamy, D., 1739), II. 143, 261, 297

Perjur'd Husband (Centlivre, Mrs S., 1700), II. 159, 166, 220–1, 303

Perjur'd Lover = Cælia

Perjured Nun (?1680), I. 444

Perjured Prince (1728), II. 380

Per-Juror (Bullock, C., 1717), II. 190, 212, 301

Perkin Warbeck (1836), IV. 518

Perla (Manuel, E., 1875), V. 475

Permit (1831), IV. 518

Perola (1883), V. 732

Perolla and Izadora (Cibber, C., 1705), II. 27, 31, 102–3, 310

Perourou, the Bellows Mender (Moncrieff, W. T., 1842), IV. 175, 361

Perouse (Fawcett, J., 1801), IV. 311

— (1846), IV. 518

Per Parcel's Post (Fox, G. D. and Morton, W. E., 1883), V. 371

Perpetual Motion (1855), V. 843

Perplex'd Couple (Molloy, C., 1715), II. 145, 157, 173, 345, 441

Perplex'd Husband (1748), II. 381

Perplex'd Lovers (Centlivre, Mrs S., 1712), II. 22, 168, 305

Perplexed Husband (Clarke, S., 1811) = Kiss, IV. 518, 636

Perplexed Lovers (1776), III. 339

Perplexities (Hull, T., 1767), III. 114, 274

Persecuted Wife = Needle of Agony

Persecution (1864), V. 732

— (1866), V. 732

— = Don Carlos

Perseus (Suter, W. E., 1864), V. 732, 843

Perseus and Andromeda (Brough, W., 1861), V. 279

— (Theobald, L., 1730), II. 137, 254, 359, 381

— (Weaver, J., 1716), II. 134, 252, 254, 319, 381, 446

— (1765), III. 339

— = (1) Deep Deep Sea; (2) Shipwreck

Perseverance (Oulton, W. C., 1789), III. 296

— (1802), IV. 518

Persian Ambassador and the Beautiful Circassian (1819), IV. 518

Persian Festival (1812), IV. 518

Persian Hero (1741), II. 452

Persian Heroine (Jodrell, R. P., 1786), III. 277

— (Jodrell, R. P., 1819), IV. 333, 590

— (Thornton, B., 1820), IV. 614

Persian Hunters (Noble, T., 1817), IV. 518, 636

Persian Prince = Loyal Brother

Persian Prince and the Moorish Boy (1836), IV. 518

Persian Princess (Theobald, L., 1708), II. 31, 78, 264, 358

Personal Adventures of David Copperfield = Born with a Caul

Personation (Dibdin, T. J., 1828), IV. 305

— (Kemble, M.-T., 1805), IV. 335

Pert (1886), V. 732

Peruvian (Naucaze, A. de, 1891), V. 501

— (1786) = Fair Peruvian, III. 32, 113, 206, 339, 403

Peruvian Boy = Zamor and Zamora

Peruvian Chief = Rolla

Peruvian Clemency = Inca

Peruvian Hero = Rolla

Peruvian Heroes (1825), IV. 519

Peruvian Lovers (1827), IV. 519

Peruvian Nuptials = Telesco and Amgahi

Peruvians (Parker, L. N., 1895), V. 513

Peruvian Virgin = Incas

Peruviens = Zulica

Pestilence of Marseilles (Moncrieff, W. T., 1829), IV. 82, 359

Pest, the Patriot and the Pippin = Tell Re-told

Pet (1855), V. 732

Pet Dove (1870), V. 732

Peter and Paul (Planché, J. R., 1821), IV. 377

— (Webster, B. N., 1842), IV. 418

Peter Bell (Buckstone, J. B., 1836), IV. 519, 636

Peter Bell the Waggoner (Buckstone, J. B., 1829), IV. 273

Peter Fin (Jones, R., 1822), IV. 334, 591

Peter Fin's Trip to Brighton = Peter Fin

Peter Jenkyns (1845), IV. 519

Peterkin (Ladislaw, W., 1893), V. 446

Peter Monk's Dream of the Marble Heart (1851), V. 732

Peter of the Castle = Pahdre na Mouhl

Peter Parley's Pantomime = Harlequin Gulliver

Peter Piper (1846), IV. 519

Peter Priggins (Stirling, E., 1842), IV. 519, 636

Peter Proteus (1831), IV. 519

Peter Pry (1821), IV. 519

Peter Smink (Payne, J. H., 1826), IV. 369

Peter's Pride (1880), v. 732

Peter Spyk (Planché, J. R., 1870), v. 811

Peter Stuyvesant (1899), v. 732

Peter the Beauty (1832), IV. 519

Peter the Cruel (1813), IV. 519

— (1829), IV. 519

+Peter the Emperor and Paul the Sailor (Cob. 1823)

Peter the Great (Cherry, A., 1807) = Wooden Walls, IV. 280, 556, 576, 643

— (Fitzball, E., 1852), v. 368

— (Irving, L. B., 1898), v. 432

— (Morton, T. and Kenney, J., 1829), IV. 364

Peter the Shipwright (Maddox, J. M., 1871), v. 732, 805, 843

Peter Wilkins (À Beckett, G. A. and Lemon, M., 1846), IV. 250

— (Blanchard, E. L., 1860), v. 263

— (Dibdin, C. I. M., 1800), IV. 290

— (1827), IV. 519

— (1860), v. 732

— (1883), v. 732

— (1889), v. 732

Peter Wilkins and the Flying Indians (Spry, H. and Conquest, G., 1857), v. 732, 785, 817, 843

Pet Heiress (1864), v. 732

Petite folle (1825), IV. 519

Petite Mademoiselle (Reece, R. and Leigh, H. S., 1879), v. 539, 813

Petites braconniers (1815), IV. 519

Petites Danaïdes (1831), IV. 519

Petit Faust (Farnie, H. B., 1870), v. 361, 790

Petition to the Muses = Apollo's Holiday

Pet Lamb (Selby, C., 1860), v. 560

Pet of Newmarket (Mooney, H., 1881), v. 491

Pet of the Petticoats (Buckstone, J. B., 1833), IV. 274

— = Convent

Pet of the Public (Stirling, E., 1853), v. 584

— (1897), v. 732

Petraki Germano (Dobbs, J., 1823), IV. 519

Petrarch and Laura (1843), IV. 519

Petrolengro (1891), v. 732

Petrona (Courtney, J., 1839), IV. 578

Petrovna (Hodges, F. S., 1885), v. 423

Petruccio (1895), v. 732

Pets (Ellis, B., 1889), v. 357

— (Graham, H., 1899), v. 386

Pets of the Ballet (1854), v. 732

Pets of the Parterre (Coyne, J. S., 1860), v. 328

Pet, the Patriot and the Pippin = William Tell with a Vengeance

Petticoat Captains = Going to Chobham

Petticoat Colonel (Wilson, Mrs C. B., 1832) = Hussars = Venus in Arms, IV. 481, 519, 618, 636

Petticoat Government (Dance, G., 1832), IV. 288, 579

— (1839), IV. 519

— = Barren Island

Petticoat Lancers = Greenwich Fair

Petticoat Management = Neglected Wives

Petticoat Parliament (Lemon, M., 1867), v. 455

Petticoat Perfidy (Young, Sir C. L., 1885), v. 149, 636

Petticoat Plotter (Hamilton, N., 1712), II. 334

— (Ward, H., 1746), II. 363

Petticoat Service (Lancaster, E. R.), IV. 593

Peveril of the Peak (Fitzball, E., 1823), IV. 94, 312, 584

— (Pocock, I., 1826), IV. 94, 385

— (1823), IV. 94, 519

Phadrig the Bocaun (Werner, C. J., 1879), v. 619

Phaedra (Morris, T., 1793), III. 339, 392, 403

— (1776), III. 60, 339

Phaedra and Hippolitus (1753), III. 399

— (Sherburn, Sir E., 1701), I. 432

— (Smith, E., 1707), II. 72, 80, 232, 355, 444

Phillip II (Bliss, H. Q. C., 1849), IV. 573

Phillip IV (Pitt, G. D., 1847), IV. 375

Phillip Quarl (1861), V. 732

Phillis = Nightingale

Phillis at Court (1767), III. 339

Phillis Mayburn (Hazlewood, C. H., 1873), V. 414

Philoclea (Morgan, M., 1754), III. 49, 288

Philoctetes (Sheridan, T., 1725), II. 355, 444

— (Warren, J. L., 1871), V. 615

Philoctetes in Lemnos (Monro, T., 1795), III. 339, 392

Philodamus (Bentley, R., 1767), III. 82, 236

Philomel (Craven, H. T., 1870), V. 329

Philosophe Moderne (Craven, E., 1790), III. 249

Philosopher (?Milner, H. M., 1819), IV. 356, 599

— (1795), III. 339

— = Wheel of Fortune

Philosopher Outwitted = Too Learned by Half

Philosopher Puzzled = Family Party

Philosophers of Berlin (Bernard, W. B., 1841), IV. 266

Philosopher's Opera (Maclaurin, J.), III. 285

— (1757), III. 339

Philosopher's Stone (Taylor, T., 1850), V. 592

Philosophic Whim (Hiffernan, P., 1774), III. 268

Philosophy no Defence against Love = Solon

Philotas (Frowde, P., 1731), II. 29, 34, 70, 75, 92, 329

Philpot and Co. (1827), IV. 519

Phil's Folly (Haywell, F., 1877), V. 412

Phobus' Fix (1870), V. 733

Phoebe (Hoadly, J., 1748), II. 260, 337

Phoebe at Court (Arne, T. A., 1776), III. 200, 234

Phoebe Hersel (Eburne, W. H., 1860), V. 789

Phoebe Hersell (Johnstone, J. B., 1847), IV. 519, 636

Phœnix (Astley, P., Jr., 1802), IV. 257

Phonograph (Wood, A. C. F., 1889), V. 630

Phormio (Rant, H., ?1674), I. 425

Photograph (1861), V. 733

Photographic Fix (Hay, F., 1865), V. 411

Photographic Fog (1898), V. 733

Photographic Fright (Soden, J. E., 1881), V. 817

Photographs (1884), V. 733

Photographs and Ices (Robertson, T. W.), V. 547

Photography (1876), V. 733

Phrenological Philanthropy = Shifts of Genius

Phrenologist (Coyne, J. S., 1835), IV. 284

— (1825), IV. 636

Phrenologists (Wade, T., 1830), IV. 415

Phroso (1898), V. 733

Phunnygraph (Bowyer, F. and Sparling, H., 1894), V. 271

Phyllis (Blatchford, M., 1890), V. 265

— (Burnett, Mrs F. H., 1889), V. 292

— = Double Deception

Phyllis Thorpe (Hazlewood, C. H., 1855), V. 733, 796, 843

Physic (1888), V. 733

Physical Metamorphosis (Streeter, F., 1778), III. 310

Physician (Jones, H. A., 1897), V. 167, 440

— = Dr and Mrs Neill

Physician against his Will (?1667), I. 444

Physician's Daughter = Cruel Kindness

Physician's Wife (Webb, C., 1858), V. 733, 823, 843

— (1845), IV. 519

Physick lies a Bleeding (Brown, T., 1697), I. 394

Pia di Tolomei (Williams, T. J.), V. 824

Piccadilloes (Macfarren, G., 1831), IV. 350

Piccolino (Samuel, S., 1878), V. 815

Piccolomini (Coleridge, S. T., 1800), III. 63, 245; IV. 86, 281

— (Moir, G., 1827), IV. 86, 358

Piccolomini's (1805), IV. 86, 519

Picked up at Sea = Found at Sea

Picking up the Pieces (Sturgis, J., 1882), V. 586

Pickles (Meritt, P., 1879), V. 486

— (Mills, H. and Charles, T. W., 1894), V. 489

Picklock of Paris (1866), V. 733

Pitman's Daughter (Springate, H. S., 1879), v. 576

Pitman's Secret = Wealth

Pit of Acheron (Bennett, J., 1795), III. 377

Pit's Mouth (Lewis, J., 1895), v. 459

Pity (Shirley, A., 1882), v. 453

Pity is akin to Love (Jerome, J. K., 1888), v. 436

Pity of it (Robertson, I., 1896), v. 545

Pity Poddlechock (Allen, O., 1881), v. 239

Pity the Poor Blind (1858), v. 733

Pity the Sorrows of a Poor Old Man (1866), v. 733

Pizarro (Buckingham, L. S., 1862), v. 286

— (Collins, C. J., 1856), v. 733, 785, 843

— (Geisweiler, C., 1800), III. 264

— (Helme, E., 1800), IV. 324

— (Heron, R., 1799), III. 64, 268, 387

— (Sheridan, R. B., 1799), III. 64, 68, 306, 396

— (Thompson, B., 1800), IV. 412

— (West, M., 1799), III. 64, 315, 398

Pizarro in Peru (Dutton, T., 1799), III. 64, 258, 383

Pizarro, the Great Tyrant (Marchant, F., 1861), v. 733, 805, 843

Pizarro, the Rolla-King Spanish Tyrant = Pizarro, the Great Tyrant

P.L. (Lemon, M., 1836), IV. 343

Place du Palais = Eugenia

Place Hunter (Webster, F., 1840), IV. 520, 637

Place Hunters (1819), IV. 520

Plagiarist Detected (McLaren, A., 1820), IV. 352

Plague (Robertson, I., 1896), v. 545

Plague and the Fire = Woman's Revenge

Plague, Fire and Water = This and the other Hand

Plague o' both your Houses (1856), v. 733

Plague of a Wanton Wife = (1) Amorous Adventure; (2) Harlequin's Contrivance

Plague of Envy = Suspicious Husband Criticized

Plague of Florence (1837), IV. 637

Plague of Marseilles (Raymond, R. J., 1828), IV. 82, 520, 637

Plague of Marseilles (1828), IV. 82, 520

Plague of Plymouth (1845), IV. 520

Plague of Riches = Farmer

Plague of the Family (1854), v. 733

Plagues of Mankind = Pandora's Box

Plaguy Good-natured Friend (1807) = Too Friendly by Half, IV. 520, 637

Plain Cook on the Strand (Stirling, E., 1852), v. 584

Plain Dealer (Bickerstaffe, I., 1765), III. 237, 377

— (Kemble, J. P., 1796), III. 279, 389

— (Wycherley, W., 1676), I. 2, 3, 14, 68, 82, 188, 191, 200, 238–40, 308, 346, 350, 439; III. 389

Plain English (Morton, T., Jr., 1869), v. 497

Plainest Man in France = Ugly Lover

Planchette (1890), v. 733

Plank across the Street (Wilks, T. E., 1848), IV. 617

Planter (Yardley, W., 1891), v. 634

Planter and his Dog (1830), IV. 520

Planters of the Vineyard (1750–1800), III. 340

Planter's Wife (1885), v. 733

Plants and Planets (Dibdin, C. I. M., 1816), IV. 294

Platonic Attachment (Phillpotts, E., 1889), v. 524

Platonic Attachments (Bernard, W. B., 1850), v. 259

Platonic Friendship (Barrie, J. M., 1898), v. 251

Platonick Lady (Centlivre, Mrs S., 1706), II. 166–7, 304

Platonic Wife (Griffith, Mrs E., 1765), III. 121, 266

Play (Robertson, T. W., 1868), v. 125, 128–9, 546

Play-Actress (Dyce-Scott, R., 1896), v. 353

Played and Lost (Wild, W. J., 1887), v. 622

Player Queen (Farren, W., 1892), v. 363

Player's Looking Glass (1751), III. 403

Play Ground and the Battle Field = Wait till I'm a Man

Playhouse hissing Hot = Damnation

Play-House to be Let = Rival Theatres

Play-House to be Lett (D'Avenant, Sir W., 1663), I. 95, 97, 186, 248, 401

Play-House to be Lett = Stage Mutineers

Play-House Wedding = City-Ramble

Playing at Loo Loo (Macdermott, G. H., 1871), v. 468

Playing at Lovers = Mrs Jollybutt's Out

Playing at Marbles = Marble Maiden

Playing First Fiddle (1850), v. 733

Playing the Game (Younge, W. and Flaxman, A. J., 1896), v. 637

Playing their Game = Found in London

Playing with Fire (Brougham, J., 1861), v. 280

Playing with Water (1862), v. 733

Play in Little (Robertson, I., 1892), v. 545

Play in the Pleasure Grounds = Actors al Fresco

Play is Over (Holcroft, T., 1804), IV. 326

Play is the Plot (Breval, J., 1718), II. 213, 266, 299, 300

Playmates (Warburton, H., 1888), v. 613

Play of Genoa = Vandyck

Play's the Thing (Drew, E., 1889), v. 350

Play without a Plot = Cat let out of the Bag

Pleasant Adventures at Brussels = Campaigners

Pleasant and merrye humor off a roge (Cavendish, W., ?1660), I. 396

Pleasant Dreams (Dance, G., 1834), IV. 288, 579

Pleasant Hour (Robbins, A. F., 1878), v. 544

Pleasant Neighbour (Planché, Mrs J. R., 1836), IV. 383

Pleasant Time of it (Buckingham, L. S., 1858), v. 733, 781, 843

Please Copy the Address (Blanchard, E. L., 1859), v. 263

Please to remember the Grotto (Oxenford, J., 1865), v. 510, 809

Pleasure (Meritt, P. and Harris, Sir A., 1887), v. 487

Pleasures of a Country Life = Haymaking

Pleasures of Anarchy (Newnham, F., 1852), v. 503

— (1809), IV. 520

Pleasures of Housekeeping and Horsekeeping = Mr Briggs

Pleasures of London = London Chimes

Pleasures of Memory = Man without a Head

Pleasures of the Town (Fielding, H., 1730), II. 323

— (1757), III. 403

— = Punch's Oratory

Plebeian (Costello, Miss, 1891), v. 325

Plebeian Daughter = Merchant's Honour

Plebeians (Derrick, J., 1886), v. 343

Pledge (Kenney, J., 1831), IV. 337

— (1847), IV. 520

Pledge of Love (1843), IV. 520

Plighted Troth (Darley, C., 1842), IV. 289, 579

Plot (Kelly, J., 1735), II. 237, 256, 340

Plot against Plot (Wilson, T., 1821), IV. 618

Plot and Counterplot (Kemble, C., 1808), IV. 334

Plot, and No Plot (Dennis, J., 1697), I. 32, 59, 337, 402; III. 114, 173

Plot and Passion (Taylor, T. and Lang, J., 1853), v. 98, 592

Plot Discover'd = Venice Preserv'd

Plot for Plot (Young, Sir C. L., 1881), v. 636

Plot of his Story (Beringer, Mrs O., 1899), v. 259

+ Plot of Potzentausend (French)

Plots (Arnold, S. J., 1810) = Bad Neighbours, IV. 255, 429, 569, 620

— (1831), IV. 520

Plots and Plans = Cloris

Plots for Petticoats (Wooler, J. P., 1849), IV. 422

Plots in Madrid (1824), IV. 520

Plots in Spain = Adventurer

Plots of Harlequin (1724), II. 381

Plot Spoil'd = Fatal Mistake

Plotters (1722), II. 448

Plotting Lovers (Shadwell, C., 1720), II. 354, 444

Plotting Managers (?1787), III. 340

Plotting Sisters = Fond Husband

Plotting Wives (Linnecar, R., 1789), III. 282

Ploughman turned Lord = Fortune's Frolic

Plowdens (Rose, E., 1892), v. 550

Pluck: A Story of £50,000 (Pettitt, H. and Harris, Sir A., 1882), v. 521

Poison Tree (1831), IV. 520
Polar Star (1829), IV. 520
Pole-faces and the Put-em-in-the Cauldron Indians = Ever-so-little Bear
Pole, the Patriot and the Pippin = Tale of Tell
Policeman (Helmore, W. and Phillpotts, E., 1887), V. 416
Police Spy = Spy of the Republic
Polichinel Vampire (1828), IV. 520
Policy (Robertson, T. W., 1871), V. 546
— (Siddons, H., 1814), IV. 401
Polidus (Browne, M.,1723), II. 68, 84, 300
Polish Jew (Emery, S., 1872), V. 358
— (Ware, J. R., 1872), V. 614
Polish Jew polished off = Mathias
Polish Patriot = Siege of Dantzig
Polish Squabble = King and No King
Polish Tyrant (1806), IV. 520
Polite Conversation (Miller, J., 1740), II. 381, 441, 448
Polite Gamester (1753), III. 340
Political Humbug = Sham Fight
Political Pair (Godbold, E. H., 1899), V. 382
Political Woman (1894), V. 734
Politician (1758) = No Matter What, III. 340, 403
— = Polititian
Politician Reformed (1774), III. 340
Politick Whore (1680), I. 443
Politic Queen, I. 388
Politics in Petticoats = Two Queens
Politics on Both Sides (1735), II. 381
Polititian (1677), I. 349, 444
Polititian Cheated (Green, A., 1663), I. 412
Polka (Barnett, C. Z., 1844), IV. 260
— (Vaun, R., 1895), V. 607
Polkamania (Stocqueler, H., 1844), IV. 520, 637
Polka, Polka, Polka (1844), IV. 520
Poll and Partner Joe (Burnand, F. C., 1871), V. 290
Poll Practice (1852), V. 734
Polly (Colman, G., 1777), III. 246
— (Gay, J., 1729), II. 22, 182, 233, 240-1, 332, 437, 447; III. 47
— (Mortimer, J., 1884), V. 494
Polly and Joe Stubbs (1876), V. 734
Polly Honeycombe (Colman, G., 1760), III. 182, 245

Polly in India = Macheath turn'd Pyrate
Polly Middles (1892), V. 734
Polly of Plympton = Constant Maid
Polly of Portsea and Joe the Marine (1831), IV. 520
Polly Plumtree = All a Mistake
Polly's Birthday (Fawcett, C. S., 1884), V. 364
Polly's Venture (Watson, T. M., 1888), V. 616
Poluscenion (1789), III. 340
Polynchinel Vampire (Dibdin, C. I. M., 1823), IV. 295
Polyphonus (Killick, J. M., 1872), V. 444
Polysceine Pasticcio = Egrirophadron
Pomona (Towers, E., 1877), V. 601
Pompadour (Wills, W. G. and Grundy, S., 1888), V. 627
Pompeii (1858), V. 734
Pompey (Philips, K., 1663), I. 98, 106, 347, 423
Pompey the Great (Waller, E., 1663), I. 98, 106, 436
Pong Wong (Mathews, C. J., 1826), IV. 354, 520, 598, 637
Ponsonby Hall (Cartwright, G. L., 1892), V. 305
Ponteach (Rogers, R., 1766), III. 303
Pool of the Four Willows = Who's to win?
Poonowing Kewang (1851), V. 734
Poor and Content (1836), IV. 520
Poor Andrew of the Tyrol = Falling Star
Poor Bess and Little Dick = Outcasts
Poor but honest (1870), V. 734
Poor Carpenter and his Family (1859), V. 734
Poor Cousin Walter (Simpson, J. P., 1850), V. 567
Poor Covent Garden (1792), III. 340
Poor Dick (1890), V. 734
Poor Dog Tray = (1) My Poor Dog Tray; (2) Omadhaun
Poor Em'ly (Ellis, B., 1870), V. 356
Poor Gentleman (Colman, G., the Younger, 1801), IV. 52, 184, 282
— (1812), IV. 520
Poor Gentlewoman (Isdell, S., 1811), IV. 330
Poor Girl (Young, Mrs H., 1863), V. 734, 843

Popish Impostor = King Henry VII

Popocatapetl (Robson, F., 1871), v. 547

Popolino (1841), IV. 521

Poppleton Court Plot = Number Two versus Number One

Poppleton's Predicaments (Rae, C. M., 1870), v. 532

Popping the Question (Buckstone, J. B., 1830), IV. 273, 521

— (1830), IV. 521

Popsey Wopsey (Grundy, S., 1880), v. 396

Popsy (Dabbs, G. H. R., 1888), v. 332

Popular Felons (Jerrold, D. W., 1826), IV. 331

Popularity (Moncrieff, W. T., 1839), IV. 521, 637 .

Pork Chops (Blanchard, E. L., 1843), IV. 268

Poro, Re dell' Indie (Humphreys, S., 1731), II. 397, 439

Porsenna's Invasion (1748), II. 381

Port Admiral (Bowles, T. G.), v. 271

— (1835), IV. 521 [The probability is that these entries refer to the same play]

Porter of Havre (Oxenford, J., 1875), v. 511, 809

Porter's Knot (Carton, R. C., 1892), v. 305

— (Oxenford, J., 1858), v. 509, 809

Portfolio (Kenney, J., 1816), IV. 336

Portmanteau Predicament (Bingham, F., 1881), v. 261

Port of London (Blake, T. G., 1851), v. 262

Portrait (Colman, G., 1770), III. 121, 195, 207-8, 246, 379

— (Sapte, W., Jr., 1888), v. 556

— (1784), III. 340

— = Love laughs at Locksmiths

Portrait of Cervantes (Greffulhe, 1808), IV. 321, 586

— (Hamilton, W. H., 1810), IV. 324

Portrait of Michael Cervantes = Plot and Counterplot

Portraits (1838), IV. 521

Portraits of Cervantes = Plots

Portsmouth Heiress (1704), II. 170, 381

Poses = Worship of Plutus

Positive and Negative (1899), v. 734

Positive Man (O'Keeffe, J., 1782), III. 292

Possessed = Dominique, the Resolute

Possession (Browne, G. W., 1890) v. 283

— = Nine Points of the Law

Possession Nine Points of the Law = MacCarthy More

Possible Case (1888), v. 734

Possible Exception (1873), v. 734

Postal Card (1871), v. 734

Post Boy (Craven, H. T., 1860), v. 328

Post Captain (Bosworth, J., 1838), IV. 573

— (Townsend, W. T., 1849), IV. 521, 614, 637

Post-chaise Companion (1835), IV. 521

Post-chaise of St Agnes = Wrecker of Cornwall

Posterity (Moore, A. M., 1884), v. 491

Post Haste (Robertson, T. W.), v. 547

Postheen Phewn (Grover, J. H., 1872), v. 395

Post House (1819), IV. 521

Posthumous Man = Lost Life

Postillion (À Beckett, G. A., 1837), IV. 249, 567

— (Hart, J. P., 1837), IV. 521, 637

— (1843), IV. 521, 637

Postillion of Longjumeau (1892), v. 734

Postman (Pemberton, T. E., 1892), v. 519

Postman's Knock (Thornton, L. M., 1856), v. 599

Postmaster's Wife, and the Mayor's Daughter = Diamond Arrow

Post Office Frauds (1870), v. 734

Post of Honour (Mildenhall, T., 1844), IV. 355

Post of Peril (Rede, W. L., 1848), IV. 607

Postscript (Knight, F. H., 1888), v. 445

Potentate (1898), v. 734

Pothooks (1883), v. 734

Potocatapelto (1877), v. 734

Pot of Money (Swift, J., 1881), v. 589

Potpourri (Tanner, J. T., 1899), v. 591

Poul a Dhoil (Hazlewood, C. H., 1865), v. 413

Poule aux Œufs d'or (Hall, F., 1878), v. 399

Pounds, Shillings and Pence (Thompson, Mrs G. and Sinclair, K., 1892), v. 597

Poupée (Sturgess, A., 1897), v. 586, 818

Pouter's Wedding (Morton, J. M., 1865), v. 496

Pouvoir de l'amour = Adolphe et Matilde

Poverty (Blake, T. G., 1844), IV. 268

— (De la Pasture, Mrs H.), v. 341

Poverty and Crime = Two Locksmiths

Poverty and Nobleness of Mind (Geisweiler, M., 1799), III. 65, 138, 264, 385

Poverty and Pride (Reade, C., 1857), v. 536

Poverty and Splendour = Molly Sullivan

Poverty and Temptation (1849), IV. 521

Poverty and Wealth (Wilson, C. H., 1799), III. 69, 316

Poverty, Competence and Riches = Ambition

Poverty Enobled by Virtue = True Patriotism

Poverty of Gold = Incognito

Poverty of Riches (Hendrie, E. and Wood, M., 1899), v. 417

Powder and Ball (Selby, C., 1845), IV. 399

Powder and Shot (Chandler, B., 1896), v. 307

Powder for Peeping = Curiosity Cured

Power and Principle (Barnett, M., 1850), v. 249

— = André the Miner

Power and the Glory (Darrell, C., 1898), v. 337

Powerful Party (1862), v. 734

Power of Conscience (Rutter, R. P., 1891), v. 553

Power of Drink = Del. Trem.

Power of England (Dering, C. E., 1885), v. 343

Power of Gold (Osman, W. R., 1865), v. 734, 808

— (Osman, W. R., 1870), v. 508

— (Sandford, W., 1897), v. 555

Power of Love (Lindley, H., 1888), v. 459

— (1881), v. 734

— = (1) Hercules and Omphale; (2) Satanella

Power of Magic (1783), III. 403

Power of the Heart (Davis, A., 1873), v. 338

Power of the Press (Pitou, A. and Jessop, G. H., 1896), v. 525

Power of Truth (1861), v. 734

Power of Will = Mehalah

P.P. (Parry, T., 1833), IV. 368

P.Q. (1832), IV. 521

Prabod'h Chandro'daya (Taylor), IV. 410

Practical Joker (Hulme, C. L., 1895), v. 430

Practical Jokes (1825), IV. 521

Practical Man (Bernard, W. B., 1849), IV. 266

Practice of a Modern Comic Entertainment = Monstrum Horrendum

Pragmatical Jesuit New-leven'd (Carpenter, R., ?1661), I. 395

Prairie Flower (Ellis, B. and Carlton, A., 1895), v. 357

— (1860), v. 734

Prancing Girl (Rae-Brown, C., 1891), v. 533

Pranks of Puck with the Elfin King (1844), IV. 521

Prawns and Pommery (1884), v. 734

Prayer (Child, H., 1898), v. 309

Prayer in the Storm = Thirst of Gold

Prayer of the Wrecked = Sea of Ice

Precept against Practice = Love's Frailties

Precept without Practice = Gamester Father

Preceptor (Hammond, W., 1739), II. 334

— (Warboys, T., 1777), III. 117, 315

Preciosa, the Spanish Gipsy (?Soane, G. or ?Ball, W., 1825), IV. 521, 637

— (1824), IV. 521

Preciosita (Dorisi, L., 1893), v. 347

Precious Little Crusoe (1894), v. 734

Precious Relics (1796), III. 340

Predestination = Alwyn and Bertholdy

Prediction (1844), IV. 521

— = Second Sight

Predilection (1830), IV. 521

Preference Bond (Maclaren, J. B., 1887), v. 471

Prejudice (Phillips, E., 1848) = Bachelor's Vow, IV. 372, 429, 604

— = Sons of Erin

Prejudice of Fashion (1779), III. 340

Prejudices (Cherensi, B. F., 1796), III. 243

Preludio to the Beggar's Opera (Colman, G., 1781), III. 247

Prentice (1895), V. 735

'Prentice Pillar (Eden, G., 1895), V. 353

Presbyterian Lash (Kirkman, F., 1661), I. 417

Prescription (1833), IV. 521

Presence (Cavendish, M., 1668), I. 396

Presence of Mind (Scudamore, F. A., 1881), V. 558

Presented at Court (Coyne, J. S., 1851), V. 327

Present, Past and Future = White Chateau

President (Fisher, J. M. and Turner, E., 1896), V. 367

President and the Peasant's Daughter (Dibdin, T. J., 1819), IV. 302, 581

Pressed for the Navy = Dead Reckoning

Pressed into the Service = Our Volunteers

Press Gang (Jerrold, D. W., 1830), IV. 332

— (1755), III. 340

— = Nancy

Press Gang at Billingsgate = Nancy

Pres St Gervais (Reece, R., 1874), V. 538

Preston Guild = Jubilee of 1802

Preston in the Olden Time = Cotton Famine

Presumption (Peake, R. B., 1823), IV. 369

Presumptive Evidence (Boucicault, D., 1869), V. 269

— (Buckstone, J. B., 1828), IV. 273

— = Card-Drawing

Presumptuous Love (?Taverner, W., 1716), II. 260, 358, 381

Pretence (Lawrence, S. B., 1891), V. 451

— (1896), V. 735

Pretended Puritan (Horde, T., 1779), III. 273

Pretender (Duncan, G., 1876), V. 352

— (Stafford, J. J., 1828), IV. 405

Pretenders (Dilke, T., 1698), I. 218, 403

— = Kensington-Gardens

Pretender's Flight (Philips, J., 1716), II. 348

Pretty Alice of Portsmouth (Rayner, J., 1852), V. 535

Pretty Bequest (Watson, T. M., 1885), V. 616

Pretty Blue Belle and the Ugly Beast (Hazlewood, C. H., 1860), V. 735, 796, 843

Pretty Couple (Addison, H. R., 1848), IV. 251

Pretty Druidess (Gilbert, W. S., 1869), V. 379

Pretty Esmeralda and Captain Phoebus of Ours (Byron, H. J., 1879), V. 299

Pretty Gipsey and the Bullfighter (1855), V. 735

Pretty Girl of Dundee (1802), IV. 521

Pretty Girl of Stilberg = Regiment of Tartars

Pretty Girls of Stilberg (Webster, B. N., 1842), IV. 616

— (Webster, B., 1855), V. 735, 823, 843

Pretty Horsebreaker (Brough, W. and Halliday, A., 1861), V. 279

Pretty Hunchback = Baden Baden

Pretty Milliners = Trois Fetes de Bois

Pretty Mollie (Rae, J. and Sidney, T., 1892), V. 533

Pretty Perfumeress (Byron, H. J., 1874), V. 298, 782

Pretty Piece of Business (Morton, T., Jr., 1853), V. 497

Pretty Poll (Reece, R., 1876), V. 538

Pretty Poll of Paddington (Coleman, H., 1852), V. 316

Pretty Poll of Portsea, and the Captain with his Whiskers = Mendacious Mariner

Pretty Polly = Our Polly

Pretty Polly, the Farmer's Daughter = Our Polly

Pretty Predicaments (Phipps, A. J., 1876), V. 524

Pretty Princess and the Ugly Beast = Pretty Blue Belle and the Ugly Beast

Pretty Purchase = Love the Leveller

Pretty Request (1885), V. 735

Pretty Sicilian (Blasis, 1847), IV. 521, 637

Pretty White Horn = Bold Robin Hood

Pretty White Mouse (1844), IV. 521

Preux Chevalier (1853), V. 735

Preventive Service (Milner, H. M., 1824), IV. 357

Priceless Jewels = Imperial Guard

Priceless Wife = Devotion

Price of Empire (Hope, A., 1896), v. 425
Price of Existence (Hazlewood, C. H., 1872), v. 414
Price of Freedom = Petrovna
Price of Life = Seventh Hour
Pride (Albery, J., 1874), v. 237
— (Hillyard, J., 1851), v. 422
— (Towers, E., 1872), v. 601
Pride and its Fall (Wilkins, J. H., 1849), IV. 419
Pride and Passion = Honour of the House
Pride and Patience (Pitt, G. D., 1850), v. 526
— (1859), v. 735
— = (1) Twin Brothers; (2) Witches' Weeds
Pride and Poverty = Poacher's Wife + Pride and Vanity (*French*)
Pride of Birth (Rodwell, G. H., 1843), IV. 395
— = Belphegor the Mountebank
Pride of Fallen Pine (1894), v. 735
Pride of Jerrico (1899), v. 735
Pride of Kildare (1844), IV. 521
Pride of Life (1863), v. 735
Pride of Poverty (Barnett, B. and Johnstone, J. B., 1857), v. 249
Pride of the Alhambra = Zana + Pride of the Blood; or, The Child of Mystery (Moncrieff, W. T.; Garrick, 15/10/1832)
Pride of the Family (Parry, A., 1878), v. 514
Pride of the Market (Planché, J. R., 1847), IV. 382
Pride, Poverty and Splendour = Seamstress and the Duchess
Pride's Cure = John Woodvil
Pride shall have a Fall (Croly, G., 1824), 174, 285
— (Soane, G., 1832), IV. 30, 404
Priest and the Convict = Out of Evil cometh Good, v. 735
Priest Hunter (O'Grady, H., 1892), v. 506
Priest of Saragossa = De l'Orme
Priest of the Parish = Spanish Dollars
Priest or Painter (Poel, W., 1884), v. 529
Priest's Daughter (Serle, T. J., 1845), IV. 400
Prig of Pimlico = Newgate Ned

Prima Donna (Boucicault, D., 1852), v. 267
— (Farnie, H. B. and Murray, A., 1888), v. 363
Prime Minister (1887), v. 735
Prime Minister a prim-in-a-stir = Eudora
Primitive Wife and Modern Maid = Wives as they Were and Maids as they Are
Primrose Farm (Harvey, F., 1885), v. 408
— (Major, H. A., 1871), v. 472
Primrose Green (1790), III. 340
Primrose Hall (Lacy, M. R., 1863), v. 446
Primrose of Ireland (Pitt, G. D., 1845), IV. 374 [This is the same as Irish Molly: see IV. 483]
Primrose Path (Findon, B. W., 1892), v. 366
Prince (Dibdin, C. I. M., 1812), IV. 292, 521, 580, 637
Prince Amabel (Brough, W., 1862), v. 279
Prince Amabel, Mother Goose (1873), v. 735
Prince and No Prince = German Blunder
Prince and Peasant (1881), v. 735
Prince and the Breeches = Court of Queen Anne
Prince and the Fairy (1857), v. 735
Prince and the Lion King (Suter, W. E., 1863), v. 735, 843
Prince and the Mandarin = Timour Khan
Prince and the Mermaiden = Pearl of the Ocean
Prince and the Ogre (Marchant, F., 1860), v. 735, 805, 844
Prince and the Pauper (Beringer, Mrs O., 1890), v. 259
— (Hatton, J., 1891), v. 409
Prince and the Peasant = Maurice the Woodcutter
Prince and the Peri (O'Neill, J. R., v. 808
Prince and the Piper = King of the Merrows
Prince and the Pirate = Sicilian
Prince and the Player (1823), IV. 521

Prince Blue Cap (1876), v. 735

Prince Brilliantino (1888), v. 735

Prince Camaralzaman (Bellingham, H. and Best, W., 1865), v. 257

Prince Carlo's Party (1887), v. 735

Prince Caruso (1833), IV. 521

Prince Charles Edward Stuart (Crawford, J., 1868), v. 329

Prince Charlie (1830), IV. 637

Prince Cherry and Princess Fair Star (Collins, C. J., 1855), v. 735, 785

Prince Cherrystar (Saunders, T., 1893), v. 556

Prince Chimney-Sweeper, and Chimney-Sweeper Prince = Adventures of the Prince of Seville

Prince Dorus (Taylor, T., 1850), IV. 521, 637; v. 592

+ Prince Edward (Mitford, E. L., in *Poems*, 1869)

Prince et le jardinier (1813), IV. 521

Prince Firoaz, Schah of Persia and the Princess of Bengal = Enchanted Horse

Prince for an Hour (Morton, J. M., 1856), v. 495

Prince Fortune and Prince Fatal (1854), v. 735

Prince in Conceit (Kirkman, F., 1662), I. 417

Prince Karatoff (Dam, H. J. W., 1892), v. 334

Prince Karl (Gunter, A. C., 1888), v. 397

Prince Lardi-Dardi and the Radiant Rosetta = White Cat

Prince Lee Boo (1833), IV. 521

Prince Love (Vandervell, W. F., 1870), v. 606

Prince Lucifer (Austin, A., 1887), v. 245

Princely Peasant and Peasant King = Shepherd King

Princely Shepherd = Royal Revenge

Prince Methuselem (Leigh, H. S., 1883), v. 454, 803

+ Prince Nysey Nosey (Keating, Miss, *French*)

Prince of Agra (Addington, Sir W., 1774), III. 58, 232, 389

Prince of Angola (Ferriar, J., 1788), III. 55, 58, 259, 383

Prince of Arragon = Birth-Day

Prince of Borneo (Herbert, J. W., 1899), v. 418

Prince of Cambria = Welshman

Prince of Cyprus (Broadfoot, J. W., 1846), IV. 271

— (1847), IV. 521

Prince of Darkness (Henry, S. C., 1896), v. 418

Prince of Egypt (Squier, C., 1882), v. 577

Prince of Happy Land (Planché, J. R., 1851), v. 527, 811

Prince of Jerusalem (1899), v. 735

Prince of Madagascar (1884), v. 735

Prince of Mischance (1897), v. 735

Prince of Pearls (1855), v. 735

Prince of Pimlico = Rumfustian Innamorato

Prince of Sauerkrautenberg (Boyce, W., 1895), v. 272

Prince of the Black Mountains = Dinas Bran

Prince of the Lakes = Thierna-na-Oge

Prince of the Orange Islands = Silver Tower

Prince of the Peaceful Islands (Cheatham, F. G., 1863), v. 735, 844

Prince of Tunis (Mackenzie, H., 1773), III. 90, 283

Prince of Wales's Visit (1869), v. 735

Prince Otto (Thalberg, T. B. and Gurney, G., 1888), v. 595

Prince Peacock and the Queen of Spite (1859), v. 735

Prince Pedrillo (Saull, J. A., 1893), v. 556

Prince Peerless (1860), v. 844

Prince Pigmy and Gorillacum (1862), v. 735

Prince Pippo and the Fair Mayde of Islington (Hazlewood, C. H., 1866), v. 735, 796, 844

Prince Pretty-Pet and the Butterfly (Brough, W., 1854), v. 279

Prince's Ball (?1682), I. 447

Prince's Nap and the Snip's Snap = La Ba Kan

Princes of Persia = Zadoc the Sorcerer

Prince Sohobazar (Bowles, E. W., 1885), v. 271

Prince's Park and Scotland Row (Elphinstone, J., 1867), v. 790

Prince's Present = Match-breaking
Princess (Gilbert, W. S., 1870), v. 379
— (Killigrew, T., 1661), I. 416
Princess Amaswazee (Paulton, T., 1895), v. 517
Princess and no Princess = Forest of Hermanstadt
Princess and the Butterfly (Pinero, Sir A. W., 1897), v. 180, 525, 810
Princess and the Swineherd (Hood, B., 1897), v. 425
Princess Badoura (1887), v. 735
Princess Battledore and Harlequin Shuttlecock (De Hayes, W., 1843), IV. 522, 637
Princess Carlo's Plot (Hilton, H., 1887), v. 422
Princess Charming (Arnold, H. T., 1867), v. 243
— (1877), v. 735
Princess Diana (Jones, J. W., 1889), v. 441
Princess Fairlocks (1857), v. 844
Princess Fair Star = Fair Star
Princess George (1885), v. 736
Princess Ida (Gilbert, W. S., 1884), v. 144, 380
Princess in the Tower (Talfourd, F. and Hale, W. P., 1850), v. 590, 819
Princess Liza's Fairy (Wurm, J., 1893), v. 633
Princess of Ashantee = King Coffee
Princess of Cleve (Lee, N., 1681), I. 96, 147, 272, 419
Princess of Georgia (Craven, E., 1799) = Georgian Princess, III. 249, 380
Princess of Orange (James, F., 1896), v. 433
Princess of Parma (Cumberland, R., 1778), III. 78, 251, 381
— (Smith, H., 1699), I. 432
Princess of Parmesan (Millais, W. H., 1898), v. 488
Princess of Persia = Distress'd Innocence
Princess of Poland = Juliana
Princess of Tarento (McDonald, A., 1791), III. 283
Princess of the Burning Eyes (1854), v. 736
Princess of the Pearl Island (Hazlewood, C. H., 1866), v. 736, 796, 844

Princess of Trebizonde (Kenney, C. L., 1870), v. 443, 801
Princess of Zanfara (1789), III. 340
Princess Pansy (1891), v. 736
Princess Pocahontas (1894), v. 736
Princess Primrose and the Four Pretty Princes (Bellingham, H. and Best, W., 1866), v. 257
Princess Radiant (Brough, W. and Brough, R. B., 1851), v. 278
Princess's Idea (Moore, T., 1892), v. 492
Princess Springtime (Byron, H. J., 1864), v. 297, 782
Princess Tarakanoff (Graves, C., 1897), v. 389
Princess, the Peri and the Troubadour = Lalla Rookh
Princess Toto (Gilbert, W. S., 1876), v. 380
Prince's Stratagem = Citizen of Paris
Princess Verita (Cockburn, Mrs T., 1896), v. 315
Princess who lost her Head (1857), v. 736
Princess who was changed into a Deer (1845), IV. 522
Princess with the Raven Locks = Barber and the Bravo
Prince's Trumpeter (Campbell, A. V., 1849), IV. 279
Prince, the Pirate and the Pearl = Bride of Abydos
Prince, the Princess and the Mandarin = Chang Ching Fow, Cream of Tartar
Prince troubadour (1815), IV. 522
— = Joconde
Principal and Interest (1881), v. 736
Principal Boy (D'Lanor, G., 1899), v. 346
Principle and Genius = Edmund Kean
Principle and Practice Combined (1792), III. 340
Printer's Devil (Planché, J. R., 1838), IV. 381
— (1832), IV. 522
Printers' Squabbles (1852), v. 736
Prior Claim (Pye, H. J. and Arnold, S. J., 1805), III. 300; IV. 388
Priscella (1889), v. 736
Prison and Palace (Simpson, J. P., 1853), v. 567, 816
Prison Breaker (1725), II. 244, 381

Prodigal Son (Willett, E. N., 1896), v. 624

—— (Young, H., 1864), v. 825

— (1724), II. 381

Professional Beauty (Ambrose, V., 1880), v. 240

Professionals Puzzled (Rede, W. L., 1832), IV. 389

Professor (Barrington, R., 1895), v. 251

— (Maxwell, G., 1894), v. 482

— (1868), v. 736

— (1883), v. 736

— (1891), v. 736

Professor of Folly (1718), II. 381

Professor—of what? (1866), v. 736

Professor Sick War (1898), v. 736

Professor's Love Story (Barrie, J. M., 1894), v. 251

Professor's Novel (1896), v. 736

Professor's Venture = On 'Change

Professor's Wooing (Gillette, W., 1881), v. 381

Professor Wiggles (1870), v. 736

Profligate (Pinero, Sir A. W., 1889), v. 160, 525

— (Rede, W. L., 1844), IV. 522, 637

— (Taylor, G. W., 1820), IV. 410

— = Ellen Trent

Profligate of Memphis = Azael the Arab

Profligate Reclaimed = Dwarf

Profligates (1829), IV. 522

Profligate's Career (1862), v. 736

Progress (Robertson, T. W., 1869), v. 546

Progress of a Harlot = Jew Decoy'd

Progress of a Lawsuit (1830), IV. 522

Progress of Ambition = Mystic Cavern

Progress of a Rake (1833), IV. 522

Progress of a Scamp = Raby Rattler

Progress of Crime (1868), v. 736

— = (1) Jack Sheppard; (2) Marie de Roux

Progress of Vice (1828), IV. 522

Projecting Ginger-bread Maker = Rehearsal of Kings

Projector (1803), IV. 522

Projectors (Wilson, J., 1664), I. 212, 438

— (1737), II. 381

— (1788), III. 340

Projects = Female Officer

Prologue = Nell Gwynne

Promessi Sposi (Hersee, H., 1881), v. 797

Prometheus (Reece, R., 1865), v. 537

— (1775), III. 340

Prometheus and Pandora = Olympic Revels

Prometheus Bound (Browning, E. B., 1833), IV. 272

— (Medwin, T., 1827), IV. 598

— (Webster, A., 1866), v. 617

Prometheus Britannicus (Brereton, J. L., 1840), IV. 574

Prometheus in Chains (Morell, T., 1773), III. 288

Prometheus the Fire Bringer (Horne, R. H., 1864), v. 426

Prometheus Unbound (Shelley, P. B., 1820), IV. 79, 191, 401

Promise (Lawrence, S. B., 1889), v. 451

Promised in Pique (1885), v. 736

Promised Land (Pettitt, G., 1875), v. 520

Promise of May (Tennyson, Alfred Lord, 1883), v. 594

Promissory Note (Beazley, S., 1820), IV. 522, 571

Promotion (Planché, J. R., 1833), IV. 379

Prompter Puzzled = Management

Prompter's Box (Byron, H. J., 1870), v. 115, 297, 782

Prompter's Story = Honor Bright: A Story of the Stage

Proof (Burnand, F. C., 1878), v. 291

Proof Impression = Cousin Matthew

Proof of Love (Byrne, J., 1813), IV. 522, 637

Proof of the Pudding (Bayly, T. H., 1832), IV. 522, 637

Proof Positive (Burnand, F. C., 1875), v. 290

Proof Presumptive (Kemble, C., 1818), IV. 522, 637

Proper Fairy (1883), v. 736

Prophecy (Dibdin, T. J., 1820), IV. 302

— (1801), IV. 522

Prophet (Bentley, R., 1788), III. 236

— (Fitzball, E., 1849), IV. 84, 317

— (Greville, E. E., 1893), v. 394

— (Wilkins, J. H., 1849), IV. 419

— (1849), IV. 522

— (1851), v. 736

— (1854), v. 736, 844

— (1892), v. 736

Prophet and Loss of Troy = Agamemnon and Cassandra

Prophetess (Dryden, J., 1690), I. 48, 55, 82, 83, 337, 352, 406–7; II. 413
— (Galt, J., 1814), IV. 318, 635

Prophetess of Ordsall Cave = Guido Fawkes

Prophet of Stonehenge = Mad Ruth of Wilton

Prophet of the Caucasus = (1) Questor's Steed; (2) Conqueror's Steed

Prophetess of the Glen = Two Drovers

Prophet of the Moor = Fire Raiser

Prophet of the Rock = Lonely Lighthouse

Prophet's Curse (Markwell, W. R., 1862), V. 477

Prophet's Priest = Maid of Venice

Proposals (Gilmore, J. F., 1887), V. 381

Proscribed (Stanford, G., 1889), V. 578
— = John Wilson

Proscribed Royalist (Seymour, F., 1881), V. 561

Prospect of Peace (Dibdin, T. J., ?1795), III. 382

Prospero (1883), V. 736

Protean Bandit = Reprobate

+Protector at Houghall; or, The Lily and the Rose (Brayshay, J. (Durham, 10/7/1851), 8° (1851; Groombridge))

Protector's Oath = Stanfield Hall

Proteus (Woodward, H., 1755), III. 209, 317
— (1833), IV. 522

Proud Prudence (Atkyns, S., 1849), IV. 257

Proud Shepherd's Tragedy (Downes, J., 1823), IV. 582

Proud Young Porter and the Fair Sophia = Lord Bateman

Proved True (Murdoch, J. M., 1883), V. 499

Provisional Government (Stocqueler, J. H., 1848), IV. 522, 637

Provision for the Convent = Monks and Smugglers

Provocation (1790), III. 340

Provok'd Husband (Cibber, C. and Vanbrugh, Sir J., 1728), II. 10, 15, 40, 134, 135, 137, 138, 152, 158, 183, 189, 190–1, 312, 434

Provok'd Wife (Vanbrugh, Sir J., 1697), I. 244–5, 436

Provoking Predicament = Love Limited

Provost of Bruges (Lovell, G. W., 1836), IV. 347, 596
— (1837), IV. 522

Provost of Paris (1837), IV. 523

Provost's Daughter (Ballantyne, J., 1852), V. 247

Prude (Ryves, E., 1777), III. 304
— (Weeks, J. E., 1791), III. 315
— = Cariboo

Prudes and Pro's (Votieri, A., 1891), V. 609

Prude's Progress (Jerome, J. K. and Phillpotts, E., 1895), V. 436

Prunella (Estcourt, R., 1708), II. 266, 320

Prussian Brothers (Pitt, G. D., 1847), IV. 375

Prussian Camp (1758), III. 340

Prussian Discipline (Abbott, W., 1817) = Youthful Days of Frederick the Great, IV. 249, 523, 567

Prussian Dragoon (1788), III. 340

Prussian Festival (1791), III. 340

Prussian Soldiers = Friendship, Love and Duty

"P.S. Come to Dinner" (Raymond, R. J., 1830), IV. 388

+Prying Little Girl (French)

Psyche (Shadwell, T., 1675), I. 37, 40, 42, 133, 135, 205, 337, 348, 430–1

Psyche Debauch'd (Duffett, T., 1675), I. 37, 135, 249, 407

Psychic Force (1872), V. 736

Public (Maclaurin, J., 1798), III. 285

Public Dinner in aid of a Philanthropic Object (Reece, R., 1868), V. 537

Public House (1787), III. 340

Public Men in Private Life = State Secrets

Public Wooing (Cavendish, M., 1662), I. 396

Pucelle = Maid of Orleans

Puck (Webb, M. G., 1883), V. 617
— (1890), V. 736

Puck in a Pucker = Frolics of the Fairies

Puck's Pantomime (Morton, J. M., 1844), IV. 523

Puddinhead (Mayo, F., 1895), V. 483

Puff of Smoke (Rowe, C. J., 1876), V. 552

Puff! Puff!! Puff!!! = London Characters

Pug (1836), IV. 523

Pugilist Matched = Dreamer Awake

Pull Devil, Pull Baker (1849), IV. 523

Pump (Clowes, W. L., 1886), v. 315

Punch (Byron, H. J., 1881), v. 299

— (Selby, C., 1841), IV. 398

Punch à la Romaine (1852), v. 736

Punch and Fun (Rhys, H., 1862), v. 542

Punch and his Little Dog Toby = Show Folks

Punch and Judy (Collins, C. J., 1859), v. 736, 785, 844

— (Conquest, G. and Spry, H., 1864), v. 736, 844

— (Willard, Mrs E. S., 1893), v. 623

— (1837), IV. 523

— (1853), v. 736

Punch Bowl (Ford, T. M., 1887), v. 370

Punchinello (Dabbs, G. H. R., 1890), v. 332

— (Farnie, H. B., 1864), v. 361

— (?1666), I. 446

— (1843), IV. 523

Punchinello and his Wife Judy (Barlas, J., 1886), v. 249

Punch in Italy (Euston, J. H., 1849), IV. 523, 637

Punch in Naples (1858), v. 736

Punch in Paris (1851), v. 844

Punch's Defeat (1748), II. 381

Punch's Festival (1813), IV. 523

Punch's Oratory (1730), II. 381

Punch's Pantomime (by the writers of *Punch*, 1842), IV. 523, 637

Punch's Politics (1730), II. 381

Punch turn'd Quaker = Town Rake

Punishment in Six Stages (Melville, H., 1849), IV. 355

Punishment of Sacrilege = Blue Man

Puns in Plenty = Will, or the Widow

Pup (1883), v. 736

P.U.P. (Moss, H., 1883), v. 497

Pupil of an Architect (1871), v. 736

Pupil of da Vinci (Lemon, M., 1839), IV. 523, 595, 637

Pupil of Nature = Paulina

Puppet (1897), v. 736

Puppets (McArdle, J. F., 1893), v. 467

Puppet Town (1899), v. 736

Pure as Driven Snow (Hazlewood, C. H., 1869), v. 1, 414

Pure as Snow (Berrie, E., 1873), v. 259

Pure Gold (Marston, J. W., 1863), v. 479

Purely Platonic (De Smart, Mrs A., 1898), v. 343

— = Cocum

Puritan (Murray, D. C. and Shine, J. L., 1894), v. 500

Puritan Girl = In the Days of the Siege

Puritani (À Beckett, G. A., 1843), IV. 523, 637

Puritanical Justice (1698), I. 444

Puritans (Mathews, 1856), v. 806

Puritan's Bride = Queen's Jewels

Puritan's Daughter (Bridgeman, J. V., 1861), v. 275

— (Lavington, W. F., 1875), v. 449

Puritan's Plot (1838), IV. 523

Puritan's Romance (1897), v. 736

Puritan's Sister (1835), IV. 523

Purpose of Life = Patience

Purrah (Moser, J., 1808), IV. 364

Purse (Cross, J. C., 1794), III. 98, 102, 249

+Purse; or, Falstaff (Lewes, L.; Stourbridge, 8/1799)

Purse of Almo (Lunn, J., 1834), IV. 523, 637

Purser (Day, J. T., 1897), v. 340

Pursuit of Vengeance = Vendetta

Puss (1859), v. 736

Puss in a New Pair of Boots (Byron, H. J., 1861), v. 296, 782

Puss in Boots (Blanchard, E. L., 1873), v. 264

— (Blanchard, E. L., 1887), v. 265

— (Bridgeman, J. V., 1859), v. 736, 780, 844

— (Conquest, G. and Spry, H., 1892), v. 322

— (Craven, E., 1799), III. 249

— (Daly, B. and East, J. M., 1898), v. 334

— (Dance, C. and Planché, J. R., 1837), IV. 152, 288, 381, 578, 605

— (Graves, C., 1888), v. 794, 844

— (Hazlewood, C. H., 1859), v. 796

— (Lonsdale, M., 1801), IV. 347

— (Marchant, F., 1873), v. 476

— (Rice, C., 1877), v. 542

Quarter of an Hour before Dinner (Rose, J., 1788), III. 303

Quarters (1887), v. 737

Quarter to Nine (Peake, R. B., 1837), IV. 370

Quartette (1828), IV. 523

Quasimodo (Fitzball, E., 1836), IV. 315

Quasimodo, the Deformed (Spry, H., 1870), V. 576

Quatre Bras (Rice, C., 1853), v. 542

Quatres Fils d'Hemons (1788), III. 341

Quavers and Capers (1817), IV. 523

Queen (Swarbreck, J. W., 1879), v. 589

Queen and Cardinal (Raleigh, W. S., 1881), v. 534

Queen and the Cardinal (1836), IV. 523

Queen and the Knave (1862), v. 737

Queen and the Yeoman (1862), v. 737

Queen Anne's Farthing and the Three Kingdoms of Copper, Silver and Gold (1859), v. 737

Queen Bee (Barrymore, W., 1828), IV. 262

— (1839), IV. 523

— (1869), v. 844

Queen Catharine (Pix, M., 1698), I. 424

Queen Catherine and Cardinal Wolsey (1828), IV. 524

Queen Cock-a-doodle-do, the Dame who lost her Shoe (1866), v. 737

Queen, Crown and Country = Headsman's Axe

Queen Dido (1792), III. 341

Queen Elizabeth (Gregg, T. D., 1872), v. 794

— (1869), v. 737

Queen Elizabeth and the Knight of Sheppey = Sea Horse

Queen Elizabeth's Trumpets = Fame

Queen Elizabeth's Visit to Reading (1862), v. 737

Queen Ellinor (1875), v. 737

Queen! God bless her (1838), IV. 524

Queen Hortensia's Shoe (Krasinski, H., 1857), v. 801

Queen Lady Bird and her Children (1860), v. 737

Queen Lucidora the Fair One with the Golden Locks (Planché, J. R., 1868), v. 528

Queen Mab (Dalby, 1857), v. 332

— (Godfrey, G. W., 1874), v. 382

Queen Mab (Somerset, C. A., 1851), v. 574

— (Vandervell, W. F., 1857), v. 822

— (Woodward, H., 1748), II. 446; III. 209, 317

— (1850), v. 737

— (1851, 1860), v. 844

Queen Mary (Stirling, E., 1840), IV. 80, 524

— (Tennyson, Alfred Lord, 1876), v. 208, 594

— = Tower of London

Queen Mary's Bower (Planché, J. R., 1846), IV. 382

Queen-Mother (Swinburne, A. C., 1860), v. 589

Queen o' Diamonds (Brabner, W. A., 1894), v. 272

Queen of a Day (Haines, J. T., 1841), IV. 323, 587

— (Moncrieff, W. T., 1840), IV. 600

— (1851), v. 738

— = Court of Spain

Queen of an Hour (Douglass, J. T. and Stainforth, F., 1877), v. 348

Queen of Aragon (Paul, H. M., 1854), v. 515, 809

Queen of Argos (Bell, W. B., 1823), IV. 572

Queen of Arts (1884), v. 738

Queen of Beauty = Second Calender

Queen of Bohemia (Blanchard, E. L., 1845), IV. 268

Queen of Brilliants (Thomas, B., 1894), v. 596

Queen of Carthage (Hoare, P., 1792), III. 269

— (1797), III. 341

Queen of Connaught (Jay, H., 1877), v. 738, 799, 844

— (Buchanan, R., 1887), v. 285

Queen of Cyprus (Beazley, S., Jr., 1842), IV. 264

— (Stirling, E., 1842), IV. 613

Queen of Diamonds (Brunton, A., 1882), v. 284

— = Hand of Fate

Queen of England (Clarke, C. A., 1898), v. 312

Queen of Fashion (Cannam, T. and Preston, J. F., 1887), v. 302

Queen of France and England = Eleanor the Amazon

Queen of Golconda (Dibdin, T. J., 1817), IV. 301

Queen of Hearts (Roe, J. E., 1863), v. 814

— (Thomas, C., 1877), v. 596

— (1833), IV. 524

— (1883), v. 738

— (1884), v. 738

— (1894), v. 738

Queen of Hungary = Gertrude and Beatrice

Queen of Hungary Triumphant = Universal Monarch Defeated

Queen of Manoa (Chambers, C. H. and Tristram, W. O., 1892), v. 307

Queen of May (1851), v. 738

Queen of Poland (1847), IV. 524

Queen of Spades (Boucicault, D., 1851), v. 267

— (Worsdale, J., 1744), II. 364

— (1852), v. 738

Queen of the Abruzzi (1846), IV. 524

Queen of the Beggars (Serle, T. J., 1837), IV. 400

Queen of the Butterfly Tower (1828), IV. 524

Queen of the Cannibal Islands = Africaine

Queen of the Clover Field (Lee, N., 1833), IV. 524

Queen of the Frogs (Planché, J. R., 1851), v. 527

Queen of the Hills (Wilkins, J. H.), IV. 420

— = Corsican Maid

Queen of the Market (Coape, H. C. and Webster, B. N., 1852), v. 315

Queen of the May (Legg, F. W., 1896), v. 453

Queen of the Moor (1899), v. 738

Queen of the Night (Tracey, F. T. and Berlin, I., 1897), v. 602

Queen of the Roses (1850), v. 738

Queen of the Silver Lakes = Rodolph and Rosa

Queen of the Thames (Fitzball, E., 1843), IV. 316

Queen of the Vintage and the Courier Prince (1854), v. 738

Queen of Wales = Love's Victim

Queen o' May (1884), v. 738

+ Queen's Ball (À Beckett, G. A., 1838), [Under this title, À Beckett's *Black Domino* was printed in the Duncombe series]

Queen's Bench (Rede, W. L., 1848), IV. 391

Queensberry Fête = Who's your Friend?

Queen's Bounty = Sport

Queen's Bouquet and the Three Cards = Red House

Queen's Champion (Gore, Mrs C. G. F., 1834), IV. 319

Queen's Colours (Conquest, G. and Pettitt, H., 1879), v. 321

Queen's Command ("William Shakespeare", i.e. Walton, 1838), IV. 524, 637

Queen's Counsel (Mortimer, J., 1890), v. 494

Queen's Court = John Duddlestone, the Breeches Maker of Bristol

Queen's Court of Conscience = Royal Twelfth Cake

Queen's Evidence (Conquest, G. and Pettitt, H., 1876), v. 321

Queen's Favourite (Grundy, S., 1883), v. 396

— = Lady of the Louvre

Queen's First Move = Check to the King

Queen's Horse (Planché, J. R. and Honan, M. B., 1838), IV. 381

Queen's Jewel (Collier, W., 1835), IV. 281

Queen's Jewels (Dodson, R., 1876), v. 346

Queen's Lieutenant = Laura

Queen's Love (Hilles, M. W., 1879), v. 421

— = St Bartholomew

Queen's Lover (1834), IV. 524

— = (1) Marie Antoinette; (2) Salvoisy

Queen's Masque (Osborn, H., 1842), IV. 602

Queen's Messenger (Manners, J. H., 1899), v. 474

Queen's Musketeers (1856), v. 844

Queen's Necklace (Ford, D. M., 1899), v. 370

— = Marie Antoinette

Railway Belle (Lemon, M., 1854), v. 455
Railway Bubbles (Coyne, J. S., 1845), IV. 524, 578, 638
Railway King (Stirling, E., 1845), IV. 408
— (1845), IV. 524
— (1851), v. 738
Railway Mania (1845), IV. 524
Railway Train (1840), IV. 524
Raiment and Agonies of that most Amiable Pair, Raimond and Agnes (Marchant, F., 1860), v. 738, 805, 844
Rain Clouds (Walkes, W. R., 1894), v. 612
Rainy Day (Smith, Miss A., 1868), v. 571
Raised from the Ashes (Fuller, F., 1879), v. 374
Raising the Wind (Kenney, J., 1803), IV. 131, 336
— (1811), IV. 524
— = Enchanted Isle
Raitchpoot (1876), v. 738
Rajah of Chutneypore = Nautch Girl
Rajah of Nagpore (1846), IV. 524
— (1862), v. 738
Rajah of Ram Jain Poore = Indian Prince
Rajah's Daughter = Cataract of the Ganges
Rajah's Vengeance = Farmer's Daughter
Rake = Suspicious Husband
Rake and his Pupil (Buckstone, J. B., 1833), IV. 70. 182-3, 274
Rake Demolish'd = Bawdy-House School
Rake Husband = Giovanni in the Country
Rake Reclaimed = Love at a Venture
Rake's Progress (Dibdin, C. I. M., 1826), IV. 296
— (Rede, W. L., 1833), IV. 389
— (Rede, W. L., 1841), IV. 390
— = Peasant Ruffian
Rake's Will (Grattan, H. P., 1889), v. 389
+ Raleigh's Queer Dream (Croft; R. Polytechnic, 1873; 8° [1873])
Ralph de Bigod, Earl of Norwich (Smith, J., 1829), IV. 403
Ralph Gaston (1860), v. 738
Ralph's London (1766), III. 404
Ramah Droog (Cobb, J., 1798), III. 205, 244 [The entry of a Dublin edition should be deleted]

Ramblers (1836), IV. 524
Rambles in Bagdad = Caliph and the Cadi
Rambles in Dorsetshire = London Hermit
Rambles of Covent Garden = Harlequin's Frolics
Ramble through London = Touch at the Times
Ramble to Bath (1796) = Jacob's Ramble, III. 404
Ramble to Oxford = Humours of the Road
Rambling Justice (Leanerd, J., 1678), I. 23, 43, 57, 269, 418-19
Rambling Lady = Sir Anthony Love
Rambling Shepheard = Constant Nymph
Ramiro (Clarke, J. B., 1822), IV. 576
Rampant Alderman (1685), I. 217, 444
Ramsbottoms at Rheims (Peake, R. B., 1825), IV. 524
Ranache King (1891), v. 738
Randall's Thumb (Gilbert, W. S., 1871), v. 136, 379
Ran-Dan Club (Worrell, 1840), IV. 618 [This is the same as The Female Waterman's Society, see IV. 460]
Randolph the Reckless (Stephens, V., 1888), v. 581
Random Shot (1898), v. 738
Random Shots (1830), IV. 524
Randy the (W)Reckless and the Grand Old Man of the Sea = People's William
Ranelagh (Simpson, J. P. and Wray, C., 1854), v. 567
Ranger in Wedlock (Silvester, 1788), III. 307
Ranger of the Forest = Mysterious Murder
Ranger's Daughter (Fitzball, E., 1843), IV. 316
Rank (1871), v. 738
Rank and Fame (Rae, L. and Stainforth, F., 1875), v. 533
Rank and Riches (Collins, W. W., 1883), v. 318
Ransom (Planché, Mrs J. R., 1836), IV. 383
Ransom of Manilla (Lee, R. G., 1793), III. 281

Ransom of the Rose Diamond = Mine Girl of Kebal

Ranting Roaring Willie (Ebsworth, J.), IV. 309

Ranz des Vaches = Home Sweet Home!

Rape (Brady, N., 1692), I. 170-1, 394
— (1729), II. 381

Rape of Europa by Jupiter (1694), I. 444

Rape of Helen (Breval, J., 1733), II. 266, 300

Rape of Proserpine (Theobald, L., 1727), II. 135, 137, 235, 252, 254, 359, 443

Rape of the Lock (Oxenford, J., 1837), IV. 99, 367, 603

Rape of Virginia = Titus Andronicus

Rape upon Rape (Fielding, H., 1730), II. 177, 324

Raphael's Dream (1830), IV. 524
— (1834), IV. 524

Raphelina (1879), V. 738

Rapid Thaw (Robertson, T. W., 1867), V. 546
— = Adonis Vanquished

Rapparee (Boucicault, D., 1870), v 269

Rapparee's Bride = Moyna a-Roon

Rapparee's Mystery = Spirit Trapper

Rappings and Table Movings (Paul, H. M., 1853), V. 515

Rare en Tout (Roche-Guilhen, Mme, 1677), I. 133-4, 356, 427

Raree Show (Paterson, J., 1739), II. 347

Rash Marriage (Pinkerton, J., 1813), IV. 525, 604, 638

Rasselas (1835), IV. 525

Rasselas, Prince of Abyssinia (Brough, W., 1862), V. 279
— (1864), V. 738

Rat-catcher's Daughter (1855), V. 739

Rathac the Fisherman = Lake of Lugano

Rathboys (Buchanan, R. and Gibbon, C., 1862), V. 284, 781
— (1863), V. 739

Ratheil Sullivan (Campbell, A. V., 1829), IV. 278

Rather too Bad! (Dibdin, T. J., 1818), IV. 301

Ratification = Olive Branch

Rat of Rat's Castle (Johnstone, J. B., 1864), V. 438

Rat of the Hold = Archy Insore

Rats of the Rigmerole = Rougemont the French Robber

Rats of the Seine (James, C. S., 1852), V. 433
— = Pierre Brouillard

Rattlin the Reefer (Haines, J. T., 1836), IV. 322

Rat-Trap (Milner, H. M., 1827), IV. 525, 638

Rauberbraut (Fitzball, E., 1829), IV. 313, 584

Ravencourt (Wynn, H. W., 1843), IV. 618

Ravenna (Clarke, J. B., 1824), IV. 87, 280

Ravens (Pocock, I., 1817), IV. 384, 606

Raven's Nest (Wilks, T. E., 1835), IV. 420

Raven's Oak (Wheatcroft, N., 1882), V. 619

Ravens of Orleans (Moncrieff, W. T., 1820), IV. 359

Ravenswood (Merivale, H. C., 1890), V. 487

Ravin the Reefer = Sixteen String Jack

Ravin the Savage (1807), IV. 525

Raw Carotte (Thorne, G., 1873), V. 599

Raw Recruit (Bellamy, C., 1889), V. 256

Raw Recruits = Omnia vincit Amor

Raykisnah the Outcast (Scott, J. M., 1813), IV. 525, 638

Raymond (1793), III. 341

Raymond and Agnes (Fitzball, E., 1855), V. 368, 792
— (Grosett, H. W.), IV. 586
— (Lewis, M. G., 1809), IV. 346
— (1797) = Don Raymond, III. 341, 400

Raymond de Percy (Harvey, M., 1822), IV. 324

Raymonde (1892), V. 739

Raymond in Agonies (Mowbray, T., 1860), V. 498

Raymond Remington (Ashdown, W., 1893), V. 244

Raymond the Betrayer = Arbabance the Hebrew

Raymond the Rebel (Wilks, T. E., 1835), IV. 420

Rayner (Baillie, J., 1804), IV. 258

Ray of Light (1876), V. 739

Ray of Sunlight (Newte, H. C. W., 1896), V. 503

Reading for the Bar (Grundy, S., 1876), v. 205, 396

Reading of the Will = Forgery

Ready and Willing (Towers, E., 1867), v. 600, 821

— (1880), v. 739

Ready Money Mortiboy (Maurice, W. and Rice, J., 1874) = My Son Dick, v. 482, 723, 806, 841

Real and Ideal (Wigan, H., 1862), v. 622

Real Case of Hide and Seekyl (Grossmith, G., 1888), v. 395

Realities of Life (Conquest, G., 1862), v. 739, 785, 844

Reality (Rogers, C., 1889), v. 548

Real John Bull (1822), IV. 525

— = Mysteries and Miseries

Real Lady Macbeth (Copping, E., 1889), v. 324

Real Life (Bleakley, E. O., 1872), v. 265

— (Dodson, R., 1882), v. 347

Real Life in London (Amherst, J. H.), IV. 254

Real Little Lord Fauntleroy (Burnett, Mrs F. H., 1888), v. 292, 782

Realm of Joy (Gilbert, W. S., 1873), v. 379

Real Mr Potter of Texas (1890), v. 739

Real Poor of London = Pride of Poverty

Real Prince (Greet, D. V., 1894), v. 393

Real Truth about Ivanhoe (Nugent, E. C., 1889), v. 506

Reapers (Pritt, S., 1897), v. 531

— (Stirling, E., 1856), v. 584, 818

— (1770), III. 121, 341

Reaping the Harvest = (1) Life's Harvest; (2) True Grit

Reaping the Whirlwind (Lennard, H., 1884), v. 455

Rear Admiral (Emden, W. S., 1839), IV. 310

— (1866), v. 739

Reasonable Animals (1780), III. 341

Reasonable Fool (1789), III. 341

— (1811), IV. 525

Reasonable Lover (Kelly, H., 1776) = Man of Reason, III. 341, 389, 404

Rebecca (Barber, J., 1845), IV. 259

— (Halliday, A., 1871), v. 401

Rebecca and her Daughters (1843), IV. 525

Rebecca of York (1874), v. 739

Rebecca, the Jewish Wanderer (Garthwaite, F., 1864), v. 739, 844

Rebel (1849), IV. 525

Rebel Chief (Grattan, H. P., 1836), IV. 525, 586, 638

Rebel for Love = Waverley

Rebellion (Bromley, G. P., 1815), IV. 271

— (1819), IV. 525 [The date is 1819, not 1809]

Rebellion Defeated (Cutts, J., 1745), II. 317

Rebellion of Lowland's Creek = Armourer's Forge

Rebellion of Norwich in 1549 (1815), IV. 525

Rebel of 1745 = Life of James Dawson

Rebel Rose (1899), v. 739

Rebels (Fagan, J. B., 1899), v. 359

Rebels and Guerillas = Spain and Portugal

Rebel's Gauntlet = Students

Rebel's Heir = Haunted Hulk

Rebel Spirits (1894), v. 739

Rebel's Wife (Jarman, F., 1898), v. 434

Recalled to Life (Hewson, J. J., 1885), v. 420

Receipt for Beauty = Blind Girl

Receipt for Mirth (Burton, 1811) = Right and Wrong, IV. 277, 525, 636

Receipt Tax (Dent, C., 1783), III. 254

Receipt to make a Benefit = Hodge Podge

Recent Event (1832), IV. 525

Reception (1799), III. 341

Reckless Temple (1890), v. 739

Reckoning (Dauncy, S., 1891), v. 337

— (Genet, E., 1891), v. 377

Reckoning Day (1885), v. 739

Reclaimed (Mortimer, J., 1881), v. 494

— = Nance

Recluse (Feist, C., 1823), IV. 525, 638

— (1825), IV. 95, 525, 638

— = Misanthropy and Repentance

Recluse of the Alps = Solitaire

Recluse of the Cavern (1830), IV. 525

Recluse of the Forest (1863), v. 739

Recluse of the Monastery = Caledonian Assassin

Recluta por Fuerza (1832), IV. 525

Recollections which may or may not have happened = Strand-ed Actor

Recommendations (1823), IV. 525

Recommended to Mercy (Jones, J. W., 1882), V. 440

Recompense = Louise

Reconciled (Gwynne, P. and Harrison, C., 1888), V. 398

— = Howard Howard

Reconciliation (Ludger, C., 1799), III. 65, 283, 391

— (Neville, G. F., 1876), V. 502

+ — (Render, W., 8°, 1799)

— (1813), IV. 525

Recrimination (Clarke, C., 1813), IV. 280

Recruit (1788), III. 341

— (1794), III. 341

— (1829), IV. 525

— (1892), V. 739

Recruiting Manager (Oulton, W. C., 1785), III. 296

Recruiting Officer (Farquhar, G., 1706), II. 4, 21, 37, 41, 131, 132, 133, 134, 135, 136, 137, 138, 149, 157, 322

Recruiting Party (Kilmorey, Earl of, 1895), V. 444

Recruiting Serjeant (Bickerstaffe, I., 1770), III. 199, 237

Recruits for the King of Prussia = She Gallant

Recruits for the Queen of Hungary = Prodigal

Rector (Pinero, Sir A. W., 1883), V. 525

Rector's Daughter (Strettell, J. D. C., 1898), V. 585

Rectory (1673), I. 348, 444

Red and Blue (Fanshaw, F., 1892), v. 361

— = Passing Fancies

Red and White (André, R., 1891), V. 241

Red Banner (1831), IV. 525

Red Barn (Mildenhall, T., 1829), IV. 598

— (Comer, G. and Ellis, L., 1892), V. 319

— (1830), IV. 638

Red Bob the Coiner (Towers, E., 1863), V. 821

Red Bridge (Suter, W. E., 1860), V. 739, 819, 844

Red Brigade (1856), V. 739

Red Buoy (1851), V. 739

Red Cap (Archer, T., 1846), IV. 255

Redcliff (1845), IV. 525

Red Coat (Williams, B., 1899), V. 624

Red-Cross Knights (Holman, J. G., 1799), III. 62, 272

— = Harold the Renegade

Red Cross of Burgundy = Perinet Leclerc

Red Crow (Wilks, T. E., 1834), IV. 420

Red Daemon of the Harz Forest (1821), IV. 525

Red Dick (1873), V. 739

Red Dwarf (1871), V. 739

— (1873), V. 739

Redeemed (Coggan, J., 1883), V. 316

Redeeming Spark = Honour

Redemption (1882), V. 739

— (1897), V. 739

Red Eric, the Sea King (1837), IV. 638

Red Farm (Moncrieff, W. T., 1842), IV. 361

Redgauntlet (Murray, W. H., 1825), IV. 94, 365

— (1824), IV. 94, 525

— (1835), IV. 94, 525

Red Hand (Lyon, T., 1865), V. 739, 845

— = (1) Brian, the Probationer; (2) Desmore; (3) Desmoro; (4) Exiled

Red Hand of Fontainebleau (1857), V. 739

Red Hand of Justice (1878), V. 739

Red Hands (À Beckett, G. A., 1869), V. 233

— (Dibdin, C. I. M., 1805), IV. 291

— (Dibdin, C. I. M., 1815), IV. 291

Red House (1849), IV. 525

— (1850), V. 739

Red Huntsman (1858), V. 739

Red Hussar (Stephens, H. P., 1889), V. 580

Red Indian (1822), IV. 525

— (1824), IV. 525

Red John the Daring (1861), V. 739

Red Josephine (Lane, Mrs S., 1880), V. 448

Red Knave (Drinkwater, A. E., 1892), V. 351

Red Lamp (Travers, W., 1862), V. 739, 821, 845

— (Tristram, W. O., 1887), V. 604

Red Lance (Lancaster, E. R., 1841), IV. 593

Redland the Robber (1833), IV. 525

Red Light (Stanley, H. J., 1874), V. 579

Red Maid (1834), IV. 525

Red Man (Phillips, F. L., 1844), IV. 372

Retort Courteous (1834), IV. 526
Retour de Corsair = Bazzard d'Algier
Retour du printemps = Zéphyr
Retreat of the Mountains (Ebsworth, J., 1824), IV. 308
Retribution (Bennett, G. J., 1850), V. 258
— (Dillon, J., 1818), IV. 306
— (Taylor, T., 1856), V. 100, 593
— (1859), V. 740
— = Justifiable Homicide
Retributive Justice (Ashton, J., 1813), IV. 256
— (Burton, E. G., 1863), V. 740, 782
Returned (Pitt, H. M., 1869), V. 526
Returned Captive = Don Rafaelle
Returned from India (1859), V. 741
Returned from Trafalgar (1811), IV. 526
Returned Killed (Planché, J. R., 1826), IV. 378
Returned Outcast (Lee, N., Jr., 1859), V. 802
Return from Navarino = Welcome Home
Return from Siberia = Forced Marriage
Return from Slavery = Native Land
Return from the Baltic (1855), V. 740
Return from Victory = Relief of Williamstadt
Returning the Compliment (Waldan, O. and Palmer, F. G., 1890), V. 610
Return of a Ticket-of-Leave (1863), V. 741
Return of Peace = Speed the Plough
Return of Perouse (1836), IV. 526
Return of the Druses (Browning, R., 1843), IV. 272
Return of the Season = Invitation
Return of the Wanderer = Jessy Vere
Return of Ulysses (Bridges, R. S., 1890), V. 275
— = Patient Penelope
Return Ticket to the International Exhibition (Spencer, G. and James, W., 1862), V. 119, 576
Return to Ithaca = Adventures of Ulysses
Reuben Blight (Panton, J., 1861), V. 741, 809, 845
Reunited (1888), V. 741
Revanche des Cigales (1897), V. 741

Revelations of London (Stevenson, 1868), V. 583
— = Elixir of Life
Revell of Aldford = Countrey Revell
Revels by Moonlight = Millers
Revenge (?Behn, A., 1680), I. 65, 391, 392
— (Chatterton, T., 1770), III. 243
— (Kemble, J. P., 1814), IV. 335
— (Parlby, B. B., 1818), IV. 368
— (Young, E., 1721), II. 59, 70, 71, 113, 264, 364
Revenge and Love = Ellie Brandon
Revengeful Queen (Phillips, W., 1698), I. 170, 266, 423
Revenge of Athridates (1765), III. 341
Revenge of Ceres (Moser, J., 1810), IV. 364
Revenge of Taran (Fitzball, E., IV. 584
Revenge of the Blighted One = Alice Home
Reverse of a Day = Ups and Downs
Reverses (Farnie, H. B., 1867), V. 361
— = Shepherd of Derwent Vale
Review (Colman, G., 1800), IV. 282
— (1837), IV. 526
— = Clump and Cudden
Revolt at Cabul and British Triumphs in India = Afghanistan War
Revolt at Naples = Masaniello
Revolt at Sea (1847), IV. 526
Revolt in the East (1859). V. 741
Revolt of Bruges (Smith, A. R., 1842), IV. 526, 638
Revolt of Flanders (Robinson, E., 1848), IV. 526, 638
Revolt of Genoa = (1) Fiesco; (2) Republican Duke
Revolt of Moscow = Emissary
Revolt of Surinam (1825), IV. 526
Revolt of the Angels (Reade, E., 1830), IV. 607
Revolt of the Chummies (Lighterness, W. B.), IV. 595
— = "Sweep Sweep Sweep!"
Revolt of the Greeks (Walker, C. E., 1824), IV. 526, 638
Revolt of the Harem (1834), IV. 526
Revolt of the Naiades = Lurline
Revolt of the Players = Night Rehearsal

427

Rival Soldiers (1814), IV. 527

Rival Sorcerers (1790), III. 342

Rival's Rendezvous (1861), v. 742

Rival's Revenge = Patrick's Vow

Rival Statues (Cross, J. C., 1803), IV. 286

Rival Tars (Dibdin, C. I. M., 1802), IV. 290

Rival Theatres (Stayley, G., 1759), III. 309 [This was acted Smock Alley, Dublin, 21/2/1759]

Rival Tinkers (Ward, H. R., 1848), IV. 416

Rival Valets (Ebsworth, J., 1825), IV. 308

— = Painter's Study

Rival Widows (Cooper, Mrs E., 1735), II. 142, 205–6, 316

Riven Clouds (1880), v. 742

River God (1835), IV. 527

River of Life (Shirley, A. and Landeck, B., 1894), v. 564

— = Great Temptation

Riverside Story (Bancroft, Lady, 1890), v. 248

River Sprite (Linley, G., 1865), v. 460

Rizpah Misery (Campbell, Mrs V., 1894), v. 301

Rizzio (Graham, D., 1898), v. 386

Road and the Riders = Scarlet Dick

Road of Life (Blanchard, E. L., 1843), IV. 268

— = Up and Down

Roadside Cottage = Day after the Fair

Roadside Inn (Douglass, J. T.), v. 789

— (Simpson, J. P., 1865), v. 576

Roadside Inn turned inside out = Robert Macaire

Road, the River and the Rail (Spencer, G., 1868), v. 576

Road to Bath = Night's Adventures

Road to Blue Ruin = Miss Formosa

Road to Fame (White, A. and Grunfeld, P., 1885), v. 620

Road to Fortune (Dering, C. E., 1893), v. 343

Road to Happiness (Melville, H., 1848), IV. 355

— = Forget and Forgive

Road to Odiham = 'Tis an ill Wind that blows nobody good

Road to Ridicule (Streatfield, T., 1799), III. 310

Road to Ruin (Holcroft, T., 1792), III. 49, 55, 136, 141, 271

— (1897), v. 742

— = High-mettled Racer

Road to Transportation (Courtney, J., 1862), v. 786

Road to Yaroslaf = Narensky

Roaring Dick & Co. (1896), v. 742

Roasted Emperor = Jenny's Whim

Roasting a Rogue (Palmer, T. A., 1882), v. 512

Robber (Cumberland, R., 1809), IV. 287

Robber Knight = Hans von Stein

Robber of Epping Forest (1831), IV. 527

Robber of Genoa = Great Devil

Robber of the Alps (Nicholson, J., 1820), IV. 366

Robber of the Rhine (Almar, G., 1833), IV. 252

Robbers (Anderson, J. R., 1851), IV. 254; v. 240

— (Render, W., 1799), III. 62, 301

— (Thompson, B., 1800), III. 62, 311, 397; IV. 412

— (Tytler, A. F., 1800), III. 62, 313; IV. 615

— (1724), II. 382

— (1797), III. 62, 342, 404

— (1820), IV. 527

— = Cartouche

Robber's Bride (Pocock, I., 1829), IV. 115–16, 385

— = (1) Abelino; (2) Rauberbraut

Robber's Mother = Band of Death

Robbers of Normandy = Florence Montaubon

Robbers of the Caucasus = Zulema the Circassian Beauty

Robbers of the Mail Post = Courier of Lyons

Robbers of the Pyrenees (Suter, W. E., 1862), v. 588

— = Gallant Moriscoes

Robber's Sister (Fitzball, E., 1841), IV. 316

Robber's Wife (1831), IV. 527

— = Robber's Bride

Robber's Wife of the Apennines = Sparbuto

Robbery at the Tower of London = Colonel Blood

Robbery of the Cape Diamonds = Kimberley Mail

Robbery of the Mail = Courier of Lyons

Robbery under Arms (Dampier, A. and Walch, G., 1894), v. 335

Robbing Robin Hood (1890), v. 742

Robbing Roy (Burnand, F. C., 1879), v. 291

Robbing the Mail = Arrah-ma-Beg

Robers Rob'd = Bouncing Knight

Robert and Bertram (Horton, S. G., 1887), v. 427

Robert and Bertrand (1845), iv. 527

Robert Burns (Lemon, M., 1842), iv. 344

— (1896), v. 742

Robert Emmet (Digges, W., 1881), v. 345

Robert Emmett (Boucicault, D., 1884), v. 269

Robert Emmett, the Irish Patriot of 1803 (1873), v. 742

Robert La Grange (1861), v. 742

Robert le Diable (Fitzball, E. and Buckstone, J. B., 1832), iv. 83, 314

— (1832), iv. 83, 527

Robert le Grange (Webb, C., 1843), iv. 417

Robert Macaire (Byron, H. J., 1870), v. 297

— (Selby, C., 1835), iv. 397, 610

— (Simpson, C. and Simpson, J. P., 1867), v. 816

— (1887), v. 742

Robert Macaire Renovated (Clarance, L., 1884), v. 311

Robert of Normandy = Fiend Father

Robert Rabagas (Fiske, S., 1873), v. 367

Robert Richborne (1871), v. 742

Robert Ryland (Glynn, G., 1849), iv. 319

Robert the Bruce (1819), iv. 92, 527

— (1834), iv. 92, 528

Robert the Devil (Beazley, S., Jr.), iv. 264

— (Gilbert, W. S., 1868), v. 379

— (?Lacy, M. R., 1830), iv. 340, 592

— (Raymond, R. J., 1830), iv. 388

— (1830), iv. 528

— (1888), v. 742

Robespierre (Bernard, W. B., 1840), iv. 266

— (Bliss, H., 1854), v. 265

— (Irving, L. B., 1899), v. 210, 432

— (Patterson, R. H., 1877), v. 809

— (Springate, H. S., 1879), v. 576

Robin and Marion (1819), iv. 528

Robin Bullcalf's Readings (1785), iii. 342

Robin Goodfellow (Carton, R. C., 1893), v. 305

— (Loder, E. J., 1848), iv. 346

— (1738), ii. 136, 382, 448

Robin Gray (1814), iv. 528

Robin Hood (Barri, H., 1890), v. 251

— (Blanchard, E. L., 1858), v. 742, 779, 845

— (Burnand, F. C., 1862), v. 288

— (Douglass, J. T., 1878), v. 348

— (Fitzball, E., 1860), v. 368

— (Hall, F., 1880), v. 399

— (Jones, R. S., 1848), iv. 591

— (McCardle, J. F., 1880), v. 742, 804, 845

— (Macnally, L., 1784), iii. 285

— (Mendez, M., 1750), iii. 287

— (Mills, H. and Horton, S. G., 1888), v. 798, 807, 845

— (Oxenford, J., 1860), v. 510

— (1730), ii. 448

+ — (D.L., 1750), ii. 260

— (1810), iv. 528

— (1857, 1859), v. 845

— (1861), v. 742

— (1876), v. 742

— (1878), v. 845

— (1879, 1881, 1896), v. 742

Robin Hood and his Merry Little Men (Blanchard, E. L., 1877), v. 265

Robin Hood and his Merry Men (Hazlewood, C. H., 1867), v. 413

— (1867), v. 742

Robin Hood and Little John (1730), ii. 365

— (1896), v. 742

Robin Hood and Maid Marion (Hood, B., 1899), v. 425

Robin Hood and Richard Cœur de Lion! (Stocqueler, J. H., Brooks, C. W. S. and Kenney, C., 1846), v. 528, 591

Robin Hood and ye Curtall Fryer (Dawtrey, R. A., 1892), v. 339

Rob Roy, the Gregarach (Soane, G., 1818), IV. 403

Robson's Academy (Campbell, A. V., 1849), IV. 279

Rob the Ranter (1820), IV. 528

Robur Ragabas (1873), V. 744

Robust Invalid (Reade, C., 1857), V. 536, 812

Rocambole (Suter, W. E., 1866), V. 588

Rocco Salvioni (1862), V. 744

Rochester (Moncrieff, W. T., 1818), IV. 17, 143, 358; V. 100

Rocket (Pinero, Sir A. W., 1883), V. 525

Rockleys (Hoffman, A. A., 1887), V. 423

Rock of Annaboa = Descart, the French Buccaneer

Rock of Arpennaz (1824), IV. 528

Rock of Beauty (1847), IV. 528

Rock of Death = (1) Amalderac, the Black Pirate; (2) Glendwyr of Snowdon

Rock of La Charbonniere = Father and Son

Rock of Rome (Knowles, J. S., 1849), IV. 339

Rock of St Helena = Death of Napoleon

Rock of Skulls (1837), IV. 528

Rocks and Shoals in the Voyage of Life = Harry Hawser

Rocky Road to travel = Perseus.

Rodar the Raven (Campbell, A. V., 1831), IV. 528, 638

Roderic (1853), V. 744

Roderick of Ravenscliff (1832), IV. 528

Roderick Random (Ryley, S. W., 1789), III. 304

Roderick the Goth (1820), IV. 528

Roderick vich Alpine = Lady of the Lake

Rodogune (Aspinwall, S., 1765), III. 60, 234

Rodolph and Rosa (1807), IV. 528

Rodolph the Wolf (Planché, J. R., 1818), IV. 376, 604

Rodrigo (Albo, E. J., c. 1846), IV. 567

Roebuck (Peake, R. B., 1823) = Poachers, IV. 528, 638

— (Somerset, C. A., 1827), IV. 404

Roger and Joan (1739), II. 237, 260, 346, 382

Roger-la-Honte (Buchanan, R., 1888), V. 285

Roger O'Hare (Everett, H., 1865), V. 744, 790, 845

Roger's Wedding (1710), II. 382

Rogue and Vagabond (Eldridge, H. W., 1895), V. 356

Rogueries of Nicholas = Adventures of a Ventriloquist

Rogue Riley (Matthews, E. C., 1894), V. 481

Rogue's a Fool = Beggar my Neighbour

Rogues All! (1814), IV. 528

Rogues and Vagabonds (Hill-Mitchelson, E. and Benton, F., 1897), V. 422

Rogue's Comedy (Jones, H. A., 1896), V. 167-8, 170, 182, 440

Rogues of Paris = Bohemians

Rogue's Paradise (1895), V. 744

Roi Carotte (Leigh, H. S., 1872), V. 454

Roi l'a dit (Temple, R., 1894), V. 820

Rokeby (Macready, W. C., 1814), IV. 92, 352

— (Thompson, C. P., 1814), IV. 92, 413

Rokeby Castle (Dibdin, C. I. M., 1813), IV. 293

Roland (1835), IV. 528

Roland and his Steed (Suter, W. E., 1858) = White Palfrey, V. 744, 767, 819, 845, 849

Roland for an Oliver (Morton, T., 1819), IV. 84, 131, 364

— (1819), IV. 528

Roland the Rider (Courtney, J., 1851), V. 326

Roley Poley (Conquest, G. and Spry, H., 1877), V. 321

Rolla (Lewis, M. G., 1799), III. 281, 390

— (Thompson, B., 1800), IV. 412

— (1810), IV. 528

Rolla in a Sensation Role = Great Sensation

Rolling Stone (1856), V. 744

— (1896), V. 744

Rolling Stone sometimes gathers Moss (Marchant, F., 1870), V. 476

Roll of the Drum (Hatton, J., 1896), V. 409

— (Wilks, T. W., 1843), IV. 421

— (1894), V. 744

Rollo, the Minstrel (1843), IV. 528

Roma (Lubimoff, A., 1885), V. 464

Roman (Dobell, S. T., 1850), IV. 581; V. 346

Romany Lore (Vincent, G. F., 1894), v.
  609
Romany Revels = Romany Lore
Romany Rye (Sims, G. R., 1882), v. 568
Romany's Revenge = Zamet
Rome Excis'd (1733), II. 382
Romeo and Juliet (Cibber, T., 1744),
  II. 7, 24, 69, 314
— (Dowling, M. C., 1837), IV. 91, 307,
  582
— (Farnie, H. B., 1890), v. 363
— (Garrick, D., 1748), II. 330
— (Gurney, R., 1812), IV. 91, 322
— (Halliday, A., 1859), v. 400
— (Howard, J., ?1665), I. 137, 172, 414
— (Kemble, J. P., 1814), IV. 335
— (Lee, J., 1777), III. 280, 390
— (Lee, N., 1852), v. 452
— (Marsh, C.), III. 286
— (Sheridan, T., 1746), III. 306
— (1770), III. 70, 342, 404
— (1813), IV. 88, 528
— = Lovers of Verona
Romeo and Juliet, as the Law Directs =
  Romeo and Juliet
Romeo and Juliet Up-to-date (Henry,
  S. C., 1893), v. 418
Romeo and Juliet up-to-larks (Cane, C.,
  1893), v. 302
Romeo Revised = Modern Juliet
Romeo the Radical and Juliet the Jingo
  (Emery, C. P., 1882), v. 358
Romeo Travestie (1841), IV. 91, 528
Rome Preserv'd = Porsenna's Invasion
Rome Preserved (1760), III. 342, 404
Rome's Follies (1681), I. 445
Romiero (Baillie, J., 1836), IV. 157, 162,
  258
Romp (Lloyd, 1778), III. 207, 282
— (1817), IV. 528
Romp in Disguise = Frolick
Romp Reclaimed = All her own Way
Romulus (Johnson, H., 1724), II. 340
— (1854), v. 744
Romulus and Hersilia (Hoole, J., 1800),
  III. 388
— (Schomberg, R.), III. 304
— (1682), I. 57, 101, 156, 445
Romulus and Remus (Reece, R., 1872),
  v. 537
Ronald Dhu (Pitt, G. D., 1847), IV. 375
Ronald the Reaper = Broken Chain

Ronald the Reiver (1823), IV. 528
Roof Scrambler (À Beckett, G. A.,
  1835), IV. 249
Rook and the Cause = Flamingo
Rooks Pigeoned = Game at Commerce
Rookwood (Atkyns, S., 1850), v. 245
— (Conquest, G., 1859), v. 744, 785,
  845
— (Pitt, G. D., 1840), IV. 373
— (Roberts, G. and Gerald, F., 1895),
  v. 545
— (1855) = Turpin's Ride to York, v.
  744, 760
Room for the Ladies (Wooler, J. P.,
  1869), v. 632
Room 70 (Fitzgerald, P., 1878), v. 369
Root of All Evil (1864), v. 744
— (1876), v. 744
Rope Ladder (1822), IV. 529
Rope Merchant (Melford, M., 1890), v.
  484
Rory O'More (Lover, S., 1837), IV. 347
Rosabelle = Houp-la!
Rosalia (1860), v. 744
Rosalie (Ebsworth, J., 1823), IV. 308
— (Rede, W. L., 1838), IV. 390
— (1864), v. 744
Rosalie Mortimer (1857), v. 744
Rosalinda (Lockman, J., 1740), II. 236,
  342, 440
Rosalinde (1892), v. 745
Rosamond (Addison, J., 1707), II. 31,
  223, 228, 233, 235, 294
— (Holcroft, F., 1805), IV. 326
— (1767), III. 342, 404
Rosamund (Baildon, H. B., 1875), v. 247
— (Swinburne, A. C., 1860), v. 589
— (1829), IV. 638
Rosamunda (Williams, T. J.), v. 824
Rosamund, Queen of the Lombards
  (Swinburne, A. C., 1899), v. 589
Roscius in Spirits (O'Neil, J. R., 1852),
  v. 507
Roscius of the Fleet = Jolly Jack
Rose (Arne, T. A., 1772), III. 199,
  234
— (Edwards, H. S., 1864), v. 355
— (1819), IV. 529
Roseallan's Daughter (McGilchrist, J.,
  1861), v. 469
Rose among Thorns (Damerell, S.,
  1898), v. 335

Rose and Colin (Dibdin, C., 1778), III.
255, 381
Rose and the Lily (1873), V. 745
Rose and the Ring (Clarke, H. S., 1890),
V. 313
— (Heyne, M., 1878), V. 420
— =Ambassador's Lady
Rose and Thistle=Rights of Woman
Rose Ashford (1848), IV. 529
Rose Brilliant (1899), V. 745
Rosebud of Stinging-nettle Farm
(Byron, H. J., 1863), V. 296
Rosebuds (Bradley, C., 1885), V. 273
Rose Clinton (Courtney, J., 1848), IV.
284; V. 845
— (1854), V. 745, 845
Rosedale (Arnold, C., 1893), V. 243
— (Wallack, L., 1876), V. 612
Rose d'Amour (1818), IV. 529
Rose Graham (1860), V. 745
Rose Lendin (1842), IV. 529
Rosemary (Parker, L. N. and Carson,
S. M., 1896), V. 513
+ Rose Maythorn (Lee, N., Jr., 1867)
Rose Michel (Clarke, C., 1875), V. 311
— (Millward, C., 1886), V. 489
Rosenberg (1828), IV. 529
Rosencrantz and Guildenstern (Gilbert,
W. S., 1891), V. 381
Rose of Alvey=Pretender
Rose of Altenheim=Hunter's Bride
Rose of Amiens=Our Wife
Rose of Arragon (Knowles, J. S., 1842),
IV. 339
Rose of Auvergne (Farnie, H. B., 1869),
V. 790
Rose of Balsora=Noureddin and the
Tartar Robbers
Rose of Blarney (Rhys, H., 1862), V. 542
Rose of Castile (Harris, A. G. and
Falconer, E., 1857), V. 405
Rose of Castille=Queen and the Knave
Rose of Corbeil (Stirling, E., 1837), IV.
406
Rose of Devon (Jourdain, J., 1889), V.
442
Rose of Ettrick Vale (Lynch, T. J.,
1825), IV. 92, 529, 596
Rose of Gurgistan=Persian Hunters
Rose of Ireland and the Fairies of
O'Donoghue's Lakes=Brother's
Revenge

Rose of Ispahan (1897), V. 745
Rose of Kerry=Ireland
Rose of Killarney (1894), V. 745
— =Aline
Rose of Morven=Beautiful Insane
Rose of Persia (Hood, B., 1899), V. 425
Rose of Rathboy (Fitzgerald, D., 1899),
V. 368
Rose of Romford (Martin, J. R., 1885),
V. 479
Rose of St Fleur (1867), V. 745
Rose of Salency (1866), V. 745
Rose of Stepney (1838), IV. 529
Rose of the Alhambra (Fitzball, E.,
1836), IV. 315
— (Parker, C. S., 1891), V. 513
Rose of the Ferry (1860), V. 745
Rose of the Village (1856), V. 745
Rose of Tuscany=Three Dons
Rose of Windsor (Parke, W., 1889), V.
512
— =Herne's Oak
Rose Queen (1898), V. 745
— =Philandering
Rose Roy (Pitt, G. D., 1835), IV. 372
— (1835), IV. 529
Roses (Valpy, R., 1795), III. 313
Roses and Thorns (Lunn, J., 1825), IV.
348
Rose, Shamrock and Thistle (Lee, N.,
Jr., 1865), V. 803
— (1845), IV. 529
— =Frolics of the Fairies
Roses of Shadow (Raffalovich, A.,
1893), V. 533
Rose's Victory (1871), V. 745
Rose, Thistle and Shamrock (Edge-
worth, M., 1817), IV. 209, 309
Rose without a Thorn=Chrystabelle
Rose Wreath (?Palmer, J., 1781), III.
342, 393, 404
Rosicrucian Student=Daemon Owl
Rosière (Monkhouse, H., 1892), V. 491
Rosimunda (Preston, W., 1793), III. 300
Rosina (Brooke, F., 1782), III. 206, 240,
378
Rosine (1836), IV. 529
Roslin Castle (Ebsworth, J.), IV. 309
Rosmer of Rosmersholm (1891), V. 79,
745
Rosmersholm (Archer, C., 1891), V. 79,
187, 242

Rosmersholm (1893), v. 745

Rosamunda (1856), v. 745

Rossignol (1825), IV. 529

Roth (Ross, C. H. and Richards, P., 1871), v. 551

Rotherhithe in the Olden Time (1854), v. 745

Rotherick O'Connor, King of Connaught (Shadwell, J., 1720), II. 354

Rothomago (Farnie, H. B., 1879), v. 362

Roué Brother = Adèle

Roué Reformed = Jupiter and Juno

Rouge et Noir (Ebsworth, J., 1838), IV. 308

— (Leslie, H. T., 1866), v. 745, 803, 845

— (1838), IV. 529

Rougemont = French Libertine

Rougemont the French Robber (Johnstone, J. B., 1860), v. 800

Rough and Ready (Glendinning, J., 1897), v. 382

— (Meritt, P., 1873), v. 485

— (1860), v. 745

Rough and Smooth (1827), IV. 529

Rough Diamond (Buckstone, J. B., 1847), IV. 130, 275

— (1836), IV. 529

Rough Hands and Honest Hearts (1873), v. 745

Rough Honesty (Pitt, W. H., 1877), v. 527

Roughly Woo'd and Gently Won (1878), v. 745

Rough Road tests the Mettle = Adversity

Rough Road to a Golden Land = Tiger of Mexico

Rough Rob, the Gipsy Thief of Hangman's Hollow (Thorne, R. L., 1850), v. 599

Round a Tree (Risque, W. H., 1896), v. 544

Roundhead (Bussy, B. F. and Blackmore, W. T., 1883), v. 294

Roundheads (Behn, A., 1681), I. 79, 224, 391

Round of Intrigue (Clarance, J., 1847), IV. 280

Round of Wrong (Bernard, W. B., 1846), IV. 266

Round Robin (Dibdin, C. I. M., 1811), IV. 292

Round the Clock (McArdle, J. F., 1878), v. 466

Round the Globe (McArdle, J. F., 1875), v. 466

Round the Globe in Eighty Days (1875), v. 745

Round the Links (Overbeck, E., 1895), v. 509

Round the Ring (Meritt, P., 1891), v. 487

Round the World (Murray, A., 1886), v. 499

Round the World in Eighty Days (1875), v. 745

Round the World in W'Eighty Days (FitzGeorge, Capt., 1877), v. 368

Round Tower (Cross, J. C., 1797), III. 250, 342, 380, 404 [The date on p. 250 should be 1797]

— (McCarthy, J. H., 1892), v. 467

Roused Lion (Webster, B. N., 1847), IV. 418

Rout (Hill, Sir J., 1758), III. 269

Rout Routed (1800), IV. 529

Rover (Behn, A., 1677, 1681), I. 57, 222–3, 231, 252, 348, 349, 350, 351, 352, 390, 391; III. 114

— (Boyce, S., 1752), III. 239

— (1757), III. 114, 342

Rover from Many Lands = Bitter Reckoning

Rover of the Isles (1833), IV. 529

Rover of the North Sea = False Earl

Rover Reclaim'd = (1) Damon and Phillida; (2) Lady's Revenge

Rover Reclaimed = Breakfast of Love

Rovers (Canning, G., 1798), III. 67, 241

Rover's Bride (Almar, G., 1830), IV. 252

Rover's Cruise = Wapping Old Stairs

Rovers of Weimar = Quadrupeds of Quedlinburgh

Rover's Secret (Stirling, E., 1845), IV. 408

— (1860), v. 745

Roving Commission (Besemeres, J., 1869), v. 260

Roving Husband Reclaim'd (1706), II. 182, 382

Roving Meg (Clarke, A. H., 1899), v. 311

Row in the Buildings (Greenwood, T., 1844), IV. 321

Row in the House (Robertson, T. W., 1883), v. 547

Rowland for an Oliver = Roland for an Oliver

Rowley and Chatterton in the Shades (1782), III. 342

Row of Ballynavogue (Scott, J. M., 1817), IV. 529

Row on the Premises (1859), v. 745

Rows of Castille (Edwardes, C. T. M., 1872), v. 354

Roxalana (1819), IV. 529

Roy = Forgery

Royal Academicians (Williams, J., 1786), III. 316

Royal Amazon = Thomyris, Queen of Scythia

Royal Baker (1830), IV. 529

Royal Berkshire Regiment (Laun, H. T. Van and Remo, F., 1886), v. 449

Royal Box (Coghlan, C. F.), v. 316

Royal Brew = Punch Bowl

Royal Bull-fight = Crichton

Royal Captive (Maxwell, J., 1745), II. 344

Royal Captives (1729), II. 382

— = Troades

Royal Chace (Phillips, E., 1736), II. 137, 138, 349

Royal Champion (1728), II. 382

Royal Charlie (1845), IV. 529

Royal Choice (Stapylton, Sir R., 1653), I. 433

Royal Clemency = Deserter

Royal Commission from Paris (1840), IV. 529

Royal Convert (Rowe, N., 1707), II. 28, 31, 58, 100, 116, 352, 443

Royal Crusader (1846), IV. 638

Royal Cuckold (1693), I. 445

Royal Dane (1827), IV. 90, 529

Royal Delinquent (1834), IV. 529

Royal Divorce (Wills, W. G., 1891), v. 628

Royal Elephant = Siamovaindainaboo, Princess of Siam

Royal Escape (Coghlan, C. F., 1861), v. 745, 784, 845

Royal Example = Sprigs of Laurel

Royal Exiles = Fall of Portugal

Royal Family (Marshall, R., 1899), v. 478

Royal Federation = Champ de Mars

Royal Flight (1690), I. 445

Royal Foxhunt (Moncrieff, W. T., 1847) = Favourite of the Derby, IV. 460, 529, 600, 625

Royal Fugitive = (1) Sobieski; (2) Wanderer

Royal Fugitives (1791), III. 342

Royal Garland (Bickerstaffe, I., 1768), III. 237

Royal Heroe (1744), II. 382

Royal Hostages (1793), III. 404

Royal Impostor = Innocence Betray'd

Royalist (D'Urfey, T., 1682), I. 79, 274, 349, 408

+ — (Nichol, C. J. S.: Ampthill, 10/1892; 8°, n.d.)

— (1850), v. 745

— (1879), v. 745

Royalist and Republican (1855), v. 745

Royalists of Paris (Webb, C., 1862), v. 823

Royal Jubilee (Hogg, J., 1822), IV. 588

— (1809), IV. 529

Royal Lovers = Britannia

Royal Mail (Douglass, J. T., 1887), v. 349

Royal Marriage (Douglass, J. T., 1868), v. 348

— (1736), II. 382

Royal Martyr = Tyrannick Love

Royal Martyr, K. Charles I (Fyfe, A., 1705), I. 100; II. 78, 329

Royal Menagerie (Blanchard, E. L., 1853), v. 263

Royal Merchant (Hull, T., 1767), III. 113, 274

— (Norris, H., 1705), II. 132, 134, 138, 346

Royal Message (Boyd, H., 1793), III. 239

Royal Mischief (Manley, M., 1696), I. 55, 75, 157, 266, 420

Royal Mistress (1838), IV. 529

Royal Nuptials (1816), IV. 529

Royal Oak (Dimond, W., 1811), IV. 306

— (Hamilton, H. and Harris, Sir A., 1889), v. 402

— = Boscabel

Royal Pardon (Conquest, G. and Pettitt, H., 1878), v. 321

Royal Penitent (Bentley, J., 1803), IV. 265

Royal Penitents = Innocence Distress'd

Royal Precedence = Shakespeare and Burbage

Royal Prisoners (1793), III. 342

Royal Resentment = Cruel Gift

Royal Revenge (1722), II. 382

Royal Riddle (Mills, H., 1887), v. 489

Royal Roundhead (Seton, H., 1893), v. 561

Royal Salute = Milliner to the King

Royal Scots Fusileers (1835), IV. 529

Royal Scout (Comer, G., 1892), v. 319

Royal Seat = Forester

Royal Shepherd (Rolt, R., 1764), III. 69, 197, 303

Royal Shepherdess (Shadwell, T., 1668), I. 138, 204, 264, 430

— = (1) Dorastus and Fawnia; (2) Faithful Couple

Royal Shepherds (Cunningham, J., 1765), III. 253

Royal Slave = (1) Nuvian Captive; (2) Oroonoko

Royal Stag Hunt of Windsor Forest = Herne the Hunter

Royal Star (Richardson, F., 1898), v. 543

Royal Sufferers = Annira

Royal Suppliants (Delap, J., 1781), III. 71, 80, 253

Royal Twelfth Cake (1833), IV. 529

Royal Twins = Man in the Iron Mask

Royalty in Disguise = Sesostris

Royal Union = Love's Triumph

Royal Vagrants (Hurst, C., 1899), v. 431

Royal Villain = Persian Princess

Royal Visit (McLaren, A., 1822), IV. 352

Royal Visit to Edinburgh = Far Off

Royal Voyage (1690), I. 11, 445

Royal Waggery = Charles the Second

Royal Ward (Hersee, H., 1883), v. 420, 797

Royal Watchman (Boosey, W., 1887), v. 267

Royal William = Adelaide

Royal Woes and Royal Wooing = Cupid's Diplomacy

Roy's Wife (1825), IV. 93, 529

Rubber of Life (Bagot, A. G. and Bagot, F. R., 1885), v. 247

— (Stirling, E., 1841), IV. 407

Rube the Showman (Calvert, C. and Coleman, J., 1870), v. 300

— (1862), v. 745

Ruby (France, E. S., 1885), v. 372

Ruby Cross (1829), IV. 530

— = Child of Mystery

Ruby Cross and the Last of the Magi = Fiend King

Ruby Heart (Rae, J. and Sidney, T., 1892), v. 533

Ruby Ring (Wilks, T. E., 1840), IV. 421

— (1858), v. 845

Ruby Ruins (1842), IV. 530

Ruddigore = Ruddygore

Ruddy George (Taylor, H. G. F., 1887), v. 591

Ruddygore (Gilbert, W. S., 1887), v. 145, 380

Rudeus (Echard, E., 1693), I. 410

Rudolph of Hapsburg (1841), IV. 530

Rudolph of Varosnay (Blackwell, J. A., 1841), IV. 267

Rudolpho the Hungarian (Mead, T., 1871), v. 483

Rudolph the Wolf (1818), IV. 530

Ruffian Boy (Dibdin, T. J., 1819), IV. 301

— (Fitzball, E., 1819), IV. 312

— (Frimbley, 1823), IV. 585

Ruffian of Prague = Ruffian Boy

Rugantino (Lewis, M. G., 1805), IV. 82, 345, 595

Rugantino, the Bravo of Venice (1831), IV. 82, 530

Ruin, Degradation and Death = Three Warnings

Ruined House at Milbank (1846), IV. 530

Ruined Life (Goodrich, A. and Crauford, J. R., 1884), v. 384

Ruined Merchant (Twigg, J., 1851), v. 605

Ruines of Love = Queen Catharine

Ruins of Athens (Bartholomew, B., 1846), IV. 530, 638

Ruins of Paluzzi (Dibdin, T. J., ?1796), III. 382

Ruins of St Paul = Cardillac, the Terror of Paris

Ruins of St Pierre (1832), IV. 530

Ruins of the Mill = Soldier's Widow

Rule a Wife and Have a Wife (Kemble, J. P., 1811), v. 325

Rule a Wife and Have a Wife (Love, J., 1776), III. 283, 391

Rule Britannia (Becher, M., 1870), v. 254

— (Campbell, A. V. 1836), IV. 278, 575

— (Roberts, J., 1794), III. 302

— (1846), IV. 530

— (1868), v. 745

— (1895), v. 745

Rule of Contrary = Sayings and Doings

Rule of Three (Le Clercq, P., 1891), v. 452

— (Talfourd, F., 1858), v. 590

Ruling Passion (Macnally, L., 1778), III. 285 [This was acted on 24/2/1778 at Crow-street, not Capel-street, Dublin]

— (Willing, J., 1882), v. 626

Rumbelow (1888), v. 745

Rum Duke and the Queer Duke (1730), II. 382

Rumfuskin King of Bythnyphorbia (1818), IV. 530

Rumfustian Innamorato (Walker, C. E., 1824), IV. 416, 615

Rummin's Reputation (Rae, C. M., 1879), v. 532

Rummio and Judy (Logan, W. H., 1841), IV. 595

Rum Ones (1822), IV. 530

Rumour (Stannard, Mrs, 1889), v. 579

Rump (Tatham, J., 1660), I. 211, 224, 292, 391, 434

Rumpelstiltskin and the Maid (Burnand, F. C., 1864), v. 288

Rumpus in Ashan-T = King Koffee

Rum'uns from Rome (1881), v. 745

Runaway (Cowley, Mrs H., 1776), III. 248

Runaway Bride (McLaren, A., 1823), IV. 352

Runaway Girl (Hicks, Sir S. and Nichols, H., 1898), v. 421

Runaway Goddess and the Enchanted Daffodil = Diana's Chase

Runaway Horse = Hut of Valais

Runaway Husbands (Jackson, W. H., 1893), v. 432

— (1849), IV. 530

— = Ladies of St Cyr

Runaway Match (Mayne, A., 1872), v. 483

Runaway Match (1854), v. 745

— (1880), v. 745

Runaways (Aria, E., 1898), v. 243

— (Broughton, F. W., 1880), v. 281

— (1894), v. 745

Run down to Brighton (Meadows, A. M., 1893), v. 483

Run for your Life (1820), IV. 530

Run in (Gaskell, Mrs P., 1899), v. 376

Runnamede (Logan, J., 1784), III. 61, 282, 391

Running of the Rat = Brisket Family

Runnymede (Richards, A. B., 1846), IV. 608

Run of Luck (Pettitt, H. and Harris, Sir A., 1886), v. 521

— (1877), v. 745

Run to Earth (Macdonough, G. F., 1874), v. 469

— (Roberts, G., 1887), v. 544

— (Saunders, C., 1873), v. 556

— = (1) Day at Boulogne; (2) Scarlet Sins

Run wild (Coffin, E., 1888), v. 316

Rupert Dreadnought (Beverley, H. R., 1871), v. 261

Rupert of Hentzau (Hope, A., 1898), v. 425

Rural Felicity (Buckstone, J. B., 1834), IV. 274

Ruralising (Carlyle, G., 1872), v. 303

Rural Love (1732), II. 382

— (1764), III. 342

Rural Sports (1740), II. 382

Rural Visitors (1807), IV. 530

Ruse de guerre (Selby, C., 1835), IV. 610

Ruse de Guerre on the Banks of the Tagus = Lisbon

Rushford's Last Ruse (Lawrence, W., 1878), v. 451

Rush Light (1795), III. 404

Russell (1839), IV. 638

Russia (Farnie, H. B. and Reece, R., 1877), v. 362

Russia against Turkey, now on Trial at Cook's Arena of Chivalry before Britannia assisted by immortal Punch (1854), v. 745

Russian (Sheridan, T., 1813), IV. 401

Russian Ambassador (Shield, H., 1871), v. 563

Russian Brothers = Serf

Russian Bride (Hazlewood, C. H., 1874), v. 415

Russian Captive (Haines, J. T., 1831), IV. 530, 639

Russian Daughter (1820), IV. 530

— = Zelma

Russian Festival (Noble, 1817), IV. 530, 639

Russian Impostor (Siddons, H., 1809), IV. 401

Russian Mandate = Ivan Daniloff

Russian Perfidy = Boor's Hut

Russian Sacrifice (Code, H. B., 1813), IV. 281

Russian Slaves = Day in Turkey

Russian Stratagem = Love in Wrinkles

Russian Tyranny (1854), v. 845

— (1884), v. 745

— = Nadeshta, the Slave Girl

Russian Village (Brown, C. A., 1813) = Narensky, IV. 530, 639

Rustic (Halley, W. F., 1896), v. 400

— (Siedle, A. E., 1888), v. 566

Rustic Adonis (1837), IV. 530

Rustic Chivalry (Weatherley, F. E., 1892), v. 617

Rustic Heroine = Loyal Shepherds

Rusticity (1750–1800), III. 342

Rustic Maiden (Gordon, G. L., 1882), v. 385

Rustic Roses (1873), v. 745

Ruth (Bright, A. A. and Jerome, J. K., 1890), v. 275

— (Haines, J. T., 1843), IV. 323

— (Lancaster, E. R.), IV. 593

— (Moore, R., 1868), v. 492

— (1840), IV. 530

— (1883), v. 745

Ruth Lee (Waldron, W. R., 1869), v. 611

Ruth Martin, the Fatal Dreamer (Barnett, C. Z., 1846), IV. 261

Ruth Oakley (Harris, A. G. and Williams, T. J., 1856), v. 405

Ruth of Rosedale (1848), IV. 530

Ruth's Lovers (1898), v. 745

Ruth's Romance (Broughton, F. W., 1876), v. 152, 281

Ruth the Jewess = Ruth

Ruth the Mountain Rose = When the Clock strikes Nine

Ruth Tudor (1837), IV. 530

Ruth Underwood (Mitchell, L. E., 1892), v. 490

Ruthven (Harris, A. G., 1859), v. 405

Ruy Blas (Alexander, W. D. S., 1890), v. 238

— (Crosland Mrs N., 1887), v. 787

— (Falconer, E., 1860), v. 360

— (Gilbert, W. S., 1866), v. 379

— (Glover, W. H., 1861), v. 793

— (Grist, W., 1886), v. 395, 795

— (Leslie, F. and Clark, H. F., 1889), v. 456

— (O'Rourke, E., ?1861), v. 808

— (1860), v. 745

— (1861), v. 745

Ruy Blas Righted (Reece, R., 1874), v. 538

Rye House Plot (Haines, J. T., 1838), IV. 322

— (1861), v. 745

— (1865), v. 745

Sabbioneta (1896), v. 746

Sabine War = Romulus and Remus

Sabotiers (1806), IV. 530

Sachem's Vow = Red Man

Sacontalá (Jones, W., 1789), III. 70, 277

— (1870), v. 746

Sacrament of Judas (Parker, L. N., 1899), v. 514

Sacred Elephants of the Pagoda = Rajah of Nagpore

Sacred Standard and the Chinese Prince (Milner, H. M., 1828), IV. 530, 639

Sacred Trust (Faucquez, A., 1861), v. 746, 791, 845

Sacrifice (Fane, Sir F., 1686), I. 101, 410

— (Victor, B., 1776), III. 313

— (1857), v. 746

Sacrificed (Lloyd, M. F., 1891), v. 461

Sacrifice of Iphigenia (1750), III. 342

Sadak and Kalasrade (Dibdin, T. J., 1797), III. 342, 382

— (Mitford, M. R., 1835), IV. 358

— (1814), IV. 530

Saddled for the Field = White Surrey

Saddler of Bantry = Black Tom of Tyburn

Sad Memories (Withers, F., 1895), v. 630

Saint Cecily (Medbourne, M., 1666), I. 420

St Clair of the Isles (Polack, E., 1838), IV. 385

St Clara's Eve = Conquest of Taranto

St Clare and the Happy Days of Uncle Tom = Slave Hunt

St Clement's Eve (Taylor, Sir H., 1862), v. 820

St Cupid (Jerrold, D. W., 1853), v. 69, 104, 436

St Cuthbert's Eve (1820), IV. 530

St Cyr = Ninon

St David's Day (Dibdin, T. J., 1800), IV. 297

St Dru, the Accused (1836), IV. 530

St George and the Dragon (À Beckett, G. A. and Lemon, M., 1845), IV. 250

— (Bayliff, R. L., 1891), v. 253

— (Bernard, W. B., 1833), IV. 572

— (Blanchard, E. L. and Greenwood, T. L., 1877), v. 265

— (Cheetham, G. F., 1864), v. 746, 783, 846

— (Dibdin, C. I. M., 1802), IV. 290

— (Dibdin, C. I. M., 1822), IV. 295

— (Ducrow, A., 1833), IV. 307

— (Henry, A., 1884), v. 417

— (Lee, N., 1843), IV. 530, 639

— (Osman, W. R., 1869), v. 508

— (?1688), I. 447

— (1822), IV. 530

— (1855, 1857), v. 746

— (1857), v. 846

— (1883, 1884, 1888, 1896), v. 746

St George for England = Royal Champion

St George's Day (1789), III. 342

— = Knights of the Garter

St Giles's Scrutiny (1785), III. 342

St Gothard's Mount (1824), IV. 530, 639

St Helena (Thompson, E., 1776), III. 311

St Hilda's Cave (1824), IV. 530, 639

St James's and St Giles's (Wilkins, J. H., 1853), v. 623

— = Rubber of Life

St James's Park (1733), II. 382

— = Love in a Wood

St John's Priory (1839), IV. 530

St Kilda in Edinburgh (Heron, R., 1798), III. 268 [The date 1728 for the Larpent MS. is given in error]

St Leger (Fox, G. D., 1877), v. 371

St Leon (Caunter, J. H., 1835), IV. 576

St Marc (Wilkins, J. H., 1853), v. 623

St Margaret's Cave (Carr, G. C., 1804), IV. 279

St Mark's Day = Zenaldi

St Mark's Eve (À Beckett, G. A., 1834), IV. 249

St Mary's Eve (Bernard, W. B., 1838), IV. 266

St Monday (1788), III. 343

Saint or Sinner? (Dampier, A., 1881), v. 335

St Patrick's Day (Sheridan, R. B., 1775), III. 184, 305, 395

— = Shamrock

St Patrick's Eve (Power, T., 1832), IV. 387

— = (1) Kathleen Mavourneen; (2) Lost Bride of Garryowen

St Patrick's Oak = Devil's Punch Bowl

St Robert's Cave = Eugene Aram

St Ronan's Well (Davey, R. and Pollock, W. H., 1893), v. 338

— (Fisher, D., 1876), v. 367

— (McNeill, A. D., 1871), v. 472

— (Planché, J. R., 1824), IV. 95, 377

— (1824), IV. 95, 530

Saints and Sinners (Jones, H. A., 1884), v. 71, 163–5, 172, 439

St Stephen's Green (Phillips, W., 1700), II. 176, 349

St Stephen's Well (1844), IV. 530

St Swithin's Chair = Night Hag

St Tibb's Eve = Powder and Ball

St Valentine (Sharpe, G. F., 1892), v. 562

St Valentine's (Aitken, J. E. M. and Bergne, H. à C., 1897), v. 236

St Valentine's Day (McCabe, C. W., 1891), v. 467

— (Travers, W., 1869), v. 603

St Valentine's Eve (Milner, H. M., 1828), IV. 95, 357

Sakuntala (1899), v. 746

Salamanca Doctor Outplotted = Stolen Heiress

Salamandrine (1847), IV. 530

Salammbo (1885), v. 746

Salammbo, the Lovely Queen of Carthage (1871), v. 746

Salem's Sorrow (1872), v. 746

Sally Cavanagh (Mansfield, J. G., 1871), v. 475

Sally in our Alley (Jerrold, D. W., 1830), IV. 332

— (Lyster, F. and Heriot, P., 1888), v. 466

Sally Smart (1855), v. 746

Salmagundi (Dibdin, C. I. M., 1818), IV. 294

Salomé (Wilde, O. F. O'F. W., 1893), v. 190, 622

Saloon (Dibdin, C.), IV. 290

Saloon and Cellar (Rede, W. L., 1845), IV. 390

Saloons of Paris = Ecarté

Salopian Esquire (Dower, E., 1739), II. 44, 215, 319

Salthello Ovini (1875), v. 746

Saltimbanco (Sicklemore, R., 1797), III. 307

Salt Mine of Cracow = Zorinski

Salt Tears (Speight, T. W., 1873), v. 576

Salvator (Heraud, J. A., 1845), IV. 588

— (1820), IV. 531

Salvatori (Barnett, M., 1853), v. 250

Salvator Rosa (1866), v. 746

Salve (Beringer, Mrs O., 1895), v. 259

Salviniana (Gordon, G. L., 1877), v. 385

+Salvoisy; or, The Queen's Lover (8°, 1834)

Sambodampalus (Tully, J. H., 1853), v. 604

Sam Carr, the Man in Possession (1872), v. 746

Sam'l of Posen (Jessop, G. H., 1895), v. 437

Samor (Milman, H. H., 1818), IV. 356

Sam Patch (1844), IV. 531

— (1855), v. 746

Sample versus Pattern (Sapte, Walter, Jr., 1887), v. 556

Sampson's Wedding (Rowe, G. F., 1869), v. 552

Sampson the Serjeant = May Queen

Sam's Arrival (Oxenford, J., 1862), v. 510

Sam Scud (1842), IV. 531

Samson (Hamilton, N., 1743), II. 398, 437

Samson Agonistes (Milton, J., 1670), I. 420

Samuel in Search of Himself (Coyne, J. S. and Coape, H. C., 1858), v. 328, 784, 786

Sam Weller (Moncrieff, W. T., 1837), IV. 97, 360

Sam Weller's Tour (Moncrieff, W. T., 1838), IV. 97, 531, 639

Sancho at Court (Ayres, J., 1742), II. 44, 233, 237, 247, 296

Sancho the Great (1799), III. 343

Sancho turn'd Governor = Barataria

Sanctuary (Carpenter, J. E., 1855), v. 303

Sandford and Merton (Burnand, F. C., 1893), v. 292

Sandford and Merton's Christmas Party (Burnand, F. C., 1880), v. 291

Sands of Time (Jenkins, T. J. P., 1894), v. 436

Sang Bleu (Yeldham, Major, 1888), v. 635

San Lin (Blau, H., 1899), v. 265

Sans Culottes and the Grand Culottes (1793), III. 343

Santa Claus (Daly, C., 1898), v. 334

— (Lennard, H., 1894), v. 456, 803

Santon's Cave = Greek Amazon

San Toy (Morton, E. A., 1899), v. 495

Santuzza (1897), v. 746

+Sapho and Phao (Didelot, music Mazzinghi; H¹ 6/4/1797; 8°, 1797)

Sappho (Braunsen, J., 1820), IV. 270, 574

— (Collingham, G. G., 1899) = Idol of an Hour, v. 317, 746, 785, 846

— (Lee, E. B., 1846), IV. 594

— (Lobb, H., 1886), v. 461

— (Mason, W., 1796), III. 286

— (Serle, T. J., 1843), IV. 400

— (Wills, W. G., 1875), v. 627

— (1866), v. 746

Saracen's Head (1814), IV. 531

Saracen's Head removed from Snow Hill (Beazley, S., 1818) = Bull's Head, IV. 531, 571

Sarah (Jarman, F., 1892), v. 434

— = Warranted Burglar Proof

Sarah Blange (Barnett, M., 1852), v. 250

Sarah Jane in the Harem (Akhurst, W. M., 1875), v. 237

Sarah's Young Man (Suter, W. E., 1856), v. 587

Sarah the Creole = Sarah Blange

Sarah, the Fair Maiden of the Rhine (Bluth, R. J., 1879), v. 266

Sarah the Jewess (1861), v. 746

— = Dream of Fate

Saratoga = Brighton

Sardanapalus (Byron, Lord G. G., 1821), IV. 169–70, 278

— (Granville, H. S., 1868), v. 388

Sardanapalus, the "Fast" King of Assyria (À Beckett, G. A. and Lemon, M., 1853), v. 233

Satan (Grattan, H. and Jones, E., 1899), v. 389

— (1844), IV. 531

— (1897), v. 746

Satanas and the Spirit of Beauty (Coyne, J. S., 1841), IV. 284

Satan Bound (Boulding, J. W., 1881), v. 270

Satanella (Harris, A. G. and Falconer, E., 1858), v. 405

Satan's Daughter (Avondale, W., 1882), v. 246

Satisfaction (Blake, T. G., 1845), IV. 268

— (Bridgman, C., 1880), v. 275

Satisfactory Settlement = Business is Business

Satisfied (1831), IV. 531 [Presumably the same as Not more than I want, see IV. 512]

Saturday Night = Quarter Deck

Saturday Night and Sunday Morning = Touch and Take

Saturday Night at Sea = Armstrong the Shipwright

Saturday Night at Sea = Forecastle Fun

Saturday Night in London (Wilkinson, M., 1899), v. 623

Saturnalia (1873), v. 746

Sauce of Old Nile = Cheek and Plant

Saucy Housemaid = Robust Invalid

Saucy Lass (Haines, J. T., 1843), IV. 587

Saucy May (1884), v. 746

Saucy Nabob (1886), v. 746

Saucy Sally (Burnand, F. C., 1892), v. 292

Saucy Sultana (Stephens, V., 1894), v. 581

Saul (Heavysege, C., 1859), v. 416

Saul (Hill, A., 1760), II. 438; III. 268

— (1738), II. 398

— (1820), IV. 639

Saul and Jonathan (Crane, E., 1761), III. 249

Saul Braintree the Poacher (Ebsworth, J., 1831), IV. 308

Saul of Tarsus (Paley, G. B., 1885), v. 511

Saul the Servant (Almar, G., 1841), IV. 568

Sauny the Scott (Lacy, J., 1667), I. 69, 172, 212, 288, 418

Savage (1727), II. 383

Savage and Civilization (Anderson, J. R. and Wilkins, J. H., 1864), v. 746, 777, 823, 846

— = Huron Chief

Savage and the Maiden (Horncastle, J. H., 1844), IV. 328

Savage as a Bear (Wigan, H., 1860), v. 622

Savage Chieftain (Eyre, E. J., 1814), IV. 310

— (1816), IV. 531

Savage Lovers (Dibdin, C. I. M., 1826), IV. 296, 531, 580, 639

Savages (1792), III. 343

Savages of America = Ponteach

Savannah (Douglass, J. T., 1861), v. 788

— (Mathews, C. J., 1861), v. 746, 806, 846

Saved (Douglass, J. T.), v. 789

— (Granville, H. S., 1868), v. 388

— (Shirley, A., 1833), v. 563

— (1889), v. 746

Saved by a Child = Bab

Saved by an Irishman's Pluck = In the Hands of the Redskins

Saved by a Song (Addison, H. R., 1868), v. 236

Saved by a Word (Newbound, E., 1877), v. 502

Saved by the Sword = Life Boat

Saved from Death = Woman's Peril

Saved from Sin (Selby, H. C., 1884), v. 560

— (1891), v. 746

Saved from the Jaws of Death = Balaclava Joe

Saved from the Scaffold (Carson, L., 1897), v. 304

Saved from the Scaffold = Missing

Saved from the Sea (Shirley, A., 1895), v. 564

— = Not Dead

Saved from the Streets (Conquest, G. and Eaton, R. H., 1886), v. 322

Saved from the Wreck (1869), v. 746

Saved from the Yardarm (1890), v. 746

Saved on the Post (Fenton, C., 1893), v. 365

Savonarola (À Beckett, G. A., 1884), v. 234

— (Austin, A., 1881), v. 245

Savourneen Deelish (Blake, T. G., 1839), IV. 268

— = Peep o' Day

Savourneen Delishus = Peep of Day by a new (Lime) light

Savoyard (1815), IV. 531, 636

Savoyard Assassin = Lelia the Betrothed

Savoyard Travellers (1749), II. 383

Sawney Beane (1839), IV. 531

Sawney Bean, the Cannibal (1864), v. 746

Sawney Bean, the Terror of the North (1823), IV. 531

Saw ye Bony coming? (McLaren, A., 1804), IV. 350

Saxon Chief = Ivanhoe

Saxon King = Enchanted Raven

Saxon Maid (1842), IV. 639

Saxon Outlaw = Osric the Lion

Saxon Princes = Offa and Ethelbert

Saxons and Normans in England = Isaac of York

Saxon Slave = (1) Walsha; (2) Warlsha

Sayings and Doings (Morton, J. M., 1839), IV. 362

Sayings and Doings of Sam Weller = Pickwick

Scalded Back (Yardley, W., 1884), v. 634

Scales of Justice (Waldron, W. R., 1894), v. 611

— (1857), v. 746

— = Cotton King

Scalp Hunters (Wilkins, J. H., 1861), v. 823

Scamp = Wild Goose

Scamps of London (Moncrieff, W. T., 1843), IV. 103-4, 118-19, 361

— (1843), IV. 531

Scamps of London (1877), v. 746

— = Ups and Downs of Life

Scamps of Society (Carte, C., 1896), v. 305

Scamp, the Tramp and the Lamp = Aladdin

Scandal (Matthison, A., 1878), v. 481

Scandinavian Sketch (1851), v. 746

Scanderbeg (Dibdin, T. J., 1819), IV. 302

— (Havard, W., 1733), II. 17, 74, 75, 83, 334

— (Whincop, T., 1747), II. 84, 364

Scan. Mag. (Pocock, I., 1833), IV. 385

Scapegoat (Jones, J. W., 1891), v. 161, 441

— (Lawrence, W., 1890), v. 451

— (Poole, J., 1825), IV. 386

Scapegrace (Beazley, S., Jr., 1832), IV. 255, 571

— (Miller, W. F., 1893), v. 489

— (1828), IV. 531

Scapegrace of Paris (1844), IV. 531

— (1855), v. 746

Scapin (1753), III. 343

Scapin in Masquerade (1803), IV. 531

Scaramouch a Philosopher (Ravenscroft, E., 1677), I. 188, 252, 255, 346, 426

Scaramouch in Naxos (Davidson, J., 1889), v. 338

Scaramouch Scapin (1742), II. 383

Scaramuccia (Fitzball, E., 1839), IV. 316

Scarecrow (Thomas, C., 1889), v. 596

— (1848), IV. 531

Scarf of Flight and the Mirror of Light = Dragon's Gift

Scarlet Brotherhood (Darbey, E. and Manning, W., 1893), v. 336

Scarlet Coat (Grogan, W. E., 1899), v. 395

Scarlet Dick (Howe, J. B., 1867), v. 428

Scarlet Dye (Masters, J. C., 1887), v. 480

Scarlet Feather (Greenbank, H., 1897), v. 392, 794

Scarlet Flower (1862), v. 746

Scarlet Letter (Aveling, E. B., 1888), v. 246

— (Coleridge, S. and Forbes, N., 1888), v. 317

— (Rayner, A., 1863), v. 535

Scarlet Letter = (1) Corsican Brothers; (2) Hester Prynne

Scarlet Mark (Hazlewood, C. H., 1868), v. 413

Scarlet Sins (Crozier, C. and Milton, P., 1888), v. 331

Scar on the Wrist (Simpson, J. P. and Templar, C., 1878), v. 568

Scattered Leaves (Lingham, R. H., 1861), v. 747, 804

Scellés (Masters, J. C., 1888), v. 480

Scene at the Siege = Gay City

Scene in Germany = Man-Trap

Scene in the Life of an Unprotected Female (1850), v. 747

Scene of Confusion (Wilks, T. E., 1839), IV. 421

— = New Farce

Scene Rehearsed = Poor Covent Garden!

Scenes at Home and Abroad = Fifteen Years of a Soldier's Life

Scenes from an unfinished Drama (Hunt, L., 1820), IV. 329

Scenes from the Rejected Comedies (À Beckett, G. A., 1844), IV. 148, 181, 250

Scenes in Fashionable Life = Zorayda

Scenes in Imitation of the Rehearsal (Moser, J., 1809), IV. 364

Scenes in London (1821), IV. 531

Scenes in the Life of an Actress = Life of an Actress

Sceptic (Hill, H., 1896), v. 421

Sceptre and the Cross (Wright, M., 1898), v. 633

Schamyl (Anderson, J. R., 1854), v. 240

Schamyl, the Warrior Prophet (Simpson, J. P., 1854), v. 567

Scheme (Clyne, H., 1880), v. 315

Schemer (Stanhope, W., 1887), v. 579

— (1823), IV. 531

— (1894), v. 747

Schemers (Bromfield, W., 1755), III. 113, 240

Schemes of Harlequin (1746), II. 383, 452

Scheming and Seeming (Lunn, J., 1830), IV. 348

Scheming Butler = They've bit the old one

Scheming Dog Fancier = Marrying for Money

Scheming Lieutenant = St Patrick's Day

Scheming Valet (1776), III. 343

Schinderhannes of the Owl Forest = Robber of the Rhine

Schneider (Shirley, A. and Ripleby, R., 1892), v. 564

Schniederkins (Dibdin, T. J., 1812), IV. 299

Scholar (Buckstone, J. B., 1835), IV. 274

Scholar's Mate (Kennedy, H. A., 1893), v. 443

School (Robertson, T. W., 1869), v. 1, 129, 546

+ School Bored (Heighway, W., French)

School-Boy (Cibber, C., 1702), II. 129, 134, 137, 138, 209, 308

Schoolboy Frolics (1847), IV. 531

School Boy's Frolic = Holiday Time

School-Boy's Mask (Spateman, T., 1742), II. 356

School-Boy's Opera = Chuck

School Drudge (1881), v. 747, 846

Schoolfellows (Jerrold, D. W., 1835), IV. 332

Schoolfellows' Pleasure = Brown, Jones and Robinson

School for Arrogance (Holcroft, T., 1791), III. 118, 271, 387

— = Riches

School for Authors (Tobin, J., 1808), IV. 164, 413

School for a Wife = (1) Female Innocence; (2) Love in a Labyrinth

School for Cookery (Gattie, W. M., 1879), v. 377

School for Coquettes (Gore, Mrs C. G. F., 1831), IV. 319

— (Simpson, J. P., 1859), v. 567

School for Cowards = Greek Slave

School for Daughters (Lawler, D., 1808), IV. 342

School for Diffidence (Nation, W., 1789), III. 290

School for Eloquence (Cowley, Mrs H., 1780), III. 248

School for Fathers (Bickerstaffe, I., 1770), III. 199, 237

— (1812), IV. 531

School for Friends (Chambers, M., 1805), IV. 31, 183-4, 279

School for Gallantry (1828), IV. 531

Scotch (Dawson, F., 1895), v. 339

Scotched and Kilt = Robbing Roy

Scotch Figaries (1747), II. 383

Scotch Ghost (1796), III. 343

— (1800), IV. 531

— (1801), IV. 531

Scotch Lovers (1800), IV. 531

Scotch Marriage = Man and Wife

Scotch Marriage Laws (Jones, 1823), IV. 531, 590, 639

Scotch Mist (Shepherd, E., 1886), v. 562

— (Wills, H., 1842), IV. 531, 639

Scotch Œconomy (1750–1800), III. 404

Scotch Reformation = Assembly

Scotch Regalia = Oliver Cromwell

Scotch Sisters (1863), v. 747

Scotch Tocsin sounded = Philistines

Scotland and Algiers = Vacant Chair

Scotland's Ancient Days = Weird Woman of the Isles

Scotland's Patriot King (1820), IV. 531

Scotland Yard (1895), v. 747

Scotsman in London = Conjuror

Scots wha ha'e wi' Wallace bled (Stevens, E., 1895), v. 583

Scottish Chief and the Maid of Ellerslie (Anderson, J. R., 1863), v. 240

Scottish Chiefs (Egan, F. B., 1868), v. 356

Scottish Chiefs (not Miss Porter's) (Stirling, E., 1839), IV. 531, 639

Scottish Gentleman who was good all round = Crichton

Scottish Gold Mine = Belford Castle

Scottish Outlaw = Jonnie Armstrong

Scottish Outlaws = Gordon Gray

Scottish Volunteers (McLaren, A., 1795), III. 284, 391

— = Highland Drover

Scott Scotched = Real Truth about Ivanhoe

Scourged Page = Castle Cauldron

Scourge of Denmark = Rodar the Raven

Scourge of the North = Alabama, Privateer

Scowrers (Shadwell, T., 1691), I. 209, 431

Scrap of Paper (Simpson, J. P., 1861), v. 567

Scraps (Dibdin, T. J., 1818), IV. 301

Screw Loose (Melford, M., 1893), v. 484

Scribe (Hayman, P., 1891), v. 411

— (Hope, P., 1899), v. 426

— (1899), v. 747

Scribler (1751), III. 343

Scrivener's Daughter = Spendthrift

Scrooge the Miser's Dream (1844), IV. 97, 531

Scrub's Trip to the Jubilee (Gentleman, F., 1769), III. 264

Sculptor (Warren, T. G. and Craft, J., 1893), v. 615

— (1821), IV. 531

Sculptor of Frankfort (1849), IV. 532

— (1850), v. 846

Sculptor's Dream: A Romance of Real Life = Marble Heart

Sculptor's Workshop (1837), IV. 532

Scuttled Ship (Reade, C., 1874), v. 536, 812

Sea (Somerset, C. A., 1842), IV. 405

Sea and Land (Lemon, M., 1852), v. 455

Sea Bathing a Cure for Roguery = Voyage to Margate

Sea-Captain (Lytton, Lord, 1839), IV. 349

Sea Captain of Dundee = Grizzel Jamphray

Sea Captains (1674), I. 445

Sea Devil (Moreton, 1822), IV. 601

— (1830), IV. 532

— (1839), IV. 532

Sea Flower (Law, A., 1898), v. 450

Sea Fruit (Moss, H., 1893), v. 498

— (1887), v. 747

Sea-girt Cliff (Douglass, J. T.), v. 789

Seagull Rock (Gunton, R. T., 1895), v. 397

Sea Gulls (Maltby, A. and Stainforth, F., 1869), v. 473

Sea Horse (1839), IV. 532

Sea is England's Glory (Marchant, F., 1875), v. 476

Sea-King's Daughter = Frozen Hands

Sea King's Vow (Stirling, E., 1846), IV. 408

Sealed (1876), v. 747

Sealed Lips (1888), v. 747

Sealed Packet = Prisoner of Ham

Sealed Sentence (Stirling, E., 1844), IV. 407

— (1857), v. 747

Sealed to Silence (Bussy, F. M. and Holles, H. M., 1896), v. 294
— (Rees, H. V. and Norton, S., 1896), v. 540
Sea Lion (Pitt, G. D., 1849), IV. 376
— (1825), IV. 532
Sea Lion's Den (1835), IV. 532
Seaman and la Belle Sauvage (Dibdin, C. I. M., 1825), IV. 296
Seaman and the Savage (Dibdin, C. I. M., 1818), IV. 294
Seaman's Chest = Wreck of the Royal George
Seaman's Destiny = Lone Star
Seaman's Duty = Gunpowder Tom
Seaman's Fireside = (1) Captain Bertram; (2) Jack Junk
Seaman's Log = Breakers Ahead
Seaman's Oath = Greenwich Pensioner
Seaman's Return (Price, J., 1795), III. 300
Seaman's Star = Anchor of Hope
Seamstress and the Duchess (1856), v. 747
Sea Nymph and the Sallee Rovers = Beautiful Haydee
Sea Nymphs (Farnie, H. B. and Reece, R.), 1877, v. 362.
Sea-nymph's Cave (1854), v. 747
Sea of Ice (Robertson, T. W., 1867), v. 546
— = Omoo
Search after Happiness (More, Mrs H., 1765), III. 213, 217, 288, 392
Search after Perfection (1815), IV. 636
Search for the Southern Star = Promised Land
Search for Two Fathers = Pedrillo
Sea Serpent (Dibdin, T. J., 1818), IV. 301
— (Fitzball, E. and Buckstone, J. B., 1831), IV. 314
Seaside Girl = Sport
Sea-side Hero (Carr, Sir J., 1804), IV. 279
Seaside Holiday (1885), v. 747
Seaside Mania (Grain, R. C., 1890), v. 388
Sea-side Story (Dimond, W., 1801), IV. 12, 27, 141, 306
— (1819), IV. 532
— (1828), IV. 532

Sea-side Story = Ambrose Gwinett
Seaside Studies (Brough, W., 1859), v. 279
Seaside Swells (1889), v. 747
Season at Cheltenham = Fashionable Life
Seasons (Courtney, J., 1852), v. 326
— (Taylor, T., 1860), v. 593
— (Woodward, H.), III. 317
Seasons (not Thomson's) (Holl, H., 1836), IV. 326
Sea! the Sea! (1834), IV. 532
Seats of the Mighty (Parker, G., 1897), v. 513
Seaweed Hall (Johnstone, J. B., 1870), v. 438
Sea Witch (1839), IV. 532
Sebastian (Toosey, G. P., 1772), III. 312
Sebastian IV (1821), IV. 532
+ Sebastian of Portugal (Hemans, Felicia: a "fragment" printed in Works, 8°, 1844, vol. III)
Sebastopol (1854), v. 747
Second Brutus (1855), v. 747
Second Calender (Brough, R. B. and Brough, W., 1850), v. 278
Second Love (Simpson, J. P., 1856), v. 103, 567
Second Marriage (Baillie, J., 1802), IV. 208, 258
Second Mrs Tanqueray (Pinero, Sir A. W., 1893), v. 163, 173-4, 180-2, 187, 191, 197, 525
Second Sight (Goff, H., 1828), IV. 319
— (McLaren, A., 1817), IV. 351
— (Ryan, R., 1836), IV. 532, 639
— = (1) Dead Letter; (2) Montrose
Second Thought is Best (Hough, J., 1778), III. 273
Second Thoughts (Buckstone, J. B., 1832), IV. 274
— (Herbert, G. C., 1874), v. 418
Second Thoughts are Best (Cowley, Mrs H., 1781) = World as it Goes, III. 248, 380
— (1847), IV. 532
Second to None (1864), v. 747, 846
Second Volume (Orres, F., 1895), v. 508
Second Witness = Abigail
Secours Imprevu = Unfeeling Parent
Secrecy and Truth = Afrancesado
Secret (Barrymore, W., 1824), IV. 262

Secret (Beerbohm, C., 1888), v. 255
— (Moncrieff, W. T., 1823), IV. 359, 600
— (Morris, E., 1799), III. 138–9, 288; IV. 112
— = Haydee
Secret Agent (Coyne, J. S., 1855), v. 327
Secret Agreement (Gregory, E., 1886), v. 394
Secret Arch = Highgate Tunnel
Secretary (Knowles, J. S., 1843), IV. 339
— (Webb, C., 1848), IV. 417
Secretary and the Cook (1821), IV. 532
Secret Avengers = Rinaldo Rinaldini
Secret Blabbed = Female Freemason
Secret Castle (1799), III. 343
Secret Crime (Dobson, M. S., 1892), v. 346
Secret Death Union of South America = Ku-Klux-Klan
Secret Discovered = Masonry
Secret Enemy = (1) Banished Brother; (2) Brave Cossack
Secret Expedition (1757), III. 343
Secret Foe (Stevens, J. A., 1887), v. 583
— (Stirling, E., 1845), IV. 407
Secret-Love (Dryden, J., 1667), I. 27, 140, 186, 192, 227–8, 231, 307, 343, 344, 346, 351, 404; II. 142
Secret Marriage (1842), IV. 532
— (1860), v. 747
— (1877), v. 747
— = (1) Philippe; (2) Proof Presumptive
Secret Memoirs (Webb, C.), IV. 616
Secret Mine (Dibdin, T. J. and Fawcett, J., 1812), IV. 299
Secret Mission (1877), v. 747
Secret Mission and the Signet Ring = Raffaelle the Reprobate
Secret Muse (1814), IV. 532
Secret Nuptials = Louisa of Lombardy
Secret of a Life (Williams, A. and Roberts, G., 1886), v. 624
— = Adrienne
Secret of Life = Bridal Phantom
Secret of State (Anstruther, E., 1898), v. 241
Secret of the Five Masks = Night Guard
Secret of the Guilde Court = Musette
Secret of the Holly Bough = Bitter Cold
Secret of the Iron Cabinet = Dead Hand

Secret of the Keep (Raleigh, C., 1898), v. 534
Secret of the Lodge Room = Freemason
Secret of the Sea (Muskerry, W., 1870), v. 500
Secret of Twenty Years = Leonard
Secret Pass (Fitzball, E., 1852), v. 368
Secret Passion (1858), v. 747
Secret Plot (Green, R., 1777), III. 266
Secrets (?D'Avenant, Sir W.), I. 402
Secrets at Court = Hush!
Secret Service (Gillette, W., 1895), v. 381
— (Planché, J. R., 1834), IV. 182, 380
Secret Society (Hannan, C., 1895), v. 402
Secrets of an Old Iron Safe = Foundered Fortune
Secrets of a Palace = Doubtful Son
Secrets of Office = Alcaid
Secrets of the Abbey = Eugenio
Secrets of the Bastille = Man in the Iron Mask
Secrets of the Devil (Osman, W. R. and Fenton, F., 1864), v. 747, 792, 808, 846
Secrets of the Harem (Goldberg, M., 1896), v. 383
Secrets of the Night (1821), IV. 532
Secrets of the Past = Travers' Secret
Secrets of the Police (Melford, M., 1886), v. 484
Secrets of Thornfield Manor = Jane Eyre
Secrets of Thornfield Manor House = Jane Eyre
Secrets of War (1855), v. 747
Secret Sorrow (Dowse, G. D., 1890), v. 350
Secret Springs (1811), IV. 532
Secrets Worth Knowing (Morton, T., 1797), III. 142–3, 289
Secret Tribunal (Boaden, J., 1795), III. 238
— = Vehme Gericht
Secret Twelve (1855), v. 747
Secret Vault and the Voice of Death = Will and the Way
Secret Vaults of Tilney Castle (1806), IV. 639
Secular Masque (Dryden, J., 1700), I. 407

Senekos the Greek (1833), IV. 532
+ Senior Wranglers (Whitmore, E. H., *French*)
Sensational Novel in Three Volumes (Clay, F., 1871), V. 313
+ Sensation Dramas for the Back Drawing Room (Byron, H. J., *Lacy*)
"Sensation" Goat = Esmeralda
Sensation Hunt (1868), V. 747
Sensation Novel (Gilbert, W. S., 1871), V. 379
Sensation Scene = Brumley's Wife
Sensations of the Past Season = 1863
Sense and Sensation (Taylor, T., 1864), V. 593
Sensualist (Buenn, M. and Laidlaw, F. A., 1891), V. 287
Sentence (Webster, A., 1887), V. 617
Sentenced, but not Guilty (1876), V. 747
Sentenced to Death (Conquest, G. and Pettitt, H., 1875), V. 321
— (Stanley, H. J., 1873), V. 579
Sentimental Mother (Baretti, J., 1789), III. 235
Sentimental Waiter = Animal Sympathy
Sentinel (Boucicault, D., 1853), V. 267, 779
— (Morton, J. M., 1837), IV. 362
Sentinel of the Alma (Lover, S., 1854), V. 463
Sentry (Rémo, F. and Watson, T. M., 1890), V. 541
Sentry-Go (1896), V. 747
Sent to the Tower (Morton, J. M., 1850), V. 495
Separate Maintenance (Colman, G., 1779), III. 246
— (Coyne, J. S., 1849), IV. 285
Separation (Baillie, J., 1836), IV. 258
— (Roberts, Sir R., 1886), V. 545
Separation and Reparation (Morton, T., 1830), IV. 364
Sequel (Parker, L. N., 1891), V. 161, 513
Sequel to Nicholas Nickleby = Fortunes of Smike
Sequel to the Bottle = Drunkard's Children
Sequin the Scalp-hunter (1853), V. 747
Seraglio (Dibdin, C., 1776), III. 255
— (Dimond, W., 1827), IV. 307, 581
— (Noble, 1816), V. 522
Seraglio in an Uproar = British Beauty

Seraphina the Fair (Laidlaw, C. W., 1874), V. 446
Seraphine (Boucicault, D., 1869), V. 269
Serbelloni (1833), IV. 532
Serenade (Taylor, S., 1669), I. 435
— (1894), V. 747
Serenaders (Harris, Sir A. H. G. and Parker, W., 1892), V. 406
Serenading (Rede, T. L., 1836), IV. 532
Serenata (Machale, L., 1888), V. 469
Serf (Talbot, R., 1828), IV. 410
— (Taylor, T., 1865), V. 593
Sergeant's Daughter (Massinger, G., 1888), V. 480
Serge Panine (Thorp, J. H., 1891), V. 599
— = Justifiable Homicide
Serious Family (Barnett, M., 1849), IV. 131, 261
Serious Mistake = Lay Figure
Serious Youth (Suter, W. E., 1857), V. 819
Serjeant's Wedding (Wilks, T. E., 1840), IV. 421
Serjeant's Whim (Dibdin, C. I. M., 1804), IV. 291
Serjeant's Wife (Arnold, S. J., 1835), IV. 256
— (Banim, J., 1827), IV. 258
— (1840), IV. 532
Serpent and the Doves = Gipsy Boy
Serpent Lady (1833), IV. 532
Serpent of the Jungle = Attar Gull
Serpent of the Nile (Stirling, E., 1840), IV. 407
Serpent on the Hearth (Mead, T., 1861), V. 747, 806
— (Simpson, J. P., 1869), V. 568
Serpent Play (Hake, T. G., 1883), V. 795
Serpent's Coil = Victims of Power
Sertorius (Bancroft, J., 1679), I. 143, 388
Servant Mistress (1770), III. 123, 343
— = (1) Maid the Mistress; (2) Serva Padrona
Servant of All Work (Bernard, W. B., 1830), IV. 532, 572, 639
Servant or Suitor (1872), V. 747
Servant with Two Masters = Hotel
Serva Padrona (Baker, D. E., 1763), III. 235
— (Storace, S., 1758), III. 123, 310, 396

Serve him right (Barnett, M. and Mathews, C. J., 1850), v. 249

Service in London = Martha Willis, the Servant Maid

Serving the Queen (Leonard, H., 1898), v. 456

Sesostris (Sturmy, J., 1728), II. 90, 358

— (Williams, G. H., 1853), v. 823

— (1899), v. 747

Seth Green (1884), v. 748

Sethona (Dow, A., 1774), III. 257

Seth Slope (1839), IV. 532

Set of Horses (1792), III. 122, 325

Set of Rogues (1899), v. 748

Setting of the Sun (Hannan, C., 1892), v. 402

Setting Sun (Hogg, C., 1809), IV. 326

Settled in Full (Maxwell, H. B., 1898), v. 482

Settled out of Court (Burney, E., 1897), v. 293

Settlers and Natives = Van Dieman's Land

Settlers in America = Omala

Settler's Perils = Red John the Daring

Settler's Struggles = Indian Maid

Settling Day (Scudamore, F. A., 1893), v. 559

— (Taylor, T., 1865), v. 593

+ Settling the Verdict (*French*)

Seven Adventures = Carl Carlsruhe

Seven Ages (Jerrold, D. W., 1823), IV. 331

Seven Ages of Man (Webb, T. H., 1844), IV. 532, 639, 846

— (Webb, T. H., 1859), v. 748, 823

Seven Ages of Woman (Blanchard, E. L., 1855), v. 779

— = Maids and Matrons

Seven Brazen Towers of Tepelini = Aslan the Lion

Seven Capes (1808), IV. 532

Seven Castles of the Passions (Stirling, E., 1844), IV. 532, 612, 639

Seven Champions of Christendom (Dibdin, T. J., 1821), IV. 303

— (Osman, W. R., 1870), v. 508

— (Planché, J. R., 1849), IV. 383

— (Stocqueler, J. H., 1845), IV. 532, 639

— (1829), IV. 532

— (1853), v. 748

— = St George and the Dragon

Seven Champions of Christendom and the Storm Demon (1844), IV. 532

Seven Charmed Spuds (Quayle, C., 1872), v. 532

Seven Clerks (Wilks, T. E., 1834), IV. 420

Seven Clerks of Marseilles = Denouncer

Seven Dials (James, C. S., 1849), IV. 330

Seven Fairies of the Grotto = Doctor Faustus and the Black Demon

Seven Gifted Servants = Fortunio

Seven in One (1822), IV. 533

Seven Islands = Seven Capes

Seven Maids of Munich (Rodwell, G. H., 1846), IV. 395

Seven Mannikins and the Magic Mirror = Snowdrop

Seven Merry Maids of Marylebone = Light and Shade

Seven or Seventeen [IV. 533 should be Seventy or Seventeen]

Seven Poor Travellers (Duval, C., 1869), v. 353

— (Johnstone, J. B., 1855), v. 748, 800, 846

— (1855), v. 748

Seven Saints of Thule = Sense and Sensation

Seven Sins (Meritt, P. and Conquest, G., 1874), v. 486

Seven Sisters (Almar, G., 1835), IV. 253

Seven Steps to Ruin (1859), v. 748

— = Man

Seven's the Main = Winning a Husband

Seven Swan Princes and the Fair Melusine = Wittikind and his Brothers

Seventeen and Seventy (1837), IV. 533

Seventeen Hundred and Eighty One (1781), III. 343

Seventeen Hundred and Ninety (Hunt, H., 1894), v. 430

Seventeen Hundred Fifty Seven = Male Coquette

Seventeen Hundred Years Ago = Last Days of Pompeii

1792 = Robur Ragabas

Seven Temptations (Howitt, M., 1834), IV. 589

Seventh Bullet = Freischutz

Seventh Hour (Hughes, B. and Faucquez, A., 1861), v. 748, 792, 846

Seventh Night = Daft Meg of the Cliff

Seven Towers of Constantinople = London Apprentice

Seven Towers of Jaba = Arab's Faith

Seven Twenty Eight = Casting the Boomerang

Seventy or Seventeen (1837), IV. 533 [wrongly cited as Seven or Seventeen: apparently by C. Dance]

Seven Wise Men of Gotham = Academic Sportsmen

Seven Years Ago (Grattan, H. P., 1879), v. 389

Seven Years' Secret (Hazlewood, C. H., 1870), v. 414

Seven Years Since = Matter of Doubt

Several Wits (Cavendish, M., 1662), I. 396

Severed = Pilgrims

Severed Ties (1889), v. 748

Severine (1885), v. 748

Sewing Machine on Easy Terms (Hayman, H., 1876), v. 411

Sexes Mismatch'd (1742), II. 384

Sexton (Kirkman, F., 1662), I. 417

Sexton of Cologne (Fitzball, E., 1836), IV. 315

Sexton of Stepney (Pitt, G. D., 1847), IV. 533, 639

— (1862), v. 748

Sexton's Bird (1855), v. 748

Sexton's Prophecy = Dead Guest

Sganarelle (1709), II. 383

Shade (Thompson, C. P., 1829), IV. 413

Shades (Thompson, H., 1884), v. 598

Shades of Logic, Tom and Jerry = Death of Giovanni

Shades of Night (Marshall, R., 1896), v. 211–13, 478

— (1894), v. 748

Shadow (Almar, G., 1835), IV. 253, 568

Shadow and Sunshine (Palgrave, R., 1883), v. 511

Shadowed (1890), v. 748

Shadow Hand (Austen-Lee, C., 1893), v. 245

Shadow Hunt (Davey, R. and Pollock, W. H., 1891), v. 338

Shadowless Man (1833), IV. 533

— = Devil's Elixir

Shadowless Man and the Poor Student of Hildeburgh = Gold Fiend of the Black Forest

Shadow of a Crime (Ward, E., 1887), v. 613

— = Grace Holden

Shadow of Crime = (1) Double Life; (2) On the Verge

Shadow of Death (Somerset, C. A., 1846), IV. 405

— (Walrond, J. R., 1876), v. 612

— = (1) Fisher Girl; (2) Willow Pool

Shadow of Sin (Jarman, F., 1893), v. 434

— (1884), v. 748

Shadow of the Cross (Ward, A. H., 1898), v. 613

Shadow of the Deep = Death Hand

Shadow of the Mill (Burnley, J., 1885), v. 293

Shadow of the Rope = Day will come

Shadow of the Scaffold = Crime and Justice

Shadow of the Sword (Buchanan, R., 1881), v. 284

Shadow of Wrong (Conquest, G., 1863), v. 748, 785, 846

— (Mead, T., 1872), v. 483

Shadow on the Heart (Hazlewood, C. H., 1874), v. 415

Shadow on the Hearth (Bolton, C., 1863), v. 748, 779, 846

— (Maynard, W., 1887), v. 483

— = Workman

Shadow on the Wall (Serle, T. J., 1835), IV. 400, 610

Shadows (Young, Sir C. L., 1871), v. 149, 635

Shadows and Sunshine of Life = Village Story

Shadow Sceptre (Hamilton, H., 1882), v. 401

Shadows of a Great City (Jefferson, J. and Shewell, L. R., 1887), v. 435

Shadows of Crime (1856), v. 748

Shadows of Life (1872), v. 748

— = Hand of Fate

Shadows of the Dead = Crime and Remorse

Shadows of the Past (Simpson, J. P., 1867), v. 104, 567

— (1897), v. 748

Shadows on the Blind (Darnley, J. H. and Bruce, H. P., 1897), v. 337

Shadows on the Water (1845), IV. 533

Shadow-tree Shaft (Robertson, T. W., 1867), v. 546

Shadrack (1805), IV. 533

Shadragh the Hunchback (Williamson, H. W., 1878), v. 626

Shadragh the Shingawn (1862), v. 748

Shadroch the Shingawn and Ailleen the Rose of Kilkenny = Rathboys

Shaft No. 2 (1897), v. 748

Shah (Hall, K. E., 1873), v. 399

Shah's Festival = Night in Persia

Shake Hands (Buckingham, L. S., 1864), v. 748, 846

Shakers and Quakers = Rival Artistes

Shakespeare (Greville, E. E., 1891), v. 394

Shakespeare and Burbage (Moncrieff, W. T., 1838), IV. 91, 533, 639

Shakespeare and the Fairies = Midsummer Night

Shakespeare Converted into Bacon (Cox, S. A., 1899), v. 786

Shakespeare, his Life and Times (1847), IV. 533

Shakespeare-ience Teaches = What's it on?

Shakespeare in the Shades (Cumberland, R., ?1744), III. 251

Shakespeare Jubilee = Man and Wife

Shakespeare's Choice Spirits (1768), III. 343

Shakespeare's Dream (Maynard, M., 1861), v. 806

— (1831), IV. 91, 533

Shakespeare's Early Days (Somerset, C. A., 1829), IV. 91, 404

Shakespeare's Festival (Moncrieff, W. T., 1830), IV. 91, 360

Shakespeare's House (Coyne, J. S., 1864), v. 786

Shakespeare's Jubilee (Carey, G. S., 1769), III. 242

Shakespeare Versus Harlequin (Dibdin, C. I. M. or Dibdin, T. J., 1820), IV. 91, 294, 580

Shakespearian Reverie (Brough, W., 1864), v. 279

Shakespear's Garland = Jubilee

Shakey Page, more Funkey than Flunkey = Don Giovanni Jr.

Shakspeare's Dream (Brougham, J., 1858), v. 280

Shakspere and Company (Bradshaw, C. B., 1845), IV. 573

Shall he forgive her? (Harvey, F., 1894), v. 408

Shall I Kill Myself? (Dibdin, T. J., 1826), IV. 305

Shall we remember? (Turnbull, W. and Ellis, R. C., 1893), v. 604

Shamacda (1814), IV. 533

Sham Beggar (1756), III. 343

Sham Captain (1848), IV. 533

— = Boarding School

Sham Conjurer (1741), II. 383

Sham Doctor (1740), II. 383

— = Anatomist

Sham Duke (1896), v. 748

Shame (Chapin, A. and Oliphant, E. H. C., 1892), v. 308

— (Noble, C., 1883), v. 504

Shameful Behaviour (Troughton, A. C., 1859), v. 604

Sham Fight (1756), III. 343

— (1836), IV. 533

Sham Funeral = Two English Gentlemen

Sham Ghost (1790), III. 343

Sham Lawyer (Drake, J., 1697), I. 63, 337, 403

Sham Marquis = Younger Brother

Sham Pilgrims (1734), II. 140, 383

Sham Prince (Shadwell, C., 1719), II. 354 [This was acted Smock Alley, Dublin about June 1719]

— (1836), IV. 533

Shamrock (O'Keeffe, J., 1777), III. 292

Shamrock and the Rose (Reynolds, W., 1891), v. 541

Shamrock of Chelsea = Fine Old British Veterans

Shamrock of Ireland (Howe, J. B., 1867), v. 428

Sham Solicitor (Tabrar, J., 1883), v. 589

Shamus-na-Glanna (Aylmer, B., 1876), v. 246

Shamus-na-Lena (Towers, E., 1876), v. 601

Shamus O'Brien (Jessop, G. H., 1896), v. 437

— (Maeder, F. and Vernon, C., 1897), v. 472

Sham Van Voght (O'Neil, J. R., 1862), v. 8ɔ8

Sham Wedding = Apparition

Shandy the Spalpeen (Hayward, A., 1879), v. 412

Shane-na-Lawn (Roche, J. C. and Knox, J. A., 1885), v. 547

Shank's Mare (Vicars, W. A., 1878), v. 6ɔ8

Shares (1873), v. 748

Shark of the Atlantic (1843), IV. 533

Sharks Alongshore = Laid up in Port

Sharp and Flat (Lawler, D., 1813), IV. 342

Sharper (Clancy, M., 1738), II. 314
+ — [Douglas, J.: Smock Alley, Dublin, ?1782: in *Travelling Anecdotes*, 1782 (*Rochester*)]

Sharper of High Life = Modern Honour

Sharpers (Gardiner, M., 1740), II. 329, 437 [This was acted Aungier-street, Dublin, 21/2/1740]

Sharpers Outwitted = Squire Burlesqued

Sharper's Progress = Heart of London!

Sharp Practice (Lunn, J., 1843), IV. 348

Sharps and Dupes = Life's Highway

Sharps and Flats (Marchant, F., 1870), v. 476
— (Mills, J., 1846), IV. 356

Sharp Set (1809), IV. 533

Sharps, Flats and Naturals (1831), IV. 533
— = Musical Bob

Sharps or Flats? (Wright, E., 1895), v. 633

Sharp Way to catch a Wife (Barrett, R., 1869), v. 250

Shatchem (Doblin, H. and Dickson, C., 1890), v. 788

Shattered Fetters (Earlesmere, H., 1894), v. 353

Shattered Idol (Cimino, 1877), v. 310
— (1895), v. 748

Shattered Lives (Parry, A. W., 1890), v. 514

Shattered 'Un (Chevalier, A., 1891), v. 3ɔ9

Shaughraun (Boucicault, D., 1874), v. 45, 91–3, 269

Shave you directly (Brooks, C. W. S., 1849), IV. 271, 531, 574, 639

Shawn Long and the Fairies (Kertland, W., 1835), IV. 592

Shaw, the Lifeguardsman (1859), v. 748

She (Preston, J. F., 1888), v. 530
— (Rose, E., Sidney, W. and Graves, C., 1888), v. 550

Shebeen (Harvey, F., 1896), v. 409

She Dragon of Irwell (1875), v. 748

Sheelah's Choice = Rival Loyalists

Sheep in Wolf's Clothing (Taylor, T., 1857), v. 98, 593

Sheep Shearing (Colman, G., 1777), III. 246, 379
— (Morgan, M., 1754), III. 213, 288
— = Southwark Fair

Sheep Stealer (1828), IV. 533

Sheep's Trotter (1841), IV. 533

Sheep, the Duck and the Cock (1783), III. 343

Sheet Anchor of Albion (1806), IV. 533

She Gallant (O'Keeffe, J., 1767), III. 292, 393
— (1759), III. 343

She-Gallants (Granville, G., 1695), I. 43, 191, 246–7, 412

Shelah from Cork (Seaman, W., 1856), v. 748, 815, 846

She Lives! (Goldsmith, M., 1803), IV. 319, 533, 585, 639

Shell Spirit = Coquilla

Shelter (Goldsmith, W. H., 1890), v. 383

Shepherd and Shepherdess (1843), IV. 533

Shepherd Boy (1825), IV. 533

Shepherdess of Cheapside (Cobb, J., 1796), III. 244

Shepherdess of the Alps (Dibdin, C., 1780), III. 255

Shepherd King (1832), IV. 533

Shepherd of Cournouailles (March, M. G., 1879), v. 475

Shepherd of Derwent Vale (Lunn, J., 1825), IV. 348
— (1831), IV. 533

Shepherd's Artifice (Dibdin, C., 1764), III. 254

Shepherd's Heir = Blighted Willow

Shepherd's Holiday (1729), II. 383

Silvia (Lillo, G., 1730), II. 237, 248, 341, 440

Silvio (1894), v. 749

Simeon Pouter's Wedding = Pouter's Wedding

Simms in Long Clothes Again = Grand Baby Show

Simon (Hazlewood, C. H., 1876), v. 415
— (Spackman, J. S., 1875), v. 575

Simon Lee (Pitt, G. D., 1839), IV. 373

Simon Moneypenny (Gower, J., 1888), v. 386

Simon the Smith (Bowles, E. W., 1890), v. 271

Simon the Tanner (1856), v. 749

Simon the Thief (1866), v. 749

Simple Bess of Billingsgate = Deeds and Doings of the Dark House

Simple Hearts (Lorenzo, C. H., 1888), v. 463

Simple Historie (1834), IV. 535

Simple Simon (Wallace, J., 1805), IV. 416

Simple Squire and the Evil Eye = Marigold Farm

Simple Sweep (Broughton, F. W., 1882), v. 281

Simply an Advertisement (1863), v. 749

Simpson and Co. (Poole, J., 1823), IV. 386
— (1839), IV. 535

Simpson and Delilah (Edwards, H. S., 1882), v. 355

Simpson's Little Holiday (Nichols, H., 1884), v. 504

Sin, and its Shadow = Dead Witness

Sin and its Shadows (Lemon, H., 1885), v. 454

Sin and the Sorrow (Leslie, H. T., 1866), v. 457

Sinbad (Horner, J., 1884), v. 427
— (Jones, J. W. and Melville, W., 1897), v. 441

Sinbad and the Little Old Man of the Sea (Conquest, G. and Spry, H., 1887), v. 322

Sinbad the Sailor (Allen, O., 1885), v. 239
— (Blanchard, E. L., 1882), v. 265
— (Blanchard, E. L. and Greenwood, T. L., 1876), v. 264
— (Clay, T. L., 1878), v. 313

Sinbad the Sailor (Conquest, G. and Spry, H., 1896), v. 323
— (Denny, J. T., 1885), v. 342
— (Grattan, H. P., 1874), v. 389
— (Grattan, H. P., 1875), v. 389
— (Green, F. W., 1879), v. 391
— (Green, F. W. and McArdle, J. F., 1880), v. 391
— (Hazlewood, C. H., 1866), v. 797
— (Horsman, C., 1863), v. 798
— (Lee, N., Jr., 1870), v. 453
— (McArdle, J. F., Byam, M. and Melville, A., 1889), v. 467
— (Pemberton, T. E. and Hewson, J. J., 1886), v. 750, 798, 810, 846
— (Somerset, C. A., 1854), v. 574
— (Tabrar, J., 1893), v. 589
— (Thorne, G. and Palmer, F. G., 1885), v. 820
— (Young, J., 1896), v. 636
— (Younge, H., 1838), IV. 535, 639
— (1805), IV. 535
— (1857), v. 846
— (1866, 1871), v. 750
— (1871), v. 846
— (1872), v. 750
— (1875, 1876, 1877, 1878, 1879), v. 749
— (1880), v. 846
— (1881), v. 749
— (1882, 1883, 1884), v. 750
— (1884), v. 846
— (1885, 1886, 1887, 1888), v. 750
— (1888), v. 846
— (1889, 1890, 1891, 1892, 1893, 1894, 1895, 1896, 1898, 1899), v. 750
— = Mission to Borneo

Sinbad the Sailor and the Old Man of the Sea (Green, F. W., 1883), v. 391

Sinbad the Sailor, the Genii of the Deep (1812), IV. 535

Sing a Song of Sixpence (1857), v. 750

Sing a Song of Sixpence, a Pocket full of Rye, Four and Twenty Black Birds Baked in a Pie (Lee, N., Jr., 1862), v. 750, 802, 846

Singing Apple and the Dancing Waters = Fair Star

Singing in One Lesson = Psychic Force

Single Heart and Double Face (Reade, C., 1882), v. 536

Single Life (Buckstone, J. B., 1839), IV. 275

Sir Politick Ribband = State Juggler
Sir Popular Wisdom = Polititian
Sir Reginald (Taylor, T. M. and Ray, L., 1894), v. 591
Sir Richard Whittington (1895), v. 751
Sir Richard Whittington, Thrice Lord Mayor of London (1711), II. 384
Sir Roger de Coverley (Corri, M., ?1844), IV. 578
— (Dorman, J., 1740), II. 206, 319, 435
— (Smith, J. F., 1836), IV. 403
— (Taylor, T., 1851), v. 592
Sir Rupert the Fearless (Talfourd, F., 1848), IV. 410
Sir Salomon (Caryll, J., ?1669), I. 188, 269, 347, 395‾
Sir Salomon Single = Sir Salomon
Sir Sidney Smith (1830), IV. 535
Sir Solomon Squat, the City Vampire (1824), IV. 535
Sir Thomas Callicoe (1758), III. 114, 344
Sir Thomas More (Hurdis, J., 1792), III. 86, 274
Sir Thomas Overbury (Savage, R., 1723), II. 53, 353
— (Woodfall, W., 1777), III. 86–7, 317
Sir Timothy Tawdrey = Town-Fopp
Sir Timothy Treat-all = City Heiress
Sir Walter Raleigh (Sewell, G., 1719), II. 6, 20, 43, 61, 106, 190, 354
Sir William Crichton (Smith, W., 1846), IV. 612
Sir William Wallace, of Ellerslie (Jackson, J., 1780), III. 86, 276
Sir William Wallace the Scots Champion = Siege of Perth
Si Slocum (Tayleure, C. W., 1876), v. 591
Sister (Lennox, C., 1769), III. 8, 281
Sister and I (Mildenhall, T., 1846), IV. 355
Sister Grace (Battams, J. S., 1884), v. 253
— = Her Release
Sisterly Service (Wooler, J. P., 1860), v. 632
Sister Mary (Barrett, W. and Scott, C., 1886), v. 250
Sister of Charity (Baynem, 1829), IV. 535, 636
Sisters (Barrymore, W., 1817), IV. 535, 639

Sisters (Courtenay, E., 1893), v. 326
— (Foote, S., 1762), III. 384
— (Hazlewood, C. H., 1878), v. 415
— (Pettitt, H. and Broughton, F. W., 1883), v. 521
— (Swinburne, A. C., 1892), v. 589
— (1792), III. 325
— (1864), v. 751
— (1875), v. 751
Sister's Honour (1889), v. 751
Sister's Love (Youle, H. F., 1867), v. 635
— = (1) Countess; (2) Gipsy Bride
Sisters of Chatillon (Courtney, J., 1844), IV. 283
Sisters of St Leonard = Effie and Jeannie Deans
Sisters of Segoria (1879), v. 751
Sisters of Switzerland (Blanchard, E. L., 1840), IV. 573
Sister's Penance (Taylor, T. and Dubourg, A. W., 1866), v. 593
Sister's Sacrifice (French, S., 1859), v. 751, 793, 846
— = Love's Pledge
Sisters Saved (1824), IV. 535
Sisters Three = Family Peculiarities
Sister's Vow (Stanhope, W., 1888), v. 579
— = Eugénie
Sister's Wrongs (1855), v. 751
Sithors to Grind (Walker, G. R., 1873) = Coming Home, v. 611, 822
Six and Eightpence (1884), v. 751
Six-and-Six (Hughes, T. B., 1880), v. 430
Six and Six when suited = Matrimony
Six Brigands of the Monastery de l'Annonciade (1820), IV. 535
Six Days Adventure (Howard, E., 1671), I. 35, 60, 214, 414
Six Degrees of Crime (Barnett, C. Z., 1844), IV. 260
— (1860), v. 751
Sixes (Lindsay, A., 1893), v. 460
— (1835), IV. 535
Sixes and Sevens (Whitmore, H. E., 1894), v. 621
Six Escapes of a Robber = Cartouche
Six Hours More (Dibdin, C. I. M., 1825), IV. 295
Six Miles from Glasgow (1830), IV. 535

Six Months Ago (Dale, F., 1867), v. 106, 332

Sixpenny Telegram (Bell, Mrs H.), v. 256

Sixpenny Wire (Rae-Brown, C., 1887), v. 533

Six Persons (Zangwill, I., 1893), v. 637

Six Physicians (1818), IV. 535

Six Simpletons (Amherst, J. H., 1825), IV. 254

Six Spaniards (1787), III. 344

Six Steps of Punishment (1849), IV. 535

Sixteen and Sixty (1815), IV. 535, 636

Sixteen and Sixty-three = Modern Misses

Sixteen—not out (Blair, J., 1892), v. 262

1679 (Webb, C., 1872), v. 617

Sixteen String Jack (Rede, W. L., 1823), 389, 607

— (Rede, W. L., 1841), IV. 18, 390

— (Wilks, T. E., 1842), IV. 421

Sixteen Years Ago (Wolff, J., 1871), v. 630

Sixteen Years Since = (1) Eleventh Hour; (2) Leontine; (2) Horrors of War

Sixth Commandment (Buchanan, R., 1890), v. 285

6000 a Year = German Silver

Sixth Victim = Necromancer

Six to Four on the Colonel (Dance, G., 1832), IV. 579

Six to One against you = Transformation

Sixtus V (Boucicault, D. and Bridgeman, J. V., 1851), v. 267

— (Phillips, F. L., 1860), v. 810

Sixty-Six (1876), v. 751

Sixty-third Letter (Oulton, W. C., 1802), IV. 366

Sixty Years Ago (1852), v. 751

Sixty Years Since = Waverley

Six Voyages of Sinbad the Eastern Mariner (1820), IV. 535

Six Years After (Cheltnam, C. S., 1866), v. 309

Six Years More = Hearts at Fault

Skeleton (Stephens, Y. and Graves, C., 1887), v. 581

Skeleton Crew (Hazlewood, C. H., 1867) = Wilfred Ned, v. 768, 850

Skeleton Hand (Barnett, C. Z., 1833), IV. 259, 570

Skeleton in the Cupboard (1885), v. 751

— = Zenobia

Skeleton Lover (1830), IV. 535

— = Love and Anatomy

Skeleton of the Wave (1852), v. 751

Skeleton Robber (1861), v. 751

Skeleton Steed (Ramsay, T. J., 1843), IV. 388

Skeleton Witness (Rede, W. L., 1835), IV. 390

Sketches from Life (Frome, S. B., 1809), IV. 318

— (Sicklemore, R., 1802), IV. 401

Sketches in 1840 = Devil in London

Sketches in India (1846), IV. 535

— (1854), v. 751

Sketches of Character = Proteus

Sketches of Northern Mythology (Sawyers, F., 1789), III. 304

Sketch from the Louvre (Major, H. A., 1860), v. 805, 846

— (1867), v. 751, 805

Sketch of a Fine Lady's Return from a Rout (Clive, C., 1763), III. 243

Sketch of the Times = Detection

Skilful Practitioner (1861), v. 751

— (1868), v. 751

Skimmer of the Sea (1830), IV. 535

— = Water Witch

Skip Jack Joe (Evans, F., 1874), v. 790

Skipper of the Two Sisters (1884), v, 751

Skipper's Secret (1878), v. 751

Skirt Dancer (Ridgwell, G., Mansell, E. and Mackay, R. F., 1898), v. 543

Skirts of the Camp = Hartford-Bridge

Skittles Limited (Thompson, R. H., 1895), v. 598

Skyward Guide (Bradshaw, Mrs A. and Melford, M., 1895), v. 273

Slander (Wyke, E. B., 1878), v. 633

— (1882), v. 751

Slanderer (Wallace, J., 1823), IV. 416

Slasher & Crasher (Morton, J. M., 1848), IV. 363

Slate Pencillings (Hay, F., 1876), v. 411

Slave (Morton, T., 1816) = Freedom and Slavery, IV. 364, 464, 601, 626

— = Gambia

Slave Bride (Young, H., 1861), v. 825

Soft Sex (Mathews, C. J., 1861), v. 480

Soft Soap (Jourdain, J., 1888), v. 442

Softy of Merrington (Stephens, W., 1878), v. 581

Soggarth Aroon (Coleman, J., 1897), v. 316

Soiree Dramatique = Lady Lovington

Sold (1873), v. 752

— (1879), v. 752

— (1898), v. 752

Sold again (Soutar, R., 1876), v. 575

Sold for a Song (Bailey, W., 1829), IV. 257

— = Carmen

Soldier and a Man = British Hero

Soldier and a Sailor (McLaren, A., 1805), IV. 351

Soldier and the Tinder Box (Hood, B., 1897), v. 425

Soldier for the Ladies = Beau's Duel

Soldier Girl (1822), IV. 536

Soldier of Fortune (Anderson, J. R., 1864), v. 241

— (Boucicault, D., 1845), IV. 270

— (Broughton, F. W., 1889), v. 281

— (Dwyer, P. W., 1805), IV. 308

— (1846), IV. 536

Soldier of Vietri = Bride of the Bleeding Heart

Soldiers at Home—Heroes abroad = Love and Honour

Soldier's Bride (1854), v. 752

— = (1) Austerlitz; (2) French War; (3) Savourneen Deelish

Soldier's Courtship (Poole, J., 1833), IV. 387

Soldier's Daughter (Cherry, A., 1804), IV. 279

— (Cobham, E. M., 1897), v. 315

— (1815), IV. 536

— = Virginia

Soldier's Dream (1826), IV. 536, 640

Soldier's Father = Bertha and Durimel

Soldiers' Festival (1790), III. 344

Soldier's Fortune (Pearce, G., 1878), v. 518

— (1748), II. 384

— = (1) Fan-Fan the Tulip; (2) Siege of Barcelona; (3) Souldiers Fortune

Soldier's Frolic (1811), IV. 536

Soldier's Gift (1848), IV. 640

Soldier's Gratitude = (1) Annette Carline; (2) England's King

Soldier's Grave = Last Kiss

Soldier's Honour (1826), IV. 536

— = (1) Death Doom; (2) Saved from Sin

Soldier's Legacy (Oxenford, J. and McFarren, G. A., 1863), v. 510

— (1864), v. 752

— = Marcelline

Soldier's Life = On Service

Soldier's Love = Imperial Guard

Soldier's March from the Cradle to the Grave = First Friendship

Soldier's Motto "Life for Life" = Red Ribbon

Soldier's Oath (Pitt, G. D., 1844), IV. 373

— = Coiner

Soldiers of the Queen (Goldberg, M., 1898), v. 383

Soldier's Opera (Ewing, P., 1791), III. 258

Soldier's Orphan (Bennett, G. J., 1844), IV. 265

Soldier's Peril = False Accusation

Soldier's Pledge of Love = Tobacco Box

Soldier's Progress (Courtney, J., 1849), IV. 284

Soldier's Return (Hook, T. E., 1805) = Garland, IV. 327, 466, 589

— (1809), IV. 536

— (1886), v. 752

— = Antonio

Soldier's Sister (1847), IV. 536

Soldier's Son (Newton, C. and Boyne, W., 1899), v. 503

Soldier's Stratagem (Dibdin, T. J., 1822), IV. 303

— (1719), II. 384

— (1830), IV. 536

Soldier's Stratagems (Lacy, M. R., 1828), IV. 340

Soldier's Trust = Millions of Money

Soldier's Vow (1837), IV. 536

Soldier's Welcome Home = Native Land

Soldier's Wife (Cooper, F. F., 1854), v. 752, 786, 847

— (Dalgleish, S. and Peacock, W., 1898), v. 332

— (Whitmore, H. E., 1899), v. 621

— (1853), v. 752

Soldier's Widow (Fitzball, E., 1833), IV. 314 [This was printed in the Cumberland series as The Deserted Mill]
— (McLaren, A., 1800), III. 284; IV. 350
Soldier, the Monk and the Assassin = Secret Marriage
Sold to Advantage (Wooler, J. P., 1853), V. 632
Sold Up (Goldberg, M., 1890), V. 383
Sole Survivor (Conquest, G. and Pettitt, H., 1876), V. 321
Sol Gandy (Bellingham, H. and Best, W., 1887), V. 257
Solicitor (Darnley, J. H., 1890), V. 337
Solid Silver (1880), V. 752
Solitaire (Planché, J. R., 1821), IV. 377, 604
Solitary of Lambeth (1849), IV. 536
Solitary of Mount Savage (1822), IV. 82, 536
Solitary of the Desert Mountains = Solitaire
Solitary of the Heath (1830), IV. 536
Solomon (Morell, T., 1749), II. 399
Solomon's Twins (Peile, F. K., 1897), V. 518
Solon (Bladen, M., 1705), II. 298
Solon Shingle (Owens, J. E., 1865), V. 752, 809, 847
Solway Mariner = Paul Jones
Solyman (1807), IV. 536
Some Bells that ring the Old Year out and a New One in (Hazlewood, C. H., 1862), V. 752, 796, 847
Somebody Else (Planché, J. R., 1844), IV. 382, 605
Somebody's in the House with Dinah (1847), IV. 536
Somebody's Sweetheart = Sunny Florida
Some Day (Phillips, Mrs N. and Tresahar, J., 1889), V. 523
Some Passages in the Diary of a Physician (1847), IV. 640
Some Passages in the Life of Love = Cupid in London
Something Forgotten (1874), V. 752
Something like a Nugget (1869), V. 752
Something like History = Charles II
Something New (Dibdin, T. J., 1792), III. 382; IV. 297, 580

Something of All Sorts (1871), V. 752
Something Singular = Is She his Wife?
Something to Do (Hoare, P., 1808), IV. 326
— (Morton, J. M., French)
Something to live for = Reuben Blight
Somewhat (Barnard, E., 1757), III. 235
Somnambula (Beazley, S., Jr., 1833), IV. 84, 264
— (Greenwood, T., 1841), IV. 321
— (Rede, W. L., 1844), IV. 391
— (1835), IV. 536
— (1854), V. 752
Somnambulist (Moncrieff, W. T., 1828), IV. 84, 359
— = Somnambula
Somnambulistic Knickerbockers = Rip Van Winkle
Somnambulists = Village Phantom
Somnambulo and Lively Little Alessio (Byron, H. J., 1878), V. 299
Sonambula (1859), V. 752
Son and Stranger (Chorley, H. F., 1851), V. 310
— (1896), V. 752
Songe d'Ossian (1824), IV. 536
Song of Fortunis (1876), V. 847
Song of Solomon (Bland, J., 1750), III. 238
Song of the River (Loader, M. and Ellis, F. R., 1898), V. 461
Songs of the Birds (Fitzball, E.), IV. 313
Sonia (Overbeck, E., 1895), V. 509
Son-in-Law (O'Keeffe, J., 1779), III. 42, 292, 393
Son of a Sailor = False Light
Son of a Sinner (Forshaw, F., 1896), V. 371
Son of Clanronald = Infant Heir
Son of Erin (Burges, G., 1823), IV. 575
Son of Neptune (1791), III. 344
Son of Night (1856), V. 752
— (1857), V. 752
— (1872), V. 752
Son of the Desert (Charlton, W. H., 1858), V. 783
— (Rede, W. L., 1843), IV. 390
Son of the Navy (1848), IV. 536
Son of the Night = Del Ombra
Son of the Sea (1866), V. 753

Spectre on the White Horse = Conlath of the Isles
Spectre Pilot (1829), IV. 537
Spectre's Compact = Red Marine
Spectresheim (Reece, R., 1875), v. 538
Spectres of the Past (Whitbread, J. W., 1893), v. 620
+ Speculation (Farrell, J.; Pav. 10/11/1828)
— (Freeman, 1830), IV. 537, 640
— (Reynolds, F., 1795), III. 132, 301
— (Sapte, W., Jr., 1886), v. 555
Speechless Wife (1794) = Colin and Susan, III. 344, 404
Speech of the Dumb Restored = Torrent of the Valley
Speed the Plough (Dibdin, C. I. M., 1802), IV. 290
— (Morton, T., 1800), III. 142-4, 289; IV. 184, 363
Speedy Settlement (1896), v. 753
Speidhair = Shamus-na-Lena
Speidhoir = Shamas-na-Glanna
Spell (1756), III. 404
Spell-bound (Faucit, H. S., 1871), v. 363
— (Mackay, R. F., 1892), v. 470
Spell-bound Garden (Parker, L. N. and Carson, S. M., 1896), v. 513
Spelling Bee (Reece, R., 1876), v. 538
Spell of the Cloud King = Bronze Horse
Spells of Love = Truth
Spendthrift (Albery, J., 1875), v. 155, 237
— (Blake, T. G., 1844), IV. 537, 640
— (Draper, M., 1731), II. 178-9, 319
— (Foote, S., 1762), III. 384
— (Jerrold, D. W., 1839, 1850), IV. 333; v. 436
— (Kenrick, W., 1778), III. 113, 279
— = Legacy
Spendthrift Husband = Frank Wildeye
Spendthrift's Folly and Fortune (1751), III. 404
Sphinx (Boult, W., 1872), v. 270
— (Brough, W. and Brough, R. B., 1849), IV. 271
— (Clarke, C., 1874), v. 311
Spider and the Fly (Addison, J., 1890), v. 236
— (Conquest, G. and Spry, H., 1862) = Number Nip, v. 320, 753, 785, 847

Spider and the Fly (1862), v. 753
Spider King = Tarantula
Spiders and Flies (Galer, E. J. N., 1868), v. 375
Spider's Web (Henry, B., 1876), v. 417
— (1881), v. 753
— = In the Spider's Web
Spider, the Fly and the Butterfly = Village Nightingale
Spightful Sister (Bailey, A., 1667), I. 388
Spindlepops (1854), v. 753
Spin for Life (Carriden, W., 1897), v. 304
Spinster (Gwynne, P. and Harrison, C., 1887), v. 398
— (1883), v. 753
Spinsters Beware! (1873), v. 753
Spirit Bride (1850), v. 753
Spirit Captain (Holt, C., 1864), v. 798
Spirit Child's Prayer (Travers, W., 1865) = Neglected Home, v. 724, 753, 821, 841, 847
Spirit Haunted (Townsend, W. T., 1845), IV. 414
Spirit Medium (1862), v. 753
Spirit of Air (1838), IV. 537
Spirit of Avarice = Devil of Marseilles
Spirit of Avenel = White Lady
Spirit of Beauty (1841), IV. 537
Spirit of Conscience = Old Shadow
Spirit of Contradiction (Rich, J., 1760), III. 301, 394
Spirit of Death (Suter, W. E., 1861) = Angel of Midnight, v. 588, 753, 819, 847
Spirit of Evil = Legend of the Headless Man
Spirit of Gold (1848), IV. 537
Spirit of Good and Evil = Doom of Morana
Spirit of Liberty (Hazlewood, C. H., 1859), v. 753, 796, 847
Spirit of Mercy (1863), v. 753
Spirit of Peace = Angel's Whisper
Spirit of Punch = Arcadian Brothers
Spirit of Revenge (Suter, W. E., 1860), v. 753, 819, 847
Spirit of the Air = Étoile
Spirit of the Bell (Kenney, J., 1835), IV. 338
Spirit of the Black Mantle = Wenlock of Wenlock

Spirit of the Boreen = Banshee

Spirit of the Chimes = Bell Ringer

Spirit of the Elbe = Blackenberg

Spirit of the Fountain (Courtney, J., 1843), IV. 537, 640

Spirit of the Grotto (1796), III. 344

Spirit of the Haunted Room (1855), v. 753

Spirit of the Hill (1828), IV. 537

Spirit of the Lake = All Hallows' Eve

Spirit of the Loom (1848), IV. 538

— = Mary of Manchester

Spirit of the Mist (Keppell, 1831), IV. 538, 640

Spirit of the Moon (Farley, C., 1824), IV. 538, 640

— (1830), IV. 538

Spirit of the Reclining Stone = Ombra

Spirit of the Rhine (Barnett, M., 1835), IV. 261

Spirit of the Star = Zoroaster

Spirit of the Valley (Markwell, H., 1853), v. 476

Spirit of the Vault = Palace of Geneva

Spirit of the Waters (Milner, H. M., 1829), IV. 357

— = Undine

Spirit of Water = Demon of the Drachenfels

Spirit Rappers (Pitt, G. D., 1853), v. 526

Spirit Rapping and Table Moving (1853), v. 753

Spirit Rappings and Table Moving (1853), v. 753

Spirits and Water (Reynoldson, T. H., 1845), IV. 393

Spirits in Bond = Bottle Imp

Spirits of Donan the Goblin Page = Water Queen

Spirits of Good and Evil (1857), v. 753

Spirits of the Departed (1863) = Wishing Glen, v. 753, 769, 847, 850

Spirits of the Night (Markwell, W. R., 1853), v. 477

Spirit's Song (Haines, J. T., 1843), IV. 323

Spirit Trapper (1853), v. 753

Spiritualist (Durez, H., 1891), v. 352

Spiritual Minor (1762), III. 344

Spiritual Mountebank Detected = Female Enthusiast

Spirit Warning (Brougham, J., 1863), v. 780

Spirit World (1888), v. 753

Spitalfields Weaver (Bayly, T. H., 1838), IV. 263

Spite and Malice (McLaren, A., 1811), IV. 351

Spitfire (Morton, J. M., 1837), IV. 362

Spitz-Spitze (Conquest, G. and Spry, H., 1875), v. 321

Spleen (Colman, G., 1776), III. 12, 117, 183, 246, 379

Splendid Investment (Bernard, W. B., 1857), v. 259

Splendid Mrs Wichels (1898), v. 753

Spoglioni (1832), IV. 538

Spoil'd Child (Bickerstaffe, I., 1790), III. 238

Spoiled Child (1836), IV. 538

Spoiled Children (Dibdin, T. J., 1819), IV. 302

Spoilt Spree (1892), v. 753

Sponge in the Country = No Dinner Yet

Sponge out of Town = No Dinner Yet

Spoons (Lowe, W., 1881), v. 464

Sport (Nicholson, G. A., 1876), v. 504

— (Turner, M. and Edwardes-Sprange, W., 1895), v. 605

— (1883), v. 753

Sport after Rain = Angler

Sporting Boots of the Inn = Lad of the Village

Sporting Intelligence Extraordinary (1861), v. 753

Sporting in the Dark (1855), v. 753

Sporting Life (Raleigh, C. and Hicks, Sir S., 1897), v. 534

— = St Leger

Sporting Youth from the Counting House to the Hulks = Grand National

Sport of Fate (1895), v. 753

Sport of Kings = Favourite

Sports and Pastimes of London 200 Years Ago = City Games

Sportsman (Lestocq, W., 1892), v. 457

Sportsman and the Shepherd (1816), IV. 538

— = Dinner of Madelon [Evidently a revised title of the above]

Sportsman Pearl = Derry Driscoll

Sport upon Sport = Mad Lovers

State Secrets (Wilks, T. E., 1836), IV. 420

Statesman (Dent, J., 1782), III. 254

Statesman Foil'd (Dossie, R., 1768) = Trial of Skill, III. 257, 383

Statesman's Opera = Patron

State Tower = Unknown Guest

State Trial (Irving, L. B., 1896), v. 432

Station House (Dance, G., 1833), IV. 288, 579

— (1854), v. 754

Station Master's Daughter = Last Express

Statue (Dibdin, C.), IV. 290

— = Evadne

Statue Blanche (1856), v. 847

Statue Bride (Amcotts, V., 1868), v. 240

— = Elves

Statue Feast (Craven, E., 1782), III. 117, 249, 366, 380

Statue in the Wood = Red Robber

Statue Lover (Jerrold, D. W., 1828), IV. 331

— (1854), v. 754

Statue of Clay (1892), v. 754

Statue Shop = Helen of Troy up-to-date

Statue Steed (1832), IV. 538

Statute (1777), III. 344

Statute Fair = Lady Henrietta

Statute of Albemarle (Whishaw, Mrs B., 1892), v. 620

Statutory Duel = Grand Duke

Stay at Home (Lewes, G. H., 1856), v. 459

Steamboating on the Mississippi = Down the River

Steed of the Silver Star and the Last Struggle of the Moors = Conquest of Granada

Steel Castle (1845), IV. 538

Steel Hand and his Nine Thieves (1857), v. 754

Steel Pavilion (Peake, R. B., 1836), IV. 370

Steeple Chase (Morton, J. M., 1865), v. 496

Steeple Jack (Pemberton, T. E., 1888), v. 519

Stella (Findon, B. W., 1889), v. 366

— (Shoberl, F., 1804), IV. 86, 401

— (Thompson, B., 1800), IV. 86, 412

— (1798), III. 344, 404

Stella (1852), v. 754

Stella and Leatherlungs (Colman, G., 1823), IV. 282

Stella de Rittersdorf (Barnett, C. Z., 1844), IV. 260

Stella Gordon (1893), v. 754

Stella, the Female Pirate (1859), v. 754

Step Brothers = Actor

Step by Step (1862), v. 754

— = Sybilla

Stephania (Field, M., 1892), v. 366

Stephen (Denny, J., 1851), v. 788

Stephen Arncliffe = Honour among Thieves

Stephen Digges (Oxenford, J., 1864), v. 510

Stepmother (Gillies, R. P., 1814), IV. 538, 585

— (Howard, F., 1800), III. 273; IV. 329

— (Jones, J., 1829), IV. 333

— (Lacy, M. R., 1828), IV. 84, 340

— (Sketchley, A., 1880), v. 571

— (Stapylton, Sir R., 1663), I. 38, 139–40, 264, 433

— (1882), v. 754

— = Forced from Home

Stepmothers (1877), v. 754

Stepmother's Vengeance = Belinda the Blind

Stepping Stones (Fox, G. D., 1887), v. 371

Step-Sister (Sapte, Walter, Jr., 1887), v. 556

Stern Resolve (Masterton, C., 1837), IV. 353

Steward (Beazley, S., Jr., 1819), IV. 263, 571

— (Spicer, H., 1844), IV. 405

Stick, the Pole and the Tartar = Mazourka

Still Alarm (Arthur, J. and Wheeler, A. C., 1888), v. 244

Still Waters run deep (Taylor, T., 1855), v. 100–101, 592

+ Stirring the Pudding (Planché, J. R.: Dicks (1868, in Pieces of Pleasantry))

Stirring Times (Celli, F. H. and Daly, B., 1897), v. 307

Stock Exchange (Dance, C., 1858), v. 335

Stock-Jobbers (Chetwood, W., 1720), II. 214, 306

Story of a Pocket-book = (1) Lost and Found; (2) Lost Fortune

Story of a Sin (Thorpe, C., 1895), v. 599

Story of Aymere = Nana Sahib

Story of Babylon (1898), v. 754

Story of Chicken Hazard = Fowl Play

Story of Country Lanes and London Streets = Summer and Winter of Life

Story of Four Seasons = Rich and Poor

Story of London (À Beckett, G. A., 1844), IV. 250

Story of Love and Trial = Kate Kearney

Story of Orestes (Warr, 1886), v. 614

Story of Procida (1867), v. 754

Story of the Boat Race = Go to Putney

Story of the Commune = Love's Sacrifice

Story of the '45 (Phillips, W., 1860), v. 523

Story of the Four Seasons = Rich and Poor

Story of the Heart (1860), v. 754

Story of the Mayflower = Princess Radiant

Story of the Skull = Howlet's Haunt

Story of the Solway = St Mary's Eve

Story of Troy (Warr, 1886), v. 614

Story of Venice = Bravo

Story of Waterloo (Doyle, Sir A. C., 1894), v. 350

Story-Telling (Planché, J. R., 1846), IV. 382

Stout Gentleman (Bayly, T. H. adap. Peake, R. B., 1825), IV. 538, 640

Stowaway (Craven, T., 1884), v. 329

Stradella (Bunn, A., 1846), IV. 276, 575

Strafford (Browning, R., 1837), IV. 178, 272

— (Sterling, J., 1843), IV. 612

Straight and Narrow Paths of Life = Crooked Ways

Straight from the Heart (Vane, S. and Shirley, A., 1896), v. 606

Straight Tip (1873), v. 754

— = Keen Blades

Strand-ed Actor! (Dibdin, T. J., 1833), IV. 538, 640

Strange Adventures of a French Pianist (Darâle, F., 1891), v. 336

Strange Adventures of Miss Brown (Buchanan, R. and Jay, H., 1895), v. 285

Strange Arrivals in 1851 = First Floor to Let

— = Registered Lodging House

Strange but True (1866), v. 754

Strange Case of a Hyde and Seekyll (1886), v. 754

Strange Conclusions (1848), IV. 539

Strange Gentleman (Dickens, C., 1836), IV. 146, 305

Strange Guest (Lange, F., 1892), v. 448

Strange History in Nine Chapters (Lewes, G. H. and Mathews, C. J., 1852), v. 458

Strange Host (Law, A., 1882) = Happy New Year, v. 450, 687, 802

Strange Intruder (Archer, T., 1844), IV. 255

— (1844), IV. 539

Strange Legacy (Wilks, T. E., 1847), IV. 421

— (1888), v. 755

Stranger (Papendick, G., 1798), III. 64, 296

— (Schink, A., 1798), III. 16, 64, 304

— (Thompson, B., 1798), III. 220, 311, 373, 397; IV. 140, 412

— (1812), IV. 140, 539

Strange Relation (Compton, E., 1876), v. 319

— (Montague, L. A. D.), v. 491

Stranger in a Strange Land (1899), v. 755

Stranger in Black = Esperanza

Stranger in New York (Hoyt, C. H., 1897), v. 429

Strangers at Home (Cobb, J., 1785), III. 205, 244

Stranger—stranger than ever (Reece, R., 1868), v. 537

Strangers Yet (Allen, O., 1872), v. 239

Stranger to Himself (Holcroft, G., 1889), v. 424

Stranglers of Paris (Shirley, A., 1887), v. 564

+ Stratagem (Dibdin, C. I. M.; R.A., 1797–8)

— (1761), III. 344, 404

— (1830), IV. 539

Stratagem = (1) Juan Fernandez; (2) Stratagemma

Stratagem for Stratagem = Hamlet and Zelina

Stratagemma (1759), III. 404

Stratagem of Harlequin (1732), II. 384

Stratagem on Stratagem = Witchcraft of Love

Stratagems (1816), IV. 539

Stratagems of Harlequin (1730), II. 384

Stratford Jubilee (Garrick, D., 1769), III. 264

Stratford Wake = Man like himself

Strathlogan (Overton, C. and Moss, H., 1892), V. 509

Strathmore (Marston, J. W., 1849), IV. 93, 353

Strawberries and Cream (De Banzie and Grant, J., 1890), V. 340

Strawberry Girl = Fashion and Famine

Strawberry Pickers (1796), III. 344

Straw Hat (1873), V. 755

Strayed Away (Travers, W., 1870), V. 603

Strayed from the Fold (Murdoch, J. M., 1878), V. 499

Streak o' Sunshine (Don, L., 1888), V. 347

Streaks of Gold (Randford, M., 1878), V. 534

Streanshall Abbey (Gibson, F., 1799), III. 264; IV. 319

Street Arab = Outcast Joe

Street Ballad Singer = Stolen

Street Juggler = Grimaldi

Streets (Gordon, G. L., 1884), V. 385

Street-singer, the Sailor, and the Noble = Little Ned

Streets of London (Boucicault, D., 1857), V. 85, 92–3, 268

— = Poor of Liverpool

Streets of New York = Streets of London

Streets to the Hulks (Conquest, G., 1869), V. 320

Stricken Oak (1863), V. 755

Stricken Down (Dillon, C., 1870), V. 345

Strike (Herbert, L., 1873), V. 418

— (Stanley, H. J., 1875), V. 579

— (1885), V. 755

Strike = Long Strike

Strike at Arlingford (Moore, G., 1893), V. 161, 187, 492

Strike at the Mill and the Mutineers = Lashed to the Helm

Strike of the Cantons = William Tell

Striking Beauty (1836), IV. 539

Striking Feature = Man in the Moon

Striking Similarity (Hay, F., 1870), V. 411

Striking the Hour (Pitt, W. H., 1867), V. 527

Striking Widow (1858), V. 755

String of Pearls (Clarke, C. A. and Silva, H. R., 1892), V. 312

— (Pitt, G. D., 1847), IV. 374

— (Young, Mrs H., 1862), V. 755, 825, 847

— (1861), V. 755

— = Sweeney Todd, the Barber of Fleet Street

Stripling (Baillie, J., 1836), IV. 162, 258

Stroke of Luck (Bagot, A. E. and Murray, J. K., 1899), V. 247

Stroke of the Pen = Fool's Fidelity

Strolers (Breval, J., 1723), II. 49, 134, 213, 299, 432

Strolers Pacquet open'd (1742), II. 4, 172, 211, 216, 384, 385

Stroller (Dick, C., 1887), V. 344

— (Logan, Mrs O., 1878), V. 462

Strollers (Glenny, G. W., 1888), V. 382

Strolling and Stratagem = Counter Attractions

Strolling Country Actors = Country Actors

Strolling Gentleman = Wild Oats

Strolling Players (1823), IV. 539

Strong as Death (Ford, D. M., 1899), V. 370

Strongbow (French, W. P., 1892), V. 373

Stronger than Hate = Zola

Stronger than Love (1894), V. 755

Strong Man of the West = Trapper of the Hills

Strozzi (1824), IV. 539

Struck in the Dark (Moore, R., 1875), V. 492

Struck Oil (1876), V. 755

Struck Oil at Last = Seth Green

Struggle for a Crown (1846), IV. 539

Struggle for Gold and the Orphan of the Frozen Sea (Stirling, E., 1854), v. 584, 755, 818, 847

Struggle for Liberty = (1) Sea King's Vow; (2) Spy of Paris; (3) War in Turkey

Struggle for Life (Buchanan, R. and Horner, F., 1890), v. 285

— (Drayton, E., 1884), v. 350

Struggle of Seventy Years = Phoebe Hersell

Struggles at Starting = Professionals Puzzled

Struggles of a Poor Engineer = Dora's Love

Struggles of the Poor (Hazlewood, C. H., 1857), v. 755, 796, 847

Struggling for Wealth (Gosnay, W. A., 1880), v. 386

Student (1823), IV. 539

Student of Blackfriars (1836), IV. 539

Student of Bonn = Blind Wife

Student of Gottingen = Death Fetch

Student of Jena (Cooper, W., 1842), IV. 539, 640

Students (Courtney, J., 1861), v. 755, 786, 847

— (Smith, G., 1837), IV. 539

— (Stewart, J., 1777), III. 309

— (1762), III. 344

— (1779), III. 344

Student's Dream (Blake, T. G., 1845), IV. 268

— = Pandemonium

Student's Frolic (Molloy, J. L., 1864), v. 807

Student's Grave (Seaman, W., 1853), v. 559

Students of Bonn (Rodwell, G. H., 1842), IV. 395

Students of Jena (Planché, J. R., 1833), IV. 379

Students of Salamanca (Jameson, R. F., 1813), IV. 330

Students Whim = Don Sancho

Study of Two Women (Wilton, Mrs, 1898), v. 629

Stuffed Dog (Knox, J. A. and Atwell, E., 1889), v. 446

Sturdy Beggars (1733), II. 385

Sub-Editor (Payne, E. and Harrison, C., 1896), v. 518

Subject's Joy for the King's Restoration (Sadler, A., 1660), I. 427

Sublime and Beautiful (Morton, T., 1828), IV. 364

Substance and the Shadow (Mullen, F. and Atkinson, T., 1894), v. 499

Substitute (Bell, M., 1893), v. 256

— (Payn, J., 1876), v. 518

Subterfuge (1857), v. 755

Suburban Spectre (1898), v. 755

Suburb-Justice = Town-Shifts

Success (Hyde, H. F., 1879), v. 431, 846

— (Knight, F. H., 1892), v. 445

— (Planché, J. R., 1825), IV. 12, 78, 135-6, 149, 378; v. 133

— = Stowaway

Successful Mission (1894), v. 755

Successful Pyrate (Johnson, C., 1712), II. 45, 142, 221-2, 339

Successful Straingers (Mountfort, W., 1689), I. 225, 421

Such a Good Man (Besant, W. and Rice, J., 1879), v. 260

Such a Guy Mannering (Strachan, W., Jr., 1868), v. 585

Such is Life (Rignold, H. H., 1893), v. 543

— (Young, H., 1864), v. 755, 847

— (1885), v. 755

Such is Love (Mond, A. M., 1894), v. 491

Such is the Law (Taylor, T. and Merritt, P., 1878), v. 594

Such Stuff as Dreams are made of (Fitzgerald, E., 1899), v. 368

Such Things Are (Inchbald, Mrs E., 1787), III. 55, 145-7, 148, 150, 275

Such Things Have Been (Ryder, W., 1789), III. 304

Such Things Were (Hoare, P., 1787), III. 269

— = Highland Robbers

+ Sudden Arrival (Hay, F., French)

Sudden Arrivals (Cobb, J., 1809) = Man of Business, IV. 281, 500, 577, 632

Sudden Attack (1863), v. 755

Sudden Shower (1895), v. 755

+ Sudden Squall (Lancaster-Wallis, E., French)

Sunny Side (Rae, C. M., 1885), v. 532

Sunny South (Darrell, G., 1884), v. 337

Sunny Vale Farm (Bridgeman, J. V., 1864), v. 275, 780

Sun Picture = Quadroon

Sunset (Jerome, J. K., 1888), v. 186, 436

Sunshine (Broughton, F. W., 1880), v. 281

Sunshine after Rain = (1) Cry To-day and Laugh To-morrow; (2) Mad Guardian

Sunshine and Shade (Rede, W. L., 1843) = Faith and Falsehood, IV. 539, 607, 640

Sunshine and Shadow (Thomson, A., 1867), v. 598, 820

— = Sunlight and Shadow

Sunshine in Season = Happy Hours

Sunshine through the Clouds (Lewes, G. H., 1854), v. 458

Sunshine through the Mist = My Wife

Super (Heathcote, A. M., 1894), v. 415

Superannuated Gallant (Reed, J., 1745), II. 351; III. 300

Superfluous Lady (Bell, Mrs H., 1891), v. 255

Super-Natural = Hurlothrumbo

Supernatural Warning = Death Fetch

Supper (Binyon, R. L., 1877), v. 261

Supper Dances (Young, Sir W. L., 1891), v. 637

Supper for Three = Tourists

Supper for Two (Gifford, J. W., 1883), v. 184, 378

Supper Gratis (Reeve, W., 1871), v. 540

Supper Party (1861), v. 755

Supper's Over (Barnett, M., 1830), IV. 261

Supper the Night before the Coronation (1831), IV. 539

Supper, the Sleeper and the Merry Swiss Boy = La! Somnambula

Supreme Moment (Clifford, Mrs W. K., 1899), v. 755, 784, 847

Sure Aim (1807), IV. 539

Sure Bait for a Good Husband = Female Angler

Sure to Win (Goldsmith, W. H., 1896), v. 383

— (1876), v. 755

Surgeon of Paris (Jones, J., 1849), IV. 334

Surooj Seeing (1820), IV. 539

Surprisal (Howard, Sir R., 1662), I. 55, 214, 414

Surprise (Calvert, W., 1897), v. 300

— (Kirkman, F., 1662), I. 418

— (1899), v. 755

Surprises (Burnette, C., 1890), v. 293

Surrender of Calais (Colman, G., the Younger, 1791), III. 247

— (1801), IV. 539

Surrender of Conde (1793), III. 344

Surrender of Trinidad (1797), III. 344

Surrender of Valenciennes (1793), III. 344

Surrey Toll-Gate = Stoney Batter

Surrounded = War—the Fugitives

Susan Hapley (Denvil, Mrs, 1841), IV. 579

Susan Hopley (Pitt, G. D., 1841), IV. 373

Susanna (Tollet, E., 1755), III. 312

Susan's Lovers (1878), v. 755

Susan Smith (Harris, A. G., 1860), v. 405

Susian Captive = Panthea

Suspicion (1843), IV. 539

— (1875), v. 755

Suspicious Brother (1789) = Try Again, III. 344, 405

Suspicious Husband (Hoadly, B., 1747), II. 137, 206, 207–8, 337, 439

Suspicious Husband Criticized (Macklin, C., 1747), II. 207, 342

Suzanne (Leigh, H. S., 1884), v. 454, 803

— (Lucas, W. J., 1838), IV. 539, 640

Suzette (1832), IV. 539

Swallows' Nest (Young, Mrs H., 1863) = Ben Child, v. 648, 755, 827, 847

Swallows of Paris = Game of Life

Swamp Hall (Jerrold, D. W., 1833), IV. 332

Swan and Edgar (Edwards, H. S. and Kenney, C., 1859), v. 755, 789, 801, 847

Swansea Castle in 1327 = Regicide

Swarry Dansong (Barrington, R., 1890), v. 251

Swedish Ferryman (Poole, J., 1843), IV. 539, 640

Swedish Nightingale = Jenny Lind at Last

Taken Up and Taken In = Disagreeable Surprise

Take that Girl Away (Buckingham, L. S., 1855), v. 286

Take Warning! (1805), IV. 540

Take your Choice (1839), IV. 540

Taking by Storm (Lewes, G. H., 1852), v. 458, 804

Taking it easy (1882), v. 756

Taking of the Bastille (1844), IV. 540

Taking of the Pledge (1844), IV. 540

Taking Possession (1845), IV. 540

Takings and Mistakings = Married and Single

Taking the Bull by the Horns (Newte, H. C. W., 1889), v. 503

Taking the Census (Blanchard, E. L., 1851), v. 262

Taking the Veil (Hazlewood, C. H., 1870), v. 414

Taking the Waters (1886), v. 756

Talbot's Trust (Tharp, T. A., 1875), v. 595

Tale in a Tub (Reiss, F. R., 1893), v. 541

Tale of a Coat (Brough, W. and Franck, 1858), v. 756, 780, 793, 847

Tale of a Comet (Horne, F. L., 1873), v. 426

Tale of a Copper (1871), v. 756

Tale of Africa = Gorilla Hunt in the Forest of Gabon

Tale of a Palace = Ladies at Court

Tale of a Reaper's Fireside = Our Own Hearth at Home

Tale of a Tar = Gale Breezeley

Tale of a Telegram (1888), v. 756

Tale of a Telephone (Clarke, H. S., 1879), v. 312

Tale of a Tub (Gore, Mrs C. G. F., 1837), IV. 319

— (Vaun, R., Atwood, A. and Booth, W., 1896), v. 607

— = Marforio

Tale of a Tubb (Girnot, H. and Meritt, P., 1876), v. 382

Tale of a Wig = Professor Wiggles

Tale of Blood = (1) Idiot Witness; (2) Solitary of the Heath

Tale of Dartmoor (1891), v. 756

Tale of Eighteen Hundred and Five = Days we live in

Tale of India = Fugitives

Tale of Malkin Tower = Witch-Wife

Tale of Manchester Life = Mary Barton

Tale of Mantua = Wife

Tale of Mystery (Holcroft, T., 1802), IV. 81, 326

— (1812), IV. 540

— = Cœlina

Tale of New Zealand = Emigrant Family

Tale of Old China (Burnand, F. C. and Molloy, J. L., 1875), v. 290

Tale of Other Days = Second Sight

Tale of Other Times (Dibdin, T. J., 1822) = Minstrel Maid, IV. 303, 581

Tale of Pisa = Italian Boys

Tale of Seville = Loretta

Tale of Sorrows = Mary Graham

Tale of Tell (Clarance, L., 1883), v. 310

Tale of Terror (Siddons, H., 1803), IV. 401

Tale of the Abruzzi = Francesca Doria

Tale of the Castle (1793) = Who is she like? III. 345, 406

Tale of the Commune = No. 50

Tale of the Eleventh Century = Old Man of the Mountain

Tale of the French Police = Dutch Anna

Tale of the Goodwin Sands = Sole Survivor

Tale of the Highlands = Second Sight

Tale of the Irish Rebellion = Raymond the Rebel

Tale of the Kitchen (1862), v. 756

Tale of the Neutral Ground = Emigrant's Daughter

Tale of the O'Hara Family (1827), IV. 540

Tale of the Old and New Year = Right and Wrong

Tale of the Past = Mark Drummond

Tale of the Sea = Pilot

Tale of the Seaside = Broadsea Cliffs

Tale of the Spanish War (Lee, N., 1854), v. 452

Tale of the Thames (Conquest, G. and Shirley, A., 1895), v. 323

— = Pilot

Tale of the Thames Valley = Dark Secret

Tale of the Times = Counterfeit

Tarantula (Scott, M. A., 1897), V. 558
— (Talfourd, F. and Smith, A., 1850), V. 590
— (1831), IV. 540
Tarare (James, C., 1787), III. 119, 276, 388
Tar Ashore and Afloat = Life on the Ocean Wave
Tarempon and Serinda (1810), IV. 540
Tares (Beringer, Mrs O., 1888), V. 259
Tar for All Weathers = Blue Anchor
Tarnation Strange (Moncrieff, W. T., 1838), IV. 131, 361
Tar of Trinidad and the Spirit of the Ocean = Red Buoy
Tarquin and Lucretia = Judgment of Brutus
Tarquin's Overthrow = Tuscan Treaty
Tarrare, the Tartar Chief (Arnold, S. J., 1825), IV. 540, 640
'Tars at Anchor = Jolly Crew
Tars at Torbay (1799), III. 345
Tars in Port (1801), IV. 540
Tars of England (1852), V. 756
Tars of Old England = Reprisal
Tars on Shore (1818), IV. 540
Tars regaling = Rendezvous
Tar's Revenge = Jeffery the Seaman
Tartar Hordes = Adalna
Tartars Tartar'd = Baghran-Ho
Tartærs Tarter'd = One Foot by Land and One Foot by Sea
Tartar's Vengeance = Black Tower
Tartar Witch and the Pedlar Boy (1832), IV. 540
Tartar Woman (1829), IV. 540
Tar that was "pitched" into = Sinbad the Sailor
Tartuffe (Medbourne, M., 1670), I. 188, 258–9, 420
— (Oxenford, J., 1851), V. 509
Tarugo's Wiles (St Serfe, Sir T., 1667), I. 192, 220, 250, 271, 346, 427
Tasso (Neil, R., 1879), V. 502
Taste (Foote, S., 1752, 1761) = Virtuoso, III. 172, 259, 260, 383
Taste a la Mode = (1) Fall of Phæton; (2) Tittle Tattle
Taste and Feeling (1790), III. 345
Taste in the Upper Story = High Life
Taste of the Age = Fool's Opera
Tasting Order (1854), V. 756

Tatlers (Hoadley, B., 1797), III. 269
Tatterley (Shirley, A. and Gallon, T., 1898), V. 565
Taunton Vale (Parker, L. N., 1890), V. 513
Tavern Bilkers (Weaver, J., 1702), II. 252, 385, 425, 446
— = Cheats
Tawno's Bride (Bowles, E. W. and Phillips, G. R., 1892), V. 271
Taxes (Bacon, P., 1757), III. 235
Taylor made a Man = Humours of Greenock Fair
Taylor of Brussels (Neil, R., 1874), V. 501
— = Duke for a Day
Taylors, to Arms! = Volunteers
Tea (Noel, M., 1887), V. 505 [The entry IV. 366 is in error, and should be deleted]
Tea and Turn Out (1823), IV. 541
Teacher Taught (Stirling, E., 1850), V. 584
Teaching made Easy (1823), IV. 541
Teague (1821), IV. 541
Teague's Ramble to London (1770), III. 345
Teaman's Car = Brown Fanny
Tea-Room (1811), IV. 541
Tears (Scott, C. W. and Stephenson, B. C., 1874), V. 557
Tears and Smiles (Eyre, E. J., 1809) = Vintagers, IV. 541, 640
Tears and Triumphs of Parnassus (Lloyd, R., 1760), III. 282
Tears, idle Tears (Scott, C. W., 1872), V. 557
Tears of Britain (Eyre, E. J.), IV. 310
Tears of Virtue = Such Things Were
Teasing made Easy (Jameson, R. F., 1817), IV. 331
Tea's the Twaddle = Twisting and Twining
Tea-totallers versus Witcelers (1840), IV. 541
Tecalco (Spicer, M. H., 1889), V. 576
Teddy O'Connor (1876), V. 756
Teddy Roe (Stirling, E., 1841), IV. 407
Teddy's Wives (Hume, F., 1896), V. 430
Teddy the Rollicker = Foster Sisters of Wicklow
Teddy the Tiler (Rodwell, G. H., 1830), IV. 395

Tempter (Jones, H. A., 1893), v. 165–6, 169, 172, 440

— (Lee, N., Jr., 1859), v. 756, 802, 847

Tempter and the Betrayer = Belinda Seagrave

Tempter and the Disowned (1860), v. 756

Tempter and the Tempted = Annie Tyrell

Tempting Bait (Austin, W. J., 1875), v. 246

Tenant for Life (Phelps, W., 1858), v. 756, 810, 847

Tenant of the Tomb (1830), IV. 541

— = (1) Hour of Retribution; (2) Raymond de Percy; (3) Vampire Bride

Tenants (James, H., 1894), v. 433

Tenants in Common (1885), v. 756

Ten Daughters and No Husband (1871), v. 756

Tender Chord (Maltby, A., 1899), v. 473

— (Mortimer, J., 1873), v. 494

— (Somerset, C. A., 1853), v. 574

Tender Husband (Steele, Sir R., 1705), II. 129, 130, 131, 132, 134, 135, 136, 144, 157, 183, 192, 231, 356, 444

Tender Precautions (Serle, T. J., 1851), v. 561

Tender Sisters (Gilbert, 1805), IV. 319

Ten Minutes for Refreshments (Mansfield, R., 1882), v. 475

Ten Nights in a Bar-room (Pratt, W., 1867), v. 530

Tennis (Eastwood, L. B., 1893), v. 353

Ten of 'em (Matthison, A., 1874), v. 481, 806

+ Ten Pounds (Emson, F. E., 8°, 1873)

Tenterhooks (Paull, H. M., 1889), v. 516

10.30 Down Express (Stanley, H., 1899), v. 579

10th of October = Threepence a Pot

£10,000 a Year (Peake, R. B., 1844), IV. 371

— (Somerset, C. A., 1841), IV. 612

Ten Thousand Pounds for a Pregnancy = Wanton Countess

Ten Thousand Top-sail Sheet Blocks (Bosworth, J., 1838), IV. 573

Ten Thousand Years (1841), IV. 541

Ten to One = Nettlewig Hall

+ Ten Tortured Tutors (Heighway, W., French)

Ten Years' Blunder (1824), IV. 541

— = Botheration

+ Ten Years Hence (Seymour, M., French)

Ten Years of a Woman's Life (1834), IV. 541

Teraminta (Carey, H., 1732), II. 30, 31, 235–6, 302

Teresa (Bancroft, G. P., 1897), v. 248

Teresa Tomkins (Moncrieff, W. T., 1821), IV. 359

Termagant (Parker, L. N. and Carson, S. M., 1899), v. 514

Termagant Mistress = Prussian Dragoon

Termagant tam'd = Gingerbread Nut

Termagant Wife (1793), III. 345

Term Day (Houston, T., 1803), IV. 329

Terpsichore (McCarthy, J. H., 1894), v. 467

— (1855), v. 756

Terpsichore's Return (Degville, 1805), IV. 579

Terrible Fright (Law, A., 1884), v. 450

Terrible Hymen (À Beckett, G. A., 1866), v. 233

Terrible Peak (Dibdin, C. I. M., 1817), IV. 294

Terrible Revenge = Cruel Father

Terrible Secret (Coyne, J. S., 1861), v. 328

— (Waldron, W. R., 1889), v. 611

Terrible Tinker (Williams, T. J., 1869), v. 626

Terrible Trilby (Pleon, H., 1895), v. 528

Terrible Twins = Oliver Grumble

Terrible Unknown (1836), IV. 541

Terrific Brothers = Zambo and Cadjoc

Terrific Horn = Mountain Robbers

Terrific Register (1824), IV. 541

Territor of St Faust = Desrues the Deceiver

Terror of France = Gabrielle the Girondist

Terror of London (James, W. and Whyte, H., 1879), v. 434

— = Spring-heeled Jack

Terror of Normandy = Robert the Devil

Terror of Paris (Hill-Mitchelson, E. and Longden, C. H., 1894), v. 422

They've bit the old one (Cross, J. C., 1798), III. 345, 380, 405

They were Friends (1889), v. 757

They were married (Crauford, J. R. and Hawley, F., 1892), v. 328

They would if they could (1803), IV. 542

Thief Maker (Towers, E., 1878), v. 601

Thief's Shoe = Ankle Jack

Thief-taker of Paris = Vidcoq

Thief, the Artist, the Doctor and the Banker = Realities of Life

Thierna-na-Oge (Planché, J. R., 1829), IV. 378

Thieves' House (Atkyns, S., 1844), IV. 19, 257

Thieves of Dijon = Beggar and the Soldier

Thieves of Paris (Stirling, E., 1853), v. 584

— = Bohemians

Thieves! Thieves! (1857), v. 757

Thimble Rig (Buckstone, J. B., 1844), IV. 275

Thimble's Flight from his Shopboard (1789), III. 345

Things that happen every Hour = How Time flies

Third Class and First Class (Seaman, W., 1859), v. 757, 815, 848

Third Day = Hussars of Hesse

Third Time (Dickinson, C. H., 1896), v. 344

Third Time the Best = Perseverance

Thirst of Gold (Webster, B. N., 1853), v. 618

1395 (1855), v. 848

Thirteenth Chime (1859), v. 757

1313 (Desprez, F., 1879), v. 343

Thirteen to the Dozen (Kenney, J., 1826), IV. 337

Thirteen Years' Labour Lost (Bennett, J. M., 1821), IV. 265 [The correct title is as here, not Thirteen Years of Labour Lost]

— (1855), v. 757

Thirty Nine Thieves (1863), v. 757

— (1877), v. 757

— = Ali Baba

30 Strand = P.L.

Thirty Thousand (Dibdin, C. I. M., 1808), IV. 292

— (Dibdin, T. J., 1804), IV. 52, 298

Thirty Thousand Pounds (Harleigh, L. W., 1875), v. 404

Thirty Three Next Birthday (Morton, J. M., 1858), v. 496

Thirty Years (1827), IV. 542

Thirty Years of a Gambler's Life (1827), IV. 542

— (1831), IV. 542

— = Hut of the Red Mountains

Thirty Years of a Rattler's Life = Elbow Shakers

Thirty Years of a Woman's Life = Isabelle

This and the other Hand (1863), v. 757

Thisbe and Pyramus (1889), v. 757

This Horse will be sold to pay the Expenses, if not claimed within Fourteen Days (1854), v. 757

This House to be Sold (Coyne, J. S., 1847) = Old House at Home, IV. 285

This House to let (Oxenford, E., 1884) = In Ladbroke Square, v. 509, 696, 809, 836

— (Towers, E., 1869), v. 601

This is the House that Jack built (Akhurst, W. M., 1871), v. 236

This Little Back Parlour (Mowbray, T., 1857), v. 498

This Plot of Ground to let, a Capital Site for a Theatre (1874), v. 757

This Side of the Water = Champion's Belt

This Side Up (Rae, L., 1874), v. 757, 811, 848

Thistle and the Rampant Lion (1872), v. 757

Thistle and the Rose = Caledonia

This Woman and That (Le Clercq, P., 1890), v. 452

This World of Ours (Hicks, Sir S., 1891), v. 420

Thomas à Becket (Darley, G., 1840), IV. 289

— (Jerrold, D. W., 1829), IV. 180, 332

Thomas and Sally (Bickerstaffe, I., 1760), III. 197–8, 237

Thomas and Susan (1787), III. 345

Thomaso (Killigrew, T., 1663), I. 416

Thomas the Rhymer (Thomas, E. L., 1894), v. 596

Thompkins in North-Street (Rennell, C. R. 1865), v. 813

Thompson and Co. (1831), IV. 542

Thompson's Visit (Douglass, J. T., 1872), V. 348

Thomyris, Queen of Scythia (Motteux, P. A., 1707), II. 58, 228–9, 399

Thorgrim (Bennett, J., 1890), V. 258

Thorneycroft Cousins (Thorneycroft, Lieut-Col., 1888), V. 599

Thorney, Laben and Dobin (Carey, G. S., 1770), III. 242

Thorough Base (Pemberton, T. E., 1884), V. 519

Thorough-bred (Lumley, R. R., 1895), V. 465

Those Dear Blacks! (Brough, W., 1852), V. 278

Those Horrid Garotters (1873), V. 757

Those Landladies (Cassilis, I. L.), V. 306

Those Mysterious Shots (Deane, C., 1894), V. 340

Those...put asunder (Trevelyan, C., 1897), V. 603

Those Terrible Twins (1899), V. 757

Those Volunteers (Ellis, B., 1875), V. 357

Tho' Strange 'Tis True (1732), II. 385

Though out of Sight, ne'er out of Mind = Constant Couple

£1000 Reward = (1) Condemned; (2) Legacy

Thou shalt not kill (Scudamore, F. A., 1899), V. 559

— = Two Christmas Eves

Thread of Silk (Matthison, A., 1881), V. 481

Threatening Eye (Knight, E. F. and Jourdain, J., 1885), V. 445

Threat for Threat = Shadow of Wrong

Three Adventures = Day well Spent

Three Ambassadors = Czar of Muscovy

Three and One (1839), IV. 542

Three and the Ace (Dibdin, C. I. M., 1810), IV. 292

Three and the Deuce (Hoare, P., 1795), III. 270

— (Lawler, D., 1810), IV. 542, 641

— (1862), V. 757

Three Bachelors (1862), V. 848

Three Banished Men of Milan = Gaspardo the Gondolier

Three Beauties of Dresden (1831), IV. 542

Three Beggars (Dunn, S., 1883), V. 352

Three Black Seals (Stirling, E., 1864), V. 584

Three Blind Eyes (Amherst, J. H.), IV. 254

Three Blind Mice (Ellis, B., 1883), V. 357

— (French, H. P., 1896), V. 373

Three Brothers = Black King

Three Brothers of Bagdad = Golden Lily

Three Brothers of Brevannes (Mead, T., 1863), V. 757, 806, 848

Three Brothers of Mystery (Suter, W. E., 1861), V. 757, 819, 848

Three Brothers of Normandy (1859), V. 757

Three Brothers of Paris (Rayner, A., 1858), V. 812

Three Brothers of the Old Chateau (Rayner, E., 1860), V. 757, 812, 848

Three Caskets (1827), IV. 542

— = Courtship

Three Charcoal Burners = (1) Fire Goblin; (2) Red Daemon of the Harz Forest

Three Cheers for Charity (1853), V. 757

Three Clerks (Oxberry, W. H.), IV. 602

Three Cloaks = Sparks in the Dark

Three Conjurers (1767), III. 345

Three Conscripts = Weaver of Lyons

Three Conspirators (Thompson, A., 1874), V. 597

Three Criminals = Two Men

Three Cripples and the Queen of Billingsgate (Amherst, J. H., 1822), IV. 253, 542, 568, 641

Three Crumpies (Dibdin, T. J., 1825), IV. 304

Three Crumps (1818), IV. 542

Three Cuckoos (Morton, J. M., 1850), V. 107, 495

Three Days at a Well-known Hotel = Incog.

Three Days at Hatchett's = (1) Exeter Mail; (2) Incog.

Three Days at Long's = Arrivals

Three Days' Trial = Magic Car

Three Deep (Lunn, J., 1826), IV. 348

Three Degrees of Crime = Progress of a Rake

Three Doctors (Gammon, R. T., 1896), V. 375

Three Doctors (Peacock, T. L.), IV. 369.

Three Dons (1828), IV. 542

Three Dukes of Dunstable = Fool's Preferment

Three Dummies (1859), V. 757

Three Entertainments (Thurmond, J., 1727), II. 360

Three Fairy Gifts (Adams, F. D., 1896), V. 235

Three Fast Men (1860), V. 757

Three Fathers and One Son (1827), IV. 542

Three-Fingered Jack (1860), V. 757

— = (1) Karfa the Slave; (2) Obi

Three Fishermen (1822), IV. 542

Three Fives (1812), IV. 542

Three Flats (1880), V. 757

Three Fra Diavolos (Stocqueler, J. H., 1844), IV. 542

Three Furies (Roberts, G., 1865), V. 544

Three Generations (1830), IV. 542

— = Rogues All!

Three Glass Distaffs = Discreet Princess

Three Golden Apples = Atalanta

Three Golden Lamps (1825), IV. 542

Three Graces (À Beckett, G. A., 1843), IV. 250

— (Collins, H. B., 1898), V. 318

— (1859), V. 848

— (1891), V. 757

— = Hobbs, Dodds and Stubbs

Three Great Worthies (Anderson, J. R., 1866), V. 241

Three Hats (Dove, O. and Maltby, A. 1883), V. 349

— (Woodrow, H. C., 1896), V. 631

Three Hours after Marriage (Gay, J., 1717), II. 13, 25, 29, 41–2, 144, 213–14, 331, 423

Three Hunchbacks (De Frece, M., 1872), V. 341

— (Fitzball, E., 1826), IV. 313, 584

Three Hundred a Year (1863), V. 758

Three Jacks (1883), V. 759

Three Johns (1819), IV. 542

Three Keys (Hiller, H. C., 1888), V. 421

Three Legs, King of Man (1853), V. 848

Three Lives (Hazlewood, C. H., 1860), V. 758, 796, 848

— = (1) Fair Lilias; (2) Ralph Gaston

Three Magic Wands (Amherst, J. H.), IV. 254

Three Merry Boyes (Kirkman, F., 1662), I. 417

Three Miles from Paris (Dibdin, C. I. M., 1818), IV. 294

Three Millions of Money (Lyster, F. and Mackay, J., 1876), V. 466

Three Moorish Princesses = Alhambra

Three Musket Dears, and a Little One In (Paulton, J. and Paulton, H., 1871), V. 517

Three Musketeers (Brown, W. H., 1898), V. 210, 282

— (Carl, F., 1899), V. 303

— (Daly, B. and East, J. M., 1898), V. 210, 334

— (Goldberg, M., 1892), V. 383

— (Hamilton, H., 1898), V. 210, 402

— (Rice, C., 1850), V. 210, 542, 813

— (Saintsbury, H. A., 1898), V. 210, 554

— (Whitney, H., 1899), V. 621

Three Musqueteers (1899), V. 758

Three Mutineers (1828), IV. 542

Three Naughty Boys = Brown, Jones and Robinson

Three O'Clock = Camelford

Three of a Kind (1894), V. 758

Three of Them (Dibdin, T. J., 1821), IV. 303

Three Old Women Weatherwise = Old Women Weatherwise

Three Paddies (Dibdin, T. J., 1817), IV. 300

Three Pairs of Lovers (1852), V. 758

Threepence a Pot (1830), IV. 542

Threepenny Bit (Morton, J. M. and Young, A. W., 1870), V. 496

Threepenny Bits (Zangwill, I., 1895), V. 637

Three Per Cents (Reynolds, F., 1803), IV. 391

Three Perils (Marchant, F., 1870), V. 476

Three Perils of Man (Blanchard, E. L., 1852), V. 262

Three Phases of a Life = Marlborough

Three Princes (Kingdom, J. M., 1850), V. 444

Three Red Men (Archer, T., 1848), IV. 255

— (1848), IV. 542

Three Secrets (Lemon, M., 1840), IV. 344

Three Secrets (1849), IV. 345, 595

Three Shots from a Carbine (Suter, W. E., 1865), V. 758, 819

Three Singles (1862), V. 758

Three Smugglers of Kent (Barnett, C. Z., 1843), IV. 260

Three Spectres (1831), IV. 542

Three Spectres of the Castle of St Valori = Man and the Marquis

Three Strangers (Lee, H., 1825), IV. 342

Three Suitors (1805), IV. 542

Three Sultanas (1826), IV. 542

Three Talismans (Dibdin, T. J., 1818), IV. 301

Three Temptations = (1) Better Self; (2) Demon of Darkness

Three Tenants (À Beckett, G. A. and Reed, G., 1874), V. 234

Three Thieves and the Dreamer = Seven Clerks

Three Thieves of Lambetti (1854), V. 758

Three Times Three (Dibdin, T. J., 1816), IV. 300

Three to One (1831), IV. 542

— (1850), V. 848

— (1853), V. 758

— (1893), V. 758

— = (1) I'm Puzzled; (2) What would the Man be at?

Three Transformed Princes = Enchanted Wood

Three Travellers of the Tyrol = Accusing Spirit

Three Trials = (1) Bianca; (2) Woman's Worth

Three Turkish Razor Grinders (1854), V. 758

Three Vampires (1823), IV. 542

Three Warnings (Rayner, A., 1872), V. 535

— (Warner, A., 1873), V. 614

Three Wayfarers (Hardy, T., 1893), V. 404

Three Ways of Living = Lesson of Life

Three Weavers (Pitt, G. D., 1851), V. 526

Three Weeks After Marriage (Murphy, A., 1776), III. 15, 181–2, 290

— (1812), IV. 542

Three Weeks at a Well-known Hotel = Incog.

Three Wishes (McLaren, A., 1823), IV. 352

— (1819), IV. 542

— = (1) Court of Oberon; (2) Don't you wish you may get it?

Three Wives of Madrid (Peake, R. B., 1844), IV. 33, 371

Three Women (1866), V. 758

Three Yards of Broadcloth (1826), IV. 542

Three Years in a Man Trap (Morton, C. H., 1879), V. 494

— (Stephens, W., 1874), V. 581

Three Years' System (Maynard, W., 1887), V. 483

Thrice Married (Paul, H. M., 1854), V. 515

— = Escaped

Thrillby (Muskerry, W., 1896), V. 501

Throne and the Tomb = Ambition

Throne, the Tomb and the Cottage = Rudolpho the Hungarian

Through a Glass, darkly (Seymour, E. M., 1896), V. 561

Through Fire and Snow (Goldberg, M., 1886), V. 383

Through Fire and Water (Gordon, W., 1865), V. 385

Through Life = Deceived

Through my Heart First (Campbell, J. M., 1884), V. 301

Through Shot and Shell (1896), V. 758

Through the Fire (Hastings, G., 1879), V. 409

— (Lestocq, W. and Stephens, Y. 1888), V. 457

Through the Furnace (Howell-Poole, W., 1885), V. 429

Through the Looking Glass (Stephens, H. P., 1882), V. 580

Through the World (Wray, C., 1874), V. 633

Thrown on the World = Cruel Destiny

Thrown Together (Greet, D. V.), V. 393

Throw of the Dice (Kennedy, H. A., 1890), V. 443

Throw Physic to the Dogs (Lee, H. 1798), III. 280, 390

Throwster's Opera (1731), II. 385

Thugs of Paris (Ellis, B., 1887), V. 357

Thumbscrew (Byron, H. J., 1874), V. 298

Times (1831), IV. 543

Time's a Tell-Tale (Siddons, H., 1807) = Mark the End On't, IV. 142, 401, 500, 611, 632

Times of Oliver Cromwell = Esdale Hall

Time's Revenge (Edwardes-Sprange, W., 1890), V. 354

— (Henry, S. C., 1898), V. 418

— (1875), V. 758

Time's Story = Heir of Ashmore

Time's Triumph (Byron, H. J., 1872), V. 298

— (1889), V. 758

Times we live in = Gin and Water

Time Tells Tales = Devil's Gap

Time the Avenger (Craven, T., 1892), V. 329

— (1877), V. 758

Time tries all (Courtney, J., 1848), IV. 284

Time Turned Occulist = Albion Restored

Time will tell (Gardner, H., 1882), V. 376

— = Father's Sin

Time Works Wonders (Jerrold, D. W., 1845), IV. 185-6, 333

Timoleon (Jameson, R. W., 1852), V. 799

— (Martyn, B., 1730), II. 31, 63, 68, 81, 233, 343

— (Southby, 1697), I. 171, 432

Timon in Love (Kelly, J., 1733), II. 145, 249, 340, 440

Timon of Athens (Cumberland, R., 1771), III. 57, 78, 251

— (Hull, T., 1786), III. 57, 86, 274

— (Lambe, G., 1816), IV. 341

— (Love, J., 1768), III. 57, 283

— (Shadwell, T., 1678), I. 85, 173, 337, 431

Timothy to the Rescue (Byron, H. J., 1864), V. 296

Timour Khan (1826), IV. 543

Timour the Cream of all the Tartars (À Beckett, G. A., 1845), IV. 250, 567

Timour the Tartar (Chamberlaine, E., 1869), V. 307

— (Lewis, M. G., 1811), IV. 346

— (Oxenford, J. and Brooks, C. W. S., 1860), V. 510

— (1829), IV. 543

Timson's Little Holiday (+ Nicholls, H., 1884: *French*), V. 758

Tin Box (Fenn, G. M., 1892), V. 365

Tinder Box (1823), IV. 543

Tinker (1791), III. 345

Tinker and his Son = Mountain Hut

Tinker's Holiday (1886), V. 758

Tinker's Son = Mountain Hut

Tinsel Queen (Morton, W. E., 1883), V. 497

Tinted Venus (Bessle, E., 1889), V. 260

Tipperary Legacy (Coyne, J. S., 1847), V. 275

Tippitywitchet (1845), IV. 543

Tipplers (1730), II. 452

Tippoo Sahib (Milner, H. M., 1823), IV. 599

— (1791), III. 345

— (1792), III. 345

Tipster (Fitzhamon, L., 1898), V. 369

— = Round the Links

Tipsy Gipsy and the Pipsy Wipsy = Merry Zingara

'Tis All a Farce (Allingham, J. T., 1800), III. 232; IV. 251

'Tis all a Mistake = See if you like it

'Tis an Ill Wind that Blows nobody Good (Markwell, W. R.), V. 477

— (1788), III. 345

'Tis a strange World (Holcroft, T., 1795) = Deserted Daughter, III. 345, 387, 405

'Tis a Wise Child knowns his own Father (Waldron, F. G., 1795), III. 314

'Tis a Wise Child that knows its own Father = Match-making

'Tis better than it was (Digby, G., 1662-5), I. 192, 403

'Tis She (Wilks, T. E., 1838), IV. 420

'Tis so reported = Law for Ladies

'Tis Well if it Take = Amorous Old-woman

'Tis Well if it Takes (Taverner, W., 1719), II. 133, 358

'Tis Well it's no Worse (Bickerstaffe, I., 1770), III. 123, 178, 237

— = Haunted Chamber

'Tis well they are married (1804), IV. 543

Tita in Tibet (Desprez, F., 1879), V. 343

Tit Bit for a nice Palate = Top of the Tree

Tit-Bits (Gordon, G. L., 1883), v. 385

Tit for Tat (Arnold, S. J., 1828), IV. 543, 641

— (Charke, Mrs C., 1743), II. 138, 306

— (Colman, G., 1786), III. 177, 247

— (Talfourd, F. and Wigan, A. S., 1855), v. 590

— (Woodward, H., 1748), II. 446; III. 317

— (1766), III. 345

— (1777), III. 345

— (1858), v. 758

— (1862), v. 758

— =(1) Bachelors' Wives; (2) Night's Frolic

Tithe Sheaf (1828), IV. 543

Tithonus and Aurora (1748), II. 385

Title (Pemberton, T. E., 1885), v. 519

Title Deeds (Peake, R. B., 1847), IV. 187, 371

Titled Grisette = Oak Leaves and Emeralds

Tit Tat Toe (Cusnie, W., 1858), v. 787

— (1847), IV. 543

Tit, Tat, Toe—My First Go (Frost, F., 1856) = Fairy Elves, v. 374, 674, 793, 831

Tittle Tattle (1749), II. 67, 69, 267, 385

Titus (Hoole, J., 1767), III. 387

Titus and Berenice (Otway, T. 1676), I. 98, 422

Titus Andronicus (Ravenscroft, E., ?1678), I. 83, 137, 173, 255, 426

Titus Caesar (1839), IV. 543

Titus Vespasian (Cleland, J., 1754), III. 70, 243, 378

+Toads and Diamonds; or, The Fairy's Gift (Conquest, B. and Gomersal, E.; Garrick, Christmas, 1837)

To Arms (Hurlstone, T., 1793), III. 275

Tobacco Box (1782), III. 345

Tobacco Jars (Monckton, Lady, 1889), v. 490

Tobacconist (Gentleman, F., 1760), III. 112, 264, 385

Tobacconist of Bishopsgate Street = Short Cuts and Returns

To be continued in our next (James, W., 1867), v. 434

To be Let by Auction (1820), IV. 543

To Be or Not to Be (Lonergan, Mrs E. A., 1894), v. 462

— (1811), IV. 543

— = Love's Telegraph

Tobin and Nannette (1859), v. 758

"Tobit's Dog!" (Moncrieff, W. T., 1838), IV. 185, 361

To Call her Mine (Landeck, B., 1893), v. 447

To-day (Brookfield, C. H. E., 1892), v. 277

— (Vieson, C., 1895), v. 608

Toddles and Togg (1855), v. 758

Toilers of the Thames (Waldron, W. R., 1869), v. 611

Toiling up the Hill = Thief Maker

Token = Halfpenny Club

Token of Love, Faith and Death = Scarlet Flower

Toledo (1896), v. 758

Tollcross (Campbell, H., 1877), v. 301

Tom (Dalroy, H. and Bearne, A., 1893), v. 333

Tom and Jerry (Egan, P., 1822), IV. 96, 309 [The exact date of acting was Exeter, 8/4/1822]

— (Moncrieff, W. T., 1821), IV. 96, 137, 359

— (1823), IV. 96, 543

Tom and Jerry in Edinburgh (1823), IV. 97, 543

Tom and Jerry in France (Macfarren, G., 1822), IV. 97, 349, 597

Tom and Jerry's Funeral = Death of Life in London

Tom and Jerry's Tour = Green in France

Tom and the Boy = Champion of England

To Marry, or Not to Marry (Inchbald, Mrs E., 1805), III. 147, 150; IV. 16, 185, 329

Tombo-Chiqui (Cleland, J., 1758), III. 120, 243, 378

Tomb of Monteith = St Cuthbert's Eve

Tomb of St Aubin = Black Valley

Tomb of Sigismond (1823), IV. 543

Tom Bowling (Campbell, A. V., 1830), IV. 278

Tom Bowling's Will = Poor Jack

Tom Boy (1811), IV. 543

— (1888), v. 758

Too Careful by Half (Ebsworth, J., 1838), IV. 543

Too Civil by Half (Dent, J., 1782), III. 254

Too Clever (1876), v. 759

Too Clever by Half (1868), v. 759

— = Much too clever

Too Curious by Half (Planché, J. R., 1823) = Marplot in Spain, IV. 377, 500, 605, 632

Toodles (?Raymond, R.J., 1832), IV. 543

— (1862), v. 759

Too Fatiguing (1885), v. 759

Too Friendly by Half (1807) = Plaguy Good-natured Friend, IV. 543, 641

Too Handsome for Anything = Cousin Adonis

Too Happy by Half (Field, J., 1895), v. 365

— (Simpson, J. P.), v. 816

Too Kind (Fenibond, P., 1876), v. 364

Too Late (Quayle, C., 1876), v. 532

— (Thompson, G. F., 1881), v. 597

— (1868), v. 759

— = Shall we remember?

Too Late for Dinner (Jones, R., 1820), IV. 334, 591

— (1835), IV. 543

— (1844), IV. 543

Too late for the Train (Morton, J. M., 1852), v. 495

Too late to save (Palmer, T. A., 1861), v. 511

Too Learned by Half (Sharpe, J., 1793), III. 305

Toole at Sea (Reece, R., 1875), v. 538

Toole up-to-date = Ibsen's Ghost

Toolooloo and Woolooloo (1858), v. 759

Too Lovely Black-Eyed Susan (Lennard, H., 1888), v. 455

Too Loving by Half (Robson, H., 1784), III. 302

Too Many by One (Burnand, F. C. and Cowan, F., 1865), v. 288

Too many Cooks (Kenney, J., 1805), IV. 336

— (Reed, G., 1863), v. 759, 813, 848

Too many Cooks spoil the Broth (1846), IV. 543

Too much for Friendship = Joke's a Joke

Too much for Good Nature (Falconer, E., 1858), v. 360

Too much Johnson (Gillette, W., 1898), v. 759, 793, 848

Too much married (Melford, M., 1886), v. 484

Too much of a good thing (Harris, A. G., 1855), v. 404

Too much the Way of the World (Herbert, J., 1817), IV. 325

Too too far from the Madding Crowd = Squire's Maria

Too True (Craven, H. T., 1876), v. 329

Tootsie (Townley, A. H., 1888), v. 602

Tootsie's Lovers (Le Quex, W. T., 1886), v. 456

To Parents and Guardians (Taylor, T., 1846), IV. 411; v. 592, 820

To Paris and back for Five Pounds (Morton, J. M., 1853), v. 495

Top Boots (1834), IV. 543

To Persons about to Marry (1844), IV. 543

Top of the Ladder = Man of the People

Top of the Tree (1739), II. 385

Topsail Sheet Blocks (Townsend, W. T., 1838), IV. 414

Topsy Turvy (1885), v. 759

Topsey Turveydom (Gilbert, W. S., 1874), v. 380

Topsy Turvey Hotel (Sturgess, A., 1898), v. 586

Topsyturvydom (Byford, R., 1895), v. 295

Toretta [By error this appears at IV. 543 for Loretta, see IV. 276]

Tornado (Carter, L. J., 1899), v. 305

Torneo (1838), IV. 544, 641

Torquato (Swanwick, C., 1850), v. 819

Torrendal (Cumberland, R., 1813), IV. 287

Torrent of La Charbonnière = Forest Savage

Torrent of the Valley (1816), IV. 544

— (1821), IV. 544

Torrid Zone (Clarke, S., 1809), IV. 280

Tortesa the Usurer (Wilks, T. E., 1839), IV. 421

Torture of Shame (Gannon, J., 1896), v. 376

Tosca (Grove, F. C. and Hamilton, H., 1889), v. 395

Toss up (Addison, J., 1876), v. 236

— (1897), v. 759

Tradesman's Son (Shepherd, R., 1862),
v. 563
Trafalgar (Campbell, A. V., 1845), IV.
279
— (1807), IV. 544
— (1849), IV. 544
Trafalgar Medal (Buckstone, J. B.,
1863), v. 781
Tragedy (Fawcett, C. S., 1887), v. 364
Tragedy à la Mode = (1) First Act of
Taste; (2) Lindamira
Tragedy Expell'd = Art of Management
Tragedy for Warm Weather = Devil
among the Tailors
Tragedy in Trousers = Irvingmania
Tragedy in True Taste = Distress upon
Distress
Tragedy of Amidea = Traytor
Tragedy of Love = Cyrus the Great
Tragedy of Ovid (Cockain, Sir A.,
1662), I. 397
Tragedy of Tragedies = Tom Thumb
Tragedy of Vortigern Rehearsed =
Precious Relics
Tragedy Queen (Oxenford, J., 1855), v.
759, 848
— (Robson, W., 1847), IV. 395
Tragedy rehearsed = Critic
Tragical Actors (1660), I. 445
Tragic Mary (Field, M., 1890), v.
366
Tragopodagra (Francklin, T., 1780), III.
261
Traill the Anarchist (1896), v. 759
Trail of Sin (Leslie, H. T., 1863), v.
457
Trail of the Serpent (Lander, G., 1879),
v. 448
— (Walker, W., 1881), v. 611
— (Watson, F. M., 1896), v. 616
Trained to Crime (Towers, E., 1878), v.
601
Training a Husband (Dening, Mrs C.,
1892), v. 342
Traitor = (1) Maurice the Woodcutter;
(2) Traytor
Traitor Doubts (1887), v. 759
Traitor's Doom = Destiny
Traitor's Gate (Lucas, W. J., 1834), IV.
347
Traitors of Ferrara = Florinda Salviati,
the White Devil

Traitor's Touch = Wedding Eve
Traitor, the Jew and the Gypsey =
Casper Duverade
Traitor to Himself (Johns, W., 1678), I.
101, 415
Traits of Ancient Superstition = Test of
Guilt
Tra-la-la Tosca (Burnand, F. C., 1890),
v. 291
Tramp (Harrison, C., 1889), v. 407
Tramp and the Treasure of the Seven
Seas = Pauper of Lambeth
Tramps (Stephens, W. and McCul-
lough, B., 1896), v. 581
Tramp's Adventure (Phillips, F. L.,
1860) = Dying Gift, v. 522, 671, 810,
831
Trances of Nourjahad = Illusion
Transferred Ghost (Lynn, N., 1894), v.
465
Transferring a Licence (1852), v. 759
Transformation (Allingham, J. T.,
1810), IV. 252, 568
— (1787), III. 346
— (1816), IV. 544
— (1822), IV. 544
Transformations (1821), IV. 544
Transformations in Olympus = Low
Life below Stairs
Transformed (1854), v. 759
Transformed Lover (1850), v. 848
Transgressor (Gattie, A. W., 1894), v.
377
Transit of Venus (Tanner, J. T., 1898),
v. 591
Transmogrification = Crockery's Mis-
fortunes
Transported for Life (Murdoch, J. M.,
1880), v. 499
Trap of Gold (Higgie, T. H., 1864), v.
421
Trapolin's Vagaries = Devil of a Duke
Trapped (1885), v. 759
— (1898), v. 759
Trapped at Last (Neville, G. F., 1882),
v. 502
Trapper (Roberts, G., 1888), v. 545
Trapper of the Hills (1845), IV. 544
Trappers of the Mountains = Year and a
Day
Trapper Trapped = Caught in his own
Trap

Trial of Love (Lovell, G. W., 1852), IV.
347; v. 463
— (Soane, G., 1827), IV. 545, 641
Trial of Poverty = Love Gift
Trial of Skill (Dossie, R., 1768) =
Statesman Foil'd, III. 346, 383, 405
— (Wilcox, W. T. W., 1837), IV. 419
— (1835), IV. 545
Trials and Triumphs of Temperance
(Pitt, G. D., 1851), v. 526
Trials and Troubles of Claude and
Pauline = Extraordinary Version of
the Lady of Lyons
Trials of a Fond Papa = Virginius
Trials of a Merry-Andrew = Belphegor
Trials of Life = Wealth and Poverty
Trials of Love = Angel's Visit
Trials of Poverty (1843), IV. 545
Trials of the Heart (1799), III. 346
— = (1) Avalanche; (2) Woman's Life
Trials of the Poor (1887), v. 759
Trials of Tomkins (Williams, T. J.,
1863), v. 625
Trials of Youth = Resolution
Tribulation (Poole, J., 1825), IV. 184,
386
Tribunal of Blood = Black Banner
Tribunal of Death = Maid of Grenada
Tribute of a Hundred Virgins (Mon-
crieff, W. T., 1840), IV. 600
Trick and Trap (1859), v. 759
Tricked (Dalrymple, L., 1884), v. 333
Trick for Trick (Dibdin, T. J., 1817),
IV. 300
— (D'Urfey, T., 1678), I. 273, 408
— (Fabian, R., 1735), II. 321
— (Forrest, A., 1889), v. 370
— (Gathercole, Mrs, 1877), v. 376
— (Stanley, H. J., 1874), v. 579
— (1812), IV. 545, 641
— (1827), IV. 545
— = Comical Resentment
Tricking a 'Tec (Drew, E., 1891), v. 350
Tricking's Fair in Love (1814), IV. 545
Tricks (Field, W. F., 1889), v. 366
— (Wyke, E. B., 1878), v. 633
Tricks and Blunders (Dobbs, J., 1823),
IV. 545
— (1822), IV. 545
— (1825), IV. 545
Tricks and Honours (Gray, L., 1897), v.
390

Tricks and Trials (1850), v. 759
Tricksey Monarch and the Wicksey
Warrior = Louis XI
Tricks of Harlequin (Downing, G.,
1739), II. 319
Tricks of London (McLaren, A., 1812)
= Ways of London, IV. 351
Tricks of the Turf (1867), v. 759
Tricks of Timothy = Castle of Lausanne
Tricks upon Travellers (Brassington,
R., Jr., 1816), IV. 270
— (Burges, Sir J. B., 1810), IV. 276
Trick to Cheat the Devil = Imposture
Defeated
Trick upon Trick (Yarrow, J., 1742), II.
364, 385, 386
— (1739), II. 364, 385, 447–8
— = (1) Hymen's Triumph; (2) Sor-
ceress; (3) Squire Brainless
Tricky Esmeralda (Bailey, W. E. and
Ward, E., 1897), v. 247
Tried and True = Patriot's Daughter
Tried for Life (1896), v. 759
Tried in the Fire = Mary Warner
Triermain (Ellerton, J. L., 1831), IV.
92, 309
Trifles light as Air (1850), v. 759
Trifling Mistake = Prince and the
Player
Trilby (Potter, P. M., 1895), v. 530
— (1896), v. 759
Trilby the Model (1896), v. 759
Trinummi Imitated (Barnes, J., ?1684),
I. 389
Trip across the Herring Pond = Paris
and London
Trip by Railway = Look to your Lug-
gage
Trip from the North = Lowland Lassie
in London
Triple Alliance (Oxenford, J., 1862), v.
510
— (1897), v. 759
— = Poor Tommy
Triple Bill (Adams-Acton, Mrs, 1894),
v. 235
Triple Dilemma (1863), v. 759
Triple Discovery (1800), IV. 545
Triple Marriage (Foote, S., 1762), III.
384
Triple Revenge = Spouter
Triple Wedding = Pill for the Doctor

Troubadour (1831), IV. 545

— = Laura et Linza

Troubadours (Planché, J. R., 1819), IV. 376

Trouble at the Court of King Bulbous (1896), v. 760

Troubled Hearts (1866), v. 760

Troubled Waters (Brock, F., 1899), v. 276

— (Hume, H., 1864), v. 760, 799, 848

— (1878), v. 760

— (1893), v. 760

Troubles (Findon, B. W., 1888), v. 366

Troubles of a Tourist (Grain, R. C., 1884), v. 387

Troublesome Lodger (Mayhew, H. and Baylis, H., 1839), IV. 545, 641

Troublesome Twins = Corsican "Bothers"

Trovatore (Byron, H. J., 1880), v., 299

— (Suter, W. E. and Travers, W., 1855), v. 587

Troy Again (Bowles, E. W., 1888), v. 271

Truant Chief (?Oxberry, W. H., 1837), IV. 367, 602, 603

— = Provost of Paris

Trudge and Wowski (Knight, T., 1790), III. 279

True as Steel (Hazlewood, C. H., 1869), v. 414

— (Reeve, W., 1871), v. 540

— (Romaine, E., 1871), v. 549

True as Truth (Drinkwater, A. E., 1891), v. 351

True at Last (Reynoldson, T. H., 1866) = Gitano Boy, v. 683, 813, 833

True Blue (Outram, L. S. and Gordon, S., 1896), v. 509

— (1787), III. 346

— = Nancy

True Blue for Ever = Spaniards dismayed

True-born Irishman (Macklin, C., 1762), III. 284, 391

True-born Scotsman (Macklin, C., 1764), III. 284 [This seems to have been acted first at Smock Alley, Dublin, 10/7/1764]

True British Tar (Hull, T., 1786), III. 274

True Briton (Cranke, 1782), III. 249

True Colours (Hartley, C., 1889), v. 408

— (Hurst, J. P., 1888), v. 431

True Friends (Dibdin, T. J., 1800), IV. 297

True Grit (Pettitt, H. and Flaxman, A. J., 1894), v. 521

— (Stafford, A., 1887), v. 578

True Heart (Byatt, H. and Magnay, W., 1889), v. 295

True Hearts (Bell, F., 1874), v. 255

True Irish Girl = Kathleen

True Lesson of Life = Temperance Pledge

True Life in the Brickfields = Bright Beam at Last

True Love (Goodrich, A., 1885), v. 384

True Lovers' Knots (Pettitt, H., 1874), v. 520

True Nobility (Ford, T. M., 1892), v. 370

True Patriot = Vortimer

True Patriotism (1799), III. 346

True Revenge = Abbot of San Martino

True Ring of the Genuine Metal = Gold and Guilt

True Satisfaction (1815), IV. 545

True Story told in Two Cities (Galer, E. J. N., 1884), v. 375

True Tale of the Twelfth Century = Who's the Murderer?

True Test of Gold = Voyage to California

True till Death (Dix, F., 1896), v. 345

— (Marston, H., 1876), v. 478

— = Lord Darcy

True to his Colours (Bean, F., 1892), v. 254

True to his Trust = Terry

True to the Core (Slous, A. R., 1866), v. 571

— = Will Tell

True to the Corps = Vivandière

True to the Last (Whitbread, J. W., 1888), v. 620

— = Tramp's Adventure

True Touch of the Times = Harlequin's Whim

True Virgin Prophetess = Virgin Prophetess

True Way to be Happy = Darby and Joan

True Widow (Shadwell, T., 1678), I. 12, 23, 193, 207, 431

True Woman (Dodson, R., 1878), v. 346

— (Wild, W. J., 1897), v. 622

— (1883), v. 760

True Woman's Heart = Twixt Gold and Love

True Women (Braekstad, H. L., 1890), v. 780

Trulla's Triumph = Hudibras

Trump Card (Broughton, F. W. and Jones, J. W., 1882), v. 281

— (1878), v. 760

Trumpet Call (Sims, G. R. and Buchanan, R., 1891), v. 569

Trumpeter's Daughter (Coyne, J. S., 1843), IV. 284, 578

— (Webster, B., the Younger, 1863), v. 618

Trumpeter's Wedding (Morton, J. M., 1849), IV. 363

Trumps in the Dumps (1823), IV. 545

Trust (Breck, C., 1808), IV. 270

— (Newte, H. C. W., 1891), v. 503

— (1871), v. 760

— (1877), v. 760

Trust and Trial (Calmour, A. C., 1880), v. 300

Trust Each Other = Joe and Nolly Stubbs

Trustee (Allingham, J. T., 1809) = Independence, IV. 545, 641

— (Lovel, G. W., 1841), IV. 347

— (1854), v. 760

— = Noah's Ark

Trust to Luck (Clarke, C. A., 1891), v. 312

Truth (Howard, B., 1879), v. 428

— (Mathews, C. J., 1834), IV. 354

— (Pitt, W. H., 1871), v. 527

— (1821), IV. 545

Truth against the World (Spencer, G., 1870), v. 576

Truth and Fiction (Williams, T. J. and Harris, A. G., 1861), v. 625, 824

— = Romance and Reality

Truth and Filial Love (1797), III. 346

Truth and Treachery = Angiolina del' Albano

Truth and Treason = Foresters

Truth Found too Late = Troilus and Cressida

Truthful James (Mortimer, J. and Klein, C. H., 1894), v. 494

Truth is a lie = 'Twas I

Truth may be blamed but cannot be shamed = Family Treason

Truth Will Out = All-Hallows' Eve

Try Again (1821), IV. 545

— (1790) = Suspicious Brother, III. 346, 405

— = Jack Mingo, the London Street-Boy

Tryal (Baillie, J., 1798), III. 224, 235

Tryal of Conjugal Love (Jacob, H., 1738), II. 205, 338

Tryall of Samuel Foote, Esq. for a Libel on Peter Paragraph (Foote, S., 1763), III. 260

Tryal of Abraham (1790), III. 346

Tryal of the Time-Killers (Bacon, P., 1757), III. 235

Tryal's All (Herbert, 1802), IV. 325

Try before you Buy (1806), IV. 545

Try Before You Trust (?1660-1700), I. 445

Trying a Magistrate (Toole, J. L., 1877), v. 600

Trying it on (Brough, W., 1853), v. 278

Trying Scenes of Life (Gardner, C., 1876), v. 376

Tryphon (Boyle, R., 1668), I. 38, 39, 55, 99, 107-8, 393

T.T.S. (1829), IV. 545

T.T.T.—Tom Trimmer's Trials = My Husband's Wife

Tuckitomba (Pocock, I., 1828), IV. 385

Tufelhausen (Johnstone, J. B., 1856), v. 438

Tully's Rambles (1794), III. 405

Tumble-Down Dick (Fielding, H., 1736), II. 34, 67, 255-6, 263, 328

Tumble Down Naps = Man in the Moon

Tummus and Meary (1773), III. 346

Tunbridge-Walks (Baker, T., 1703), II. 60, 129, 135, 143, 175, 216, 231, 296, 432

Tunbridge-Wells (Rawlins, 1678), I. 216, 234, 426

Tuppins and Co. (Watson, T. M., 1889), v. 616

Turandot, Princess of China (Gurney, A. T., 1836), IV. 322; v. 397

Turf (Lemon, H., 1884), v. 454

Twelve Months and a Day = Unhallowed Templar

Twelve Month's Honeymoon = Living
too fast

Twelve Months Since = Larboard Fin

Twelve O'Clock (Bennett, 1814), IV.
572

— (1823), IV. 546

— (1884), V. 760

Twelve O'Clock and the Midnight
Angel = Spirit of Death

Twelve Pages (1826), IV. 546

Twelve P.P.s. = Matrimonial Advertisement

Twelve Precisely (Milner, H. M., 1821),
IV. 356, 599

Twelve Wishes and the Charmed Bit =
Demon Horse

Twentieth-Century Girl (Trevelyan,
C., 1895), V. 603

Twenty-five Years Since = Foresters

Twenty Four Hours in Algiers = Dey
and a Knight

24th Geo. II (Crofton, E., 1866), V. 330

24th of May (Reynoldson, T. H., 1844),
IV. 393, 546, 608, 641

Twenty Maids and One Bachelor (1825),
IV. 546

Twenty Minutes' Conversation under
an Umbrella (Dubourg, A. W., 1873),
V. 351

Twenty Minutes with an Impudent
Puppy (1856), V. 760

Twenty Minutes with a Tiger (1855),
V. 760

Twenty Minutes with H.P. (1860), V.
760

Twenty One Metamorphoses (1788),
III. 346

Twenty per Cent (Dibdin, T. J., 1815),
IV. 300

£20 a Year, all found (Byron, H. J.,
1876), V. 298

£20 Reward = Stolen

Twenty Six Shillings = Pay Me

Twenty Straws (Hazlewood, C. H.,
1865), V. 760, 796, 848

— (Henry, B., 1873), V. 417, 825

— (Young, Mrs H., 1865), V. 760,
848

Twenty Thieves (Ebsworth, J.), IV. 309

£20,000 (1833), IV. 546

Twenty Thousand Pounds a Year
(Towers, E., 1871), V. 601

Twenty Years Ago! (Pocock, I., 1810),
IV. 111–12, 383, 606

— = Father's Curse

Twenty Years in a Debtor's Prison
(Wilkins, J. H., 1858), V. 623

Twenty Years of a Soldier's Life =
Order of the Night

Twice Fooled (1895), V. 760

Twice Killed (Oxenford, J., 1835), IV.
367

Twice Killed—Good Night, Signor
Pantalon

Twice Married (O'Neil, C. and Silvester, H., 1887), V. 507

— (1865), V. 760

Twice Married and a Maid Still (1717),
II. 386

Twice the Dagger Struck = Foundling
of the Forest

Twice Told Tale (Wooler, J. P., 1858),
V. 632

Twice Wedded (Horn, J., 1882), V.
426

Twig Folly (Dodson, R., 1878), V. 346

Twilight (Barrett, W., 1871), V. 250

— (Dalroy, H., 1893), V. 333

— (Geary, W., 1887), V. 377

— (Swears, H., 1896), V. 589

Twilight to Dawn (1885), V. 760

Twin Brothers (Paul, W., 1874), V. 516

— (1830), IV. 546

— = Widow's Son

Twine the Plaidon (Walker, G. R.,
1877), V. 611

Twinkle, Twinkle, Little Star (Green,
F. W., 1875), V. 760, 794, 848

— (Hall, F., 1876), V. 399

— (Strachan, J. S., 1876), V. 585

— (1875, 1898, 1899), V. 760

Twin-Rivals (Farquhar, G., 1702), II.
133, 135, 136, 148, 321; III. 115

Twins (Derrick, J., 1884), V. 343

— (Hull, T., 1762), III. 111, 274

— (Lewis, M. G., 1799), III. 281

— (Woods, W., 1780), III. 317

Twin Sisters (Lemain, B., 1877), V. 454

— (Schiff, E., 1870), V. 557

— = (1) Open House; (2) Sleepwalker

Twins of the Tyrol = Black Musket

Twins of Warsaw (1833), IV. 641

Two Roses (Albery, J., 1870), v. 69, 153–5, 237

Two Rubies (Kingsley, C., 1894), v. 444

Two Rum 'uns = Romulus and Remus

Two's Company (Andreæ, P., 1895), v. 241

Two Seconds! (Peake, R. B., 1827), iv. 370

Two Shades of Life (1888), v. 761

Two Sides of the Gutter = Poor Old Haymarket

Two Sides of the Question (Dibdin, T. J., ?1797), iii. 383

Two Sisters (Raymond, C. F. M., 1843), iv. 388

— (1875), v. 761

— = Sisters

Two Socias (1792), iii. 346

— = Amphitryon

Two Sons (Manuel, E., 1877), v. 474

Two Sosias = Amphitryon

Two Spanish Valets (Scott, J. M., 1818) = Lie upon Lie, iv. 492, 547, 631, 641

Two Stages from Gretna (1828), iv. 547

— = Disguises

Two Stars = Prompter's Box

Two Strings to a Beau = Cupid

Two Strings to your Bow (Cherry, A., 1814), iv. 280

— (Jephson, R., 1791), iii. 277

Two Students (1861), v. 761

Two Suicides (Doone, N., 1891), v. 347

Two Thieves (1823), iv. 547

Two Thompsons = Lunatic Asylum

Two Thorns (Albery, J., 1871), v. 237

Two Thumbs (Neale, F., 1849), iv. 366

Two to One (Colman, G., the Younger, 1783), iii. 247

— (1806), iv. 547

— = Irish Footman

Two to One, bar One (1894), v. 761

Two to One on the Winner = Greenwich Railway

'Twould Puzzle a Conjuror (Poole, J., 1824), iv. 386

Two Valets (1822), iv. 547

Two Violettas = Don John

Two Waiters (1849), iv. 547

Two Ways of Telling a Story = Bannister's Budget

Two Ways to Bring up a Son = Leading Strings

Two Wedding Rings (Bellamy, G. S. and Romer, F., 1882), v. 256

Two Wild Flowers = Lost and Found

Two Winters (1859), v. 761

Two Wives! (Parry, J., 1821) = Cabinet and Two Wives = Master Key, iv. 547, 603, 641

Two Wives of Clitheroe = Kate Wynsley

Two Women (Rose, E., 1885), v. 550

— (1895), v. 761

Two Words (Arnold, S. J., 1816), iv. 256

Two Young Wives (1892), v. 761

Type of the Old One = Printer's Devil

Typewriter (East, J. M., 1892), v. 353

Tyrannick Love (Dryden, J., 1669), i. 42, 81, 92, 96, 99, 113–14, 322, 346, 404

Tyranny: A Tale of the Press-gang of 1810 (1884), v. 761

Tyranny of Tears (Chambers, C. H., 1899), v. 189, 205, 307

Tyranny Triumphant! and Liberty Lost (1743), ii. 386

Tyrant (1722), ii. 386

Tyrant and Parrasite (Kenney, J., 1812) = Turn Him Out! iv. 547, 641

Tyrant King of Crete (Sedley, Sir C., 1722), i. 428

Tyrant of Algiers (1838), iv. 547

Tyrant of New Orleans = Confederate's Daughter

Tyrant of Padua = Angelo

Tyrant of Syracuse (1827), iv. 547

Tyrant Saracen and the Noble Moor (1811), iv. 547

Tyrolese Peasant (1832), iv. 547

Tyrrel (Tait, E. and Menzies, K., 1841), iv. 355, 598, 613

Tythe Pig (1795), iii. 346

Tythe Sheaf (1791), iii. 346

— = Harvest Home

Tzigane (Smith, H. B., 1895), v. 572

Uanita (Newland, H. C., 1894), v. 503

Ugly Club (Iliffe, 1798), iii. 347, 388, 405

Ugly Customer (Williams, T. J., 1860), v. 625

Ugly Duckling (Grain, R. C., 1893), v. 388

Under the Star = Nicksey
Under the Stars (Banks, W., 1879), v. 248
Under the Thumb = Joseph Chavigny
Under the Tricolour (1886), v. 762
Under the Union Jack (1897), v. 762
Under Two Flags (Abel, W. H., 1870), v. 234
— (Daventry, G., 1882), v. 338
— (1869), v. 762
— (1883), v. 762
Under Two Reigns (Percival, W. and Willing, J., 1879), v. 520
Under which Flag? (1899), v. 762
Undine (Buckstone, J. B., 1858), v. 762, 781, 848
— (Courtney, J., 1857), v. 786
— (Reece, R., 1870), v. 537
— (1821), IV. 547
— (1883), v. 762
Undine and the Goblin Page = Spirit of the Waters
Undine, the Spirit of the Waters (Blanchard, E. L., 1852), v. 263
Undine Undone (1873), v. 762
Undutiful Father = Completely Successful
Unearthly Bride = Këolanthè
Uneasy Man (1771), III. 347, 405
Uneasy Shaving = No. 70
Unequally Sentenced (1876) = Clergy, v. 660, 762, 848
Unequal Match (Taylor, T., 1857), v. 593, 820
— = Injured Princess
Unequal Rivals (Learmont, J., 1791), III. 280
Unexpected (1870), v. 762
Unexpected Marriage = Seaman's Return
Unexpected Visit (Archer, D., 1898), v. 242
Unfeeling Parent (1793), III. 347
Unfinished Gentleman (Selby, C., 1834), IV. 397
Unfinished Story (Cassilis, I. L., 1891), v. 306
Unfit for Service (1833), IV. 547
Unfortunate Beau (Williams, J., 1784), III. 116, 316
Unfortunate Brothers = Unfortunate Duchess of Malfy

Unfortunate Couple (Filmer, E., 1697), I. 421
Unfortunate Duchess of Malfy (1707), II. 386, 448
Unfortunate Lovers = Pyramus and Thisbe
Unfortunate Miss Bailey (À Beckett, G. A., 1835), IV. 249
Unfortunate Propensity (1853), v. 762
Unfortunate Shepherd (Tutchin, J., 1685), I. 435
Unfortunate Youth (MᶜLaren, A., 1821), IV. 352
— (Webster, B. N., 1840), IV. 417
Ungrateful Favourite (Southland, T., 1664), I. 233, 433
Ungrateful Lovers (1667)? = Unfortunate Lovers, I. 445
Ungrateful Spaniard = American Heroine
Unhallowed Sepulchre = Valmondi
Unhallowed Templar (Haines, J. T., 1827), IV. 548, 641
Unhappy Conqueror = Neglected Virtue
Unhappy Father (Leapor, M., 1751), III. 280
Unhappy Favourite (Banks, J., 1681), I. 2, 165–6, 272, 389
Unhappy Kindness (Scott, T., 1697), I. 12, 170, 427
Unhappy Marriage = (1) Bateman; (2) Orphan
Unhappy Penitent (Trotter, Mrs C., 1700), II. xi, 104, 361
Unhappy Rescue = Fatal Inconstancy
Uniform (1841), IV. 548
Uninhabited Island (Williams, A., 1766), III. 70, 316
Uninhabited Isle (Hoole, J., 1800), III. 387
Union (Wilson, R., 1790), III. 347, 398, 405
Union des Nations (Conquest, Mrs G., 1852), v. 323
Unionist (Cleaton, E. R., 1890), v. 313
Union Jack (Pettitt, H. and Grundy, S., 1888), v. 521
— (Somerset, C. A., 1842), IV. 405
+Union Jack; or, The Crew of the Bright Blue Wave (Rogers, W.; Pav. 1843)

Very Good Wife (Powell, G., 1693), I.
261, 425

Very Grand Dutch—s (Bernard, C.,
1869), v. 763, 778, 849

Very Last Days of Pompeii (Reece, R.,
1872), v. 537

Very Latest Edition of the Gathering of
the Clans (Hunt, G. W., 1873), v. 430

Very Latest Edition of the Lady of
Lyons (Byron, H. J., 1859), v. 295

Very Little Faust and More Mephistopheles (Burnand, F. C., 1869), v. 289

Very Little Hamlet (Yardley, W., 1884),
v. 634

Very Low Spirits (Bourne, W., 1876), v.
270

Very much above Pa = Under Proof

Very Picture = Speaking Likeness

Very Pleasant Living (Suter, W. E.),
v. 588

Very Queer Lover (1884), v. 763

Very Serious Affair (Harris, A. G.,
1857), v. 405

Very Suspicious (Simpson, J. P., 1852),
v. 567

— = Decorum

Very, very much engaged (Haworth, J.
and Buchanan, R. C., 1895), v. 410

Very Wilful Maid of Venice = Count
Tremolio

Vesper Bell = Lodovic the Corsican

Vespers of Palermo (Hemans, Mrs F. D.,
1823), IV. 324

Vesta (Farnie, H. B., 1871), v. 361

Vestal Virgin (Brooke, H., 1778), III. 240

— (Howard, Sir R., 1665), I. 40, 99, 126,
127, 137, 414–15

Vesta's Temple (1872), v. 763

Vetah (Santley, K., 1886), v. 555

Veteran (1804), IV. 549

— (1827), IV. 549

— = Veteran Soldier

Veteran and his Dog = Conscript

Veteran and his Progeny (1865), v. 763

— = 102

Veteran and his Son (1860), v. 763

— = Ben Block

Veteran Ashore (1851), v. 763

+Veteran of 102 (Milner, H. M.,
French)

Veteran of the Old Guard (1847), IV.
642

Veterans (Dibdin, T. J., 1821), IV. 303

— (1888), v. 763

— = Veteran Soldier

Veteran Serjeant (1839), IV. 549

Veteran Soldier (Knight, E. P., 1822),
IV. 338 [This was printed 8°, 1822 as
The Veteran]

Veteran Tar (Arnold, S. J., 1801), IV.
255

Veva (O'Neil, C., 1883), v. 507

Vicar (Hannan, C., 1893), v. 402

— (Hatton, J. and Albery, J., 1885), v.
409

Vicarage (Scott, C. W., 1877), v. 557

Vicar of Bray (Grundy, S., 1882), v. 396

Vicar of Wakefield (Coyne, J. S., 1850),
v. 763, 786, 849

— (Dibdin, T. J., 1817), IV. 301, 549,
642

— (Douglass, J. T., 1870), v. 348

— (Farren, W., 1888), v. 363

— (Taylor, T., 1850), v. 592

— (1850), v. 764

Vicar of Wideawakefield (Stephens,
H. P. and Yardley, W., 1885), v. 580

Vicar Primrose = Vicar of Wakefield

Vicar's Daughter (Corney, M., 1896),
v. 325

— (Drew, E., 1889), v. 350

— = Betrayed

Vicar's Dilemma (Vicarson, A., 1898),
v. 608

Vicar's Fireside = Strayed from the Fold

Vice and its Consequences = Red
Brigade

Vice in Liverpool = Prince's Park and
Scotland Row

Vice Reclaim'd (Wilkinson, R., 1703),
II. 171, 233, 364

Viceroy (Dibdin, C. I. M., 1817), IV.
294, 549, 580, 642

— (Hayley, W., 1811), IV. 324

Vices of the Age Displayed (1711), II.
386

Vice Versa (Rose, E., 1883), v. 550

Vice versus Virtue (Barker, J., 1891), v.
249

Vicissitudes (Sicklemore, R., 1817), IV.
611

Vicissitudes of a Servant Girl = Susan
Hopley

Vicissitudes of Life = George Vernet

Village Blacksmith (1857), V. 764

Village Cobbler = Port Admiral

Village Conjurer (1767), III. 120, 347, 405

Village Coquette (Simon, 1792), III. 307

— (1884), V. 764

— = Love Charm

Village Coquettes (Dickens, C., 1836), IV. 146, 305

Village Doctor (Cross, J. C., 1796), III. 250

— (Montignani, F. A., 1810), IV. 600

— = Alcantara

Village Festival (1855), V. 764

— = Chip of the Old Block

Village Fete (Cumberland, R., 1797), III. 252

— (1802), IV. 549

— (1810), IV. 549, 642

Village Forge (Conquest, G. and Craven, T., 1890), V. 322

Village Frolics = (1) Goody Two Shoes; (2) Serjeant's Whim

Village Ghost (Dibdin, T. J., ?1794), III. 382

Village Gossip = Scan. Mag.

Village Heiress (Dibdin, C. I. M., 1814), IV. 293

Village Hotel = Sharp Set

Village Inn and the Count Out = Allario and Adelina

Village Lawyer (Macready, W., 1787), III. 285, 391

Village Life in France (1837), IV. 549

Village Madcap (Mervyn, E., 1898), V. 488

Village Maid (1792), III. 347

Village Nightingale (Craven, H. T., 1851), V. 328

Village of Youth (Hatton, B., 1899), V. 409

Village Opera (Johnson, C., 1729), II. 134, 242, 339; III. 116

Village Outcast (Taylor, T. P., 1846), IV. 411

— (1844), IV. 549

+ Village Pearl (Wilson, J. C.)

Village Phantom (1833), IV. 549

— (1839), IV. 549

— = White Spectre

Village Politicians = (1) Electioneering; (2) Wealth and Want

Village Post-Office (Dabbs, G. H. R. 1889), V. 332

Village Practitioner (1824), IV. 549

Village Pride = Jeannette and Jeannot

Village Priest (Grundy, S., 1890), V. 397

Village Rejoicing Day = Prize of Industry

Village Rivals = Pierette

Village Romps (1765), III. 347

Villagers (Earle, W.), III. 258

— (Worgan, T. D., 1808), IV. 422

— (1756), III. 347

— = Augustus and Gulielmus

Villagers of San Quintino = Scaramuccia

Village Smithy (1894), V. 764

Village Somnambulist = Spirit of the Hill

Village Story (Raymond, R. J., 1838), IV. 389

— (Serle, T. J., 1859), V. 561

Village Tale (Reade, C., 1852), V. 535

— (Younge, A. 1850), V. 637

— = Rachel the Reaper

Village Theatre = Scraps

Village, the Voyage and the Bush = Emigration

Village Torment (1870), V. 849

Village Vauxhall = How to take up a Bill

Village Venus (Stephens, V. and Birch, A., 1895), V. 581

+ Village Virtue; or, The Libertine Lord, and the Damsel of Daisy Farm (Byron, H. J.: *Dicks* (in *Sensation Dramas*))

Village Virtues (Lewis, M. G., 1796), III. 281

Village Washerwoman = Bubbles in the Sudds

Village Wedding (Love, J., 1767), III. 283

Villain (Porter, T., 1662), I. 38, 62, 69, 136, 346, 351, 425

Villain and Victim (Walkes, W. R., 1894), V. 612

Villainous Squire and the Village Rose (Byron, H. J., 1882), V. 299

Villainous Squire and the Virtuous Villager = Rosebud of Stinging-nettle Farm

Villain Reclaimed = Chance of War

Villain Unmask'd = Lost Child

Volcano (Lumley, R. R., 1891), v. 464

Volcano of Italy (Hazlewood, C. H., 1865), v. 764, 796, 849

Vologese (Gallet, 1803), IV. 585

Voltaire's Wager (Wingfield, L., 1875), v. 629

Vol. III (Ellis, W., 1891), v. 357

Voluntary Contributions (Porter, W., 1798), III. 299

Volunteer Corps (1859), v. 764

Volunteer Returned (1784), III. 347

Volunteer Review = Young Man in Green

Volunteers (Bayly, T. H., 1835), IV. 571
— (Downing, G., 1780), III. 257
— (Shadwell, T., 1692), I. 2, 23, 209–10, 431
— (Woods, W., 1778), III. 317, 398
— (1748), II. 386

Volunteer's Ball (Burnand, F. C. and Williams, M., 1860), v. 288, 781

Von Orenburg (Bryant, M., 1824), IV. 574

Voorn the Tiger (1812), IV. 550

Vortigern (Ireland, S. W. H., 1796), III. 276, 367

Vortimer (Portal, A., 1796), III. 299

Votaries of the Ruby Cross (Milner, H. M., 1829), IV. 550, 642

Votary of Wealth (Holman, J. G., 1799), III. 272

Vote for Griggs (1892), v. 764

Vow (Macartney, C. J., 1800?), III. 283 [The entry at IV. 349 under Macarthy should be deleted]

Vow of Silence (Barnett, C. Z., 1834), IV. 570
— (1854), v. 764
— = Shipwrecked Mother

Vow of the Three Avengers = Irene, the Greek Girl of Janina

Vow of Vengeance (Amherst, J. H., 1821), IV. 550, 642
— (1897), v. 764

Voyage dans la Lune (Leigh, H. S., 1876), v. 454

Voyage en Suisse (Reece, R., 1880), v. 539

Voyage of Love = Sword of Peace

Voyage to California (1849), IV. 550

Voyage to India (1807), IV. 550

Voyage to Margate (1820), IV. 550

Voyage to Poland = John du Bart

Voyage to the Gold Mines (1849), IV. 550

Voyage to the North (1833), IV. 550

Voyage to the North Pole (1823), IV. 550

V.R. (1887), v. 764

Vulcan (1882), v. 764

Vulcan and Co. Ltd. = Olympus

Vulcan's Wedding = Momus turn'd Fabulist

Vultures (Landeck, B., 1888), v. 447
— (1899), v. 764

Vulture of the Apennines = Belmonti

Vulture's Nest = Drip, drop, Drip drop

Waconsta (1849), IV. 550

Wag = Confusion

Wager (Halliday, G. B., 1879), v. 401
— (Kappey, J. A., 1871), v. 442
— (Lancaster, E. R., 1839), IV. 593
— (Parry, J., 1837), IV. 550, 642
— (1780), III. 347
— (1808), IV. 550
— (1825), IV. 550
— (1840), IV. 550
— (1867), v. 764

Wager Lost = Twelve O'Clock

Wages of Sin (Harvey, F., 1882), v. 408

Waggery in Wapping (Dibdin, T. J., 1816), IV. 300

Waggoner of Westmoreland (Moncrieff, W. T., 1834), IV. 360

Wagner and Abericot (1726 or 1727), II. 253, 386 [This = The Miser (II. 360)]

Wagner Mania (1884), v. 764

Wagner Out-wagged (1881), v. 764

Wags (Dibdin, C., 1790), III. 256

Wags of Wapping (1846), IV. 550

Wags of Windsor (1810), IV. 550
— = Review

Wagustavus (À Beckett, G. A., 1834), IV. 567

Waif (Pyat, F., 1873), v. 531
— = (1) Forger; (2) Stroller; (3) Such is Life

Waif of the Streets (1877), v. 764

Waifs (Murdoch, J. M., 1869), v. 499

Waifs and Strays = Saved from the Streets

Waifs of New York (Collins, O. B., 1878), v. 318
— (Raymond, C. F. M., 1875), v. 535

Wait a Little Longer = Hard Times

Wait and Hope (Byron, H. J., 1871), v. 297

— (Nanton, L., 1869), v. 501

— = Checkmated

Waiter (Henry, R., 1887), v. 417

— (Pleon, H., 1891), v. 528

Waiter at Cremorne (Suter, W. E., 1855), v. 107, 587

Waiter at the Eagle = Waiter at Cremorne

Wait for an Answer (Lemon, H., 1869), v. 454

Wait for a Year and a Day (1876), v. 764

Wait for the End (1877), v. 764

Waiting (1887), v. 764

— (1899), v. 764

Waiting Consent (Fairbairn, Mrs R., 1881), v. 359

Waiting for an Omnibus in Lowther Arcade on a Rainy Day (Morton, J. M., 1854), v. 495

Waiting for an Omnibus on a Rainy Day = Lowther Arcade

Waiting for Dead Men's Shoes (1875), v. 764

Waiting for Death (Robertson, L. and Comerford, M., 1877), v. 545

Waiting for the Coach (Clement, F. A., 1891), v. 314

Waiting for the Dawn (Moore, R., 1870), v. 492

Waiting for the Train (Fitzgerald, S. J. A., 1899), v. 369

— (Wilmot, A. A., 1891), v. 628

Waiting for the Underground (Du Terreaux, L. H., 1866), v. 765, 789, 849

Waiting for the Verdict (Hazlewood, C. H., 1859), v. 97, 412

Waiting Game (1891), v. 765

Waits (Taylor, T. P., 1849), iv. 411

Wait till I'm a Man (Hazlewood, C. H., 1868), v. 413

Wake not the Dead (Almar, G., 1824), iv. 550, 642

+ Walberg; or, Temptation (Smith, Sophia Mary: printed in *The Eastern Princess and Other Poems*)

Walcot Castle (Goldsmith, M., 1804) = Angelina, iv. 550, 642

Waldeck (Slous, A. R., 1852), v. 816

+ Waldemar, surnamed Seir (Chapman, J. F., 12° 1841 [Translated from a play by B. S. Ingemann]

Walker, London (Barrie, J. M., 1892), v. 187, 211, 251

Walker's Trunks (1837), iv. 550

Walk for a Wager! (Peake, R. B., 1819), iv. 369

Walking Statue (Hill, A., 1710), ii. 133, 336

— = Devil in the Wine-Cellar

Wallace (Buchanan, R., 1856), v. 284

— (Grahame, J., 1799), iii. 347; iv. 586

— (Waddie, C., 1898), v. 610

— (Walker, C. E., 1820), iv. 416

— (1833), iv. 550

— = (1) Caledon's Tears; (2) Patriot

Wallace and Bruce (Robe, 1869), v. 544

Wallace the Brave (McLaren, A., 1819), iv. 352

Wallace, the Hero of Scotland (Barrymore, W., 1817), iv. 262, 570

Wallachian (1854), v. 765

Wallenstein (1799, 1800), iv. 87, 550

— = Piccolomini

Wallenstein's Camp (Gower, Lord F. L., 1830), iv. 320

Wall of China (Matthison, A., 1876), v. 481

Walls have Ears (Grain, R. C., 1894), v, 388

Walloons (Cumberland, R., 1782), iii. 126, 251

Walooka and Noomahee (1825), iv. 550

Walpole (Lytton, Baron, 1869), v. 466, 804

Walpurghi's Eve (1830), iv. 550

Walpurgis Night (Atkyns, S., 1844), iv. 257

— (1859), v. 849

Walsha (Haines, J. T., 1841) = Warlsha, iv. 551, 587 [The title appears both as Warlsha and Walsha: the correct date is 26/4/41]

— (1837), iv. 550, 587

Walter (Warmington, G., 1846), iv. 616

Walter Brand (Fitzball, E., 1833), iv. 314

Walter Lorimer (1845), iv. 550

Walter, the Mechanic (1854), v. 765

35

Wanted, Husbands for Six (Kenney, C. L., 1867), v. 443

Wanted Immediately (1895), v. 765

Wanted 1000 Spirited Young Milliners (Coyne, J. S., 1852), v. 327

Wanted to Marry (Sawyer, W., 1849), IV. 397

Wanton Countess (1733), II. 386

Wanton Jesuit (1731), II. 387

Wanton Trick'd (1743), II. 387

Wanton Wife = Amorous Widow

Wants and Superfluities = Azim

Wapping Landlady (1748), II. 387

— = (1) All Alive at Liverpool; (2) Sailor's Wedding

Wapping Old Stairs (Blake, T. G., 1834), IV. 268

— (Faucit, J. S., 1837), IV. 311

— (Holl, H., 1834), IV. 326

— (Robertson, S., 1894), v. 545

War (Daly, C., 1871), v. 334

— (Robertson, T. W., 1871), v. 129–31, 546

War and Peace (Barrymore, W., 1814), IV. 261

— (1855), v. 765

War Balloon (Lovegrove, W., 1871), v. 463

War Cloud (Barrs, H., 1895), v. 252

War Correspondent (Corbett, Mrs G. and Boyne, W., 1898), v. 324

Ward and Brother = Outwitted at Last

Warden (1855), v. 765

Warden of Galway (Groves, E., 1831), IV. 321, 586

— = Lynch Law

Wardock Kennilson (Fitzball, E., 1824), IV. 312, 584

Ward of France (1897), v. 765

Ward of the Castle (Burke, Miss, 1793) III. 241, 378

Wards and Wardens (1830), IV. 551

Wards in Chancery = Irish Dragoon

War in Abyssinia (1868), v. 765

War in India = (1) Burmese War; (2) Sikh's Invasion

War in Syria (1840), IV. 551

War in Turkey (1854), v. 765

War in Zululand (1879), v. 765

Warlock (Smythe, A., 1892), v. 573

Warlock of the Glen (Walker, C. E., 1820), IV. 416, 615

Warlock of the Glen (1827), IV. 551

Warlocks of the Border = Chevy Chase

War, Love and Duty = Africans

War, Love and Peace (Lee, N., 1848), IV. 343

Warlsha (Harris, J. T., 1841) = Walsha, IV. 587 [The title appears both as Warlsha and Walsha: the correct date is 26/4/41]

Warming Pan = My Lord

Warm Member (Seaton, P., 1898), v. 559

— = Ballyhooley

Warm Members (1891), v. 765

Warm Reception = Bobby No. 1

Warning Bell of Ronguerall = Memoirs of the D—l

Warning Dream (Pitt, G. D., 1851), v. 526

Warning Spirit = Lady Anne's Well

Warning to Bachelors (Mortimer, J., 1871), v. 494

Warning to Mesmerists = Baby

Warning to Parents (Roberts, G., 1877), v. 544

Warning to Wives (1849), IV. 551

Warning Vision = Twin Brothers

Warning Voice (Lee, N., Jr., 1864), v. 765, 849

— = Bletchington House

War of Paris in 1649 = Partisans

War of Wealth (Dazey, C. T. and Vane, S., 1898), v. 340

War of Wits = Midnight Hour

Warranted (1875), v. 765

Warranted Burglar Proof (Stephenson, B. C., 1888), v. 582

Warranted Sound and Quiet in Harness (Douglass, J. T., 1871), v. 348

Warrior and his Child (1843) IV. 642

Warrior and the Crescent = Enchanted Palfrey

Warrior Bold (1879), v. 765

Warrior Boy (Burton, E. G., 1851), v. 294

Warrior Kings (1835), IV. 551

Warrior of the Sun = Storming of Quito

Warrior Peasant (1847), IV. 642

Warrior's Career = Emperor's Decree

Warrior's Faith (1834), IV. 551

Warrior Slaves (1841), IV. 551

Warrior's Steed = Corasco

Warrior Women = Last of the Race
Wars in China = Chinese War
Wars in Spain (Corn, G. E., 1844), IV.
283
— (1837), IV. 551
Wars in Wedlock = Spanish Bonds
Wars of the Jews (Blake, T. G., 1848),
IV. 551, 642
Wars of the Punjab (1846), IV. 551
Wars of the Roses = King Maker
Wars of Wellington (Amherst, J. H.,
1834), IV. 551, 642
War—the Fugitives (Abel, W. H., 1871),
V. 234
War Time (1867), v. 765
War to the Knife (Byron, H. J., 1865),
v. 297
War Trail (Townsend, W. T., 1857), v.
765, 821, 849
War versus Art (Wilson, M., 1898), v.
628
War versus Law = Quits
War Whoop = Americans
Warwickshire Jubilee = Shakespear's
Garland
Warwick the Kingmaker (Lancaster,
E. R.), IV. 593
Warwick the King Maker and the Battle
of Barnet = Last of the Barons
+ War with the Danes; or, Wild Eric of
the Hills (Pav. 15/2/1864) [A revised
version of The Sea King's Vow, by
E. Stirling]
War with the Waves (Stirling, E., 1864),
v. 584
War Wolf = Zapolyta
War Woolf of Tlascala (1828) IV. 551
Wary Widow (Higden, R., 1693), I.
13, 16, 18, 27, 218, 413
Washed Ashore (1894), v. 765
Washerwoman of St Remy (1846), IV.
551
Was he the Man? (1870), v. 765
Washington Watts (Schonberg, J.,
1879), v. 557
Was it a Dream? (Staples, E. B., 1896),
v. 579
Was I to blame? (Rodwell, G. H., 1830),
IV. 395
Wasted Life (Osmond, L. and Herbert,
F. H., 1894), v. 508
Wasted Lives (France, E. S.), v. 792

Wasted Lives (1875), v. 765
— = Nell Snooks
Wastrel (Byatt, H. and Moss, H., 1894),
v. 295
Watch and Wait (Higgie, T. H. and
Shepherd, R., 1871),
Watch and Ward (Wigan, A. S., 1844),
IV. 419, 617
Watch Cry (Simpson, J. P., 1865), v.
110, 567
Watchdog (1854), v. 765
— = Carlo
Watchdog of the Castle (1844). IV. 551
Watchdog of the Walsinghams (Simp-
son, J. P., 1869), v. 568
Watchers on the Longships (1885), v.
765
Watchful Mother Duped = Kate of
Brockmoor
Watch-house (Galt, J., 1814), IV. 318,
635
Watching and Waiting (Hodgson, A. H.
and Hodgson, A. C., 1891), v. 423
Watching and Winning = Brought to
Light
Watching the Body (1848), IV. 551
Watchmaker of Clerkenwell (Wilks,
T. E., 1843), IV. 421
Watchman (1829), IV. 551
Watchman of New York (1856), v. 765
Watchman's Secret = Found Dying
Watch Tower (1859), v. 849
Watch-word (Bell, R., 1816) = Assassin,
IV. 112, 264, 428, 572
Watchwords of Old London = Young
Apprentice
Water and Fire = Drenched and Dried
Water Babes (Bowles, E. W., 1887), v.
271
Water Carnival (1890), v. 765
Water Carrier (1875), v. 765
— = Escapes
Water-carrier and the Beauty (1831), IV.
551
Watercress Girl (Travers, W., 1865), v.
765, 821, 849
Water Cure (Felix, A., 1883), v. 364
Water Kelpie (1844), IV. 551
Water King = Flying Fish
Waterloo (Akhurst, W. M., 1876), v. 237
Waterloo Bridge (Dibdin, T. J., 1817),
IV. 300

Weak Woman (Byron, H. J., 1875), v. 114, 298

We all have our little Faults (Suter, W. E., 1864), v. 588

Weal or Woe (Vaughan, A., 1878), v. 607

Wealth (Jones, H. A., 1889), v. 160, 439

— (Lacy, M. R., 1870), v. 446

— (Wright, F., 1877), v. 633

Wealth and Poverty (Denvil, Mrs, 1841), IV. 579

— (1855), v. 766

Wealth and Pride = Merchant's Daughter

Wealth and Want (Newton, E., 1884), v. 503

— (Rede, W. L., 1835), IV. 390

Wealth Got and Lost (Hazlewood, C. H., 1870), v. 414

Wealth of Shylock (1851), v. 766

Wealth of the World (Lampard, E. J., 1891), v. 446

Wealth Outwitted = Money is an Asse

Wealthy Widow (Poole, J., 1827), IV. 386

We are seven = Sir George and a Dragon

Wearing of the Green = (1) Cannie Soogah; (2) Lover's Leap

Wearin' o' the Green (Howard, W., 1896), v. 428

— (Matthews, E. C., 1896), v. 481

Weary of Bondage = Sybyle

Weary of Waiting = Lily's Love

Weathercock (Allingham, J. T., 1805), IV. 132, 252

— (Forrest, T., 1775), III. 261

— (1811), IV. 552

Weather Hen (Thomas, B. W. and Barker, H. G., 1899), v. 595

Weathering the Admiral = Barrington's Busby

Weather or No (Ross, A. and Beach, W., 1896), v. 551

Weather Permitting (Snow, W. R., 1872), v. 573

Weatherwise (Newton, H. C., 1893), v. 503

Weaver's Daughter (Darlington, W., 1883), v. 336

Weaver of Lyons (Barber, J., 1844), IV. 259

Weaver's Distress = Mary Barton

Weaver's Wife (Pitt, G. D., 1845), IV. 374

Webb worried by Wyndham (Webb, C., 1852), v. 617

Web of Fate (Tullock, A., 1899), v. 604

Webster at Home (Lemon, M., 1853), v. 455

Webster's Royal Red Book (1849), IV. 552

Webster's Wallet of Whims and Waggaries (Webster, B. N., 1836), IV. 417

Wedded (1884), v. 766

Wedded and Lost (Travers, W., 1868), v. 603

Wedded and Wooed = Lady Clancarty

Wedded Bliss (Gordon, G. L., 1871), v. 384

— (Paulton, H., 1882), v. 516

Wedded, not Wived (Coleman, J., 1886), v. 316

Wedded to Crime (Jarman, F. and Selwyn, W., 1891), v. 434

Wedding (Hawker, E., 1729), II. 237, 242, 334

— (1734), II. 387

Wedding Bells (Merton, C., 1876), v. 488

Wedding Breakfast (Morton, J. M., 1843), IV. 362

— (Parry, J., 1866), v. 514

Wedding Day (Fielding, H., 1743), II. 178, 328, 436

— (Inchbald, Mrs E., 1794), III. 185, 190, 275

— (Logan, J.), III. 282

Wedding Dinner = Cook

Wedding Eve (Hazlewood, C. H., 1864), v. 766, 796, 849

— (Howe, J. B., 1867), v. 428, 798

— (Yardley, W., 1892), v. 634

Wedding Gown (Jerrold, D. W., 1834), IV. 332

Wedding Guest (Jones, H. A., 1882), v. 439

Wedding March (Gilbert, W. S., 1873), v. 379

— = Haste to the Wedding

Wedding Night (Cobb, J., 1780), III. 243, 379

— (1740), II. 448

— = Marriage Night

Wedding Present (Arthur, A., 1888), v. 244
— (Kenney, J., 1825), IV. 337
— (1881), v. 766
Wedding Ring (Dibdin, C., 1773), III. 122, 202, 254, 381
Wedding Supper (1834), IV. 552
Wedlock = Ariane
Wee Curly (1883), v. 766
Weeds (Pemberton, T. E., 1874), v. 519
— (Walford, H. L., 1871), v. 611
— = Idol
Weeds and Flowers (Abel, W. H., 1870), v. 234
Weeds and Flowers of Erin (Macdermott, G. H., 1870), v. 468
Week at Holyrood (1832), IV. 552
Week in Turkey = Sultan and the Slave
Weekly Journalist = Craftsman
"Weel may the Keel row" = Jessie, the Flower of Dumblane
Weeping Cross = Dick Wilder
Weeping Willow (Davey, P., Linford, H. and Ram, H. S., 1886), v. 338
We Fly by Night (Colman, G., the Younger, 1806), IV. 282, 577
— (1813), IV. 552
We have all our Deserts (Woodfall, H. S.), III. 317
Wehr Wolves of St Grieux (1833), IV. 552
Weighed in the Balance (Hoskins, W. H., 1881), v. 427
Weird Destiny (Stanhope, W., 1888), v. 579
Weird Experience (Marriott, G. M., 1895), v. 477
Weird Sisters (Dibdin, C. I. M., 1819), v. 284
— (1793), III. 347
— (1802), IV. 552
— (1804), IV. 552
Weirds of the Rhine = Rudolph of Hapsburg
Weird Wanderer of Jutland = Elfrid
Weird Woman of the Isles (Milner, H. M., 1824), IV. 552, 642
Weir Wolf (Slight, H., 1844), IV. 611
Welch Chieftains = Red Hands
Welch Heiress (Jerningham, E., 1795), III. 7, 169–70, 196, 277

Welch Rabbits, Rarebits (Johnstone, J. B., 1863), v. 766, 849
Welcome and Farewell (Harness, W., 1837), IV. 587
Welcome Home (Wilks, T. E., 1842), IV. 421
— (1827), IV. 552
— (1860), v. 766
— = Paternal Affection
Welcome Little Stranger (Albery, J., 1890), v. 238
— (Lemon, M., 1857), v. 766, 803, 849
Welcome Messenger (1885), v. 766
Welcome Visit (Norwood, E., 1887), v. 505
Well and the Treasure = Punch in Paris
Weller Family (+ Emson, F. E., 1878: 8°, 1878), v. 766
Wellington (1852), v. 766
Wellington and Waterloo (1852), v. 766
Wellington, Nelson and Napoleon (1852), v. 766
Wellington's Laurels = Vittoria
Well Matched (Havard, P., 1887), v. 410
Well of Love = Eveline
Well of Marble Water = Giant's Castle
Well of St Marie = Red Farm
Well of Wishes (Brook, B., 1889), v. 276
Well Paired (Morley, F. G., 1879), v. 493
Well Played (Knight, A. F., 1888), v. 445
Wells in the Days of Queen Bess = Old Sadler's Ghost
We'll Watch (1859), v. 766
Well Won = Fleurs de Lys
Welsh Dairy (Byrne, J., 1802), IV. 575
Welsh Feuds = Owen, Prince of Powys
Welsh Girl (Planché, Mrs J. R., 1833), IV. 130, 383
— (1855), v. 766
Welsh Heiress (Cullum, W. T., 1893), v. 331 [An advertisement in The Era for 1897 claims a play of this name for Theodore A. Sharp]
Welshman (Milner, H. M., 1826), IV. 552, 642
Welsh Opera (Fielding, H., 1731), II. 245, 324
Welsh Orphan (Cavendish, P., 1894), v. 306
Welsh Rabbits (Summers, K. and Reece, R., 1881), v. 587
Welsh Wolf (Pitt, G. D., 1851), v. 526

What's bred in the Bone = Who's to Father Her?

What shall I do for a Ticket? = Bal Masqué

What shall I sing? (Blunt, R., 1892), v. 266

What's in a Name? (Green, K., 1895), v. 392

— (Moncrieff, W. T., 1835), IV. 552, 642

— (1829), IV. 552

— (1880), v. 766

What's in the Wind? = (1) Up the Flue; (2) Who did it?

What's it on? (Routledge, W., 1870), v. 552

What's the Clock? = Mysterious Murder

What's the Matter? (Oulton, W. C., 1789), III. 296

What's the News? = Old Quizzes

What's the Odds? (Jones, J. W., 1882), v. 440

What's the Result? = All in One

What's to be Seen? = Bill of Fare

What's your Game? (Bruton, H., 1858), v. 284

What! The Devil Again! (Murray, W. H., 1833), IV. 552, 642

What to Eat, Drink and Avoid (1848), IV. 552

What was found in a Celebrated Case = Over-Proof

What We Have Been and What We May Be (Siddons, H., 1796), III. 307

What We Must All Come To (Murphy, A., 1763), III. 7, 181, 290, 392

— = Three Weeks after Marriage

What will become of him? (Marchant, F., 1872), v. 476

What Will be the End of It? = Emmeline of Hungary

What will he do next? (1825), IV. 552

What will he do with it? (Lightfoot, 1871), v. 459

— (Phillips, F. L., 1859), v. 766, 810, 849

What will my Aunt say? (1850) = Forbidden Fruit, v. 679, 766, 832, 849

What will my Lady say? = Knight of the Boots

What will my Wife say? = Assignation

What will the Neighbours say? (Douglass, J. T., 1873), v. 348

What will the World say? (Bancroft, G. P., 1899), v. 248

— (Gillum, W., 1787), III. 265

— (Lemon, M., 1841), IV. 344

— = Captain Tarradiddle

What will they say at Brompton? (Coyne, J. S., 1857), v. 328

What Women will do (Jerome, J. K., 1890), v. 436

What won't a Woman do? = Venus in Arms

What Would She Not? (Ross, W., 1790), III. 303

What would the Man be at? (1801), IV. 552

What you please (1750–1800), III. 405

— (1788), III. 347

— = Crisis

Wheedling (Lunn, J., 1832), IV. 552, 642

Wheel of Death = Black Vulture

Wheel of Fortune (Collier, H., 1883), v. 317

— (Cumberland, R., 1795), III. 128–9, 252, 381

— (Howell-Poole, W., 1890), v. 429

— = Fool's Expectation

Wheel of Life (1856), v. 766

Wheel of Time (Bannister, T. B., 1892), v. 248

Wheels within Wheels (Carton, R. C., 1899), v. 305

— (Dibdin, T. J., 1820), IV. 302

— (1873), v. 766

When a Man's in Love (Hope, A. and Rose, E., 1898), v. 425

— = Man in Love

When George was King = Master of Hope

When George III was King (Rimington, C., 1893), v. 543

When George IV was King (Moore, F. W., 1896), v. 492

When Greek meets Greek = Roll of the Drum

When it takes Place (1820), IV. 552

When London Sleeps (Darrell, C., 1896), v. 337

When one Door shuts another opens (Thomas, C., 1885), v. 596

When Poverty comes in at the Door = Love and Poverty

When Rogues fall out (1898), v. 766

When the Bell Tolls (1819), IV. 552

When the Cat's Away (Matthews, A. K., 1896), V. 480

When the Clock Strikes (1820), IV. 552

— = Golden Farmer

When the Clock strikes Nine (Hazlewood, C. H., 1869), V. 413

When the Lamps are lighted (Sims, G. R. and Merrick, L., 1897), V. 570

When the Wheels run down (Rogers, M. M., 1899), V. 548

When Widows wooed (Chevalier, A., 1899), V. 309

Where are you going to, my Pretty Maid? = Naomi's Sin

Where did the Money come from? = Two Gregories

Where have you been? (1888), V. 766

Where is Eliza? (1847), IV. 552

Where is She? = Who Wants a Guinea

Where is she gone? (Baron-Wilson, Mrs C., 1832), IV. 570

Where is the Note? = Miss Pop

Where's Brown? (Legg, J., 1859), V. 766, 803, 835, 849

— (1859), V. 766

Where's Crevelli? (Howard, J. and Cooper, F. F., 1854), V. 766, 786, 798, 849

Where's Eliza? (James, C. S., 1847), IV. 330, 552, 590, 642

Where shall I dine? (Rodwell, G. H., 1819), IV. 395

Where's Mr Smith (Conquest, G., 1858), V. 766, 785, 849

Where's Prodgers? (Hester, E., 1896), V. 420

Where's the Cat? (Albery, J., 1880), V. 238

Where's the Child? = Philip and his Dog

Where's the Wig? = Sportsman and the Shepherd

Where's your Wife? (Bridgeman, J. V., 1863), V. 275

Where there's a Will = My Great Aunt

Where there's a Will there's a Way (Morton, J. M., 1849), IV. 363

— = Black Squire

Where to find a Friend (Leigh, R., 1811), IV. 343, 553, 594

Which? (Bagot, A. G., 1886), V. 247

Which can be the Man? (1821), IV. 553

Which is He? = (1) Snake in the Grass; (2) William Thompson

Which is it? (Robertson, T. W., 1881), V. 546

— (Tully, J. H., 1862), V. 604, 822

Which is Mine? = Old Soldier

Which is my Cousin? (Raymond, R. J., 1825), IV. 388

— = Love and Mystery

Which is my Husband? (1861), V. 766

— = Giralda

Which is my Love? (1846), IV. 553

Which is my Son? = (1) Middle Temple; (2) Tricks and Blunders

Which is the Bride? = Tale of Other Times

Which is the Dandy? = Ultra Exquisite

Which is the Girl? = Irish Tar

Which is the King? (Watts, W., 1848), IV. 417

Which is the Lady? = Sleepwalker

Which is the Man (Cowley, Mrs H., 1782), III. 141, 166-7, 248

Which is the Manager? = Odds and Ends

Which is the Miller? = Peter Smink

Which is the Real Dog (1799), III. 347

Which is the Right One? = Round of Intrigue

Which is the Thief? (Barber, J., 1843), IV. 259

— = Maid and the Magpye

Which is the Uncle? (Watts, W., 1841), IV. 417, 616

Which is the Woman? (1833), IV. 553

Which is Thomas? = Black and White

Which is which? (Smith, S. T., 1871), V. 573

— (1810), IV. 553

— (1878), V. 766

— = (1) Fire of London; (2) King and the Duke; (3) Twins

Which Mr Smith? (Reach, A. B., 1846), IV. 389

Which of the Two? (Morton, J. M., 1859), V. 496

Which shall I marry? = Whom shall I marry?

While there's Life there's Hope = False Accusation

Which wins? (Piggott, J. W., 1889), V. 524

Whiffin and Co. (1893), V. 766

Whig and Tory (Griffin, B., 1720), II.
37, 140, 198-9, 333
While it's to be had (Collette, C., 1874),
V. 317
While there's Life there's Hope
(Brougham, J., 1863), v. 280
While the Snow is falling (1873), v. 766
Whim (Macklin, C., 1764), III. 284
— (Wallace, Lady E., 1795), III. 19,
314, 397
— (1734), II. 387
— (1741), II. 387, 448
Whim of the Moment (1797), III. 347
— = Love's Vagaries
Whims and Fancies = Self-Tormentor
Whims and Wonders = Table Talk
Whimsicality (McLaren, A., 1810), IV.
351
Whimsical Ladies = Bristol Sailor
Whimsical Lovers (Foote, S., 1762), III.
384
Whimsical Serenade (Horde, T., 1781),
III. 273
Whims of Love = Automaton
Whines from the Wood = Babes
W[h]ines from the Wood = Madeira
Whip Hand (Merivale, H. C. and Dale,
C., 1885), v. 487
Whipping Post (France, E. S., 1884), v.
372
Whips of Steel (Dilley, J. J. and Row-
sell, M. C., 1889), v. 345
Whirligig (Hardwicke, P., 1875), v. 795
Whirlwind (Rosenfeld, S., 1890), v. 550
Whiskey and Water (1854), v. 849
Whiskey Demon (1867), v. 766
Whisky and Water (Shands, G. W.,
1854), v. 561, 849
Whisperer = Redmond of the Hills
Whist (Wilson, F., 1879), v. 628
Whistle (1836), IV. 553
Whistle for it (Lambe, G., 1807), IV. 341
Whistler (Pitt, G. D., 1833), IV. 93, 372,
604
— (Pitt, G. D., 1841), IV. 373, 604
White and Red Roses, and the Robber
Woodcutters = Margaret of Anjou
Whitebait at Cremorne (1865), v. 766
Whitebait at Greenwich (Morton,
J. M., 1853), v. 495
White Bard's Tower (1820), IV. 553
White Bear (1898), v. 766

White Bear = Captain MacShane
White Blackbird (Bowyer, F. and
Edwardes-Sprange, W., 1898), v. 272
White Boy (Taylor, T., 1866), v. 593
White Boys (Towers, E., 1862), v. 766,
820, 849
— = Rebel Chief
White Boys: A Tale of the Irish Rebel-
lion of 1798 (Plunkett, H. G., 1862),
v. 766, 794, 811, 849
White Boys of Ireland = Black Hugh the
Outlaw
White Boys of Kerry (Grattan, H. P.,
1872), v. 389
White Cat (Blanchard, E. L., 1877), v.
265, 779
— (Burnand, F. C., 1870), v. 289
— (Leigh, H. S., 1875), v. 454
— (Planché, J. R., 1842), IV. 381
— (1811), IV. 553
— (1813), IV. 553
Whitechapel in 1740 = Murder of the
Mount
White Chateau (Conquest, G., 1861), v.
767, 785
— (1852), v. 849
White Chief (1866), v. 767
White Cliffs (Meritt, P. and Pettitt, H.,
1880), v. 486
White Cliffs of Albion = White Cliffs
White Cockade (Barnett, R. W. and
Harris, C., 1895), v. 250
— (Cook, D., 1892), v. 323
— (Phillips, W., 1871), v. 523
— (Taylor, T., 1874), v. 594
— = Vive le Roi
White Cross Knight (1834), IV. 553
White Cuirassier (Simonton, H. W.,
1895), v. 566
White Devil (Freeman, C., 1893), v. 373
White Eagle (1828), IV. 553
White Elephant (Carton, R. C., 1896),
v. 305
— (Hayman, H., 1875), v. 411
— (Heathcote, A. M., 1894), v. 415
White Fairy (1830), IV. 553
White Farm (Lucas, W. J., 1856), v. 464
— (1847), IV. 553
— = Assassin Labourer
White Fawn (Burnand, F. C., 1868), v.
289
White Feather (1844), IV. 553

Whitefeet (1832), IV. 553

White Fox (1779), III. 406

Whitefriars (Townsend, W. T., 1844), IV. 414, 615

— (1838), IV. 643

White Goat = Fifteenth Carbineers

White-Hands (Spicer, H., 1856), V. 817

White Hat (1873), V. 767

White Hawk Lady (Bew, C., 1831) = Brighton Cliff, IV. 572, 436, 621

White Heather (Raleigh, C. and Hamilton, H., 1897), V. 534

White Hood (Planché, J. R., 1850), V. 527

White Hoods (1838), IV. 553

White Horse = Mrs H.

White Horse of Nick of the Woods = Jibbenainosay

White Horse of the Peppers (Lover, S., 1838), IV. 347

White Hypocrite (Mackenzie, H.), III. 284

White Indian (Towers, E., 1860), V. 767, 821, 849

White Joke (1730), II. 387

White Knight (Ogilvie, G. S., 1898), V. 506

White Lady (Beazley, S., 1826), IV. 84, 93, 553, 642

— (1892), V. 767

— (1893), V. 767

White Lie (Grundy, S., 1889), V. 397

— (Mortimer, J., 1888), V. 494

White Lies (Lunn, J., 1826), IV. 348

— (Stones-Davidson, T. W., 1896) = Taradiddles, V. 585, 767, 818, 849

— (1886), V. 767

White Lily (1891), V. 767

White Lion (1833), IV. 553

White Magic (Chorley, H. F., 1852), V. 310, 783

White Maid (Payne, J. H., 1827), IV. 84, 93, 369

White Maid of Avenel = Monastery

White Maiden of California (Fitzball, E., 1849), IV. 317

White Maiden of Tiernaboul = Cluricanne's Tower

White Mask = May Dudley

White Milliner (Jerrold, D. W., 1841), IV. 333

White Nun (1831), IV. 553

White Nun of Wakefield (Pitt, G. D., 1849), IV. 376

White of the Prairie = War Trail

White Palfrey (Suter, W. E., 1858) = Roland and his Steed, V. 744, 767, 819, 845, 849

White Passport (1869), V. 767

White Phantom (Pitt, C., 1867), V. 525

White Pilgrim (Merivale, H. C., 1874), V. 487

White Pilgrims (1820), IV. 553

White Plume (Dibdin, T. J., 1806), IV. 52, 298

White Queen (Boulding, J. W., 1883), V. 270

— (1889), V. 767

White Rabbit of Edinburgh = Royal Scots Fusiliers

White Rose (Sims, G. R. and Buchanan, R., 1892), V. 569

— = Housekeeper

White Rose and the Red Rose (1835), IV. 553

+ White Rose of the Plantation; or, Lubly Rosa, Sambo don't come (Byron, H. J.: Dicks (in Sensation Dramas))

White Roses (Gilbert, E., 1891), V. 378

Whiter than Snow (Lee, K., 1885), V. 452

White Scarf (1864), V. 767

— = Louise

White Serjeants (Selby, C., 1850) = Buttermilk Volunteers, V. 560, 654

White Silk Dress (Dam, H. J. W., 1896), V. 334

White Slave (Campbell, B., 1882), V. 301

— (Pitt, G. D., 1845), IV. 374

— (Stirling, E., 1849), IV. 409

White Slave of Guadeloupe = Ship Boy

White Spectre (Amherst, J. H., 1828), IV. 254

White Spirit (Burton, E. G., 1850), V. 294

White Squall (Haines, J. T.?, 1839), IV. 553, 643

White Star (1891), V. 767

White Stocking (Ferris, E. and Stewart, A., 1896), V. 365

White Stockings (Hannon, G. W., 1888), V. 403

White Surrey (Dibdin, C. I. M., 1825), IV. 295, 553, 580, 643

White Warrior = Zameo

White Witch (Dibdin, C. I. M., 1808), IV. 292

White Wolf (Dibdin, T. J., 1827), IV. 305

— (Rayner, B. F., 1841), IV. 389

— (1840), IV. 553

White Wreath (1840), IV. 553

Whitson Holidays (1749), II. 387

Whitsun Eve (Lancaster, E. R.?, 1839), IV. 553, 643; V. 849

Whitsun Monday (1788), III. 347

Whitsuntide (1851), V. 767, 849

Whittington (Farnie, H. B., 1874), V. 362

— (?1668), I. 446

— (1876, 1881), V. 767

Whittington and his Cat (Akhurst, W. M., 1877), V. 237

— (Blanchard, E. L., 1875), V. 264

— (Blanchard, E. L., 1884), V. 265

— (Burnand, F. C., 1881), V. 291

— (Byron, H. J., 1861), V. 296

— (Davey, S., ?1739), II. 317

— (Douglass, J. T., 1873), V. 348

— (Glover, E., 1853), V. 382

— (Henry, A., 1882), V. 417

— (James, D. S., 1892), V. 433

— (Lennard, H., 1890), V. 455

— (Muskerry, W., 1888), V. 501

— (+Smith, A., Taylor, T. and Kenney, C., 1845), IV. 553

— (Soutar, R., 1868), V. 575

— (Thorne, G., 1887), V. 598

— (Thorne, G., 1891), V. 599

— (1795), III. 347

— (1835, 1837, 1849), IV. 553

— (1859), V. 849

— (1865, 1870, 1877, 1881, 1885, 1886, 1895), V. 767

Whittington Junior and his Sensation Cat (Reece, R., 1870), V. 537

Who am I? (1819), IV. 553

— = Asleep or Awake

Who Bids Most? = Wife to be Sold

Who but he? = Dash

Who can have taken it? = Mysterious Theft

Who can help it? = C'est l'amour, l'amour, l'amour

Who can I be? (1818), IV. 553

Who dare Sneeze? = O.P. Victorious

Who'd be a Manager? (1876), V. 767

Who'd have thought it? (Cobb, J., 1781), III. 243

— (1763), III. 406

Who did it? (Vollaire, H., 1875), V. 609

— (1846), IV. 554

— (1867), V. 767

Who did you take me for? (Morton, J. M., 1847), IV. 363

Who has seen Tommy Toddle? (1850), V. 767

Who is he? (1873), V. 767

Who is Sarah? (McCabe, C. W., 1889), V. 467

Who is She? (Simpson, J. P., 1871), V. 568

— (Stirling, E., 1845), IV. 408

— = Deuce is in Her

Who is she like? (1793) = Tale of the Castle, III. 345, 347, 406

Who is Sylvia? (Fryers, W., 1887), V. 374

Who is that knocking at the Door? (1847), IV. 554

Who is to Marry Princess Royal? = Comedy of Terrors

Who is who? = (1) All in a Fog; (2) Transformation

Who is who and which is which? = King Kokatoo

Who killed Cock Robin? (Mathews, C. J., 1829), IV. 554, 643

— (Mathews, C. J., 1865), V. 480

— = Stage Dora

Who killed the —? = Very Earliest Edition of Il Trovatore

Who kissed Jeannette? (1819), IV. 554

Whole Hog (1844), IV. 554

Who lives at Number Nine? (1849), IV. 554

Who'll buy a Duck? = Geoffrey Dunstan

Who'll lend me a Wife? (Millingen, J. G., 1834), IV. 356

Who'll serve the Queen? (1855), V. 767

Who lodges at No. 1? (1853), V. 767

Whom shall I Marry? (Suter, W. E., 1863), V. 588, 819

Whom the Gods love (1882), V. 767

Who Owns the Hand? = Monk, the Mask and the Murderer

Who Owns the Head? (1821), IV. 554

Who Pays the Bill? = Blind Man's Buff

Who Pays the Piper? (1803) = Bad Customers, IV. 554, 643

— (1810), IV. 554

— = Blind Man's Buff

Who Pays the Reckoning? (Arnold, S. J., 1795), III. 234, 377

Who pays the Rent? (1797), III. 347

— = Quarter Day

Who Rules? = Sultan and the Slave

Who's Afraid? (Carr, Sir J., 1805), IV. 279

— (Jodrell, R. P., 1787), III. 277

— = Hop

Who's Afraid? Ha! Ha! Ha! = Who's Afraid

Who's at Home? (1825), IV. 554

Who's a Traveller? (Howard, J. and Cooper, F. F., 1854), V. 767, 786, 798, 849

Who's Drowned? = Hoax

Whose Baby? (1885), V. 767

Whose Wife? (Horridge, F., 1898), V. 427

— = Spiritualist

Who's for India? = Drapery Question

Who Shot the Dog? = Frightful Hair

Who's Married? (Adams-Acton, Mrs, 1893), V. 235

Who's my Father? (Morton, T., 1818), IV. 364

Who's my Husband? (Morton, J. M., 1847), IV. 363

— (1861), V. 767

Who's my Papa? (1845), IV. 554

Who speaks first? (Dance, C., 1849), IV. 289

Who's the Composer? (Morton, J. M., 1845), IV. 362

Who's the Dupe? (Cowley, Mrs H., 1779), III. 115, 186, 248

Who's the Heir? (March, M. G., 1869), V. 475

— = Prince Pedrillo

Who's the Murderer? (Dibdin, T. J., 1816), IV. 300

— = (1) Angeline; (2) Martin Faber

Who's the Richest? = Thirty Thousand

Who's the Rogue? (1801), IV. 554, 643

Who's the Victim? (Hazlewood, C. H., 1856), V. 797

Who's the Winner? = Game and Game

Who's to be Master? (1886), V. 767

Who's to Blame? (Meadows, T., 1805), IV. 355

— (1880), V. 767

Who stole the Pocketbook? (Morton, J. M., 1852), V. 495

Who stole the Tarts? (Silvester, F., 1894), V. 566

Who's to Father Her! (Planché, J. R., 1820), IV. 376

Who's to have her? (Dibdin, T. J., 1813), IV. 299

— (Sharpe, J., 1791) = Laura, III. 348, 395, 406

Who's to have him? (1831), IV. 554

— = Woman's Wit

Who's to inherit? = Poor Relations

+ Who Stole the Clock? (Lucas, W. J., French)

Who stole the Ducks? = Proscribed Royalist

Who Stole the Partridge? = Man and the Monkey

Who's to Teach? = Polka, Polka, Polka

Who's to win? (Branson, W. S., 1877), V. 274

— (1878), V. 767

Who's to Win her? = Woman's Whims

Who's to win him? (Williams, T. J., 1868), V. 118–19, 625

Who's who? (Poole, J., 1815), IV. 386

— (1853), V. 767

Who's Wife is She? (O'Neil, J. R., 1852), V. 507

Who's your Friend? (Planché, J. R., 1843), IV. 382

Who's your Hatter? (1855), V. 767

Who wants a Guinea? (Colman, G. the Younger, 1805), IV. 52, 282, 577

Who wants a Wife (Bishop, Sir H. R., 1816), IV. 267

Who will get her out? = Veteran

Who will he have? = Rifles

Who Wins? (Allingham, J. T., 1808) = Widow's Choice, IV. 252, 568

— (1866), V. 767

— = Loyal Lovers

Who would be married? (Addison, H. R., 1833), IV. 251

Who would have thought it? = Too Careful by Half

Will and No Will (Macklin, C., 1746, 1748), II. 342, 387, 440
— (1799), III. 348
Will and the Deed (Reynolds, F., 1797) = Will, III. 348, 394, 406
Will and the Way (Brown, W. M., 1853), v. 282, 787
— (Davis, S., 1854), v. 787
— (Hall, Mrs C., 1853), v. 399
— (McCarthy, J. H., 1890), v. 467
— (Pitt, G. D., 1853), v. 526
— (Seaman, W., 1853), v. 559
— (Waldron, W. R., 1860), v. 610
— (1853), v. 768
Will and the Word (1860), v. 768
— = Variety
Will Brockman (1831), IV. 555
Will for the Deed (Dibdin, T. J., 1804), IV. 298
— = Summer Flies
Will he come home again? = Two or One
Will he win her? = Britomart
William (Parker, L. N., 1892), v. 513
William II and ye Fayre Maid of Harrow (Lee, N., 1857), v. 452
William and Adelaide (Fitzball, E., 1830), IV. 313
William and Lucy (Paton, 1780), III. 296
William and Nancy = Cottagers
William and Nanny = Cottagers
William and Susan (Reynoldson, T. H., 1859), v. 542
— (Wills, W. G., 1880), v. 627
— (1785), III. 348
William March (1859), v. 768
William Rufus (Field, M., 1885), v. 366
William Simpson (Fitzgerald, P., 1872), v. 369
William's London Recollections (1830), IV. 555
William's Morsels of Mirth (1831), IV. 555
William's Return (1811), IV. 555
William Tell (Banfield, T. C., 1831), IV. 86, 258
— (Buckingham, L. S., 1857), v. 20, 286
— (Grosett, H. W., 1812), IV. 86, 321, 586
— (Knowles, J. S., 1825), IV. 172, 339
— (Molini, Miss, 1846), IV. 87, 358

William Tell (O'Keeffe, J.), III. 295
— (O'Neil, A., 1867), v. 507
— (Peter, W., 1839), IV. 86, 371
— (Robinson, S., 1825), IV. 86, 394
— (Roche, E., 1808), IV. 86, 395
— (Talbot, R., 1829), IV. 86, 410
— (Taylor, T., Smith, A. R., Talfourd, F. and Hale, W. P., 1856), v. 593
— (Thompson, H., 1845), IV. 86, 413
— (Vœux, C. de, 1827), IV. 86, 415
— (1794), III. 348
— (1856), v. 768
— (1882), v. 768
William Tell, the Hero of Switzerland (1802), IV. 555
— (1821), IV. 87, 555
William Tell Told Again (Reece, R., 1876), v. 538
William Tell with a Vengeance (Byron, H. J., 1867), v. 297
William that married Susan (1859), v. 768
William the Conqueror (Blanchard, E. L., 1848), IV. 269
— (Fitzball, E., 1824), IV. 555, 643
William the Conqueror's Invasion of England (Courtney, J., 1844) = Invasion of England by William the Conqueror, IV. 555, 643
William the Great and Miguel the Little = Pills for Portugals
William Thompson (Boaden, C., 1829), IV. 269
Willie Armstrong (Poole, R., 1829), IV. 555
Willie the Wanderer (Rogers, F., 1866), v. 768, 814, 850
Willikind and his Dinah (Coyne, J. S., 1854), v. 327
Willing Sacrifice, v. 768
Willing Slave (Melford, M., 1883), v. 484
Will made in a Snowdrift on the Flyleaf of a Rake's Diary = Found Dying in the Streets
Will Nobody Marry Her? (Campbell, A. V., 1848), IV. 279
Will of Fate (1807), IV. 555
Will of the Wisp (Dibdin, C., 1795), III. 256
Will of Wise King Kino (Albery, J., 1873), v. 155–6, 237

Will, or the Widow (Hook, T. E., 1810), IV. 328

Will o' the Wisp (Addison, J., 1897), V. 236

— (Johnstone, J. B., 1859), V. 768, 800, 850

— (Seaman, W., 1859), V. 768, 815, 850

— (1869), V. 768

— (1879), V. 768

— (1890), V. 768

— =(1) Fanchette; (2) Fanchonette the Cricket; (3) Zelma

Willow Copse (Boucicault, D., 1849), IV. 270

Willow Grove (1824), IV. 555

— (1850), V. 768

Willow Marsh (Faucquez, A., 1862)= Forced Marriage, V. 768, 792, 832, 850

Willow Pattern Plate (Bowkett, S. and Day, G. D., 1897), V. 271

— (Hale, W. P. and Talfourd, F., 1851), V. 398

Willow Pool (1870), V. 769

Will Pontypridd (1875), V. 769

Will Reckless (1836), IV. 555

Will Tell (1895), V. 769

Will Watch (Amherst, J. H., ?1825), IV. 568

Will Watch, the Bold Smuggler=Blood demands its Victim

Will with a Vengeance (Hay, F., 1876), V. 411

Willy Reilly and his Own Dear Colleen Bawn (Brady, F., 1861), V. 273

Wilmore Castle (Houlton, R., 1800), III. 273; IV. 329

Wiltshire Tom (Kirkman, F., 1673), I. 418

Win and Wear (Berwick, E. L. A., 1859), V. 779

Wind and Wave (Moore, R., 1868), V. 492

Windmill (Morton, T., Jr., 1842), IV. 364, 601

Windmill Hill=Merry Pranks

Windmill Turrett=Bonifacio and Bridgetina

Window Curtain (1849), IV. 555

Windsor Castle (Burnand, F. C. and Williams, M., 1865), V. 288

— (Marchant, F., 1873), V. 476

Windsor Castle (Pearce, W., 1795), III. 297

— (1838), IV. 555

Windsor Installation=Knights of St George

Wind Up=Ghosts of Tom and Jerry

Wine and Passion=Amour

Wine does Wonders (1820), IV. 555

— =Ramah Droog

Wine Dresser's Daughter=Village Life in France

Wine Drinkers of Paris=Isabel Bertrand

Wine House (Taylor, T. P., 1839), IV. 411

Wine, Women and Gambling=Three Perils

Wings of the Storm (Barlow, R. J. and North, W., 1891), V. 249

Wings of Wealth (Clarke, A. H., 1894), V. 311

Win her and Take her (Smythe, J., 1691), I. 260, 432

Win Her and Wear Her (1832), IV. 555

— =Race for a Wife

Winifred's Vow (Douglass, J. T., 1892), V. 349

Winkelried (McAlister, J., 1837), IV. 349

Winkhopper's Plot (Rolfe, V. C., 1897), V. 549

Winki the Witch and the Ladies of Samarcand=Enchanted Girdles

Winkle's Waxworks (1883), V. 769

Winner (1894), V. 769

Winning a Husband (Macfarren, G., 1819), V. 339

Winning a Widow (1856), V. 769

Winning a Wife (1888), V. 769

Winning Card (Wood, A., 1867), V. 630

Winning Defeat (Campbell, D. and Quaire, M., 1891), V. 301

Winning Hand (Conquest, G. and Miller, St A., 1895), V. 323

Winning Hazard (Wooler, J. P., 1865), V. 119, 632

Winning Post (1885), V. 769

Winning Suit (Filmore, L., 1863), V. 366

Winning the Winner=Jockey

Winona, the Sioux Queen (1880), V. 769

Winterbottoms (Moncrieff, W. T., 1837), IV. 131-2, 360

— (1859), V. 769

Winter in London (1854), V. 769

Without a Home = Alone in the World·
Without Encumbrance (1895), v. 769
Without Incumbrances (Simpson, J. P.,
    1850), v. 567
Without Love (Yates, E. and Dubourg,
    A. W., 1872), v. 635
Without Money or Friends (Ellis, B.,
    1874), v. 357
With Safety Pins (1899), v. 769
With the Colours (Galer, E. J. N. and
    Mew, J., 1886), v. 375
Wit in Necessity = Fashionable Lover
Witness (Bayley, 1829), IV. 262
— (Galt, J., 1814) = Appeal, IV. 318,
    585, 635
— = Her Own Witness
Witness from the Grave (1859), v. 769
Wit of a Woman (Walker, T., 1704), II.
    209, 363
— = Love at First Sight
Wits (Kirkman, F., 1662, 1672), I. 2,
    417–18
Wit's Cabal (Cavendish, M., 1662), I.
    396
Wit's Last Stake (King, T., 1768), III.
    118, 279, 389
— = Will and no Will
Wits Led by the Nose (Chamberlayne,
    W., 1677), I. 396–7
Witt above Crowns = Love's Martyr
Wittikind and his Brothers (Taylor, T.,
    1852), v. 592
Witty Combat (Porter, T., 1663), I. 220,
    425
Witty False One = Madam Fickle
Witty Wife (1791), III. 348
Wives (Calmour, A. C., 1883), v. 300
Wives and Partners (1828), IV. 556
Wives as they Were and Maids as they
    Are (Inchbald, Mrs E., 1797), III. 46,
    145, 146, 149, 275, 388
Wives by Advertisement (Jerrold, D. W.,
    1828), IV. 331
Wives Excuse (Southerne, T., 1691), I.
    57, 240–1, 250, 433
Wives Incog. = Zulieman
Wives in Plenty (1793), III. 116, 348
Wives Metamorphos'd = Devil to Pay
Wives of Whitechapel (1850), v. 769
Wives Revenged (Dibdin, C., 1778), III.
    255, 381
Wizard (Arnold, S. J., 1817), IV. 95, 256

Wizard (Baylie, S., ?1680), I. 390
— (1777), III. 348
Wizard and the Winds = Sea Serpent
Wizard of Peru (1835), IV. 556
Wizard of the Black Moor = Graeme
Wizard of the Moor (Gott, H.), v. 386
— = Elshie
Wizard of the Nile (Smith, H. B., 1897),
    v. 572
+ The Wizard of the Silver Rocks; or,
    Harlequin's Release (S.W. Easter
    M., 1781)
Wizard of the Wave (Haines, J. T.,
    1840), IV. 323, 587
Wizard of the Wilderness (Reece, R.,
    1873), v. 537
Wizard of Venice = Golden Dream
Wizard Priest (Walker, J., 1833), IV.
    556, 615, 643
Wizard Schooner (Pitt, G. D., 1843),
    IV. 604
Wizard's Dream = Silver Swan
Wizard Skiff (Haines, J. T., 1831), IV.
    322
Wizards of the Rocks (1768), III. 348
Wizard's Ring = Robert the Devil
Wizard's Wake (Dibdin, C. I. M.,
    1802), IV. 290
Wizard Tree = Death Omen
Woggles' Waxworks (Capel, G., 1879),
    v. 302
Wolf and the Lamb (Wilks, T. E. or
    Mathews, C. J., 1832), IV. 420, 597, 617
— (1877), v. 769
— = (1) Brothers in Arms; (2) Supper
    for Two
Wolfe Tone (Whitbread, J. W., 1898),
    v. 620
Wolf-hunter of the Haitzberg = Wal-
    purgis Night
Wolf of Hornsey Wood (1851), v. 769
Wolf of St Ange = Marinette
Wolf of the Pyrenees (Travers, W.,
    1868), v. 603
Wolf Rock (1834), IV. 556
Wolowski (Magnus, T., 1838), IV. 597
Wolsey (Smith, J. F., 1845), IV. 403,
    556, 611, 643
Wolves (Coyne, G., 1882), v. 327
— (1870), v. 769
Wolves and Waifs (Cox, A., 1891), v.
    327

Woman (Boucicault, D., 1843), IV. 269
— (Falconer, E., 1861), V. 360
— (Thackeray, T. J., 1835), IV. 556, 643
— (Webb, C., 1852), V. 617
Woman against Woman (Harvey, F., 1883), V. 408
Woman and her Master (Davis, S., 1855), V. 787
— (Seaman, W., 1853), V. 559
— (Waldron, W. R., 1854), V. 610
Woman and Philosophy (Pinkerton, J., 1813), IV. 556, 643
Woman and the Law (1884), V. 769
Woman at the Wheel = Rumpelstiltskin and the Maid
Woman—Beware of Woman! (1835), IV. 556
Woman from the People (1882), V. 769
Woman-Captain (Shadwell, T., 1679), I. 14, 191, 207, 431; II. 142
Woman Hater (Bernard, W. B., 1842), IV. 266
— (Godfrey, G. W., 1895), V. 383
— (Lloyd, D. D. and Terry, E., 1886), V. 461
Woman he loved (Daly, C., 1872), V. 334
Woman he married = Shall he forgive her?
Woman—her Rise and Fall in Life (Pitt, W. H., 1871), V. 527
Woman I adore (Morton, J. M., 1852), V. 495
Woman in Black (Adams-Acton, Mrs, 1895), V. 235
— = Haunted Lives
Woman in Mauve (Phillips, W., 1864), V. 523
Woman in my Dust Hole (Buckingham, L. S., 1858), V. 769, 781, 850
Woman in 1900 (1894), V. 769
Woman in Red (Coyne, J. S., 1864), V. 328
Woman in the Wood = White Wolf
Woman in White (Collins, W. W., 1871), V. 318
— (Ware, J. M., 1860), V. 769, 823, 850
— (1861), V. 769
Woman is a Devil (Gazul, C., 1825), IV. 318
Woman is a Riddle (Bullock, C., 1716), II. 16, 133, 146, 160, 172, 212, 301, 385; III. 116

Woman Keeps a Secret = Wonder
Woman keeps the Secret = Ton of Gold
Woman made a Justice (Betterton, T., 1670), I. 259, 392
Woman Never Vexed = Injured General
Woman never Vext (Planché, J. R., 1824), IV. 30, 377, 605
Woman of Business (Webster, B., the Younger, 1864), V. 618
Woman of Colour (Williams, Capt., 1853), V. 624
Woman of Dreams (1841), IV. 556
Woman of No Importance (Wilde, O. F. O'F. W., 1893), V. 190, 192, 622
Woman of Spirit (Chatterton, T., 1803), III. 243
Woman of Taste (1738), II. 387
— = Female Rake
Woman of Ten Thousand = Polish Tyrant
Woman of the Future = Josiah's Dream
Woman of the People (Webster, B., the Younger, 1877), V. 618
— = Marie Jeanne
Woman of the Tree (Bass, C., 1829), IV. 571
Woman of the World (Cavendish, Lady C., 1858), V. 306
— (Coyne, J. S., 1868), V. 328
— (Lee, N., Jr., 1858), V. 452
— (Stephenson, B. C., 1886), V. 582
— (Suter, W. E., 1866), V. 588
— (1858), V. 769
Woman of Uncommon Scents = Dora and Diplunacy
Woman Once in the Right = Richmond Heiress
Woman Outwitted (Drew, E. and Henry, D. M., 1886), V. 350
Woman Pays = None but the Brave
Woman's Advocate = Contented Cuckold
Woman's Ambition = Catherine Howard
Woman's Caprice and Man's Obstinacy (Lewis, H. M., 1895), V. 459
Woman's Constancy = Eloise
Woman scorned (Pringle, W., 1898), V. 531
Woman's Devotion (Faucquez, A., 1863), V. 769, 791, 850
— = Gambler's Wife

Woman's Error (Glen, I., 1876) = Stolen Diamonds, v. 382, 754, 793, 847
— (Murray, J. K., 1898), v. 500
Woman's Faith (Bernard, W. B., 1835), IV. 265
— (1855), v. 769
Woman's Fate = Mother's Dying Child
Woman's First Fault = Fatal Error
Woman's Fools (1897), v. 769
Woman's Freak (Thompson, A., 1882), v. 597
Woman's Glory = Judge Not
Woman's Guilt (Copping, B., 1896), v. 324
Woman's Heart (Bell, R. S. W., 1897), v. 255
— (Calmour, A. C., 1881), v. 300
— (Vandenhoff, Miss, 1852), v. 606
— (1841), IV. 643
— (1858), v. 769
Woman's Idol (Daly, C. and Raphael, C., 1891), v. 334
Woman's Life (Pitt, G. D., 1844), IV. 373
— (1834), IV. 556
— = Isabelle
Woman's Love (Alleyn, A., 1881), v. 239
— (Bird, F. W., 1890), v. 261
— (Cleveland, H., 1875), v. 314
— (Wade, T., 1828), IV. 415
— (Wilks, T. E., 1841), IV. 421, 617
— (Woodville, H., 1899), v. 631
— (1881), v. 769
— (1894), v. 769
— = (1) Ernestine; (2) Rose Ashford; (3) Soldier's Honour
Woman's No (Gibney, S., 1895), v. 769, 793, 850
Woman's Peril (Suter, W. E. and Crofte, A., 1877), v. 588
— = Tried for Life
Woman's Proper Place (Jones, J. W. and Warden, G., 1896), v. 441
Woman's Reason (Brookfield, C. H. E. and Philips, F. C., 1895), v. 277
Woman's Reputation (1894), v. 769
Woman's Revenge (Bullock, C., 1715), II. 133, 135, 141, 211, 300, 385
— (Jordan, L., 1882), v. 441
— (Payne, J. H., 1832), IV. 369
— (Pettitt, H., 1893), v. 521
— (1860), v. 769

Woman's Rights (Marchant, F., 1876), v. 476
— (Palmer, T. A., 1882), v. 512
— (1848), IV. 556
— (1869), v. 769
Woman's Sacrifice (Chapin, A., 1899), v. 308
— = Lost Love
Woman's Secret (Argent-Lonergau, E., 1894), v. 242
— (Conquest, G., 1853), v. 320
Woman's Sin = On the Verge
Woman's Tears (Bourchier, A., 1889), v. 270
Woman's the Devil (Stirling, E., 1837), IV. 406, 556, 613, 643
Woman's Trials (Parry, T., 1839), IV. 368
Woman's Trust (Towers, E., 1872), v. 601
Woman's Truth (Reynolds, W., 1886), v. 541
Woman's Vengeance (Harvey, F., 1888), v. 408
— (Savile-Clark, C., 1892), v. 557
— (Swinerd, H., 1889), v. 589
— = Red Josephine
Woman's Victory (Brabner, W. A., 1895), v. 272
— (Dodson, R., 1885), v. 347
Woman's War (1860), v. 769
Woman's Whim = Phantom Love
+ Woman's Whims (Hallett, Mrs, 12°, 1838)
— (Stephens, W., 1867), v. 581
Woman's Will (1815), IV. 636
— = Woman's Word
Woman's Will—a Riddle (Swift, E. L., 1820), IV. 556, 613, 643
Woman's Wit (Adams-Acton, Mrs, 1893), v. 235
— (Cibber, C., 1696), I. 218, 279, 397
— (Knowles, J. S., 1838), IV. 17, 339
— (Milner, H. M., 1829), IV. 357
— (1843), IV. 556
— = (1) Angela; (2) Tricky Esmeralda
Woman's Word (1820), IV. 556
Woman's Work = Marcelle
Woman's World (Hurst, J. P., 1896), v. 431
Woman's Worth (Howe, J. B., 1863), v. 770, 850

Woman's Worth (Whitehead, D. C., 1846), IV. 419

Woman's Worth and Woman's Ways = Four Sisters

Woman's Wrongs (Courtney, J., 1859), v. 786

— (Heathcote, A. M., 1887), v. 415

— = Felon's Son

Woman Tamer (Doone, N., 1896), v. 347

Woman that was a Cat (Suter, W. E., 1859), v. 587

Woman turn'd Bully (1675), I. 216, 446

Woman wears the Breeches = Semiramis, Queen of Babylon

Woman who wooed (Ashlyn, Q., 1897), v. 245

+ Duologue. A Woman will be a Woman (Ware, J. R.: *Dicks*)

Woman will have her Will (1713), II. 387

Woman wronged by Woman = Madeline Martel

Women and Men (Dubourg, A. W., 1871), v. 351

Women and Wine (Landeck, B. and Shirley, A., 1897), v. 447

— (1834), IV. 556

Women of Shunem = Elisha

Womens Conquest (Howard, E., 1670), I. 61, 138, 414

Women Three (1866), v. 770

Won at Last (Reeve, W., 1869), v. 118, 540

Won by a Head (Clarke, C. A., 1887), v. 311

— (Taylor, T., 1869), v. 593

— (1897), v. 770

Won by a Neck (Horsman, C., 1879), v. 427

— (1880), v. 770

Won by a Trick (Wilson, S., 1885), v. 770, 824, 850

Won by Honours (Brunton, A., 1882), v. 284

Won by Wit (Attenborough, F. G., 1895), v. 245

Wonder = Honest Yorkshire-Man

Wonder: A Woman Keeps a Secret (Centlivre, Mrs S., 1714), II. 20, 142, 168, 305, 433; III. 205

Wonderful Adventures of Daddy Daddles = Great Metropolis

Wonderful Cousin (1874), v. 770

+ Wonderful Cure (*French*)

Wonderful Duck (Kenney, C. L., 1873), v. 443, 801

Wonderful Lamp (1830), IV. 556

Wonderful Lamp in a New Light (À Beckett, G. A., 1844), IV. 250

Wonderful Lamp of Aladdin (1827), IV. 556

Wonderful Travels of Gulliver (Byron, H. J., 1867), v. 782

Wonderful Visit (Wells, H. S., 1896), v. 619

Wonderful Wall and the Wise Elephants of the East = Chinese Insurrection

Wonderful Water Cure (Webster, B. N., 1846), IV. 418, 616

Wonderful Woman (Dance, C., 1849), IV. 289

Wonders in St Helena = Napoleon's Glory

Wonders in the Sun (D'Urfey, T., 1706), II. 233, 320

Wonders of Derbyshire (1779), III. 27, 29, 348, 367

Wonders of Wales = Penmaenmawr

Wonder-Worker (Cumberland, S., 1894), v. 331

Wonga of the Branded Hand (Atkyns, S., 1844), IV. 257

Won, not Wooed (Lodge, A., 1874), v. 462, 804

Woodbarrow Farm (Jerome, J. K., 1888), v. 436

Wood Carver of Bruges = Midnight

Woodcock's Little Game (Morton, J. M., 1864), v. 496

Wood Daemon (Lewis, M. G., 1807) = Demon of the Woods, IV. 345, 346, 450

Wood Demon (Conquest, G. and Spry, H., 1873), v. 321

— (Kenney, C. and Smith, A. R., 1847), IV. 556, 643

— (Marchant, F., 1867), v. 475

— (1813), IV. 556

Wood Devil (Fitzball, E., 1836), IV. 315

Wooden Spoon (Burgess, G., 1892), v. 287

Wooden Spoon Maker (Halliday, A. and Brough, W., 1863), v. 400

Wooden Walls (Cherry, A., 1806) =
Peter the Great, IV. 556, 643
Woodin's Carpet-bag and Sketchbook (1854), V. 770
Woodleigh (1883), V. 770
Woodman (Bate, H., 1791), III. 236
Woodman and his Ass (1835), IV. 643
Woodman and his Dog = Bruin the Brave
Woodman Prince (1817), IV. 556
Woodman's Daughter = Zittau, the Cruel
Woodman's Dream = Lesson of Life
Woodman's Horse (1854), V. 770
Woodman's Hut (Arnold, S. J., 1814), IV. 256
Woodman's Spell (Stirling, E., 1850), V. 584
Woodriffe (Dibdin, C. I. M., 1822), IV. 295
Woodstock (?Pocock, I. or Dibdin, C. I. M., 1826), IV. 33, 94, 296, 385
— (1826), IV. 94, 556
Woodstock Bower = (1) Fair Rosamond; (2) Fall of Fair Rosamond
Wood Wolf of the Black Mountains (Moncrieff, W. T., 1842), IV. 361
Wooer, the Waitress and the Willain = Belle of the Barley Mow
Wooing = Florentine Wedding
Wooing and Waiting (Levy, E. L., 1895), V. 458
Wooing a Widow (Bernard, W. B., 1832), IV. 265
— (1833), IV. 556
— (1836), IV. 556
Wooing in Jest and Loving in Earnest (Troughton, A. C., 1858), V. 604
Wooing One's Wife (Morton, J. M., 1861), V. 496
— (1870), V. 770
Wooings and Weddings = Look before you Leap
Wool (Linden, H., 1878), V. 459
Woolcomber's Progress (1879), V. 770
Wool-gathering (Brayley, 1826), IV. 270
— (Longride, A., 1888), V. 463
Worcester Fight (Dalton, M., 1890), V. 333
Worcester Sauce (1872), V. 770
Word for Nature (Cumberland, R., 1798), III. 252

Word for the Ladies (Kenney, J., 1818), IV. 337
Word of Honour (Meritt, P., 1874), V. 486
— (Skeffington, L. S., 1802), IV. 402
— (1814), IV. 635
— = Seigneur's Daughter
Words made visible (Shaw, S., 1679), I. 432
Word to the Wise (Kelly, H., 1770), III. 7, 18, 130–1, 132, 155, 278, 389
— = Historical Register
Worga (Haines, J. T., 1824), IV. 556, 643
Work and Wages (Bourne, W., 1890), V. 161, 270
Workbox (Craven, T., 1890), V. 329
Work for the Bailiffs = Broken Stock-Jobbers
Work for the Upholders = Bickerstaff's Burying
Work Girl (Conquest, G. and Shirley, A., 1895), V. 323
Work Girl of Cardiff = Welsh Orphan
Workgirls of London (Hazlewood, C. H., 1864), V. 770, 796, 850
Workhouse Life = Casual Ward
Workhouse, the Palace and the Grave (Seaman, W., 1858), V. 770, 815, 850
Working in the Dark = Waifs
Working Man (Hardy, H., 1890), V. 403
— (1852), V. 770
Working Man's Story = Ready and Willing
Working the Oracle (1862), V. 770
Workman (Harvey, F., 1880), V. 408
— (Towers, E., 1880), V. 601
Workman's Dream = Rich and Poor
Workman's Wife (1875), V. 770
Workmen of Paris (1864), V. 770
Work of Mercy (Racer, F., 1892), V. 532
World (Meritt, P., Pettitt, H. and Harris, Sir A., 1880), V. 486
— (Kenney, J., 1808), IV. 184, 336
World against her (Harvey, F., 1887), V. 408
World and Stage (Simpson, J. P., 1859), V. 567
World as it Goes (Colls, J. H., 1792), III. 245
— (Cowley, Mrs H., 1781) = Second Thoughts are Best, III. 248, 380
— = (1) Fashion; (2) Touchstone

Yachting Cruise (Burnand, F. C., 1866), v. 288

Yachting Trip = Bombay to Henley

Yager's Rest = Bier Kroeg

Yahrmanka nal Dhu (1832), IV. 557

Yaldo the Remorseless = Lion of the Jungle

Yaller Seal = Gore

Yamun Dhuv (1830), IV. 557

Yankee = Lucifer Matches

Yankee Courtship (1858), v. 770

Yankee Doodle upon his Little Pony (Lee, N., 1848) = Harlequin and Yankee Doodle, IV. 557, 643

Yankee Housekeeper (1856), v. 770

Yankee Land (Logan, C. A., 1844), IV. 557

Yankee Legacy (1862), v. 771

Yankee Notes for English Circulation (Stirling, E., 1842), IV. 407

Yankee Notions (1889), v. 771

Yankee Pedlar (Bernard, W. B., 1836), IV. 266

Yard Arm and Yard Farm (1812), IV. 557

Yaromeer the Yager (1831), IV. 557

— (1851), v. 771

Yarra (Dibdin, C. I. M., 1822), IV. 295

Yashmak (Raleigh, C. and Hicks, Sir S., 1897), v. 534

Year and a Day (Dicks, J., 1864), v. 788

— (1879), v. 771

— = Cain

Year in an Hour (Poole, J., 1824), IV. 386

Year One = A.D. 1

Ye Battel of Bosworth Field = King Richard ye Third

Ye Belle Alliance (?Sala, G. A., or Brough, W. and Brough, R. B.), v. 279, 780

Ye Childe of Hale (1880), v. 771

Ye Dagger and ye Poisoned Bowl = Fayre Rosamond

Ye Days of ye Good Queen Bess (1879), v. 771

Ye Evil Spirits and Dickie Sam (Vickery, S., 1858), v. 822

Ye Faire Maide of Merrie Islington (Cheatham, F. G., 1869), v. 308

Ye Fair One with ye Golden Locks (Grattan, H. P. and Garston, L., 1872), v. 389

Ye Fancy Fayre (Grain, R. C., 1881), v. 387

Ye Faust and Marguerite (Osman, W. R., 1873), v. 508

Ye Good Old Days (Raymond, E., 1897), v. 535

Ye Ladye of Coventry and the Exiled Fairy = Godiva

Ye Ladye of Lyons (Lewis-Clifton, A., 1882), v. 459

Ye Legende (Grattan, H. P., 1883), v. 389

Yell of Doom (1857), v. 771

Yellow Admiral (1845), IV. 557

Yellow Boy (1883), v. 771

— = Fire King

Yellow Dwarf (À Beckett, G. A., 1842), IV. 250

— (Blanchard, E. L. and Greenwood, T. L., 1875), v. 264, 779

— (Browne, G. W., 1879), v. 282

— (Byron, H. J., 1869), v. 297, 782

— (Conquest, G. and Spry, H., 1897), v. 323

— (Doyle, T. F., 1888), v. 771, 789, 850

— (Hall, F., 1880), v. 399

+ — (Keating, Miss. *French*)

— (Pitt, G. D., 1847), IV. 375

— (Reece, R. and Thompson, A., 1882), v. 539, 813

— (Roe, J. E., 1868), v. 814

— (Woolfe, J. H., 1897), v. 771, 824, 850

— (1820, 1829), IV. 557

— (1860, 1865), v. 850

— (1876, 1878, 1879, 1898), v. 771

Yellow Dwarf and the King of the Gold Mines (Planché, J. R., 1854), v. 527

Yellow Fiend (Dibdin, C. I. M., 1825), IV. 296

Yellow Frigate (1861), v. 850

Yellow Husband (Lemon, M., 1843), IV. 344

— (1842), IV. 557

Yellow Joke (1730), II. 387

Yellow Kids (Barnett, M., 1835), IV. 261

Yellow Passport (Neville, H., 1868), v. 502

Yellow Roses (Young, Sir C. L., 1878), v. 149, 635

Yelva (Bishop, Sir H. R., 1829), IV. 267, 572

Ye Merrie Days of Olde Englande ⇌
  Good Queen Bess
Ye Merrie England (Webb, G., 1877),
  v. 617
— = Merrie England
Ye Miller and hys Man (Thorne, G.,
  1893), v. 599
Ye Mysseltoe Boughe (1861), v. 771
Yeoman of Kent = Tunbridge-Walks
Yeoman's Daughter (Serle, T. J., 1833),
  IV. 399
— (1833), IV. 557
— (1834), IV. 557
Yeoman's Service (Pemberton, T. E.,
  1885), v. 519
Yeomen of the Guard (Gilbert, W. S.,
  1888), v. 145, 380
Ye Queene, ye Earle and ye Maydenne
  = Kenilworth
"Yes!" (Somerset, C. A., 1829), IV. 145,
  404
Ye Siege of Liverpool (Millward, C.,
  1852), v. 807
Ye Signe of ye Golden Ship (1881), v.
  771
Yes or No (Beauchamp, E., 1877), v.
  254
— (Pocock, I., 1808), IV. 144, 383
— (Poel, W., 1892), v. 771, 811
Yew Tree Ruins (Haines, J. T., 1841),
  IV. 323
Ye Wyn-Wyn-Wyn (McArdle, J. F.,
  1875), v. 466
Y'lang, Y'lang (Cohen, G. M., 1893), v.
  316
Yogi's Daughter (Hopkins, J. B., 1854),
  v. 426
Yolande (1877), v. 771
Yorick's Love (Howells, W. D., 1878),
  v. 429
Yorick, the King's Jester (Somerset,
  C. A., 1836), v. 394
York and Lancaster (Hood, T., 1829),
  IV. 327
York Roses (Markwell, W. R.), v.
  477
Yorkshire Attorney = (1) Sheep Stealer;
  (2) Three Yards of Broadcloth
Yorkshire Bonfire = Make a Noise Tom
Yorkshire Brothers (1852), v. 771
Yorkshire Ghost (Craven, E., 1794), III.
  249

Yorkshire Grey (1833), IV. 557
Yorkshire Highwayman and the Twin
  Brothers = Nat Graves
Yorkshire Hoyden (1797), III. 406
Yorkshire Lady = (1) Female Rake;
  (2) Woman of Taste
Yorkshire Lass (Jones, J. W., 1891), v.
  441
— = Luck
Yorkshire Lover = Change upon Change
Yorkshire-Man   Bit = Industrious
  Lovers
Yorkshire Miller = Ellen and Alberto
Yorkshire School (Pitt, G. D., 1847),
  IV. 374
York, you are not wanted = Lubin Log's
  Journey to London
You can't marry your Grandmother
  (Bayly, T. H., 1838), IV. 14, 263
You know what (Beazley, S., Jr., 1842),
  IV. 14, 264
You know who (Morton, J. M., 1864), v.
  496
You may like it, or let it alone (1791),
  III. 348
You May Say That = Fortune Hunters
You must be buried (Planché, J. R.,
  1827), IV. 378
You must be married (Selby, C., 1846),
  IV. 399
You mustn't laugh (Lubimoff, A.,
  1892), v. 464
You Never Can Tell (Shaw, G. B.,
  1899), v. 195, 562
You Never Know (Dale, G., 1899), v.
  332
Young Actress (Boucicault, D., 1853),
  v. 268
— (1860), v. 771
Young America (1897), v. 771
Young and Handsome (Planché, J. R.,
  1856), v. 527
Young Apprentice (Hazlewood, C. H.,
  1868), v. 413
Young at Sixty (1829), IV. 557
Young Burglar (1891), v. 771
Young Chasseur = Romance of the
  Pyrenees
Young Colonel = Military Promotion
Young Coquette (1705), II. 387, 448
Young Country Widow (Gray, S.,
  1839), IV. 321